1 MONTH OF FREE READING

at
www.ForgottenBooks.com

By purchasing this book you are eligible for one month membership to ForgottenBooks.com, giving you unlimited access to our entire collection of over 1,000,000 titles via our web site and mobile apps.

To claim your free month visit:
www.forgottenbooks.com/free514747

* Offer is valid for 45 days from date of purchase. Terms and conditions apply.

ISBN 978-0-364-96166-7
PIBN 10514747

This book is a reproduction of an important historical work. Forgotten Books uses state-of-the-art technology to digitally reconstruct the work, preserving the original format whilst repairing imperfections present in the aged copy. In rare cases, an imperfection in the original, such as a blemish or missing page, may be replicated in our edition. We do, however, repair the vast majority of imperfections successfully; any imperfections that remain are intentionally left to preserve the state of such historical works.

Forgotten Books is a registered trademark of FB &c Ltd.
Copyright © 2018 FB &c Ltd.
FB &c Ltd, Dalton House, 60 Windsor Avenue, London, SW19 2RR.
Company number 08720141. Registered in England and Wales.

For support please visit www.forgottenbooks.com

THE

Connecticut Quarterly.

AN ILLUSTRATED MAGAZINE.

Devoted to the Literature, History and Picturesque Features of

CONNECTICUT.

Vol. I.

January, 1895, to December, 1895

HARTFORD, CONN.:
COPYRIGHT BY THE CONNECTICUT QUARTERLY COMPANY.
1895.

Contents of Volume No. 1.

JANUARY—DECEMBER, 1895.

	Page
Aaron Burr, (Old Colonial Characters III,) with portrait. "Felix Oldmixon."	374
Anæsthesia, the History of, *Illustrated.* James McManus, D. D. S.	56
Ancient and Modern Norwalk. *Illustrated.* Hon. A. H. Byington	281
Argonauts of 1849, The "Henry Lee," *Illustrated.* Frank Lorenzo Hamilton	229
"Autumn Morning," (Frontispiece I,) from a Painting by D. F. Wentworth	314
Bits from Great Grand Mother's Journal. Mrs. Ellen Strong Bartlett	265
Bungalow Bay. (Frontispiece III.) Gardner Arnold Reckard	216
Bungalow, Ella Wheeler Wilcox and The, *Illustrated.* Gardner Arnold Reckard	219
Bushnell Park, (The Hartford Park System I, II.) *Illustrated,* Sherman W. Adams	67, 173
Campbell's Falls, View of, (Frontispiece II.) Mrs. Marie H. Kendall	108
Canton. *Illustrated.* Hon. William Edgar Simonds	239
Center Church Burying Ground, and its Associations, The, *Illustrated.* Miss Mary K. Talcott	43
Clinton, once Killingworth. *Illustrated.* Miss Ellen Brainerd Peck	233
Colonial Characters, Old, "Felix Oldmixon."	33, 155, 374
Ella Wheeler Wilcox and the Bungalow. *Illustrated.* Gardner Arnold Reckard	219
Farmington, Tunxis which is, *Illustrated.* Martha Stanley	15
Frontispieces—"The Twilight Hour." Gardner A. Reckard	2
View of Campbell's Falls, Norfolk, Conn.	108
"Bungalow Bay," Gardner A. Reckard	218
"Autumn Morning," D. F. Wentworth	314
Girl from Massachusetts, The, Miss Pauline Phelps	362
Granby, Scenes in and around, *Illustrated.* Howard W. Benjamin	134
Green, The New Haven, *Illustrated.* Miss Ellen Strong Bartlett	315
Hartford Park System, The, (Bushnell Park.) *Illustrated.* Sherman W. Adams	67, 173
(The Pope and Pond Parks.) *Illustrated.* Howard W. Benjamin	337
"Henry Lee" Argonauts of 1849, The, *Illustrated.* Frank Lorenzo Hamilton	229
Highland Park, Manchester. *Illustrated.* Marie De Valcherville	298
Historic Homes, (Hartford.) *Illustrated.* W. Farrand Felch	3, 123, 288
History of Anæsthesia, The, *Illustrated.* James McManus, D. D. S.	56
Hospital Rock, The, (at Farmington, Conn.) *Illustrated.* James Shepard	50
In and Around Granby, Scenes, *Illustrated.* Howard W. Benjamin	134
Jonathan Edwards, (Old Colonial Characters I, II.) "Felix Oldmixon,"	33, 155
Last Century, Yale Boys of the, Miss Ellen D. Larned	355
Letter from a Repentant Royalist. Miss Ellen D. Larned	399
Lost Library, Scrope, or the, Frederick Beecher Perkins	74, 195, 303
Massachusetts, The Girl from, Miss Pauline Phelps	362
Memories of Meriden, I. Mrs. Frances A. Breckenridge	352
Modern Norwalk, Ancient and, *Illustrated.* Hon. A. H. Byington	281
Musical Melange, (see Departments.) The Editor	
Music and Musicans, Old Time, Prof. N. H. Allen	274
Native Orchids, Some, *Illustrated.* Miss C. Antoinette Shepard	345
New Britain in the Days of the Revolution. *Illustrated.* Mrs. C. J. Parker	379
New Haven Green, The, *Illustrated.* Miss Ellen Stong Bartlett	315
Norfolk and that Neighborhood. *Illustrated.* Miss Adele Greene	109
Norwalk, Ancient and Modern. *Illustrated.* Hon. A. H. Byington	281
Notes and Queries, (see Departments.) The Editor	
Old Colonial Characters. "Felix Oldmixon,"	33, 155, 374
Old Time Music and Musicians. Prof. N. H. Allen	274, 368
Orchids, Some Native, *Illustrated.* Miss C. Antoinette Shepard	345

CONTENTS.

	Page
Parks,—Bushnell Park I, II. *Illustrated.* Sherman W. Adams	67, 173
The Pope and Pond Parks III. *Illustrated.* H. W. Benjamin	337
Highland, Manchester. *Illustrated.* Marie De Valcherville	298
Queries, Notes and, (see Departments.) The Editor	
Reginald Roxdale: A Study of Heredity. Franklin E. Denton	39
Repentant Royalist, A Letter from a, Miss Ellen D. Larned	271
Revolutionary Boycott, A, Miss Ellen D. Larned	153
Round Table, The, (see Departments.) The Editor	
Scenes in and around Granby. *Illustrated.* Howard W. Benjamin	134
Scrope, or the Lost Library. Frederic Beecher Perkins	74, 195, 303
"Ships that Pass in the Night." (Frontispiece III.) G. A. Reckard	218
Simsbury. *Illustrated.* Rev. John B. McLean	141
Small Pox Hospital Rock, The, (Farmington, Conn.) *Illustrated.* James Shepard	50
Sociology and Civics, (see Departments,) The Editor	
Some Native Orchids. *Illustrated.* Miss C. Antoinette Shepard	345
Suffield: A Sketch. *Illustrated.* Prof. Martin H. Smith	165
Talcott Mountain, The Towers of, *Illustrated.* S. C. Wadsworth	180
"The Bungalow," Ella Wheeler Wilcox, and, *Illustrated.* Gardner A. Reckard	219
The Thomas Hooker of To-day, (Abstract of Sermon.) Rev. Geo. Leon Walker	72
"The Thomas Hooker of To-day," (Round Table.) Rodney Dennis	84
Three Dates, The, Franklin E. Denton	160
Towers of Talcott Mountain, The, *Illustrated.* S. C. Wadsworth	180
Treasure Trove, (see Departments.) The Editor	
Trio and Tripod. *Illustrated.* Geo. H. Carrington	23, 188, 250, 391
Tunxis, which is Farmington. *Illustrated.* Mrs. Martha Stanley	15
"Twilight Hour, The," (Frontispiece I.) G. A. Reckard	2
View of Campbell's Falls, near Norfolk, Conn. (Frontispiece II.) Mrs. Marie H. Kendall	108
Visit to Mrs. Sigourney, A, *Illustrated.* Mrs. Louise J. R. Chapman	47
"Wide Awakes," The, *Illustrated.* Major Julius G. Rathbun	327
Yale Boys of the Last Century, I. Miss Ellen D. Larned	355

POETRY.   686540

An Autumn Rondeau. Ellen Brainerd Peck	354
A Retrospect. Florence Carver Davis	172
Atalanta. Fanny Driscoll	179
A Tribute to our Dead Poets. Louis E. Thayer	270
A Typical Easter. *Illustrated.* W. Farrand Felch	163
Autumn Rondeau, An, Ellen Brainerd Peck	354
Burning of Simsbury, The, Albert Lewis Thayer	151
Charter Oak, The, *Illustrated.* Ellen Brainerd Peck	22
Connecticut. Louis E. Thayer	46
Cousin Lucrece, (selected,) Edmund Clarence Stedman	66
Daughter of the Dawn, A, Will. Farrand Felch	326
Day Dream, A, Clement C. Calverley	302
Departure (Double Sonnet.) Robert Clarkson Tongue	361
Elizabeth, Her Belt. (Anonymous)	71
Fame. Louis E. Thayer	152
First Love. John Rossiter	55
Gentian. Joseph Archer	367
Harp and a Soul, A, Henry Mason Chadwick	154
House and Home. (Anonymous.)	13
In a Fragrant Garden, (in "Clinton.") Ellen Brainerd Peck	236
I Read of Algol, When, Franklin E. Denton	162
Midsummer Dream, A, Willard Warner	280
Monte-Video, (selection.) John Greenleaf Whittier	187
Nasturtiums. (Anonymous.)	21

CONTENTS.

	Page
Nature Poems. John Rossiter	55
New Haven Elms. Herbert Randall	402
Norfolk Hills, (in "Norfolk" and that Neighborhood.) Adele Greene	122
Over the River, (selection.) *Illustrated.* Rose Terry Cooke	248
Retrospect, A, Florence Carver Davis	172
Rondeau Redouble. John Payne	287
Rondeau, An Autumn, Ellen Brainerd Peck	354
Schubert's Unfinished Symphony. (Musical Melange.)	92
Sea Glow. Rev. Dr. F. C. H. Wendel	228
Secrets. John Rossiter	55
Simsbury, The Burning of, Albert Lewis Thayer	151
Sonnets. F. E. Denton, 162; Stockton Bates, 194; R. C. Tongue	361
The Old Farm Home, (selected.)	390
The Old Place. Joseph Truman	297
The One Shall be Taken, the Other Left. Stockton Bates	194
The Pennyroyal Hymn, (selected.)	279
The Spinet, (Musical Melange.) Ellen Brainerd Peck	210
The Spirit of Beauty. Rufus Dawes	373
The Trouter's Paradise. *Illustrated.* Will. Farrand Felch	264
To the Bard of the Bungalow. John Payne	287
Tribute to our Dead Poets. Louis E. Thayer	270
Typical Easter, A, *Illustrated.* W. Farrand Felch	163
Unafraid, (selection.) Richard E. Burton	49
Your Native Town, (see Note in "Round Table.") "Josephine Canning."	301

DEPARTMENTS.

The Round Table. 83, 204, 307, 403.
    An Adequate State History.—A Contretemps.—A Word of Promise.—A Word of Praise.—A Word of Welcome.—A Word of Retrospect.—A Year Old.—A Former State Magazine.—"Civic Beings."—Every Man an Antiquity.—Fore-Words.—It Smacks of the Soil.—Love of Nature.—Personal Journalism.—The American Type.—The Charm of the Commonplace.—"The Thos. Hooker of To-day."—The Growth of Humane Sentiment.—"Uncut Leaves."

Musical Melange. 88, 210.
    A New Music Hall.—A Public Musical Library.—Chopin and Tennyson.—Individuality in Music.—Hartford Musical Culture.—New Worship.—New York Notations.—Rubinstein: Requiescat.—Schubert's Unfinished Symphony.—The Messiah.—The Spinet.

Treasure Trove. 94, 212, 310.
    Connecticut "Colloures."—Conn. Society of the Sons of the American Revolution.—Conn. Society of the Daughters of the American Revolution.—Conn. Society of Colonial Wars.—Conn. Society of the War for the Union.—Conn. Historical Society.—Conn. Historical Society's Collections.—Ignorance of Ancestry.—Patriotic Societies.—The Half-way Covenant.—The Last of the Blue Laws.—The Loyal Legion.—The New Haven Colony Historical Society.

Sociology and Civics. 99, 207, 313.
    Charity Organization and Medicine.—Conn. Humane Society.—Conn. Society of University Extension.—Our School of Sociology.—School of Sociology.—Science of Duty.—The Fabian Essays.—The Messiah of the Apostles.—University Extension.

A Free Lance in the Field of Life and Letters. "Felix Oldmixon." 103.

Notes and Queries. 98, 214, 313, 408.
    Abbott, Arms, Baldwin, Backus, Batterson, Benjamin, Birdseye, Blackney, Blakesley, Camp, Chapman, Dayton, Dickinson, Edwards, Farrand, Francis, Gardner, Gorham, Graves, Hale, Hoadly, Holt, Ledyard, Lincoln, Mason, Mallory, McDonough, Miller, Peck, Porter, Preston, Prince, Sanford, Shepard, Swords, Talcott, Tuttle, Walton, Ware, White, Williams, Winthrop.

Vol. 1   Jan., Feb., Mch., 1895.   No. 1

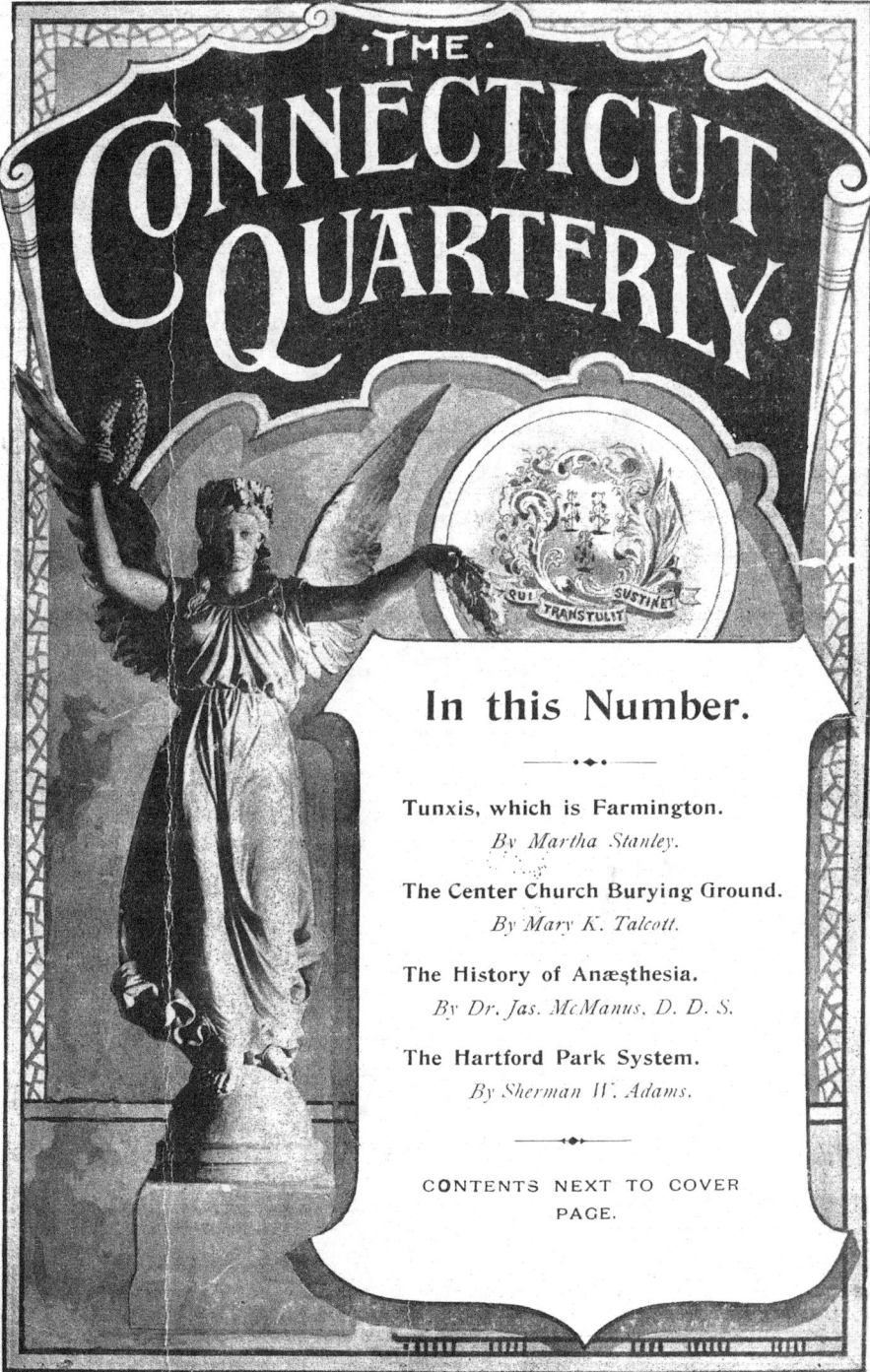

THE CONNECTICUT QUARTERLY.

In this Number.

Tunxis, which is Farmington.
  By Martha Stanley.

The Center Church Burying Ground.
  By Mary K. Talcott.

The History of Anæsthesia.
  By Dr. Jas. McManus, D. D. S.

The Hartford Park System.
  By Sherman W. Adams.

CONTENTS NEXT TO COVER PAGE.

50c. a Year   Hartford, Conn.   15c. a Copy

WEBSTER'S INTERNATIONAL DICTIONARY

Entirely New.
Abreast of the Times.
A Grand Educator.

Successor of the "*Unabridged.*"

Standard of the U. S. Gov't Printing Office, the U. S. Supreme Court and of nearly all the Schoolbooks. Warmly commended by every State Superintendent of Schools, and other Educators almost without number.

A College President writes: "For ease "with which the eye finds the word sought, "for accuracy of definition, for effective "methods in indicating pronunciation, for "terse yet comprehensive statements of facts, "and for practical use as a working diction-"ary, 'Webster's International' excels any "other single volume."

The One Great Standard Authority,
So writes Hon. D. J. Brewer, Justice U. S. Supreme Court.

G. & C. MERRIAM CO., Publishers,
Springfield, Mass., U. S. A.

☞ Send to the publishers for free pamphlet.
Do not buy cheap reprints of ancient editions.

CONNECTICUT CORRESPONDENCE COLLEGE

OF

Modern Languages.

**FRENCH,
GERMAN,
ITALIAN,
SPANISH.**

By the NATURAL METHOD only.

The proper way to learn any spoken language is to learn *to think in it*, gradually acquiring its idioms, forms, and practices. The best course to pursue is to learn it *by the ear*, not by the eye alone. Our **New Natural Method** is constructed on the above lines, can be thoroughly mastered by any person, even a child, speaking fluently in an incredibly short time, colloquially and grammatically.

Our Natural FRENCH Method, giving the true Parisian accent to every word, ensures correct, thorough knowledge in 25 or more lessons.

Our HANOVERIAN GERMAN Method, will accomplish as much in the same time.

ITALIAN, "the language of songs." A special course for singers and others; and

SPANISH, "the language of chivalry," are in preparation by native teachers, by the Natural Method.

Being taught by mail the pupil keeps up his interest to the end, each pupil being treated separately, and in a **short time can surprise his friends.** Sample Lessons, Terms, and Full Information sent for ten cents, silver or stamps.

Address as above: **Box 142, Hartford, Conn.**

WE ARE NOW PUBLISHING

A NEW BOOK,

UNDER THE TITLE OF

A CONTINUOUS FAMILY GENEALOGY

On an **ENTIRELY ORIGINAL PLAN.**

It contains a newly devised system of Charts, Tables, and Special Blanks conveniently arranged for keeping a

Complete Family Record,

Case with Book inclosed.

including a history of the Ancestors of the Family and their Descendants, thus providing a continuous record of

PAST, PRESENT, AND FUTURE GENERATIONS.

These books are of a convenient size, printed on linen paper and bound in attractive and durable styles.

Handsome Leather-Covered Cases stamped in Gold, are provided for holding and preserving the book, as shown in cut above.

They are in every respect fully adapted to meet the wants of all who desire to keep a Family Record.

Send for Descriptive Circular and Price List containing full information.

ARMS PUBLISHING CO.,

336 Asylum Street,   HARTFORD, CONN.

...THE...
Connecticut Quarterly.

50 Cents a Year.   15 Cents a Copy.

HARTFORD, CONN.

WEBSTER'S
I
Entirely
Abreast of t
A Grand E

A Coll
" with w
" for ac
" methoc
" terse ye
" and for
" ary, ' V
" other s

The Or
So

G. & C.

Sen
Do

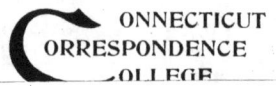

The Connecticut Qua

—— WHAT IT IS ——

An Illustrated Magazine devoted to Connecticut phases of History, Literature, Science a

During the past year the four hundred pages of t of THE QUARTERLY have contained many articles by illustrated with over *three hundred engravings*.

Concerning the October, November and Decemb *Hartford Times* published the following:—

The Connecticut Quarterly.

This excellent magazine, devoted chiefly to Connecticut subj illustrated, continues to grow in public favor. The number for Oct December has just appeared. It justifies the publisher's characteri scope and character of the magazine, as a publication devoted to the and picturesque features of Connecticut." In it the "New Have matter for a pleasant leading illustrated paper by Ellen Strong Bartlett old green and its local accessories is well calculated to awaken a corre the subject among those of her readers whose homes are not in New not, therefore, fully share her local enthusiasm for the square and its b

Case

PA

These be
attractive and
Handson
and preservin
They are
to keep a Fa
Send for

G. Rathbun contributes an interesting article on "The 'Wide-Awake lican organization of 1860, which originated in Hartford, and be election of the November of that year had spread into other States til

...THE...
Connecticut Quarterly.

Another interesting paper in this number of the *Quarterly* is Howard W. Benjamin's illustrated article on "The Pope and Pond Parks and Their Donors"—a good sketch of the important donations of Hartford's proposed park system.

Miss C. Antoinette Shepard, of New Brtiain, one of our best botanists, contributes a valuable article on "Some Native Orchids." It shows, both in the text and in the illustrations, something of the wealth of floral beauty in our northern orchids—of which Connecticut has nearly fifty species. Frances A. Breckenridge contributes a paper on "Memories of Meriden."

There is in this number a collection of extracts from the journal of Elijah Backus, edited by Miss Larned, on the "Yale Boys of the Last Century," which will be read with much interest.

There are other good things in this number of the *Quarterly*, particularly Mrs. Parker's paper on "New Britain in the Days or the Revolution," and Mr. Carrington's continuation of his illustrated papers about rambles along the western border of Hartford county. The magazine is a credit to Connecticut. It is published by the Connecticut Quarterly Company, and costs but 50 cents a year.

The foregoing is but one of the many testimonials we have received.

Each of the other numbers for 1895 were of uniform excellence, and for 1896 we shall produce a better magazine in every respect than we have in 1895. Improvement is our constant aim.

It needs to be seen to be appreciated.

Send 15 cents for single copy, either No. 3 or No. 4.

☞ Nos. 1 and 2 of Volume I are out of print.

We can begin subscriptions as far back as No. 3 (the July-August-September number) if desired.

WEBSTER'S

CONNECTICUT CORRESPONDENCE COLLEGE

For 1896

Our plans include representation of very rich and interesting historical fields New Haven, Fairfield and Litchfield counti not forgetting to continue in Hartford cou and taking as much as possible of other pa of the State into consideration.

From the abundant material at hand is our purpose to so represent the State that the bound volumes of *Quarterly* will be the most interesting and valuable books on Connecti ever published. Illustrated articles on "The History of Mining in C necticut," "The Quarries of the State," "The Evolution of Towns," "The Early Highways and Stage Coaching Days," besi other matters pertaining to the early history of different parts of State will appear. Among the more modern topics, an important arti for which we are now planning, is a finely illustrated one on "C necticut at the Atlanta Exposition."

Numerous other valuable features we shall bring to your attent as the numbers appear.

For further information address

THE CONNECTICUT QUARTERLY,

66 State St., Courant Bldg.,

HARTFORD, CONN.,

or see your newsdealer or local agent.

Case

PA

These b attractive an Handsor and preservii They ar to keep a Fa Send for

… THE …

Connecticut Quarterly.

An Illustrated Magazine.

DEVOTED TO THE LITERATURE, HISTORY, AND PICTURESQUE FEATURES OF CONNECTICUT.

PUBLISHED QUARTERLY
By THE CONNECTICUT QUARTERLY COMPANY,
66 State Street, Courant Building,
HARTFORD, CONN.

GEO. C. ATWELL, General Manager.   W. FARRAND FELCH, Editor.

CONTENTS.

Vol. 1.   January, February, March, 1895.   No. 1.

Frontispiece. "THE TWILIGHT HOUR."		2
From a painting by Gardner A. Reckard.		
Historic Homes. 1. HOMES OF GENIUS. Illustrated.	W. Farrand Felch.	3
House and Home. Poem. Selected.		13
Tunxis, Which is Farmington. Illustrated.	Martha Stanley.	15
Nasturtiums. Poem. Selected.		21
The Charter Oak. Poem. Illustrated.	Ellen Brainerd Peck.	22
Trio and Tripod. 1. IN THE TUNXIS VALLEY. Illustrated.	George H. Carrington.	23
Old Colonial Characters. 1. JONATHAN EDWARDS.	Felix Oldmixon.	33
Reginald Roxdale. A STUDY OF HEREDITY.	Franklin E. Denton.	39
The Center Church Burying Ground, and its Associations. Illustrated.	Mary K. Talcott.	43
Connecticut. Poem.	Louis E. Thayer.	46
A Visit to Mrs. Sigourney. Illustrated.	Louise J. R. Chapman.	47
Unafraid. Poem. Selected.	Richard E. Burton.	49
The Small-Pox Hospital Rock, at Farmington, Conn. Illustrated.	James Shepard.	50
Nature Poems.	John Rossiter.	55
The History of Anæsthesia. Illustrated.	James McManus, D. D. S.	56
Cousin Lucrece. Poem. Selected.	Edmund Clarence Stedman.	66
The Hartford Park System. 1. BUSHNELL PARK. Illustrated.	Sherman W. Adams.	67
Elizabeth; Her Belt. Poem. Selected.		71
The Thomas Hooker of To-day. (Abstract of Sermon.)	Rev. Geo. Leon Walker, D.D.	72
Scrope; or the Lost Library: A Novel of New York and Hartford.	Frederic Beecher Perkins.	74

DEPARTMENTS.

The Round Table.	The Editor.	83
Fore-Words.—"The Thomas Hooker of To-day." (Contributed.)—"Uncut Leaves."—An Adequate State History.—Personal Journalism.—A Word of Promise.		
Musical Melange.	"Minerva."	88
New York Notations: Edwin Warren DeLeon, of New York City.—"The Messiah," by Prof. Charles H. Johnson, of Hartford.—Hartford Musical Culture. (Contributed.)—Rubenstein: Requiescat. (Selected.)—Chopin and Tennyson. (Selected.)—Schubert's Unfinished Symphony. (Sonnet.)—New Worship.—A New Music Hall.—A Public Musical Library.		
Treasure Trove.	"Algernon."	94
Patriotic Societies; Ignorance of Ancestry; Connecticut Society of the Sons of the American Revolution; Society of Colonial Wars in Connecticut; Society of the Daughters of the Revolution in Connecticut; Connecticut Historical Society.		
Notes and Queries.		98
Sociology and Civics.	"Solon."	99
Our School of Sociology; Science of Duty; School of Sociology; Connecticut Society of University Extension; Connecticut Humane Society.		
A Free Lance in the Field of Life and Letters.	Felix Oldmixon.	103

Copyright 1895 by THE CONNECTICUT QUARTERLY Co. (*All rights reserved.*)
Price 50 cents per year, 15 cents a number. Remittances should be made by P. O. order or registered letter. Money by mail at sender's risk. The Connecticut Quarterly Co., Box 565, Hartford, Conn.

CAUTION.—Do not pay money to agents unknown to you personally, unless they have authority signed by the manager of the Company to collect such money, and give you a receipt also signed by the manager of the Company and countersigned by themselves.

IN THE LINE OF ANNOUNCEMENTS:

For the Second Quarter we can now mention the following attractive papers:

NORFOLK AND THAT NEIGHBORHOOD, BY MISS ADELE GREENE,
of Brooklyn, N. Y., which will be illustrated from photographs by Mrs. Marie H. Kendall, of Norfolk. This article gives a graphic survey of the picturesque hill-top resort of Connecticut.

TRIO AND TRIPOD, BY GEORGE H. CARRINGTON,
an engaging chronicle of the adventures and exploits of our "trio" of artists, in the Tunxis Valley, while passing through the towns of Avon, Simsbury and the Granbys.

SIMSBURY, BY REV. JOHN B. MCLEAN,
the principal of the McLean Seminary, is an article that has been carefully prepared by one of the ablest writers in Connecticut, and is fully illustrated by some fine views of the elm-lined highways and byways, and of the historic spots of one of the most beautiful villages in the Tunxis valley. It will be appropriately supplemented by a historical ballad:

THE BURNING OF SIMSBURY, BY ALBERT LEWIS THAYER,
of Collinsville, describing the destruction of the primitive village by King Philip, on Sunday, March 26th, 1676, the ancient warrior witnessing its downfall from the top of Talcott Mountain.

THE THREE DATES, BY FRANKLIN E. DENTON,
a new story by the author of "Reginald Roxdale" in this issue, in his peculiar, weird, Poesque style.

SCENES IN AND AROUND GRANBY, BY HOWARD W. BENJAMIN.
This graphic chronicle will be liberally interspersed with half-tone engravings from photographs by the author, and drawings by F. L. Stanton.

AN EASTER POEM,
will be an appropriate feature of the April issue, illustrated by a young artist of this State who has recently returned from abroad.

SUFFIELD, BY PROF. MARTIN H. SMITH,
for years Principal of the Conn. Literary Institution, a ready and fluent writer, will be welcomed by all lovers of that pleasant village of classic shades.

OLD COLONIAL CHARACTERS, II,
by "Felix Oldmixon" will be continued in this and ensuing numbers, the second chapter containing an account of Jonathan Edwards's home, and the childhood of Aaron Burr.

HISTORIC HOMES, II, HOMES OF WEALTH,
will deal with the residences of wealthy and well-to-do people of this city, who have done so much to beautify, adorn, and benefit the city.

THE HARTFORD PARK SYSTEM, II, BY JUDGE S. W. ADAMS,
President of the Board of Park Commissioners, will be continued, the second chapter treating of Bushnell Park under the Commissioners, bringing the record down to the present day.

A REVOLUTIONARY BOYCOTT, BY MISS ELLEN D. LARNED,
the historian of Windham County, well and favorably known throughout the State for rare historical acumen, fidelity and enthusiasm.

THE MIDSUMMER ISSUE

will be an especially bright and pleasing number. It will deal largely with the hill-top and sea-side resorts of the State, giving a fair selection from an already large list.

CANTON, BY HON. WILLIAM EDGAR SIMONDS,
ex-Speaker of the House, ex-U. S. Commissioner of Patents, and ex-President of the Copyright League, will treat of the town he has chosen for his summer home, in all its virginal summer beauty.

NORWALK AS A SUMMER RESIDENCE, BY HON. A. H. BYINGTON,
editor of the Norwalk Gazette for nearly half a century, the well-known war correspondent in "the late unpleasantness" and intimate friend of Lincoln, Seward, Greeley and many others, will write of his home for years, and its attractive and pleasant environment.

CLINTON, BY MISS ELLEN BRAINERD PECK,
whose reputation as a poet is increasing, and whose dainty verses "remind one of old china cups over-flowing with *riant* Jacqueminot roses," as a friend declares, will write of this beautiful town.

THE OLD HOUSES OF STONINGTON, BY HON. RICHARD A. WHEELER,
the venerable historian of Stonington, who will write of his own town and its quaint old residences.

POMFRET, BY HON. JOHN ADDISON PORTER,
editor of the Hartford Post, who will treat of the town he has selected as his own summer home. Besides all these we are promised a number of others that will appear in early numbers.

ROCKY HILL, BY DR. RUFUS W. GRISWOLD.

VERNON, BY REV. E. PAYSON HAMMOND.

NIANTIC, BY A YOUNG SOLDIER, **NOROTON**, BY AN OLD SOLDIER,
and numerous others are in preparation.

TESTIMONIALS.

We have received tributes, "almost too numerous to mention," of which we give a few:

From Prof. Nathan H. Allen: "I like the scheme as you outline it, and certainly wish you all success."

From the Hon. Henry Barnard, LL. D.: "I am quite sure from your specimen signature and your table of contents you will *stay*, but *progress* through pastures and fields new, from year to year. God speed your plough, your reaper and your rake."

From Mrs. Louise J. R. Chapman, Chicago: "I thankfully acknowledge the receipt of prospectus of THE CONN. QUARTERLY. I am so much pleased with its appearance, its attractive cover and charming 'interior,' its chaste and clear typography, artistic illustrations and undivided pages that I make haste to express my pleasure upon its combined merits.

From Prof. D. N. Camp, New Britain: "I congratulate you upon the auspicious undertaking, and I shall expect to find much in it that will interest and instruct."

From Mrs. Elizabeth Champion Lathrop, West Springfield, Mass.: "I am very much pleased with it. I would not care if I did not read anything else than articles of this kind. I like very much your plan for THE QUARTERLY."

From Miss Ellen D. Larned: "I was very pleased to receive your prospectus. Have long wished that our State could have such a mouthpiece. I am very sure that there is sufficient material and competent writers to fill such a magazine with great credit."

From Prof. John B. McLean, of McLean Seminary: "I wish to say that I am delighted with it, and anticipate much pleasure and profit in the future in the companionship of this very artistic and instructive magazine. I have often wished for something of the kind for our State."

From Matthews and Wilberforce, Heraldry and Genealogy, Phila.: "We think it promises to be a valuable and interesting work."

From Hon. John Addison Porter, editor of Hartford Post: "You have my best wishes for success in the undertaking. If rightfully managed the magazine ought to reflect credit on this city and prove a good financial investment."

From Prof. Francis T. Russell, principal St. Margaret's School, Waterbury: "Success to you in your historical enterprise."

From Miss Russell: "My brother and myself were very much interested in the prospectus. My dear sister, Mrs. Russell, would have felt a tender interest in Mrs. Chapman's article, but she is no longer with us. She departed this life the 20th of August, 1889." (Mrs. Sigourney's only daughter.)

These are but a small number of those we are receiving. We are always glad to get warm testimonials from those living outside of their native State or descended from Connecticut people. There are many such yet to hear from.

This issue will reach over ten thousand people.

Our first subscriber was from Havana, Cuba. Good news spreads fast.

Subscribe for yourself. Subscribe for your friends. See premium list on next page.

We want ten thousand more subscribers within the next six months; and feel sure we will get them.

We wisely make no pretense of competing with the leading magazines of general trend and wide scope.

We desire to make our magazine more original and brilliant in time and to present as many features as the larger magazines.

Will you help us to get a large subscription list. Every one can win a premium, as nearly every one subscribes who sees the magazine.

We apologize for the lateness of the present issue for reasons explained in the editorial columns. The second number will appear April first.

This is in no sense an experiment, nor a sample issue only, for every number will be as good as the first issue, and the general average as high.

We want to reach those who have lived in Connecticut or are otherwise interested in the State. Addresses of such will be thankfully received that we may send circulars.

Lastly we have made little effort to secure advertising for the first number, not being certain until type was all received when it would appear. We solicit a good class of advertising for future numbers.

THE PUBLISHERS.

A PARTIAL LIST OF PREMIUMS.

I. FOR CLUBS, SCHOOLS, SOCIETIES, ETC.

	No. of subs.
The International Encyclopedia (the best American work), 15 vols., 900 pages each, 14,000 pages, 50,000 subjects, $3 to $5 a vol., according to style of binding,	450 to 750
The Webster's International Dictionary, revised edition, ten years in revision; cost $300,000; 100 editors; from	100 to 200
The Standard Dictionary, (the very latest; out Nov. 28;) weighs 19 pounds. More words than the Century Dictionary,	120 to 220
Larned's History for General Reference and Topical Reading. A history compiled from all histories; 5 vols.,	250
The Life of Christ represented in Art. Canon F. W. Farrar,	60
The Oxford Bible; flexible leather binding; for teachers,	35
Wood's Dictionary of Quotations; 30,000 references; for the Clergy, Lawyers, Literary Workers, Teachers, etc.,	25 to 45

II. FOR SHAKESPERE-LOVERS, SCHOLARS, STUDENTS.

Bartlett's Shakesperian Concordance; 1910 pages; 1 vol.,	140
The Rolfe Shakespere; 6 subs. for each vol.; all 26 vols.,	156
The Henry Irving Shakespere; 8 vols; small quarto; 600 illustrations in the text and 37 etchings; edited by Henry Irving and the late Frank A. Marshall,	240 to 300
English History in Shakespere's plays; B. E. Warner, M. A.,	18
William Shakespere, a study, by Barrett Wendell, M. A.,	20

III. FOR ANTIQUARIANS, PATRIOTS, SOCIETIES, ETC.

The Discovery of America, by John Fiske; 11th thousand,	40
The American Revolution, by John Fiske, 2 vols.,	40
The Critical Period of American History, by John Fiske, (1783-89); 1 vol., 12th edition,	40
The Beginnings of New England, by John Fiske, 9th edition, 1 vol.,	20
Civil Government in the U. S., by John Fiske; 59th thousand,	10
The War of Independence, by John Fiske,	8
The Makers of America, John Winthrop, by Rev. J. H. Twichell,	8
Thomas Hooker, by Rev. George Leon Walker, D. D.,	8
Cotton Mather, by Prof. Barrett Wendell, (or others in the set)	8
Colonial Days and Dames, and Through Colonial Doorways, Edition de Luxe; 2 vols., in a box,	25
Through Evangeline's Country; 30 half tone engravings,	20
Three Heroines of New England; 80 illustrations,	20
Costume in Colonial Times,	13
Our Colonial Homes, by Samuel Adams Drake,	10
The Oliver Wendell Holmes Year-book, with fine portrait,	10
American Book Plates, by Charles Dexter Allen, Hartford,	35

IV. BOOKS OF ADVENTURE, FOR CHILDREN AND "GROWN-UPS."

Mrs. Burnett's Juveniles: 1, Little Lord Fauntleroy,	20
2, Sara Crewe,	10
3, Little Saint Elizabeth,	15
4, Giovanni and the other,	15
5, Piccino,	15
The Count of Monte Cristo and Three Musketeers, each 30 subs,	60
Stanley J. Weyman's New Books: 1, My Lady Rotha; 2, Under the Red Robe; 3, A Gentleman of France; 4, The House of the Wolf; 4 vols., by the Prince of Modern Romance,	50
The Norseland Series, by H. H. Boyesen: 1, Norseland Tales; 2, Against Heavy Odds; 3, Boyhood in Norway; 4, The Modern Vikings; 4 vols. in a box,	50
Three New Henty Books: 1, In the Heart of the Rockies; 2, Wulf, the Saxon; 3, When London Burned; (15 each,)	45
The Kombi Camera, a midget Camera. All other makes of Cameras at proportionate rates,	35
Sandow's Method of Physical Culture,	20
The Jungle Book, by Rudyard Kipling, (13th thousand,)	15
The Brownies Around the World, by Palmer Cox,	15
The Century Book for Young Americans,	15
Little Men and Women, for 1895; for your little ones,	10
Babyland, the babies' own magazine, for 1895,	5

Silver and Gold Library; pub. at $1.25 each; extra English cloth, marbled sides.
The Century Library, large type, fine paper.
The Chandos Classics, 6,000,000 sold.
The World's Best Books, extra cloth, and
The Home Library. We offer any one volume (500 books) of either of these five series for 5 subs.
Send for full catalogue.

THE CONNECTICUT QUARTERLY CO.,
Box 565, Hartford, Conn.

From a painting by G. A. Reckard.

"THE CLOSING HOUR OF DAY CAME ONWARD, MANTLED O'ER WITH SOBER GRAY."

The Connecticut Quarterly.

"Leave not your native land behind."—Thoreau.

FIRST QUARTER.

Vol. 1   January, February and March, 1895.   No. 1

I. HOMES OF GENIUS.

BY W. FARRAND FELCH.

Not every home is historic. It is seldom that a house is greater than its present occupants. Being simply a shell or shelter, and not carried around like the snail's, it acquires little individuality. But if, by force of past associations and inherent interest, it attains to greater consideration than its present occupants, it surely is as much entitled to the historic increment as if it actually lived, moved, and had a being. There are those among us who are so thoroughly attached to the houses in which we had birth, wherein we lived in childhood, where we acquired manhood, or have led calm, contented, marital careers for long years past, that we learn to love them as if they were human and possessed personal attributes.

Such a sentiment cannot be translated and written on paper. Your home or mine may be of the simplest and humblest description, but it is our own;

and while it may be regarded cavalierly by others, as only one of a multitude, to us it is hedged almost with divinity. But it is not of such that we write. The homes of culture, refinement, luxury, and picturesque beauty attract the most attention. But above and beyond all these, the home of genius possesses the greatest fascination, be it a sturdy cotter's hovel, a lordly castle, a plain exterior, or a gaudy facade decorated with tablet or emblazoned with armorial bearings.

It is our especial privilege to be able to present to the curious reader a group of pictures of the exteriors of homes of genius that are not in any sense displeasing or disenchanting; all possessing a quiet dignity appropriate to their environment, and with no evidence that their builders sought for extraneous details or decorations out of keeping with the character of the occupants. In

HOME OF MRS. SIGOURNEY.

fact, it would be extremely inappropriate in "the land of steady habits" to overstep the bounds of propriety in this as in any other case.

It is a common saying that "one cannot throw a stone in Hartford without hitting an author." And, indeed, in certain sections, this is no doubt true, provided one is not an expert marksman. There appears to be a universal tendency in every city or large congeries of people for folk of each vocation to "flock by themselves." So that all trades, all professions even, have their select haunts and habitats, as if they had been sieved and winnowed and fallen in allotted spots. It is not remarkable in the lesser walks of life that competition should force tradesmen together; but authors are not a gregarious class, and prefer isolation and self-communing. So that it seems singular to find, really within a stone's throw of one another, the homes of some of the leading lights in our literature, their occupants dwelling together in unity of spirit and interests, while around, in near proximity, naturally congregate a lesser coterie

HISTORIC HOMES.

growing in strength and grace. It is in fact almost a literary colony — not, however, on the plan of the famous Brook Farm experiment.

It is not our purpose to delve in the past literary history of the city, where we should find an embarrassment of riches, in the days of the "Hartford Wits," a century or less ago, but to give a glimpse of the homes of the present contingency. One naturally reverts to Mrs. Sigourney as almost of this latter generation of writers, and yet so much of the past that she has gained already a reputation in directions that she could not have anticipated.

The home of Mrs. Sigourney was on Asylum street, now overlooking the railroad embankment that separates it from the Capitol grounds and Bushnell Park. It was originally owned by Charles Sigourney, her husband, and was built in the old Colonial style, with massive Ionic columns to the two-story "portico," which is surmounted by a wide cornice. South of the house is a brick barn, on which the letters "C. S." (the proprietor's initials) appear in ironwork, on the Capitol side of the building. In this barn was set apart for years a room in which traveling indigents — not of our common genus "tramp" in that early day — could find shelter and comfort for the night; and it was always open to those of that class of men who were not objectionable. In our degenerate day, when the "common tramp" marks your front gate with all sorts of cabalistic signs, to denote to the next comer of his ilk the degree of your hospitality and the prowess of your watch-dog, such "Open Hearth" receptions are not thought of for a moment.

Mrs. Sigourney came to this home as a bride, and much of her literary work was accomplished here. It is not even a trifle poetic in appearance to-day, albeit the outlook is over the beautiful park; and it would be a very modern and *fin de siecle* muse that could find inspiration, tormented with momentary interruptions of noisy locomotive leviathans almost at the front door.

The house is surrounded by many of the old forest trees, and part of the original orchard still remains. It stands back from the street at some distance, and would not attract more than passing notice if it were not pointed out to the stranger. Ex-Lieutenant Governor Julius Catlin spent a large part of his life in this house, dying there a few years since. The railroad has despoiled the place of its poetic suggestions and attractiveness, and it is fast becoming a forgotten, or at least a neglected, landmark.

A later writer, one who was intimately acquainted with the poet, writes of her literary friendships:

"In the words of S. G. Goodrich, the historian, Lydia Huntley soon became 'the presiding genius of the young social circle of Hartford; and as the years went by she gathered about her a circle of distinguished people such as any woman might feel honored to consider her *salon*.' After her marriage to Charles Sigourney, her beautiful home . . . . became the place most sought for by literary and artistic men and women who came to Hartford. It was also the scene of her greatest literary activity. David Clark was her friend and financial adviser. Mr. Wadsworth encouraged and aided her literary work

Whittier, whom she intensely admired, was a frequent visitor, during his sojourn in this city, while connected with the *New England Weekly Review*, subsequently merged with the *Courant*.

William Cullen Bryant was an intimate friend of our Hartford queen of song, and I have before me, as I write, a volume of his 'Thirty Poems,' which he gave to Mrs. Sigourney, with an autograph inscription to her. Every one was pleased to be numbered among her friends. She was a constant attendant at Christ Church, where she was a communicant. There stands a beautiful memorial tablet of her, erected by her friends and admirers. Bishop Williams, who was her trusted friend, has given it a suitable inscription, and the epitaph is from the pen of Whittier. This, it has been said, practically embodies a biography of the poetess:

> 'She sang alone, ere womanhood had known
> The gift of song which fills the air to-day;
> Tender and sweet, a music all her own
> May fitly linger where she knelt to pray.'"

One of the most attractive streets in the city has been honored with the poet's name, and a new park adjoining it bids fair to achieve a like distinction. It is amusing, to one who cares to notice the humorous side of illiterate life,

HOME OF MRS. STOWE.

how varied the pronunciation of the name of this street has become with those who do not seem to be capable of pronouncing, much less spelling it, and perhaps have never heard of the poet — ringing all the changes, "Siggernay," "Signerary," "Siggernerary," "Singery," "Sijourney," "Sy-gourney"—with the accent on the second syllable — and many other tortuous permutations of a not unmusical and honest old Huguenot name.

Perhaps of more interest in the eyes of the present generation of sightseers is the home of Mrs. Harriet Beecher Stowe, a name that has become a household word in every home in the land. It is on Forest street, which derives its name, as one may readily suppose ("guess," we had almost said), from being hewn out of the forest primeval at no distant bygone year. It is a plain unpretending home, as one may see, but is so distinctly homelike, broadside to the street and near it, — indicating open and abundant hospitality within, as well as a desire on their part to be near to and in touch with the world without. There is no attempt to hide from the public gaze; and perhaps one may have the rare

HISTORIC HOMES.

good fortune now and then to see the aged occupant herself in a stolen glimpse. It is no impious motive that leads the curious to seek for this boon, and perhaps it is more or less pardonable; besides, she seldom goes abroad now, except in the best weather and at rare intervals.

Mrs. Stowe was born June 14, 1811, in Litchfield, Conn., and is now nearly 84 years of age. Her eldest sister, Catharine, was born in 1800; then came William, Edward, Mary, George, Harriet, who died at the age of a month, Harriet Elizabeth (herself, named after the one who had just died before her birth, according to the old Puritan precedent); two years younger was Henry Ward, and next came Charles. These were the children of the first wife of Rev. Lyman Beecher, named Roxanna Foote, of the almost as famous Foote family. Of the other members of these families we may have something to say anon.

Harriet Beecher first came to Hartford at the age of thirteen, to attend a school recently established by her sister Catharine. Of this period she wrote later: "When I entered the school there were not more than twenty-five scholars in it, but it afterwards numbered its pupils by the hundreds. The schoolroom was on Main street, nearly opposite Christ Church, over Sheldon & Colton's harness store, at the sign of the two white horses." February 26, 1827, Catharine wrote to her father, Dr. Beecher: "My affairs go on well. The stock is all taken up, and next week I hope to have out the prospectus of the Hartford Female Seminary." In this Harriet remained as pupil and teacher until 1832.

In 1832 Dr. Beecher received a call to become President of the Lane Theological Seminary, in Cincinnati, and thither also went his daughters (excepting Mary, who had married Mr. Thomas Perkins of Hartford, and remained here) to establish another ladies' seminary. In 1836 Harriet became the second wife of Prof. Calvin E. Stowe of the Lane Theological Seminary. Mrs. Stowe had her first introduction to slavery while on a visit in Kentucky, on an estate which afterwards figured as that of "Mr. Shelby" in "Uncle Tom's Cabin."

We cannot linger over the portrayal of her later literary career in the short space given us, but must perforce speak of her return to Hartford in 1863, when Prof. Stowe's long and pleasant Andover connection ended. They occupied a house in Hartford built on the bank of Park river, in a grove of oaks that had been a favorite resort in her girlhood; she had declared then if she ever built a house it should stand in that spot. It was then beyond the city limits and a beautiful location, but the family occupied it only a few years, as factories sprang up in the near vicinity, and to escape their encroachments the Stowes removed to their present home, which we have pictured, on Forest street, in 1873. The first house, the only one ever planned by Mrs. Stowe, is now occupied by several families as a tenement house.

Mr. and Mrs. Stowe resided in Florida, at Mandarin, for several winters, from 1866 onward. Here they had a many gabled cottage overlooking the St. Johns river, which is at this place five miles wide, in a grove of moss-grown live-oaks, and with a well-tended orange grove in the rear. On the broad veranda the aged professor spent many quiet hours, in that absolute peace and restful calm which his scholarly nature delighted in; at almost any hour the patriarchal figure might be seen sitting on the broad veranda, with a basket of books close at hand, many of them in the dead languages. The last winter spent in their southern home was that of 1883-84, as the professor's health was too precarious to permit the long journey thither the next winter. He died in Hartford, in August, 1886, full of years and honors. He was the original of "Harry" in "Old Town Folks," a book which embodies many of his strange experiences.

None of the incidents or characters in the Old Town series are ideal; they are true to nature not only, but actually happened. Sam Lawson was a real

HOME OF CHARLES DUDLEY WARNER.

character. Mrs. Stowe began writing in 1833, and ended in 1881, in that time publishing thirty-two works, besides an incredible amount of short stories, letters of travel, essays, and other matter; her literary life really began in 1852, with "Uncle Tom's Cabin," and the twenty-six years that ended in 1878 with "Poganuc People" were crowded with hard work. Her public life ended soon after that, and she has rested from her arduous labors since. To a friend she writes, later: "I have thought much lately of the possibility of my leaving you all and going home. I am come to that stage of my pilgrimage that is within sight of the River of Death, and I feel that now I must have all in readiness day and night for the messenger of the King."

The homes of the three most noted of the Hartford *literati* of the present day are in speaking distance of one another, in an odd-shaped triangle. Mr. Warner's home is situated somewhat back from Forest street, while Mr. Clemens' home faces, or should face, Farmington Avenue, which intersects Forest street, but in point of fact the rear or side of the house is presented to the avenue, so that it is a constant source of gossip with passers-by that "Mark Twain built his kitchen in front of his house, facing the street." But this is hardly the truth, as one may see by closer examination, and a knowledge of the bizarre order of architecture adopted for the purpose, conforming to the rolling contour of the ground on which the house stands. Mr. Warner's home is in the rear of both Mrs. Stowe's and Mr. Clemens' homes, and has the distinction of being on a lot which contains more of the original monarchs of the forest than any other lot in the city. It is an imposing structure, especially when seen from a distance.

The golden age of Hartford literature, at least as far as the present century is concerned, was in the "seventies" and "eighties." Mr. Warner came to Hartford in 1860, as one of the editors of the *Press*, and later became one of the editors and proprietors of the *Courant*, with which he is still connected; but he did not begin to write books until 1871, when "My Summer in a Garden" appeared. Mrs. Stowe returned to Hartford in 1864, and several of her works were published prior to the "seventies," notably "The Minister's Wooing" and "Old Town Folks," both in 1868. Mr. Clemens has lived in Hartford since 1871, at which time only his "Innocents Abroad" had appeared in book form, in 1869.

It is with the advent of the last of the famous trio that their most productive period began, continuing almost uninterruptedly for two decades. In 1871 appeared Mrs. Stowe's "Pink and White Tyranny," and "My Wife and I;" Mr. Warner's "Summer in a Garden," which had been originally printed in the columns of the *Courant*, and attracted considerable attention, was published the same year. In 1872 came Mr. Clemens' "Roughing It," and Mr. Warner's "Saunterings" and his inimitable "Back Log Studies." In 1873, Mrs. Stowe's "Palmetto Leaves;" in 1874 Mr. Warner's "Baddeck," and Mr. Perkins' "Scrope;" in 1875 Mrs. Stowe's "We and Our Neighbors," and the next year Mr. Clemens' "Mark Twain Sketches," and his first boy's book, the delightful "Tom Sawyer," while Mr. Warner produced the first of his transatlantic saunterings, "My Winter On the Nile," following it the next year with "In the Levant." In 1877 also, Mr. Perkins collected a number of his stories into a volume called "Devil Puzzlers and Other Stories." In 1878 Mr. Warner published "Being a Boy," and "In the Wilderness," and the same year appeared Mrs. Stowe's "Poganuc People." This is but the record of one decade. In the next decade Mrs. Stowe's pen became inactive and she retired from public life, as already noted. But Mr. Clemens inaugurated his fascinating series of Don Quixotic romances, located abroad, "The Prince and the Pauper" and others, while Mr. Warner continued his conquests of unexplored territory, and still has "other worlds to conquer."

CHARLES DUDLEY WARNER.

Mr. Warner was born in Plainfield, Massachusetts, Sept. 12, 1829, and as Dr. Twichell says of him, "the ink began to stir in his veins when he was a boy." He has embodied in his charming volume, "Being a Boy," his recollections of his boyhood, in a typical Calvinistic New England village of fifty years ago. While in college he contributed to *Putnam's* and the "*Knickerbocker*" magazines, and edited a "Book of Eloquence" soon after graduating in 1851 from Hamilton College. He subsequently graduated from the law department of the University of Pennsylvania in 1856, and practiced his profession in Chicago until 1860, when he was called east to become assistant editor of the *Press*, which was subsequently merged into the *Courant* of which he became co-editor with Gen. Hawley, and subsequently editor. In 1884 he became one of the editors of Harper's *Monthly Magazine* and has continued in that connection to the present, during which time his most important work has been published in its pages, as for instance "Studies in the South," followed by some Mexican papers, and by "Studies in the Great West." His later work has been in similar lines and fully as successful, in particular, "Their Pilgrimage" and the present year "The Golden House," — a study of socialistic tendencies. He was for several years a member of the Connecticut State Committee on Prisons, and of the National Prison Association, and also for a number of years a member of the Park Commission of Hartford. Yale gave him the degree of Master of Arts in 1872 and Dartmouth in 1884.

In this connection we cannot well refrain from quoting from a felicitous sketch of his home, by his neighbor and friend, Rev. Dr. Joseph H. Twichell, which appeared in *The Critic* several years ago, and afterwards in a book called "Authors at Home," published in 1888 :

"It stands unenclosed, several rods back from the street in a grove of noble chestnuts, having no other grounds nor needing any either. Close behind, at the foot of a steep, bushy bank sweeps a bend of a considerable stream. 'The Garden,' which Mr. Warner has made so famous, will be looked for in vain on the premises. . . . . It pertained to another house where Mr. Warner lived when 'My Summer in a Garden' was written; the fireside of it, also, is celebrated in his 'Back-Log Studies,' to not a few of his readers the most delightful of his books, — a house dear to the recollection of many a friend and guest. . . . . As one would anticipate, the interior of Mr. Warner's house is genial and homelike. The cheerful drawing-room opens into a wide, bright, music-room, making, with it, one shapely apartment of generous, hospitable proportions. The furnishing is simple, but in every item pleasing. A hint of modern decorative art is there, though under rational restraint. A chimney-piece of Oriental design rises above the fireplace of the music-room set with antique tiles brought by Mr. Warner from Damascus. Other spoils of travel are displayed here and there, with pictures and engravings of the best. In the nook of a bow-window is a lovely cast of the Venus of Milo, which, when it was made a birthday present in the family, was inscribed 'The Venus of My-h' eye.' The house is full of books. Every part of it is more or less of a library. Laden shelves flank the landings of the broad stairway, and so on all the way up to the workroom in the third story, where a statuette of Thackeray, on our author's table seems to survey with amusement the accumulated miscellaneous mass of literature stacked and piled around. . . . . Upon any volume of this collection Mr. Warner can lay his hand in an instant — when he has found where it is. . . . . His home is a thoroughly charming one in every way, and whoever may have the pleasure of an evening there will come away wishing he might write an article on the mistress of that house."

Mrs. Warner is considered to be the most accomplished amateur musician in New England. Most of the able musical criticisms so prominent throughout Mr. Warner's writings are due to her influence.

Mr. Frederic B. Perkins is not now a resident of Hartford, but born here and closely allied in many ways with this city. He is a year older than Mr. Warner, to the month. He is a grandson of Lyman Beecher, a son of Thomas C. Perkins who married Mary Beecher, and is also a brother-in-law of Rev. Dr. Edward Everett Hale, of Boston. He does not approve of sketches of authors, on general principles, and of himself in particular; but from his associations with Hartford, we shall perhaps be forgiven if we give the barest outline of his literary career. He was a member of the Class of '50 at Yale, but left college in '48 to begin the study of law. In 1851 he was admitted, at Hartford, and a year later he entered the Connecticut State Normal School, where he graduated the same year. He held various positions in Hartford until 1854, in which year he went to New York, remaining until 1857; then returning to Hartford, he became assistant editor of Barnard's *American Journal of Education*, and was also appointed librarian of the Connecticut Historical Society. Later he became secretary of the Boston Public Library, and from '80-'87 he was librarian of the San Francisco free public library, and still later was employed in the Sutro library. In '81 he published his "Rational Classification of Books," and a revised edition the next year. He has also been editorially connected with various papers and magazines. Among his writings are "Scrope" (Boston, 1874), "My Three Conversations with Miss Chester" (1877), "Devil Puzzlers and other studies" (1877), "Charles Dickens, his Life and Works" (1877). He also compiled a "Check-List of American Local History" (Boston, 1876), and the fourth edition of his "Best Reading" appeared in 1877, the first edition, in collaboration with the late George P. Putnam, having appeared in '72. He has contributed to various periodicals sundry sketches and some fifty stories, the best known of which is perhaps "The Minister Manufactory." In his "Devil Puzzlers," his sketch entitled "Childhood" possesses some local interest, being to some extent autobiographic.

FREDERIC B. PERKINS.

"Mark Twain's" life has been so often told that it seems a work of supererogation to repeat; as our space is limited we will only give a few salient points in his career, such as relate to this city. In 1868-9 Mr. Clemens was in New York city looking around for a publisher for his recently completed "Innocents Abroad." The late Albert D. Richardson, having had several books published in Hartford, offered to place the manuscript in the hands of his publishers here. Mark had previously been to Hartford in August, conferring with a publisher but met little encouragement. As he expressed himself to his friends, "These publishers have astonished as much conceit out of me as a long siege of sea-sickness.' The result is well known; Mr. Bliss publishing the book on his own account, against the advice and objections of the other officers and directors. The sale, including pirated editions, reached 200,000 copies. Mark was crazed with joy, and wrote to an old steamboat friend, "Thirty tons of paper have been used in publishing my book, 'Innocents Abroad.' It has met with a greater sale than any book ever published, except 'Uncle Tom's Cabin.' . . . Not so bad for a scrub pilot, is it?"

On the occasion of his first visit to Hartford he wrote in one of his newspaper letters, at the close, his impressions of the city which was afterward to become his home:

"I have been about ten days in Hartford, and shall return there before very long. I think it must be the handsomest city in the Union in summer. It is the moneyed center of the State; and one of its capitals, also, for Connecticut is so law-abiding, and so addicted to law, that there is not room enough in one

HISTORIC HOMES.

city to manufacture all the articles they need. Hartford is the place where the insurance companies all live. They use some of the houses for dwellings. The others are for insurance offices. So it is easy to see that there is quite a spirit of speculative enterprise there. Many of the inhabitants have retired from business, but the others labor along in the old customary way, as presidents of insurance companies."

HOME OF SAMUEL L. CLEMENS.

At a Hartford dinner party one day, the subject of eternal life and future punishment came up for a lengthy discussion, in which Mark Twain took no part. A lady near him, turned suddenly and inquired:

SAMUEL L. CLEMENS.

"Why do you not say anything? I want your opinion."

Mr. Clemens replied gravely: "Madam, you must excuse me, I am silent of necessity. I have friends in both places."

His daughter at one time kept a diary, which was brought to the attention of her father. After this Clemens did and said several things that were intended to attract the child's attention, and found them duly noted afterward. But one day the following entry occurred:

"I don't think I'll put down anything about father, for I think he does things to have me notice him, and I believe he reads this diary."

This is perhaps the same daughter who in London, quite recently, was asked about one of her father's latest books, and replied:

"Really, I can't give an opinion. Papa's books bore me terribly. I haven't read half of them. Papa is the nicest thing in the world, but, oh dear! I do wish he was not a famous funny man."

Probably no one would laugh more heartily over such a criticism and from such a source than Mr. Clemens himself.

HOUSE AND HOME.

Where is the house, the house we love?
By field or river, square or street,
The house our hearts go dreaming of,
That lonely waits our hurrying feet;
The house to which we come, we come,
To make that happy house our home.

Oh dear dream house! for you I store
A medley of such curious things,
As a wise thrush goes counting o'er,
Ere the glad morn of songs and wings,
When a small nest makes all her heaven,
And a true mate that sings at even.

Up those dim stairs my heart will steal,
And quietly through the listening rooms,
And long in prayerful love will kneel,
And in the sweet-aired twilight glooms,
Will set a curtain straight, or chair,
And dust and order, and make fair.

Oh, tarrying Time, hasten, until
You light our hearth-fires, dear and warm,
Set pictures on these walls so chill,
And draw our curtains 'gainst the storm,
And shut us in together, Time,
In a new world, a happier clime!

Whether our house be new or old
We care not; we will drive away
From last year's nest its memories cold,
And all be gold that once was gray,
Oh dear dream-house, for which we pray,
Our feet come slowly up your way.

FARMINGTON STREET.

TUNXIS, WHICH IS FARMINGTON.

BY MARTHA STANLEY.

Ever since the time when the ancient people came to Elim, where were twelve wells of water and three score and ten palm trees, water and trees have stood as symbols of rest and refreshment.

From the standpoint of every true New Englander, all country without is desert; but once within the magic border, the traveler finds a region abundant in groves and well-springs, a veritable Elim wherein to pitch his tent. Nor need one travel far to find these spots. Only the difference which distance makes lies between them and the cities. Especially is this true of Farmington, near to Hartford on the one hand and to New Britain on the other. It is as remote from each as though impenetrable forests lay between.

There are modern ways of reaching Farmington, but he who travels for pleasure will forego the convenience of the railroad and come by stage from Hartford; thus entering the town from the hill, where the great elm tree stands, and the Inn which bears its name bids the traveler welcome.

What a charm there is in being a stranger! letting imagination take the place of knowledge and so creating a dream-village, out of which one may pass into reality as gradually as out of sleep. In this way nothing is forced upon us. We walk up and down the long street until we feel at home beneath its trees. At sunset, when we turn our faces westward, the winding course of the willows and

---

NOTE—The historical side of Farmington has been so well treated in the article by Ex-President Porter in the Memorial History of Hartford County, and an address by Mr. Julius Gay, that it is not dealt with here. This does not preclude the possibility that an historical article may appear in these pages at another time in regard to Farmington.—ED.

alders tells of the pleasant river that they guard. We become acquainted with the mountains round about; and soon the houses, grown familiar to us, begin to give up their secrets.

It is held that appearances are deceitful; nevertheless, nettles and thorns proclaim sloth now as truly as they did in Solomon's time; while on the other hand a flower or a curtained window proclaim thrift and hospitality, and may be our open sesame. The scent of burning wood and the curling line of smoke tell their story night after night, until we know where are the cosiest firesides. So we begin to feel in touch with the life around us. Our dream-village resolves itself into individual homes, and we are seized with that human interest which, sooner or later, under all circumstances, must assert itself.

This is no place for Shakesperian discussion as to what is in a name, but it

ELM TREE INN.

may be noted that after settling the points of the compass, the first question asked by the stranger is: "Who lives in the house across the way?" and having received an answer, he repeats the name with a satisfaction which is genuine if not understandable, albeit he probably will never exchange a word with the owner of the place.

So in our village of Farmington we begin to ask questions. Indeed we do not so much ask them as we get them answered; for once having shown proper interest, information comes — sometimes we know not how.

There is a little store at the end of the street, near the Inn, where one may find things both "old and new." Perchance, if on a summer evening, one joins the little group which sits outside with chairs atilt, he may learn much which will serve him in his next day's walk. Let him who would have a happy mixture of truth and fiction hire a horse, and so obtain converse with that encyclopædic individual, the liveryman. What a fund is his! One

THE STORE.

can almost fancy that the patient plodding horses have caught the secret of many a quiet drive and confided the same, as at evening they responded to the master's caress.

Be this as it may, knowledge comes, and what we have known as "the Colonial house within the gate" becomes the Thomas Cowles' place, and gives us our first hint of the part played by Farmington in the War of the Revolution. It was a young officer in Burgoyne's army, of clever brain and cunning hand,

THOMAS COWLES' HOUSE.

who designed this house; and so left one evidence that the British, had they been so minded, could have built up as effectually as they tore down.

So we walk the street, and in time call the houses all by name. To the oldest house in town we pay the respect that age demands. It is the lilac-bush at the corner that gives the touch that makes the picture typical of old New England homes. The traveler through the country must have noticed how truly the lilac is a part of the oldest homes, and oftentimes when the house has fallen away, these trees gently cover the ruin and mark the spot where once was life.

THE OLDEST HOUSE.

There is such a strong week-day attraction in a country church that in most cases one prefers to obtain the key and enter alone, to waiting until such time as stated service gives entrance. Why do we imagine that worship waits only upon the assembling of ourselves together? How thoroughly Charles Lamb understood when he wrote: "Wouldst thou know the beauty of holiness? Go alone on some weekday; traverse the cool aisles of some country church; think of the piety that has kneeled there. With no disturbing emotions, no cross conflicting comparisons, drink in the tranquility of the place.' The associations of more than a hundred years are centered in this place; and yet this house is but the child of the one which was before, and that in turn points backward to those earlier days when the first little meeting house planted in the forest, was the sign of the cloud and the fire to our forefathers, dwelling amid the dangers of an unsettled country. All the reverence we are wont to give to historic places, all the homage due to heroes, should be given here; for what is written history but the evidence of all that is unwritten, and what is a hero but the representative of many?

THE CHURCH.

It would seem from the exceeding plainness of this old house of worship that our elders thought not of beauty as the hand-maide of truth; and yet we find it crowned with a spire of most delicate design. Once having seen this spire against its background of blue sky or green hill, it becomes the central feature in the landscape, and from every point of view is the guide to the village in the valley.

It is in full harmony with the New England spirit that we find in Farmington a school, which may be said to be the distinctive feature of the place. The very name, Porter, has an educational sound to New England ears, and Miss Porter's school has long been the embodiment of that wisdom whose ways are ways of pleasantness. This institution, planted in 1844, has taken deep root in the little village and brought forth fruit, as do all beneficent things. There is also the "Art and Music Hall" on the hillside, built and presented to Miss Porter by "her girls."

MISS PORTER'S SCHOOL.

At the south end of the street may be seen the "Lodge," owned by the pupils past and present, and maintained by them for the benefit and pleasure of working girls who fill the house during the summer months. It is when we visit the cemetery, overlooking the Farmington river, and have read the inscription on the Indian monument, that we become interested in the original tenants of this ground. Modern title deeds lose their value, and

> "Owners and occupants of earlier dates
> From graves forgotten stretch their dusty hands
> And hold in mortmain still their old estates."

We are taken back to the year 1640, when the Tunxis tribe of Indians fished in these waters and hunted in the great forests beyond; food there was sufficient, — salmon and venison. Along the river banks were the wigwam homes of the living; on this grassy slope above were resting places of their dead. Then the white man came through the woods from Hartford and made a treaty with Sequasson, the sachem, and the land was divided.

After five years Tunxis was called Farmington and, in like manner, time removed the remnant of the tribe which bore the name. They were not exterminated however, but as the forests were open and travel became less dangerous, they naturally became absorbed in other tribes. For many years after their departure they made yearly pilgrimages to this spot, and held midnight dances around the graves of their ancestors. Farmington has the reputation of comparatively happy relations with the Indian tribes. Very rarely do we read of treachery or advantage on either side.

There will be those who will be attracted by the inscription, "Memento Mori," over the gateway which leads into the old burying ground. Not alone in this enclosure, but everywhere, as we learn of the past, do the words come again, "Memento Mori," and we ask concerning the fathers of this good land.

The story is like many another of brave, true men who separated themselves from the parent colony and pushed farther on into the wilderness, to replenish the earth and subdue it. We know how, for fear of enemies and wild beasts, and for desire of being near the meeting house, they built near each other on one long street.

ART AND MUSIC HALL.

To us who sit in peace and plenty, those days are of romantic interest. We live in towns that are made for us. But think of laying out a town! The record has all the flavor of patriarchal times. They came to Round Hill in the meadow and measured,—To the north three miles, to the south five miles, to the east two miles, to the west two miles. Such lands as were not held by the proprietors were reserved for the purposes of public comfort and convenience. All lands without were likewise measured and divided into shares; to every man a share according to his wordly possessions. But, to the Rev. Samuel Hooker, first pastor of the Farmington church, was given a double portion, no doubt because they loved him, for he is remembered in written history as an "animated and pious Divine."

The town increased and was prospered, keeping in touch the while with all political questions of the day, and the growth of the country; and failing not at the appointed time to send her sons forth into battle. The little town furnished enough men for a regiment, and this statement interpreted is: "That every young man worthy of consideration was at some time in the field."

The village street formed a part of the highway from Boston to New York, and General Washington often passed through it, and sometimes halted to refresh himself at one of the hospitable inns. Perchance if one makes acquaintance with those of ancient heritage in the town, he may be shown some dainty china or rare bits of silk, which were once imported by Farmington merchants. You smile and scarcely believe that in this quiet place were once flourishing business houses? Even so, there were. The sign on the stores, "East India and West India Goods" bore witness, and the rustle of silks on Sunday gave testimony that foreign invasion had taken place and put to flight the homespun; while in the harbor of New Haven, and at Wethersfield, floated the vessels which were owned by these merchantmen.

VILLAGE HALL.

If the visitor to Farmington cares to inquire further into the history of the town, he will find information sure and plentiful from other sources. If he is but a passer-by, content to know the little here set forth, let him recognize what this little stands for, a tribute to a typical New England village; and in parting lift his hat in reverence thereto.

NASTURTIUMS.

The whole little hill town blazed with them,
    Of strangest scarlet and oddest pink.
If you walked through the streets your garment's hem
Brushed by the flower and bent the stem
    That leaned from the gray fence chink.

And every gay little girl one met
    Had their colors glowing against her hair,
Or had daintily in her bosom set
Some faded tint like a pink regret,
    Or a little rose-flushed despair.

And through the open, bountiful doors,
    Down the glimmering dusk of ancient halls,
In the old blue ware of orient shores,
You saw them grouped on the shining floors,
    Or shelved on the paneled walls.

For the whole little hill-town blazed with them
    And every girl had a flower to wear,
Hued like a star or hued like a gem,
Or a scarlet flame on a flickering stem,
    Or gold as her own gold hair.

THE CHARTER OAK.

ELLEN BRAINERD PECK.

Time's shadows thronging, gather fast
   About the deeds of storied years;
The fact that lived in sacred past,
   Now as a legend re-appears.

A lofty oak up-reared its head,
   With stately branches spreading wide
To this the red-man pointing, said,
   'To us it is a silent guide,

That shows us that the spring draws near,
   For when its tender leaves are born —
No larger than the grey-mouse ear —
   It then is time to plant the corn.

Oh, white man, let our totem be
   And let the listening Indian hark
Unto its whispering boughs and see
   Its opening buds — the spring-tide mark.'

And so the old tree held its place,
   And felt the seasons ebb and flow,
As stalwart as the conquering race
   Beneath its boughs — a passing show.

Until at last, it chanced to be
   A safe that guarded, as if gold,
The charter of our liberty —
   In those grand, earnest days of old.

The red man's form dim memories fold;
   Across the past his shadow wan
Flits on, to silences untold,
   Long since; the old tree too has gone, —

Has vanished: for, by Nature's hand
   Forever was its hand laid low;
Its story, on Time's way will stand,
   A mile-stone, while the ages go.

TRIO AND TRIPOD

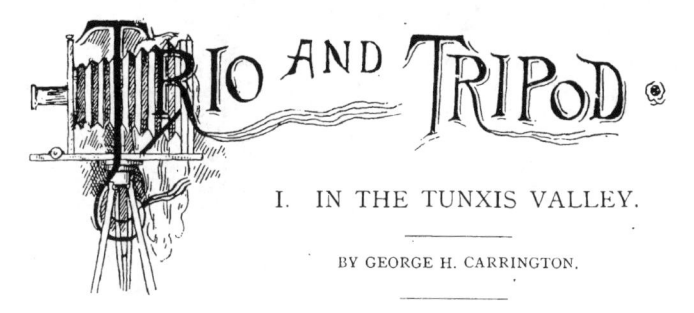

I. IN THE TUNXIS VALLEY.

BY GEORGE H. CARRINGTON.

"With a trio of tripods, a coach and a span,
And with cameras four, two boys and a man,
Made a start, quite intent to photo creation,
For profit and pleasure and art recreation.
They "exposed" on the towns, on the mountains and ridges,
The people, the meadows, the brooks and the bridges.
And though pictures obtained counted up by the score
They lamented when, passing, they lost one or more.

Now, the nags of this team had a deep chestnut hue,
And the natives considered a "chestnut," the crew.
They called them the mail, and gypsies and drummers,
Surveyors and burglars, map-makers and bummers.
The boy was called John — he was such a good waiter;
And t'other was "Huggins"— on account of his natur';
And the man was, from facts that ought not to be told,
Soon named "Sir Philip," and "the boy that was old"—

So sang "Sir Philip" himself,—as he had been dubbed by "the boys,"

SIR PHILIP'S PEPPERIDGE TREE.

who deemed that his majestic presence, enhanced by his flowing beard, merited a title that became his appearance.

We were on the mountain road from New Britain to Farmington, when Sir Philip pointed to an umbrella-like tree, upon a hill-side pasture, and told how he had photographed it and given it an honored place in his collection for years, labelled "Pepperidge Tree," until "the other day I was up there after pepperidge blossoms, and found that it was a hornbeam. Of course we all make mistakes sometimes, *especially* the best of us," sighed he.

At the top of the hill, just before descending into the quiet village, a glimpse was caught of the beautiful Farmington valley. Flanked by Talcott mountain on the right, the broad meadows, with a most picturesque setting, stretch away to the northern line of hills where the "barn-doors" peep up in the blue distance. Along the central part of the field, the line of trees marks the course of the river that flows through and gives its name to the valley. Here, then, was the enchanted land through which we were to pass.

Sir Philip recalled how, long years ago, he had traversed the region in the capacity of a commercial traveler, seeking whom he could sell, and he anticipated the delights of comparing the then and the now.

Huggins, in turn, well remembered the time when, one summer afternoon, he strolled along the banks of the Farmington. He had copied the inscriptions on the Indian monument, in the cemetery by the river, and photographed both of them. He had sat in the shade and dozed and dreamed, as he watched the haymakers in the distant fields, wishing that he too was a farmer and could lead such a happy life. He had wandered along to where the piers of the old aqueduct were still standing and sat there musing on the glory of that by-gone time in the palmy days of canal life, when the boats glided over them and the boatman's horn resounded through the vale. As he mused, his mind recurred to the time when the red man inhabited the land, and he repeated to himself that refrain from Channing:

"Thus, perchance, some Indian hunter,
Many a lagging year agone,
Gliding o'er thy rippling waters,
Lowly hummed a natural song.

Now the sun's behind the willows,
Now he gleams along the waves,
Faintly o'er the wearied billows,
Come the spirits of the braves."

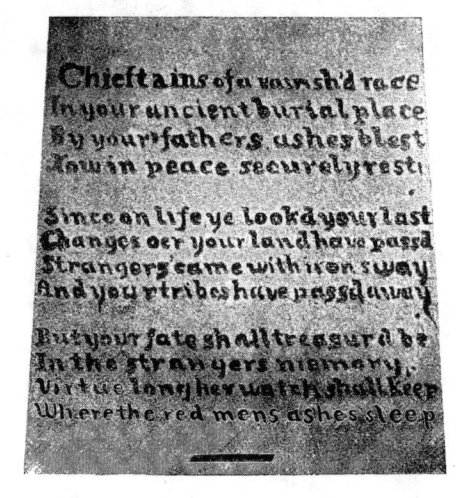

He had dozed off thus into a quiet sleep, and was dreaming that the Indian was crossing the river in his birch-bark, and was bearing down upon him, when the scene changed — and somehow he was transported to the home of his boyhood and the school-mates of his youth. Who, among them all, should be remembered more clearly than Clara — the little girl with wavy blonde hair and laughing blue eyes — to whom he addressed his first *billet-doux* and hence became the victim of school-boy teasing. Well, he did like her pretty well, and now she had grown to be a young lady and was a school teacher holding forth in the little school house near at hand, and had come down to see him and talk over old times. He was having a delightful time, sitting beside her on the bank, talking of the old home in the Green Mountain state and what had transpired since leaving there — when, as the conversation was at a most interesting point, he awoke, and "'twas but a dream!" As "the closing hour of day came onward, mantled o'er with sober gray," he reluctantly departed, resolved to soon revisit the scene, for "perchance," said he "it was thought transmission. She *may* live there—who knows?"

And even as Sir Philip and Huggins knew somewhat of this country, so John had been into the edge of it and had spent a Sabbath beneath the classic shades of Talcott Mountain. The minister, in the church he attended, removed his heavy coat and donned a light one, the better to emphasize his remarks by impressions on the pulpit cushion. The impression on the audience was that the sermon was original with some other man. Why need they object, if it was a better one than he could have prepared? Yet they hated to see his salary come so easy, and proceeded to cut it down before next Sunday. The elderly deacon, a pillar of the church leaning against another, the singer who hung on to the last notes, the women who looked pious and chewed fennell, the pretty girls in "the singers' seats" and elsewhere, the boys lining the vestibule after service, the small size of the church, where it seemed that you could shake hands from corner to corner, which made one feel so conspicuous, — all these reminded John of "going to meeting" in earlier times. On this trip, John would get a picture of that church. So each of the trio had plans for commemorating "Auld Lang Syne" pictorially.

And knowing not what treasury the golden rays of Phœbus had in store for us, we, the trio, went forth into the land of promise. We descended the hill and drove through one of the most beautiful of village streets. The long shady road and sidewalks, the large trees, the old, rich-looking houses, lend a charm to Farmington that is its own. Quaint and restful, yet full of thought is its atmosphere, a fitting place for philosophers to live. So much there was of interest here that it is left for abler ones to tell.

THE MONUMENT.

IN THE PASTURE.

We crossed the river, drove through fragrant pine woods where the bright Philadelphicum lilies blossomed by the roadside, stopped " to take " some horses in a pasture, turned into a by-road and lo! were at the aqueduct. Is it any wonder that many recollections illumined the soul of Huggins as he gazed upon the scene? For, since he had there dreamed what he could not forget, he had often visited the place, and once found, upon conversing with a neighboring farmer that a flaxen-haired girl from somewhere in the northern part of New England had taught school near there a year or so before. This made Huggins hopeful. Perhaps he would find her yet.

Sir Philip sat regarding the thirty-foot piers with a reminiscent, far-away look in his eyes, and finally said: "That would seem a queer structure to a stranger in this vicinity, unacquainted with its origin and former use. It has been nearly fifty years since a boat has been through the huge wooden trough that once rested upon the piers, yet they are firm to-day. They built for all time in those days, as you can observe by the solidity of the abutments. The tow-path here was evidently on the south side, as the top projections of the piers are wider on that edge. Many traces of this old water-way are yet visible. The bed can be traced much of its course from New Haven,—where the tracks of the Consolidated railroad now run,— through Hamden, Cheshire, Southington, Plainville, Farmington, Avon, Granby, and southern Massachusetts to Northampton. Much of it is overgrown with brush, and often containing good-sized trees; but there are stretches of it as clear as in the days of its use. Riding along the highway near its course, we notice the partially filled in and somewhat obscured "ditch," crossing and recrossing the road, or having the latter follow the bed or tow-path for short distances. Here and there we find a culvert, and in places the remains of locks with the lock-keeper's house near by, still in good repair and occupied, as at Granby and Cheshire. The stone-work of the lock at Cheshire, near Brooksvale, which was known to the Canal Company as Lock number 12, is in almost as good condition as when built—a rare thing to find, for the stone has been carted away from most of them for other uses. The course of the large feeder built from the Farmington river, and emptying into the Canal a

LOCK NO. 12.

THE AQUEDUCT.

little northwest of here, is very plain, and a part of the feeder-dam can be seen at the river in Unionville."

We little realize in these days of railroads, what a problem transportation was but a short fifty years ago. Land carriage, by all then known contrivances, was too costly, and when the Erie Canal was completed and became successful, the problem was considered solved. Certainly nothing could be considered so suitable as artificial waterways. Canals were proposed from Boston, Dover, and Portland to the Connecticut River, and in 1826 there was much talk of improving the Connecticut River, so as to make it navigable to Barnet, Vermont, thus opening to northern New England and even lower Canada, the markets of Hartford, New Haven, and New York.

As this Farmington Canal was put under construction in 1825, naturally enough, interested parties wanted the traffic to come this way to Farmington and New Haven, instead of the river route to Hartford, and much controversy ensued. Surveys and estimates were made by both sides, and petitions were presented to the Legislatures of Connecticut, Massachusetts, New Hampshire, and Vermont, and aid solicited from Congress.

We read in the histories that the Farmington Canal was chartered in 1822, begun in 1825, finished as far as Farmington in 1828, to Westfield in 1829, and carried to Northampton in 1835. The canal was begun by two companies. The Farmington Canal Company, from New Haven to the State line, and the Hampshire and Hampden Canal Company, from the State line to Northampton. The companies were consolidated in 1826. Ten years later, they conveyed all their rights and franchises to another organization known as the New Haven and Northampton Canal Company, on the condition that the latter should assume the debts. The original stock was a total loss, and the new company put over $120,000 more into the business, but was unsuccessful, owing to the expensive repairs necessitated by freshets, a long drought in 1844 which suspended navigation entirely for a time, and the growing competition of railroads. The total sum sunk was over one million, three hundred and seventy-seven thousand dollars. The cost of construction was considerable, the most expensive item being lockage. There were twenty-eight locks in this State and thirty-two more in Massachusetts. It was estimated that the cost of building a lock was six hundred dollars a foot lift, and as there were five hundred and twenty feet rise and fall between New Haven and Northampton, the locks alone must have cost over three hundred thousand dollars. The remainder of the sum, more than a million dollars, was necessary for the building and maintenance for twenty years, as the income never came anywhere near paying running expenses. The heaviest losses were caused by freshets. Storms would wash away the banks, and were often aided by muskrats making the first opening.

A CULVERT.

"I remember," said Sir Philip, "that, at one freshet a boat got through a breach into the river at Farmington, broke the tow-line, and reached Avon before it was stopped. I have been told that two deacons who had a mill-pond in Cheshire, complained about the Canal Company taking water from their stream; something like tradition states that, on dark nights, they took a long iron rod and tested the bank, which hence often washed away there, and the deacons then had plenty of water to grind with."

"Almost every one who lived near the canal in the days of its use, has an incident to relate. One remembers when his father had loaded a hogshead of molasses on his cart, the steers became frightened and ran, the hogshead fell off and burst, and the molasses ran into the canal. Another tells about his father hitching up the team one nice morning, and saying, 'Boys, I must go down to the Basin to-day on very important business, and, after you've hoed that seventeen-acre field of corn, you can dig post-holes until chore-time. I may not be home till after dark,' going away without any pangs of conscience for the tasks imposed, for a quiet day's fishing. One man relates how the families from Plainville went to church by boat to Farmington, and while the old folks were singing psalms in front, the boys were trolling for bull-heads and catching pollywogs from the stern. Some will tell you how well they remember hearing the horn and going out to see them unload freight at the stations. Perhaps they had made the trip from up in the country, to New Haven on one of the packet boats. They could go from Plainville to New Haven in a day and made three round-trips a week between these places and one round-trip a week from Northampton to New Haven. I well recall the time when we schoolboys would rush up to the storehouse, after a boat had left some freight. It was often sugar or molasses, and we each had a spoon. Sammy Jones was an active boy, usually the first. His motto of the early bird and the worm was verified, once, for instead of sugar he found out that it was fertilizer; he found it out after his mouth was full. The boys learned to swim in the canal in summer, and there was usually enough water left in it, in the fall, to freeze and furnish skating in winter."

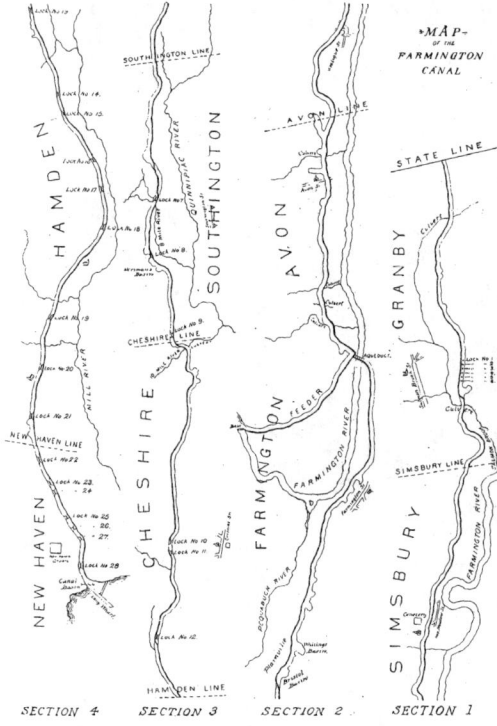

"We can imagine the interest which the people in the vicinity took in their only means of freight transportation to tide water. The towns along the route, Granby, Simsbury, Avon, Farmington, Plainville, and those further south thought their era of great prosperity had come and made preparations. It did help Avon trade, but was not of so much benefit to Farmington, because Plainville was nearer to the surrounding population of Bristol and Terryville, and took that trade.

"When the canal was opened to navigation, the interest was intense all along the line. Bonfires and other manifestations proclaimed the event. One who remembers the scene in Farmington writes the following: 'Major Dickinson was captain of the James Hillhouse, the first boat on the Farmington Canal. When the boat went up the canal, all Farmington turned out to see the wonderful sight. On the bridge, at the north end of the town, among many others, stood old John North, then some eighty years old; as the boat came along, horses covered with ribbons, flags flying, band playing and guns banging, Old John North lifted up his hands and said, 'My God, what would our fathers have

OLD TIMERS.
From a painting by G. A. Reckard.

said!' The scenes and excitement were similar at all points. Said one old lady, 'Who'd a-thought of a boat going across the great plain!' It was regarded by some as the fulfillment of a prophecy made by a foolish fellow who had some years before insisted that the Connecticut River would some time come down through here."

But in spite of the money expended, the help from the city of New Haven, which voted to pay the company three thousand dollars per year for the use of the water, and the Mechanics Bank of New Haven subscribing to $200,000 worth of stock under a condition of their charter exempting them forever from taxation, the Company finally decided that the only way to save its property from utter loss was to build a railroad upon the line of the canal, and thus save grading and acquiring a new right of way. The plan was to build the railroad to Plainville and use the canal temporarily the rest of the way; so a few boats were left at Plainville and above.

The railroad was begun in January, 1847, and finished as far as Plainville in January, 1848, but the boat plan did not prove feasible and only a few trips were made. Then the boats were sold to the farmers, for small sums, and used for chicken-coops and storehouses. The revenue derived from the sale of these boats must have gone to swell the proceeds of the sale of the hay from the banks and the muskrat-hides — said to be the only sources of profit to the

Company. The toll collected from private boats, and the freight receipts of their own boats were small, compared with expenses, and they could not hope for much, if any, passenger traffic on account of slowness. Just think of spending a week to go from New Haven to Northampton and back, — on urgent business! It must have been in gentle sarcasm that they referred to the "Raging Canawl" and named one of the boats "Wild-fire." "The Rising Sun," "Ceres," and "Henry Farnam" were other names. The "James Hillhouse" was built in Farmington, in Pitkin Basin, west of where Miss Porter's house now stands. Some of the first boats were built in Clinton.

And yet those times, between 1825 and 1828 were not so different from the present. All was stir and energy. Men were digging "the Big Ditch;" they were building bridges for the property owners, while the latter were building the fencing; for the charter compelled the Company to furnish a bridge to every one who owned land on both sides of the Canal. So each man had his bridge, many of which were seldom used. The land owners built the fences as the cost of them was supposed to be included in the damages allowed by the commissioners. And men and teams in this vicinity were busy for some time carting stone, — probably from the red-sandstone quarry east of Farmington depot, — for these piers and abutments. At other places they were building the locks.

"It was a big undertaking," continued Sir Philip. "The price of land jumped right up, similar to the booms now-a-days when an electric road starts through the country. But, alas! for those 'best laid plans of mice and men!' The general public favored the Canal and opposed the railroads, predicting the failure of the latter. What is now the Consolidated railroad had the most bitter opposition to overcome at the start. It would never pay, was the general verdict. But there was money in the Canal. So there proved to be: over one and one-quarter million of dollars in it, and no one able to get it out. The Consolidated road, I believe, is still able to keep going in a modest manner, and the old, once new, Canal has passed away. Well, boys, how would you like to have taken a vacation trip on the Canal?"

"First rate," said John.

But Huggins only murmured abstractedly,

> "The moon in gentle radiance shone,
> O'er ruined pile and armed tower,
> O'er lowly roof and lordly bower,
> And danced upon the Farmington."

Ah! Huggins was dreaming again, or thinking of — who knows? Visions of a moonlight night and congenial company are apt to inspire poetic thoughts.

(TO BE CONTINUED.)

OLD COLONIAL CHARACTERS.

BY FELIX OLDMIXON.

I. JONATHAN EDWARDS.

In heredity and environment Darwin finds the evolution of man. The influence of environment works slowly and with continually diminishing force; while heredity, being the sum of the accretions of uncounted centuries and tending constantly to greater fixity in its forms, is well nigh omnipotent in the determination of individual character. Darwin's theory is that:

> "Gemmules of innumerable qualities derived from innumerable ancestral sources, circulate in the blood and propagate themselves generation after generation. The vastly greater number remain undeveloped, for want of favorable conditions and by reason of the overmastery of the more potent in the struggle for points of attachment. Hence there is a vastly larger number of capabilities in every human being than ever had expression, and for every patent element there are countless latent ones — the latter counting for naught as to the individual."

This theory explains that strange phenomenon called Atavism, which is forever playing hide and seek in human organisms, — the recurrence of remarkable traits or peculiarities of remote ancestors, skipping over the intermediate generations, like those streams which sink into the soil and again come to light. There are, however, those who cavil at birth-right as a means of determining capabilities of a given rising generation or individual of such generation. Even so profound a thinker as Thomas Carlyle, in *Sartor Resartus*, says, "In a psychological point of view it is, perhaps, questionable whether from birth and genealogy, how closely scrutinized soever, much insight is to be gained. It is a wise mother that knows her own child."

The theories and speculations of Darwin, of Galton, of Herbert Spencer, of Ribot, and others which have been widely circulated among the masses, are too well known to need extended mention. According to Galton, we may anticipate from the same strain of blood other minds and characters of exceptional power and dignity in the future, whenever the necessary conditions shall exist.

"Man's natural abilities are derived by inheritance under exactly the same limitations as are the forms and physical features of the whole organic world," is the axiom laid down by Galton; while Ruskin supplements it with this sentiment:

> "Both moral and physical qualities are communicated by descent far more than they are developed by education and there is no ascertained limit to the nobleness of form and mind which the human creature may attain by persevering obedience to the laws of God respecting birth and training."

"How shall a man escape from his ancestors?" asks Emerson. Like begets like; the renal calculus of Montaigne, the historical instinct of St. Simon, are well-known instances. Victor Hugo says, "The good humor of Louis XVII was inherited from Henry IV." In a school of thirty boys at Stratford-on-Avon, William Howitt easily identified "the Shakespere boy" (a descendant of Shakespere's sister) by his likeness to the portraits and busts of the poet. "To come of respectable parentage is *prima facie* evidence of worth, in a belief, as in a person," says Herbert Spencer.

Man's traits of all evil sorts come mainly from inheritance, and the most he can do is to accept the Divine helps and make himself what he may be. Men are like trees; all are trees, but some are pine, others oak, and still others crab-apples, and so they will always remain. Traits of character are not discovered until a man is old enough to look within and discover what he is. In childhood he suspects nothing and is happy, yet heredity is doing its work. Stripped of hereditary drawbacks, man with his experience of troubles in life here will be better off in the life to come than if he had been born an angel; he will thereby better preserve his personality, and be known by his trials here, in the other world.

Rev. A. J. Gordon, in a sermon at Princeton College, the *alma mater* of Aaron Burr, said;

"When I was here before, I went into the grave-yard and saw close together the tombs of Jonathan Edwards and Aaron Burr; and it set me thinking of the vast gulf between those two careers, one of the seraphic life of a soul whose intellect and affections were aflame with Divine love and holiness; the other, estranged from God, going on from sin to sin till his hands were imbrued in the blood of murder."

And yet these two were of the same blood descent. It is wonderful, says a late writer, how much of the grace and culture of American society has sprung from this root. The same pursuits, continued generation after generation in the same families, originally set apart by nature for a chosen work, has resulted in a heritage of confirmed aptitudes, enlarged mental capacity, delicacy and refinement of physical organization, manners, sentiments, and tastes: a sort of "Brahmin caste in New England" as Dr. Holmes puts it; of which the Edwards family forms a considerable proportion, and in which it holds a high rank.

Let us trace back the ancestors of Jonathan Edwards and of his grandson, Aaron Burr, and endeavor to discover a similitude of tastes and of strains of blood to produce two such dissimilar characters.

On the paternal side, Jonathan Edwards' father was Rev. Timothy Edwards, son of Richard, the son of William the emigrant, who was said to be son of a Rev. Richard Edwards. Rev. Timothy Edwards was for over fifty years pastor of the church at East Windsor, Conn., and married Esther, daughter of Rev. Solomon Stoddard, son of Anthony Stoddard, of Boston, by wife, Mary Downing, of notable antecedents. Rev. Solomon Stoddard was pastor of the church at Northampton, Massachusetts, and married Esther, daughter of Rev. John Warham, and the widow of Rev. Eleazer Mather, his predecessor at Northampton. *

Anthony Stoddard of Boston, his father, married Mary Downing, daughter of Emmanuel and Lucy (Winthrop) Downing, and sister of Sir George Downing who was called "An arrant Downing." Lucy Winthrop, the mother, was daughter of Gov. John Winthrop of Massachusetts.

Rev. John Warham was from Exeter, England, and was pastor of the church at Windsor, Conn., where he died in 1670, afflicted with melancholia, — perhaps a sign of insanity, and perhaps not, but at any rate a strain of idiosyncracy in the blood of the Edwards family.

The Congregational Church of Windsor, which has proven its claim time and again, to be the oldest society of the kind in this country, excepting the churches of Plymouth and Salem, had for the first thirty-five years of its existence the godly John Warham as its spiritual teacher. As originally organized and perfected at Plymouth, England, in 1630, prior to their departure for Dor-

---

* Among the descendants of this distinguished lineage may be named: Rev. Timothy Dwight, D. D.; Judge John Trumbull, LL. D.; William Williams, signer of the Declaration of Independence; Hon. John Sherman of our day; Rev. Samuel A. Worcester, D. D.; ex-president Woolsey of Yale; Rev. R. S. Storrs, D. D.; Stoddard, the missionary; "Grace Greenwood;" "Susan Coolidge;" Elizabeth Stuart Phelps-Ward; Bishop Williams; the Rev. Dr. Todd, of New Haven, and many others, in male and female lines. We are indebted largely for genealogical and other data herein to the venerable genealogist, Geo. Frederick Tuttle, of New Haven.

chester, Mass., whence they moved in a body to Windsor, Mr. John Maverick had been chosen as Mr. Warham's colleague, but he died before their removal from Dorchester. Mr. Warham was thoroughly identified with the material development of Windsor, established the "Old Warham Mill" and dealt largely in real estate in the infant years of the Colony. He was of a strong, active temperament, but given to melancholia, perhaps through dyspepsia, or mayhap real mental aberration. In reference to this matter Cotton Mather in his *Magnalia*, throws a strong side-light upon the minister:

> "I suppose the first preacher that ever preached with notes, in our New England, was the Rev. Warham, who though he was sometimes faulted for it by some judicious men who had never heard him, yet when once they came to hear him, they could not but admire the notable energy of his ministry. But I have one thing to relate concerning him which I would not mention, if I did not by the mention thereof propound and expect the advantage, of some that may be my readers. Know then that though our Warham were as pious a man as most that were out of Heaven, yet Satan often threw him into those deadly pangs of melancholy that made him despair of ever getting thither. Such were the terrible temptations and horrible buffetings undergone sometimes by the soul of this holy man that when he has administered the Lord's Supper to his flock whom he durst not starve by omitting to administer that ordinance, yet he has forborne himself to partake at the same time in the ordinance, through the fearful dejections of his mind, which persuaded him that those blessed seals did not belong to him. The dreadful darkness which overwhelmed this child of light in his life did not wholly leave him till his death. 'Tis reported that he did even set in a cloud, when he retired into the Glorified Society of those Righteous ones that are to shine forth as the Sun in the Kingdom of their Father, though some have asserted that the cloud was dispelled before he expired."

Mr. Warham died in 1670 leaving a large estate over which his heirs contended for some time, and the Court could not decide which of the three wills he left was valid; so his estate was distributed "according to law." Mrs. Warham died worth considerable property, several years later, and had impatient relatives who awaited her death; her will was a peculiar compilation made by these relatives and showed her to be of penurious and peculiar disposition; she declares "that she had formerly given her Cousin, Miles Merwin, such a Multitude that if she had thousands she would not give him a penny. No not a pinn's poynt;" she further said that "things were so with her now in regard to her long sickness and expense thereupon that she could not tell whether she had anything to give away."

The origin of the Edwards family is veiled in obscurity, so far as the remote ancestors of the American family are concerned. Burke, the heraldist, mentions two Edwards' families of Welsh origin, one of which bore on their arms the Welsh motto: "Heb Dduw Dwim Dww Adigon," which translated means "Everything with God, Nothing without God." The above motto seems doubly significant as applied to the American line, with its distinguished representatives. But the story or tradition of the Rev. Richard Edwards is doubted by Rev. I. N. Tarbox, a late acute authority, who considered him "too shadowy a personage for history."

The original Edwards attained little prominence in this country, and only in his son, Richard, did the family assume any prominence in its early history, prior to Rev. Timothy and Jonathan. Richard, only child of William and Agnes (Spencer) Edwards was born in Hartford in 1647. Richard Edwards was twice married; first to Elizabeth Tuttle, or Tuthill, of New Haven, in 1667, when he was aged twenty, and from whom he was divorced in 1691, twenty-four years later. He married, second, Mary, daughter of Lt.-Col. John Talcott, in 1692. Mr. Richard Edwards had by his first wife six children whom he recognized as his own; and one, the first after their marriage, a daughter, of whom there is no trace aside from the record of her birth, whom Mr. Edwards did not own as his child; he was fined by the Colonial Court, for fornication, on account of this daughter, but earnestly protested his innocence, and the subsequent conduct of the mother would lead to the inference that he was indeed innocent of its paternity. Timothy, the eldest son of Richard, seems not to have inherited his mother's propensities, being quiet, studious, and later, a firm, thoughtful man at maturity. But through him were undoubtedly transmitted many traits inherited from her, which cropped out later in his remote posterity. The branch of the Tuttle family from which Elizabeth Tuttle came was erratic to the degree of insanity, and is so to a certain extent to the present day. This family taint was restrained by the strong will and great spirituality and intellectual vigor of Rev. Timothy and Rev. Jonathan, only to crop out again in renewed activity in the son, (Pierpont Edwards,) and the grandson, (Aaron Burr,) of the "divine Jonathan," both of whom were profligate, vicious and licentious. Mrs. Richard Edwards' brother was found guilty of slaying his sister, by the Colonial Court, and executed; and another sister was found guilty of killing her own son, but through the confusion existing at that time, she escaped the penalty of the law, — the trouble arising from the usurpation of Sir Edwin Andross, — there being in fact no government that could execute her. The plea of emotional insanity, or pure insanity, had not then been favored in the early courts. The divorce obtained by Richard Edwards was largely grounded on insanity. Martha, daughter of Rev. Timothy Edwards, who married Rev. Moses Tuttle, of Granville, Mass., was a woman of a very peculiar disposition, and led him an unquiet life. She had two daughters who inherited her peculiarities and died confirmed opium-eaters, both unmarried.

William Edwards and Agnes	Spencer	William Tuttle and Elizabeth	Anthony Stoddard Mary Downing	Rev. John Warham,	John of Ipswich, Mass	Jno. Stowe Eliz. Bigg	Rev. Thos. Hooker	Capt. Thos. Mary Brown dau of Jno. Brown
Richard Edwards	Elizab. Tuttle	Rev. Solomon Stoddard	Esther Warham	John Pierpont	Thankful Stowe	Rev. Sam'l Hooker	Mary Willet
Rev. Timothy Edwards		Esther Stoddard		Rev. James Pierpont		Mary Hooker	

Jonathan Edwards married Sarah Pierpont

From this rapid summary it will be seen that Jonathan Edwards was exceptionally favored in his direct lineage, as he was also in the line of the Pierponts into which he married. His father was a minister for fifty years; his maternal grand-father was a minister who married the daughter of a minister, widow of another.

Jonathan Edwards' wife was the daughter of a minister, and grand-daughter and great-grand-daughter of others, in the Hooker line. Jonathan Edwards, married Sarah Pierpont, the daughter of Rev. James Pierpont, second pastor of the church at New Haven by his wife Mary, the daughter of Rev. Samuel Hooker, who was son of Thomas Hooker, the founder of the Connecticut Colony at Hartford, and called the "light of the Western churches." So that, on his mother's side, Aaron Burr came of a strong clerical strain, and of eminently good blood. Rev. Samuel Hooker married Mary, the daughter of Captain Thomas Willett, a leading spirit in the settlement of Connecticut, and a sort of Miles Standish in that Colony, giving a martial tinge to the blood, added to the valorous and brave Thomas Hooker's strain. *

---

* Capt. Willett, was of the Leyden Pilgrims at Kennebec where he was sent as agent of the trading house, by the Plymouth Colony: he succeeded Miles Standish, 1647, as commissioner of the military company at Plymouth and became an assistant to the Governor, 1661-'65. He was afterwards twice or three times Mayor of New York, and died in 1674, aged 64; his grandson, Francis Willett, was prominent in Rhode Island, while his great-grand-son, Col. Marinus Willett, was like himself, Mayor of N. Y. City. Capt. Thomas Willett, married Mary Brown, of Rhode Island, daughter of "the worthy John Brown, esquire," (ancestor of Capt. John Brown, whose "soul goes marching on.") So that it will be seen that a certain dominant strain of blood and martial ardor distinguished her ancestry, together with great tenacity of purpose and aggressive ideas and practices.

Rev. James Pierpont was son of John Pierpont who lived in Roxbury, (the ancestor of John Pierpont the poet, the Hon. Edwards Pierpont and all the Connecticut Pierponts, a notable family to-day.) John Pierpont married Thankful Stow, daughter of John Stow of Maidstone, Kent, who was nearly related to the Antiquary Stow, the "man of infinite remembrance." This John Stow came over, in 1631, to Roxbury, Mass., and married Elizabeth Bigg, the daughter of Rachel Bigg whose will is among the first recorded in Boston records, a descendant of an ancient family in Kent, located there before the Conquest, which has held its own for over one thousand years.

John Pierpont was son of James Pierpont, of Ipswich, Mass., descended from an ancient family whose founder came over with the Conqueror, one branch of which attained to the Dukedom of Kingston. The Pierponts were a simple, sturdy stock, and not notable in clerical or martial lines.

The children of the Rev. Timothy Edwards (and of Jonathan as well) were widely noted for fine forms and features, which came, tradition says, to the Edwards lineage from the Stoddards. They inherited their clear, fine, expressive features from their mother, Esther Stoddard, taking their physical and in a great degree their mental proportions from her. Her son, Jonathan, was nearly six feet high, and her ten daughters used sometimes to be spoken of as "Mr. Edwards' sixty feet of daughters;" an exaggerated statement, although they were remarkably tall. The descendants of all the daughters so far as we can learn, were tall, finely-formed men and women, inclined to be spare and somewhat angular, akin to their uncle Jonathan in this respect.

The sisters of Jonathan Edwards were well educated and "early pious," their minds disciplined by classical studies, and possessing many of the accomplishments upon which our modern belles pride themselves. Specimens of their drawings, paintings, and needle-work still remain, — rather stiff to be sure, but looking probably as well as will the fancy articles of our daughters to the third and fourth generations of their descendants. Better remembrances, however, exist in the influences which they exerted upon the families into which they were transplanted, upon the children which they nurtured, and which is still felt by their descendants at this hour. They married into the best families in the Eastern States and brought to their husbands the richest dower a wife can bring — piety, refinement and intelligence.

An early attachment was formed between the college tutor, Jonathan Edwards, and the beautiful daughter of the New Haven pastor, Rev. James Pierpont; yet we hardly ever think of Jonathan Edwards as a youthful lover beneath the sighing elms of New Haven, nor of the accomplished Sarah Pierpont as a bashful bride. Her wedding dress was handed down as a relic to her grand-daughter, corresponding with our ideas of the plain and simple vestments of our Puritan ancestors; and we can look upon her portrait still and fancy how the bride of 1727 looked in her bridal outfit, as she plighted troth to the embryo metaphysician. Her dark hair was parted plainly on her forehead, her dark eyes hid by long lashes, her cheek pensive and yet mantled by varying color, as she stood slight and youthful, before her father, to receive the nuptial and parental benediction. Edwards we can see with his calm features, his high intellectual forehead, and his quiet reserved manner. At this wedding probably met the Hookers, the Mathers, the Stoddards, the Davenports, and many more of the descendants of the first Colonists, connected either by blood or marriage with the two families. There was the father of President Edwards, a man of no mean note, and a scholar and Christian gentleman; there was the mother, a woman, refined, dignified, superior to her husband in intellectual endowments, and commanding at once affection and respect. The bride's father, the popular and pious Pierpont, of course officiated, and we can not forget the mother, of no less patriarchal lineage — the grand-daughter of the venerable Hooker of Hartford, (who had led his flock from the shores of the Atlantic to the healthful Connecticut valley, through the untrodden wilderness, with his wife, traditionally the daughter of Davenport, his first bride, carried this long distance in a litter to survive her nuptials only six weeks.) This latter bridal was no less auspicious — for it was the union of two equal in circumstances, similar in habits, of the same faith and principles: he, calm, dignified, studious, with a tinge of constitutional melancholy; and she a creature of light and gladness, warmth, affection, and buoyancy which rose above every care. From the record which her contemporaries have kept of her, from the manner in which her husband speaks of her, from the traditions still remaining among her descendants, she may be regarded as the model of a virtuous wife and mother; she relieved her husband from all domestic care; she instructed her children; she cheerfully met all the claims which a large congregation made upon the time and patience of a minister's wife; and she gracefully dispensed the liberal yet simple hospitality which the New England pastor still delights to show. Herself a model of conjugal deference, the spirit of filial reverence was early instilled into her children; and we can testify to the respect and veneration which their children, when themselves aged and feeble, still looked back upon the parents from whom they derived their being. They were taught to rise when either of their parents entered the room; never to sit while their parents stood, and however they might be engaged in conversation, to stop and remain silent while their parents spoke. Such habits would exert a powerful influence on a family. These forms are rapidly passing away from our family government, and in but a few do traces still remain. But it has been thought that the principles by which our ancestors regulated their families were too rigid, that they exacted too much, and infused into the minds of their children rather a servile fear than a wholesome veneration. It might have been so, and the family of President Edwards was not altogether an exception; there have been those among his immediate descendants who have felt that the parental influence was not so happily exerted as it might have been had the children of the family come more into familiar contact with their parents. The great secret of domestic influence seems to be to unite firmness with authority and affection with kindness, and thus secure both the respect and love of the child; but this idea was not a part of the dominant doctrine of Jonathan Edwards, the rigid discipline which he inculcated, perpetuated even to the present day and generation.

With every abatement which we may be required to make, we may still believe that Mrs. Edwards was both skillful and successful in the education of her family. The daughters she lived to educate were intellectual, dignified, and pious women. One, the betrothed of Brainerd, soon followed him to an early grave and rests by his side, without a stone or inscription, as if it were enough for her woman's heart to watch over him while he lived and lie by him when she died. Mrs. Burr was no ordinary woman, and the mother of President Dwight will not soon be forgotten. The sons of President Edwards are not unknown; and although their parents were not spared to complete the education of all their children or witness their conversion, a blessing seemed still to follow them; and their descendants still believe that they yet receive rich spiritual blessings in answer to the prayers of those who have so long slumbered in their graves. As we have known the scattered branches of this family, we have been pleased to note common maxims, habits, and principles, which, like the traditions of different nations may be traced to one stock, and which originating with their pilgrim ancestors, have been handed down from generation to generation.

(TO BE CONTINUED.)

REGINALD ROXDALE.

A STUDY OF HEREDITY.

"How the Living Memory of a Dead Man Detected His Crime."

BY FRANKLIN E. DENTON.

"Before he was born he had been living for thousands of years."—*Renan at Turguenéff's Funeral.*

I am wasting with fatal disease. Soon life's candle will have flickered to the socket and I shall be—where? Surely, no worse fate can befall me than once did, for I (my personality) was annihilated forever before I was born, and forevers are equal. I am dying. Yet what of it? To what do the best of us amount? We (individually) are here by the merest chance. Of course, the race is not. Men are nothing; man is everything. We are huddled into a few paltry summers and winters, but the coffers of humanity are full of glittering centuries. If twenty tandem lives ago some Saxon swain had won another maid, where would myriads be? Where would we be? Fellows fully as good would do our little task, but where these beloved, these infinitely precious selves? Why this all-absorbing I, this hub of the wheel of the whole, this insulated cogitation, of which Proclus says the universe is the statue? If naught, why seem we of such vast account? It may be because every man is, in a sense, all humanity, You and I are compendiums of all the buried generations, synopses of all the untravailed epochs. We began to breathe with Adam, and our hearts will not wholly cease to throb till the last of his sorrowing progeny lies down to his eternal sleep.

I know you do not deem it wise for me to talk. I know the doctor has left express word for me not to do so. But it is only a matter of a little while at the most. What odds to the man just dead whether he saw twenty or a hundred springs? There are a few things I wish to say to you. They are not so very important, still I would have you know them before I go. Do not divulge them, for others of my blood are yet living. I feel that I can trust you, for we have been fast friends from the very morning.

I am a very unique man. You know this. I am sure you will overlook a little egotism from the lips of an old friend so soon to be no more. My peculiar power lies in my subjectivity. There are two types of introspectors. (All men of mind are introspectors. Their ability is proportioned in their capacity for spiritual vivisection). One type, like Shakespere, Calderon, Moliere, learn all the world out of themselves. The other, of which Poe, Hawthorne and Byron are perhaps conspicuous examples, learn themselves out of all the world. To this latter type I belong. I see backwards. Since I have made a study of myself, incessant, indefatigable, is it at all unreasonable that I should have learned some things of which others are ignorant, pertaining, it may be, as much to them as to me? I am going to tell you a fact, and how I came to know it to be a fact. I am very weak. Listen attentively, as neither you nor any one will ever know it, should my faltering lips refuse to utter it.

Now do not deem me out of my head. My mind is fully as sound as your own. I have striven to live a pure life. I undoubtedly have done wrong, else inconsistent with my humanity, but I never committed a crime. Nevertheless, I have suffered remorse. I have suffered remorse for a crime that I never committed. I know who did commit it, however. His own living memory detected him, after he had been in his grave many years.

Did you never, perhaps at bustling noon, have a sudden and subtle recollection of something seeming to have occurred, some time in your career, and yet so dim, so vague, it seemed as if it must have been the experience of some pre-natal life? Did you never dream of being in places the like of which you never saw in your waking hours, and yet they appeared as familiar as if you had spent years there? If you have not, you are the first one who has told me so. These unrecollected recollections, playing hide-and-seek in the by-ways of our beings, Plato would tell you, and Vaughn, and Wordsworth, and many minds of poetic cast, that they are the memories of a life we have lived previous to this terrestrial one. It is a very beautiful idea, but it has no foundation in fact. I will admit that my theory is not so beautiful, but it has this redeeming feature — it is based on absolute fact; it is true. I will state it in the form of a proposition: These unrecollected recollections, these incomprehensible paroxysms of association, in which something in the heavens above or earth beneath reminds us of something we have experienced we know not when or where, are fragments of inherited memory. Do you hear me? *Fragments of inherited memory.* Sleep often materializes these wrecks of remembrance, and when in dreams, we visit a familiar place unfamiliar to us, the descended impression some place (native village, perhaps) made upon some ancestral mind, revives for the time.

I cannot remember when I did not, every few weeks, perhaps oftener, dream of being in a little village that I never saw when awake. It was a lovely village. I love little country-villages, and when I see their white church-spires gleaming in the blue and green of the summer distance, I am moved to tears. I abhor the frightful desolation of populous cities, the spiritual Andersonvilles of mighty towns. No fairer place was ever roofed by the inverted blue-bell of the sky, yet never, save in great sadness, did I somnambulate gentle streets. I had wondered why I should so incessantly redream this town, but, given as I was to hypothesizing, could never weave any satisfactory theory.

I had a conception of the town only in a general way, but one house therein I knew to the minutest detail. I had been in every room. It was a huge, square, undecorated house, with three front chamber windows, and one small attic window above them, in close proximity to the flat roof. To the left of the attic window there was a piece of clapboard gone. Strange that an insignificant detail like a broken clapboard should be noticed in a dream. I am quite sure that we forget not anything. We are coral-reefs of memory, and the insects who pile us up are moments.

Often in the daytime, inexplicable feelings would flash over me, in some way related to the dream, and whenever I beheld the moon obscured by a cloud, a mood of gloom and remorse possessed me — a feeling of defiant despair, and a feeling as if I had committed some dreadful act mingled in one. I had ever supposed that these experiences were only the taints of insanity that haunt even the healthiest and best-balanced minds.

Until past my majority, no individual took part in my dream. I never saw a person in that village until I dreamed one night that I was passing by the house. (It was close to the road.) It seemed to be a glorious night in May, not far from half-past eight. The air was full of the fragrance of the resurrected flowers. The daffodil light of the "sunken sun" and the spiritual azure of the zenith were still commingling like the purposes of loving hearts, while the lonely only cloud in all the illimitable heavens was saturated with the pure, sweet light of the ascending moon, like an innocent heart with the spirit of Jesus. Just as I reached the front of the house the cloud passed directly across its disk. Simultaneously, a terrific shriek proceeded from the middle chamber window directly above me, and a female voice exclaimed, (there was something in the tone of voice like mine) " Reginald, you have killed me !" Then, all clad in flowing white, she fell from the window at my feet. I caught but one glimpse of her features, but enough to stamp their ineffaceable photography upon my consciousness. The contour of her face bore a striking resemblance to that of mine. Mark this. But I digress.

Upon waking I tried to formulate some hypothesis as to my diabolical vision. It could hardly have arisen from gastric disorders, for my digestion was well nigh perfect those days, and I was very abstemious. Then bad dreams resulting from bodily ills are usually so incongruous in their extravagance of horror that their impressions flee with the dark and the stars, but this incubus was so consistent from beginning to end that it clung to my consciousness with all the pertinacity of a noon-day reality. What troubled me most was the word Reginald. That was the name of my father, of my poor, dead father, who died June 8, 1852, the week before my birth. I had been thinking much of him the evening previous, of all my dead mother had told me concerning him. I had wondered, in the moonlight, whence he came, what his history, who his kin, why silent as a stone about his past, why he came to the town of my birth in the night. Perhaps the word Reginald occurred in the dream because I had been revolving it in mind before retiring. This was plausible, but I could gain no satisfaction therefrom. It would not do.

Though there was no repetition of the terrible vision, I continued, as usual, at intervals, to dream of the same old house, of the chamber windows and the attic window above them and the broken clapboard.

The next autumn — the autumn I was twenty-two — I took a pleasure trip into an adjoining State. It was sufficiently leavened with business to cover expenses, else I could not have taken it. One of the towns that I had to visit was that of S————. It was off the line of the railroad, and to reach it a hack-ride of ten miles was needful. It was a fine region over which I rode, and a grander October day never chased the darkness round the world. Nature is the most intellectual in autumn, and on that pure, calm, golden day, from the archipelago of clouds to the aged flower, from the blue infinity to the gray rock that had not moved for an hundred centuries, all things exhaled a beautifully awful contemplation. The forests crowning the environing hills ringed the horizon with a round sunset. If the soul of Shelley could be made into a day I know it would be exactly such an one. The commonplace chatter of the passengers, the enervating heat and the snail-like pace of the consumptive steeds, tugging us through the dust, had at last lulled me to a semi-doze, when I was aroused by hearing a little child of one of the passengers say that we are entering town. Looking out, sure enough, there we were, right in the town. Looking out, I felt my heart leap into my very throat. Why, not fifty feet away, loomed the huge, square, undecorated house. There could be no mistaking it, for there were the three front chamber windows, the small attic window above them in close proximity to the flat roof, and the broken clapboard. I concealed my emotion as best I could, although the unwonted pallor of my face drew the sympathy of one corpulent, motherly old lady, who sat on the seat beside me.

Reaching the hotel, I registered my name, and was immediately shown my room. I was ill. It is a peculiarity of my make-up that any excitement attacks my stomach. I ate no supper, but went directly to bed. There was no sleep in my eyes, however. I did not sleep a wink that night, but spent it in feverish and involuntary hypothesizing concerning the developments of the previous day.

Bad things are as transitory as good, and the miserable night at length became a portion of the past. The morning broke cold and foggy. As I stood arranging my necktie, I cast a glance outdoors.—When my eyes fell upon the lurid foliage of the maples through the aerial pearl of the fog, a dark theory flashed across my brain. Could it be true? If so, it would cast a shadow over my future; but, if so, it would give me a new truth, not new alone to me; new to everybody. I would be the Columbus of it.

Knowing that the village was the county-seat, after the ceremony of breakfast, I went directly to the court-house. Obtaining permission of the proper officials, I searched in the records of the town.—On the 101st page of a huge volume (I never forget isolated numbers and dates), the very legible writing informed me that August 5, 1818, a son was born to Reginald and Mary Roxdale. My father's name was Reginald Roxdale, and he died in 1852, aged 34 years; therefore, I was certain that that son was my father, who bore the first name of his father. Making further search, I discovered that, in the year 1840, Reginald Roxdale cast his first vote. This must have been that son, as 1840 would have found him a little past his majority. But how could all this account for the hideous dream?

I returned to the hotel. It was fifteen minutes before dinner was ready. Picking up a paper in the bar-room — a local one — I thought I would accelerate the moments by browsing in its columns. I began at the first one, looking through each in order. At the top of the second column of the editorial page was an article entitled, "The Crimes of the County," wherein some rural Gibbon discoursed of the demoniac deeds which had stained the annals of that county since its settlement. What do you think was one of the facts that I read? This: On a moonlight evening in May, 1846, Reginald Roxdale hurled the beautiful Helen Morrison, his affianced, from a chamber window of her home on Summer street, in the town of S——, from the effects of which violence she died the following day, and the criminal fled and was never heard of thereafter. It was very plain to me now. My theory was substantiated. I had inherited the memory of my father. He had destroyed the beautiful Helen Morrison, and all his recollections of the affair, even to the aspects of nature at the time, had descended to me. Thus did the living memory of a dead man detect his crime, after he had been in the grave many years.

But the strangest of all is yet to come. The article further described the girl.— She was the most lovely of maidens for leagues around. Her hair was raven-black. Her eyes were large, and dark and lustrous. Her form was slight and willowy. I inquired of an old man who sat near me, whom I took for the hostler, if he remembered the event. He said he did, related the circumstances substantially as I had read them, and told me he had a picture of the unfortunate girl.— He asked me if I was a relative of hers.— I told him that I did not know that I was. He said that I looked very much like her. In the afternoon, he brought to me the picture. Sure enough, she bore a striking resemblance to me. The general configuration of her head was like mine. She had the same Grecian nose, the same development of the forehead between the eyes, the same dimple in the chin! Furthermore, my hair was black, my eyes, large and dark, and my form slender. Then the idea flashed across my mind, which will be universally true to me until disproven — the first-born of a household bears a strong resemblance to her to whom the father should have been wedded, the vicissitudes of life preventing; thus showing that, while the earthly nuptials have never been consummated, the spiritual union has.

But I am very weary, and must sleep a few more hours, before that deeper sleep steals over me. Do not divulge my statements. I would that I had strength to tell you other weird truths, the knowledge of which must be snuffed out with me.

THE CENTER CHURCH BURYING-GROUND AND ITS ASSOCIATIONS.

BY MARY K. TALCOTT.

The old Center burying-ground contains much honored dust, and this paper is written in the endeavor to call to mind some of these forgotten worthies. Thomas Hooker, "the Light of the Western Churches," lies there, and his successors in the ministry, Stone, Haynes, Foster, Woodbridge, Dorr, all lie under table monuments, in two rows, not far from the gate. Near them rest two Governors of Connecticut, John Haynes, the first Governor of the Colony, and Joseph Talcott. Governor Leete is also buried in the yard, and a modern obelisk has been erected to his memory by a descendant. He was the last Governor of the New Haven Colony, and the first from it, of Connecticut, elected in 1676.

As the visitor enters the gate he sees before him a broken column. erected in memory of Jeremiah Wadsworth, the friend of Washington, and the commissary-general of our French allies during their campaigns. Members of his family lie near him. Then there are Stanleys, Seymours, Lawrences, Chenevards, Bulls, Goodwins, Whitings, Ellerys, Olcotts, and many other names prominent in Hartford's history.

CENTER CHURCH.

The Wyllyses lie in the center of the ground in unmarked graves, a fact significant of family pride quite as much as if they had stones emblazoned with heraldic emblems. One of the family is reported to have said that if

Connecticut could not remember the Wyllyses without gravestones their memory might rot!

It is needless to say that many stones bear dates between 1660 and 1700. The oldest is probably that of Susannah Wolterton, who died in 1662. Among the older stones is one bearing the name of John Allyn, who "served his generation in the quality of Magistrate and Secretary of the Colony for thirty-four years," dying in 1696. "Mr. Secretary Stanley" is also there, whose memory has been perpetuated more thoroughly by his recipe for black ink than by his modest gravestone. Nathaniel Stanley and John Lawrence, both Treasurers of the Colony, sleep their last sleep here. The Rev. Elnathan Whitman and the Rev. Benjamin Boardman, "Big Gun of the Gospel Boardman," both pastors of the South Church, are buried here.

Lyon Gardiner, the first Lord of Gardiner's Island, is buried here, having died while in Hartford on a visit. Other strangers are buried here, as Dr.

TABLE MONUMENTS.

Langrell, who was drowned in the Connecticut River. In those days, when the difficulties of transportation were so great, people were almost universally buried where they died. Hearses were not introduced until late in the last century, and in the earlier days the dead were borne painfully on biers, on the shoulders of their friends and neighbors, often over rough roads, to the nearest burying-ground.

There are many stones in memory of the Lord family, once very prominent in Hartford, and still recalled by the name Lord's Hill, bestowed on Asylum Hill by old residents even yet. One of the most notable members of the family, though not a Lord by birth, was Mrs. Abigail (Warren) Lord, wife of the third Richard Lord, who married for her second husband, Rev. Timothy Woodbridge. She survived Mr. Woodbridge many years, and was one of the largest land owners in the Colony, and an excellent woman of business.

Among the many table monuments is one to the memory of John Ledyard, Esquire, a prominent merchant, and the ancestor of a distinguished progeny; among them, Colonel William Ledyard, murdered by the English officer to whom he surrendered, September 7' 1781; the brave and dashing Light Dragoon, Thomas Youngs Seymour, who figures prominently in Trumbull's painting of Burgoyne's surrender; and the famous African traveler, John Ledyard, who made his first essay in voyaging in a birch-bark canoe down the Connecticut, from Hanover, New Hampshire, to his grandfather's house on the banks of the Little River, in Hartford.

The remains of many who served their country well in the French and Indian wars, and in the Revolution, are in this graveyard, and it would be well to do for them what has been done in the old cemetery at historic Concord, by the Sons of the American Revolution, for those who fought for independence, viz: place bronze crosses, suitably inscribed, at the head of each soldier's resting place.

The yard contains the grave of one of Hartford's literary celebrities, Dr. Lemuel Hopkins, not only a skillful physician but the author of clever satires, social and political. The most famous of these was the "Echo," a travesty on political and current events, written in collaboration by Hopkins, Dwight, Alsop, and Mason F. Cogswell.

A tall gray slab attracts attention. It marks the grave of the fair Maria Trumbull, daughter of the second Governor Trumbull, and the first wife of Mayor Henry Hudson, who died at the early age of twenty-one. A contemporary poet thus describes her:

> "Light as the gossamer, with fairy feet,
> Maria moves, with gracefulness replete.
> Artless as truth she seems — and oft bestows
> The modest smile which softens as she goes."

All that remains of what was once goodness, bravery, learning, wit, beauty, lies here. Does it not behoove us to preserve carefully these relics, and the place where they lie, to see that no vandal disturbs the memorials erected by loving hands now dust, and that no desecration of any kind be allowed?

CONNECTICUT.

LOUIS E. THAYER.

Let others sing of states that teem
With mines in which the gold-veins gleam;
Of states that boast King Cotton's reign,
Or vaunt of iron, coal, or grain.
Aye, singers, sing; sing as you will—
Connecticut is my song still.

Thy sons, oh State, are men of toil
That praise thy name, and love thy soil.
They're humble men, yet courage know,
And at their country's call they go;
While bearing arms against the foe,
The humble man transformed is, lo!
Throughout the livelong bloody day
Leads in the thickest of the fray.

What state with you dare boast in wealth
Of strength, ambition, vigor, health?
What firmer foot has ever trod
The path that leads from earth to God,
Than feet of those who showed the way,
You taught to love, you taught to pray?

Connecticut owns honest men;
Some guide the plough, some hold the pen.
The world gives some an honored name;
Some wear the laurel-wreath of fame.
Aye, noble state, though others rise
To dwarf you by their greater size,
Yet, on the old red, white and blue,
The brightest star shines out for you.

A VISIT TO MRS. SIGOURNEY.

BY LOUISE J. R. CHAPMAN.

A careful appreciative biography of Mrs. Sigourney has yet to be written, perhaps it may sometime appear, but it is my light and pleasant task to chat of the woman as she appeared to a young friend, to whom she gave graceful friendship and encouragement. My acquaintance with Mrs. Sigourney began through an event conducted by the late Dr. J. G. Barnett, who was her friend and my musical instructor. It was Commencement of the Hartford Female Seminary, June 25, 1857, and Mrs. Sigourney wrote the words which Dr. Barnett used in the program, while the writer of "An Ode to Education" was a young woman who felt very much honored to appear associated with the celebrated poetess in the musical and literary exercises of the day. Mrs. Sigourney was very kind in praising my effort, and invited me to her home. This was the beginning of a very precious experience as her devoted friend.

The many pictures extant in various publications represent Mrs. Sigourney as a rather large woman. She was small, dainty, a perfect picture of sweet womanhood — in her own personality, a poem. She always wore soft gowns, quite in the modern æsthetic style, with rare laces about her neck. Her jewels, of which she had many, were choice, not large, but rare, and in her taper fingers she usually carried a cobwebby handkerchief.

The *carte de visite*, elsewhere reproduced, was given to me during one of the many quiet visits which it was my privilege to enjoy. It, of course, fails to give even a hint of the exquisite tints of her complexion, the rare, sweet look in her blue eyes, and the soft flaxen curls, which seemed like those of a child, though they were then fading into gray. Her love of dress will be apparent, although the awkward "fixing" of the photographist has evidently interfered with her pretty, graceful poses, and stiffened up her soft, patrician hands, of which she was unaffectedly vain. A sculptor once made a model of her hand, in marble. This rested upon a table in the drawing-room.

She met her friends with a little "curtsy," and ushered them into her drawing-room with an air which seemed like that of a tiny princess. There was her piano, of old-time style, always ornamented with vases of flowers and bits of china and glass and silver bric-a-brac, which the women of that time called a "clutter," but which would have delighted the taste of a collector of to-day.

She would always take you by the hand and lead you to her favorite sofa, upon which were pretty cushions, in silk and embroidery, for which she sometimes apologized, as it was not the fashion to "loll" three or four decades ago.

She was a pronounced blonde, with light curls which were always arranged in a becoming coiffure. Her hair was surmounted by a cap, in choice lace, and one, which was my special admiration, had wide, pink satin strings, which were permitted to float at either side.

Her voice was low and flexible, and her language simple, but remarkably well chosen. One cannot obtain any correct idea of her charm in conversation from the stilted manner which she generally assumed when writing. It was one of the literary mannerisms of the day, which she quite discarded in speech.

To be invited to "take tea" with Mrs. Sigourney was a privilege of which any young lady felt proud, and one day in particular remains a most precious memory, as I was then enabled to see and know the rare woman as never before.

MRS. SIGOURNEY'S HIGH STREET HOME.

Let me give a description of the "tea." As we entered the dining-room I saw the table. Daintily, spotless, even shining white, was the heavy damask. It seemed almost bare to me, who was not then used to the custom of serving in courses, but the silver was shining, the china delicate and the glass brilliant. She bowed her head in silent blessing, then the waitress presented a salver upon which to serve the viands. This maid was a colored woman of quiet dignity, who seemed to anticipate every want, to be always "alert, but aloof," which, Howells says, is the most desirable trait in a table waiter. The servant emerged from the shadows of the dimly-lighted room, which seemed so quiet and restful to one who came from a home filled with childish voices and merry clatter, and placed upon the board a silver tureen, from which Mrs. Sigourney — her rings flashing in the candlelight — served creamed oysters. After this was removed, came another, more massive, of solid silver, which, being, uncovered, showed a delicious dish of baked beans, golden brown, and sending forth a most appetizing aroma. The poet smiled at me as she served them, saying: "My dear young friend, I have always preserved the good old-fashioned custom of having baked beans Saturday night, and I hope you will enjoy them as much as I do." They were baked beans idealized, really made poetical by the manner of their serving, and the accessories of pickles and sauces, contained in pretty bits of table-ware, which greeted my beauty-loving eyes.

Her pieces of china did not "match;" instead, they were of odd and different design in decoration and shape. It was a revelation, for it had not seemed possible to use such things to eat from, any "good housekeeper" considering her "set" spoiled if one piece was broken and could not be perfectly reproduced. She gracefully referred to the various bits of rare porcelain, saying they were gifts, and telling, in the most fascinating manner, of their social history. Then the spoons! I wonder where they are now? — if they have been kept together in these days, when our daughters are "collecting" so enthusiastically and do tease so witchingly for the rare heirlooms and relics of the past?

These, with their long handles and queer little bowls, the small tea cups, the cream pitcher and sugar bowl, the plates of brown bread and white, the succeeding course of quince sauce, raised cake and tiny caraway cookies, the whole "tea" seemed so dainty and quaint and "old-fashioned" that it remained a memory, of which the minutest details cling to my mind. Now it does not seem old-fashioned, but modern, and in the most exquisite taste, and so we finally come around again to æsthetic beauty and good taste, which she imported from the drawing-rooms of England, and made her custom in advance of our later education. Could we now possess the brass-mounted, claw-legged tables, the *papier-mache* covered desks and rare, carved cabinets, which furnished her rooms, we should be rich indeed, but Hartford people then thought them queer, and supposed she kept them only because they had been given to her by foreign friends and admirers, not realizing their beauty as she did.

Mrs. Sigourney had been presented "at court" in England, and among her treasures was a diamond bracelet from Queen Victoria. She sincerely admired the queen of England, and spoke of her as a good, true "sister woman."

She was the peer of any queen, a woman who was in advance of her time in literary possibilities, in æsthetic taste, in gracious manners and spontaneous heartfulness. She was an honor to the little practical commonwealth, which was her native state, an ornament and a blessing to the city which became her adopted home. Feeling that she may not always have been worthily appreciated by the young school of *litterateurs*, and that the present dwellers in Hartford should occasionally pause and think of her who left so much that is refining and cultivating to them, the writer, who knew and loved her well, offers this small flower of memory as a tribute to her matchless personality.

UNAFRAID.

(From Harper's Magazine.)

A dialect beyond our ken,
   The accents of an unknown tongue,
Life speaks,—this world of passing men
That is incomparably old
And sad with sinning manifold,
   Yet, with each morning, sweet and young,

Yea, sweet and young it is, and plain
   Its meaning,—for a girl's light breath
Outwits the wisdom that has lain
Long centuries stored in reverend books,
They doubt and dream; she, by her looks,
   Laughs down the lie of churlish death.
            —Richard E. Burton.

THE SMALL-POX HOSPITAL ROCK *

AT FARMINGTON, CONN.

BY JAMES SHEPARD.

Dr. Eli Todd, the first superintendent of the Connecticut Retreat for the Insane, was for many years settled in Farmington, and before he began to practice there, Dr. Theodore Wadsworth was a practicing physician of Southington. The town of Farmington, December 12, 1791, "Upon the petition of Theodore Wadsworth of Southington and Eli Todd of Farmington, physicians, requesting permission of the town to establish and open a Hospital at some convenient place within the limits of the town and near the Southington line, which shall be approved of by the Authority and Selectmen, for the purpose of inoculating for the Small Pox during the ensuing Autumn," voted to grant said petition.

THE BROWN TRACT.

On the mountain southeasterly from Farmington, where the trap rock that largely composes the mountain itself comes to the surface and slightly projects above the surrounding soil, the rock has many inscriptions, representing at least sixty-six individuals, together with dates ranging from 1792 to 1794. From these dates we may infer that the hospital established in pursuance of this vote was near this rock. About fifty years ago an intimate friend of Dr. Todd pointed out this rock to a son, who is now living and then told him that Dr. Todd's

---

* The writer acknowledges his indebtedness to Mr. Julius Gay, Commander Edward Hooker, Mr. Wm. L. Cook, and all others who have kindly rendered him valuable assistance in the preparation of this paper.

Hospital was near this rock. There are men now living, who on returning home in their boyhood days, after a visit to this rock, remember hearing their father tell of incidents of hospital life that happened while he was a patient there. Time passed, vegetation flourished, until the rock in its wild seclusion was nearly hidden and seemingly forgotten.

But it was not wholly forgotten; a few, and only a few now well along in years and some who have only recently passed away, have talked about the days when their relatives had the small pox there and called to mind the many incidents connected therewith, how father told of the things that his mother sent him and other incidents preserved only in treacherous memories. A few years ago that son of Dr. Todd's friend determined to rediscover this rock, although he had not seen it for nearly fifty years. His first efforts were unsuccessful, but at length he found it, nearly covered with turf which he rolled away, and again brought to light many of the hidden inscriptions. Hunters from New Britain

HOSPITAL ROCK.

soon found it and the papers were full of many strange conjectures as to its significance.

Following the old mountain road that runs from Farmington to New Britain and passes a little to the east of Will Warren's den, keeping on by the summit over the eastern slope of the mountain until about one hundred and fifty feet lower than the summit, we come to an abrupt angle where the road turns easterly, as shown in our illustration of what is locally known as the "Brown Tract." Elias Brown lived here for many years including the years inscribed upon the rock. Here, leaving the road and entering the field through the grassy path between the cedars, in continuation of the Farmington arm of this angle in the road, passing by the old cellar hole half hidden amid the clustering lilac bushes at the right, and continuing on through the bushy pasture, we reach a little brooklet in the edge of the woods when the path soon forks, and between its two branches is "hospital rock." Cedar trees were growing on its margin, but they have been overturned to peel their masses of roots from the rock in order to lay bare inscriptions which nature had concealed. Our view of the rock shows some of these overturned trees and the surface on which most of the inscriptions appear, although on too small a scale to show the carving.

The work is mostly well done and appears to have been made by persons of tact or by those skilled in the use of hammer and chisel. One of our cuts shows a group of six names just as they appear on the rock, and these with the name of Edward Hooker also shown by a cut, represent the average style of inscription. We also show the name of Salmon Clark in the ground story of

MARY A NORTON
LEMIRA WHITMAN AGE 20
CALEB BACON. AGE 20 oct '1794
CYRUS CURTIS 23
AROXCY HART AGE 23
Anson Curtis AGE 21 1794

ONE-FOURTH ACTUAL SIZE.

the house — like figure which borders it, while John C—— appears tucked away in the attic. John's surname cannot be determined although faint traces of the letters after the "C" appear. It is difficult to say whether or not John's name is a part of the original plan, but evidently a trespasser left the initials "W. H." with the "W" just outside the roof and the "H" within it, before the word

EDWARD HOOKER
AGED NINE 1794

ONE-FOURTH ACTUAL SIZE.

John C
SALMON CLARK
AGE 28 1792

ONE-EIGHTH ACTUAL SIZE.

"John." We omit this trespassing H from our cut as not belonging to the original design. The most elaborate inscriptions are those showing the name of J. Bronson in several forms, two of which are illustrated. It is not at all probable that such lettering could have been by Bronson himself who was then only ten years old. Many other names are duplicated on the rock, both in full and by initials. The following is a full list of the names and initials in so far as they are legible, excluding duplicates, and all initials that correspond with the full names and ages elsewhere given.

Kesia Allvord, 21. Timothy Arnold, age 12. J. Bishop Andrews, Ae,
Shubael Brownson, age 9. J. Bronson, 10 y Sep. 1792. Sophia Bull. Laura Bull. Caleb Bacon, age 29, Oct. 1794.
Cyrus Curtis, age 20, Oct. 1794. Rebecca Curtis, Ae. 25 y. Thirza Curtis, 18. Anson Curtis, age 21, 1794. Salmon Clark, age 28, 1792. Sally Cowles, 33. T. Cowles, 1794. Claramond Cowles, 16. Rena Cowles, 10. Daniel Cornwell. G. Cowle. Chester Case. Timothy C——. John C——.
L. D. D. D.
Eunice Gleason, 27. Nancy Gleason.

Edward Hooker, aged nine, 1794. Sally Hooker. Wm. Hooker, 1792. John Hull, 23, 1793. Peter Hull, age 18, 1794. George Hull. Amos Hull. Nimrod Hull. Amos Hawley, age 20. Aroxcy Hart, age 23. P. H. Zenas Hart.
Amasa K——. M. K. S. L.
William Mathews. Anna Mix, 10, 1794. Betsy Mix, 12.
Mary A. Norton. R. S. Norton. (Reuben.) Nathan North, 15, 1794.
M. C. Pitkin. James Richard, age 10, 1794. Timothy Root, age 12. Roxana Root, 18. S. R. L. R. 1794.
Luther Seymour, of Hartford, Ct. 22. Anne Street, 19. A. S. 24. Abigail Scott, age 26. 1794. Norris Stanley, age 20. A. Stanley, 1793. J. B. R. Samuel Scott, October 1794. Age 21. P. Stanley.
Lemira Whitman, age 26. R. W. 16. C. W. Amos Wilkinson, Age 16.

There are various figures, borders, and embellishments which we can neither show nor describe, and the numerals 1 to 35 inclusive are strung in a continuous row across the rock, excepting where the rough surface caused the sculptor to skip a space. For the same reason blank spaces appear in many of the inscriptions.

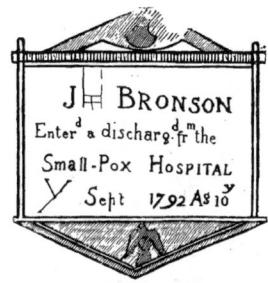

ONE-FOURTH ACTUAL SIZE.

In these days of vaccination and anti-vaccination, inoculation for small pox is not a familiar subject. For over four thousand years small-pox was unknown, the first known cases having appeared in the sixth century. A person once having it is generally protected for life against a second attack, but not always, as cases have occurred where persons have had it three times. Formerly it proved fatal to about one-fourth, or one-fifth of all who were attacked. Inoculation is the introduction under the cuticle of a minute portion of the virus of the real small pox, and it is remarkable that when thus communicated the disease is far less violent than if communicated by natural contagion, and yet a second attack after a person has had small-pox by inoculation is as improbable as in cases where persons take the disease in any other way. When taken by inoculation in some retired hospital, every thing could be prepared for, and the physician in charge could begin with the proper treatment without waiting for symptoms upon which to base a diagnosis and without any liability of making a mistake. The mortality was rarely greater than one in six or seven hundred, and no doubt, with young people as shown by the ages given on the rock, the danger of fatal results was very small. Danger was also largely avoided by selecting the cooler months, the heat of summer being one of the conditions that greatly enhance the terror of the disease. It was for this reason that the vote of permit was not to take effect until "the ensuing autumn" and that in other permits it was "provided that no person be allowed to take the infection after the 12th day of May next." The operation was introduced into Europe from the East by Lady Mary Wortley Montagu and was first performed in London in 1721.

ONE-FOURTH ACTUAL SIZE.

Probably most or all of those whose names appear on this rock came to Dr. Todd's Hospital for inoculation. This was from two to four years before Dr. Edward Jenner learned that those who caught the cow pox by the act of milking diseased cows, were supposed to be incapable of taking the small-pox, and acting on this clue, he performed vaccination upon a human subject for the first time in 1796. The protective influence of vaccination cannot be greater than that of the small pox itself, nor that of inoculation, both of which are sometimes ineffectual. Mr. Erastus Scott, of Farmington, had small-pox by inoculation and when in after years, while as one of the selectmen, he had to look after a small-pox patient, he caught the disease again. He recovered, and lived many years after this second attack, but he first gave the disease to one of the other selectmen, Mr. Stanley, of Plainville; yet Mr. Stanley had been successfully vaccinated in his youth and in after years he had been repeatedly vaccinated with no effect. A vaccinated person having the varioloid may communicate by contagion the most virulent form of small-pox. For a number of years Dr. Jenner's practice was not looked upon with that favor with which it is received by modern school boards, and so, not only in the last century, but in the beginning of the present century, the only known preventative was by inoculation.

The dread of the disease was then so great that those who had the means were willing to undergo the trials of banishment from society for a time, to take small-pox by inoculation, rather than be exposed to its natural ravages.

It is not probable that this rock marks the site of the hospital which would not have been located so near Mr. Brown's house nor even so near a frequented public road. This old road was then the only road over the mountain between New Britain and Farmington. Mr. Adna Hart of New Britain, now ninety-one years old, says he has known the site of the hospital for eighty years. He points it out as on a little knoll about one-third of a mile southerly from the rock. There are probable traces of a building here and by the brook; a little east are plenty of good springs, while all the surroundings indicate that this was just an ideal place for a hospital. Although it is now covered with hemlock trees of considerable size, it was an open lot when Mr. Hart first knew it. Tradition says that there was a flat rock which was the meeting-place of the hospital attendants and messengers from the town, who frequently came with supplies and to take back messages, and perhaps some convalescent patient. One who remembers many incidents of the hospital as told him in his younger days, conjectures with reasonable probability that this inscribed rock is the traditional meeting-place. September, 1792, is the oldest date on the rock and what discharged patient, when waiting for the messengers from town and seeing the name J. Bronson inscribed on the banner and emblazoned with the battle-axe and eagle, could resist saying to the skillful carver, "please put down my name;" and thus, no doubt, if all the inscriptions there could now be read, we would find the names of nearly if not all of the patients treated at this hospital. From 1792 to 1794 may have been the only years that the hospital was in use. For various reasons they changed from place to place and there were many other places for inoculation. At least three permits to establish such hospitals were voted by the town of Farmington within the ten years previous to granting the permit for this hospital.

Various private correspondence shows the existence of such places near Farmington in 1798 and 1799. One letter says "Fanny and Julia Cowles I believe will come out of the pest house this week a Saturday or Monday." Another says " J. Grand, S. W. and L. N. and M. A. S. are going to have the small-pox to Ben Sweet's. They are a going to-morrow and Mr. Thomas Smith's wife and Col. Norton's wife too. Ben is not a going to take any boys or men." A young man writes to a friend that "The young girls here are all in the pest house. I have been up to Goat Pasture to see them. They are as thick as toads after a rain. Nancy Hooker and Fanny Cowles have it the hardest but they will all do well I believe." The writer of this letter must have had the small-pox in some way or he would not have dared to make this visit. "Goat Pasture" was farther to the north than is our hospital rock.

Many have supposed that the names on this rock were those who had died of the small-pox, but this is a great mistake. Every name on the rock is that of a person who was living when the name was placed there. Norris Stanley lived to own ships which were captured in the war of 1812 by Algerian pirates, and still later to receive from the United States an indemnity therefor amounting to a large sum. These names represent the best of families and were mostly from Farmington, New Britain, Kensington and Southington, while Luther Seymour, the only one whose "residence" appears on the rock, was from Hartford. They were mostly children and young people, only one age being recorded as over thirty and the fact that this person was a woman, indicates that some one else put down the name and age. Eunice Gleason is recorded as twenty-seven, but she had no reason to conceal her age as she was already a married woman. A small-pox hospital would seem a strange place for courtships, but I am informed that at least three marriages resulted from acquaintances formed there.

Among the living representatives of those whose names appear on the rock I may mention Commander Edward Hooker of the U. S. Navy, now of Brooklyn, New York, and his brother, John Hooker of Hartford, who married Isabella Beecher, both children of Edward Hooker of the rock. His brother William Hooker, also of the rock, was the Dr. William G. Hooker who died in New Haven Sept. 19, 1850, leaving highly respected descendants. There are many others on the list whose subsequent history is more or less known, and which may be further pursued with pleasure by those who are especially interested. It is also not improbable that by turning back from the rock more of the overgrowing sod, or by a closer study of the surface now exposed, still other names may be discovered.

NATURE POEMS.

BY JOHN ROSSITER.

SECRETS.

The west wind knows what the birches say,
And the robins listen every day;
You and I, indeed, may never know
Whether they murmur of weal or woe.

And who has caught the speech of the waves,
In the depths of sounding ocean-caves?
Have the strange wild sea-birds stopped to hear
A message unknown to mortal ear?

But, farthest of all, beyond our ken,
Are hid the unfathomed souls of men;
And none there are who may read aright,
Save He who fashioned in love and might.

FIRST LOVE.

A sunny dawn that lights the field and wood;
A village street, a bridge above the brook,
Whereon a maiden stands, with happy look,
As one whose thought foreshadows naught but good.

And this is all — for more I would not pray,
Since from that time my wistful gaze was bent
Upon this scene, and rested well content, —
It has lent grace and gladness to my day!

THE HISTORY OF ANÆSTHESIA.

BY JAS. McMANUS, D. D. S.

The history of modern anæsthesia has been given to the world by many writers, for both medical and literary magazines, as well as through the newspapers, in such a careless, ignorant, and untruthful manner, that it is not to be wondered at that the public is befogged and uncertain as to who should be given the credit and honor as the discoverer. A true and concise statement of a few facts, that tell of the discovery, and by whom it was made, will no doubt be of interest at this time, as the dental profession of the country has recently held commemorative exercises in honor of the fiftieth anniversary of the discovery, December 11, 1844, by Dr. Horace Wells, a dentist, of Hartford, Connecticut.

In looking up the records of the centuries we find mention of various medicines that have been used for the purpose of rendering patients insensible to pain during surgical operations. Homer mentions the anæsthetic effects of nepenthe. Dioscorides and Pliny allude to the use of mandragora. Lucius Apuleius, who lived 125 A. D., and whose works were published in the fourteenth century, says that "if a man has to have a limb mutilated or burnt, he may take half an ounce of mandragora wine and whilst he sleeps, the member may be cut off without pain." A Chinese physician who lived in the third century, named Hoatho, gave his patients a preparation of hemp, whereby they were made insensible during surgical operations. The soporific effects of mandrake are mentioned by Shakespeare, as well as other draughts the composition of which is not given. It is on record that the ancient Chinese, Greeks, and Scythians used preparations of mandragora and hemp with some success during surgical operations; but their preparation and use were abandoned. For centuries, opium and alcoholic stimulants were the only agents that the surgeons could rely on, to help their patients endure the pain of an operation.

After the discovery of nitrous oxide gas by Dr. Priestly, Sir Humphrey Davy made a series of experiments, the results of which were published in 1800, in his volume of "Researches in Nitrous Oxide Gas." He states that April 11,

1799, he made his first inspiration of pure nitrous oxide gas, and for a year after, he made an exhaustive study of the gas, and also many experiments with it, both on himself, and medical and other friends. He states on page 276 that one day while suffering pain, caused by cutting a wisdom tooth, he found that while breathing the gas, he got relief from pain. He also says that he once imagined that the pain was more severe after the experiment than before. On the last page but one of his book, he made this suggestion: "As nitrous oxide gas appears capable of destroying physical pain, it may probably be used to advantage during surgical operations, in which no great effusion of blood takes place."

The closing paragraph in his book states: "That pneumatic chemistry in its application to medicine, is an art in infancy; weak, almost useless, but apparently possessed of capabilities of improvement. To be rendered strong and mature, she must be nourished by facts, strengthened by exercise, and cautiously directed in the application of her powers by rational scepticism." Many of the famous surgeons of Europe must have been more or less familiar with his published work, yet there is no record that any surgeon dared to act on his suggestion or that any one had confidence enough in his statement to advise any sufferer to do so. Sir Humphrey Davy lived for many years after the publication of his book, attaining both wealth and distinguished honors, and it is only fair to presume that he did not even think that he had made a great discovery, for if he had, he certainly would have put it to a trial.

The anxiety that oppressed the surgeon was in no way lessened by the suggestion of Sir Humphrey Davy, and the dreaded operating day at the hospital often taxed the moral and physical courage of the surgeon to a greater degree than it did the agonized yet hopeful patient that awaited the operation. It was only a few years previous to 1844, that the celebrated French surgeon, Velpeau, published the following hopeless statement in his work on surgery: "To avoid pain under incisions is a chimera, which is no longer pursued by any one. A cutting instrument and pain in operative surgery are two words, which never present themselves separately to the mind of the patient; and of which he must of necessity admit the inevitable association." This statement was accepted by many as authoritative and final; and the few, who still hoped that some agent would yet be found that would lessen the horrors of surgical operations, were looked upon by the majority of surgeons as idle dreamers; and for this reason, every surgeon was ambitious to rank as a rapid operator: "The quicker the surgeon, the greater the surgeon," was the professional and popular belief during the first half of the present century.

HOUSE IN WHICH DR. WELLS LIVED, IN HARTFORD.

Fortunately the number of severe surgical cases are comparatively few, while we all know that every member of the human family, sooner or later, must submit to having one or more teeth extracted. As the demands for dental operations were of daily occurrence, the dental practitioner had constant evidence that all patients showed more or less fear and dread of the operation, and the great need for some safe agent to give relief, was constantly impressed on the mind of the dentist.

We have the testimony of Linus P. Brockett, M. D., of Hartford, Conn., that in the summer of 1840, while conversing with Dr. Wells, he found him deeply impressed with the idea, that some discovery, would yet be made by which dental and other operations might be performed without any pain. For forty-four years medical and chemical professors, and popular lecturers were experimenting with the gas; and not one of them caught the idea, or dared put to the test the suggestion made by Sir Humphrey Davy in 1800.

Professor G. Q. Colton gave a course of lectures on chemistry and natural philosophy in Hartford, early in December, 1844. To popularize as well as amuse the audience at these lectures, the exhibition of the effects of laughing-gas on willing subjects was made a special feature of the entertainments. Dr. Horace Wells, well known in Hartford as a skillful dentist, attended with his wife the lecture given the evening of December 10th, 1844. Dr. Wells inhaled the gas: the effect not being as pleasant as his wife wished, for she reproached him on the way home for taking it, and making himself ridiculous before a public assembly. Dr. Wells went to that lecture to see, hear, and learn. He inhaled the gas, and subsequently watched its effects on others. The exciting incident to him at the entertainment was when Mr. Samuel A. Cooley, a well-known Hartford citizen, gave a lively exhibition of the effects of the gas by running and jumping about, and falling, striking his legs against the wooden settees, and acting apparently perfectly unconscious of possible danger. After the effects of the gas had passed off, Dr. Wells asked him if he was not hurt, and he replied that he did not know it at the time, but on looking at his legs found them bleeding from the injuries he had received. Dr. Wells turning to Mr. David Clark said, " I believe a man by taking that gas, could have a tooth extracted or a limb amputated and not feel the pain."

Before leaving the lecture hall, Dr. Wells asked Professor Colton whether one could inhale the gas, and have a tooth extracted without feeling any pain, and he replied that he had not given the subject any thought, that he had been giving the laughing-gas for over a year, and such an idea had not occurred to him and he could not express an opinion. Dr. Wells said that he was inclined to try the experiment on himself, and have a troublesome tooth extracted if he would bring a bag of the gas to his office the next day. Late that evening Dr. Wells called on Dr. Riggs to tell him of his experience at the lecture, and that Mr. Cooley had injured himself and was not conscious of it; adding, " if he did not feel pain, why cannot the gas be used in extracting teeth." A long discussion followed as to whether it would be right, or safe, for them to make such a trial, with possible danger to health and life; but Dr. Wells was so confident and fearless, that he agreed to take the gas and have a tooth extracted the next day if Dr. Riggs would perform the operation,. As requested, Prof. Colton the next morning brought a bag of the gas to the office of Dr. Wells. There were present Drs. Wells and Riggs, and as onlookers a Mr. Colton and Mr. Cooley, the star performer of the night previous.

Dr. Wells sat down in the operating chair, took the bag into his hands and at the possible risk of his life, inhaled the gas until he was insensible, when Dr. Riggs extracted an upper wisdom tooth. Dr. Wells remained unconscious a short time and on recovering exclaimed, " I did not feel it so much as the prick of a pin;" "A new era in tooth pulling." "It is the greatest discovery ever made," and other remarks of a similar nature, being perfectly delighted with his successful experiment. It was at his own suggestion and desire that he deliberately

DR. G. Q. COLTON.

THE HISTORY OF ANÆSTHESIA.

took the gas, and its value as suggested by Sir Humphrey Davy in 1800, was proved a certainty Dec. 11th, 1844, when the first surgical operation was successfully performed on Dr. Horace Wells while under its influence. On that day *Modern Anæsthesia* was given to the world, and nitrous oxide gas proved to be a blessing to suffering humanity and the forerunner of all other anæsthetics.

We have the testimony of Dr. J. M. Riggs, "that we were so elated by the success of this experiment that we turned our attention to the extraction of teeth by means of this agent, and continued to devote ourselves to this for several weeks almost exclusively." With ample evidence to substantiate his claim, a few weeks later, in January, 1845, Dr. Wells went to Boston to make generally known and to demonstrate his great discovery. He obtained permission of the elder Dr. Warren to address his class in the medical college, and at the close of his remarks he gave the gas to a boy and extracted a tooth. The boy made an outcry and the students hissed and cried humbug, although the boy on recovering said he did not know when the tooth was drawn. The first and only trial allowed Dr. Wells was denounced as a failure. If the surgeons of the Massachusetts General Hospital or any of the medical and scientific men of Boston or the country ever knew of the suggestion made by Sir Humphrey Davy, they evidently had forgotten it, or had no faith in his statement.

Dr. Wm. T. G. Morton had been a student of dentistry with Dr. Wells in 1841 and 1842, but was living in Boston and renting an office of Dr. Charles T. Jackson. These gentlemen tried to dissuade Dr. Wells, having no faith in his statements, and advised him to give up the use of the gas. Dr. Jackson, noted then as a chemist, treated the subject as increduously as did the surgeons and students, calling it a humbug. That a dentist from a country town could appear in Boston, and announce to the world that he had made such a grand discovery, was not to be credited, and Dr. Wells soon learned that not one of the influential medical or scientific men of Boston could be induced to interest themselves in investigating the properties of the gas, or to assist him in any way while he remained in that city. They preferred to hiss and cry humbug rather than to give Dr. Wells a second chance to prove the value of his discovery. Dr. Wells returned to Hartford, disappointed and discouraged at the lack of interest shown by the medical profession and especially at their ignoring the testimony which he offered, of reputable citizens of Hartford who had had operations performed painlessly, while under the influence of the gas.

DR. J. M. RIGGS.

In the Boston *Medical and Surgical Journal* of June 18th, 1845, there was an article written by P. W. Ellsworth, M. D., of Hartford, Connecticut, on the "Modus Operandi of Medicine," in which he states, "that the nitrous oxide gas has been used in a number of cases by our dentists and has been found to perfectly destroy pain and no unpleasant effects follow its use.' The unjust assumption of the Boston surgeons, that he had made a complete failure in the single experiment allowed him, and their contemptuous treatment of him and his claims gave a set-back for two years to the general introduction of surgical anæsthesia, and millions of sufferers were deprived of the use of a safe anæsthetic for nearly twenty years. At this time Hartford had no hospital or medical journal to push the introduction of this discovery, and for a time Hartford people alone realized that such a discovery had been made.

Dr. Wm. T. G. Morton, while studying dentistry, lived in Farmington, Conn., and made frequent visits to Hartford as a student to recite to Dr. Wells. He was present when Dr. Wells gave his demonstration before the surgeons and class in Boston, and had frequent talks with him while he remained in the city. During the summer of 1845, he visited Hartford and called with Dr. Wells on Dr. Riggs to talk about the gas and he wanted them to give him some, and tell him how it was prepared. Dr. Wells referred him back to Dr. Jackson, who he said could prepare it for him, or tell him how it should be done as he knew all about it. In the summer of 1846, Miss Elizabeth Williams, of Hartford, met Dr. Morton in Stafford Springs, Connecticut; learning that he was a dentist, she told him her experience with the gas and that Dr. Wells had extracted a tooth for her on the 6th of March, 1845. He asked her about the effect and operation of the gas, and gave no intimation to her that he had any knowledge of the gas, or any other anæsthetic. Drs. Wells, Riggs and Terry continued to give the gas in their practice with success, and they were greatly surprised, when they learned that Drs. Jackson and Morton were heralded in the Boston papers, in the fall of 1846, as the discoverers and inventors of a compound which they stated, by breathing into the lungs, induced so deep a slumber as to enable them to perform the most painful surgical operations with entire unconsciousness on the part of the patient. Dr. Morton made his so-called discovery, September 30th, 1846, when he extracted a tooth for Mr. Eben. Frost, while he was under the influence of his pretended compound. Soon after he called on Dr. Warren, who arranged for him to test his compound, on the 16th of October, when he made his first experiment at the hospital in a surgical case. Boston surgeons were at last convinced that anæsthesia had been discovered, and Boston men were the discoverers. The managers of the Massachusetts General Hospital were now ready to claim for their institution the honor and credit of first demonstrating this great fact to the world, and Boston surgeons, Boston newspapers, and the public, were now very much interested and only too ready and anxious to assist the assumed discoverers in introducing their pretended discovery, and advising its use in general surgery.

The possible money value that might accrue to them from a vigorous pushing of the discovery, set the doctor and dentist to figuring out futures, and they decided to take out a patent, which was applied for October 27th, 1846. Before the patent was granted, Dr. Jackson, fearing he might be censured, or even expelled from the Medical Society, if he took out a patent, made an assignment which apparently gave to Dr. Morton all his right, title, and interest in the then assumed invention; but for which act he obligated Dr. Morton to pay him ten per cent. of all he made out of it, and later on, through his counsel, he demanded twenty-five per cent. of all the profits both at home and abroad, which Dr. Morton refused to give. The patent was granted Nov. 12th, 1846, circulars were sent out with the names of Drs. Jackson and Morton as the discoverers and inventors of a compound that later proved to be the well known fluid, Sulphuric Ether. Agents were sent out to sell rights. The doctor, dentist, or anybody qualified or not, who would pay the price could buy the right to use this wonderful and powerful agent. The scale of prices being: for cities of over one hundred and fifty thousand inhabitants, two hundred dollars; fifty thousand and under, one hundred and fifty dollars; cities, under five thousand, thirty-seven dollars, for seven years, the life of the patent. Soon after there was a bitter controversy between the Boston discoverers, and the public then learned that each one denied that the other had any just claim for the credit of the discovery.

Late in the year 1848 chloroform was introduced by Prof. James Y. Simpson, M. D., of Edinburgh, Scotland, and that for a time seemed to supplant

Sulphuric Ether. Drs. Jackson and Morton from the start had persistently stated that nitrous oxide gas was a failure and that it was not an anæsthetic. The death of Dr. Wells, January 24th, 1848, left the field open for them, and as the new agent, chloroform, was making a successful record, it soon became so popular that the use of the gas was given up and by many forgotten. Hartford had no medical schools, hospital surgeons of national reputations, or professional journals, to compete with Boston, while all these influences were freely given to aid the Boston claimants in their attempt to rob Dr. Wells of the honor and credit of his discovery. Boston influence aided them in their successful appeals to the rich, and the profession for remuneration; and Boston money helped them, in wining and dining a memorable lobby influence in its attempts to get through Congress a bill granting them one hundred thousand dollars, for the use of their pretended discovery by the Army and Navy. Through the efforts of the Hon. Truman Smith, United States Senator, and the members of Congress from Connecticut, the passage of the bill was defeated.

The surgeons and the public were soon convinced that chloroform and ether were uncertain and dangerous agents. The frequent deaths reported, and the ill effects that often followed their use, caused a feeling of dread on the part of both patient and operator so that comparatively few cared or dared to risk taking or giving either of them. From 1848 until 1863, the longing for a safe anæsthetic was universal. Again, Professor Colton appeared before the public as a lecturer and exhibitor of laughing gas. In his lectures he related the history of the discovery of anæsthesia by Dr. Wells, and after his lecture in New Britain in 1862, he gave instructions to Dr. R. C. Dunham, and he introduced the use of gas in his practice there, and in Hartford. Later, Dr. Joseph H. Smith, of New Haven, revived the use of the gas in that city, and from that time on its use has been general all over the world. It is only those who have had to undergo severe surgical operations that can fully realize what a great blessing the discovery and introduction of anæsthesia is to the world, and it is only the surgeons now living that were in practice over fifty years ago, that can fully appreciate and realize the blessing this discovery is to the profession.

Several years after Dr. Wells had proclaimed and demonstrated his discovery, Dr. Crawford W. Long, of Georgia, discovered—*that he had discovered*—as early as 1842, the properties of Sulphuric Ether, and had performed an operation on a patient while under its infinence. This information was not given to the public until December, 1849. He says, in referring to his delay in making the fact known: "I leave it with an enlightened medical profession, to say whether or not my claim to the discovery of anæsthesia is forfeited by not being presented earlier; and with the decision which may be made, I shall be content." It is possible, that many surgeons in different parts of the world, at nearly the same time, or in the remote past, may, with the aid of some agent, have performed surgical operations painlessly as claimed by Dr. Long, but failing to publicly announce their success, the world gained no benefit. Dr. Wells discovered, demonstrated and proclaimed the fact at once; and then within one month's time, traveled over one hundred miles to Boston to make it generally known. The public should not be allowed to forget that the simple, honest Christian desire of this dentist was to give his discovery to all, to be "free as the air we breathe." The motive that actuated Drs. Jackson and Morton, when they put their assumed invention on the market, was to get money. Its commercial value was the dominant idea, and it was well worked up. Dr. Jackson sneaking behind the cover of an assignment of his rights, in order to hold his membership in the Medical Society, demanded twenty-five per cent. of all the profits, both at home and abroad, from Dr. Morton. This resulted in a Kilkenny fight, each denouncing the other as a fraud. A bitter controversy followed, each claimant having friends enough to furnish the Medical Journals and newspapers with lively reading for years after.

Dr. James Y. Simpson, of Edinburgh, Scotland, was the only man connected with the introduction of anæsthesia who had a remarkably fortunate life. He was eminently successful in his profession, acquired wealth, was created a baronet, and was probably better known all over the world, than any one else connected with the discovery. The last professional article he gave to the public was written by dictation, while on his sick bed, in reply to a bitter and unjust attack made upon him by Dr. Jacob Bigelow, of Boston. It was published in the Boston Gynæcological Journal for May, 1870. He writes:

"An American dentist works out to its practical results, the suggestion published in England half a century before, by Sir Humphrey Davy, and which you seem to wish to efface from anæsthetic records; and he travels a long distance to place the important result before the Medical School at Boston, and some surgeons at the Massachusetts Hospital. There is a slip in the single experiment allowed him. He is spurned and hooted away. In doing this, the Medical School of Boston thus delays the whole subject of artificial surgical anæsthesia for a couple of years. Was not the Medical School of Boston, then, in your violent language, 'chargeable with the continuance of operative tortures,' for that period much more than Sir Humphrey Davy? Did not your school stamp out — and thus prevent for two years more the most beneficent discovery which has blessed humanity since the primeval days of paradise?'"

Sir Benjamin Ward Richardson says in his recent monograph, "The Mastery of Pain":

"It was fortunate that ether came in before chloroform; because if chloroform had come in first, the number of deaths from it would probably have put a stop to anæsthesia at once."

STATUE OF DR. WELLS IN BUSHNELL PARK.
Inscription.—"Horace Wells, the Discoverer of Anæsthesia, December, 1844."

It is infinitely more fortunate that gas came in before ether, for the demands for its use are more urgent and general, and the deaths from it, do not number more than one in over a million. There is no doubt if Dr. Wells had been a resident of Boston, an M. D., and a member of the staff of the Massachusetts General Hospital, his discovery in 1844 would have been quickly accepted. As a stranger and a dentist, his claim as a discoverer, and the evidence he had to sustain it, could not awaken enough interest in the minds of the stupid, stubborn, and jealous men that he appeared before, to induce them to make another trial of the gas. They condemned it as a humbug and suffering humanity was deprived of the blessing of an agreeable and safe anæsthetic for over twenty years.

THE HISTORY OF ANÆSTHESIA.

The introduction of modern anæsthesia in all its varied modes of administration, is undeniably the result of a dentist's heroic experiment and discovery. It is true, that it was two years after the discovery, and after repeated successful operations in the hands of Hartford dentists, before Boston surgeons could be induced to accept the fact that an anæsthetic had been discovered.

The record is now well up in the millions of successful operations performed while under the influence of the gas; and there is abundant testimony that Dr. Wells was the first to submit to a surgical operation while under its influence. The General Assembly of Connecticut, in 1847, passed resolutions in favor of Dr. Wells as the discoverer of anæsthesia and declared that he was entitled to the favorable consideration of his fellow citizens, and to the high station of a public benefactor. The Court of Common Council of the city of Hartford passed resolutions to the same effect. The physicians and surgeons of the city of Hartford, united in a testimonial declaring their belief in the justice of the claims of Dr. Wells. The Medical Society of Paris, France, in January, 1848, voted that to Dr. Horace Wells, of Hartford, Connecticut, is due all the honor of having first discovered anæsthesia. On Bushnell Park in Hartford there stands a monument erected by the State of Connecticut, and the city and citizens of Hartford, commemorating this great discovery of anæsthesia first given to the world in Hartford in 1844, with the name inscribed and a portrait statue of Dr. Horace Wells, to whom alone belongs the honor of the discovery. When it was proposed, some months ago, to celebrate the 50th anniversary, it was decided that there could be no more fitting testimonial than for his

E. S. WOODS.

brother dentists to place a tablet, and mark the very spot where his discovery was made. It was fortunate that it could be placed in a most conspicuous position, to be a perpetual reminder to the public of the great obligation they are under to this dentist. Hereafter no one can visit Hartford without having the truth of this discovery brought very visibly before him. In the light of recent publications in the magazines, it would seem as if the tablet in this respect alone would have a mission.

THE FIFTIETH ANNIVERSARY.

The tablet is a fine piece of bronze work from the foundry of Mr. Mossman, of Chicopee, Mass. It is five feet long by twenty-nine inches wide and bears the following inscription:

To the memory of
HORACE WELLS, DENTIST
who upon this spot
DECEMBER 11TH, 1844
Submitted to a surgical operation
DISCOVERED
Demonstrated and Proclaimed
the blessings of
ANÆSTHESIA

It is probably the largest out-door Memorial Tablet placed on the front of a public building in this country. The committee were very fortunate in their selection of the sculptor, Mr. E. S. Woods, of Hartford. He has made a beautiful and artistic tablet that will attract for years to come, the attention of all lovers of the true and beautiful in art.

The fiftieth anniversary of the discovery of anæsthesia by Dr. Horace Wells in this city, December 11, 1844, was formally observed by a banquet at Habenstein's cafe. The banquet was given under the auspices of the Connecticut Dental Association and was presided over by its president, Dr. Charles P. Graham of Middletown.

At the right of the toastmaster sat Governor-elect Coffin, of Middletown, Dr. G. W. Russell, of this city, Dr. G. Q. Colton, of New York, Dr. Henry Barnard, Judge Thos. McManus, and Dr. John Dwyer, of this

1815 1848

TO THE MEMORY OF
HORACE WELLS
DENTIST
WHO UPON THIS SPOT
DECEMBER 11 1844
SUBMITTED TO A SURGICAL OPERATION
DISCOVERED
DEMONSTRATED AND PROCLAIMED
THE BLESSING OF
ANÆSTHESIA

city. On his left were seated Charles T. Wells, John Addison Porter, Mayor Leverett Brainard, President G. W. Smith, of Trinity College, Rowland Swift, and Dr. C. C. Barker.

The divine blessing was invoked by President Smith. An elaborate menu was served.

As it was necessary for him to take the 10:05 train for home, Hon. O. V. Coffin made a brief speech thanking the members for their kindness in sending him an invitation and congratulating them on their worthy enterprise. Cheers were given as the governor-elect left the room.

President Graham in opening the post-prandial exercises referred to the beneficent effects on humanity of Dr. Wells's discovery. He introduced the several speakers of the evening in a felicitous manner, who were Mr. Chas. T Wells, the only living descendant and son of Dr. Horace Wells. Mayor Leverett Brainard, Dr. C. C. Barker, of Meriden, President of the Connecticut Valley Dental Society, Dr. G. Q. Colton, of New York, eighty-one years of age, and who as a young man was associated with Dr. Wells at the time of his experimenting fifty years ago. He retold the story of the discovery. Dr. G. W. Russell, Dr. P. W. Ellsworth, Dr. H. P. Stearns, superintendent of the Hartford Insane Retreat, President G. Williamson Smith of Trinity College, Henry Barnard, LL. D., Judge Thomas McManus, and Mr. E. S. Woods, the sculptor.

Dr. James McManus referred to the sincere regret of all that Dr. Parmele was unable to be present. "Up to this noon he expected to be with us but to-night he was unable to come out," he said. "He has worked hard to make this movement a success and it is a great disappointment to him not to be with us to-night. To-morrow the anniversary will be celebrated at Philadelphia where three dental colleges will participate. The formal celebration will be held there, but this banquet to-night is the introductory celebration of the anniversary. The tablet that has been erected has been provided by only practicing dentists and the contributors are located all over the country from Portland, Maine, to Portland, Oregon. The erection of the tablet is no local act, but is a friendly tribute from the entire country.

President Graham then read telegrams and letters of regret from Governor Morris and Lieut.-Gov. Cady, Senator Joseph R. Hawley, Maj.-Gen. Wm. B. Franklin, Chas. J. Hoadley, LL. D., Hon. A. E. Burr, Charles Dudley Warner, Col. A. A. Pope, Richard Burton, Dr. C. T. Stockwell, of Springfield, Mass., Chas. Hopkins Clark, and Col. Samuel A. Cooley, at the conclusion of the speeches.

Dr. James McManus moved that the tablet be presented to the city of Hartford and the members voted unanimously to make the presentation. After a rising vote of thanks had been extended to Sculptor Woods, the party marched up Pratt street and down Main, stopping in front of the building of the D. F. Robinson estate on which the tablet is erected. Here at 12:40 o'clock Sculptor E. S. Woods cut the cord that upheld the veil and the son of Dr. Wells, Charles T. Wells of this city, unveiled the tablet.

Dr. James McManus in a brief and fitting speech presented the tablet to the city, and Mayor Brainard made a patriotic response accepting the tablet in behalf of the city and assuring the Connecticut Dental Association of the approval of his action by the Common Council. The unveiling and presentation to the city at this hour of the night made the scene extremely impressive. The party then broke up after a hearty clapping of hands at the completion of the enterprise.

COMMITTEE OF ARRANGEMENTS.

The committee for arranging all details for the memorial tablet and the dinner were: Dr. George L. Parmele, chairman; Dr. James McManus, treasurer, and Dr. Civilian Fones. Others present at the banquet were: John Addison Porter, Dr. William J. Rider, dental commissioner, of Danbury; Dr. R. Wentworth Browne, commissioner of New London; Dr. James McManus of Hartford, Dr. Edward S. Gaylord of New Haven, Dr. R. C. Dunham of New Britain, Dr. N. Morgan of Springfield, Dr. George A. Maxfield of Holyoke, Dr. L. C. Taylor, Dr. Charles McManus, Dr. Henry McManus, Dr. N. J. Goodwin, Dr. Joel F. Wright, Dr. A. E. Wales, of New Britain, Dr. Monroe Griswold, Dr. Edward Eberle, Rowland Swift, Ernst Schall, H. C. Ney, R. A. Wadsworth and Dr. John Dwyer, all of this city; Dr. Alfred Fones, of Bridgeport, Dr. Daniel A. Jones, of New Haven, Dr. William H. Rider, of Danbury, Dr. E. M. Smith, of Newtown, Dr. J. Tenney Barker, of Wallingford, Dr. G. M. Griswold, of Manchester, Dr. F. W. Murless, Jr., of Windsor Locks, and Dr. M. M. Maine, of South Manchester.

The stranger visiting Hartford or passing through on the cars from the south, is attracted first by the massive and beautiful buildings of Trinity College, the towers of St. Joseph's, one of the most beautiful and grand specimens of cathedral architecture on this continent, and the gilded dome of the State Capitol building on the heights of Bushnell park. The statues of historic men on the east front of the Capitol, and the bas-relief pictures of early incidents in the history of the state; with the statues of Nathan Hale, the martyr spy of the Revolution, and Wm. A. Buckingham, the war Governor, during the rebellion, within the building—these all give but a meagre idea of what the Commissioners have suggested and planned for the future artistic ornamentation of the building and Capitol grounds. The unique and beautiful Soldiers' and Sailors' Memorial Arch, that as the years roll on, will be even more admired and appreciated than it is to-day. The statues of Bishop Brownell on the College Campus, and Dr. Horace Wells, General Israel Putnam and Governor R. D. Hubbard on Bushnell Park, and the heroic statue of Nathan Hale, by our Hartford sculptor, Mr. E. S. Woods, that stands on the lawn in front of the

COUSIN LUCRECE.
Edmund Clarence Stedman in St. Nicholas.

Here where the curfew
  Still, they say, rings,
Time rested long ago,
  Folded his wings;
Here, on old Norwich's
  Out-along road.
Cousin Lucretia.
  Had her abode.

Norridge, not Nor-wich
  (See Mother Goose),
Good enough English
  For a song's use,
Side and roof shingled,
  All of a piece,
Here was the cottage of
  Cousin Lucrece.

Living forlornly on
  Nothing a year,
How she took comfort
  Does not appear;
How kept her body,
  On what they gave,
Out of the poorhouse.
  Out of the grave.

Highly connected?
  Straight as the Nile
Down from "the Gard'ners" of
  Gardiner's Isle
(Three bugles, chevron gules,
  Hand upon sword),
Great-great-granddaughter
  Of the third lord.

Bent almost double,
  Deaf as a witch,
Gout her chief trouble—
  Just as if rich;
Vain of her ancestry,
  Mouth all agrin,
Nose half-way meeting her
  Sky-pointed chin;

Ducking her forehead-top,
  Wrinkled and bare,
With a Colonial
  Furbelowed air;
Greeting her next-of-kin,
  Nephew and niece—
Foolish old, prating old
  Cousin Lucrece.

Once every year she had
  All she could eat,
Turkey and cranberries,
  Pudding and sweet;
Every Thanksgiving
  Up to the great
House of her kinsman was
  Driven in state.

Oh, what a sight to see,
  Rigged in her best!
Wearing the famous gown
  Drawn from her chest—
Worn, ere King George's reign
  Here chanced to cease,
Once by a forbear of
  Cousin Lucrece.

Damask brocaded,
  Cut very low,
Short sleeves and finger-mitts
  Fit for a show;
Palsied neck shaking her
  Rust-yellow curls,
Rattling its roundabout
  String of mock pearls.

Over her noddle,
  Draggled and stark,
Two ostrich feathers—
  Brought from the ark;
Shoes of frayed satin,
  All heel and toe,
On her crippled feet
  Hobbled below.

My! how the Justice's
  Sons and their wives
Laughed; while the little folk
  Ran for their lives,
Asking if beldames
  Out of the past,
Old fairy-godmothers
  Always could last?

No! One Thanksgiving,
  Bitterly cold,
After they took her home
  (Ever so old),
In her gray chair she sank,
  There to find peace:
Died in her ancient dress—
  Poor old Lucrece.

THE HARTFORD PARK SYSTEM.

I. BUSHNELL PARK.

BY SHERMAN W. ADAMS.

In the United States, the establishment of public parks in urban situations, is a matter of but recent introduction. Even Central Park, in New York city, (probably the oldest one in this country), was not definitely planned until 1858; although authority to take the lands required for the purpose was granted in 1853. The ancient Common, at Boston, is not an exception, for it was never a park, in any proper sense of the word. Like many another town common, it was originally set apart as a public pasture for cattle and sheep and it has never been dedicated, or used, exclusively as a park area.

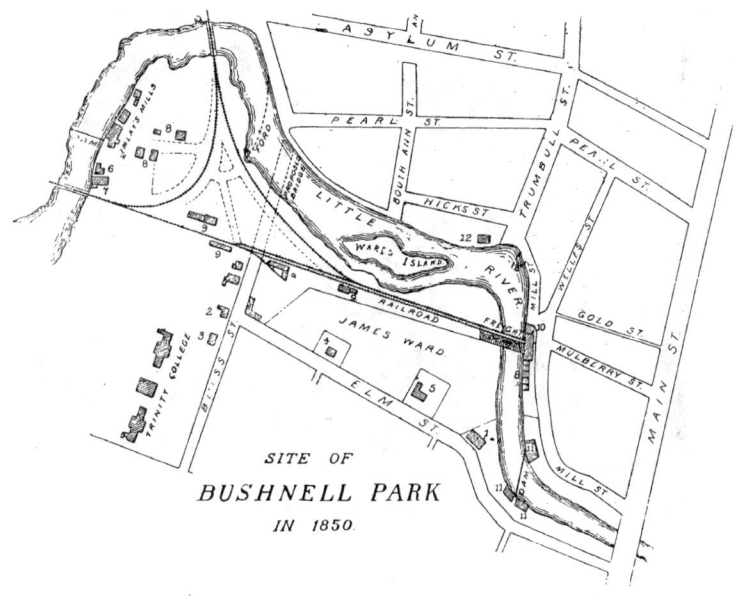

SITE OF BUSHNELL PARK IN 1850.

1. Morocco Factory. 2. Bliss House. 3. Webb House. 4. 5. James Ward's Houses. 6. Cooper Shop. 7. Ice House. 8. Dwellings. 9. Railroad Buildings. 10. Soap Factory. 11. Daniels' Mill. 12. Blacksmith Shop. 13. Watering Place.

Bushnell Park, in Hartford, may therefore truly claim to be one of the oldest in this country; perhaps, next to Central Park, the oldest. It was in November, 1853, that a committee of the Court of Common Council reported in favor of a public park for Hartford. This was pursuant to a scheme devised and earnestly advocated, in the face of strong opposition — by a man possessed of great intellect and foresight, the late Rev. Horace Bushnell, D. D. The committee (but two members of which are living) consisted of: David S. Robinson, James L. Howard, Chauncey Howard, James Bolter, William L. Wright, Edwin Merritt, and John W. Danforth. Its estimate of the probable cost of the lands required to be taken, was $115,000. The project did not contemplate the taking of any land on the left bank of Little (now Park) River.

In December, 1853, the same committee reported in favor of a new, and more southern line for Elm street, so as to bring more area within the proposed park. The Common Council, by a vote of seventeen to three, adopted the report. Other meetings, subsequently held by that board, resulted in a submission of the question of the establishment of the Park to a popular vote of the

THE ISAAC BLISS HOUSE, which stood on the west side of the present Trinity street. From a painting in possession of Mrs. Robert E. Day.

city, held January 5th, 1854. The vote was 1,005 in favor of the Park, and 682 in opposition to it.

But a decision to have a public park is one thing, and the having it, is, or may be, quite a different one. A committee (Dennison Morgan, Hiram Bissell and Wm. W. House) was chosen to appraise the required lands; and its appraisal amounted to $121,000. Progress in obtaining these lands was slow. At the end of 1854, but two contracts of purchase had been closed. One of these, was the purchase of Henry French's (formerly William Imlay's) grist-mill and water privilege, for $28,000; possession to be given April 1st, 1855. The other, was the purchase of road-bed, etc., of the Hartford and New Haven R. R. Co., at the price of $25,000; the right of possession to commence April 1st, 1856. This last sale included land and buildings on Welles street, and land on Asylum street.

Neither of these were included in the original scheme; and the cost of them was $7,000.

In the limited time at my command, I have not been able to compile a statement of the names of the proprietors whose lands were taken, nor of the amounts each received. In the eastern section, the largest area taken belonged to Col. James Ward. He was paid for it (including two dwelling-houses) $32,000. Several large and noble elm trees, near Elm street, stand by the sites of these departed dwellings. East of these, and near to Daniels' mill, on Elm street, stood Skinner's morocco-leather works. The land was taken, and the buildings removed. Farther up the same street, and on its south side, was the African Methodist Episcopal Zion's Church. This, with two or three dwellings belonging to colored occupants, gave way to the new location of Elm street.

At the head of Elm street, and west of the present Trinity street, was the

View looking southwest from a point near foot of Trumbull street. It shows the Island (that was); Trinity College Buildings; also a railway car, standing near the site of the present Park Pond. From a painting in possession of the Conn. Historical Society. Artist unknown.

residence of Maj. N. Seymour Webb. He professed a strong attachment to the old homestead, and strongly opposed the Park project, but his efforts did not avail to prevent the taking of his land. North of the Webb place, was the venerable mansion of the Isaac Bliss estate, with sundry buildings, remnants of his tannery. These were taken; but the ancient elm tree, with several less ancient but grand specimens, besides — were spared, and still cast their welcome shade upon that section. The noted spring, on the same premises, appears to have had its waters diverted to some subterranean drain or passage.

Going now to the extreme western limit, on the river bank, a railway bridge crossed the stream at the point where the Park tool-house now stands. In fact, the rear wall of that building rests upon the old eastern abutment of the bridge. North of this was an ice-house; next, a cooper shop; next, Imlay's dam (said to have been twelve feet high); and close below the dam was the flouring mill belonging to Henry French, but formerly Wm. H. Imlay's. Below the mill, were three other buildings on the river bank. Where the Terrace is, was a ledge of rock, which had been worked, and was known as the Quarry. A little north of this were railroad repair shops. Still further north, was a collection of buildings; some being dwelling-houses, and some sheds, etc. Another railway bridge crossed the river, to the depot north of Asylum street. It was a little below the present stepping-stones' dam. This depot (built in 1849) was for passengers; whilst the old one, at the foot of Mulberry street, had been given up to freight purposes.

East of the river, adjoining the west side of Mill (now Welles) street, was a row of five or six dwelling-houses. These were south of the depot. North of the depot, and opposite to the site of the present Hotel Heublein, was the soap factory of R. S. & G. Seyms. They were paid for their property $10,000. Considering the nature of the property, it seems as though very liberal prices were paid to these riparian owners. Among other lots south of the Mulberry street bridge, those of Hungerford & Cone, Bernard Sceery, and Jeremiah Howard, were bought for $5,015, $4,255, and $2,300, respectively. And the City is still paying ground-rent to Trinity College for some of these parcels.

IMLAY'S MILL AND DAM; from a sketch now in possession of the Conn. Historical Society. Artist unknown.

Excepting the railroad land, none was taken on the left bank of the river, until after the laying out of Jewell street, and the new line of Mill street, which was made to end at Trumbull street. By the vote establishing Jewell street (passed in 1861) land was acquired north of the river, from Ford street to Trumbull. The latter terminated,

Foot-bridge, that stood near the Ford, at foot of Pearl street. Sketched (from memory) by Frederick B. Perkins; the original now in possession of the Conn. Historical Society.

south, at the river bank; and a little east of this terminus was, or had been, a watering place for horses, and a immersion place for the Baptists. A vote, also passed in 1861, provided for taking the land on the west side of Mill street, including the Daniels' mill property on that street. Why this property (so desirable for park purposes) was not acquired — is past comprehension. Perhaps the burdens of the Civil War, prevented the appropriation of the requisite funds for that purpose. It was not till 1867, that the new street and embankment were completed.

In the river, off the foot of South Ann street, was an Island, (Ward's) of considerable size; so large, in fact, that it had served as the site of a tannery. It was now occupied by somewhat large trees. This Island was some years later graded down, and is now mainly a shoal, in the widest part of the river. South of the river, at this point, was a slough, whose site is now occupied by the Park Pond. Imlay's dam, heretofore mentioned, disappeared during a freshet in 1856. A deep "hole" in its pond had been the scene of many a drowning; and Col. "Sam" Cooley recovered many bodies, and rescued many people from its darksome depths.

About the only structure antedating the Park, and now within it, is Ford street bridge, built in 1856. Its five elliptical arches have been since surmounted by battlemented parapets, and made to harmonize architecturally with the Memorial Arch which dominates its southern approach. Prior to 1850, there was a "ford," near the foot of Pearl street. Bliss street (now Trinity) did not extend across the river; and the ford was mainly used by teams bound to or from Imlay's mill. Access to the mill from the south, was had by a path curving northwesterly from Bliss street. Besides grain, ginger-root, dyewoods, etc., were ground at this mill. A ship's mast, on high supports, lay athwart the stream, below the ford; for the accommodation of such pedestrians as would venture to cross thereby. Of the railway bridge at Mulberry street, only the abutments and pier remain; and these support the present foot-bridge at that point. The Trumbull street bridge was not built until 1864. Nor was there a bridge-crossing opposite to Union Place, before 1859. These last two are foot-bridges, only.

These explanations will serve to show the situation in 1860, when, for the first time, a board of park commissioners was constituted, thenceforth to assume the management of the parks of Hartford.

ELIZABETH—HER BELT.

Ye dainte, pinkie silken bande,
  I warn ye, be not ower bolde,
Because in alle the sunlit lande
  There be no taske like thyne—to holde
    My ladie's waiste.

Your prettie colour is not seen
  Beside the rose-blush in her cheeke.
And silver buckles pale, I ween,
  Before the loving lights which seeke
    Her swete browne eyes.

And let me whisper, silken belte,
  That to ye nowe is tribute paide
Because prime favorite art thou helt,
  Forsoothe, by that coquettish maide.
    Elizabeth.

Yet, 'tis but passing honour. Soon
  Ye will give place to newer thing
That takes her fancy—a fresh tune,—
  And alle the joys your day shall bring
    I envy not.

For, look ye, while in useful guise
Ye clasp her waiste, e'en this shorte tyme,
Her two redde lippes, her swete browne eyes
  And alle her tender love are myne,—
    I holde her heart.

THE THOMAS HOOKER OF TO-DAY.

POSITION AND INFLUENCE WHICH HE WOULD HAVE IN THE PULPIT AT PRESENT.

The Rev. Dr. Walker preached an able discourse, Sunday morning, October 14th, at the Center Church, relative to the life and influence of Thomas Hooker, the founder of that church. The historical facts of the great founder's career were depicted in a few brilliant passages. Dr. Walker's idea was not to present the history of the man so much as to indicate what his position and influence would be were he the occupant of the pulpit at the present time. One thing then, said Dr. Walker, that Thomas Hooker would stand for, were he pastor of this church at the present hour, would be the largest attainable intelligence in this pulpit, in this congregation, and in the community generally. Mr. Hooker was himself a man of an extraordinary, alert and instructed intelligence, attained against many adverse circumstances. Plainly, were he living at the present time, he would be open-eyed to see, and open-minded to accept, all new light on doctrine, life and behavior which the progress of time might have brought. Only I must insist, that that acute intelligence would demand that the "new light" should be really light. I see no evidence that he ever loved the new because it was new or change because it was change. He was indeed progressive and innovative in his time; but he progressed only where he thought the truth led him, and innovated only against what his reason and conscience pronounced wrong. Just where in any theological divisions of the present time Mr. Hooker would be found, I do not pretend to know or to conjecture. But sure I am, his position would be assumed with full intelligence of the facts and arguments in the case; and once assumed would be as clearly and powerfully maintained. As steadfast for the true, as resolute against the false, he would be to-day no weather-cock of every whiffling wind, but a man to be reckoned with and relied upon, as one sympathizing with all that is good; accepting all that is clearly proved; rejoicing in everything enlightening and enlarging in human thought; as a scholar, catholic, generous, honest; as a minister, wise, inspiring and uplifting toward the beautiful, good and true.

Another thing Thomas Hooker would stand for, were he in the Hartford pulpit or in Hartford citizenship to-day, would be the largest scope of individual privilege and opportunity compatible with public order and social welfare.

The needy and the down-trodden would have in him a champion always. He would have been an anti-slavery man in days when anti-slavery views were not as fashionable as they after a while came to be. He would be a temperance man, and would not relish having a licensed dram shop standing within a hundred feet of the door of the First Church of Hartford; and almost equally close to his grave. He would be an opposer of tyranny and injustice of all kinds; whether the tyranny and injustice of capital, class-distinction, birth privilege, or the subtler, but sometimes equally arrogant injustice and tyranny of Pharisaic virtue and dilletanti scholarship. This is quite plain. But equally plain is it that the liberty he would claim for every man is a liberty subject to law. The privilege he would demand for all would be a privilege compatible with the welfare of all. No anarchist he; no socialist. No wild doctrinaire declaiming against property, and loosening by his influence the stern demands of industry and self-control and prudence, as the recognized conditions of success. How he would brush aside with a whiff of clear, bracing common-sense a great deal of the self-meant twaddle that has of late found utterance in many of our pulpits, whose effect has been to intensify rather than to ameliorate the antagonism between employers and employed; to encourage the idea that anywhere in this world anything lastingly good can be got by anything but honest labor; and which has dissimulated broadcast the idea among those all too ready to welcome it, that the Church of Christ is and has been a hindrance rather than a helper to the welfare of mankind! No, this man, was a democrat, but not a fanatic. He was a statesman, not a demagogue.

Another thing Thomas Hooker would stand for were he in his pulpit to-day is the free, unformalistic conduct of church government and worship.

One is almost tempted to wish that Thomas Hooker and John Cotton might come back from whatsoever place they now are, and behold the development of the seed they so arduously sowed and nurtured two centuries and a half ago.

What if now they could see what meets our eyes to-day! More than five thousand churches explicitly of our Congregational connection, confederated in one body on precisely those principles of local independency and mutual fellowship so clearly defined in Cotton's Keys and Hooker's Survey, and stretching through every county, almost, from our eastern to western sea! What if they could see also the fundamental principle of unhierarchic church government and free unprescribed worship for which they contended, illustrated not alone by Congregational churches, so-called, but by other great bodies of Christian believers not bearing our name—Baptists, Unitarians, Christians, Plymouth Brethren, as well as several smaller religious fraternities; so that in a fair estimate about 38 per cent. of American Christianity to-day, spite of the vast importation of Romanism in the last fifty years, is essentially Congregational!

As a last suggestion in the line of our present inquiry I remark that another thing which Thomas Hooker would stand for and represent were he living now, would be earnestness and spirituality in personal religion. I put this last, not as being least, but as being greatest, in the things Mr. Hooker represented two centuries and a half ago; and which, being the man he was, we may believe he would represent were he in this pulpit to-day.

Mr. Hooker's clear title to his eminence as the author of the outline of the Connecticut Constitution, and so of his repute as a statesman, rests on twenty-six lines of a report of one of his sermons by Henry Wolcot of Windsor. But he left about thirty volumes, great and small, written in his character of shepherd of human souls, and dealing only with morals and religion. His repute as a definer and expounder of Congregationalism stands on the single, but sufficient, basis of one book. This well expresses his sense of the proportion of things as they stood in his conception of his life and appointed work. What he did other than as a Gospel minister he did as it were accidently and by the way. His scholarship, of which he had so much, was a thing to make his ministry more effective and useful. His influence and views in political affairs were employed that the State might be the harmonious fellow-worker with the Church in the welfare of men. Even his studies and endeavors in framing a church polity were to the end that religion might the better flourish. Religion was the uppermost thing always. A spiritual earnest piety in human hearts; that was the one great thing he was set to promote, and to it, above all else, he gave himself.

A preacher so intent on helping men was certain to enkindle men's sympathies. And such a preacher was sure of hearers whether in city or in frontier wilderness. Indeed, with all due respect to any of the long succession of this church's pastors, living or dead — and some of them have been quite eminent men — I doubt if this church ever had preaching so acute, vivacious and inherently stirring, as it had from the first pastor's lips, in the old log meeting-house, down on what we call state house square.

INTRODUCTORY.

The editor of the Connecticut Quarterly Magazine has done me the honor to ask me to write something in the nature of an introduction to his proppsed re-issue in the magazine of my story of "Scrope." He suggested anything which I might wish to add about the Scrope family, and also any observations about the origin and development of the story itself. He justifies his reprint of the story by saying that after twenty years from its first appearance (in "Old and New," in 1874), it will now be practically an unknown and therefore a new book. It always was somewhat that way, and doubtless is so still.

I take pleasure in acceding to his wish as well as I can; but I doubt whether I shall greatly gratify either him or his readers. I am not able to add anything to the statements made in the story about the Scrope and Throop families. The Scropes were a very old and honorable English family, as is very well known, and their history is well established for nearly a thousand years, with a good deal of detail. But I have never made out exactly the relationship of the regicide, Adrian Scrope or Scroope to that Adrian Scroope, whose signature is in the archives of the State of Connecticut; and the question of the change of his name to Throop is at least equally obscure.

It remains to speak of the origin of the story itself. A story is often hatched out of one original germ or central idea, as a butterfly is hatched out of an egg. This original idea comes of itself into the writer's mind, and no other account of its source can be given, so far as I know. Indeed, all those operations of the mind which we call thinking, take place beyond the reach of any scrutiny or observation of ours. When we desire any result of thought, such for instance as to remember something, to devise some means to an end, or some theme for a story, we appeal to our minds, as one does to the hidden mechanism of a "slot machine." We drop our request into the slot, and wait. The actual thinking is done in a region both near and far—within our head, yet as utterly beyond our reach as if it were done in the planet Neptune. And then, if there is to be any answer, all at once there it is, within our consciousness. From time to time, moreover, the machine furnishes information of itself, without our asking for it; and we describe this power by saying, "It occurred to me———" or the like.

The changes and additions made by the author before publishing are like the successive developments of the egg, into caterpillar, larva, and butterfly. Thus, the original idea or germ of "Scrope" was that of a Hartford young man trying to find some books that had belonged to an ancestor of his about two hundred years before. All the other materials were added on (if I may mix ornithology with entomology in developing my metaphor) during incubation.

I made my story turn out well for the good folks and ill for the bad ones, according to justice and good literature. Stories with a melancholy ending I do most heartily despise. A little, dirty New York newsboy was once asked how he would make a story interesting, if he should set out to write one. He reflected a little, and said: "I'd have a young lady, very good and very beautiful, and then I'd just make her suffer like h———." The dirty newsboy's butcherly ideal is exactly that of all tragedy, either in novel or drama. It is the essence of vulgarity and brutality. As if there were not real sorrow enough in the world without adding a lot of counterfeit sorrow besides; as if we lived in happiness so concentrated that it required some artificial misery stirred in to dilute it! For my part, I would as soon go to see the slaughtering at a Chicago packing-house as to go to see a tragedy, or to read one!

The characters in the story are nearly all described from persons I have known. Mr. Tarbox Button, for instance, was a close study from the life, of a late successful New York subscription-book publisher. I seem to have succeeded in delineating a type in this case; for when the printers of "Old and New" came to this personage, they wanted him left out. They said I had so accurately described the person and the ways of another well-known publisher in the same line, and who was a valuable customer of theirs, that when he came to see it he would certainly be angry and would take away from them all his business; and I had some difficulty inducing them to tolerate my portrait.

Mr. Howland Ball was Mr. Merwin, of the then firm of Bangs, Merwin & Co., Mr. S. P. Quincy Anketell was the late Stephen Pearl Andrews. Mr. Stanley, the book collector, was the late George Brinley, of Hartford; Adam Welles, was Mr. Sydney Stanley of Manchester; Mr. Toomston, was the Rev. Joel Hawes, D. D., of Hartford. Olds, was Young, the detective. Van Braam and Civille were "made up;" and so on. Such of my characters as I "developed out of my inner consciousness" were, as it appears to me, comparatively vague and indistinct. The Scrope genealogy was suggested by the Stebbins genealogy, the first one printed in America.

I used to have a strong desire to be capable of writing a good lyric and of composing a good melody for it. I never wrote any lyric at all, and the best I could do towards the melody part was the airs which I set to the songs in Scrope. If I were to recommend the story as having any merit in particular, it would be for the description of the book auction in the first chapter; that of the subscription-book publisher, his character and ways of doing business, and that of old William Gowans and his catacomb of a book-store. The reception of the story at its first appearance, was quite as favorable as it deserved. I may be permitted to hope, for the sake of the present publisher, that its success in this reissue will be much greater than it deserves.
FREDERIC B. PERKINS.

Mr. Perkins's modest preface to his story will hardly do justice to its intrinsic merits, as the reader will discover as it progresses in our pages. In casting about for a suitable serial story, we accidentally fell on "Scrope," which was highly recommended by an old and tried friend, whose judgment is not to be gainsaid. As our magazine has a distinctly antiquarian flavor in the main, we conclude that we shall not be at fault in deciding to reissue it. Let the reader judge.—EDITOR.

SCROPE; OR, THE LOST LIBRARY.

A Novel of New York and Hartford.

BY FREDERIC BEECHER PERKINS.

CHAPTER I.

"Half-a-dollar, halfadollarfadollafadollafadollafadollathat's bid now, give more'f ye want it! Half-a-dollar five-eighths three-quarters — Three-quarters I'm bid: — will you say a dollar for this standard work octavo best edition harf morocker extry? Three-quarters I'm bid, three-quarters will ye give any more? Three-quarters, threequarttheequarttheequawttheequawttheequawt, one dollar shall I HAVE?"

Thus vociferated, at a quarter past five o'clock in the afternoon of Tuesday, January 9th, A. D. 186—, with the professional *accelerando* and with a final smart rising inflection, that experienced and successful auctioneer Mr. Howland Ball, a broad-shouldered, powerful-looking man of middle height, with a large head, full eyes, a bluff look, spectacles, and plenty of stiff short iron-gray hair.

A tall personage, old, gaunt and dry, but apparently strong, with dusty black clothes and a "stove-pipe" hat, pulled down over his eyes, in the front row of seats, a little to one side of Mr. Ball's desk, answered in a grave, dry, deliberate voice:

"Seven-eighths. But it's damaged."

"No tain't either," sharply answered the auctioneer, "what do ye mean, Chase?"

"Catalogue says so. It says the title-page is greasy."

Every man at once examined the catalogue he held in his hand, and a laugh arose as one and another detected the mistake that old Chase was jesting about. The printer's proof-reader — as sometimes happens even to proof-readers — had been half learned, and out of the halfness of his learning had substituted "lubricated" which he knew, for "rubricated," which he did not, and the catalogue bore that the book had a lubricated title-page. Everybody laughed except Chase, whose saturnine features did not change.

"Gentlemen," said Mr. Ball, "pay no attention to Chase's jokes, but go on with the sale. Seven-eighths I am bid. Seven-eighths, sevnatesnatesnatesnate-snate say a dollar, somebody!" implored he in his strong harsh voice. Then he paused a moment and looking around upon his hearers with an earnest expression, he slowly lifted his right hand as if about to make oath before any duly qualified justice of the peace or notary public:

"Going. Will nobody give me one dollar for that valuable and interesting work, octarvo best edition harf morocker extry, cheap at five dollars?"—A pause—"Gone! Chase at seven-eighths."

As he said "Gone," down came his hand with a slap. The hand is in these days often used for the traditional hammer, as a decent dress-coat is, instead of the judge's ermine. The following words were his announcement to his book-keeper of the customer's name and the price; and then Mr. Ball, turning again to the audience, observed with a grin and a queer chuckle—"And a good time Mister Chase'll have a gittin his money back!"

A young man in a back seat whispered to his neighbor.

"He said Chase. Isn't that Gowans?"

"What's the next line?" sung out Ball at this moment to an assistant at the side opposite to the book-keeper, always behind the long desk or counter which separates the high-priest from the votaries in such temples as this— "What's the next line? Oh yes, number ninety-three, gentlemen. 'Requeel de Divers Voyges.' Something about the pearl fisheries I guess. How much 'moffered f' th' Requeel, gentlemen? Full of valuable old copperplate illustrations; rare, catalogue says,— I 'spose that means 'tisn't well done (chuckle)— rare and interesting old book"—

"Yes. He always buys by that name," briefly answered the young man's neighbor, looking up a moment from entering "7-8 Chase" in the margin of his catalogue against No. 92.

"Do they all do so?" queried the young man.

"A good many. You see"—

"Shut up there, Sibley!" broke in the strong business voice of the auctioneer. "Order in the ranks! I can't hear myself think, you keep up such a racket!"

The words were sufficiently rough, but the speaker's bluff features wore a jolly smile, and he ended with a short chuckle. He was right, too, in substance, and the person he called Sibley did "shut up," though a kind of sniff and a meaning smile and look at his young companion intimated the dissent of superior breeding as to the manner of the request.

The sale was one which might be classed as "strictly miscellaneous." It is true that a hasty glance at the title-page of the catalogue informed the reader in "full faced display type" that there was a "valuable private library;" but a closer inspection would show that like those speakers who go at once from whisper to shout, this deluding inscription leaped from small "lower-case" to a heavy "condensed Gothic," somewhat thus:

"CATALOGUE
of books, including
A VALUABLE PRIVATE LIBRARY,
etc., etc."

No doubt it was "valuable" in a sense. So is dirt. But assuredly no human being having his wits about him, would give shelf-room to such a "mess" as this was, taking it all together, unless for purposes of commerce. It was one of those sales that are made up once in a while from odds and ends of consignments, with some luckless invoice of better books mingled in, to flavor a little, if it may be, the unpleasant mass. But the plan is sure to fail; poor Tray is judged by his company; the good books go for the price of poor ones, the poor ones for the price of "paper stock;" the account-sales ends with a small additional charge over and above receipts against the consignor to meet expenses, cataloguing and auctioneer's commissions; and the consignor, using indefensible terms of general reproach, goes through the absurd operation of paying money for the loss of his property. The auctioneer's shelves are cleared, at any rate, and ready for replenishment with those gorgeous or rare books which he loves to sell, feeling his commission rising warm in his very pockets, as the emulous calls or nods or delicate wafts of catalogues or tip-ups of fore-fingers flock up to him from every part of the room, and his voice grows round and full as he glances hither and thither, hopping up the numeration table ten dollars at a time.—

How still the room grows, when such a passage-at-purses soars aloft like the spirits of the dead soldiers in Kaulbach's "Battle of the Huns," into that rare and exhausting two-or-three-hundred-dollar atmosphere!

But there was none of that, on this occasion. The number of "lines" or lots, in the catalogue, was only two hundred and eighty-nine, in all. In the

New York book-auctions, somewhat more than a hundred lots an hour are commonly despatched; the cheaper the lots the faster they must be run off; and in the present instance a single sitting of two hours or so was deemed an ample allowance. The actual bulk, or weight, or number, whichever category you may prefer, of volumes, however, was very considerable, as the common practice had been pursued of "bunching up" five, ten or twenty of the miserable things, into parcels with a string, and cataloguing them somewhat thus:

245. Tupper's Proverbial Philosophy, etc. 5 vols.
246. Patent Reports, etc. 10 vols. Some valuable.
247. School-books. 20 vols.

Well; the sale went on, Chase buying an extraordinary number of lots, and a small, short, bushy-bearded and wonderfully dirty Israelite who sat next him, and whom the bluff auctioneer irreverently saluted when he first bid with "Hallo! you there, father Abraham?" buying a very few bundles at two cents or three cents per volume. The securing of one of these small prizes by the dirty man seemed to irritate worthy Mr. Ball; for having offered to the company the succeeding lot, and there being a moment's pause in which no one bid, the auctioneer with much gravity exclaimed,

"Put it down to Chase at five cents!"

"I won't have it!" said the old man.

"Ye *shall* have it—what's the next?" was all the auctioneer replied, with a facetious chuckle and an assumption of great violence, and down it went to Chase, while Mr. Ball, without heeding his remonstrances, went straight on with the next lot. This was a worn looking octavo volume, with what is technically called a "skiver" or "split sheep" back and old-fashioned marbled board sides.

"Number 109," cried the auctioneer; "Reverend Strong's ordination sermon and so forth. Valuable old pamphlets, and what'll you give for IT?"—with a quaint sudden stress on this seldom emphasized pronoun, as if Mr. Ball had meant that the poor neglected thing should find one at least to think it of some weight.

"Ten cents," said old Chase, in his grave dry voice—"what's the book?"

"Twenty-five," said somebody.

"Thirty," called out the young man who had asked about Chase. His voice was eager, and no doubt more than one of the sharp veterans present said to themselves, at that intonation, "Ah, I can put *him* up if I like!" But the sale was dull; as it happened no one did "put him up."

"Thirty cents I'm bid," proceeded M. Ball; "Thirty, thirty, thirty. Say thirty-five. Thirty-five shall I HAVE? And gone (slap) for thirty cents WHIZZIT?"

"Cash," was the reply to this inquiry for a name; and the buyer, stepping up to the desk, paid his money and took his book.

"Mark it delivered," resumed the auctioneer; "The next is number 110, Life of Brown. How much will you give for IT? How much for Brown? The celebrated Brown! Come, be quick, gentlemen! I can't stay here all night! One dollar one dollar one dollawundollawundolla why is that too much? What *will* you give then?"

"Two cents" timidly ventured the soiled dove of a Hebrew, who looked as if he had "lain among the pots" ever since the idea of doing so was first started.

"No you don't!" exclaimed the scandalized auctioneer, "I'll give three cents myself. Here, Chase, now I expect you to offer five cents apiece for every book on this catalogue."

"Ill do it," returned the old man promptly; and the humble hopes of the poor Jew were effectually extinguished. He rose and quietly stole out of the room, his head bent forward, with an air of exhaustion, suffering and patient endurance. No wonder; it must have been a burden to carry the real estate and perfumery together that were upon his person.

As he went out, in came Sibley in haste, from the hall outside, and resumed his seat, which nobody in particular had observed him leaving, calling out as he did so,

"What number are you selling?"

"One hundred and ten, Sibley,—five cents is bid, seven and half will you give?"

"One hundred and ten!" exclaimed Sibley, greatly discomposed—"I wanted one hundred and nine; got an unlimited order; I was only called out for a moment—who's got it?"

"Cash is his name," returned the accommodating auctioneer, chuckling; and a long thin fellow who bought books in the name of Park, and whose quiet, shrewd and rather satirical cast of features denoted much character, added briskly,

—"and cash is his nature. Be on hand next time, Sibley. 'Too late I staid, forgive the crime.'"

But Sibley paid no heed to their chaffing, and the sale went noisily on, while Mr. "Cash" civilly informed his disappointed neighbor that he had bought the book, and at the same time handed it to him for inspection. Sibley took it, and barely glancing at the title page of the first pamphlet in it, returned it with thanks;

"Thank you (then to the auctioneer)—five-eighths! (then to Cash). My customer wanted the first sermon, no doubt (then to Ball) Yes!—quarter (then to Cash) I've got a fresh uncut copy that I'll give him for the same money (then to Ball) No—let him have it (then to cash)—much obliged to you all the same."

The young man who had described himself as "Cash" now proceeded to give the volume a vicious wrench open across his knee; took out his knife and cut the twine strings at the back; then, turning the covers back together, as cruel victors pinion their captives' elbows close in behind them, he passed the knife-blade behind a smaller pamphlet bound out of sight, as it were among the full sized octavos that constituted the bulk of the volume, so as to slit it out complete, perhaps bringing with it a film of the sheepskin of the back, held to the pamphlet by the clinging dry old paste. Then he again passed the volume to his neighbor, observing

"There; that's all I wanted; I'm going, and I shall leave the rest of the volume any way; so I'll make you a present of it."

"Well," said Sibley, rather startled—"stay—however, if you say so"—

And he laid the book in his lap, for the young man had risen with sudden quickness and was already out of the room.

CHAPTER II.

There is a small oblong upland meadow, of an acre or thereabouts in extent. It is enclosed by a high but ruinous board fence, showing signs of prehistoric paint, and its line reels, as it were, every now and then, sometimes outward and sometimes inward, as if quite too drunk to be steady, but still obstinate in clinging to the general line of duty; a strange cincture for the neglected grass land within, which seems more likely to be shut in by the traditionary post-and-rail or the still more primitive "stake-and-rider" of the farm. This area is uneven, as if it had never since the removal of the first forest growth been once well levelled and cultivated; "humpy" almost, as if irregularly set with old graves; all overgrown with meadow grass, long and fine and thin, like ill kept hair of one now growing old; and looped and tangled here and there in the hollows, in dry wisps and knots, along with a scanty growth of brambles. At distant points there are a few trees. Two or three are ancient apple trees, dry-barked, thin of leafage, unhappy and starved in aspect. There is one solitary Lombardy poplar; an erect shaft, obstinately pointing upwards, though wizened and almost bare, like an energetic old-fashioned maiden aunt, good, upright, rigid and homely. The largest group is a clump, or rather a dispersed squad, of weeping willows; unexpected occupants of such high and dry and thirsty earth. Yet there they stand, with the dried, scrawny, half bald look that pertains to the very earth beneath them, and to every thing that grows outside of it; their long sad boughs trailing to the ground, so nearly destitute even of the scanty lanceolate foliage which is proper to them, as to repeat at a little distance the idea of the grass — that of long thin neglected hair.

In the middle of the space around which these dreary trees stand like a picket line, is that which they were doubtless meant to adorn; an old, comfortless-looking white wooden house. It is not ruinous, but is ill repaired and will be ruinous very soon; in a year or two more the dingy white will verge into a dingy brown; warping clapboards will have worked lose at one end, and the sloping line of only two or three of them will throw a disreputable shade over the whole front; some furious night-blast will fling those loose bricks that balance on the rim of the large old-fashioned central chimney-shaft, down with an ominous hollow bang, upon the loosened shingles of the roof, and thence to the ground; the shock will dislodge the shingles and admit the rain into the roomy old garret in streams, instead of the slow strings of drops that now make their quiet way here and there in upon the floor. When that point is reached, the destruction goes on more swiftly. Even if small boys do not break many a ready road through every old-fashioned little window-pane, the leakage through the roof itself will not require many years to loosen the faithful old plaster of the ceilings of the second story rooms, to lay it in ruin upon their floors, and to make its steady way onward to the lower floor, by a process not unlike that to which the French were forced, in penetrating the heroic city of Zaragoza.

Even to say where this desolate old house and lot is not, would never suggest where it is. Any one familiar with New England will say, "That is like an old family homestead in some ancient Connecticut or Massachusetts town, where all the young people have regularly moved away every year for the last century, and the old people have died, and the old houses are dying too."

True; it is like it. But the old house and lot is not there. It is in the heart of New York City — that is, the ground is there, and the old house too, unless it has been pulled down; which to be sure is likely enough. The place, however, is on Hudson street, a considerable distance above Canal, and nearly or quite opposite an old church. But the old church may be gone too, by this time. At any rate, so it was at the time of the auction; and the graded level of the four streets around — for this lost-looking spot occupied a whole block — contrasted stiffly with the humps and hollows within. More than one such piece of waste real estate can be found in every great city. Sometimes it is land unimproved, sometimes it is covered with ruinous shabby little hovels standing among great business houses or rich mansions, sometimes it is a costly tenement standing shut and empty year after year. The reason is commonly, either minority of heirs, a lingering law-suit, or a capitalist's whim.

The parlor of this house was a comfortably furnished well-sized room of no very particular appearance, with an open grate and a bright coal fire, a piano tables, curtains, and "tackle, apparel and furniture complete," as they say in a ship's bill of sale. Something there was however about the room, rather to be felt than seen, and which every one could not perceive at all. This something when recognized, proved to be a feeling that somebody lived in the room; that it was used; was occupied; was a home. It would be difficult to say what gave this impression. Perhaps it was that the chairs did not all stand on the meridian; that the willow work-basket at one side of the fireplace was a little too far out in the room, as if put there on purpose; and that it overflowed with the gracious little engineries and materials of feminine domestic manufacture; that a book lay carelessly over the edge of the shelf, and several others and some magazines and papers, in no order, on the table; that a curtain hung a little one side, as if some one had looked out of the window and had let the curtain fall, instead of executing a precise re-adjustment of it. The room and its contents seemed as if in process of use; not as if under effort not to use them, nor as if set apart for show, or for consecration. Some would say, no doubt, that this feeling was from the impressions or emanations or atmosphere — the persisting color or flavor or tone, or altogether — that had been dispersed about this room and printed upon its whole bounds and contents, by those who dwelt in it.

However, this may be, something of this kind there was. The room was rather dusky than light however, for the colors of wall-paper, carpet, curtains table-cover and furniture alike were chiefly of rather sombre and rusty reds and browns. A little conservatory opened from one window, which was cut down to the floor on purpose. This was filled to overflowing with strongly grown plants, most of them of the ornamental-leaved sorts that have become such favorites within the last ten or fifteen years; and among these glowed the magnificent blooms of some of the brightest and largest flowered pelargoniums and tuberous-rooted fuchsias. There was a small fountain and basin with gold fish almost buried under their leafage; and above, over it, hung from the roots by scarlet cords, a large brightly colored shell, from which grew a graceful feathery plume of green sprays.

Of ornaments or works of art, there were but very few in this room. The principal one was a large and broadly executed steel engraving, whose white "high lights" shone from its place above the grate in violent contrast to the sombre quiet of the rest of the room. Its subject was simply horrible — one of those powerful literal representations of mere agony that people seem to enjoy with a vulgar brutal appetite like that which draws a crowd to see a public death. It was called "The Dying Camel." The field of the picture was filled with two broad masses, sky and desert. Below, stretched the flat thirsty stony sand, lifeless, endless, bounded by its one heavy horizon line, and glimmering and trembling in the naked cruel stillness of the insufferable sunbeams that filled the hot white sky above. Close down in the middle of the foreground was the huge dark ungainly mass of the camel, prostrate, exhausted. His dead master lay flat on his face crowded under the shade of the beast's flank, his arms spread out at full length. An empty water flask, just beyond the dead fingers' end, protruded a mocking round vacant mouth at the spectator. The miserable camel had just strength enough left to lift its long dry neck and grotesque muzzle into the air, and the artist had imparted to the savage hairy face a horrible expression of despair, for the sunken eyes watched the circlings of a wide winged vulture from moment to moment poising himself close above for the first gripe of claw and stab of beak; and from the extreme distance there came flying low over the sand, with eager necks outstretched before them a long line of other vultures, already scenting their prey.

At the centre table of this room, on the evening of the day of the book-auction, sat an old man. He was slender and almost frail; tall, dressed in black; with long silvery curls, and a bloodlessly white face, delicately featured, and whose thoughtful spiritual intelligence was saddened by some element of sorrow which might be weakness or disappointment or dissatisfaction or pain,— any or all of them together. His forehead was high, smooth, retreating and narrow; his attitude upright; and the ease and precision of his movements, and the clearness and brightness of his eyes, although they were sunken deep under the long overgrown eyebrows, showed that he had a good deal of life still left in him. On the table under a drop-light, confused with the books and magazines, were writing materials and a disorderly pile of papers, among which he had been working—or else, as they say in the country—"puttering."

In a wadded arm-chair by the fire sat a girl, easily enough recognized as his daughter; and the next observation likely to be made was, that old as her father was, he would probably outlive her. She was of middle height, very delicately formed, but with that roundness of modeling which makes people look so much lighter than they really are. Her skin was singularly clear and thin and almost as bloodlessly white as her father's; the blue veins, here and there showing, indicated that the whiteness was not that of opaque tissue, but of deficient circulation and general condition. Her heavy black hair was coiled carelessly at the back of her head, and combed away from her forehead, and from the small white ears, so as to show the wavy line that limited the growth of the hair along the temples, and to display fully the remarkable width and fullness of the forehead. This, indeed, was so marked that the family likeness which was unmistakable upon the two faces of herself and her father, existed there in spite of the contradiction of the foreheads. Her eyes were very large, of a limpid gray, with long black lashes, and with delicate clearly pencilled eyebrows whose line was almost level for a little ways outward from the nose, and then fell on either hand in a more distant curve. The nose was fine but high, with well opened nostrils and thin, almost translucent tissues, like those of a blood horse; the mouth neither small nor large, the lips rather full than thin, and as well as the chin, beautifully modeled, with that statuesque emphasis and distinctness of cut whose absence is one of the defects of the generic American face—if such generic face there be. But these lips were much too pale for beauty of color; and they were extremely sensitive; so much so as to suggest some excessively wild and timid creature of the woods rather than a human being. And yet this vivid sensitiveness of the lips was contradicted by the serious thoughtful, fearlessness of the eyes. The character of ill health so clearly intimated by the dead whiteness of the complexion and the paleness of the lips was greatly strengthened by the dark shades under the eyes, and by an undefinable but unmistakable languor of attitude, movement, and of voice. Like her father, she was dressed in black; a heavy rich black silk, cut high in the neck, but with a small square space in front after the pretty fashion called *a la Pompadour*. A narrow border of lace at the neck, and lace cuffs to match, were the only approach to ornament in the whole costume. There was no ribbon, no bow, no ear-drops, no necklace, no bracelet, no buckle, no brooch, not even a ring. The young girl's singularly elegantly figure, the extreme quietness and even impassiveness of her perfectly composed and refined manner, were in some way intensified and set off by this rigid elderly plainness and richness of costume, which, as the French would say, "swore furiously at her youth." Thus the whole effect was a contradiction, so harsh, so violent, as to suggest at first the hateful idea of an obtruded modesty. This however quickly gave way, on a little observation, to the correct conclusion, that it was an incongruity only. But there was another effect, which the whole personality of the girl produced; it was, if one might say so, that there radiated from her, or slowly gathered about her wherever she was, not the life and light that should glow from the young, but an atmosphere — or influence — that was dark, and dreary, if not cold; perhaps not dead, but lifeless, — is there not a shade of difference? Lastly: perhaps the strongest — certainly the most obvious mark of family resemblance was a habit of eye common to her and her father. With noticeable frequency their upper eyelids came down so as to veil half the iris, and delayed there. All that this indicated was reflection, or some other mental effort. Clowns, for the purpose, scratch their heads; philosophers — and people with headaches — rest their foreheads in their hands.

A third personage sat on a sofa at the hither side of the fire — to your right hand as you came from the door towards the fire — opposite the young girl, so that the three were at the angles of a triangle; and as if the two had been chatting across the hearth while her father was busy among his papers. This third was a young man; rather tall, well made, with a noticeable quickness and liveliness of manner and movement. He was somewhat fair, with merry brown eyes, good white teeth, full lips, a nose decidedly well shaped except that it was too broad and round at the end, and too thick in the wings of the nostrils, as if the maker being in some haste, had carelessly left some surplus material there. Otherwise, the face was at first sight rather dull than bright; not nearly so sprightly as the expression of the eye and the bearing of the whole figure.

A peculiar look, which might almost be called grotesque, was given to the face, undeniably well-featured as it was, by the management of the hair and beard. The abundant crisp curls of the hair were cut at about two and a half inches in length and trained on a radiating, or what the pomologists call the fan, system. This gave the hair seen in profile the look of a crest, covering the top of the head and jutting in an enterprising manner forward and upward from the upper line of the forehead. The front view was much more glorious; for it showed a thick frizzled halo standing out within an almost circular outline about the upper part of the long oval of the face, like the solid aureoles on ancient pictures of saints; or as if he dressed his hair by giving himself an awful fright every morning. The eyebrows were rather lifted, giving a funny sort of wide-awake look, which the young gentleman was accustomed to veil in some manner, if it might be, with a double eye-glass. Truly, nature having exhausted herself in this magnificent hairy crown of glory, had come short in the matter of beard; for the chin of our friend was sparingly garnished with hair, that grew in a little thin brush or pencil, spreading outward at the ends, like the pictures of the growth of the bamboo. A like starved growth, as if a few hairs had been cruelly deserted upon some barren shore, struggled stiffly for existence upon his upper lip; and some dim prophetic glimpses of the whiskers of the future could be seen by the eye of faith, between ears and chin.

The ill-made gray suit, and the clumsy thick shoes indicated that he was an Englishman; and if this was not enough, there was a perceptible awkwardness of attitude and of manner also, such as is often seen among Englishmen even of the best social training and experience, but which in an American would be proof positive of want of such experience. Last and most of all, the cockney shibboleth of his speech ever and anon betrayed him, in spite of the sedulous watchfulness with which he tried to talk good English — a language which exists — orally — only west of the Atlantic. In England there are corrupt dialects of it only; cockney, and provincial.

(TO BE CONTINUED.)

THE ROUND TABLE.

"The Knight's bones are dust,
And his good sword rust;
His soul is with the Saints, I trust."—COLERIDGE.

"There is no grander subject in the world than King Arthur."—TENNYSON.

FORE-WORDS It is usual for an editor to make his salutatory and salaam to the public, in the initial number of his undertaking, although it is often as thankless a task as that of the callow senior on commencement day; and the average editor feels about as "vealy" as this great prototype should, who is about to set foot upon the world beneath him—or perhaps on some other world near at hand, from which coign of vantage he can, like Atlas of old, lift the burdens and sorrows of ours upon his shoulders.

In this case, however, our editor has a more modest task, as he has not set out to reform the world, nor to advance any new heresy. It is much more modest and less wearing, to be "a chronicler of small beer" than to be a hero in the van of journalism, a herald of a new crusade, or the advocate of a waning cause. We prefer to treat, chiefly, of the things of the past than of the present, not forgetting, however, that we live and move in to-day, nor that we have a future.

For this and other reasons, our magazine is removed just a trifle off the present in most respects, and has a distinctly antiquarian flavor without being at all in the sere and yellow stage itself. A few years ago it was the practice of certain magazines to avoid extended discussions of the present, and to deal with nothing raw or recent, so that we were deluged with war-papers, and later the doings of "'49ers" and "vigilantes" to more than our heart's content. But of late the opposite tack has been taken, and the present Napoleonic wave has been anticipated by more than six years' preparation,—so we are told, by the author and his publishers,—a remarkable instance of mind-reading.

It is not, however, with such large concerns or great movements that we have to deal. We only aim at a faithful reproduction of our own State,—not alone of its past, but of its present, with an occasional dip into the future. And to this end we expect to enlist the best literary talent procurable in the State, as well as the highest skill of the printer and engraver, and the impartial accuracy of the lens. In undertaking this task, we are not unmindful of its gigantic possibilities, nor yet of the multiform hindrances that lie in wait.

It is a grand responsibility, and a glorious one to be undertaken by any one, or by any coterie of persons even. We realize fully that it is not possible for a book or a play to command as large an audience as a magazine may in time. This is distinctly the magazinic age. The successful magazine circulates by thousands; hundreds of thousands in some instances. It is the arbiter of its own fate, largely, for by its intrinsic merit it wins—by careful editorial supervision and capable management. It is interesting to know how this success is attained; not by cheapness, nor by sensations which are relegated to the daily and weekly press, "read to-day, and dead to-morrow." It is perhaps due, and only due, to the fact that the successful magazine caters to the public by giving it just what it wants; by suiting the taste of the majority of its readers, and more often, sad to relate, by following every whimsey, fad, and fancy that may be passing, ready to applaud it one moment and dissect it the next. Editors thus become sensitive barometers of public opinion and public taste. The editor is in closer touch to-day with his readers than formerly, and does not set himself upon a pinnacle or a tripod, but comes down familiarly among his brothers and sisters on mother earth.

"We" are not proud. We shall welcome reasonable suggestions for making the magazine better every issue. In this way all readers and contributors will "help edit" the magazine, as a matter of state, as well as local, and personal pride. Any honest criticism will be appreciated. Do not be offended, however, if we are as free and frank with you, in editing your manuscript. The reader can not realize the value of an occasional suggestion to the average editor or publisher, nor how quickly it is acted upon.

With this brief eulogy on our undertaking, we cordially ask your co-operation and enthusiastic interest and support. We believe that our magazine possesses unique features and intrinsic interest sufficient to win your suffrages and support.

"THE THOMAS HOOKER OF TO-DAY."

We are permitted to present to our readers the following felicitous and just tribute to the merits and services of the reverend pastor emeritus of the Center Church, Dr. Walker, by one of the prominent parishioners of that church who knows whereof he writes; it was the outcome of a conviction that occurred to him, as well as to many others at that time and since, and which he has expressed in glowing words worthy to be treasured by all who know and love the doctor for his blameless daily life—an example that many follow,—and for his generally lovable qualities. We can not refrain from giving this deserved tribute its proper place, when the opportunity offers, knowing that all his friends will sanction the sentiments therein expressed:

"One who enjoyed the rare pleasure of listening, in October last, to the discourse upon the life and character of Thomas Hooker, the first pastor of the First Church in Hartford, preached by his last but one, successor, the Rev. Doctor George Leon Walker, will not fail to recognize in his tribute to the elder, the very traits and qualities which distinguish the character of the speaker himself. These are portrayed with rare felicity and fitness in the following extract from Dr. Walker's discourse:

'He was, indeed, progressive and innovative in his time; but he progressed only where he thought truth led him; and innovated only against what his reason and conscience pronounced wrong. Just where, in any theological divisions of the present time, Mr. Hooker would be found, I do not pretend to know or to conjecture. But sure I am, his position would be assumed with full intelligence of the facts and arguments of the case; and once assumed would be clearly and powerfully maintained. As steadfast for the true, as resolute against the false, he would be to-day no weather-cock of every whiffling wind, but a man to be reckoned with and relied upon, as one sympathizing with all that is good; accepting all that is clearly proved; rejoicing in everything enlightening and enlarging in human thought; as a scholar, catholic, generous, honest; as a minister, wise, inspiring, and uplifting toward the beautiful, good and true.'

"The moral and intellectual equipment of Dr. Walker, as shown by his life and his public utterances, at home and elsewhere, are illustrative and declarative of just the sort of material out of which Thomas Hooker was moulded. During the entire time of his New England ministry, Dr. Walker has been classed among the fearless and progressive men of his time; conservative, but courageous and tolerant, independent, and aggressive, but always kindly and charitable, he has gained and maintained an influence both local and general, which few men can hope to attain. Dr. Walker easily reaches the status of a great preacher. His pulpit manner is dignified and restful. One never feels that he is exploiting himself, but that he is about the work of the Master; the subject in hand engrosses and possesses him. His voice is sympathetic and commanding, like his presence. His diction is strong, direct, and persuasive. His sermons are constructed on an orderly plan, having a sequence from the beginning to the end. One conversant with the working of his mind would assume that the great preacher could as certainly win renown in the other conspicuous arenas — jurisprudence, commerce, science, or statesmanship.

"Dr. Walker is still in the prime of his mature years. The vigor of his cultured intellect is manifestly unabated. After struggling long, and heroically with some physical infirmities, he has been obliged reluctantly and to the great regret of his people, to relinquish the care and responsibility of a full pastorate. That they can still occasionally hear his voice and avail themselves of his kindly and sympathetic offices, is a source of pleasure and comfort to his friends and admirers."

"It will be gratefully remembered by the citizens of Hartford, that Dr. Bushnell and Dr. Burton, besides being faithful as pastors and teachers, were both constantly alive to the interests of the city and the State. Dr. Bushnell has left upon its landscape, for all time, an indelible imprint of utility and beauty, in the very heart of the State Capital, that entitles him to perpetual remembrance and gratitude. Dr. Burton's sympathies were as broad and unfailing as the needs and claims of humanity. Dr. Walker's watchful and sympathetic interest in the welfare of the city and the commonwealth is widely recognized; his alert, and constant championing of the oppressed and neglected among all God's creatures, is a powerful rebuke to selfishness, partisanship, and illiberality whenever manifested — always quick to assume the responsibilities of the truest and highest type of citizenship; while his prudence and true conservatism lead him to avoid extremes and sensationalism."

"UNCUT LEAVES."

A year ago the present winter, a literary club was established in New York, Boston, Chicago, and other cities large and small, entitled "Uncut Leaves," where local authors might meet and discuss their productions before publication, with that end and aim in view eventually, in order to obtain the collective criticism of their brother authors. They met only once a month, when each member read or had read for him, his best work of the month last past. Whether there were any open criticisms or not, the author could judge by its reception, tacit and unspoken though it might be, how it would affect the general public. One production from each member, or from selected members, consumed the first part of the evening; the latter part was devoted to social converse. Strangers were admitted on the invitation of members; some of them were publishers and editors, looking for new material for their periodicals, and some were simply critics and connoisseurs, while others were amateur writers.

At one time the organizer of this club arranged to have some of his "literary lights" appear in Hartford, in original unpublished readings from their own works, but for some reason they did not come. A local writer contributed to the TIMES, over the name "Yriarte" a list of Hartford writers eligible for membership in such a club, which he said was the result of a wager that he could not name fifty authors in the city. The list is curious, to say the least, and we give it place, in his own words:

"A rough classification is given, simply for purposes of comparison, and in some cases a name is given in two or three classes, showing versatility.

I. FICTION: Mrs. Stowe, Mr. Clemens, Mr. Warner, Miss Trumbull, ("Annie Elliot"), Mrs. Annie Trumbull Slosson, Mrs. Florine Thayer McCray, Miss Emily M. Morgan. II. DRAMA: Mr. William Gillette. III. HISTORY AND CRITICISM: Rev. Dr. Geo. Leon Walker, Prof. Williston Walker, Rev. Dr. E. P. Parker, Dr. J. Hammond Trumbull, Rev. Dr. Joseph H. Twichell, Prof. W. D. McCracken, Mr. Charles Hopkins Clark, Mr. Forrest Morgan. IV. POETRY: Mr. Richard E. Burton, Mrs. Caroline Wilder Paradise, Mrs. Louise J. R. Chapman, Miss Emilia Chaese. V. SCIENCE; Prof. Flavel S. Luther (astronomy), Dr. M. C. Storrs (medicine and surgery,) Rev. Dr. Kimball (evolution), Dr. T. D. Crothers (inebriety), Dr. H. P. Stearns (insanity), Dr. A. J. Wolff (microscopy). Mr. A. D. Risteen (mathematics). VI. TRANSLATIONS, CLASSICAL AND MODERN; Prof. Samuel Hart (Greek and Latin) Mr. James G. Batterson (Greek and Latin, also poems and polemics), Miss A. Howe (French; translator of Reclus' "Birdseye View of the World," etc.), Mr. Juan L. Iribas (Spanish, translator of "Ramona" and other works), Mr. Albert Hathaway (French, German, and Russian). VII. ANTIQUITIES: Dr. Irving R. Lyon (antique furniture), Rev. H. H. C. Bingham (lecturer on Mediæval Art, the Minnesingers. etc.) VIII. SOCIOLOGY: Mrs. Isabella Beecher Hooker, Prof. John J. McCook, Mr. James G. Batterson. IX. BIBLICAL STUDY AND EXEGESIS: Prof. Chester D. Hartranft (higher criticism), Prof. C. S. Beardsley (Biblical Exegesis). X. MUSIC AND HYMNOLOGY: Prof. W. S. Pratt, Dr. E. P. Parker, Prof. Samuel Hart, Dr. Geo. M. Stone, Prof. C. E. Stowe. XI. PEDAGOGICS, LITERATURE AND LANGUAGE: Prof. C. E. Johnson, Prof. C. C. Stearns, Dr. Henry Barnard, Miss C. M. Hewins. XII. TRAVELS AT HOME AND ABROAD: Frederick H. Chapin, G. R. Thayer, T. Sedgwick Steele, Mrs. Isa Carrington Cabell, Rev. E. Payson Hammond, Rev. Dr. Geo. M. Stone, and numerous lecturers.

"But to what end is all this list of Hartford's distinguished lights in the literary field, all of whom have written more or less? Simply this; if Hartford was not so exclusive and select, so formal, conservative and unprogressive, it is safe to say there are enough ability and talent, together with much that is unrecognized but able, to make a first-class literary and social club among the above named and like people, that would be not only an honor but a benefit to themselves and the city. We do not mean a mutual admiration society—for that is impossible in Hartford. . . . . Hartford has the name of a literary city. Why then should it not uphold that name, and prove it to be true?"

There is the germ of a good suggestion in the above remarks. We have looked over his list and find some have removed from the city, and some would not care to be included in the cast-iron formulæ as above, but would claim for themselves greater versatility and originality. This list will not cover half the authors in the city. A round hundred could be named, many of whom would, perhaps, be glad to belong to such a club.

Hartford is an older publishing center than New York. A hundred years ago, in the days of the "Hartford Wits," occurred the golden age of our city's literature. One of our contributors points out the second period of literary activity, "in the seventies" of the present century. But, at the present time, beyond professional literary people who do not live here much of their time, Hartford authorship is practically at a standstill, saving an occasional book or booklet. Outside of the class of fiction-writers named above, an occasional work from Dr. Walker or Dr. Twichell, (two of the best writers in New England in the line of history,) we have practically nothing to show of late years. What is the reason?

In New York, Dr. Titus M. Coan is making heroic efforts to stimulate interest in the "American Author's Guild," which is the new name for the "Association of American Authors." The last name chosen is better than the first, because the guild idea better indicates the objects of the organization, which are, to serve authors in advisory ways, co-operate with publishers, secure extensions and modifications of copyright laws, promote a fraternal spirit, and generally to advance the interests of American authors. There are a good many more authors than the general public realizes: and few of them, it must be said, are as good business men as their publishers.

The CONNECTICUT QUARTERLY offers its pages freely to Hartford writers, as to those throughout the State, under the very limited restriction that they give their best work to it; since we are determined to become, as one author expresses it, "the mouth-piece of the State," not only in a literary but in a historical way. If such a club is started in Hartford—and there is no better time than at, or near the beginning of the year—we shall cheerfully co-operate in its aims and efforts, and may; incidentally be able to offer some suggestions that will help place it on a permanent footing, to make it eventually an honor to the city, a credit to itself, and a source of delight to visiting authors from other cities who may share its hospitality or give readings under its auspices.

AN ADEQUATE STATE HISTORY.
An adequate history of the State of Connecticut, does not exist. Peters's is pugnacious and pernicious; Sanford's and Johnson's, while modern and methodical, are only handbooks suitable for schools or the shelves of the average man who does not care

much for his State; and Hollister's, while still standard, is growing passe each year and less valuable. We have, indeed, but fragments so far, barring these few general histories and others we might name. "The Memorial History of Hartford County," as well as the histories of New Haven and Windham Counties, were masterly works, but they covered only one county. Such a work, extended to other counties, would be entirely satisfactory; but there is no pecuniary inducement, nor sufficient local pride, to justify an enterprising publisher in going to such an enormous expense. Hence, a comprehensive and thorough-going history of the State has not been placed before the public. Its compilation is too gigantic a task for one man to attempt. The commonwealth is too old, too rich in details, historical, genealogical, political, and otherwise, to be compassed by one man properly, in an ordinary life-time. It must be done by concerted effort and application.

It goes without saying that our historical records are daily becoming more and more indistinct and undecipherable. and soon will be irrecoverable. But, our past has been too rich in incident, too unique in interest, too influential in the history of the country at large, to be lost, through inattention and neglect. While much has been done in preserving intact the history of the older and larger towns, many, because of later settlement, or from poverty of incident, have been passed by, but which can furnish material that when well digested, is of just as much importance as the histories of the larger towns and cities. All this material can, and should, be properly compiled, arranged, and published in attractive and readable form, for future use, and in systematic order. If it is not worth doing well it should not be attempted at all.

It is our intention to publish just such a work, covering the entire State eventually, in the pages of this magazine. It will not be in due chronological order and sequence, as one might suppose, for that would be tedious; but the history will gradually "evolve" itself from the wealth of material we shall publish; and all the small pieces of craftsmanship will gradually slip into place, as the queerly dove-tailed parts of a Chinese puzzle are assembled. In this way, we hope to treat of the entire State in all its historical, political, statistical, economic and progressive aspects and features. The whole history will be properly presented and progressively developed, provided we have sufficient encouragement and co-operation. We need the co-operation of every man, woman and child in the State (for the children will perhaps be men and women before the work is completed), to attain our objects.

We propose, first, to publish a series of descriptive articles of various places, in much the same fashion as some in this issue; these will be, for the present, sparingly interspersed with the historical papers; lastly will come a general survey of the State, and, if time and space are allowed, a genealogical history, completing Hinman "Puritan Settlers of Connecticut"; down to Revolutionary days.

PERSONAL JOURNALISM.

There are those who will criticise a new venture for being too "froward" and positive in its "make-up." This is natural, but we live in progressive days, in which if one is not self-assertive and independent, he will lag behind the procession and find it difficult to recover his place in it. While our magazine is, perhaps, unduly self-conscious in its first issue, and in its "new dress" feels rather conspicuous, and withal proud and pretty; this newness and rawness will wear off after we have had time to fully explain our raison d' etre. develop our present plans, and outline our future policy. It is necessary to be a trifle assertive in order to make ourselves heard and felt all over the State, and more than that properly understood. In this issue, however, we have simply outlined, indicated, and put in leading-strings our various departments and their conductors; we hope to show progress and improvement in future issues, and to add other features which will be of interest and value. But we will not anticipate.

One thing is noticeable; we have required all articles and contributions to be signed, as we believe in personal journalism; life is so short, art so long, opportunity so infrequent, and fame so precarious, that few really reach the reputation and reward they deserve. Thereby hangs a tale: A generation since, James Russell Lowell, then editing the ATLANTIC MONTHLY, took a prodigious fancy to a brilliant Irishman named Fitz-James O'Brien, publishing for him in the ATLANTIC, the remarkable stories: "The Lost Room," and "The Diamond Lens." At that time the Harpers would not allow American writers to append their names to their work, extending this right to English writers only. O'Brien would have none of this. A volume of HARPER'S MONTHLY for 1860, shows that Thackeray, Anthony Trollope, George Eliot, and Fitz-James O'Brien were equally honored in this respect, and American literature began to breathe freely. The privilege conceded to him is now freely recognized; many editors now insist on signed articles. This change, the working magazine and newspaper men of to-day owe to O'Brien more than to any other man.

Again, we wish to accord to all our contributors the widest liberty of expression and opinion — of course over signatures—governed by prudence, wisdom, and refinement. Wherever an evil is to be corrected, a good to be espoused, a right to be championed, there we hope to be in the midst. Whatever builds up the commonwealth or any part thereof, in a moral or intellectual aspect, that we shall advocate with heart and soul; and we ask our contributors to do likewise when writing of any place or portion of the State; if a town is slovenly and rakish, do not hesitate to say so, and cry out for a village improvement society; if it lacks mental pabulum, moral fiber, or intellectual stimulus, preach and pray for whatever is lacking to make it better; of course within the bounds of reason and moderation.

Thus, in this issue, we give considerable space to strong pleas from our musical critic for a music hall and a musical library, both of which are greatly needed. Again, Dr. McManus has also made a special plea for a new and attractive opening to our park system from the main street (and this, let us add, is not in the interest of any landlord or real estate proprietor, but wholly gratuitous and public-spirited on his part), which we hope will be heeded. Our present park is little more than a cul de sac or "vermiform appendix," with no fitting entrance from the main street. Let us have a wide and liberal opening to the present park on Main street, abutting on the famous Center Church burying ground at one side, which should be improved to correspond. A person standing on Main street can then command a lovely view of the Little river in its windings through the park; while alongside of the river should be a driveway to the Arch, and beyond to the depot. This opening or "approach" should have a new name ("Bushnell Place," perhaps), at least be changed from the unhallowed name of Gold street, which savors too much of gambling. Moreover, now that the acceptance of the park system is evident, and a new park commission ample for the purpose is to be appointed, let us caution the gentlemen thereof not to entrust the laying-out of the parks to any inexperienced landscape-gardener. The name of Frederick Law Olmsted naturally comes uppermost in one's thoughts, as the most competent in the country; and besides is not Hartford his birth-place and former home? He would certainly take great pride in beautifying his birth-place, and thus leaving a monument to his memory that will endure for ages.

Lastly, let the bicycle clubs see to it that a bicycle path or "wheel-way," be laid alongside of the boulevard, connecting the parks — and they cannot insist upon and arrange for this too early.

which is, we find, a very important element at the inception of a new magazine. Most of the work preparatory to the printers was done inside of a month—which is not a remarkable fact if we had had a settled staff of contributors and a fully developed policy. It had to be assembled out of its inchoate condition piece-meal, minds made to meet on various purposes and projects, contributions accumulated sufficient to start it; finally the editorial work was done at white-heat and the illustrations finished on short time. Add to all these unexpected balks in getting it ready, we waited for our new dress of type for nearly a month, to be cast and forwarded, as the foundry was crowded with orders which it was unable to fill. We had hoped to steal upon the public almost unannounced, in holiday times,—a sort of surprise and Christmas present to the State,—but it was not to be. At any rate we hope it will be just as gratefully received and read now as it would have been during the hurly-burly of holiday times.

We are asked various questions of late: "Will it be a success?" It is already a success—and you know "nothing succeeds like success." "Will it not 'fold its tent like the Arab, and silently steal away'?" The publishers' assurance and guarantee is sufficient answer to that. "Is it not too good to last?" No, dear reader, we have carefully provided against that, by making it just so good and no better. We have tried to make it as attractive as—for instance, a suburban car—and intrinsically as dainty, pleasant, and lovable as—old lavender, or old lace,—with a faint, all-pervasive aroma of antiquity to flavor it. We want to make it so good that all who read it will fall in love with it, and then our whole aim will have been accomplished. A glance at our announcements and list of contributors, will convince all that it will NOT be local or centralized, but that the whole boundless State is ours.

W. Farrand Felch

A WORD OF PROMISE.

A word of promise; not of apology, which is hardly ever in order; and yet if we promise too much it will be worse than apologizing for our present shortcomings. To-morrow the critics will begin; that is inevitable! Well—let them; we have done our best, under given circumstances; the chief hindrance has been the lack of time

MUSICAL MELANGE.

"Other slow arts entirely keep the brain,
And therefore, finding barren practicers,
Scarce show a harvest of their heavy toil."—SHAKESPERE.

NEW YORK NOTATIONS.

"A chiel's amang ye takin' notes
And, faith, he'll prent it."—BURNS.

NEW YORK CITY, Jan. 15, 1895.
The opera season has opened auspiciously, and continues to date successfully, with fair attendance, better indeed than last year. It is safe to gauge the success of any dramatic season by the patronage bestowed upon the opera ; but there is really little affinity between those who attend the opera and the class that prefer pure drama.

The company which sung at the Metropolitan last season was selected with great care and intelligence ; but it is not to be expected that the metropolis will accept the same thing unchanged a second time. However good the old, the public is not content, but must have novelty. A few members of the present organization have been heard in seasons past, but others are entire strangers, and this furnishes the element of novelty.

Miss Sybil Sanderson, the fair Californian, has studied under Leoncavallo, Massenet, and Marchesi. She made her debut at the Hague under the name of Ada Palmer, and her Parisian debut in Massenet's "Esclarmonde" in 1890, at the Opera Comique, and in 1891 scored a triumph in "Manon." One year later Saint-Saens wrote "Phryne" for her. Last autumn she appeared in Massenet's "Thais," taken from Anatole France's novel of the same name.

Zelie de Lussan. the CARMEN of the present company, has been here before, but went to London with the Carl Rosa Opera Company. To play "Carmen" here after Calve's triumphs in the role is tempting fortune bravely ; but she has appeared before Queen Victoria several times in "Carmen," and has met with great success in this as well as in other operas.

Miss Lucille Hill is an American, and a pupil of Mme. Marchesi. After leaving Paris she was engaged by D'Oyley Carte for the leading part in "Ivanhoe," and attracted the attention of Sir Augustus Harris (the "Abbey of London"), who engaged her for his grand opera force at Covent Garden. Mlle. Eugenie Mantelli was born in Milan. Last winter she sang in St. Petersburg, her repertoire including such parts as AMNERIS in "Aida," DALILA in "Samson and Dalila," and ORTRUD in "Lohengrin."

Victor Maurel is the one whom Verdi had in mind when he wrote "Falstaff," one of the new works to be given this season at the Metropolitan. "Otello," "Rigoletto," "Ernani," "William Tell," and "The Huguenots," are also favorite operas of his. The appearance of Francesco Tamagno, here a few seasons ago as a member of the Patti company, is still fresh in the minds of music-lovers. Mlle. Mira Heller is a native of Poland, studied in Vienna under Mme. Pauline Lucca and began her career in Italy. Mme. Libia Drog, who made such a queer contretemps from stage-fright, on her first appearance here, has since met with a decided success. She is a Venetian and has had much experience in the opera houses of the continent. So much for the personnel of the strangers ; now for their achievements so far this season.

Thus far, the season has seen the production of the operas "Otello," "Lohengrin," "Rigoletto," "Romeo et Juliette," "William Tell," "Aida," (twice), "Carmen," "Lucia di Lammermoor," "Il Trovatore," and "Faust" (twice). Last winter, the last-named opera, with the "Ideal" cast was the piece de resistance during the season. This year "Faust" has been succeeded in the popular favor, I think, by "Otello," which, with M. Maurel, Eames and Tamagno, appears to be as "Ideal" from an operatic stand-point as possible. There is probably no greater baritone living today than Maurel, and his character study of Iago is, musically, what Booth's was and Irving's is, in the dramatic domain of the world. In "Otello" Maurel has met with the most enthusiastic reception in New York, as he has from the audience of every civilized nation of the world during the past twenty-five years. Emma Eames' Desdemona is a study in grace, simplicity and sweetness. Her personality is as magnetic as when she first won our hearts, and her voice is the same limpid crystal spring of transparent beauty. Signor Tamagno is considered one of the greatest dramatic tenors in the world, and in the impassioned role of "Radames" in "Aida" he rises to heights of emotion which are wonderfully realistic.

As ARNOLDO in "William Tell," Tamagno scored a great success on the night that Mme. Drog made her embarrassing "lapsus memoriæ" in the role of

MATHILDE. Of Jean and Edouard de Reszke, I need hardly speak. The first is the acknowledged leading tenor on the operatic stage, and his work, even to the minutest details, evidences the greatest study and the genius of a master. His roles are legion and each one seems absolutely perfect until he appears in the next. This year he has thus far been heard in "Romeo et Juliette," "Faust," "Carmen" and "Lohengrin." You may remember that a grand revival of "Romeo et Juliette" took place at the Grand Opera, Paris, about seven years ago. In this notable production Mme. Adelina Patti was the JULIETTE and Jean de Reszke the ROMEO. Since then the opera has not seemed to be as popular as many others; hence we have had it sung but seldom.

M. Edouard de Reszke's repertoire is as extensive as his brother's, and his voice, a deep, sonorous basso, is thought by many to be as fine in the lower register as his brother's in the higher. MEPHISTOPHELE in "Faust" is Edouard de Reszke's great character, and a more Satanic, grim, and forbidding picture of cunning and sin would be hard to find. Of magnificent physical proportions, and with a nimble, quick action, he suggests the ruler of Milton's "Paradise Lost" to the life.

In closing, let me mention briefly the triumphs that have attended the performances of Mme. Melba, the Australian nightingale, who a few short years ago went to Mme. Marchesi unknown and left her a famous, world-renowned artist. Her greatest character with us is MARGUERITE in "Faust," and it is impossible to conceive of a gentler, lovelier, or a purer maid than she makes the unfortunate heroine of Goethe's romance. Physically and vocally she is par excellence in the part, and as the curtain descends on the prison-scene in the last act, and one sees the hosts of angels transporting the body of the sin-stained maiden who "loved not wisely but too well," there is hardly one in the audience who does not almost instinctively send up a mental prayer to Heaven that her soul may be received within the gates of that eternal kingdom where grief and sorrow are changed into notes of joy and gladness in the happy company of the elect.

In this connection it is pertinent to remark that a Mrs. Grannis, who is a former Hartford woman, has opened a crusade against the decollette gowns worn by the society leaders in the opera boxes. She contends that the display is even worse than that seen on the stage, and that the ballet is no more immodest. It is perhaps a bid for a passing notoriety, suggested perhaps by Lady Henry Somerset's crusade against the music halls and living art tableaux. At any rate, it furnishes a spicy tid-bit for society gossip.

E. W. DeLeon.

THE MESSIAH.

On December 19 the "Messiah" was given at Foot Guard Hall, by the Hosmer Hall Choral Union, under the direction of Mr. Paine. The large and enthusiastic audience was sufficient testimonial both to the popularity of the work and the excellence of its performance. It is not my intention to give any detailed criticism of the concert, but rather to call attention to the peculiar position occupied by this oratorio in the history of music.

The "Messiah" marks an epoch both in the development of the oratorio and in the life of its composer. It was written in 1741, in the fifty-sixth year of Handel's life. Until this time he had devoted himself almost exclusively to the production of operas and other secular forms of composition, and no amount of failure seemed sufficient to turn his efforts in the direction in which his peculiar genius best fitted him to succeed. The contrast between these long years of unsuccessful struggle, and the unbounded enthusiasm with which the "Messiah" was received must have shown him his mistake, for after writing it not a single opera was produced by him, but all his more important choral works, secular as well as sacred, were written in the form of oratorios. Most of these met with immediate and complete success, and gained for their author the musical pre-eminence which had so long been the object of his ambition, and which has endured to the present day.

The influence of the "Messiah" on the development of the oratorio is very significant. As originally designed and developed, in the early Italian stage of their history, oratorios had no place outside of the services of the church, being used much as the modern "praise-service,"—to draw a crowd. After its introduction into Germany and its adoption by the Lutheran church, its form assumed more definite proportions, and its artistic growth was rapid, but it was still looked upon as only an elaborate church service. This appropriation by the church was necessary for the early development of the oratorio, but had it continued, and had the oratorio never been heard outside of the church the loss to the intellectual and artistic life of the people would have been incalculable.

Handel gave to the oratorio a broader and more independent existence, and made it a part of the daily life of the people. This he accomplished chiefly by means of the "Messiah." When "Esther," his first English oratorio, was produced in 1732, the public was so ignorant of this style of writing that it was necessary to explain in the announcement that the oratorio was "to be performed by a great number of voices and instruments. . . . There will be no acting on the stage. . . . The music to be disposed after the manner of the Coronation Service."

From this time until 1741, Handel composed "Deborah," "Athaliah,' " Saul," and " Israel in Egypt," so that while none of these works were popular at the time, the public must have gained some familiarity with this form of composition. At least, when the "Messiah" was finally produced, it was considered unnecessary to explain the difference between opera and oratorio. The reception given this work, both on its first appearance in Dublin and its repetition in London, was extremely enthusiastic. It is claimed that it was upon this latter occasion that the custom of standing during the "Hallelujah Chorus" originated, the audience being so moved by the phrase, "for the Lord God omnipotent reigneth" that all present, including the king, involuntarily rose to their feet. The "Messiah" at once assumed a position in the mind of the public that is both unique and suggestive. The proceeds of the first performance, £400, was devoted entirely to charity, and from that time to this no one work has done as much for the poor and the unfortunate as the "Messiah." Handel himself presented the score to the Foundling Hospital, and from 1750 to 1759, the year of his death, conducted eleven performances of it for the benefit of this institution, the proceeds from which amounted to nearly £7,000.

The influence of the "Messiah" upon the religious life of the people, although not so easily estimated, must certainly have been very great. The sermons it preaches sink deep into the heart, and are not easily forgotten. No work was ever more divinely inspired. Its composer was a prophet charged with a distinct mission, from which he could in no wise escape, the execution of which brought him great reward, and to the rest of the world a blessing that shall endure throughout all time.

CHARLES H. JOHNSON.

HARTFORD MUSICAL CULTURE.

The recent visit of the Boston Symphony Orchestra, and some attending circumstances suggest the question as to the degree of musical culture in this city. Given a form of composition which is admittedly the loftiest and purest expression of which music is capable, and an orchestra so wonderfully organized and manned that it is reputed to be the best—save perhaps one—in the world, and it would seem that the conditions are at once established for making the test. This orchestra has been organized fourteen years, has visited Hartford four times, has always charmed its hearers, but never had a full house. It has had four conductors, and under Mr. Gericke, the second of these, it attained the remarkable finish that placed it above its competitors. Mr. Nikisch, the third conductor, infused a greater degree of warmth and passion into the playing. and then it became recognized as probably without a peer.

Three of the Hartford concerts were given by Mr. Gericke, stopping on the way to or from New Haven, where for several years a series of four concerts were given each season. The receipts were so small here that Hartford was checked off as a town not large enough, or else not musical enough to visit again ; so we were not privileged to hear the orchestra under the leadership of Mr. Nikisch. After an interval of five years, on the supposition, probably, that the city had increased its population, and had grown musically as well, the management made another attempt, but with the same result. From this point of view Hartford is given over as hopeless. On the other hand, the musicians expressed themselves as delighted with their reception, and one of their number said to the writer. "You give us more applause for the Seventh Symphony, here in Hartford, than we get in Boston."

Hartford has been getting its education in orchestral music during the last twenty-five years ; for it was in 1869 that Theodore Thomas made his first tour of the country with fifty-five men. He came here and played to an almost empty house ; but scarcely ever afterwards, for he held a very warm place in the hearts of music-lovers. Commencing with light music, such as the "Traumerei" and Strauss waltzes, he soon led up to the symphonies of Beethoven, and it is almost safe to say that every one, except the ninth, has been played here by him. The overtures of Wagner and Weber, too, were first given here by him. Season after season he came, and left some good result behind him. The elder Damrosch came once with an indifferent orchestra, which played roughly and poorly. The younger Damrosch came later, with a fine body of men ; but without the magnetism of Thomas or the impress of his marked personality, he did not attract increasing audiences. We waited long for Seidl, and when he gave his first Wagner concert, with an array of vocal artists, the house was packed and enthusiasm ran high. His subsequent visits were less successful, because of an inadequate orchestra ; but his last concert was intensely interesting, notwithstanding, for whatever he touches he ennobles by his splendid musical temperament.

The discriminating sense of concert-goers has been sharpened by comparing these different men and their work. especially in compositions that by frequent repetition have become familiar, as for example, the Seventh Symphony ; but if we give Mr. Paur and his men more applause for this work than they get in Boston, let us not forget that it was Theodore Thomas who led, not only the musical people of this city, but of the whole country, up out of the wilderness and taught them to love and reverence Beethoven.

There are about so many people—not enough to fill Foot Guard Hall—who may always be depended upon to grace with their presence every such rare occasion as was the concert by the Boston men—

a concert which stands for pure musical culture, and without the glamour of an expensively dressed female singer. There are those who easily drop into a scolding mood, and declare that Hartford is a slow town, and if one wishes to hear music, the only thing to do is to pack a grip and go to New York. This is only a partial truth, and is entirely in a wrong spirit. Let us rather set more agencies at work, at home, to create an art sentiment, which, it must be said, does not now exist to any great extent ; and out of sentiment will eventually grow a deep and abiding principle. This principle that art is worth cultivating for art's sake, is one that too many who assume leadership in musical matters are reticent about.

The Boston Orchestra sets a good example by giving us the able analytical notes by Mr. Apthorp, which it uses in all its concerts at home. They are of great educational value. The suggestion is here respectfully made that some of our daily newspapers might add to their popularity by the occasional publication of a well-edited column of musical miscellany. This service to the public is excellently done by the Springfield REPUBLICAN and the fruits are unmistakably evident in all that section. With the weekly columns of religious items and social notes, the space devoted to agriculture, the daily hints to dress-makers, amateur and professional, it would seem that a similar attention to music would be an experiment well worth making. These notes would be read in almost every household, for the interest in music is now so general that it might be said "there is music in the air"; but to say that all the people interested are well or even fairly informed is quite another thing. It is just this difference between interest and information which causes the sight now so familiar to all who attend orchestral concerts—a house only two-thirds full.

To speak of the concert of the Boston Orchestra in detail at this late day would be superfluous, as it has been freely discussed and enthusiastically praised by all who were so fortunate as to hear it. It was a generous feast of music. It is a rare pleasure to hear sixty men, and among them many great artists, some of whom play instruments that could be placed without disparagement in the Hawley Collection. It was, too, an event to be remembered because of the presence of the great Belgian artist, Cæsar Thomson. We may now hope to hear his equally great compatriot, Ysaye, before the season is over.

RUBENSTEIN : REQUIESCAT. The London SATURDAY REVIEW gives a juster estimate of Rubenstein, lately deceased, than any we have encountered. The writer remembers. as a boy, hearing the great pianist, who left an impression that time will not efface, and no later pianist has been able to eclipse, so we welcome this fair criticism to our pages :

"So much has been written and so foolishly, about Rubenstein, that our impressions of the man are likely to be a little confused. When we calmly examine his actual achievements as a pianist and a creative musician, the first thing that strikes us is that in neither capacity was he in any sense an innovator. He followed so close upon Liszt that in piano-forte technique, nothing was left him to do.

"But what Liszt had built up he used in a manner that Liszt could not have equalled. Liszt's fire—though the statement seems self-contradictory—was fire of the intellect ; indeed, we may doubt whether he possessed much fire at all, whether abnormal keenness of brain rather than heart was not his potent characteristic. At least his sympathy with the great masters was principally intellectual. He recorded them with astounding insight, it is true, but from outside ; and when he played it was to display himself much more than to interpret them.

"Not so, Rubenstein. He was an emotional giant. His emotional nature continually smouldered at a dull, red heat, but when the breath of another composer's inspiration blew upon the mass it flashed up and the conflagration was always impressive and sometimes surprising. He then saw the master-works from inside—he made us feel that here were the very thoughts and emotions of the composer, not of the virtuoso. Hence, above all things, he was a great interpreter—perhaps the greatest interpreter who has lived.

"As a composer he must be ranked much lower. He never invented a great melody. Melody he had ; it flowed in an abundant, pellucid stream, and its flavor was frequently piquant, and where piquancy without the grander qualities will satisfy, then Rubenstein is delightful. His small things—those that he probably regarded as of little account—are unique and invaluable. But his large works simply represent enormous waste of energy ; and ten years hence no one will know their names.

"Some men speak in prose and some in verse, some in marble and some in brass, some in song and some in epic, and for the epic Rubenstein had no gift, but he sang divine songs."

CHOPIN AND TENNYSON. "Chopin is, without dispute, the Tennyson of the piano. The same d e p t h, warmth and delicacy of feeling vitalize every line ; the same polish, fineness of detail and symmetry of form, the same exquisitely refined yet by no means effeminate temperament are seen in both.

"Each shows us perfect passion, beyond the ken of common men, without a touch of brutality, intense and vehement emotion with never a hint of violence in its betrayal, expressed in dainty rhythmic numbers as polished and symmetrical as if that polish and symmetry were their only raison d' etre. Superficial observers, fixing their attention on the pre-eminent delicacy, tenderness, elegance, and grace of their manner and matter, regard them as exponents of these qualities merely, and deny them broader, stronger. sterner characteristics.

"Never was a grosser wrong done true artists. No poet and no composer is more profound, passionate, and intense than Tennyson and Chopin, and none so rarely pens a line that is devoid of genuine feeling. Both had the heart and fire and tongue of gold. Tennyson wrote the modern lyrics of his language, and Chopin the model lyrics of his instrument for all posterity."—E. B. Parry, in THE ETUDE.

SCHUBERT'S UNFINISHED SYMPHONY.

Unfinished! Once I said, and could it be,
That some great soul, catching the inspired theme,
Should dare to make complete the heavenly dream
That trembles in that wondrous symphony!
For, baffled, to myself I ever ask,
How should it in its full perfection end?
Ah, well and true hast thou fulfilled thy task.
Great Schubert! Now I know thou didst intend
To show how strangely sweet one simple air
Repeated o'er and o'er may grow to be:
That air is Love's. Oh, who of us would dare
To say, for man, full ended must it be?
So list the straight that thrills along the strings,
While love unpinioned shakes his snowy wings.
—SAN FRANCISCO ARGONAUT.

A NEW MUSIC HALL.

In a recent letter to the papers, Mr. Henry Irving has drawn a careful distinction between theaters, and music halls, the latter being, he admits, "places of entertainment," and the former he assures us are not, whereupon a London journal takes him to task in this wise:

"The music hall has always existed side by side with the more seriously regarded performance of stage plays. The circus of antiquity was a music hall, and music hall entertainments were given in private houses. The modern music hall began humbly across the water. [in America]; it has had its vicissitudes but a steady progress, and now the best ones pay an annual dividend of seventy per centum. They are crowded night by night to a point to which no theater is crowded, not even the theater in which 'Charlie's Aunt' is being given. The music hall entertainment is therefore one of the accepted facts of the day which we must reckon with and endeavor to appraise justly, unless we are resolved to be deliberately out of touch with received facts. The attitude of Mr. Irving and of the conservative play-goers is an impossible attitude; it will have to be abandoned. The music hall is as certain, as serious a fact as democracy."

The music halls of London are conducted on a broader gauge than the regular theaters, hence Mr. Irving's diatribe. There is as much difference between them as between the legitimate drama and the broadest farce. They are largely responsible for the wave of farce-comedy that has overwhelmed this land; only our sense of humor differs from theirs and so our farces differ. It is not of this class of music halls that we wish to speak, but of broad, generous foundations such as the Music Hall in Boston, which is second to none in this country.

There is need of such a Music Hall in this city, and has been for years, as has frequently been pointed out in the daily press; and a decided movement is making in that direction. Where there is so much smouldering disaffection, there will sooner or later be a flame. This flame is already flickering strongly. There is a definite plan drawn for a new opera house in this city to be built at no distant date; besides, at least two churches are considering the "Auditorium plan"; and old Allyn Hall is to be remodeled, renovated, and made a comfortable theater or farce-hall probably. Surely the leaven is working in many directions, and the time seems not far distant when the crying need for large halls to accommodate growing audiences shall be satisfied.

As our last pages go to press, we learn with great pleasure and interest that negotiations, which have been for some time pending for the purchase of the present opera house, have ended in the consummation of a year's option upon the property; if a stock company can now be formed within the year, which seems certain, it will be renovated, remodeled, reseated, and changed into a ground floor theater, Mr. Walter Sanford, the artist, Mr. John B. Knox and Mr. E. W. Beardsley, prominent insurance people, are the prime movers in the enterprise, and are to be congratulated on cutting the Gordian knot, by securing this option. They are actuated by public spirited motives, believing that Hartford needs a modern theatre, and that local capital should control the field.

Hartford has had a surfeit of "circuit," attractions for years; the same hash of horse-plays and hoydenish soubrette farces, coming every year not only, but each three or four times in a season, until it has grown fearfully monotonous; for a month or two at a stretch not a notable play; and in a five or six months' season not a first-class Shakesperian or romantic-star attraction; and it has steadily grown worse. It has operated in driving away the better class of patrons and the better class of actors. Let us now hope that the new plan will be carried along to a successful termination, in spite of all obstacles, be that end, one, two, or more years' distant.

With a ground floor theater, having attractive entrances on Main, Church, and Pratt streets (like Keith's, in Boston,) and a two-story stage as in the Springfield Opera House (for people here still like to retire with the ringing of the nine o'clock "curfew bell"), it is bound to be a succcess. Add to this enterprise the new Fourth Church Auditorium (both moderate cost schemes, and worthy of cordial support), and we shall be amply equipped in the dramatic and musical fields for many years to come. We heartily commend the project as worthy of support.

NEW WORSHIP.

The growing tendency of most people is to rely too much on the verdicts of musical critics, and to attach too much importance to their opinions. The subject might be enlarged to other things in the musical world. The tendency of music-lovers towards new worship is growing and is becoming almost an evil. Several of the musical journals complain of this. It is said that last season no one talked in

London of going to hear "Carmen" or "Faust" or "Lohengrin," but it was "have you heard Jean de Reszke" in so and so? The same was the case with the great conductors Mottl and Richter, ticket issue was sold out every time their names appeared. There is, of course, not a bit of use in moralizing over this fact, but a word of warning may not be out of place.

The popular task is unstable and the popular idol is neither immortal nor inerrant. The works of art performed, owe their longevity to merits more important than mere physical dexterity, and they have been tested by severe standards. On the other hand, the great composer does not always write great music; the great singer is not always in good voice, and the great conductor sometimes makes a mistake; while there are hosts of composers, performers and conductors of lesser reputation, who can often charm the ear, if music and not new worship is the object sought, and it only requires for the public to sink personality and confess the presence of artistic merit, which often exists without a salary of $3,000 a night as a remuneration.

A PUBLIC MUSICAL LIBRARY. If there is one thing more than another that Hartford needs, outside of purely municipal affairs which will take care of themselves, if left alone long enough, it is a music hall. We have alluded to this, in another note, so will defer saying anything further. Springfield has just decided to build a fine music hall and market combined, but ours should be better. A rich Bridgeport man has lately given $650,000 to Yale to establish a conservatory or college of music which will treat of only classical music, but ours, if ever built, should be for the masses.

This is not what we started out to say, however. What we wished to say was that, secondly, in the musical line, Hartford needs, sadly too, a public musical library,—which could be a lending library of the latest popular music, the latest opera scores and librettos, and a reference library of classical music of "the Old Masters." A room can be devoted to this purpose, in the Athenæum, and even furnished with instruments, if sufficient funds are at command. It is not an experiment, but has been tried in other places, notably Brooklyn. A modest bequest for this purpose of $10,000 to $25,000 would furnish sufficient income to make the thing practicable at once, and by careful purchasing at the end of five or ten years, a large and almost complete library in most departments of music would be available to all students. It should be selected with as catholic and intelligent taste and judgment as possible, not be confined to any one class, as at Hosmer Hall, nor present any particular propaganda in the art. In a city where it is impossible to buy Beethoven's complete works, and to command any wide selection, such a library is a crying need. Moreover the donor would reap a lasting honor and glory — and it is not necessary for one to die to make such a bequest; in fact, it is better to live and enjoy it, and to know how much enthusiasm and profit others can and will derive from it. Besides it is a modest bequest — a mere bagatelle in fact — and you will not feel it, after all! It is so much better to put your money out at intellectual interest in this way. my rich friends, then to hoard and save it for lawyers to squabble over; and the rich are fast finding this out! Even Tilden, great lawyer that he was, did not form a will that could not be broken, as he boasted he should. It was only by the merest chance that New York secures the great library which is to eclipse the squeamish, conservative, close-corporation Astor library.

We like to see brains mixed with beneficence, and in most cases in equal quantities, but how seldom is this done. There are a certain number of beneficiaries that come in for a portion of the crumbs that fall when the wills of our rich men are opened, and the painful monotony of it is very depressing to other objects just as worthy. The same old list, the same old bequests, until it is all eaten up, and nothing is left for the intellectual betterment of the city, in the lines of art, music. and literature ; and if perchance anything is left it is so pitiably small that it is "only the leavings" of the residue, (the "residuum," as one of our contemporaries lately had it.)

The writer is not aiming at any one, nor yet aiming at random. It is the experience of at least ten years, perhaps more. How much have our deceased citizens done for the city in an intellectual way in the past decade or two, outside of a select few who understood its wants and needs, in their bequests? How many have even considered the wants and needs of the masses?

As masses go, let it be remembered that Hartford has invited only the better class of manufactures, and patronized only the higher grades of work, which required skilled and well-paid labor; the result is an influx of the better and brainier mechanics, who are the "bone and sinew" of the land, to quote a trite phrase. How much has been done to make them feel at home, to furnish them with mental pabulum and stimulus?

It is true we have the public library, and that is a God-send! It is true we have a new and promising science association; a small art gallery is promised; we have long had excellent schools, a college and a seminary. But, bless you, these are mostly only late beginnings! Now we have had a "rain of parks," to decorate an already showy city—plenty of parks for the poor man who can not leave the city, for the rich man who will daily drive his thorough-breds the length of our broad boulevard, and for the great middle-class, who can not often afford to drive and must perforce look on and envy. But these things are only Apples of Sodom, after all, if there are not other compensating advantages for the dwellers, and those who are attracted here to dwell,—mere "pie-crust" advantages, that will not help the city, if more and better enticements are not offered in intellectual lines.

I have perhaps gone beyond my leash, and the editor may draw me in bounds again; but he has given me the privilege of some of his own prerogatives of scolding and carping, which every editor enjoys—really enjoys too! So I may be forgiven if some of my words do some good and strike home to some hearts. If they do not, then you will perhaps forgive your music-mad

MINERVA.

TREASURE TROVE.

" Time hath, my lord, a wallet at his back,
Wherein he puts alms for oblivion."

" While place we seek or place we shun,
The soul finds happiness in none
But with a God to lead the way
'Tis equal joy to go or stay."—MADAME GUION.

PATRIOTIC SOCIETIES: In the jubilee year of our country, the "World's Fair year," we noted not only a great revival of patriotism but a steady growth of ancestral veneration amounting almost to worship. To perpetuate these sentiments as well as to revive them, several societies have sprung into existence in late years.

These societies may or may not have with them, by the nature of their organization and attributes, the permanency which may be sought for in such laudable institutions, actuated by pure patriotic zest and deep-seated reverence. It is for the future to determine whether they will stand storm and stress periods, as have the "Plymouth Society," and the "Order of the Cincinnati" (founded on the law of primogeniture as to membership), or those old and time-tried orders founded by the veterans of the civil war who are rapidly leaving the stage of action, the "Military Order of the Loyal Legion," the "Grand Army of the Republic," and other patriotic assemblies. Let us hope that their days will be long in the land. Surely when one knows the laudable motives they foster, the extended researches attempted, the spirit of fraternization and its feminine synonym among the sister orders, and the dignity and solidity of character imposed by the requirements of membership, one can not help believing that they have "builded better than they knew."

IGNORANCE OF ANCESTRY. With all these societies, and the general efforts of genealogists, there is a lamentable lack of interest among the generality of folk as to their descent from the old colonial people from whence they were derived in the first days of our fair land; the majority of the American people, it is supposed (especially outside of New England), can not, unaided, give their ancestry beyond their own grandparents. Some people, not at all ignorant in other matters either, can not tell even the names of their grand-parents. How many, indeed, know for a certainty, unless there is a well-defined tradition in the family, whether they had ancestors who fought in the Revolutionary war. If they are positive about grand-fathers and great-grandfathers in the direct paternal line, how many know anything of their ancestry to this extent in other lines than the paternal?

How many of your own grand-parents and great-grand-parents can you name off hand, without going to the records or to the family Bible? How few family Bibles give anything more than the immediate family! These strictures do not apply to the East nor to the West, nor to any section, particularly, but to the whole boundless continent, or its people rather. There is a crass and stupendous ignorance on such points. And so we say, all honor to these patriotic societies for the work they are doing in recalling some of the forgotten worthies, "the old colonial characters," who were after all like those of to-day, very human, and subject to the same faults and frailties as people of the modern, hurrying, skurrying business world.

There are those, even in staunch New England, who would throw dishonor upon these various societies and their motives and aims; but all of these detractors, we feel free to say, would be only too glad to be numbered among the membership of one or more of them. Too often it is a case of "sour grapes;" but envy should not breed malice and detraction; for if one's ancestors in all lines are carefully collated, we believe it will be found that the average American of Puritan lineage would be eligible to one or more of these societies. Indeed, we know it from researches in our family and for others who have wished to enlist in one or another of them. The writer does not seek such distinction, being a modest man, and besides can trace his ancestry not only to several ensigns, captains, lieutenants, magistrates, divines, among the puritans and pilgrims; but also into England, in many noble and royal lines back to the Conquest, and still back of that to Charlemagne, Pepin the Great, Rollo, Rurik, founder of Russia, Basil, emperor of Constantinople, the kings of Norway, Sweden, Denmark, Hungary, England, Scotland, France, Flanders, Spain, and Italy; so that all the more recent lines of descent are dwarfed by comparison! We are not one whit more proud, however, with all this weight of ancestry than if we could not trace beyond our own grand-fathers and grand-mothers. "A man's a man for a' that." Our friend Watkins insists that now a "Tory Society" should be started; or if it is too late for that, a "Society of Anglomaniacs," which would surely be popular; while our young English friend, Templeton, in the Athenæum, insists that nothing can compete with the real roast-beef Britishers. But, then every man to his taste.

We append reports of the leading state patriotic societies, or state branches of national societies, covering the past quarter, with, in some cases, an account of prior history; for which reports we are deeply grateful. One or two societies designated, failed to respond in due season for publication, and the same privilege is extended for the second issue, which we trust they will avail themselves of then.

ALGERNON.

CONNECTICUT SOCIETY OF THE SONS OF THE AMERICAN REVOLUTION.
Forty men assembled in the Capitol, at Hartford, on the second day of April, 1889, for the purpose of organizing a society to be composed of the descendants of the soldiers, sailors and statesmen of the Revolution. Among them were immediate sons of Amasa Clark and Hamilton Grant, who served under Israel Putnam. The society then organized is now known as the Connecticut Society of the Sons of the American Revolution. The objects of the Society, as officially declared are, to perpetuate the memory and spirit of the men who achieved American Independence, to encourage historical research in relation to the American revolution; to preserve documents, relics, and records of the individual services of revolutionary soldiers and patriots; to mark, by appropriate monuments, historic places within this State; to promote the celebration of patriotic anniversaries; and by these and similar means, to impress upon the present and future generations the patriotic spirit which actuated our ancestors and established the republic.

The anniversary of the capture of Ticonderoga, by an expedition set on foot by Connecticut, May 10th, was fixed upon for the beginning of the society year, and at the close of the first year, three hundred and twenty-five members had been enrolled. The roll of living members now includes between eight and nine hundred names, and this society is now by far the largest of all the societies with which it is affiliated. Connecticut men will be glad to know that their State, which, in proportion to its population, sent the greatest number of men to fight the battles of the Revolution, is again foremost in associating, to honor the deeds of the fathers and to perpetuate their spirit.

The members of the Society meet at dinner on the twenty-second of February in each year. They generally regard one another with admiration and respect. Hartford, New Haven, New London, Meriden, and Bridgeport have been visited in turn, and an invitation to dine at Norwich in 1895 has been accepted. The old war office of Governor Trumbull, at Lebanon, has been redeemed from the ignoble uses to which it had fallen, and restored, and now belongs to the Society. The flag that flies above it, invites the visitor to uncover in honor of "Brother Jonathan" and the statesmen and the generals and the common men of unknown names who also did their share, by whose feet the place has been consecrated.

The Year-Book which will include the proceedings for the period beginning May 10, 1892, and ending May 10, 1894, (the publication of the book was omitted last year), is in course of preparation. The war history of the revolutionary sires of the members constitute a conspicuous feature. Prizes, amounting to one hundred dollars have been offered to pupils in Connecticut schools for excellence in original essays, as follows:

To pupils in high schools, for essays on the share of Connecticut in the war of the Revolution, one first prize of twenty dollars; six second prizes of five dollars each. To pupils in schools below the grade of high schools, for essays on Connecticut Men of Mark in the War of the Revolution, one first prize of twenty dollars; six second prizes of five dollars each. Essays competing for these prizes are not to exceed two thousand words, and must be presented through the teachings of the respective schools before March 1, 1895. It cannot be vain to hope that the studies which these prizes may promote will tend to the proper end of all education — the building of character.

The affairs of the Society are directed by a Board of Managers, which at the present time consists of Jonathan Trumbull, Norwich, president; Ebenezer J. Hill, Norwalk, vice-president; John Clark Hollister, New Haven, treasurer; Charles Parsons Cooley, Hartford, secretary; Frank Butler Gay, Hartford, registrar; Joseph Gurley Woodward, Hartford, historian; the Rev. Edwin Stevens Lines, New Haven, chaplain; Hobart L. Hotchkiss, New Haven; H. Wales Lines, Meriden; Frank Farnsworth Starr, Middletown; Everett Edward Lord, New Haven; Franklin Henry Hart, New Haven; Edgar Jared Doolittle, Meriden; Zalmon Goodsell, Bridgeport; Rowland Bradley Lacey, Bridgeport; Rufus White Griswold, Rocky Hill; Henry Roger Jones, New Hartford; Jonathan Flynt Morris, Hartford; Frederick Miles, Salisbury; Oliver Humphrey King Risley, Willimantic; Francis Taylor Maxwell, Rockville; Albert Carlos Bates, East Granby. Delegates to the National Society: Edwin Seneca Greeley, William Erastus Chandler, New Haven; John Henry Swartwout, Stamford; Frank Julian Narramore, Bridgeport; Stephen W. Kellogg, Waterbury; Lucius Franklin Robinson, Hartford; John Hoyt Perry, Fairfield; Alfred Hebard Chappell, New London; Meigs Heyward Whaples, Hartford.

J. G. Woodward

TREASURE TROVE.

SOCIETY OF COLONIAL WARS IN THE STATE OF CONNECTICUT.

The Society of Colonial Wars in the State of Connecticut was incorporated under the laws of Connecticut, May 21st, 1893, by the following gentlemen : — Messrs. Charles S. Ward, Charles H. Trowbridge, Nathan G. Pond, Wm. Cecil Durand, George M. Gunn, Charles M. Tomlinson, Frederick L. Tibbals, Lynde Harrison, A. Heaton Robertson, and George H. Ford; pursuant to a petition for a charter, which was granted by the similar and elder Society in the State of New York on April 26th, 1893.

The first General Court of the Connecticut Society was held in New Haven on December 14, 1893, at which time most of the officers and a Council were chosen. An adjourned General Court was held in New Haven on May 26, 1894, the 257th anniversary of the attack by Captain John Mason and his forces on the Pequot fort in Mystic. At this time the rest of the officers were elected, and the constitution adopted, about thirty-one members of the Society being present. The same day the Society dined at the Ansantawae Club-house in West Haven, the Hon. Frederick J. Kingsbury reading, after dinner, an account of the Pequot War.

The officers elected at the first General Court held December 14, 1893, and by adjournment May 25, 1894 are as follows : Governor, Daniel C. Eaton ; Deputy Governor, George Bliss Sanford ; Lieutenant Governor, James Junius Goodwin ; Chaplain, the Right Rev. John Williams, D. D., LL. D. ; Secretary, Nathan Gillette Pond ; Treasurer, Charles Hotchkiss Trowbridge ; Registrar, Henry Walton Wessels ; Historian, Morris Woodruff Seymour. Gentlemen of the Council : George Hare Ford, John Edward Heaton, Evelyn Lyman Bissell, Charles Samuel Ward, Charles Edwin Brown, Charles Abraham Tomlinson, William Freeman French, Ralph William Cutler, Abram Heaton Robertson. Committee on Membership : Henry Gleason Newton, William Buddington Stoddard, Herbert Cleveland Warren, Charles Samuel Ward, Ralph William Cutler. Committee on Historical Documents : Frederick John Kingsbury, Theodore Salisbury Wolsey, Rev. Francis Goodwin, George Edward Taintor, James Lawrence Chew.

"The Society of Colonial Wars is instituted to perpetuate the memory of the events of American Colonial History, and of the men who, in the military and naval service, and in civil positions of trust and responsibility, by their acts or counsel, assisted in the establishment, defense and preservation of the American Colonies, and were in truth the founders of the nation. To this end it seeks to collect and preserve manuscripts, rolls, relics, and records ; to provide suitable commemorations or memorials of events in Colonial History ; and to inspire in its members the fraternal and patriotic spirit of their forefathers, and in the community respect and reverence for those whose public services made our freedom and unity possible." These words are taken from the constitution, and clearly declare the purport of the Society.

The second General Court of the Society was held at New Haven on Wednesday, December 12th, at 10 o'clock, in the rooms of the Governor, Quinnipiac Club, 986 Chapel Street. The officers of the previous year were re-elected, with the exception of the Secretary, deceased, and the Registrar. Charles Samuel Ward, M. D., of Bridgeport, was elected to the office of Secretary, and Mr. Frank Butler Gay, of Hartford, Registrar for the ensuing year. The gentlemen of the Council were elected as follows : Hon. Frederick J. Kingsbury, Rev. Samuel Hart, D. D., and George Hare Ford, for one year ; Hon. Abram Heaton Robertson, General Wm. Buel Franklin, U. S. A., and Charles Dudley Warner, for two years ; Ralph William Cutler, Hon. Lyman Denison Brewster and J. Lawrence Chew, for three years. Committee on Membership : Hon. Morris Woodruff Seymour, chairman, Edward Vilette Reynolds, D. C. L., Hon. Henry Gleason Newton, Hon. Wm. Hamersley, and Charles Samuel Ward, M. D. Committee on Historical Documents : Hon. Frederick John Kingsbury, Prof. Theodore Salisbury Wolsey, Rev. Francis Goodwin, Rev. George Leon Walker, D. D., Jonathan Trumbull.

About seventy-five members were present. The following are the names of the Hartford members of the Society : Hon. Leverett Brainard, Hon. Morgan G. Bulkeley, Abijah Catlin, Atwood Collins, Francis R. Cooley, Jonathan S. Curtis, M.D., Ralph W. Cutler, Gustavus P. Davis, M. D., Rodney Dennis, Gen. Wm. B. Franklin, Frank Butler Gay, Rev. Francis Goodwin, James J. Goodwin, Hon. Wm. Hamersley, Rev. Prof. Samuel Hart, D. D., Edward W. Hooker, Clarence Catlin Hungerford, Geo. L. Parmele, Henry Roberts, Lucius F. Robinson, Arthur L. Shipman, Hon. Nathaniel Shipman, Wm. Converse Skinner, Rev. Dr. Edward A. Smith, Henry Putnam Stearns, M. D., George E. Taintor, Rev. Dr. Geo. L. Walker, Rev. Prof. Williston Walker, Charles Dudley Warner, Hon. Ralph Wheeler, Jos. Gurley Woodward.

At the annual General Court, December 12th, Mr. James Junius Goodwin, of Hartford and New York, on behalf of the Hartford members, presented the Society with two large flags. One was a United States flag with a gilt eagle surmounting the pole. The other was a flag of the Society, made in accordance with the provisions of the constitution. The flag has a red cross of St. George on a back-ground of white silk. In the center is a shield with a bunch of grapes beautifully embroidered in natural colors. The flags are very handsome.

Chas. Sam'l Ward,
Secretary.

SOCIETY OF THE DAUGHTERS OF THE REVOLUTION IN CONNECTICUT.

RUTH WYLLIS CHAPTER. The organization of the Daughters of the Revolution is quite different from that of the Sons of the American Revolution, in that the different chapters receive charters and regulations from the National Society at Washington, from whence, in the main, came the influence to incorporate themselves. Applications for membership are forwarded to Washington ; an officer, called State Regent, represents the chapters as a whole, though her work has chiefly been in organizing chapters in different parts of the State. Delegates from the chapters annually represent the chapters in a conference at Washington, where the business of the order is discussed.

Some ladies of patriotic ardor had joined the Connecticut Sons of the American Revolution, and in February, 1892, others formed the "James Wadsworth Chapter" in Middletown, the second in New England, in point of time. The first chapter, under the auspices of the National Society, was formed at New London, October, 1892, and called the "Lucretia Shaw Chapter." The third in time, and second under the National Society, was at Norwalk, December, 1892. The next was the "Ruth Wyllys Chapter," in Hartford, which received its name from a lady whose husband took part in the Revolutionary War, following in patriotic service in the train of his famous ancestors.

The meeting to consider organization was in November, 1892, through the influence of Mrs. De B. R. Keim, of Washington, D. C. The ladies who answered the call, agreed to plans of business, and by December 27th, officers and charter members were elected and application made in form for a charter. The list of officers is the following:

Regent, Mrs. John M. Holcombe; Vice-regent, Miss A. R. Phelps; Secretary, Mrs. A. H. Pitkin; Treasurer, Miss M. W. Wainwright; Registrar, Miss Mary K. Talcott; Historian, Miss Julia B. Burbank.

Thus started, the chapter has grown to a membership of one hundred and twenty-five, and has increased into activity and interest which bodes well for the future. Meetings have been held with regularity, and at each a paper on some live topic has been read. The list of the topics proves this; they are as follows: 1. "Ruth Wyllys," by Miss Mary Kingsbury Talcott; 2. "On the Disappearance of the Charter," by Miss Mary Kingsbury Talcott; 3. "The Boston Tea-party," by Mrs. John H. Brocklesby. The author of the third paper was a descendant of one of the participants in that celebrated festivity, and exhibited some tea-leaves which were brought away in the shoes of the rebellious patriot. 4. "Washington and Rochambeau, in Hartford," by Miss Julia Brattle Burbank; 5. "Reminiscences of the family of Col. Jeremiah Wadsworth," by Mrs. Ellen Terry Johnson; 6. "The Origin of the Idea of Independence," by Mary Leeds Bartlett.

A pleasant incident in the chapter's history was the reception of their Charter, which was set in its frame of Charter Oak wood, decorated with acorns and oak leaves, most gracefully carved and set. On the 29th of June, 1894, the Sons of the American Revolution made an occasion of the unveiling of a tablet commemorative of the Wadsworth mansion. The house was on Main street, on the site of the Athæneum; it was the scene of hospitalities in colonial and later times. Lafayette, Rochambeau, Chatellux, and other French officers were entertained there, some of them several times; and the patriotism of Col. Wadsworth, in itself, deserved recognition; hence the tablet which was unveiled by a descendant of Col. Wadsworth, Gen. Warren, and Gen. Putnam, and the later speech-making. The ladies of the Daughters of the American Revolution assisted in the celebration by providing an entertainment for the gentlemen and their guests in the Athenæum building, which was thrown open for the occasion.

Julia Brattle Burbank

CONNECTICUT HISTORICAL SOCIETY.
The last annual meeting of this society was held in the society's rooms in the Athenæum, May 22, 1894. At this meeting the president, Hon. John W. Stedman, declining a re-election, Charles J. Hoadly, LL. D., was chosen to the office. Resolutions were passed thanking Mr. Stedman for his aid at all times so freely given, noting the vigorous growth of the society during the four years of his presidency, and requesting his portrait to place with those of its former presidents. This request was acceded to and a fine likeness of him in pastel now hangs with the portraits of Thomas Day, James B. Hosmer, Henry Barnard, and J. Hammond Trumbull. The election of Doctor Hoadly to the presidency may be considered as a noteworthy event for the society, he being no doubt the foremost student of Connecticut history. In addition to his regular duties as librarian of the State library and editor of the early records of the State, he is already doing valuable work for the society in editing the reprint of the unfortunate third volume of the society's "Collection,"—the original edition of this volume having been destroyed by fire before it was received from the printers. The volume will contain "Will and Doom," an important contribution to Connecticut's early history, written by Gershom Bulkeley two hundred years ago, and never before printed. Volume five of "Collections," the completion of the Talcott papers (begun in Volume four,) has been for some time in the press, and may be expected soon. Some work has also been done on another volume which is to consist of documents relating to Connecticut in the War of the Revolution.

The report of donations for the year presented at this meeting, showed it to have been the most important one in the history of the society; the donations of manuscripts alone amounting to almost thirty-five hundred pieces, a great majority of them being letters written to commissary Jeremiah Wadsworth during the Revolution. More than two thousand books and pamphlets were obtained from the library of the late Doctor D. Williams Patterson, for the purchase of which a large amount was subscribed by members and friends of the society. The same library also yielded a rich collection of unpublished manuscript genealogies.

The first meeting after the summer months was held October second, the new president presiding and reading a paper upon the "Case of Katherine Harrison, of Wethersfield." Doctor Hoadly's thorough knowledge of the witchcraft trials in this State enabled him to give a paper which was listened to with unusual interest. The November meeting, held on the thirteenth, was entertained with a paper by Charles S. Ensign, LL. B., on "Jonathan Gilbert, Hartford's merchant and Indian commissioner," in which Marshal Gilbert's career was traced and many items given concerning Hartford's historical spots and early local history. At the meeting on December ninth, Professor Henry Ferguson read a paper on the "Loyalists of the American Revolution." The subject was treated in an impartial manner and many facts were given showing what the loyalists suffered in support of their belief. After the reading of the paper a Bible belonging to Mr. S. W. Cowles, of Hartford, was exhibited and was remarked upon by Rev. W. De Loss Love. This Bible, as stated in notes written on the margins of many pages, was brought to this country in the "Mayflower" by Wllam White, and was later the property of Elder William Brewster. Mr. James Terry of New Haven, at the same meeting, presented to the society, the ancient records of the Separatist Church in Canterbury, Connecticut. The society is adding to its membership roll each month, and the present average attendance at its monthly meetings exceeds sixty.

Albert C Bates
Librarian.

NOTES AND QUERIES.

"When found, make a note of." — CAPT. CUTTLE.

"It is a very sad thing that nowadays there is so little useless information." — ANON.

(In this department we propose to give indefatigable genealogists a chance to settle mooted questions that arise during their researches and shall welcome all queries, doing our best to assist towards a solution, and interesting others for the same purpose. As space is valuable, a nominal charge will be made of fifty cents for each query and its answer, neither to exceed ten lines; the querist pays for the answer in this charge, and answers are solicited from all sources. We shall also welcome notes, calling attention to genealogical finds, sources of data, and new genealogies published or in preparation.)

ABBOT. — Who were Susanna Abbot's ancestors? She was daughter of Seth Abbot, said to be of Hartford at one time; married Simeon Wright, Junior, and came to Ohio early in this century. Simeon was descended supposably from the Samuel Wright, grandson of Deacon Samuel Wright of Springfield, the emigrant, who came from Massachusetts to Connecticut, and settled somewhere, but do not know where. Have the first two generations of the Abbots been straightened out satisfactorily? Susannah Abbot was somehow related to Emma Abbot, the singer, whose father was Seth. Susannah was my mother; she removed from Connecticut to Addison, Rutland County, Vt.; and when a boy I walked from there to Ohio behind a wagon. I am 86 years old and would like this matter settled while I live.

WAIT F. WRIGHT, Johnstown, Ohio.

BENJAMIN. — I want to trace up Samuel Benjamin, the Revolutionary soldier, as to his army record, etc. I want to get at the records showing when and where he was born, where his pension record can be found, etc. Would like his family record if I can get it. He was my great-grandfather. I want to be in a position to join the Sons of the American Revolution and to have my record straight and indisputable. When and where did Samuel Benjamin, Sr., die. F. H. BENJAMIN, L. & N. R. R., Louisville, Ky.

(Will some Granby friend send us a reply. Mr. J. R. Hayes or Mr. Harvey Goddard, for instance. — Ed.)

HALE. — My mother was a Miller of Wallingford, and early of East Hampton, L. I. I find her family runs into the Halls of Wallingford, and wish to trace back the line to David Hall, of Wallingford, who married Alice Hale of Connecticut. He died in 1755. On my father's side I run into the Hale family of Glastonbury, through the Samuel Hale that was early of Glastonbury and Norwalk. The Hales, of Goshen, I can not yet find. Can any one help me?

MRS. G. W. CURTIS, Hartford, Conn.

HALE. — The saddle-bags of Capt. Nathan Hale, the "martyr-spy," have been discovered in New Britain recently. Certain papers that came with them have been mislaid, but prove the authenticity of the relic. They came to the present owner recently through ex-Governor Radcliffe of Massachusetts. We may have something to say of this relic in a future issue. The editor is engaged upon the Hale family, in the interest of Rev. Dr. Edward Everett Hale, and Mr. Edward W. Hale, Sub-treasury, New York, and would be glad of any information or data bearing on the family.

HOADLY. — Mrs. William H. Hoadly, of 78 Ann street, now in her 92d year, distinctly remembers her grandmother, who was born in 1713. Mrs. Hoadly was a sister of the late Gen. Chas. T. Hillyer, and is the mother of State Librarian Hoadly and of Francis A. and George E. Hoadly.

PORTER — MALLORY — BLACKNEY — Information wanted as to the ancestors of Dr. Daniel Porter, whose daughter Elizabeth married Ard. Warner, of Wolcott, Jan. 12, 1764. Also ancestors of Thankful Mallory, who married Samuel Shepard, of Southington, Jan. 1, 1787. Also ancestors of Betsey Blackney, who married Luman Preston, of Plymouth, Dec. 25, 1800. JAMES SHEPARD, New Britain.

PRESTON — HOLT — Information wanted as to the way the first settlers of Plainfield, Conn., came from Massachusetts, whether via Stonington, and up the Thames. In this party were the Deans, Prestons and Holts; the last named families were from Salem and Andover, Mass., and soon left Plainfield for Windham.

SANFORD. — I wish to learn, if possible, names of father and mother of Mabel Sanford, who married Caleb Street (b. 1753 — —), son of Samuel and grandson of Lt. Samuel. Also information in regard to parents of Sarah Atwater, married Samuel Street (b. 1707), father of Caleb. My grandmother was Cornelia Street, granddaughter of Caleb. GUY D. PECK.

28 Broadway, N. Y., Stewart Building, Suite 90.

PRINCE. — "Silvester Prince, August 14, 1761." This is the inscription on a powder-horn in the collection of the Connecticut Historical Society at Hartford. Will the donor, or any one, who can give anything relative to the history of this horn, or its owner, please communicate with me.

FRED'K W. PRINCE,
P. O. Box 387, Hartford, Ct.

TALCOTT. — Hartford has a centenarian. Mrs. Emily Robbins Talcott, of West Hartford, who attained her 105th anniversary on Christmas, and is the oldest resident of the State. She was nine years of age when Washington died, and remembers the draping at Wethersfield, on account of that event. She was born on Wolcott Hill, Wethersfield, and was married on Christmas day, 1810, to Ansel Talcott, who died a few years ago at an advanced age. Hon. Henry Barnard, one of the oldest men in Hartford, called on the old lady on Christmas. He has seen ten centenarians in his lifetime, and he still takes an active interest in local affairs. He was greatly interested in the Wells celebration, on the 12th of December, and assisted in securing Dr. McManus' article for our pages, being a contemporary and a warm personal friend of Dr. Wells.

WALTON.— My great-grandfather, Samuel Felch, Jr., of Cambridge, born in Reading, Mass., married (1) November 24, 1743. Eunice Walton and late in life said to have married her sister, Elizabeth. Whose daughters were they? I can find nothing of them on Reading records; on Cambridge records I find, "Eunice, daughter of Jacob and Abigail, born 19th March, 1745-6: "and marriage of "James Nichols of Reading, and Eunice Walton, October 14, 1795," but no other Eunice. I think they are of some other town, and that their father was probably from inference, named Isaac.— THE EDITOR.

WHITE. — The famous "Breeches Bible" mentioned by Mr. Bates in his report, was undoubtedly brought over by William White in the Mayflower: printed in London, 1588, and in part 1586; Wm. White was the father of Peregrine White, the first white child born in New England.

WINTHROP. — WARE. — A Corrected Pedigree. — From the Times: Lucy Winthrop was not the grandmother of the Rev. Solomon Stoddard. He was the son of Anthony Stoddard, of Boston, whose first wife, Mary, was the daughter of the Hon. Emanuel Downing, of Salem, who was a brother-in-law of Governor Winthrop, it is true, but Mary was the daughter of Emanuel's first wife, Anne Ware. This Anne Ware was the daughter of Sir James Ware, who was knighted by James I, and was a member of the Irish Parliament in 1613. This correction of the usual pedigrees appears in the Massachusetts Historical Society's collections, Volume VI, fourth series, page 40, in the Winthrop letters. An error of this kind once in print is copied over and over again.

M. K. T.

We are very glad to be able to make this correct notation in our first issue, of Jonathan Edwards' ancestry (see "Old Colonial Characters") before going to press. Miss Talcott is probably the best authority on the first settlers of Hartford, in this city; she has promised the Connecticut Quarterly, the right of publication of all her additional material which did not appear in the "Memorial History of Hartford County,"—which will be gratifying news to our readers.— ED.

We beg to call attention to the handsome and unique Arms "Continuous Family Register," (see advertisement on the cover, just issued, which is certainly satisfactory for every purpose or need of the average genealogist. We have compiled two different varieties of the book, and found it adequate in every respect. It is gotten up in a dainty manner and finely bound. Mr. Arms has spent over a year in its preparation and deserves a wide patronage.

The Editor of this department has also prepared a series of blanks which enables one to trace his or her American ancestors in *all* lines, showing them at a glance; also shows *all* the descendants of one's emigrant ancestor, in compact form, giving each one only a line in which is assembled all the essential dates, (birth, death, first and second marriages), place of birth, death, burial, etc.; similar dates for the wives, and names of their parents; residence, occupation, church, army or navy services, offices held; will dated, proved, amount of inventory; *all this on one line*, so that any missing fact or date can be seen at once, and inserted at any time. It is, in fact, the most compact, accurate, and comprehensive schedule ever prepared. Sufficient blanks for a whole family history, or genealogy for 50 cents to $1.00, or sample pages for ten cents, can be had by addressing Editor Notes and Queries, Conn. Quarterly, Hartford, Conn.

The Editor of "Treasure Trove" would be pleased to undertake investigations, in England or America, at lowest rates. We have recently added to our library, Albiruni's "Chronology of Ancient Nations" (written A. D. 1000); Betham's "Royal Genealogies," published a century since, beginning with Adam if you wish; Sim's "Manual for the Genealogist," Bridger's "Index to Printed Pedigrees in England," (all of them,) and Col. Chester's "London Marriage Licenses," (1521 to 1869) 25,000 in all.)

SOCIOLOGY AND CIVICS.

"The criminal classes are so close to us that even a policeman can see them. They are so far away from us that only a poet can understand them."

"How best to help the slender store,
How mend the dwellings of the poor,
How gain in life, as life advances,
Valor and charity more and more."—TENNYSON.

OUR SCHOOL OF SOCIOLOGY.

Of the new School of Sociology, established in this city, the New York Tribune says: "Of the need of such work as this there can be no doubt. A vast amount of intellectual activity is being devoted in this country to social questions, but there is a lack of clear thinking upon them. There seems to be no limit to the interest of the people in schemes devised for the advancement of society, to the sympathy bestowed on those who are suffering real or apparent wrong, or the readiness to enter into any organization promising amelioration of anything that anybody suggests ought to be ameliorated. But it unfortunately happens that a great deal of this potential force of improvement is rendered useless or worse by being directed to wrong methods of work. What is lacking more than anything else is clear sight and trained knowledge. People need not only to think, but to think right."

"THE SCIENCE OF DUTY."

"The science of duty" is a phrase that has been heard much of late,—which is, we are told, the most important of all the sciences. We hardly know in what sense duty can be regarded as a science at all. The science of ethics we have heard about, but this is not what is meant. If the science were taught, we do not believe the children would do their duty any better. They would learn a few fine-sounding names, and that would be all. But a man is no stronger in his arms by knowing that one muscle is called flexor longa and another flexor brevis. We do not contend that each church ought not to have full liberty to teach its own creed; but why should such teaching be called the "science of duty" for have we not enough cant phrases?

Now, if church and state are to be inseparably torn asunder in this country—a creed of politics which is inviolable—what is there to take the place of ethical teaching in schools, which thereby becomes nil? All the moral agencies of churches, Sunday-schools, the Y. M. C. A , and other institutions are not sufficient to overcome the loss and ruin engendered by the deprivation of moral teaching in schools,—and for the simple reason that they do not reach all classes of society; whereas schools do, in this enlightened century, when few are illiterate. That is to say these godly institutions do not reach the entire masses, because they are not constituted and managed properly to attain that end.

This is plain talking, but we have been conscious for a decade or two that there was something lacking in their ingredients. This is borne home to us by the direct and forceful words of Rev. Frederick Stanley Root, of the Park Church in his recent resignation, offering therein a plea for the "Institutional Church." If morality and ethics can not be taught in schools, manifestly then it is the province of churches to establish schools that will teach undenominational morality, and meet the problem more than half way. THE TIMES, with its accustomed optimism in dealing with religious matters, points out the need of such an institution in this city, to supplement present facilities, and outlines a plan of work that has found favor in other cities. Such work as has been done by Dr. W. H. H. Murray, in Boston, Dr. Edward Eggleston, in New York, Dr. David Swing, in Chicago and many others we can name, is not to be gainsaid, only it too frequently happens that when the pastor or "leader" is taken away by death or otherwise, the organization dwindles and dies for want of his personal magnetism. What is needed is some strong magnetic force, compelling, drawing, far out-reaching, fertile in resources and plans, and virile and mighty in their accomplishment. With such a leader "duty" seems a pleasure, not a "science."

There is one such man in Hartford, a mighty Titan in energy and work, the President of the Theological seminary, of the School of Sociology, of the University Extension movement in this State, and of the School of Church Musicians and heart and soul in all of them. But Dr. Hartranft is accomplishing more good in his present position, and in the above lines, than he possibly could in any one church or if possible with any congeries of churches; in fact his work will have an influence in this State, as well as out of it, for years, beyond a doubt—an influence that will go on increasing in volume and effect in many after years.

We do not care to enter into a discussion of the problem stated by Dr. Root, and emphasized still more in his statement at the annual meeting of his church society, except to say that he was right, irretrievably right. in his position! He is right when he says, even in the church once occupied by Dr. Burton and Dr. Bushnell, "Sentiment, memories, æsthetics do not build a church. Work builds a church. As the OUTLOOK remarked relative to my resignation, the inquiry of a church should not be what has been, but what will best do the work that is needed now. New methods, modern conceptions, are the conditions on which churches not well situated geographically live."

Dr. Root is something of a seer. It may be another generation or two, possibly a century, before the region in which the present church is situated will be in the "slums" and subject to "university settlement;" when the backwater population from beyond Main street will overflow the ridge and precipitate itself upon the entire business section of the city,—but that time will come. Besides business houses inevitably crowd out or smother church properties— except in large cities. It would seem strange for one of the Main street churches to wish to remove to the "Lord's Hill" precincts, but it is not strange for a church located on narrow, unattractive Asylum street, (almost an alley) to want a change to a free atmosphere, and both Methodist and Park churches have long had such aspirations, which should be applauded as well as aided.

A Congregational Church on the Hill should properly be the outgrowth of the Asylum Hill Congregational Church, which is nearly "swarming" now, the hive being over-crowded. Since both this and the Park Church have the same object in view, why not combine forces and finances to make such a church as is desired, and on an ample scale and progressive ideas; then make the present Park edifice a free-seat church, not a mission church, but of a higher grade, where the poor can have the gospel free. There are too many churches with paid pews in town, already — but rich people prefer to pay for comfortable sittings with one hand and for charity and missions with the other. This inference is obvious. It is one reason why charity is so common, and why it has been so overdone in the past; a few years ago, there were in this city thirty eelymosynary institutions, until it became necessary to found a charity clearing-house. Would it not be better if charity should begin at home in some churches, in other words that the gospel should be made free, so that the poor might have a chance at least, for gospel-teaching and hearing undying truths than gradually and inevitably to become estranged, demeaned, dissolute, maybe in some degree criminal?

(3) Sociological Field Work, for training in special investigations and visitation of institutions, and (4) a special conference of friendly visitors for practical philanthropic work.

The number of students, as was expected, is small, but unusually well equipped even for college graduates for this kind of work. Nearly all of them having either taught or pursued postgraduate work in addition to the college studies. There is every indication that the number entering next year will be much larger. There are already several applications. A good beginning has been made in equipment. The students have free access to the fine Case Memorial Library, and at present the lectures are held in that building. Books suggested by the lecturers have been placed in the library, and at present the school receives between fifty and sixty periodicals bearing directly upon its work.

On the whole, the outlook for the continued and increasing prosperity of the School is hopeful. The need of such an institution is unquestioned, and thus far the hopes of the organizers have been realized.

C. M. Geer

Secretary.

THE CONNECTICUT SOCIETY FOR UNIVERSITY EXTENSION.

University extension is a comparatively new-comer in Connecticut but it has already received a warm welcome. The work of our own Hartford center, with its excellent series of lecture courses, which have been given from season to season, during the last few years, is a matter of general knowledge. It has remained for the present season, however, to witness the general diffusion of the work in different quarters of the State. At the beginning of the season, two cities only, Hartford and New London, were actively engaged in the university extension movement; this autumn, however, has witnessed the founding of new and flourishing centers at New Haven and Waterbury, while preparations are almost completed for starting the work at Meriden. In addition, the American Society is this year maintaining its own courses at Ansonia and Bridgeport,

It will thus be seen that there is a steady expansion of the movement in this state, and as each city where the work is once started, becomes a center of diffusion in its turn, it is difficult to speculate on what the ultimate possibilities may be. Of the subjects chosen as topics for lecture courses, science seems at present to occupy, by long odds, the first place. An indication of the general taste of university extension audiences is shown by the fact that Prof. E. B. Rosa's course on Electricity opens the season's work this year in no less than three centers: New London, New Haven, and Waterbury. Literature, Sociology, and Economics are, however, also upon the list of chosen subjects, and it has been the evident design of each of the centers to arrange as diversified a programme as possible. It is only by such a policy that every class of the community, each in its turn, can be interested, and the movement thus be made to accomplish its ultimate purpose.

Whatever difficulty may have originally existed of supplying a sufficient number of lecturers for our audiences, from the members of the college faculties, has long since vanished. There are now upon the staff of the State Society, forty-three lecturers, offering courses upon fifty-eight different subjects. Among this number are included representatives from every one of the higher institutions of learning within, and many from beyond, the borders of the State. The lecture courses offered cover a vast variety of subjects, including many departments of science, literature, history, philosophy, sociology, economics, and the fine arts.

The department of agricultural science is one of particular strength, nearly every member of the staff of the two Connecticut experiment stations, and the faculty of Storrs Agricultural College being represented on the lecture lists. Special attention is being devoted this year to the development of this particular branch of University extension work, and it is expected that before the end of another season, the farming communities will be fully abreast of the towns in the number and quality of their lecture courses.

If every city and town in the State should in the end desire to avail itself of the opportunities offered by the University Extension Society, it is encouraging to know that a sufficient number of college professors will volunteer their services in the work to satisfy all their needs. It is this ready and willing co-operation of the men at our principal seats of learning, which affords the brightest outlook to the future of our Society and gives us the necessary confidence to wage an aggressive campaign for the expansion of the work.

Alan C. Ruley,
Secretary.

THE CONNECTICUT HUMANE SOCIETY. The past quarter has been the most active in the history of the Connecticut Humane Society. More than three hundred complaints have been made to the central office, and nearly all were well founded. Cases of suffering families, aged and infirm people neglected by relatives and town officials, and children neglected and suffering from ill treatment by cruel parents, have been reported to this Society; and in many instances relief was furnished by calling the attention of proper officials, and of agents, and members of the Society, who rendered valuable assistance. Town authorities often use the Society as an agency for the relief of children, removing them from vicious surroundings and cruel treatment. The importance of the work among children can not be over-estimated, yet it is done—at little expense.

Within a few days, a child has been removed from a home of vice and immorality, to one of cleanliness and comfort. A boy, four years old, abandoned by both parents, was placed by us in a good home, and his father made to pay the expense. A girl of seven, subjected to immoral influences, has been rescued. Many other cases might be stated where relief has been given to children through the agency of this Society. Many cases of destitution, rather than cruelty, are referred or reported to charitable societies and town authorities. The work embraces both orders. That among animals exceeds any previous quarter. Acknowledgment is due our three hundred and fifty agents who have given time and energy to the work.

The fact that more cases have been reported, need not convey the idea that cruelty is on the increase, but rather the growth of humane sentiment, which is apparent to casual observers; for that growth is so marked that cases formerly unnoticed, will now excite attention if not indignation. The work is educational. Some offenders can only learn lessons of humanity by costly experience. The following is illustrative: A man, evidently born stubborn, owning a poor, deformed, suffering horse, repeatedly and persistently worked it, warnings and remonstrances being of no avail. He was finally arrested, yet caused the horse to work, while he was being tried for cruelty to the animal. He was found guilty, and bound over to a higher court, yet continued to work the suffering animal; when an official of this Society destroyed it, to end its suffering. The higher court has just found him guilty and imposed a fine of one hundred and fifty dollars and costs, amounting nearly to three hundred dollars.

Prosecutions follow when other resources fail. Recently a man persisted in driving a poor, lame horse twenty-four miles daily. When advised and warned, he defied the official, who left him and caused his arrest. This had a decidedly mellowing and civilizing influence. He plead guilty, paid his fine and costs, killed the horse, and learned his lesson as effectually as in the preceding case, but at much less expense. During the past quarter, every prosecution brought by the Society has resulted in a conviction.

The object in view is to create a humane public sentiment, not so much by punishment of offenders, as by dissemination of literature, which is a very important feature of the work. The publications of the society, "Our Humble Associates," by Rev. Dr. Geo. Leon Walker; "Certain other Duties," by Gurdon Trumbull; "The Checkrein," by "Ellen Snow;" "Molly Cottontail," by Miss E. V. Hallett, have been widely circulated and read. "Vivisectors and Vivisection" has been sent to every known society in the world. The latest publication of this Society, "Anna Malann," by Annie Trumbull Slosson, is of inestimable value to the cause. The work is ably presented in "the Sunday School Times," of December 1st, 1894, and has received many favorable comments by the representive press. Orders have been sent for it from all parts of the country; the first edition of one thousand copies is nearly exhausted. The story is electrotyped, and another thousand copies ordered. It is the aim of the Society to circulate through the pulpit, press, and public school, such literature, with the hope that seed thus sown will bear fruit an hundred fold.

Chandler E. Miller,
Secretary.

A FREE LANCE IN THE FIELD OF LIFE AND LETTERS

*"There stately dame and merry maid,
And Knight with visage stern,
By limner's cunning art portrayed,
Their eyes did on him turn."* — OLD SONG.

"In old days books were written by men of letters and read by the public. Nowadays books are written by the public and read by nobody."

When my son assumed editorial charge of this magazine, he extended a polite invitation to his pater-familias to take charge of a department,— "to keep it all in the family," I suppose, the sly rogue. He gave me my choice in the matter, and I replied: "Well, I am too old for any very active work, or tramping around much, but if you can give me something easy and lazy, a sort of sinecure, with lots of perquisites, you can count upon me."

"How would you like to do the book-reviews?"

"Nothing I should like better. You know I'm nothing if not critical. I like to tear a book—a bad book—to shreds, 'to tatters, to very rags,' and to praise a good book. In my old age and second childhood, I have grown very fond of romance and adventure—of knights and ladies in fiction, and like to have them all about me, in preference to the light-weight modern stuff, full of dandies in drawing-rooms. I am glad we are going back to the old days of chivalry, with Doyle and Weyman, and a host of their imitators; and you can send me all of that kind of books you wish. I like to lie at full length on the lounge, with the light at my head, and read aloud to Phillis about them, and when we find a good sensible hero we praise him, and when we don't we d-d-demolish him. Truth to tell, my son, between us, we generally manage to demolish most of your modern writers."

"Very well, so it shall be," said he, curtly, cutting off my chat and was gone on the instant.

Phillis, my "gudewife," and I have been reading "The Manxman," by Hall Caine, recently, and so we will begin with that. Phillis sits and makes "butter-doylies" and drawn-work by the hour (a thing I forbade her doing thirty years ago, when we were first wed) while I plod along through the five-hundred-and-over pages of fine type—almost as ruinous to my old eyes as her fancy-work to hers. If she becomes excited over the story and draws out a thread too many, or drops a stitch in her knitting and forgets to take it up again, the work is spoiled, of course—at least in her eyes. In like manner, if the author of the story we are reading "drops a stitch" it is spoiled, and thenceforth loses all interest in our eyes. And just here let me say that Mr. Caine has dropped several of them in this story, and has ruined a fine work, as I shall try to show.

It is a remarkable story in many respects; and in many others it is not. In the first place it is too interminably long; he lays out his work on too large a canvas, and therefore fails. The greatest sermons, songs, poems, and prayers are the shortest ones. Long-drawn-out and fine-spun work never pays in the end. Life is too short while art is altogether too long. Now, my friend Hopkinson tells me he is some day going to write the Great American Novel, and will make it 1,000 pages long, but I tell him he will never write the Great American Novel. That is the great trouble with the novels now-a-days,—their length and verbosity: as for instance Cable's "Dr. Sevier," Col. Kirkland's "Zury," Henry James' never ending yarns, Hardy's "Tess," Blackmore's "Lorna Doone," and Mrs. Ward's novels. Of course "it's English" but a bad precedent; they write nothing but three-story novels. Why should not a novel end somewhere short of a life-time, so that the attempt to read it will be worth the making?

How dreary and tiresome it is to wade through a hundred pages in which a heroine is dying of a lingering consumption (when a quick fever would have answered quite as well); or to read half of "Lorna Doone" before John Ridd gets into the den of the Doones to rescue his sweetheart; or to tramp with Cable's hero all summer over hot, blistering New Orleans streets while he searches for work which never comes, meanwhile tormented by inane platitudes in Creole patois; or to be worried to death by old miser Zury's persistent pursuit and courtship of the little New England "schoolmarm" heroine,—both before and after his wife dies until he gets her, somewhere after page 600 or 700!

Well, the author of "The Manxman" means well at any rate, if he does string out the tale almost beyond endurance. It is rumored that he goes into his writing-room, and writes almost incessantly for months, until a novel is born, and comes out almost as haggard as Haggard himself, at the end, looking wild, unkempt, distraught. Now, is it possible for a man to live in such a hothouse state, writing at white-heat all the while, and yet produce anything worthy of name and fame? And yet, this is the little man who aspires to write as his chef-d'œuvre a Life of the Christ! What a forced, ghostly, fearful thing it will be!

"The Manxman" begins well, with the death of "old Iron Christian," the disinheritance of his elder son, Tom, whose mesalliance with a shrewish, pitifully ignorant, and thoroughly vulgar wife, brings forth the alleged hero, Philip. I should not call Philip a hero—for it is impossible to love him, even after his stilted and theatrical expiation of his crime in the last pages—renouncing all his honors as Deemster and Governor, to take up with Kate, the woman he has wronged. He is not half so lovable as "Steerforth," in "David Copperfield," that prince of betrayers. Philip is as lifeless an automaton as a human can be in such a plight. He is not a villain from design or motive or desire, but by sheer accident and the temptation of an Eve; this embitters his whole life. He is a whited sepulchre through his career to power and influence, and hides his shame like the Rev. Arthur Dimmesdale because of pride and ambition,—evidently the character he was modeled upon.

He succeeds beyond his most sanguine anticipations in everything he undertakes, but it is by walking over the hearts of others, destroying and blighting nobler lives than his own; and the effort of the author to reinstate him in the reader's liking, in the last pages, is mawkish sentiment. Great-hearted "Pete" (what if he does spell his name 'peat'?) goes away, the scape-goat of all the sin, folly and wickedness of the others; but he is the true hero of the story, and as noble a hero as can be. Truly this is what Hardy would call one of "Life's Little Ironies." Pete so far over-shadows Philip and Kate, that there is no comparison.

Kate is at the start, a smart, buxom, light-hearted average girl and promises well, but Caine does not understand women at all, for he makes her change to a hysterical wife and mother, and later to a too-willing mistress of Philip—changes too abrupt for belief. She becomes colorless and insipid. We are not sorry that she practically disappears as a human sort of person before the book is half done; she becomes after that a tiresome automaton. We are of course at first as much interested in her as in any of the hoydenish heroines so common in the past decade—Rhoda Broughton's underbred "trollops," Black's "Madcaps," Grant Allen's "Maimies," or even Henry James's "Daisy Millers"—but to have her throw herself, virtue and all, at the hero's head, and then be told that this is the last resource a girl has to win the man she loves, and the fruitful cause of most betrayals—is exasperating to say the least. It is not human nature, and certainly not woman-nature.

"And more than that, Felix," chimes in Phillis at this point, "it isn't human nature or woman nature for a woman to leave her husband and child, to go with a lover without the least compunction of conscience. That may do in fiction, but women reason nowadays in real life, and besides a mother is a mother the world over." Yes, I add, you are right, but the weakest part is that Philip thinks it necessary to take Kate away from her husband, simply because he has just found out from her that their child is really his own. I don't know what the laws or customs are in the little Isle of Man, but it is not human nature for a man to assume such a responsibility on such short notice, even if duty or sentiment impel him. How he can help matters by taking her away I cannot see.

"And, Felix, to think that the hussy should leave that baby as she did! She must have been insane to think that leaving Philip's child with Pete would be expiation for her sin. Why should she not take it along with her, like any other woman would, and make Philip's expiation more complete?" That is where Hall Caine dropped another stitch that spoiled the whole fabric. Then again, Pete was altogether too wooden-headed and unsuspecting, and when he found them out, altogether too magnanimous towards them. Why, he even killed his dog, when he left the island and them to their happiness,—the only creature that had really been true to him in all his troubles. It is an uncanny tale, take it as a whole, but it is far above the average in power and description, as well as human interest until that breaks down completely. It is a pity to have to criticise so good a book, so well told a story, but it is impossible to overlook its weakness and faults. Now, I know perfectly well, Phillis, that this criticism will cause dozens of people to read the book who would not otherwise call for it. Well, let them, for I can honestly commend it as a novel above the average and one of great promise but which does not hold out to the end. There is one thing I want to commend it for—its folk-speech, knowledge of customs and of the traditions of the "right little, tight little island" of Man. The mingled simplicity and astuteness of the peasants, their quasi-Hibernian richness and "blarneyism" is delicious and admirable always.

The trouble with Mr. Caine is that he is greatly impressed with the solemnity of a novelist's career—and more impressed by his own overweening greatness. He is out now with a lecture on "Moral responsibility in the Novel and the Drama," in which he has said: "It was a frightening thought that the morality of a man's book was exactly his own morality." If this be true, how much of The Manxman is autobiographical? "There was only one thing the public demanded, and that was human nature. Undoubtedly there were subjects which it forbade; it forbade all unwholesome and unnatural passions." Then why not forbid the Manxman? Well, it is called an immoral book by some, who declare it has out-Tessed "Tess." We do not, however, think it was intended to be immoral. Mr. Caine further said he had "dreamed of a greater novel than we had ever yet seen, that should be compounded of the penny newspaper and the Sermon on the Mount—the plainest realism and the highest idealism." When he makes the two poles of thought meet in expression, in such a novel, he will have written a greater novel than his proposed Life of Christ. That will only be a novel anyway—if he writes it.

What book shall we take up next, Phillis? "Oh, anything but this erotic, neurotic stuff. Neurotic, indeed; they should call it nerve-destroying! Why can not the writers and dramatists be decent, Felix?" Well, I suppose we must put up with "adultery-dramas," or "Magdelen plays." Once upon a time they were decent, in the days of "The New Magdalen" which taught a moral, and was far above "Camille" in point and morality. But now we have "Second Mrs. Tanquery," and still later "John a' Dreams" and "Rebellious Susan" which are abominable to say the least. I suppose we will continue to have these phases of wrecked and wretched womanhood until we have had a surfeit, and audiences and readers will turn from them, for the worm will turn some time. Or, perhaps, the wrecked and wretched women will turn themselves and form a crusade against polite society in order to purify and redeem it! It would not be a bad idea, either, Phillis. This kind of reading seems to have a terrible fascination for some people,—like children playing with fire. It might be forgiven if there was any effort to state or solve a problem. But there is none. It is clear debauchery of the mind, nothing else.

"But, Trilby—what of little Trilby and her story? Is that immoral, do you think, Felix?" pleads Phillis. Am I not to make an exception of that wonderful tale, even if libraries and schoolboards have expunged and blacklisted it? For answer, I read from the critique of my friend, the editor of THE OUTLOOK, who sums it all up in a paragraph, as I have no time now to treat of Trilby at length and probably ad nauseam:

"What of Trilby and her three comrades! The latter who constitute a sort of tri-personal hero of the story, leading an artist life in the Latin Quarter of Paris, are true, genuine, chivalrous young men. Little Billee might have had Trilby as his mistress, but it does not occur to him even as a thought. That he can not have her as his wife kills him. No book in England sounds a nobler note in honor of masculine chastity. Trilby, an artist's model, child of an ignorant mother, and strangely ignorant of moral laws, yet retains her innocence. To speak more accurately, she possesses all the virtues save the one; she is simple, sincere, truthful, loving, heroically self-sacrificing; but she has lost her chastity. She has not sold herself for money or for place. She has given herself away—for love! No! rather for good nature; and knows not what she has given.

"What the Scarlet letter treats as a sacrilege in the very spirit of Paul himself, this story treats as a lache, a fault easily condoned, almost overlooked. In life, innocence is not retained after virtue is lost. A character drawing which is morally untrue is never morally wholesome. . . . To the question, Is Trilby a moral novel? we reply in the negative. Its moral standard is a purely conventional one—that of the social code of honor. The eternal sanctions of righteousness, which are never ignored in the greatest works of the greatest artists, are wholly lacking. Religion is never referred to except in its most conventional forms, and then only to be satirized, perhaps we should say travestied. It is true the story exalts all the social virtues except one. But for chastity in woman it inspires rather condonation which comes of comparative indifference than the forgiveness which comes of a pure and pitying love."

And so, Phillis, I rather think we shall have to add Trilby to the category of Tess.

Do I think that there will be any improvement or will the decadence continue? I cannot tell, Phillis. Literature is in a bad way all over the world. The nations on whom civilization depends for progress most, seem most in the slough now. The peoples that have the least literary history give the most promise. Norway puts forward a strange being named Ibsen, who is neither fish nor fowl; Belgium has a so-called original thinker in Maurice Maeterlinck, while Russia still boasts of Tolstoi—who is only a cobbler now, take him at his best. He has lately taken to "boot-makery" as he is pleased to call it, and one of his fellow shoe-makers has said of him, "Eh, eh, if he had to make his living by making boots he would fare badly, but since he only makes for himself, it doesn't matter so much." This witty saying is as true of his books as his boots. He only makes them for himself; he cobbles. He has written nothing binding him to fame except "Anne Karenina" and his "Kreutzer Sonata" is simply abominable.

Tolstoi is to Turgenef, (or Turgueneff?) the greatest Russian writer, as crash or buckram to fine linen or fine silk. In Germany we find no successor to Goethe or Schiller, in Italy no Dante, in Spain no Cervantes of to-day. The French have the exquisite Coppee, the robust Bourget, the eccentric Zola, but no Moliere nor even a Hugo in all the land. In England there is a host of writers, none of whom are good enough to wear the mantle of Thackeray or Dickens or Scott. Scott, indeed, is now easily the greatest writer of the century in England or any of the British domains. He ranks next to Shakespere as a creator of individual character of the miscellaneous human sort—such as we call "character studies," nowadays. There are a host of English writers of third or fourth class, but they are all parrots—even Mrs. Ward, the best of them is a frank imitator of George Eliot. Hardy is growing, but is a rank pessimist; Doyle is the most promising of the novelists. Du Maurier is a mere passing fashion-plate; Kipling is only for this generation, while Stevenson will last several times as long, although his last novel was a failure; he, however, reached the dignity of "collected works," and died soon after enough to save himself a niche, and to prevent his works being scattered apart again. But there is no Dickens, no Carlyle, no Thackeray; although some, like Lang, give abundant promise. It is a pity he writes only for money, not for enduring fame.

"You seem to be unusually severe, to-night, Felix. What about our American writers?" I prefer not to touch upon them now, Phillis, as it is a long story. We have a decided lull, however, on this side the water also; and now that Dr. Holmes has gone, it is too early to suggest any one to follow in the footsteps of the beginning-of-the-century group that has gone. It seems to me that we are paying altogether too little attention to one of the greatest of a younger group of writers destined to take the places of the elder group; and that one, a man born here in Hartford—Edmund Clarence Stedman—by far the most finished, scholarly, and felicitous of the now aging poets of his generation. He is one of the best critics the country affords, and a too infrequent poet; but his poetry is as good as his criticism, every whit. Hartford has every reason to honor him, and it will in time to come.

But, speaking of the decadents and impressionists, as we were but a moment ago, Phillis, I cannot help reading you the latest gibe against that school in France which plumes itself on its profundity. "Read it, and see if you understand," said one of the school, to a friend, pointing to one of his complicated sentences. The friend read it several times over and admitted that there were some glimmerings of sense in it. "Oh, I knew there was something wrong with it," answered the impressionist, sadly. Here, again is another skit, not a bad bit of humor, from the London "Satirist," on "The Pastellette."

> The pastelle is too strong, said he,
> Lo! I will make it fainter yet!
> And he wrought with tepid ecstacy
>   A pastellette.
>
> A touch — a word — a tone half caught —
> He softly felt and handled them ;
> Flavor of feeling — scent of thought —
>   Shimmer of gem, —
>
> That we may read and feel as he
> What vague, pale pleasure we can get,
> From this mild, witless mystery, —
>   The pastellette.

Contrast with this, if you please, my Phillis, this pretty "sonnet on the sonnet," by Eugene Lee-Hamilton:

> Fourteen small broidered berries on the hem
>   Of Circe's mantle, each of magic gold ;
>   Fourteen of lone Calypso's tears that roll'd
> Into the sea, for pearls to come to them ;
>
> Fourteen clear signs of omen in the gem
>   With which Medea human fate foretold ;
> Fourteen small drops, which Faustus, growing old,
> Craved of the Fiend, to water Life's dry stem.
>
> It is the pure white diamond Dante brought
>   To Beatrice ; the sapphire Laura wore
> When Petrarch cut it sparkling out of thought ;
>
> The ruby Shakespeare hewed from his heart's core:
>   The dark deep emerald that Rosetti wrought
> For his own soul, to wear forevermore.

How much better is this than the somewhat soggy sonnets which a magazine editor feels moved to offer to a patient public ; and how infinitely above the Pastellette. Well, Phillis, as we have not "the unchallenged leisure of the lilies of the field," to pursue these themes, we had best say good night to our friends.

THE DWIGHT SLATE MACHINE CO.

MANUFACTURERS OF

DRILLING MACHINES
For Light Work.
Hand and Automatic Feed.   One to Ten Spindles.

AUTOMATIC GEAR and PINION CUTTERS.

Fine Bench Lathes.

Experimental and Model Work.

SPECIAL MACHINERY.

For convenience of local trade we have established a Jobbing Department and undertake anything in the line of machine repairs. Competent men sent to any locality. Machinery moved, hangers, shafting, pulleys furnished and set in place.

GEAR CUTTING, FORGING AND PRESS WORK DONE TO ORDER.

In our warerooms we carry a full line of Machinists' Supplies. Correspondence solicited, and reasonable prices made.

Office and Warerooms,
Factory adjoining.   **13 Central Row.**

Farmington Valley Herald & Journal.

This paper has a Larger Circulation in the western part of Hartford County than any paper published.

ARE YOU A SUBSCRIBER?

If not you miss the best local news in that section.

An Ad. inserted in its columns will yield better returns, rates considered, than any other medium.

Subscription Price, $1.00 per year.

Advertising rates made known on application.

NORTH & LATE, Publishers,
23 Brown St., Hartford, Conn.

SPECIAL DESIGNS IN . . .

LETTER HEADS,	BUSINESS CARDS,	MONOGRAMS,
BILL HEADS,	CIGAR LABELS,	AUTOGRAPHS.

PLATES FOR ALL KINDS OF ILLUSTRATIONS.

We are the Recognized Leaders in this Section

IN THE LINE OF

PRINTING and WOOD ENGRAVING.

☞ *See what the Press has to say of us:*

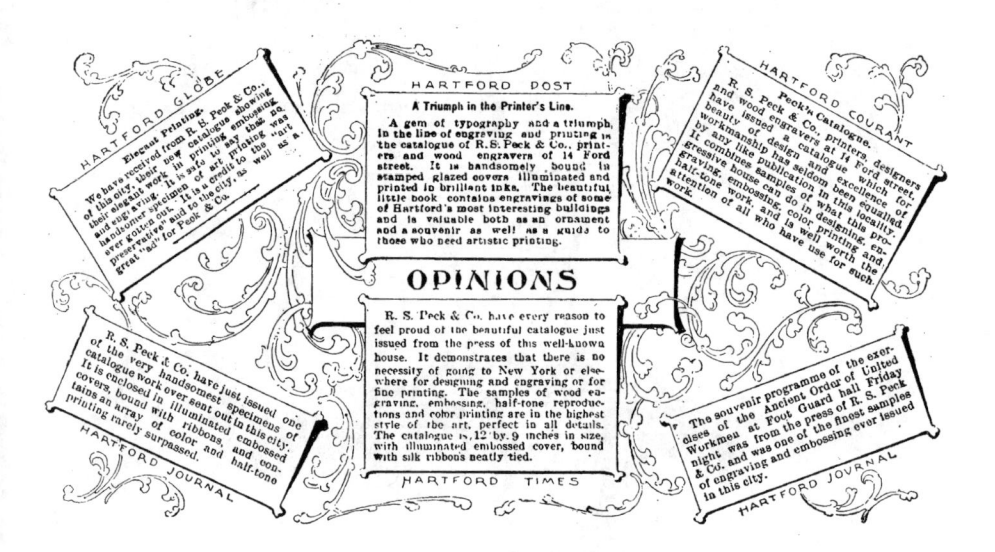

OPINIONS

HARTFORD GLOBE
Elegant Printing.—We have received from R. S. Peck & Co. showing of this city, their new printing and embossing. It is safe to say that their elegant specimens of this art is a credit to the city, their handsomest specimen sent to the city, as well as a great deal for Peck & Co.

HARTFORD POST
A Triumph in the Printer's Line.
A gem of typography and a triumph, in the line of engraving and printing is the catalogue of R. S. Peck & Co., printers and wood engravers of 14 Ford street. It is handsomely bound in stamped glazed covers illuminated and printed in brilliant inks. The beautiful little book contains engravings of some of Hartford's most interesting buildings and is valuable both as an ornament and a souvenir as well as a guide to those who need artistic printing.

HARTFORD COURANT
R. S. Peck's Catalogue.—R. S. Peck & Co., printers, designers and wood engravers at 14 Ford street, have issued a catalogue which for beauty of design and workmanship has seldom been equalled by any house in this locality. It combines publication in one samples of engraving, embossing, half-tone, color printing, etc., attention of all who have use for such work.

HARTFORD JOURNAL
R. S. Peck & Co. have just issued one of the very handsomest specimens of catalogue work ever sent out in this city. It is enclosed in illuminated embossed covers, bound with an array of ribbons, and contains an illustrated display of color and half-tone printing rarely surpassed.

HARTFORD TIMES
R. S. Peck & Co. have every reason to feel proud of the beautiful catalogue just issued from the press of this well-known house. It demonstrates that there is no necessity of going to New York or elsewhere for designing and engraving or for fine printing. The samples of wood engraving, embossing, half-tone reproductions and color printing are in the highest style of the art, perfect in all details. The catalogue is 12 by 9 inches in size, with illuminated embossed cover, bound with silk ribbons neatly tied.

HARTFORD JOURNAL
The souvenir programme of the exercises of the Ancient Order of United Workmen at Foot Guard hall Friday night, was from the press of R. S. Peck & Co. and was one of the finest samples of engraving and embossing ever issued in this city.

We Solicit your Patronage in our line, and will furnish Estimates at short notice.
Satisfaction Guaranteed.

R. S. PECK & CO.

PRINTERS AND WOOD ENGRAVERS,

No. 14 FORD STREET, - - HARTFORD, CONN.

The Hartford Engraving Co.,

66 STATE STREET,
Courant Building,
Hartford, Conn.

MANUFACTURERS OF ALL KINDS OF

RELIEF PRINTING PLATES.

SPECIAL ATTENTION

GIVEN TO

HALF TONE PHOTO-ENGRAVING.

The Illustrations in this Magazine were made by us.

Takes the Lead.

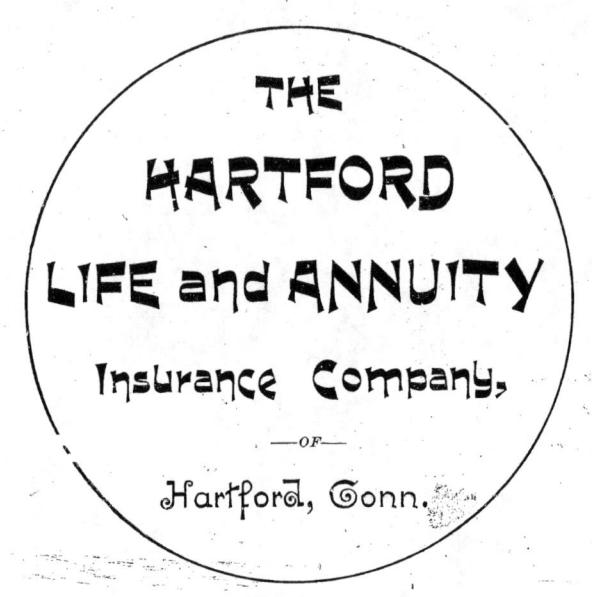

The Hartford Life and Annuity Insurance Company,

—OF—

Hartford, Conn.

In Furnishing PURE LIFE INSURANCE

AT LOWEST COST.

The Safety Fund Distribution Policy

Contains all the most desirable, up to date, features; Security beyond question, Policy conditions most liberal, Largest amount of Insurance for Least Money.

Members' Safety Fund,	$1,000,000
Paid to Beneficiaries,	9,605,086
Insurance in Force, nearly	90,000,000
Number Policy-Holders, about	45,000

First class opportunities for first class Agents.

R. B. PARKER, *President*.   STEPHEN BALL, *Secretary*.

Vol. 1   April, May, June, 1895.   No. 2

The Connecticut Quarterly.

THIS NUMBER CONTAINS

ILLUSTRATED ARTICLES

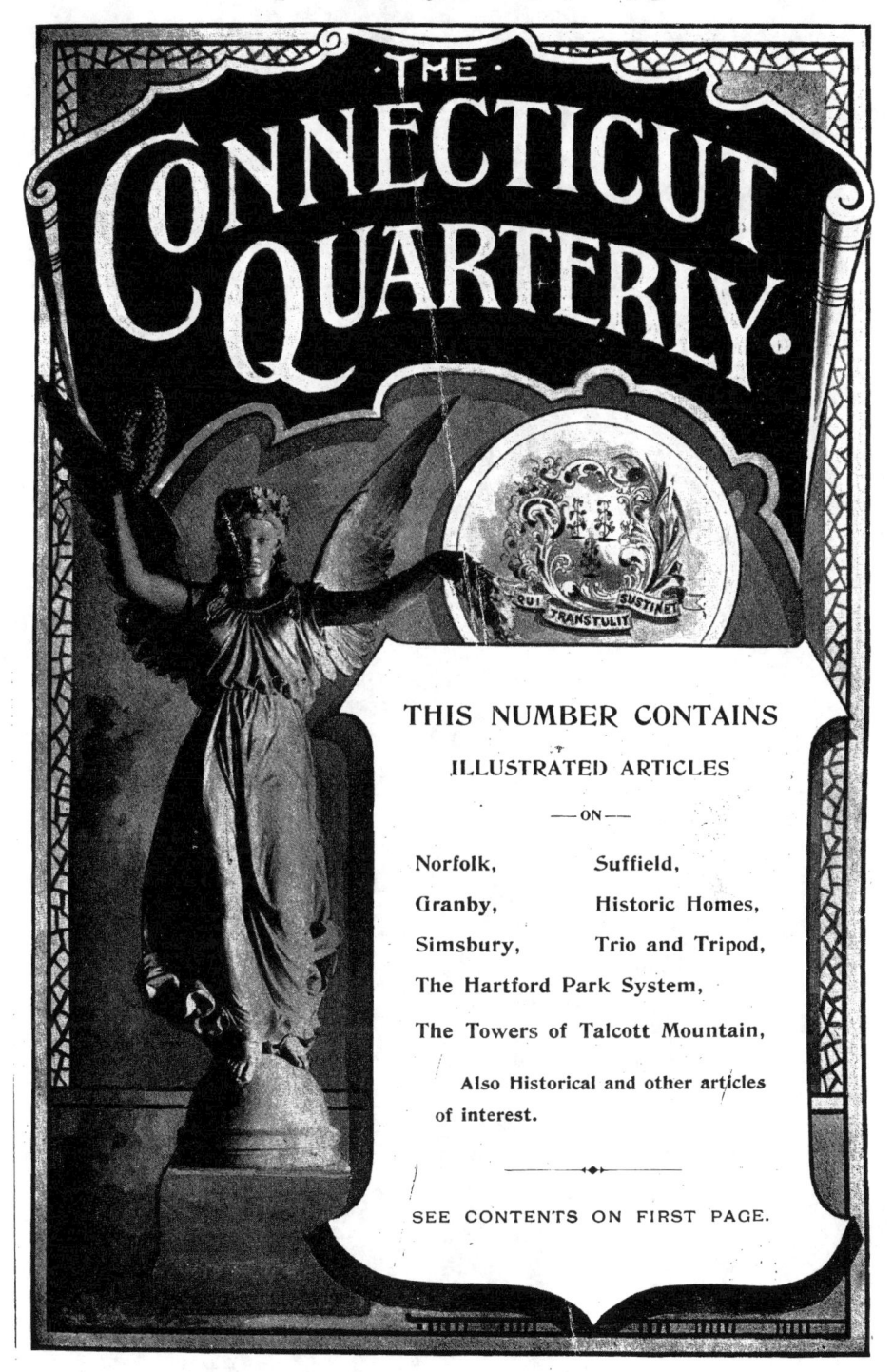

— ON —

Norfolk,   Suffield,
Granby,   Historic Homes,
Simsbury,   Trio and Tripod,
The Hartford Park System,
The Towers of Talcott Mountain,

Also Historical and other articles of interest.

SEE CONTENTS ON FIRST PAGE.

50c. a Year   Hartford, Conn.   15c. a Copy

A NEW BOOK
FOR FAMILY RECORDS.

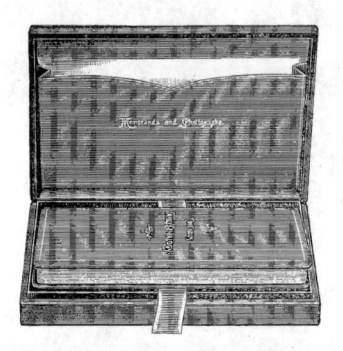

A Continuous Family Genealogy
ON AN ENTIRELY ORIGINAL PLAN
Containing a New System of Charts, Tables and Blanks for keeping a
COMPLETE FAMILY HISTORY,
OF PAST, PRESENT, AND FUTURE GENERATIONS.
In Different Styles of Binding with or without Cases.
Send for Descriptive Circular and Specimen Pages.

ARMS PUBLISHING CO.,
336 Asylum St.   HARTFORD, CONN.

HARTFORD
AGRICULTURAL WAREHOUSE AND SEED STORE.

CADWELL & JONES,
SUCCESSORS TO
R. D. HAWLEY & CO.,

Agricultural . .
. . Implements,

GARDEN, FIELD AND GRASS SEEDS,

Hardware, Wooden Ware, Etc.

498 AND 500 MAIN ST.,

HARTFORD, CONN.

Combination Outfits

For Boys, ages 4 to 15 years, consisting of a SUIT, EXTRA PAIR OF PANTS AND CAP, all of the same material and pattern, and STRICTLY ALL WOOL.

THE COMPLETE OUTFIT
ONLY COSTS YOU
$5.00.

These outfits are much improved over all former ones. The cloth being made from the PUREST LONG WOOL, (no shoddy mixtures of any kind.) Coat made up in the latest style. Double breasted only. Pants have riveted Buttons, patent elastic waistbands, seams all taped, and Double or Cavalry Knees. This is positively the best Outfit ever offered, each and every pattern of Spring 1895 make.

OVER 5000 SOLD LAST SEASON, just think of it ? a coat, two pairs of pants and cap, all of the same material and pattern and strictly all wool for $5.00.

We guarantee this outfit to be of better material and make than any Suit sold elsewhere, without the extra Pants and Cap, for $5.00, or we don't want your money.

The above will be sent you by Express, C. O. D., with the privilege of examining before paying, and if same does not come up to your expectations, you return the outfit to us at our expense. *Samples mailed free on application.*

RENNACKER & CO.,
139 and 141 Asylum St.,
HARTFORD, CONN.

Happy Boys because they have Our Combination.

...THE...
Connecticut Quarterly.

An Illustrated Magazine.
DEVOTED TO THE LITERATURE, HISTORY, AND PICTURESQUE
FEATURES OF CONNECTICUT.

PUBLISHED QUARTERLY
By THE CONNECTICUT QUARTERLY COMPANY,
66 State Street, Courant Building,
HARTFORD, CONN.

GEO. C. ATWELL, General Manager.   W. FARRAND FELCH, Editor.

CONTENTS.

Vol. 1   April, May, June, 1895.   No. 2.

Frontispiece. VIEW OF CAMPBELL'S FALLS. Near Norfolk, Conn.		108
Norfolk, and That Neighborhood, Illustrated from photographs by Mrs. Marie H. Kendall.	*Adele Greene.*	109
Historic Homes. II. HOMES OF WEALTH. Illustrated.	*W. Farrand Felch.*	123
Scenes In and Around Granby. Illustrated from photographs by the author, and drawings by Geo. F. Stanton.	*Howard W. Benjamin.*	134
Simsbury. Illustrated.	*Prof. John B. McLean.*	141
The Burning of Simsbury. Ballad.	*Albert Lewis Thayer.*	151
Fame. Poem.	*Louis E. Thayer.*	152
A Revolutionary Boycott.	*Ellen D. Larned.*	153
A Harp and a Soul. Poem.	*Henry Mason Chadwick.*	154
Old Colonial Characters. II.	*Felix Oldmixon.*	155
The Three Dates.	*Franklin E. Denton.*	160
Poems. "I READ OF ALGOL," AND SONNET.	*Franklin E. Denton.*	162
A Typical Easter. Poem. Illustrated by original drawing by Gustave A. Hoffmann.	*Will Farrand Felch.*	163
Suffield. A Sketch. Illustrated.	*Prof. Martin H. Smith.*	165
A Retrospect. Poem.	*Florence C. Davis.*	172
The Hartford Park System. II. Illustrated.	*Sherman W. Adams.*	173
Atalanta. Poem.	*Fanny Driscoll.*	179
The Towers of Talcott Mountain. Illustrated.	*S. C. Wadsworth.*	180
Trio and Tripod. II. TO SALMON BROOK. Illustrated.	*George H. Carrington.*	188
Sonnet.	*Stockton Bates.*	194
Scrope; or the Lost Library : Serial.	*Frederic Beecher Perkins.*	195

DEPARTMENTS.

The Round Table.	*The Editor.*	204

The American Type. — "It Smacks of the Soil."—The Charm of the Commonplace.—A Word of Welcome.

Sociology and Civics.	*"Solon."*	207

Charity Organization and Medicine.—School of Sociology.—University Extension.—Connecticut Humane Society.

Musical Melange.	*"Minerva."*	210

The Spinet. (Contributed.) Ellen Brainerd Peck.—Individuality in Music.—Forrest Cheney.—New York Notations, (Correspondence), Edwin Warren DeLeon.

Treasure Trove.	*"Algernon."*	212

The Last of the Blue Laws.—Connecticut Society, Sons of the American Revolution.—Connecticut Society; Daughters of the American Revolution.—Connecticut Historical Society.—New Haven Colony Historical Society.—Society of Colonial Wars.

Notes and Queries.   BOOK NOTICES.   ANNOUNCEMENTS.

Copyright 1895 by THE CONNECTICUT QUARTERLY CO. (*All rights reserved.*)
Entered at the Post Office at Hartford, Conn., as mail matter of the second class.

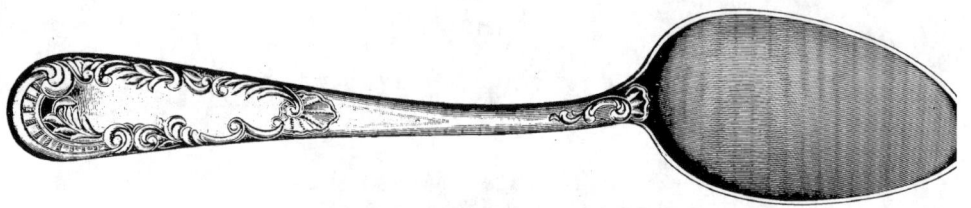

A WONDERFUL METAL.

Solid Columbian Gold: a new metal which is a perfect imitation of 18 carat gold is being manufactured into spoons, knives and forks. There is no question to-day about the merits of Columbian Gold. Wherever used, not one word of complaint any where along the line. It is no longer an experiment, as the goods are growing more popular each year.

Remember this metal is the same all through. Solid metal, No plating. With proper care they retain their color and wear the same as 18 carat gold. No one will buy silver goods when they can get Solid Columbian Gold goods.

Send 50 cents for samples and satisfy yourselves as to the quality. Your money will be refunded if not satisfactory.

PRICES AS FOLLOWS:

Tea Spoons, per set of 6,	$2.00	Dessert Forks, per set of 6,	$3.00
Dessert Spoons, per set of 6,	3.00	Medium Knives, per set of 6,	3.00
Table Spoons, per set of 6,	3.50	Dessert Knives, per set of 6,	2.50
Medium Forks, per set of 6,	3.50	Sugar Shells, each,	1.00
	Butter Knives, each,	$1.00	

Agents wanted in this State.

Address the UPSON & HART CO., Unionville, Conn.

The Hartford Engraving Co.,

66 State Street, Courant Building,

HARTFORD, CONN.

MAKERS OF

HALF TONE PRINTING PLATES.

ENGRAVERS FOR THE CONNECTICUT QUARTERLY.

THE CONNECTICUT QUARTERLY.

Price 50 cents a year, (4 numbers,) payable in advance. Single copies 15 cents.

Remittances should be by Check, P. O. Order, or Registered Letter. Money by mail at sender's risk.

Subscriptions may begin with any number. All subscriptions taken with the understanding that they expire after four numbers have been sent, unless renewed by the subscriber. When change of address is desired give both the old and new address.

Agents wanted in every town in the State to get subscriptions. Write for terms, etc.

Copies of No. 1 are already scarce, and bring double price.

The verdict of all has been, "We are delighted with it."

Advertisers: Get our rates.

THE CONNECTICUT QUARTERLY CO.,

P. O. Box, 565, HARTFORD, CONN.

CAUTION.—Do not pay money to persons unknown to you. Our authorized agents have full credentials.

CAMPBELL'S FALLS.

The Connecticut Quarterly.

"Leave not your native land behind."—Thoreau.

SECOND QUARTER.

Vol. 1   April, May and June, 1895.   No. 2.

NORFOLK, AND THAT NEIGHBORHOOD.

BY ADELE GREENE.

While the Berkshire Hills have long been a favorite resort for city folk, the Litchfield Hills, their continuation in Connecticut, have had until recent years comparatively little reputation. Litchfield, however, on its hill-top, long looked up to as one of the most beautiful towns in New England, has in its turn looked down on the world at large from its vantage ground of antiquity and culture. Excepting this town, the lovely rolling hills of Litchfield county have been greeted by no large number of visitors. But now, year by year, these hills are becoming more widely known, and increasing numbers of guests are enjoying the lovely scenery and invigorating air.

Lakeville has of late been on the lips of those interested in education, as the site of the splendidly endowed Hotchkiss School, preparatory to Yale and other universities. Also among these hills lies Washington, loved and admired as the site of the famed old "Gunnery" school, as well as for its picturesque aspect. Many other spots have been the pleasant summer haunts of the few.

In recent years, visitors in increasing numbers have been attracted to Norfolk, whose altitude, about fourteen hundred feet above tide, ensures pure air and tempers the heat with mountain breezes. It is but a few miles from the Massachusetts line. The engine which puffs arduously up to Norfolk, reaches there the highest railway station in Connecticut. This little town upon its hills, looking off on the blue Berkshires, and made glad by many streams, had doubt-

THE LIBRARY.

less still been dreaming out its sylvan life, were it not so fortunate as to be the residence of two closely connected families long noted for culture and beneficence.

A beautiful library, planned by George Keller of Hartford, has been built, perfect in every appointment, possessing even a conversation-room — for doubtless the donor of the building saw, as did the architect, the importance of a retreat for at least some of our sisters, where silvern speech might take the place of golden silence. Books may be drawn free of charge by villagers and guests. Nothing could look more charmingly cozy of a cool September or October day than the

LIBRARY HALL.

glow and flame in the open fire-place of the artistic hall; and indeed the entire furnishing of the building is a delight to the æsthetic sense. This may be said also of the fine gymnasium, from designs by H. R. Marshall, built by another member of the same family connection. There are tennis-courts on the grounds and a bowling-alley, as well as the gymnasium proper, equipped perfectly for every possible requirement. Here again, no charge is made for the many advantages. In the parlor of the building there is music, morning and evening, during the summer, and dancing in the gymnasium hall several evenings a week, to which all are welcomed. In the winter, a teacher of athletics is provided to make strong the Norfolk youth.

BOOK ROOM — LIBRARY.

Still another gift is a village fountain, which stands at the end of the village-green. This fountain, an exquisite piece of

THE GYMNASIUM.

workmanship in granite and bronze, was designed by Stanford White, the bronze being by St. Gaudens. Facing the same green is the beautiful memorial chapel of the Congregational church, built by Mrs. Urania Humphrey, in memory of her father and mother. This building, designed by Cady, is of granite, and consists of a spacious lecture-room and an adjoining parlor, which may be thrown together.

PARLOR — GYMNASIUM.

The west end of the chapel is beautified by a Tiffany window.

Close by stands the old church, a wooden structure of the New England meeting-house type, with a Wren steeple. The first house of worship was taken down and this one erected in 1813. Since then, the interior has been renovated and a fine large organ presented to the church. From the belfry, a chime of bells tells the quarter-hours, ringing out its full tune before the stroke of each hour. The latest gift is a field for athletic sports, for the young men of Norfolk.

There are numerous lakes within a few miles of Norfolk. The region abounds in springs and is noted for the purity of its water; but to insure a bountiful supply, an aqueduct, bringing water from Lake Wangum, has recently been opened. "The Hillhurst," a home-like hotel, commands a fine prospect. At this house, President Porter of Yale was wont to pass the last summers of his life. Many fine building sites are being occupied, yet the rural simplicity of the place has not been spoiled by showy ornamentation.

TENNIS COURTS.

Of the old residents of the village, the Battell and Eldridge families are notable, and to them Norfolk owes its adornments. The Rev. Dr. Joseph Eldridge was for forty-two years the beloved and honored pastor of the Norfolk church. Norfolk was indeed favored in keeping all its own a man of such marked ability and wide repute. The doors of his home were opened with large sympathy, and his hearth was sought by many, even from afar, who always found there rest and intellectual stimulus. Among his European visitors was Pere Hyacinthe, who came to this quiet nook, far away from the whirlwind of popular feeling which his sudden departure from the Church of the Madeleine had raised.

THE PIAZZA—GYMNASIUM.

The first settled pastor of Norfolk was the Rev. Ammi Ruhamah Robbins, grand-father of Mrs. Eldridge. Mr. Robbins came directly from the theological seminary to Norfolk, where his pastorate of fifty-two years ended only with his death. He came to a very different Norfolk from that of to-day, for the

BUTTERMILK FALLS.

spot was so wild — the old forests standing closely about the church — that on entering the village from the south, the building could not be seen when only a short distance away. Mr. Robbins during his long pastorate in Norfolk, is said

IN THE "GYM."

to have prepared more students for college than any other man of his time in the state. In memory of his educational work, two of his descendants — the Hon. Robbins Battell, whose recent death is so widely lamented, and his sister,

BATTELL CHAPEL.

the late Miss Anna Battell — established an academy, known as The Robbins School, a picturesque building on a wide lawn, through which a brook makes its way, singing on through school-hours and through play, is such a picture, with the hills to frame it, as one will recall with pleasure from afar. Here beauty and knowledge have locked hands. A reunion of the school, on the completion of its tenth anniversary, was recently held, when the old birds and the fledglings met together to bless the day when this "Robbins" nest was hung high up among these hills.

One of the most picturesque roads in Norfolk is the "Willows." On one side a hill rises abruptly, while on the other the venerable trees, from which the road is named, cast a dense shade, their huge trunks and twisted limbs bending devotedly over the gorge where flows their patron stream, the Blackberry river. Just above, the stream has had a fall, and with an angry turbulence is hurrying on, to serve several mills. Attracted to this lovely spot by the water advantages, these workshops stand in the midst of all this greenery, reminding us that the iron hand of civilization grasps every advantage and gives no quarter to primitive nature. The Buttermilk Falls, a series of connected tumbles, is an outflow from the Mill Pond, near by, into the Blackberry River. Here are fascinating bits for the artist. To return to the "Willows," where trees, stream, hill, and road, keep such close company — I well remember a fair September Sunday, with the Sabbath stillness over all save the restless stream, and the voices of those who like ourselves were on their way to the West Norfolk Sunday-school service, a mile and a half from Norfolk village. These services were started and are conducted during the summer, on Sunday afternoons, by one of the city visitors. On the road thither still stands the old and disused toll-gate, a curious and interesting relic of bygone days.

INTERIOR BATTELL CHAPEL.

INTERIOR BATTELL CHAPEL.

REV. JOSEPH ELDRIDGE.

The westering sun is sinking fast when we turn our faces homeward, after the service is over, and soon has dropped behind a hill, and we are in shadow. But across the road, on the opposite height, glints of sunlight linger as if loth to depart, and flickering higher and still higher, call forth here and there

CONGREGATIONAL CHURCH.

an answering glow of early autumnal color. Truly a farewell to summer are these lengthening shadows and waning September lights!

Another charming walk is the "Lover's Lane." What place would be complete without one? — and the road so called in Norfolk is well named, if a winding woodland way, with ferns on either side nod approval, and trees to whisper gently to one another, and only an occasional squirrel for third company, is what a lover's lane should be. We are reminded here of Gilder's woodland thought —

INTERIOR CONGREGATIONAL CHURCH.

"I care not if the skies are white,
  Nor if the fields are gold;
I care not whether 'tis black or bright,
  Or winds blow soft or cold;
But O the dark, dark wood,
For thee, and me, and love."

Here too, chestnuts are ripening, and late October brings no dreamers, but bright-eyed school-children who vie with the squirrels in laying in their stores.

The many drives among these hills are of great beauty and variety. Within easy driving distance are Lake Wangum, Doolittle Lake, and Campbell's Falls. Lake Wangum, about four miles from Norfolk village, is a beautiful sheet of water, high on Canaan mountain. Here an attractive little lodge has been built, open during the season, for guests who may procure meals there while passing the day in boating and fishing, and where a small party may be accommodated

REV. AMMI R. ROBBINS.

ROBBINS SCHOOL.

over night. A drive of about six miles from Norfolk, in the opposite direction, brings us to Doolittle Lake. This lake is much larger than Lake Wangum, and nestled among the hills, its indented shores are thickly wooded. At first glance one feels that here the wilderness obtains, but on closer observation one or two

THE OLD TOLL GATE WEST NORFOLK.

camps and a boat-house dispel the illusion. The fishing is said to be excellent, and a variety of the finny tribe make their uncertain home here. A surprisingly beautiful approach to this lake lies through an ancient pine forest. Surmising that this wood-way from the main road around the lake would bring us to its brink, we turned our horse's head thither, into a gloom of almost theatrical effect. The creaking of the horse's trappings emphasized the impressive stillness; voices, sounding hollow, seemed almost to desecrate the perfect quiet, and flecks of sunlight dappled the denser shade, over the soft deep carpeting, until silver glimmerings through the trees told that the lake was near — surely a startlingly charming contrast from dark to light.

The Campbell's Falls, about nine miles from Norfolk, are near the Massachusetts line. A variety of scenery is to be had on this trip by taking the road over Ball Mountain, and returning by

THE FOUNTAIN.

THE HILLHURST.

way of Canaan valley. Leaving the wagon on the roadside, a steep and wooded path winds down into a ravine, not rugged, but lined with verdure and crested with trees. From the height, at one end of the ravine, the falls, in

CENTER PUBLIC SCHOOL.

wonderful curves of beauty, bound from rock to rock, sparkling in emerald lights over mossy rocks, in the more quite nooks that flank its way, until at length they flow into a bubbling brook soon lost to sight among the trees. Nature loves this spot, and has made it glad with her best gifts of fern and moss.

LAKE WANGUM.

One should not leave Norfolk without visiting the look-out on Haystack Mountain, which stands close guard over the village and invites all to an extended and lovely view. Far to the north, against the horizon, is Greylock, the mountain which presides with such impressiveness over Williamstown, while westward is seen the Taconic range. At our feet is Norfolk, rising and falling on its hills like a billowy sea, the midmost wave crested by the old church, the spire visible from afar. Opposite, and nearer the village is Crissy Hill, which affords a somewhat more detailed outlook on the village. The soil is sandy, and malaria loves not Norfolk. So rocky is the region that many years ago when Norfolk lands were first put up at auction in Hartford, scarcely a bid was to be had for the then unhappy spot. To-day the bidders crowd one another.

RAVINE AT CAMPBELL'S FALLS.

One of the attractions of Norfolk is that, like Lenox and Stockbridge, it keeps its guests late into the autumn, and those who have seen these New England woodlands in their gorgeous autumnal tints, when a Persian mantle of color has been flung over hill and dale, will not wonder at the charm which holds the city folk long in this garden of nature. But to lovers of the hills each season

TIPPING ROCK.

THE LODGE.

brings its peculiar charm and the restful beauty of this region in midsummer

ON THE SIDE OF HAYSTACK.

verdure led to the writing of the following lines on "Norfolk Hills":*

THE NORFOLK CHIME.

Green are the hills that are rolling to meet me,
  Blue in the distance their stern brethren stand;
Flecked o'er with shadow and sunlight, they greet me —
  Peaceful, majestic, a wonderful band.

Far, far away from the soot of the city,
  Into the open, where skies arch serene;
Valley's rejoice at the brooks' tinkling ditty
  Of forested hill-tops all fluffy with green.

Away, far away from the heart's weary beating,
  Far, far away from ambition's fierce throb,
From cares that corrode, and pleasures too fleeting,
  Away from the jostling and self-seeking mob.

Here be my rest and my home for a season,
  These be my friends, and kind nature my cheer;
Peace fill the heart and sweet dreams still the reason —
  Dreams that are child-like, and joy without fear.

* Originally published in the Hartford Times.

HISTORIC HOMES.

II. HOMES OF WEALTH.

BY W. FARRAND FELCH.

Decidedly, one of the most attractive cities in New England, as far as natural beauty is concerned, is Hartford, Connecticut; and by many it is considered to be the most beautiful in the whole country. It will compare favorably with Newport, barring the ocean advantages, in points of interest and in picturesque location; with Detroit in its general topography; with Cam-

RESIDENCE OF JAMES J. GOODWIN.

bridge in historic interest,— its parent-town from whence its ecclesiastical and civil polity was derived; with New Haven, or Springfield, or Worcester, or any other New England village, in its masses of verdure and foliage. In a social sense it can be compared, in a lesser degree of course, with Boston for its culture, refinement, and advanced ideas; and with New York for its commercial spirit, business energy and perspicacity.

But, despite all these comparisons, it has its own peculiar atmosphere and environment; its own slow but thorough-going public spirit; its own devious political predilections and antagonistic elements, a parti-colored mixture of Celtic and Puritanical constitution which alternates strangely in succeeding campaigns. Like the cast of a stone in a quiet pool, causing ever-widening ripples that spread to its circumference, so the old-time "town meeting," to which recourse is still had, may start a series of circles which does not stop with the town's confines but gradually spreads over and influences the whole state.

The individual excellence of its leading citizens in all the main lines of endeavor is a source of common wonder and remark; this is because they are not merely citizens of the municipality but of the state. Some of the

ARMSMEAR.

leading literary lights of the country; some of the richest business men, who have risen from the ranks to become millionaires, (or "plutocrats" in the sense of the socialist and political demagogue); some of the shrewdest commercial and insurance men, and sharpest politicians hail from this small bailiwick. It has been called the richest city of its size in the country, per capita, in late years, and until quite recently had a per capita of $1,000 for each person in the city; not many years ago this was the per capita of every man in the State. This is all the more remarkable when the per capita of wealth of the entire United States does not exceed $50. The superabundance of wealth is largely due to the fact that Hartford is one of the chief insurance centers of the country, second only to New York city; and this branch of business always brings in more money than it sends out for immediate use or exchange. There are a dozen or more insurance companies, fire, life, and accident, and nearly or quite as many banks to contain their deposits not required for other purposes. Large sections of the far west, and the sunny south are owned, through loans and mortgages, by the insurance companies; and large blocks of railroad, manufacturing and municipal stocks and bonds are held as securities and as investments. The aggregation of wealth is in turn showered all over the country, for beneficient aims and civilizing purposes, when it is not needed for the widowed and the fatherless, the maimed and the decrepit, the homeless and impoverished, all of whose interests are protected and perpetuated. The poor western farmer is enabled by eastern capital to complete the clearing, tilling, and improvement of his new farm; the struggling tradesman, to tide over financial difficulty, or to establish a paying business on borrowed funds; and thus the great unsettled portion of the republic is gradually being filled up, if

THE LAKE,—"ARMSMEAR."

not always by the descendants of the stalwart and sturdy New England people then at least by the use and influence of good Yankee money.

Wherever there is wealth, there of course is luxury and culture and refinement. Among coarse people, luxury and style are the only things sought for, or bought with their money, and this is the characteristic of new-rich people; but with those who have enjoyed wealth for a long time, or have inherited it, we do not expect this transformation. Where a higher state of society is found than the *bourgeoise* or chrysalis stage of existence, mere luxury does not satisfy, but there must be an odor of refinement, of good breeding, of excellence, which paltry money can not of itself bestow. If we go still higher, we find society seeking, besides luxury and refinement, a certain modicum of culture and advanced ideas. Here in Hartford we have all this.

The Hartford people spend their money freely on art, on books, and especially upon music. The city has been called "music mad" by an acute observer, but that is hardly the truth; be that as it may, this is hardly the place to cavil at any short-comings. In the field of art, there are a few fine private art collections, but of course inaccessible to the general public, different customs obtaining here from those in England and on the continent where art is worshipped by the many. There is one incomplete public gallery which affords some sharp contrasts between the new and the old, the antiquarian predominant; but it is possible that a marked improvement may soon be seen and felt. In the line of architecture as sharp a contrast between the antique and the modern is afforded the beholder on nearly every street, particularly in the older portions of the city. The old colonial houses, and the later and more

THE LAWN,—"ARMSMEAR."

classical structures, (with large portico pillars reaching to the second story, upholding great pediments and classical ornamentation,) quite out of keeping with the light and airy modern habitations alongside, still exist, generally placed in the center of large lots and wide lawns which show off their massive contours. Gradually, however, these large lots are being divided and sold to house-builders with more modern tastes; so that pretty little villas and Gothic and Queen Anne cottages are now plentifully besprinkled between.

The greatest charm Hartford has in summer is the profusion of ivy which clings to and covers entire houses, from the eaves to the ground, sometimes draping, but generally trained around, each window, giving it a living frame of green, and making a bower that might have satisfied Juliet. There is no house so poor that cannot take on this coating of ivy and along with it an English air, hiding its bare walls and architectural defects and making it seem, either by sunlight or moonlight, a veritable fairy tenement. It is in fact one of the most

English looking cities, outside of Newport, in this country; but Newport is built to order, "very English, you know," with its large mansions or manors, manses or lodges, copied after British models, with timbered sides and sharp gables. Hartford, on the other hand, has not this air of newness and perhaps rawness, but like Topsy has "just growed."

Added to the ivy coverings, we find smooth-shaven lawns which look like green velvet or plush, with attractive beds of colei, cannas, caladiums, hydrangeas, and beautiful shrubbery; as well as fir, spruce, larch, maple and other trees, the larger denizens of the forest which have never been cut down in the march of improvements, and we have a good idea of Hartford homes in general. Another beauty is that fences along the main residence streets are almost entirely discarded; and in places one can look as far as the eye may penetrate along the street without encountering the sight of an ugly fence.

RESIDENCE OF FRANKLIN CHAMBERLAIN.

These were only made to keep out cows and smaller vermin; now that cows and dairies have been relegated to the country or at least to the suburbs, there is little use for fences, and they are gradually being dispensed with.

The main streets are lined with large elms, also, which hang and droop over the street, in places entirely shading it, rendering the street cool, damp, pleasant, and driving a luxury, without dust or glaring sun to dim the eyes and fret the temper of the pedestrians or people in vehicles. These drives are elegant, some new object of interest presenting itself at every turn,—some pretty side street, noble building, cozy cottage, or old rambling house of the last century.

The residence of Mrs. Samuel Colt, called "Armsmear," is one of the most attractive in the city. It is of English stucco, presenting a long irregular front on Wethersfield Avenue. Mrs. Colt is the widow of the late Samuel Colt, of Colt's revolver fame, who amassed a fortune during the war of the rebellion. A late writer, (Mr. W. A. Ayers, in the Memorial History of Hartford County) pays the following tribute to Colonel Colt:

"The improvements in the use of steam power came in rapid succession, and are largely responsible for the enormous advance in manufactures of the present century. There is no better illustration of the radical change made within one hundred years than is furnished in Colt's Armory. These works are notable not merely for the magnitude of their operations, the variety of their produce and the number of successful inventors and mechanical organizers they have produced, but also as an outgrowth of an idea which was conceived by a boy of sixteen and persistently worked out, so that at the age of twenty-one he organized a company with a capital of $300,000 for the manufacture of the product."

"Samuel Colt was born at Hartford, July 19, 1814. His father, Christopher Colt, was a manufacturer; and the boy, who had early shown a taste for mechanics, was employed for a short time in his factory at Ware, Massachusetts, when only ten years of age. Then he was sent to school, and at the age of sixteen went to sea. On this voyage he made a rough model of a revolver, which contained the germ of the idea afterwards developed in his pistol. Returning, after a voyage to Calcutta, he worked in the dyeing and bleaching department of his father's factory, obtained some chemical knowledge, and especially became interested in nitrous oxide. He conceived the idea of giving lectures, illustrating the use of this gas,— laughing gas,—and set out on a tour for this purpose, at the age of eighteen. He traveled under the name of Dr. Coult, and followed this life for some two years with such success as to obtain money for developing his invention. In 1835, he went to Europe and took out patents there, the American patents being taken out on his return. In 1836 he founded a company with a capital of $300,000 at Paterson, N. J., for the manufacture of his revolver. The money was sunk in developing the invention, and the company became insolvent in 1842, but it produced revolvers which were used in the Seminole war with such success that the experience of army men with them was what gave him a new start in business in 1847, through a Government order at the breaking out of the Mexican war . . . . The Government order was the first step in his career of success. It was for 1,000 revolvers, and he made arrangements to have them built at Whitneyville, New Haven. In the following year he became a manufacturer in Hartford, in a small building on the north side of Pearl Street, a little west of Trumbull Street; but within a few years conceived the plan of the South Meadow improvements and built the present Armory."

The rest of the story is too well known to need recapitulation. Sarah, daughter of Major Caldwell, a famous sea-captain in Hartford's early maritime days, became the wife of Christopher Colt, of Hartford, and mother of Colonel Samuel Colt. Christopher Colt was at one time in partnership with his father-in-law in his enterprises. Another daughter of Major Caldwell married Jared Scarborough, a man of prominence in the last generation but one, who owned part of the land on which the American Asylum for the Deaf and Dumb ("The American School at Hartford for the Deaf") now stands, and also land on Prospect Hill, which was known as Scarborough Hill, now Scarborough Street. Major Caldwell was a merchant in a large sense, and owned ships employed in the West India trade but occasionally making Spanish and Mediterranean voyages, and engaged to some extent in coastwise traffic. The late Commodore Caldwell H. Colt, son of Col. Colt, was named from him, and came well by his aquatic tastes, from his grand-father and father. His yacht, Dauntless, now almost dismantled and in moorings, near the mouth of the Connecticut river, was, says a late writer,

"the pet and pride of her owner, Commodore Colt, and of the yachting fleet. On every social yachting occasion the old boat was there, looking as trim and taut as the newest and finest of the fleet. The commodore's receptions and entertainments, when afloat, were on the grandest scale. No expense was spared in keeping the old yacht in sea-going trim. Her jet black hull was as smooth and glossy as a well-groomed steed; her spars were as bright as the brightest; the brass work glistened and sparkled in the morning sun; her snow-white deck was fit for a queen to walk on, and when full dressed in her cloud of white sails, reeling off 12 or 15 knots, she presented a beautiful picture." . . . . "What will eventually become of the old yacht, time only will tell. She is in charge of a keeper at present. The Commodore's mother, Mrs. Elizabeth Colt, visited the old yacht several times last summer."

Assuredly no more queenly woman ever trod the decks of the Dauntless than the Commodore's mother,—the queen indeed, of Hartford society, and first and foremost for years in all worthy charitable enterprises, not only of a general character but for the betterment of her own sex; she is the President of the Union for Home Work, for instance, and in other benevolent affairs takes a leading part. She is also President of the Society of Colonial Dames, which numbers among its members not only the descendants of the first citizens of the infant republic, but of the old Colonial Governors, magistrates, divines, doughty captains, valiant ensigns, and "high privates of the rear rank."

The "Armsmear" estate presents a frontage of nearly half a mile along one of Hartford's principal thoroughfares, Wethersfield Avenue, and extends back to the river, covering part of the South Meadows, whereon are located the extensive buildings of the "Armory." A glimpse or two into the grounds, through dense foliage, affords a delightful view of a charming lake, surrounded by statuary, fountains, and verdure; not the least notable is the statue of a colt holding a spear in its mouth, an Americanised coat-of-arms, which is certainly appropriate. It is not generally known that in England the Colt and Coutts family are the same, and that the rich London banker, Baroness Burdett-Coutts, probably the richest woman in the world, can perhaps claim distant kinship with American congeners of like name and fame.

RESIDENCE OF IRA DIMOCK.

Of equal prominence and interest, although of later origin, is the residence of the late Major James Goodwin, upon Woodland Street, known universally at Hartford as "the Castle;" says Mr. Wm. C. Brocklesby, the architect, in his technical description of its beauties:

"It is constructed of Westerly granite, with rock-face ashlar and finish of the same material, relieved by belts and courses of rose granite. The design is Gothic, and all the details are carefully executed. The characteristic feature of the principal floor plan is a wide hall, forty-five feet in length, extending entirely through the house from east to west, and displaying midway upon one of the side-walls a lofty, hooded fire-place, built of Ohio stone, enriched by carving. The stables and coachmen's quarters are so connected with the main building as to form a part in the same general design. The prominent feature of the house is the square tower, finished at its upper portion in timber work."

Major James Goodwin was born March 2, 1803, and was son of James Goodwin of Hartford, a descendant of Ozias, one of our first settlers. At the age of sixteen he became a clerk for Joseph Morgan, whose daughter Lucy he married in 1832. Before he had completed his twenty-first year he had become the proprietor of the principal line of mail stages east of Hartford. In a few years he and his associates owned and controlled all the more important lines leading out of Hartford. Between 1835 and 1840 he had, however, disposed of all his stage interests, foreseeing the coming power and extent of railways, and in 1839 he became a director of the then Hartford and New Haven Railroad.

He was one of the original incorporators of the Connecticut Mutual Life Insurance Company. In 1848 he was elected its president, and remained in that position until the time of his death, with the exception of an interregnum of three years, when Dr. Guy R. Phelps was the president.

"His name will always be closely identified with it. His courage, self-reliance, and foresight made him a leader and he had the full confidence of the community alike as to his judgment and his integrity. His shaping hand is manifest in all the affairs with which he was connected. His life was marked with constant usefulness and beneficence."

He died March 15, 1878.

We have frequently heard the remark: "What would Hartford have been if Colonel Colt and Major Goodwin had lived until now!" It is highly

MAIN HALL.—RESIDENCE OF IRA DIMOCK.

probable that these two sturdy souls, had they lived until today, or possibly either one of them alone, would have materially altered the topography and environment of the city, especially at the opposite ends of it in which they lived. It is possible also that a dearth of interest in the city's welfare, a lack of progress after the war, a lull in its industrial activity and mechanical supremacy, would have been tided over by ways and means at their command, and by their energetic example and dominant spirit. But there have been reasons for this subsidence, almost desuetude, which the wise ones will not have far to go to find. Manufacturers have not been encouraged by certain factions and interests, when they are really the sinews of civilization. Political influences have produced demoralization in certain directions; but most of all a decided inertia among the moneyed classes.

While we may not have them among us to-day, as hale and hearty octogenarian and nonogenarian Nestors, we have in their stead others who worthily and amply represent them. Of Mrs. Colt's active beneficence we have already spoken. Major Goodwin left two sons, James Junius Goodwin and Rev. Francis Goodwin, to whom Hartford owes more, directly and indirectly, than it will ever be able to repay, in a material sense. They have been prominent in church and school, in park and library affairs, for years; and we are safe in saying that the end is not yet, in any of these varied directions, if projects already gradually forming and gathering volume are any indication. Their interest in the Wadsworth Athenæum and Hartford Public Library, in Trinity parish and church, in the now rapidly evolving Hartford park system, individu-

EAST DRAWING ROOM.—RESIDENCE OF IRA DIMOCK.

ally and as trustees of the will of the late Henry Keney (empowered to purchase land for a park to be called "Keney Park") and in divers educational, historical, commercial, and municipal affairs, have endeared them to their fellow-townsmen thrice over.

Mr. James Junius Goodwin has displayed creditable interest in historical and genealogical matters, and at his instigation a history of the Goodwin family has been prepared, under the supervision of the indefatigable professional genealogist, Mr. Frank Farnsworth Starr, who was sent to England on several occasions to secure all obtainable data. It is also to the credit and honor of the same gentleman that through his aid and encouragement the genealogy of George Washington has been at last unraveled and authenticated and published in book form. Mr. Henry F. Waters, in London, the veteran genealogist achieved this work.

There are several houses of almost as imposing appearance that claim our attention, but space will not permit extended mention. On a lesser scale, and almost as beautiful, is the residence of Franklin Chamberlain, a leading lawyer, built "chiefly of broken granite, while the belt courses and finish around the windows are of red brick, giving a very rich appearance." On Albany Avenue is a spacious, but not very ornate house, crowned with a tower, the residence of the Hon. James Goodwin Batterson.

On the western edge of Hartford, over two miles from the city's center, lies Prospect Hill, along the top of which for nearly a mile, stretches the far-famed Prospect Avenue, a nearly level boulevard, on the western side of which, and just outside the city's limits which reach the middle of the street, lie the houses of some of the richest residents — not of Hartford, but of West Hartford — who do business in Hartford and yet escape that city's high taxes on their suburban homes. A strenuous effort has been made to include this

RESIDENCE OF CHARLES R. FORREST.

section within the limits of the city of Hartford, in order to take advantage of water supply, sewerage, electric lighting, and schools of the city. But the western section of the town of West Hartford is not favorable to the proposition.

For nearly a mile west of Prospect Avenue, the land rises with gentle slope, until it culminates in what is known sometimes as "Hamilton Heights" and at other times as "Vanderbilt Hill," — to the electric car men, it is simply a station yclept "Vanderbilt," dispensing with unnecessary verbiage. Between Prospect Hill and Vanderbilt Hill is a well-settled region, now known as the "Morning Slope" among its romantic denizens; the society in this section being known as "The Neighborhood," since the formation of the "Neighborhood Club" which gave the initial impetus to the foundation and building of the Prospect Casino, to afford this section a place for entertainments and social enjoyment; they were too far from the city's center to enjoy city entertainments, and reach home in good season by the slow-going horse cars, which would perhaps land them home somewhere towards the "wee, sma' hours," and the electric service was so long in coming to perfection that they chose the other horn of the dilemma and built the casino. It has but recently been opened, with pre-Lenten gaiety, by its projectors, and a distinguished social event it was. The building is a modest structure in an architectural sense, but has a fine assembly room, a well-fitted stage, parlors, card-rooms, billiard-rooms, and a bowling alley, together with a wide verandah that can be enclosed with bunting, affording a delightful promenade.

"Vanderbilt Hill" derives its name from the fact that at one time the residence of Cornelius Vanderbilt, son of "The Commodore," was built thereon especially to his tastes, but for unforeseen circumstances over which he had no control, he did not live to enjoy it long. It was then sold at auction by the administrators of the estate of the deceased, at a sacrifice, to Wm. H. Spooner, of Bristol, R. I., of whom its present owner, Mr. Ira Dimock, purchased it, in 1889, at a still further sacrifice, after having stood long vacant. The house stands on a plot of eleven acres, and the house itself, including veranda, is 100 by 110 feet, which may give a good idea of its enormous size. To be more explicit, there are three main halls, 16 by 44 feet and about thirty rooms of various sizes, eight of which are 20 by 36 feet. The billiard room, in the octagon tower is twenty-four feet in height, with a gallery around its sides, for spectators. Standing on high ground itself, the view from the house in all directions is hardly surpassed in the State. The weather-vane is about one hundred feet high above the foundation, and from that dizzy height, if it were possible to attain it, the view would be entrancing, looking down even upon the gilded dome of the capitol. The total height of the capitol, itself, is over 250 feet, and on a considerable eminence also.

There are later structures that are almost in line with those mentioned in size and structural beauty. The Charles R. Forrest home, constructed two or three years since, under the supervision of Hon. John R. Hills, as contractor, on the corner of Asylum Avenue and Gillette Street, and extending back to Niles, on a large tract, is one of the most showy houses in the city, is said to contain fifty rooms, *en suite*, and is a veritable palace inside in which one could without difficulty become lost. A few years ago this was one of the most forbidding and unattractive corners in the city, occupied by some old huts that were picturesque if not appropriate. There are several other houses, to which we wish to call attention, in future issues, but are obliged to delay the consideration until another time, owing to lack of space herein. Some of these are very old and antiquated, some recent and modern, while still others are in course of erection, and it is not fitting to treat of them while incomplete.

" Home is not merely roof and room—
　It needs something to endear it.
Home is where the heart can bloom,
　Where there's some kind lip to cheer it!
What is home with none to meet,
　None to welcome, none to greet us?
Home is sweet and only sweet,
　Where there's one who loves to meet us."

Scenes In and Around Granby.

BY HOWARD W. BENJAMIN.

Broad highways reaching about, verdure crowned hills rising from shady valleys, babbling brooks and noisy waterfalls almost hidden in luxuriant foliage, thrifty farms dotting the landscape in every direction,— such is Granby. Its aspect is always well bred; Granby is never indecorous. From the state line to the Farmington,— and this is the Dan and Beersheba of Granby,— the country is always inviting, never wearisome. Though the same rough-hewn chestnut fences zig-zag across the fields, the same white farm-houses with green blinds line the roadsides, the same Jersey cows graze in the meadows; yet, each one of the Granbys is distinct from the others and possesses a charm of its own.

From the broad expanse of fertile fields and meadows of Granby Street to the outskirts of the town among the rugged hills of Hartland is a long step, but the people are the same. The sturdy independence and shrewdness which characterize the New Englander have left their mark upon Granby. One knows the old Puritan stock at sight, wherever found. It is true that the sun never sets on New Englanders. Whether planting vineyards in northern Ohio, "punching" cattle in Texas, prospecting for gold in California, king-making at Honolulu, tasting tea at Hong Kong, speculating in oil at Baku, or photographing the midnight sun at Hammerfest, the Yankee always turns up.

Listen to the conversation at the village store at the "corners" of a Saturday evening, when the bronzed farmers gather about on benches and upturned boxes, while waiting for the mail to be sorted. The most weighty problems of the day are discussed pro and con, and decided, not always logically, but oftentimes extremely convincing. Among the hills neighbors are few, and it is only by these visits to the general store that their knowledge of the world can be aired.

It is a grand sight,— these Hartland hills in October. The deep emerald of the woods has changed to a glorious gold and red and brown, each color intensified by the crisp air and the late morning sun which breaks upon the leafy expanse in a shimmer of burnished gold. No sign of life is seen, save here and there a tiny ribbon of blue smoke curling upward which betokens the wood-chopper's hut or the pile of the charcoal burner. Verily, October is the month in which to see the hills in all their magnificence. Nature then puts forth her last and best effort, before grim Winter lays on his chilly hand. In the short space of a few weeks this riot of color will be hidden under the snow and the winds will whistle about the heads of the sturdy pines, the only green survivors of the scene before us; then, rushing down the valleys will pile the white carpet over the frozen streams and against the bare brown rocks.

One day I was riding along the slopes of the hills, enjoying the panorama of plain and valley spread out almost beneath me. The body of the wagon lurched to and fro as the wheels slid from one stone to another in the road-bed. This jolting naturally prevented any connected conversation but, notwithstanding this, my driver was giving me a glowing account of the fine country through which we were passing. I listened respectfully, and at length ventured, "Were you born here?" He stopped short in his remarks and giving me a look of unutterable pity, ejaculated, "Born here, eh?" "Why, mister, I was born *all over* this country,"—giving a magnificent sweep of his

GRANBY STREET LOOKING NORTH.

arm to indicate the extent of it. I too was born here, but only in a little cottage by the village green. So I looked at him with awe and admiration and held my peace. What an extensive personage to be sure, and how insignificant I was beside him.

Granby Center, or Granby Street as it is familiarly called, lies in the best cultivated and most fertile part of the town. The principal residences cluster about the broad street bordered with noble elms. Such a street one may see in many New England towns, but rarely elsewhere. This portion of Granby is becoming a summer resort for the city man. Away from the close proximity of railroads and the influx of foreigners, his children can run about in safety, enjoying the health-giving properties of the country air, while the man himself can come hither at the close of day, loll about on the verandah, or doze in his hammock, out among the trees, until bed-time. On the village green a monument of brown-stone has been erected in memory of the brave sons of Granby who left their farms in '61 at the country's call, to fight and die on distant battle-fields. In many instances their last resting places may be unknown but their deeds will never pass from memory.

To the westward of Granby Street is West Granby. Among the hills, we are again. Hills to the right, hills to the left, hills everywhere, with noisy brooks tumbling over the boulders in miniature eddies and cascades. The disciples of Isaac Walton may find here sport in plenty. Though the streams are difficult of access the result will well repay the fisherman. The mills sing merrily as the keen edge of the saw eats its way through the toughest monarchs of the forest, while the slow, patient water-wheel, as if knowing its power, seems loth to part with the dripping crystals so eager to rush away to the ocean. No wilder portion of Connecticut can be found than in some parts of West Granby.

SUMMER RESIDENCE OF J. B. BUNCE.

Living, here, is a synonym for toil, for the earth refuses to yield up its plenty. I have seen little fellows with bare brown legs trudging along behind a drove of cows at an age when city youngsters would be building block houses in the nursery. But what sturdy men they make; and when transplanted to other scenes, how quickly railroads are built and cities erected where before was nothing.

From almost any point in West Granby the Barn Door Hills are discernible and form a prominent part of the landscape. It is a pity that this ridiculous name should be attached to these two hills — a name which belies their beauty and shows a certain paucity of thought which could easily have been remedied. A roadway runs between the two hills while on either side rise the precipitous rocks to a great height. Nothing but a steep path and a strong pair of limbs will take you to the top, but the view of the surrounding country well repays for the effort. Granby lies all about you. Away to the north the sunlight glitters across the surface of Congamond lakes like a silver tray on a green cloth. Still further northward Mount Tom and Mount Holyoke blend their blue shapes in

THE SOLDIERS' MONUMENT.

the purple haze on the horizon. Eastward, Granby Street lies spread out, almost under your feet and then the low range of hills which slopes down to the immediate valley of the Connecticut. To the south you look down upon the smiling valley of the Farmington. As far as the eye can reach in this direction is the same and never-ending prospect of a noble river flowing through meadows of deepest green and upon whose banks cluster prosperous farming and manufacturing towns. Simsbury, Collinsville, Farmington, Avon and Granby all belong to this hierarchy. Westward, the tall hills of Hartland and Barkhamsted rise abruptly before your eyes, completely shutting out the world in this direction. Their tree-clad summits seem to say to your vision, "'Thus far shalt thou go and no farther.' Therefore be seated on yonder moss-covered rock and reflect well upon this glorious country which is shown thee, and seek not to look farther lest thou seest things which are not so beautiful."

North Granby reaches to the state line and is the oldest of the Granbys. A public library was opened here, in 1891, through the generosity of the late Frederick H. Cossitt, of New York. As a barefooted lad he had worked on a

THE "BARN DOOR HILLS," FROM WEST GRANBY.

farm in North Granby, leaving at the age of sixteen to make his fortune in the world. Mr. Cossitt afterward became a wealthy merchant in New York but never forgot the hillsides where as a boy he had lived. In his will a sum of money was left to North Granby for the erection and maintenance of a library. The building is a tasty structure, centrally located and what is better still, well patronized. The library cost about $3,500, and contains nearly three thousand volumes. Show me a town in which there is a free library liberally patronized and I will show you a community which has thrown off the trammels of a self satisfied existence while the men and women of it are living lives more valuable to themselves and the world at large. A library like this one is a blessing wherever it is located. Granby may well be proud of it and proud of the man whose generosity prompted the giving of it.

About a mile from the Cossitt Library is an old mill and a rocky gorge through which tumbles a wild mountain brook. Crag Mill Gorge it is called and the place is only saved celebrity because of its seclusion. In summer the dense green foliage almost completely hides the spot and were it not for the deep, sullen roar of the water plunging over the rocks, the wayfarer would pass it by unnoticed. To stand on the bridge over the mill-pond and watch the black water tumble and foam in the rocky depths below is well worth the notice of any one. In winter, enormous icicles hang thickly on the walls of this miniature canon, while the ice heaped up below in fantastic forms makes a veritable fairy realm. The stream soon leaves the gorge with a roar, and plunging between two huge rocks, flows blandly through the fields beyond, bearing naught but a fleck of foam on its bosom to tell of its recent struggle. This same stream flows into Cranberry Ponds at Mechanicsville, which

A BRANCH OF THE SALMON BROOK.

abound with fish and water-lilies, then out and onward again, turning the wheels of many mills, and finally adding its volume to the Farmington.

CRAG MILL GORGE.

Granby Street is oftentimes called Salmon Brook from this stream, or as the old residents say, Salmon Brook Street.

One bright spring day I was, by request, photographing the parsonage in a certain part of Granby. The good man and his wife, I had placed on the verandah, while near them, I believe, stood the two grand-children of the worthy couple. About the instrument had gathered a little semi-circle of bare-footed urchins to watch the proceedings. Most of them were munching huge slices of bread dripping with molasses,—that universal juvenile luncheon. All was ready when suddenly over the brow of the hill appeared another little chap, also with his bread and molasses, and running to join the group as fast as his brown legs could carry him. At sight of this addition to their number, the company about me set up a shout, "Hurry up, come see the telephone!" "It's goin' off!" This caused no little hilarity. After the commotion had subsided, I resumed operations, procured my picture and departed, accompanied at a respectful distance by the wondering crowd.

The ruins of Newgate prison are in East Granby, and by reason of the traditional and historical lore which lingers around the decaying walls, it demands more notice than can be given here. Perched on the side of the mountain, Newgate is visible to the eye long before one reaches the spot by the winding road. Like some feudal ruin, a thing of the past, it clings to this generation merely by its old time associations. The struggle which gave birth to this country witnessed the first years of Newgate. The prison dates from

THE RUINS OF NEWGATE PRISON.

1773 and was used for fifty-four years, or until 1827, at which time the convicts were transferred to Wethersfield and made to walk the entire distance in chains. During its palmy days the confinement was very rigorous; but later the prison discipline was relaxed and escapes became frequent. During the Revolution, troublesome Tories were brought here and allowed to reflect on patriotism. The records do not show however that this treatment cured many of them of their attachment to George III. The several buildings which composed the prison are arranged around three sides of an inclosure which formed the prison yard. A strong wall of stone, twelve feet in height incloses the yard on the side toward the road; entrance being gained through an archway which was once closed by a massive iron gate. The building which is at the south of the prison yard is yet standing but the interior has mostly decayed and fallen in a confused heap of floor timbers and partition walls. In this part were located the kitchen, shoe shop, cooper shop, and the chapel for divine worship. Adjoining this on the west is the best preserved portion of the old prison. The cells here are partly underground,—cold and damp in the hottest days of summer. From their barred windows the eye looks into, and miles up and down, the valley below. This view is a grand one and you can easily imagine the longings which would come over the poor shivering wretch within, as he pressed his haggard face against the iron rods of his window and surveyed the scene before him.

Newgate was built directly over a copper mine which was worked some years prior to the existence of the prison, and afterward by the convicts themselves. The guide takes you down a long ladder into the darkness below and then hands you a candle. You follow him as best you can, slipping along on the smooth rocks. Above ground it is ninety in the shade, but here one shivers with cold. A chamber cut into the solid rock is shown where a negro was chained and the holes in the floor show where his manacles were fastened. Barbarous punishments were common in those days and the thought makes the visitor anxious to leave hastily for the fair world above ground. One's progress outward is greatly accelerated too, for when passing through a sort of "Fat man's misery," you are compelled to bend nearly double while the icy water, dripping from the ceiling, has a pleasant way of trickling down your spine, having entered at an unguarded point between your collar and you. Volumes might be written about Newgate

IN THE COPPER MINE—NEWGATE.

—of the daring escapes, the life of the inmates, of hopes deferred and memories of the time. Only the merest sketch can of course be given here.

As you pass out through the gateway of the old prison and drive down into the valley below, one more look is cast upward at its vine-clad walls thrown into bold relief by the dark blue shale covering the precipitous side of the mountain in the background. Granby, indeed, cannot be known in a fortnight. We have merely glimpsed, as it were, at its aspect to-day, and we have explored, but hastily, the ruins of its past, so we resolve to return again at another time.

NEWGATE GATEWAY

SIMSBURY.

BY REV. JOHN B. McLEAN.

And sweet homes nestle in these dales,
And perch along these wooded swells,
And, blest beyond Arcadian vales,
They hear the sound of Sabbath bells!
Here dwells no perfect man sublime,
No woman winged before her time
But with the faults, and follies of the race,
Old home-bred virtues hold their not unhonored place."

Why Simsbury? There is much in a name notwithstanding Shakespearean philosophy. New York, Chicago, Boston. Could they have become great cities had they been blanketed with the name Simsbury? Some authentic historical reason for exchanging the musical Indian name Massaco for colorless Simsbury would make it more endurable, but the search-light of the historian reveals but conflicting guesses. The name of a place, however, with which we have no acquaintance, is but an abstraction. Knowing it, it becomes concrete,

CONGREGATIONAL CHURCH.

and the frame-work and background of a series of pictures and impressions. Though the name, Simsbury, be without suggestiveness to the strange ear, to those who have watched the seasons come and go, from her quiet homes, and to the passer-by, whose soul is touched by the beautiful, this name will turn many exquisite pages, in memory's album.

Simsbury is a mine of that wealth of which the man may possess most who has greatest capacity to receive. The great charm of the place is variety. It has some attractive features for almost every taste. Those who love mountain scenery may wander along the granite hills on the west or the trap ledges on the east. They may climb the "Pinnacle," and look down on pretty Lake "Bijou," lying like a pearl in emerald setting, or to the cedar-fringed summit of Mt. Philip, towering nearly a thousand feet above the river-ribboned meadows of Massaco. From this far famed "royal view" may be traced the old drift-"kames" by the deep green of the pines which clothe their sterile summits. Far to the north and west, Tom, Holyoke, and distant Greylock salute you through the purple haze. In the west arises that wild tumult of hills, which conceal in their bosom the grand old towns of Litchfield and Norfolk.

If the more quiet scenery of a river valley affords greater pleasure — search out and feast upon the unsung beauties of the Farmington, a stream which would have ravished the soul of Wordsworth or David Gray. For miles the road follows the river where the waters flash to the eye their fresco of over-arching elms, with background of blue sky and fleecy cloud, and where river-bank on the one hand and hedge-row on the other, seem to compete, in

METHODIST CHURCH.

wild luxuriance of flowers, grasses, and tangles of clematis and woodbine. Northward the stream winds through well-tilled meadows, where the projecting coves are almost concealed beneath a thin garment of peltate leaves, and starry lilies. At length, turning sharply eastward its tortured waters plunge wildly over the rocks of the mountain pass.

For some, the forests have peculiar charm. There are many drives through the wooded belt, running north by south nearly through the center of the township. These give cool, refreshing shelter which the fierce heat of the summer sun can scarcely penetrate, where toiling, weary brutes, and men who are not brutes, breathe gratitude. Masses of ferns, and banks of soft cool moss tempt the passer-by to recline in dreamy reverie and listen to the monotone of the wind, playing upon its mighty sylvan organ.

Simsbury offers rich enjoyment to any student who delights in reading the long story of creation, — for nowhere on the face of the earth can more formations, distinct in character, be found within the limit of a few hours' walk. Here granite, trap, sandstone and the erratic rocks chant their tragic epics for those who "have ears to hear." Not less of interest will here be found for the botanist. From showery April, when that sweet gift of the glacier smiles its greeting from beneath the leaves,— to chill November, when the deep fringed gentian seems to chide the trees for putting off their summer robes so soon, broad flower-besprinkled meadows, deep orchid-hiding woods, hedge-row, marsh, mountain cliff and glen will reward the patient seeker after Flora's gems.

Some, believing that "the proper study of mankind is man," would search the fading pages of history. No tragic scene of the world's great drama has been enacted here. The history of Simsbury is the story of a sturdy, self-dependent, God-fearing, home-loving people, who spared neither blood, nor fortune when the "drum beat" sounded to that great struggle for independence, or that more terrible death grapple with the dark demon of sin, whose voice of wild satiric laughter had ever mingled its discords with our "anthems of the free." Armed with such preparation as the "destrict school" and village

THE BACON PLACE.

lyceum afforded, her "Miltons" and "village Hamptons" have not all remained "mute and inglorious." Simsbury has given to the National Army, able officers; to Congress, wise statesmen; to the Executive, a Comptroller, a Secretary of the Treasury, and a distinguished foreign minister; to our Colleges, two Presidents; to the Episcopal Church, a Bishop; to Missouri, a Governor; to New York City, merchant princes, and to the professions prominent members.

Simsbury was the second town of the Tunxis Valley to invite the English settler. In 1643, John Griffin and Michael Humphrey came from Windsor and commenced the manufacture of tar. A certain Indian, Manahannoose, "did wittingly kindle a fire" which proved disastrous to their enterprise. The Court decreed, that "in default of payment of five hundred string of wampum," he should "serve or be shipped in exchange for neagers.' He seems to have escaped this penalty by giving the injured tar-makers a deed of Massaco. The township has several times been divided. East Granby, (where old Newgate prison is located), Granby, North Canton and Canton having, in great part, been formed from its original territory.

SIMSBURY.

Simsbury is located northwest of Hartford, in the northern part of that valley rent from the broad Connecticut by the convulsions following the Jurassic epoch. Scattered over its area, are numerous small villages, the one known as Simsbury being near the center. These are, with two or three exceptions, arranged along the streets running north and south on either side of the river. North, on the east side of the river, is located the once thriving village of Tariffville. Desolating fires, with a series of other misfortunes, have checked its prosperity. The "long road," of its misfortunes, now seems to have reached its "turning." It is wonderfully picturesque in its surroundings, and the scenery attracts many to the "Bartlett Tower," located on a mountain near by. From Tariffville southward the drive commands the most charming river and meadow scenery. Where the old Windsor road descends the mountain is a little hamlet known as "Terry's plain." Fair and delectable indeed must have seemed the virgin face of Massaco as seen first from this mountain crest, and one cannot wonder that Griffin and Humphrey (the "Caleb" and "Joshua" sent to spy out the land) resolved to settle here, notwithstanding the "Anakim."

THE OLD DISTILLERY.

THE STREET.—SOUTH END.

About two miles of road, mostly along the river bank brings us to East Weatogue, a pretty, restful hamlet. The morning sun is late in driving away the mountain shadows, but the wide westward vista lengthens out the day with glowing sunsets. Here the Hartford road winds over the mountain. From the summit of the last steep descent, the song of turbulent waters will fall upon the ear. Would you enjoy one of the daintiest bits of scenery; swing down the deep ravine and follow the laughing cascades through the gloom of the rock-walled canon.

In this village stands the oldest house of the township, known as the "Bacon Place" or "Ft. George." Built in 1717, though somewhat bowed with

RESIDENCE OF AMOS R. ENO

age, its massive timbers yield but slowly to the ravages of time. Tradition tells of wild scenes here in the old days of warfare. There also is located that fine example of colonial architecture, the "Humphrey Place," at present occupied

THE FREE LIBRARY.

by the lineal descendants of that Michael Humphrey who with John Griffin first invaded the primeval forests of Massaco.

On the opposite side of the river lies the sister village, West Weatogue, in former days the business center of the place. The "old inhabitant" still boasts of those halcyon times. Here was the village store, and the school where John Slater was, by vote of the town, authorized " to teach the youths to read, write, cypher and say the rules of arathmetack," and here another teacher of great

THE CEMETERY.

local fame taught grammar by machinery. With growth of business in another part of the town, the star of her prosperity set, but only to rise again with

THE ENSIGN HOMESTEAD.

increased splendor. Her prophet no longer chants his Jeremiads from her ruins. The "spirit of the renaissance" is sweeping over her, everywhere transforming the unsightly into the beautiful. Old farm houses burst from the chrysalis into towered mansions. An artistic granite fountain,—"in memoriam" of the beloved physician, Dr. White,—ornaments her pretty green. Even the old school house, has put off her simple gown and come out in a brand new suit, with a "Romanesque" flounce.

Separated from Weatogue by the loveliest of drives through the fragrant pines is Bushy Hill. A *bushy* hill no longer. Her ill-kept farms, where men often failed in the struggle with nature because of the heavy tribute paid "King Alcohol," have come into the possession of the Rev. D. Stuart Dodge, the Messrs Arthur, Norman, and Walter Phelps Dodge, the sons and grandson of the late William E. Dodge of New York; and her hills, commanding a wide circle of exquisite scenery, are being crowned with stately mansions. Bushy hill is honored by the association of distinguished names. In her humble farmhouses were born Anson G. Phelps the successful man of business

THE JEFFREY O. PHELPS PLACE.

and philanthropist, and John J. Phelps, the merchant prince. His son the eminent statesman and diplomat, William Walter Phelps, spent here many days of his childhood and youth.

About two miles westward, where the road from the granite mountains enters the valley between twin frowning ledges of intrusive trap, nestles the little village of West Simsbury, or "The Farms," a place lying at the threshold of the most charming and unique scenery.

About two miles north of Weatogue is the central village, which takes the township name, Simsbury. It is built along a terrace, between the wooded bluff and the river meadows. Entering from the Bushy hill or Farms road, you will pass the old Mill which still grinds the grists, and takes the toll, as in days of yore. A little down the stream stands the old distillery. It is now many years since barefoot lads and lassies, with tin pails and pennies, descended the winding path, and climbed the stile to get " a mess of emptin's," as yeast was called.

The road describes a half circle at the foot of the hill, where stands the Congregational Church, a building of classic proportions, and of a simple chaste style which harmonized with the age and worship of its time. Admire its exterior. Do not enter until a mistake of a few years since be remedied, and the sober Puritan meeting-house be disrobed of its gaudy attire. Northward for nearly a mile the street extends, straight as an arrow, broad, sentinelled by magnificent elms and sycamores. The accompanying views will give hints of its beauty. Aside from the many fine modern houses are many places of historic interest.

The Amos R. Eno mansion stands on a finely shaded eminence, overlooking the valley. Built by the Hon. Elisha Phelps,—the father of Mrs. Eno,—the recent changes in the building seem rather to emphasize its old-time dignity and atmosphere of hospitality. Here for nearly a half century, the queenly hostess won the love of high and low; and the farmer lad of fourscore years ago,—having fought life's battle in the great metropolis, and won not only "great riches," but that "good name" honored and respected by all,—has come here for quiet and rest in his declining years.

"KING ULMUS."

Simsbury numbers among her most valuable institutions, "The Free Library," a gift from Mr. Eno to his birth-place. The building is designed in harmony with its surroundings, and, within and without, is a fine expression of colonial architecture. The library,

THE DR. BARBER HOUSE.

nourished by a liberal fund, removes from the youth of Simsbury any barrier from culture.

In the center of the village, where was once the church-yard is the

Cemetery. For two and a quarter centuries, groups of people, with sad eyes, and aching hearts, have climbed this beautiful hillside, to lay away the tenement of some beloved soul. Whether the earth were covered with snow or violets, in sunshine and storm, the sad burial words have been spoken, but when the trembling voice strikes the brighter strain, "I am the resurrection and the life," the restful beauty of the scene seems to turn the thought from the

McLEAN SEMINARY.

"city of the dead," to that city whose Builder and Maker is He who giveth and taketh away. The limit of this paper forbids tarrying among the quaint headstones and quainter inscriptions. Passing the little group of stores, the old Ensign homestead stands on the left, with its lilac bushes and cinnamon roses, and nearly opposite the Jeffrey O. Phelps mansion, built in 1771,— in colonial days the famous "Phelps Tavern,". Now take off your hat and make obeisance to the monarch of the street,— King Ulmus. I can never consciously pass under this tree without a feeling of reverence. It combines, more than any other I have ever seen, great size, symmetry, grace, impressiveness of strength and character. Beautiful as it is clothed in its summer robe,— it is even more impressive when the lofty arches of its giant arms are thrown against the face of the moon or the clear blue of the winter sky.

THE STREET.—NORTH END.

The "Dr. Barber house" was built in 1762, and soon came into the possession of Major Elihu Humphrey, an ancestor of its late occupant. When Lexington roused the land, the Major gathered his company on the green before this house,—on the eve before their departure to Boston,—and here the tearful farewells were said to wives and mothers. To the shelter of this roof the wounded warrior was brought to breathe away his ebbing life.

Under the pine-covered bluff,—facing meadow and mountain is the McLean Seminary, a school founded and named in honor of the Rev. Allen McLean, for fifty-two years the beloved pastor of the Congregational Church.

The "Elizur Eno House," located in that continuation of the street called Westover plain, is the oldest but one in the town, built about 1750. It is a fine old structure, reposing under a mammoth elm of great age and beauty. Here at one time were quartered some French officers. A quarrel arising at dinner, one threw the carving knife, which missing his antagonist, buried itself in the casing, where the gash can now be seen. I have given but a glimpse of this

THE ELIZUR ENO HOUSE.

fair valley and its traditions. Would you see more? Study for yourself the tapestry of its meadows, the frescoes of its skies, the pictures on its mountain walls, and the resting-place of its children, with the names engraven there.

    From mossy mound and grassy hillock gliding,
      With noiseless step we come;
     Wishful to learn of good or ill, betiding
      The old remembered home;
     A band of brothers we, who sleep where weeping willows grow,
     Your great grand-fathers, dead and gone, one hundred years ago.

THE BURNING OF SIMSBURY.*
By the Indians under King Philip, March 26, 1676.

BY ALBERT LEWIS THAYER.

On the heights o'er the silent town,
Philip, the Chief, stood gazing down.

Folded the arms that bore no spear;
Clouded the face that knew no fear.

Might was right, and the chieftain knew
That his braves were many, his foes were few.

Quiet the hamlet that Sabbath morn;
Scarce a breeze waved the budding thorn;

While, silent and dusky as shadows, crept
Demons whose vengeance never slept.

* * * * * * *

Philip, the Chief, stood gazing down
From his lofty tower, on the doomed town,

While riot and pillage were going on,
Till day was ended and light was gone.

Then night's pall fell o'er the saddening sight,
And dense clouds covered the moon's pale light —

While from burning pyre, at the day's dark close
The stifling smoke in clouds arose.

And what was a hamlet at early morn,
With memories dear, in God's light born,

At night was a mass of ruins wide,
With sad desolation on every side.

And Philip, the Chief, smiled grimly, when
The work was done to his bidding; then

Silent and stern, he sat him down
While the smoke rose in wreaths from the ruined town.

* * * * * * *

Now strangers visit the craggy height,
Where Philip stood on that Sabbath night;

---

* NOTE: "This event took place on Sunday, the twenty-sixth of March, 1676 — the pillaging in the day-time, and the burning of the settlement in the succeeding night. Philip, it is said by tradition, seated upon a neighboring mountain, which has ever since born his name, (' Philip's Seat,' one of the Talcott range) viewed the scene, and enjoyed from its contemplation those emotions of pleasure which, it is supposed, are peculiarly agreeable to all his race, when placed under similar circumstances."—Phelps's History of Simsbury. The people being forewarned of the Indian raid, received an order to remove at once " to some of the neighboring plantations." Mr. Phelps says, " In obedience to this order, every white person was removed from the town with all possible despatch."

With pleasure they view the village fair
That sprung from the ashes of dark despair.

And thoughts go back to that fated age
That received the blows of Philip's rage;

To the many who felt his vengeance dire,
From the prattling babe to the hoary sire.

Thanks be to God, those days are past,
That cries for vengeance were heard at last:

For Philip was slain, and his warrior braves
Sleep now in scattered and unknown graves.

And though the cliff o'er some may cast
A spell of terror, from deeds long past,

Though grandsires may often tell the tale,
Sweet Peace folds her wings o'er this lovely vale.

FAME.

LOUIS E. THAYER.

You tricksy and flickering "Will o' the Wisp!"
   You dazzle, deceive us, and lead us astray.
We follow, forever, your beckoning taper
   Until we are lost, left alone, in dismay.

Pray tell us, fair spirit, who ever art sought for,
   For whom men have lived and for whom men have died —
Whom men have longed for, mourned for, and fought for —
   In what remote region you in secret abide.

How we hasten onward and struggle to catch you,
   To follow your leading; what suffering and pain
We endure in the chase, how faint and how weary
   When we find that our toil has been vain.

You fly from our grasp and still beckon us onward;
   Again in the distance your light glints and flashes.
We labor from youth for you, onward to manhood
   When nothing remains but our heart's smouldering ashes.

A REVOLUTIONARY BOYCOTT.
(July 16, 1774.)

BY ELLEN D. LARNED.

Here it is, a living document, as fresh and glowing as when it came that July day from the Sons of Liberty and Windham. Its victim was their especial pride and champion — their tallest, strongest, bravest, handsomest, most accomplished citizen — Colonel Eleazer Fitch. Descended from those old Connecticut fathers, Major John Mason and Rev. James Fitch, he had done honor to his ancestry: had served with distinction in the French war, and filled most acceptably the office of County Sheriff. In war, in business, in domestic relations, he was alike fortune's favorite. But now, just as he had passed the meridian of life, with ample means, a beautiful home, promising children, and universal respect and popularity, the tide turned. He took the wrong side in politics. He could not see things in the same light as his fellow-citizens. Those grievances against the King that so fired the wrath of great bodies of colonists, did not seem to him very serious; did not justify rebellion from the government he had served. Perhaps he sympathized with his brother Samuel, an aggressive Boston Tory, and State's Attorney of Massachusetts. Perhaps his fastidious taste was offended by the loud talk and threats of his townsmen — for Windham Green was the very hot-bed of sedition and rebellion.

And so all this noisy summer, while his neighbors and friends were making fiery speeches, and passing "red-hot" resolutions, and gathering sheep from every part of the large town to send for the relief of Boston, and making inquisitorial raids upon suspected Tories in all parts of the State, our Colonel moped at home, silent and neutral, until roused by the forcible expulsion of a Boston visitor, a tradesman collecting debts. His remarks upon this incident are best reported in the following paper, quickly framed and circulated throughout the town for signatures:

"Friends and Brethren. Ye are not unmindful that at our last meeting, we asserted our common rights and them undertook solemnly to support and maintain, in conjunction with the rest of the English settlers on this Continent, and among other things express our dissatisfaction of the cohort of Hutchinson's addressers, in their several addresses to him before his departure from Boston; whereby we undertook and engaged to and with each other — to entreat them on every occasion with the indignity they have justly deserved from us. And these our sentiments and resolutions we have published to the world.

"Nevertheless, one Francis Green, one of that odious gang, presumed, the beginning of the present month, to take this town in his tour, when he was politely and in good reason made to know that his continuance was disagreeable to the sentiments of our inhabitants — that it became him speedily to depart, which was with difficulty effected. In consequence of which he has publicly advertised and promised a reward for information, &c., with no other purpose than to render this town odious in the eyes of our enemies.

"This being thus transacte, one of our neighbors, viz: the Sheriff of the County, took it upon him to villify and reproach this our conduct at divers times and places, until yesterday morning, when in the presence of five or six, some of whom were active in that matter and some not, ridiculing and condemning the conduct of Boston, the Colonies, and this town in particular, and Green's treatment, affirmed and declared that those acting in that matter and all others who countenanced them were a pack of damned scoundrels and rascals, and ought to be discarded and reproached by all mankind; that his brother should be here uninterruptedly if he pleased; that he would blow their damned brains out if they should attempt to trouble, remove, or quiet him, and many other disgraceful, threatening, and reproachful words.

"This conduct has justly raised the indignation and resentments of the people in this part of the town, in consequence whereof, and in expectation of a visit from his ignominious brother, some forty or more assembled, seriously deliberated, and heard the evidence, and universally concluded that this man's conduct ought to be properly resented; have seriously covenanted and engaged to and with each other and all that shall join us, that we will not serve and oblige that offender with any such services and neighborly kindnesses; in a word, fully to disregard, not notice or have any farther connection with him or his, until he retracts from his above injurious sentiments and reproachful expressions (acts of humanity only excepted) with settlement of past dealings.

"In this number are included smiths, barbers, traders, millers, laborers. And of these our doings the writer was desired to make seasonable notice to our brethren in all other parts of the town, who we trust will adopt our measures and act with us in the same cause and take some particular method to bind and oblige themselves together and with us, remembering that any such matter helps our common interest. We have the pleasure to inform you that our agreement is very much approved by all denominations in this town, and that many not present last evening have engaged with us, and that one instance has already happened wherein the gentleman was denied the setting a shoe on his horse to his no small" [inconvenience].

"We have also concluded that in case any more of these addressers should come into town and dare attempt to be publicly about, that our Committee of Correspondence be desired, First, to communicate the sentiments of the town, and request their speedy departure, and if not complied with, they have them exported.

"A large number being desired, we expect your attendance at the raising of our Liberty pole.

"With prudence, unanimity, resolution, good conduct and good effect, let us act and conduct in this day of trouble.

"We are gentlemen, your obedient servants, The Sons of Liberty in this town.

"N. B. The gentleman to whom this is directed will beware of *Tories* and be careful to whom he communicates."

The recipient of this particular copy did not choose to "communicate" to any one, but laid the paper carefully aside with this endorsement: "Humanity and my ideas of good policy do not permit me to join in the proposed treatment of Col. Fitch. *E. D.* Aug. 1, 1774."

But this forbearance was exceptional. The boycott took effect. Colonel Fitch and his household were, in great measure, shut out from society and deprived of the common comforts of life. In 1776, he was deposed from the office of Sheriff. His lands were left untilled, his business ran to waste, his money depreciated in value. As his early friends passed away, Young America became more embittered against him, and he who had stood first in war, in peace, and in the popular favor, died in Canada, an ignominious exile.

A HARP AND A SOUL.

HENRY MASON CHADWICK.

I heard a harp touched by the wind,
Sound wavering notes, and purposeless,
Like faltering rain on some lake's bosom cold;
As some great mind, inert, debased
By sloth, unfashioned leaves the shapes
Of thought which lie, half-hid,— like tarnished gold.

But as I listened came along
A wind of power that tried the strings
Until forth rang a grander, purer tone.
So God will stir the dormant soul
To do His will. Then shall flash forth
Heaven's truths, until that time to him unknown.

OLD COLONIAL CHARACTERS.

II. EDWARDS AND BURR: A Series of Sorrows.

BY FELIX OLDMIXON.

The ancestors of Jonathan Edwards were eminently of a controversial turn of mind; and this was perhaps true of the original Edwards who was said to be the son of a minister. William Edwards came to Hartford in 1639, with his mother and step-father, James Cole, a cooper, whom the mother had married in England; they lived on Main street, near the South Green, running back to the street afterwards called Cole street. James Cole came to New England with his wife and her son William, and his daughter Abigail by a former wife. William Edwards married, about 1645, Agnes, widow of William Spencer, of Hartford, a man of affairs in Cambridge and Hartford, being deputy several times. William Edwards was made freeman in 1658, chimney-viewer in 1668, and died before 1672.

His son, Richard Edwards, was born May, 1647, and married Nov. 19, 1667, Elizabeth, daughter of William Tuttle, of New Haven, from whom he was divorced in 1691; he married second, about 1692, Mary, daughter of Lieut.-Col. John Talcott, of Hartford. He was an attorney-at-law and a very prominent man in his day. He died April 20, 1718; his widow, Mary, died April 19, 1723. His eldest son, Rev. Timothy Edwards, of East Windsor, was the father of the great theologian, Jonathan Edwards the elder, and through him, Richard Edwards was the ancestor of many distinguished men,— scholars, divines, statesmen. He was the ancestor of Governor Henry W. Edwards, Judge Ogden Edwards, of New York, Judge Pierpont Edwards, of Connecticut, Vice-President Aaron Burr, and others distinguished in law and theology.

In May, 1708, the office of attorney-at-law seems first to have been authorized by law in Hartford. Richard Edwards was admitted by the County Court, in September of that year, and by the Court of Assistants in October, to practice law. He was about sixty years old at that time; his grandson, the elder Jonathan Edwards, being then but five years old. When, in 1691, he had petitioned for a divorce from his wife, he had prayed that he might " have relief therein, if the law of God or man will afford it;" and "for a committee of able divines upon this charge." Upon a report submitted by certain divines, the General Court granted him a favorable decree. He had acted as an attorney as early as 1684, and in 1702-3, he had argued a fugitive slave case against Saltonstall. He was probably the first Queen's Attorney, appointed as such in April, 1705, the office having first been created in May, 1704. The act provided that there should be " in every countie, a sober, discreet and religious person, appointed by the County Courts, to be Atturney for the Queen; to prosecute and implead in the lawe all criminall offenders, and to doe all other things necessary or convenient, as an Atturney, to suppress vice and immoralitie." He held the office until 1712 or 1713, perhaps until 1717. At about the latter date, John Read of Stratford began to hold the office.

Timothy Edwards, being an only son[*] of a rich father, was given a very

Note. (*Only son of the first wife. See Notes and Queries.)

liberal education for those early times, and improved it to such a degree that when he graduated in 1691, at Harvard College, he was given the degree of A. B. in the forenoon, and of A. M. in the afternoon, the first student to bear away from those classic shades this dual distinction on one and the same day. He was, however, placed last on the list in a class of eight, perhaps on account of the standing and social prestige of his family. At that time, and for eighty years afterwards it was the custom to give the names in the ratio of social distinction of the parents; it was finally changed to the alphabetical order maintained to the present day. If, in social rank his class-mates were his superiors, surely they were inferior in scholarship, if the above is an indication.

He began his ministrations as a candidate, in East Windsor Society, in Nov. 1694, at the age of twenty-five. He came with his wife, Nov. 14, just eight days after their marriage, which was ample time to journey from Northampton, and to visit his sisters in Hartford. There he remained during a ministry of sixty-three years, which was most fruitful and satisfactory. He was formally ordained in 1698, and his ordination was followed by a *ball* in honor of the event, showing that the plain living and staid manners of that day were not so Puritanical as is generally supposed. Mr. Edwards and Mr. Warham mingled freely among their people, both being farmers also, and interested with them in their every-day dealings as well as diversions and amusements, without in the least detracting from the dignity of their sacred office.

A recent writer, in treating of the ministrations of the elder Edwards, (Timothy,) "who with such grace and simple courtesy and fervent zeal so boldly reasoned for the truth of God," says of his ethical status:

"Those who are wont to cavil and draw unfavorable comparisons between the old and new school theologians, will seek in vain for any cause of censure in the writings of Timothy Edwards. He preached no hell other than that which the Bible depicted, and drew no graphic picture of immortality that belied the precious truths of Holy Writ. Eminently a godly man, he knew of no better way to forward the cause and interests of his divine Lord than to preach the truth in Christ and lie not. 'The truth, the life, the way,' was the burden of his ministry. No sweeping words of condemnation fell on those who had no 'light;' no tesselated pave of 'infants skulls' floored the infernal vault for those who were not among the elect. But for the soul 'continued in sin' he preached naught save an eternal death. The crucial test of the Edwardean theology is found in the oft-repeated words: 'You who have sinned against your light.' This was the tenor of that ministry under which the child, Jonathan, sat. There he drank deep of unmixed truth, and fed on holy things. There that subtle intellect found its natural sustenance and finally stepped out in the richness of God-like beauty and the plentitude of a royal power to combat the things of darkness."

Jonathan Edwards the elder, was born in East Windsor, Conn., Oct. 5, 1703, and died at Princeton, N. J., March 22, 1758, and is regarded as the greatest of American theologians and metaphysicians, at least of the last century; the author of the famous essay on "The Freedom of the Will," and the hardly less famous "Treatise on Religious Affections." His literary work was mostly done at Northampton, and Stockbridge, Mass. He entered Yale in his thirteenth year, and from that time was almost continually away from home.

Dr. Emmons once said that "the senior Edwards (Timothy) had more reason than his son, but the son was a better reasoner than his father." That he was an acute reasoner, one endowed with greater mental acumen than the majority of men, anyone can clearly prove by merely dipping into his writings. In all his works, he regards self-love and natural appetite as the absolute masters of the human heart previous to regeneration, and against these he waged a ceaseless warfare. Whether we of to-day agree with, or follow him, we cannot gainsay his great ability as a theologian and thinker. He came well by his controversial ability through his father and grand-father, and perhaps the original William, though a cooper and merchant, may have been a man of solid parts and sense.

The history of the unhappy controversy which arose between the people of Northampton and their pastor, which resulted in the dismission of the latter, is well known. It stayed the plague-spot which was spreading over our land. It formed a crisis in the history of our churches. President Edwards undoubtedly felt his principles to be important, because true, and he well counted the cost before he announced his change of sentiment and his opposition to the prevailing practice and belief. But he could hardly have foreseen the extent and the bitterness of the opposition which he was to encounter. But, "truth is mighty and will prevail." The clouds passed away. The good seed sown in the storm and scattered by the whirlwind, sprung up. The name of Edwards is revered where he was bitterly opposed. His principles are adopted by that church which refused his ministrations; and strangers of other lands are led by the children of those who drove him from their presence to see the trees which he planted and the spot where he dwelt.

In all the trials of her husband, Mrs. Edwards participated; and her woman's heart might feel more acutely the desolation of leaving the early home of her married life, one of the most beautiful spots which this world can boast, for a frontier settlement; a reduced salary and a large family would not lighten her cares and trials. But we hear of no complaints. The song of praise arose in her dwelling. Her own industry and economy were doubly taxed; the accomplishments of her daughters were made to contribute to the common stock, and friends from other lands remembered them.

Another stroke followed, and the hearts of the parents were made to bleed for their widowed child, while as Christians they mourned the untimely death of President Burr, of Princeton. Then came the call to Edwards to take the place at Princeton, lately vacated by his promising son-in-law; Mrs. Edwards might have rejoiced, not only in the prospect of being restored to more congenial society, but in the sweet hope of alleviating by her presence and tenderness the sorrow of her bereaved daughter. The parting benediction of Edwards as he left to assume his new duties was touching and pathetic in the extreme, as bestowed upon his family: " I commit you to God; I doubt not if He will take a fatherly care of us if we remember Him."

Then followed his sudden death, one stroke of sorrow and affliction falling fast upon another. But the wife's constancy, the reality of her faith, her resignation and submission to the Divine will, was shown in a few lines which still remain, addressed to her daughter, Mrs. Burr, in this trying hour. Still another stroke followed in the death of this daughter, Mrs. Burr,—a woman worthy of her parents, uniting great personal beauty, feminine grace and loveliness, to deep piety and a strong mind. Mrs. Edwards left her home to take charge of her orphaned grand-children, and to be able to often visit the grave of her husband, at Princeton, some few months after the death of Mrs. Burr.

She did not reach Princeton. She died at Philadelphia, near enough to the grave of her husband to secure a place by his side. Had she been spared to watch over these children, very different might have been the character and the influence of one who inherited the talents but not the principles of his ancestors; and whose name, perpetuated as it must be in the annals of his country, will descend darkly and sadly to future generations.

There was a time of religious interest, at Princeton College, while Aaron Burr was a student, when he was almost persuaded to be a Christian. There was a particular day on which his choice seemed balancing between "I will" and "I will not." Some influence, some dissuasive speech perhaps, turned him away from the heavenly visitant, and he said, "I will not," and from what we know of his last hours, the gulf widened until the end, in darkness.

Esther Edwards, third daughter of Jonathan Edwards, married, June 29, 1752, Rev. Aaron Burr, of Fairfield, Conn., son of Daniel and Elizabeth Burr. He was one of a family of ten children. His father, Daniel Burr, was son of John or Jehu Burr, who married Mary, daughter of that veteran colonizer of many places, Andrew Ward. Daniel's grandfather, was Jehu Burr the first, a carpenter, who came with Winthrop in 1630, settled first at Roxbury, thence removed to Fairfield, Conn., and was representative there to the General Court, 1641-5. The Burr ancestry was not remarkable, like the Edwards, except for sturdy common sense, administrative abilities, and indomitable will power; these characteristics were transmitted in full measure to Aaron Burr the second, and are common to the present day.

Rev. Aaron Burr preached his first sermon in Greenfield, Conn., removed to Hanover, Morris Co., N. J., then as now merely a rural hamlet; but his talents soon promoted him to be the pastor of the First Presbyterian church in Newark, where he was ordained in 1739. In 1748 he was elected President of the College of New Jersey, then located at Newark,* and afterwards removed to Princeton. He succeeded Jonathan Dickinson, the first President. He died of nervous fever, in September, 1757; and within fourteen months of his death, four other members of the Edwards family had passed away; Rev. Timothy, died January, 1758; Rev. Jonathan, in March; and sixteen days later Mrs. Burr; while Mrs. Jonathan Edwards followed her daughter seven months later.

Rev. Aaron Burr left only two children, Sarah, three years of age, and Aaron, born Feb. 6, 1756, only twenty months of age; the mother dying soon after, left the children early orphaned, and they were placed under the stern and rigid discipline of their maternal uncle, Timothy Edwards, the eldest son of Jonathan, who had also assumed the care of his younger brother, Pierpont Edwards, born 1750, only six years older than Aaron Burr. It is said that much of the wildness of little Aaron was due to this Pierpont, but it was, we think, largely due to the perversity of the lad himself and the puritanical tenets of his uncle Timothy, as several anecdotes of his boyhood will amply illustrate.

Sarah Burr, sister of Aaron, was, with himself, placed under a private tutor, Tapping Reeve, while they resided in their Uncle Timothy's family, at Elizabethtown, New Jersey. Tapping Reeve in due time married Sarah Burr, and was as remarkable a man in his own way, as Aaron Burr. He became Chief Justice of the Superior Court of Connecticut, and was founder of the celebrated law school at Litchfield, Conn., where he resided for over fifty years. Lyman Beecher was pastor of the church at Litchfield, part of this time, and the two families became quite intimate. Harriet Beecher Stowe writes, "How well I remember Judge Reeve's house, wide, roomy, cheerful; it used to be the Eden of our imagination; I remember the great old-fashioned garden with broad alleys set with all sorts of stately bunches of flowers. It used to be my reward when I was good, to spend a Saturday afternoon there, and walk up and down among the flowers and pick currants off the bushes." While her father bears this tribute to his co-laborer. "Oh, what a man he was! When I get to Heaven and meet him there, what a shaking of hands there will be!" Dr. Samuel Hopkins, also related to the Edwards family, says of Judge Reeve,

---

* "Mr. Dickinson [Rev. Jonathan] had long felt the necessity of a Collegiate Institution, more accessible than Harvard or Yale, for the colonies this side of New England. • The course pursued by the authorities of Yale College in denying to his young friend, David Brainard, his degree, on account of a slight irregularity, and for whom he and Burr [Rev. Aaron] had both interceded in vain, determined him to establish, if possible, a College in New Jersey."— *Hatfield's History of Elizabeth, N. J.*, p. 349. The charter was granted 22, Oct., 1746 to Messrs Jonathan Dickinson, John Pierson, Eben. Pemberton and Aaron Burr, ministers. It was opened April 20, 1747; but President Dickinson died Oct. 7, 1747 * * * * The grammar school was started in Elizabethtown, 1766, by Tapping Reeve, and Eben. Pemberton, Jun. Mr. Reeve was the son of Rev. Abner Reeve, and was born at Fire Place, Brookhaven, L. I. Oct. 17, 1744.—*Ibid.*

"He was altogether an admirable man, of a purity, sincerity. and guilelessness of heart such as I have seen in but few men of this world." Mrs. Reeve was an invalid and confined to her bed for many years. A son and grandson completed this line, the latter dying while in Yale College, at the age of twenty.

Aaron Burr lived in his uncle Timothy's family until he went to college, at Princeton, at the age of twelve. When about four years of age he ran away, on account of some misunderstanding with his preceptor, Mr. Reeve, and was not found until after the third or fourth day. The family government of Mr. Edwards was strict and severe, but in the case of Aaron Burr, and Pierpont Edwards, the "rod was spared," as he is quoted as having said. A late compiler facetiously says it was however, no "maple sugar" government, for Aaron himself relates that one fine afternoon in July, he was in a cherry tree in his uncle's garden, when he observed coming up the walk an elderly lady, a guest of the house, wearing a silk dress, then a decided luxury. The prim behavior and severe morality of the old lady had disgusted the boy somewhat, and he began pelting her with cherries from his concealment; but he was caught in the act, and his bad behavior reported to his uncle. Aaron was then in his eighth year. He was summoned to the study and treated to a severe Puritanical lecture, then a fervent prayer for his reformation. But from the beginning the boy knew well that it presaged a castigation and could tell from the length and severity of the exhortation and prayer how severe would be the punishment; and as Burr expressed it, "he licked me like a sack."

At the age of ten he wanted to run away to sea, came to New York, and entered himself as a cabin-boy on a vessel, whither his uncle followed him, and he took refuge at the mast-head, from which coign of vantage he would not be dislodged until his uncle had capitulated and surrendered under a truce of peace. When eleven he was prepared for Princeton, but was not permitted to enter until the next year. He graduated with honor at the age of sixteen. It is related that while in college he won a small sum of money at his first game of billiards, and was so mortified that he never again played at any game of chance. About the time he left college, being uneasy in his mind on the subject of religion, he visited Rev. Dr. Bellamy, of Bethlehem, Conn., and with him pursued a course of religious study and conversation, from the autumn of 1773 to the spring of 1774. His conclusions on certain Calvinistic points were certainly at variance with those of his preceptor, and he henceforth avoided all religious disputation.

The beginning of the Revolutionary war led him to volunteer his services, like another Byron. In June, 1775, being a little more than nineteen years of age, he left Elizabethtown for Cambridge, and attached himself to the Arnold expedition to Quebec. At Newburyport, when the expedition sailed, he found a message from his uncle Edwards ordering his return. The two men delivering the order seemed disposed to enforce it, but were met by so plucky and determined resistance on the part of little Burr that he was allowed to proceed, and he afterwards speedily distinguished himself, sharing all the toils and privations of that arduous campaign. When Gen. Montgomery fell, on the Heights of Abraham, Burr was within six feet of him, and attempted to carry his body from the battle-field; a heavy snow-storm had fallen, and the British troops were advancing toward the dead commander, when Burr shouldered and carried the body for some distance, up to his knees in the snow, until he was compelled to drop it and escape with his life.

THE THREE DATES.

BY FRANKLIN E. DENTON.

While attending the academy at S——, a young man by the name of Philip Ripley was one of my classmates. Soon after our acquaintance began we became the most intimate of friends. He was naturally reserved and so was I, neither of us mixing more than was necessary with our fellows, but, somehow, each of us found the other's society so congenial that we were together most of the time. I do not think we had been acquainted more than three weeks when he knew my secrets and I, his.

He was a remarkable youth. In general endowment there was not his equal in the school. He was as good in one study as another, and seemed to learn by a sort of intuition. When I first knew him I felt assured of his future eminence, but I soon detected elements of weakness in his character which would render marked achievement improbable. Though royal gifts were his, I soon perceived that he had no definite purpose, and that he was the most easily discouraged person I had ever known. I came to the conclusion that he would make a failure of life and that, if ever a great sorrow overtook him, he would be broken like a reed.

Many were the hours we spent together that year, and happy ones, too. Many were the nights we talked until the crowing cocks admonished that another day was knocking for admission at the doors of the east. There were few subjects which we did not confidently grapple with, and summarily dispose of. It was a treat to hear Philip talk, his memory was such a teeming treasury, and he had such an original way of expressing himself. I seem to see him now, his face lighting up, and the far-away look coming to his large, blue eyes, as he gave eloquent utterance to some thought.

One night our conversation turned upon the universality of superstition, when he told me that from his childhood he had had the belief that there was an occult analogy between the day of his birth, the day of the most important event of his life, and the day of his death; and that from the figures of the first two dates the figures of the last date might be worked out, if the method could be discovered.

He said this with such calmness of conviction that I was deeply impressed, although it appealed to my sense of the ridiculous. I asked him if he knew the date of the most important event of his life. He answered that he did not think he had reached it. Regarding the occult analogy between the days, I asked him if he knew anything about the date of his birth, other than the simple fact of its position in a certain month of a certain year, by which he could establish the analogy when the date of the most important event should come. He answered that his mother had told him that the day of his birth — May 13, 1857 — was a cold, misty one, and that what had impressed her the most about the day was the weird appearance of the dark-green foliage of the trees in the white fog. He further answered that he had made inquiry of an old man, who was a great observer of the weather, and had kept a journal of the aspects of the days for nearly forty years, and he had substantiated his mother's statement of there having been a fog, only adding that towards night of that day

— May 13, 1857 — the weather had cleared away, and the sky became stormy, and brief copious showers had succeeded — as if the low hung clouds were huge sponges pressed at intervals by some elemental hand.

Nothing further was said upon the subject until the last day of our school life. As we parted — alas! never to meet again — I said: "Old fellow, if you get any new developments in the date line, do not fail to let me know in your letters." "I will let you know. Good-bye." These were his last words to me. As he said them, he shut the car-door behind him. A moment more and the train had turned a corner out of sight.

And so the years passed. I received letters from Philip now and then, telling me of his plans. He usually had a fresh stock in each letter. I gleaned, in substance, that, despite his vacillation, he had been admitted to the bar, and had opened an office in the growing town of G———. I had not expected even that much of him.

One day, in the fifth year since we parted, he wrote me a letter. It was shorter than any I had ever received from him, and well nigh illegible. I reproduce it (with the exception of three sentences.) Philip is dead, and I do not hesitate in making it public. It reads very strange. I should have deemed him insane, but for the odd belief I knew he held.

G———, May 21, 1880.

MY DEAR ARTHUR:

I have lived the most important day of my life — May 20, 1880: and so have date No. 2. I have lived the most important day of my life, for all of life after that day must be totally unlike all of life before it. Life was bright Life is forever more dark. * * * We parted at the midnight hour with mingling tears. But, mark you as I sobbed a good-bye, though convulsed with emotion, my eyes fell upon the moonlit night; a white fog had settled over the silent trees, and their dark green foliage had the same weird look that I know it must have had on the day of my birth. Later, when, sleepless, I paced my chamber, I heard the rain fall with copious, sudden dashes, and, going to the window, the fog had cleared, the sky become stormy and low hanging clouds seemed like huge sponges pressed at intervals by some elemental hand. Ah, do you not see now that there is an occult analogy between the date of my birth and the date of the most important event of my life? As to the method by which the date of my death may be worked out from the date of my birth and the date of the most important event of my life, I shall now make it the sole object of my remaining days to find it, as I am through chasing the phantoms other men pursue. I know that I shall die in May, for no other month of the whole year does the foliage have such a weird appearance in a fog, and the rain fall as it fell that desolate night. I am sure that the year of my death cannot be far distant.   "Yours *de profundis,*
                                                           "PHILIP RIPLEY."

I answered the letter immediately. I gave Philip the best advice of which I was capable. The drift of my two pages of foolscap may be briefly stated: I made plain to him the foolishness of allowing so promising a life as his to be blighted by any adversity. I appealed to him metaphysically. I told him that if he would analyze his passion, he would find that he had confounded the specter evoked by his soul's thirst for the unearthly beautiful with some robust and very mortal country maid.

I expected an answer soon, but none came. It was not long before the clock had ticked off one, two, and three years, and still there was no answer. I had often wondered what had become of my old friend; but, as he had not written I concluded that I could get along without him as long as he could without me.

Imagine my surprise — May 27, 1883 — to receive a dispatch to the effect that Philip could not live, and that he wished to see me before he died. He was one hundred and eighty miles distant, and the connections were such that I could not reach him before early the next morning, but I made preparations to go. At 11 A. M., I was moving westward as fast as the iron horse would take me. About 2 P. M., I observed a dense fog settling over the dark-green foliage of the trees. Ah, thought I, my trip is in vain! I shall never see Philip alive. He will die to-day. Later in the afternoon the fog cleared away, the sky became stormy, and the rain fell in copious, sudden dashes, as low-hung clouds were huge sponges pressed at intervals by some elem hand. Ah, thought I, "poor fellow, thou wast right. The occult analo complete. This is thy dying day, and thou hast already begun thy eternal sl

I reached my destination at 5 A. M. It was as I had expected, Philip dead. He had died the day before. I was at the funeral and remained the bereaved mother two days thereafter. She told me her son's history we left school, of the unfortunate most important event of his life, c shattered hopes and slow but sure decline,—all to the minutest detail. He requested her to give me a certain blank book. This was partly full of fig evidently made in the endeavor to work out the day of his death from the of his birth and the date of the most important event of his life. As his in the occult analogy had proved a correct one, as his mother asserted tha three days previous to his death he had assured her that he would die o day he did, as he wished to see me before he died, and as he left me the of calculations, I shall always feel that he had found the method he had w me he would seek.

I have been more superstitious since my experience with Philip Ripley his three dates.

POEMS.

FRANKLIN E. DENTON.

WHEN I READ OF ALGOL.

When I read of Algol in the far heavens
Algol, the demon star, him of the strangely varying beam,
How he passes upon his long journey, yet not alone;
How a dark comrade evermore attends him—
A dead orb — a sun with neither light nor heat:
Then I thought of the bright-shining faith of the heart of man,
How it, too, passes through mysterious spaces;
How it moves upon its solemn course, yet not alone;
How by ties more unyielding than those of gravity
It is fatally linked with doubt.

SONNET.

Sleep, little babe, upon thy mother's breast;
  Let the white curtains of thy lids unroll
  O'er the blue windows of thy stainless soul;
Sleep, little babe, thou can'st not always rest.
The little wren must weave itself a nest,
  The little chipmunk learn to carve its hole,
  The little seed be severed from the bole,
And thou must make thy way — for it is best.
Then sleep, my blessed baby, whilst thou can;
Yon tireless clock is ticking thee a man,
Soon will the trumpet to the battle call;
Oh, in that strife which comes to each and all,
Where but the weak and the unworthy fall,
  Be strong as Sampson, and as brave as Saul.

A TYPICAL EASTER.

WILL. FARRAND FELCH.

The Easter days, of light and warmth and splendor
  Come slowly toiling up the wintry steep;
Old Winter wakes to feign a glad surrender,
  Only to lapse into profounder sleep.
The snow-clad boughs beneath their burden quiver,
  And droop, despairing, as with weight of woe;
The blustrous winds bewailing, moan and shiver,
  And sport among the falling flakes of snow.
The sun is veiled behind the clouds, full-laden,—
  No struggling beams their ragged rifts adorn;
The gentle Spring, a coy and dainty maiden,
  Still lingers in old Winter's lap, forlorn.

How long will Nature wear her mantle dreary,
  Enshrouding her fair face from mortal ken?
How soon will April flowers, bright and cheery,
  Awaken from their winter sleep again?

We long for all the glories and the flowers
  That crown our coming Easter festival:
Are there no thorns in this great world of ours—
  And thornless roses only, crowning all!

Must Life be only valued as a wonder—
  Illusion fond, to which our fancy clings?
Are there no sober moods wherein to ponder
  The lessons that the Lenten season brings?

Are there no deeds, to others bringing gladness,
  In which our griefs can find a glad surcease?
Remember that our lives are filled with sadness—
  Echoes of sorrows of the Prince of Peace.

Then let us rest, no discontent assuming,
  Until the veil of death in twain is torn;
While Easter blossoms in our hearts are blooming:
  Fair tokens of the Resurrection morn.

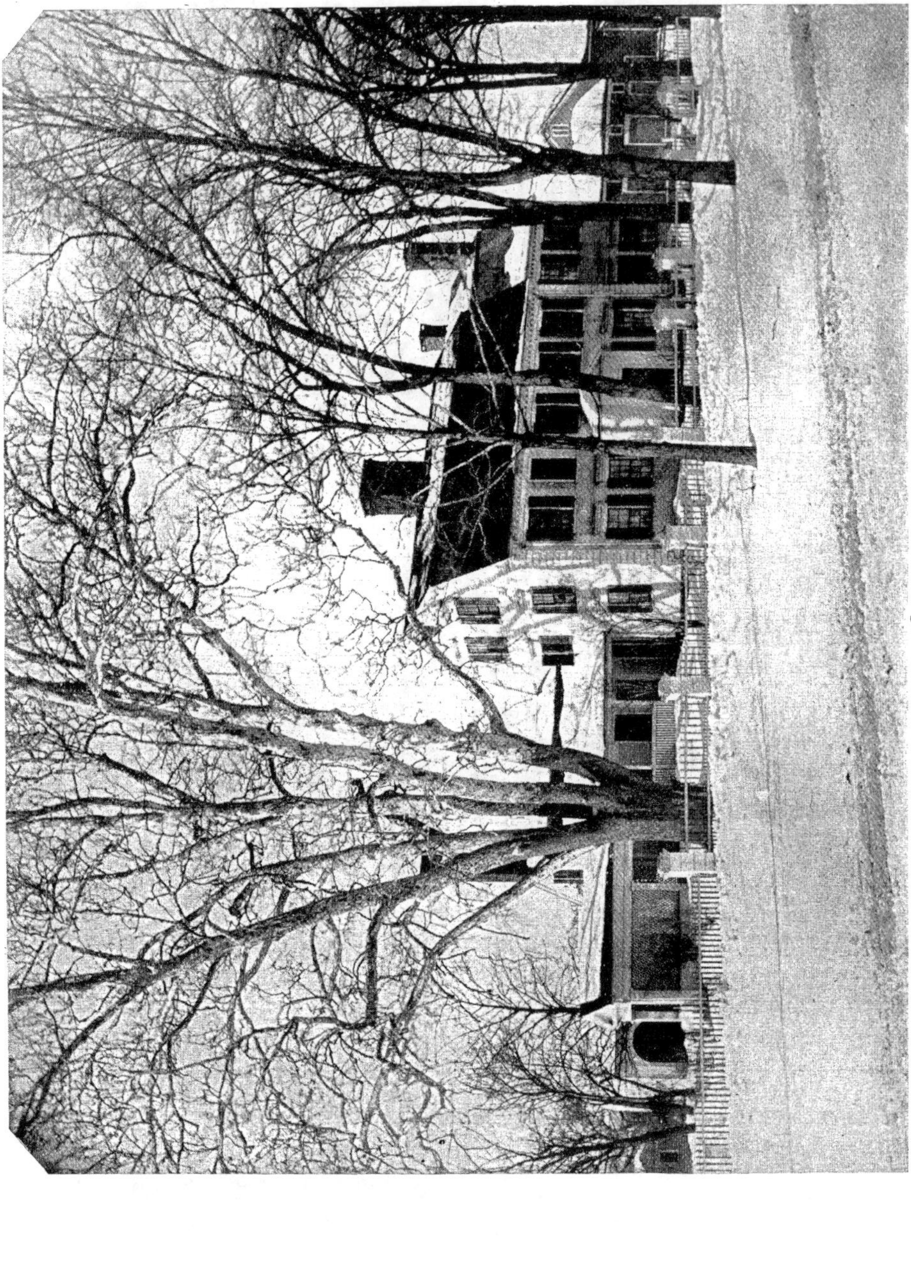

SUFFIELD.

A SKETCH.

BY PROF. MARTIN H. SMITH.

Always a conservative town was Suffield, and is now for that matter. So much so that its people actually bought the land it occupies of the Indians; and as a result not a person was killed within its limits during all the Indian wars that brought so much misery to the first settlers of New England. To be sure the price was not very large, being only thirty pounds; but as few if any of the Indians lived here, only using it for hunting ground, they were pleased with their bargain.

At first this territory, included in Springfield, was supposed to be within the Connecticut Colony, and Deputies were sent to its General Court. Later the people of Springfield concluded they were in Massachusetts, and applied to its General Court for protection. And still later, after Southfield (Suffield) had become separated from Springfield, its people petitioned for admission to the Connecticut Colony, which was granted in 1749.

The boundary between the Colonies was a subject of continued and bitter contention for many years, and was not finally settled until the adjustment of 1803. Then a tract of about two miles square was added to Suffield on the west. Windsor claimed as its northern boundary Stony River, and a bitter quarrel was kept up until 1713. There was no contention on the east for it was bounded by the Great River, nor on the west for it was an unbroken wilderness. The bounds are, north, by the State Line; east, by the River; south, by Windsor Locks, East Granby and Granby; west, by Granby and Southwick.

The fact that it was heavily timbered, with little intervale or meadow land, caused it to be settled somewhat later than the neighboring towns on the north or south. It was "hard to winne." In 1660 the General Court of

Massachusetts granted a tract seven miles square to make a plantation called Stony River, situated on both sides of the "Quonnecticut." It is probable that a settlement was attempted by the Harmons in 1664, but it was soon abandoned, and none of the original grantees ever became actual settlers of the town, so far as known. In 1670, the General Court made a grant of land six miles square on the west side of the river for a town. In the settlement of the town Major Pynchon seems to have been the master spirit, though he lived in Springfield. He purchased the land of the Indians, was the most influential of the committee of "allotments," built the first saw-mill and grist-mill, erected the first frame house, and was the constant adviser of the settlers in affairs temporal and ecclesiastical. To his account-book and letters, and so much of the "Proprietors" book as he wrote, we are indebted for the most accurate information we have of the customs and home life of the settlers; the town, county and state records being only skeletons.

TOWN HALL.

In 1670 a beginning of settlement was made by five Proprietors, to whom allotments of land had been made. In 1671 there were four allotments. In 1672, five. In 1673, one. In 1674, twenty-one. These allotments averaged about fifty acres each. The basis was for one hundred families. As there were three roads, or rather "trails," the settlements were made on them. The first led from Windsor to Northampton through Remington street and Zion's Hill. Here were the first allotments. The second trail led from the Old Factory road to the Springfield road (now "Crooked Lane"), through High Street. The third trail was along the ridge next the river, now East Street. In the allotments were each of several parcels: timber for homestead, meadow and swamp-land, and sometimes a long distance apart. There was another trail leading from Poquonock to Westfield through West Suffield by way of the "Rattley road."

FIRST CHURCH IN SUFFIELD.

Of course one of the conditions of the charter was the support of a Christian minister and a blacksmith. Mr. John Younglove came as pastor in 1679, but there is no record of his ordination. The first church building was erected in 1680, very near what is now the intersection of the West Suffield road and High Street. Mr. Younglove was succeeded by the Rev. Benjamin

Ruggles, in 1695, and he in turn by the Rev. Ebenezer Devotion, in 1710. These were the distinctive "town ministers." Their salary was sixty pounds a year, mostly in provisions, etc. The latter had a hard time with his discontented brethren. The Separatists kept up a contention, which in 1750 resulted in the establishment of the Baptist church on Zion's hill, the parent of all the Baptist churches in this vicinity, Joseph Hastyngs acting as pastor. In 1740 the Second Ecclesiastical Society (West Suffield) was formed. Its house of worship was built in 1743. The first pastor was Rev. John Graham.

BAPTIST CHURCH.

The Rev. Ebenezer Gay, D. D., became pastor of the First Congregational Church in 1741. When he first preached for the people "on trial," a characteristic incident took place. He was a devout man, highly educated and eloquent. But the kindly gossip of the day thought him too thin in stature, his legs too short and out of plumb. The Sunday after this came to the Doctor's ears, he preached a sermon on this text; "He taketh not pleasure in the legs of a man." The sermon was a success. He was pastor until 1793, when he was succeeded by his son. Father and son held the pastorate eighty-four years.

The old "Manse" was built in 1743, and is yet in good preservation. It is situated north of the Second Baptist church. Back of it stretched the "Demense" toward the river. In front, the highway, or Common, was some thirty rods wide. The Second Baptist church was constituted in 1805. The first pastor was the Rev. Caleb

CONGREGATIONAL CHURCH.

Green. The Protestant Episcopal church was organized in 1865 and the Rev. Augustus Jackson was elected pastor. The Methodist Episcopal church was organized in 1833 and Rev. Charles Chittenden was first stationed here. The first Roman Catholic service was held in this town in 1882. The above is the list of all the regularly organized churches in the town. There is of course the usual variety of unorganized " isms."

It is a loyal old town, as the Resolutions of 1774 testify, as well as its subsequent action in sending its sons to the wars. At scarcely a day's notice it started two companies, all told, one hundred and eleven men, at the giving of the Lexington alarm. Fortunately, no doubt, for the British, that speck of war was over before they had time to reach Lexington. The town cared liberally for the widows and orphans of the patriot soldiers, and when independence was gained, welcomed home the surviving heroes with such heartiness as compensated for much of the hardship undergone. The town was well represented in the war of 1812 and the

EPISCOPAL CHURCH.

CONNECTICUT LITERARY INSTITUTION.

Mexican war. One of its great jollifications was the welcoming home of a Suffield boy who had gone to the latter war a private and returned a Major by brevet. The other memorable celebrations of this generation have been the

Ruggles' one hundred and fiftieth anniversary, in 1858, the Bi-Centenial in 1870, and the dedication of the Soldiers' Monument in 1888. On each of these occasions nature favored the people with copious rains. Suffield raised more

THE GAY MANSION.

than its full quota for the war of the Rebellion, and contributed nearly seventy thousand dollars besides.

In its earliest history and up to the end of the first quarter of the present century the town was noted for its manufactories. The smelting of "bog iron" and the making of agricultural implements was quite extensively carried on. The second cotton manufactory erected in the United States was built here by Richard Crosby in 1795. A fulling mill was set up in 1796, and there were several carding mills. The town barely escaped being a great manufacturing center,

THE PEASE PLACE.

for there is no better water privilege in New England than the Connecticut river presents at its rapids east of the town. At this time a newspaper, "The Impartial Herald," was published in town, and several books were printed. There was a law school under the direction of Gideon Granger, and a number of young men were fitted for admission to the bar.

Slavery was one of the institutions of the State until abolished by the Act of 1788. There were quite a number of slaves in this town, but neither slavery nor the slave were ever very popular here. There was at one time a considerable trade with the West Indies, the vessels being loaded at the foot of the falls. Previous to the outbreak of the Civil war, hundreds of men were employed in the manufacture of cigars, and millions were shipped to California by way of Cape Horn. This industry has diminished until scarce fifty men are employed in the town.

Very soon after the settlement of the plantation the school master was sent for, in the person of Anthony Austin. He was a very satisfactory teacher, and town clerk for many years. Much attention has always been paid to the matter of education. There is to-day an excellent system of schools. In 1833 the Connecticut Literary Institution was established. It has generally held a high rank among institutions for secondary instruction. It counts its graduates by the thousand, and numbers among them some of the ablest men in the country. It has ample buildings for dormitories, class rooms, lecture rooms, laboratories, cabinets, and gymnasium, with a farm of thirty acres. The present endowment exceeds one hundred thousand dollars. So the people of the town enjoy rare educational privileges. The first school house was erected on the "Green," southeast of the Congregational church. It was moved to the site of the present town hall and was used jointly by the town and school district. Previous to this the town meetings were held in the churches, usually at the center, occasionally at West Suffield, or on the "Hill." In the reaction against "Idolatry" the descendants of the Puritans did not especially reverence wood, brick, or stone, and even if a building was principally used for religious meetings, it did not prevent its use for almost any other decent purpose. When the day appointed for training the Militia proved too inclement, they made use of the meeting-house. In 1860 the town hall and school house were burned, and before the close of the next year the present commodious building was built, and used in common by the town and school district until 1890, when the district erected a more suitable school house on Bridge street.

TRUMBULL ELM.

The old wooden bridge which unites Suffield and Enfield was built in 1832, from the proceeds of a lottery. It is an odd looking, irregular, pokish structure, seeming to invite always a contest with the wind or fire. It was then thought to be a marvelous example of what the science of civil engineering could do.

SUFFIELD. 171

The wide street in the center was early used as a "Common" pasture ground. It was an excellent place to dig gravel, and the people drove across it at will until it became unsightly enough. But in 1859 it was laid out as a park and graded. It was divided into three parts, each bordered with trees. It is one of the most beautiful features of the town, or of any town in the state for that matter.

The Great Island, or Terry's Island, as it is now more often called, is one of the most charming places in the town. For a description of it the reader is referred to an exceedingly interesting monograph written by the Hon. Hezekiah S. Sheldon. It has

THE OLD MANSE.

been claimed by both Suffield and Enfield with the preponderence of evidence in favor of Suffield. It lies at the foot of the rapids. The mass of the river flows on the east side, but the water on the west is so deep that access can seldom be had except by ferry. Its sides are abrupt, but on the top there are more than a hundred acres of land well wooded, and a part of it under cultivation. It is the "one gem" set in the waters of the Connecticut.

The town has an excellent Free Public Library which is liberally patronized by the people. It was founded in 1884, and in 1894 was reorganized under the Library Act of 1893. Connected with it is a well equipped reading room, which is

THE SOLDIERS MONUMENT.

also open every day and evening. The first license for the sale of spirituous liquors was issued in 1839. Now the burden seems to be that no such place ought to be licensed. Then the burden was that the sale ought not to be restricted. At the beginning of the century there were a dozen or more taverns in the town, and at that time an inn without a bar would have been a misnomer. It was not even beyond the dignity of the minister to join a parishioner in "a mug of flip" at a public house. Our ancestors had good stomachs for "meat, vegitables, and Rhum."

The people so violently opposed the building of the Hartford and Springfield Railroad through the town, that much to the regret of the directors of the road, they felt obliged to cross the river below the town. It is unnecessary to say that the citizens of the town have "never been sorry but once." They have since donated to that road twenty-five thousand dollars in cash, and nearly as much more in "right of way" to build an exasperating branch of four miles.

The town has an agricultural park, and a good one, belonging to a prosperous society; a Masonic lodge; an order of American Mechanics; a national bank; a savings bank; a poor house and farm which is better than most people live in; a Mutual Fire Insurance Company; a creamery company; a society for the detection of rascals; and many other useful and ornamental societies. The First School District of the First Society was incorporated into a village by an Act of the Legislature in 1893. The town was made a probate district in 1821.

"BROOKSIDE."

Suffield has produced its full share of distinguished men who have graced the history of their country. Few men ever gained a greater national reputation than Phineas Lyman, as statesman, as warrior, or as a business man. And from that time on the town has always been capably represented in the halls of legislation, in the ministry, at the bar, and on the tented field.

RETROSPECT.

FLORENCE C. DAVIS.

I backward glance adown the long, dim years,
Like a thick avenue of trees laced overhead,
Through which no little ray of light was shed,
But dews and chilling damps distilled instead
Upon me as I walked in grief and tears;
Oft pausing, now to pray, and now to weep,
As Time still drew me up the rugged steep.
But now, upon the level plain I stand,
Whose borders almost touch that other land,
And backward glance with mingled joy and pain
That I shall ne'er retrace that path again.

THE HARTFORD PARK SYSTEM.

II. BUSHNELL PARK.

BY SHERMAN W. ADAMS.

The board of Park Commissioners, as constituted for the first time, consisted of Messrs. William L. Collins, George Beach, James L. Howard, Gurdon W. Russell, and Gustavus F. Davis. This was in 1860-1. Mr. Collins was of the well-known firm of Collins Brothers & Company, wholesale merchants of dry-goods. Mr. Beach was of the equally well known house of Beach & Company, large dealers in dye-stuffs, and president of a bank. Mr. Howard was head of the firm of James L. Howard & Company, manufacturers; and has since been a Lieutenant-Governor of the State. Dr. Russell was an eminent physician, noted for his interest in the natural sciences, and has been at the head of some of our most important eelymosynary institutions. Mr. Davis was a bank president. It is a notable fact that all but one of these officials of thirty-five years ago are still living; and that Dr. Russell is still (but has not been continuously) upon the Board, and is one of its most active members. They were all cultured gentlemen, and neither was appointed as a reward for activity in politics.

REV. HORACE BUSHNELL, D. D.
Projector of the Park.

No settled policy had then become established as to the uses and line of treatment for this (at that time the only) park. They say, however, in their annual report of 1861: "It was not to be treated as a common pasture or open field;" and then they add, rather apologetically "we have no design or desire of making this a highly ornamental park; such a plan neither meets our approbation, nor do we think it would be acceptable to the public." It should be remembered that, in 1860, Mayor Henry C. Deming, in his annual message, had said, that the Park should be: "a pleasant promenade, parade, and play-ground. . . . It should remain an open, free, unprivileged *Common* for the people." The italics are his own. It is well, also, to bear in mind that there was then a deeper craze for athletic sports than now; if that were possible. And then the oncoming Civil war was over-shadowing all things else. People were timid, and so were the commissioners. It is evident that while they entertained ideas (as to park treatment) different from those of Mayor Deming, they were not inclined to disagree openly with him, and perhaps with the then prevailing public sentiment.

Any way, for reasons good or bad, progress in the development of the park was slow. It appears that, in 1858, there had been a sort of selection of a final working-plan. Gervase Wheeler, an English architect, who had formerly lived in Hartford; Seth E. Marsh, city surveyor; Thomas McClunie, a gardener from Scotland, and about a dozen others, had competed with plans.

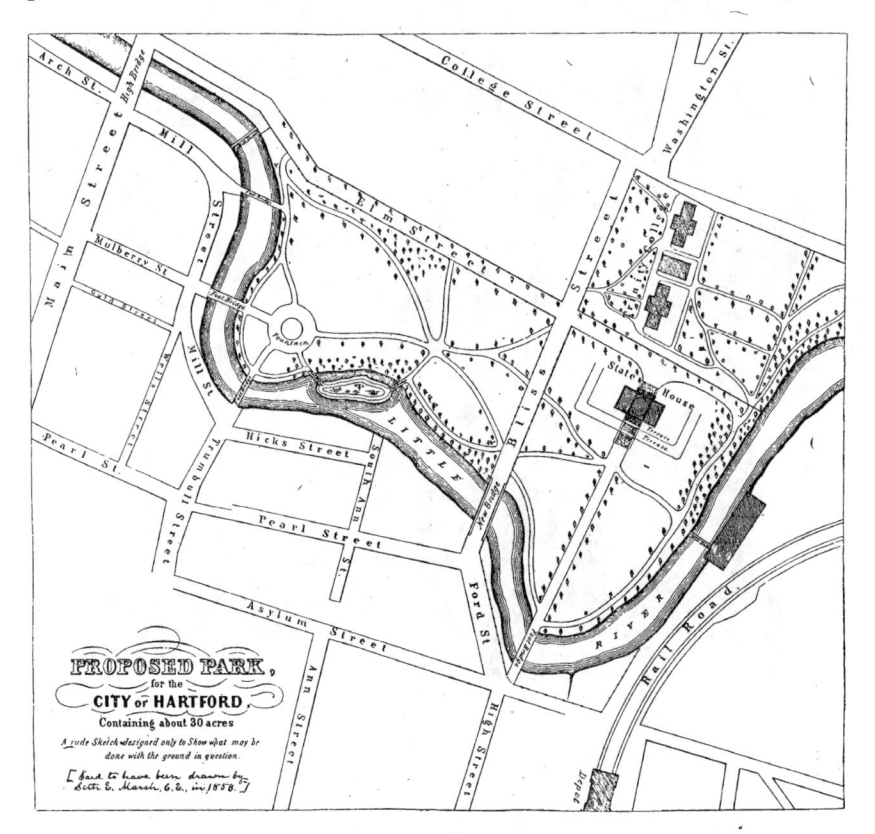

MARSH PLAN FOR BUSHNELL PARK.

Prizes were awarded to Wheeler, Marsh, and McClunie, in the order here named. It is understood that a modification, embracing some features of each of these was finally adopted, upon the advice of Mr. Fred. Law Olmsted. Probably the suggestions of Mr. Olmsted, the prince of landscape artists, were not wholly put in execution. The only one of these plans which the writer has seen, is that of Mr. Marsh. That plan contemplated: a foot-bridge close to Daniels' mill; a fountain near the main entrance, at Mulberry street; the retention and improvement of the Island, with two foot-bridges connecting it with the main-land; and a reservation of a site for a State-house, near but a little south of, the location of the present terrace. Those who are familiar with Bushnell Park need not be told that none of these features were adopted. Marsh's plan included a *straight* street for Bliss (now Trinity) street. This was not then adopted; but the straightening ensued after the erection of the Memorial Arch. He did not propose the pond, and perhaps that was entirely an after-thought.

Both Marsh and McClunie took their turns in superintending the construction of grades, walks, etc., and probably each introduced some features

VIEW SHOWING BLISS ELM
The One to the Right.

of his own. The latter, impelled by the exuberance of patriotism which characterizes many of our naturalized citizens, constructed the mound now occupied by the Wells statue, but he intended it as a site for a flag-staff.

From 1861 to 1867, inclusive, Mr. Jacob Weidenmann, a Swiss, and a regularly trained landscape architect, was employed as superintendent of the park. He was a very competent man in his line. Instances of his work may be seen in his winding road-way to the summit of Mount Royal, Montreal; in the grounds of the Hot Springs Reservation, Arkansas; and elsewhere. He died about a year ago, his last work, as I understand, having been a design for the proposed Pope Park, now the property of this city. No doubt Mr. Weidenmann was much hampered in his work here, by lack of sufficient means at his disposal; by the fact, too, that the main features of the park were already established, and that he had little latitude for the exercise of his skill and discretion, for the park was still maintained as a sort of common and parade-ground. Many games of base-ball, foot-ball, and athletic sports in general, drill-exercises, meetings of all sorts, destructive or disturbing in their nature — were permitted there; and the result was that the whole area had very much of a back-yard appearance. It was not tidy, inviting, nor restful.

PUTNAM STATUE.

It was during Mr. Weidenmann's term, in 1866, that the terrace was designed and constructed, at a cost of $4,000. It suffers by contrast, since the Capitol was erected, and is sometimes facetiously called "Howard's Tomb." In 1863, such arrangements were made that the College grounds became, practically, part of the park. A wire fence and an ornamental gate-way was set up between these adjoining tracts; the park contributing about $1,100 toward the cost of it. Through

MEMORIAL ARCH.

this gate-way, carriages were allowed to pass and have access to drive-ways then laid out on the College grounds. Here, on the river-slope was, and still is, the only primitive grove within the limits of either tract. May its venerable oaks long remain.

With the construction of the bridge at the foot of Trumbull street, in 1864 — not a highly ornamental structure — nothing artistic was added until 1869, unless the "cascade" known as the "Stepping-stones" comes within that class. But, in 1869, a statue, in bronze, of heroic size, representing the good Bishop Brownell, was set up, a little south-westerly from the terrace. It was a gift from his son-in-law, the late Gordon Webster Burnham. It stood there until after the erection of the new college buildings, when it was removed to the campus adjoining the same.

PARK POND.

With the introduction of this statue, it may be truly said that a change in the treatment and uses of the park was begun, which has more and more developed. It thereafter took on more of the character of a *public garden*, and became less and less a mere common and stamping-ground. Mr. Burnham's example was followed, in 1874, by the late Judge Joseph Pratt Allyn, whose representatives caused to be erected a bronze statue in memory of Gen. Israel Putnam. It was of heroic proportions, and cost its donor $12,000. The City of Hartford added thereto $2,000 for its pedestal. The artist of this work was John Quincy Adams Ward. In 1875, a third brazen statue was erected, upon a temporary (wooden) pedestal. It was to the memory of Dr. Horace Wells, and in honor of his discovery of anæsthesia. It was designed by the sculptor, Bartlett, and cost $10,000, the State and City of Hartford sharing equally in the expense. Its granite pedestal was added in 1890, or thereabouts — by the contributions of citizens, mostly physicians, of Hartford. An illustration of the statue may be seen in the last number of this magazine.

When and by whom the pond was contrived, is not known to the writer. It was appropriately made to assume the appearance of a natural feature; but the placing of a fountain in it, made a combination of the natural with the artificial which was incongruous, to say the least. It has been much improved in late years by the introduction of aquatic and semi-aquatic plants; and, upon its banks may be seen some of our indigenous plants and shrubs.

In 1872, the old college grounds became the "Capitol grounds," and by 1880, the hill was crowned by the new edifice, surmounted by the gilded dome; above the dome is the lantern, and still above this, at the extreme height of all, is perched the allegorical figure whereof a copy is shown on the upper cover of this magazine.

In 1876, the park was, for the first time, given a distinctive name. On February 14th, three days before his decease, the City Council named it "Bushnell Park," in honor of Horace Bushnell, to whom its origin is due. In July, 1886, the Memorial Arch was completed. It is the principal artistic feature of the park grounds. Its cost was $60,000, and the expense of the reconstruction of the Ford street bridge, originally built in 1850, to harmonize

BRIDGE OPPOSITE UNION PLACE.

with the arch, was $11,000. The addition of the six allegorical statues (completed in 1894) the lamps, change of grades, walks, etc., must have cost about $10,000 in addition, making in all about $81,000. The architect of the whole work was Mr. George Keller, of Hartford. The sculptor of the northern frieze of the Arch was Mr. John Kitson, an English artist of national repute. Mr. Kaspar Buberl, a Viennese, modeled the southern frieze, as well as the statues, and finials of the towers. Both he and Kitson had their studios in New York City, and specimens of their skill may be seen in that city, and in Washington and other places.

The foregoing is a fairly complete summary of the principal steps toward the making of the park, excepting its river walls. Quite strangely, as it seems to me, this feature, instead of being the point of beginning work, was left wholly unattended to until 1884. It then occurred to the writer (who had just become President of the Board) that, at the lowest point in the grounds (which was at the river), was the proper place of beginning; just as a builder begins and works upward therefrom. The stream traversing the park was not clear and crystalline, and was wholly unfit to be left to flow in its natural bed. Its margins were ragged, and prone to catch and hold the foul material and substances that drifted by. Progress was then begun, and has been continued, with limited means, and notwithstanding difficulties and some opposition toward defining and delineating the river's course. Retaining walls have been laid as fast and as far as authority has been given to do such work; and while they might better have been of more expensive masonry, they have, at all events, served an important purpose.

There was not a great number of species of trees and shrubs on these grounds when the park was first laid out. Most were on the college grounds, where were to be seen the elm, oak, hickory, American hornbeam, hop-hornbeam (or iron-wood), choke cherry, ash, buttonball, horse chestnut, black walnut, and linden, the last five probably planted. On the park proper were elms, oaks (three species), one pepperidge and perhaps a maple or two. Probably there were less than twenty species on both areas. Now there are probably upward of two hundred and seventy species and varieties to be seen, by far the larger number having been introduced within the last ten years. Whether they will live and flourish, will largely depend upon the respectful treatment they will receive at the hands of the public.

THE NEW CHARTER OAK;
A Seedling of 1847.

In 1867, a twenty-year old seedling of the Charter Oak was set in the triangular plat between the Mulberry and Trumbull street bridges. Now, at its age of forty-eight years, it is a flourishing, shapely and stately tree. May it thrive, and live to attain the age and proportions of its venerable and venerated parent.

ATALANTA.

FANNY DRISCOLL.

There's a bit of broken blue in the sky—
   A web of gray o'er the purple lake;
A gleam of silver along the strand
   Where the long waves break.

A dove swoops down from the upper air—
   Snowy pinion and scarlet feet;
There's a breath of spring in the orchard-aisles,
   Balmy and sweet.

This is Atalanta that comes this way—
   Bare white ankle and ripe red mouth,
Blown on the budding April winds
   Up from the South.

THE TOWERS OF TALCOTT MOUNTAIN.

BY S. C. WADSWORTH.

Undoubtedly, the first tower erected on a mountain top, in this country, for public use, was the one built on Talcott Mountain, in 1810, by Daniel Wadsworth. It was constructed of wood, fifty-five feet high, a hexagon, with spiral stairs, eighty in number; and its top was nine hundred and sixty feet above sea level. The view from it was of remarkable extent and marvelous beauty. It became noted, in this country, and even in England, (see Silliman's "Tour from Hartford to Quebec," published in London, 1819; the vignette on its title page is here reproduced.) There were many things to attract popular attention to it. The locality was unique. A beautiful lake, nearly a mile in circumference, on so narrow a mountain top, was a wonder, and the whole region adjacent was full of natural beauty and striking contrasts. Mr. Wadsworth, at that time, was the foremost citizen of Hartford in wealth and benevolence. His father, Colonel Jeremiah Wadsworth, had a national reputation, having been Commissary General in the Revolution and having been afterwards a member of the first three Congresses under the Constitution. Daniel Wadsworth married Faith Trumbull, a daughter of Jonathan Trumbull,— celebrated as having been General Washington's private secretary and *aide-de-camp*, twice speaker of the National House of Representatives, U. S. Senator, and Governor of the State of Connecticut re-elected ten times in succession. Mr. Wadsworth was something of an artist,— the engravings in Silliman's "Tour," being from his pencil,— and had a fine sense of the beautiful in nature. He had

DANIEL WADSWORTH.

accompanied his father, and uncle, John Trumbull, (the famous historic painter,) in their visits to Talcott Mountain, when that region was in its primitive state; and, soon after his marriage, he conceived the plan of making this locality his summer residence. In his peculiar, patient, thorough manner, he secured deeds of more than fifty parcels of land, comprising two hundred and fifty acres, stretching away two miles to the north from the Albany turnpike on the summit of Talcott Mountain; and, on the northern cliff of the lake, erected a tower, while near the lake, overlooking the Farmington valley, he built his residence (naming the place Monte Video). The work of converting such a wild place into excellent roads, nicely graveled walks, and velvety lawns, was not the work of a day. It is stated that at one time nearly one hundred persons were at work on the place, and it is estimated, from the accounts and papers left by Mr. Wadsworth, he must have expended nearly one hundred and seventy-five thousand dollars there, during his residence of more than thirty summers. The tower and grounds about his residence were open to the public under certain rules. No visitors were allowed on the Sabbath or on July Fourth; no carriages or horses further than the lodge, at the entrance of cultivated grounds. Outside this entrance was open level area, provided with hitching posts, for visitors' horses, and on pleasant days, they were well used by visitors from Hartford and the surrounding towns. The distance which must be walked from the lodge to the tower, was a half mile,— a very delightful walk however, over serpentine paths, beside velvety lawns, with occasional glimpses of the beautiful lake, and under the cool shade of magnificent trees, until the old boat house was reached, at the north end of the lake, where commenced the sharp climb up the steep acclivity to the tower.

COL. JEREMIAH AND DANIEL WADSWORTH.

Thousands are the feet, gone never to return, that have trodden these paths. It was here, in 1840, that Daniel Webster was Mr. Wadsworth's guest.

THE FIRST WADSWORTH TOWER AND MONTE VIDEO.

Mr. John Trumbull, Mrs. Wadsworth's uncle, whose famous paintings adorn the rotunda at Washington, the Athenæum at Hartford, and the Trumbull gallery at Yale, was often here; as was the senior Prof. Silliman, who married a sister of Mrs. Wadsworth's. The verse and prose of Whittier, Percival, Prentice, Mrs. Sigourney, and Senator Dixon testify to their visits. Miss Catherine Beecher, while in charge of the Hartford Female Seminary, was accustomed to ride out on horseback, at head of a troop of young ladies to visit the tower, being often accompanied by her assistant and sister, Harriet Beecher, now Mrs. Stowe, and a very pretty cavalcade they made. If a register had been kept at the old tower, as there has been since at the recent towers, it would show, no doubt, many a distinguished visitor. Prof. Silliman says, in his description of the place:

"The beauty and grandeur of this place depend principally upon certain general facts relating to the geological structure and consequent scenery of the middle region of Connecticut."

which he gives in "Silliman's Tour" but want of space prevents us from giving it here in full, the substance of which is this:

"That while the greater portion of the State, being composed of primitive formations, exhibits the usual aspect of such countries,—a succession of hills and hollows bounded by large curves, sometimes sinking deep, and rising high, so as to create great inequality of surface, but rarely exhibiting high naked precipices of rock; there is another region, commencing at New Haven, of secondary trap, or greenstone, which completely intersects the State, and the State of Massachusetts, like a belt, passing to the confines of Vermont and New Hampshire; through which district, as in a great valley among the ridges, flows the Connecticut River; except below Middletown, where it passes through a barrier of primitive country. This region, from New Haven to Greenfield and Gill, in Massachusetts, is one hundred miles in length, varying in breadth from three to twenty-five miles, the most conspicuous features of which are the five ridges of greenstone trap that pervade it, generally in the direction of its length; having a peculiar physiognomy, rising in bold ridges,—stretching often league after league in a continued line, or with occasional interruptions, or in parallel lines, or in spurs and branches. One front (and generally that looking westerly) is composed of precipitous cliffs of naked frowning rock, hoary with time, moss-grown and tarnished by a superficial decomposition, looking like an immense work of art,—making the beautiful and grand scenery of Monte Video without a parallel in America and probably with few in the world."

SECOND TOWER.

M. H. BARTLETT.

It is this whole region, which is in view from the towers of Talcott Mountain, the Bartlett tower at Tariffville not excepted.

The great valley of the Connecticut gives the view its tremendous sweep and extent, while the narrower valley of the Farmington adds to its beauty.

The first tower stood about thirty years and was blown down. It was replaced by Mr. Wadsworth, by a similar one, but ten feet higher, also constructed of wood. No representation of this second tower can be found, except in a wooden model, made by its builder, Mr. Nathaniel Woodhouse, now in possession of Mrs. Oliver Woodhouse, who has kindly permitted a copy. In 1848, Mr. Wadsworth died, and Monte Video and the tower passed into the ownership of David C. Collins who still allowed the public to visit it. In 1864, July 19th, the tower was burned. Much of interest concerning the old towers and Mr. Wadsworth, might be written if space allowed. His large estate, left in charge of trustees — he having no children — was finally settled, in 1882, thirty-four years after his death, by Jonathan F. Morris, in charge of the same, who paid $800,000, to thirty-two heirs under the provisions of his will.

THIRD TOWER.

BARTLETT TOWER.

In 1867, M. H. Bartlett and Charles A. Kellogg built the third tower; which was also of wood, sixty feet high, built with landings and outlook. Its was on higher ground, a quarter of a mile north of the old towers, and the only road leading to it was constructed from the north, or from the Simsbury road to Hartford. The famous "Royal·View" was on this road. A refreshment house and sheds for horses were built near the tower and an admission fee was charged. In 1868, D. W. Bartlett, Washington correspondent of the *Independent* and *Springfield Republican*, purchased "Monte Video," and a road south from the new tower was constructed around the east side of the lake connecting at the lodge with the old Wadsworth road, thus making an approach to the new tower from either Simsbury road or Albany turnpike. The new tower had visitors from all directions, sometimes a whole town having a picnic there. In 1869, M. H. Bartlett purchased the interest of Mr. Kellogg, and in 1872 he purchased "Monte Video," the next year, however, selling the lake, cultivated grounds, and old Wadsworth mansion, to Henry C. Judd, of Hartford. In 1874, Mr. Bartlett built a house near the tower for his own residence, and also to accommodate a few persons who might wish to spend

VIEW FROM EAST LEDGE.

the night or a few days; this house burned before it was occupied, but was immediately replaced by another, and for fourteen years, thousands of people enjoyed the wholesome fare, magnificent views, and bracing air.

In 1887 or 1888, Mr. Judd having sold his city residence, and purchased the Enders' place, decided to sell Monte Video and placed it in the real estate broker's hands for sale. One day, in the fall of 1888, a stranger to Mr. Bartlett was on the tower, making inquiries about Monte Video, which he was looking down upon, when he exclaimed "I wouldn't give Mr. Judd a dollar for his place unless I owned this. Do you want to sell your place?" Mr. Bartlett replied: "I don't think I do. I have lived here twenty-two years and I guess I will spend the rest of my days here." "Well, *will* you sell it?" A moment's hesitation, "Yes, I will sell it." "What do you want for it?" A round price was given, then further inquiries made, bringing out the fact that Mr. Ethan C. Ely, of Longmeadow, Mass., owned the site of the old towers and some forty acres more. Finally, Mr. Bartlett said to the stranger, "I have answered your questions. I will ask you one: Who are you?" whereupon the stranger handed his card on which was "Robert Hoe, New York." It was the millionaire printing-press manufacturer. The result was that Mr. Bartlett bought the Judd and Ely properties, and together with his own tower property, passed a deed of the whole to Mr. Hoe. Mr. Bartlett now supposed he was through with tower life, that Mr. Hoe, being immensely wealthy, might make the place more attractive than ever, and open it to the public. But when, later, he learned from Mr. Hoe, that he had purchased the place for his own private use, and saw the disappointment of his old tower friends, at the loss of their favorite resort, with Mr. Hoe's knowledge and approval, he decided to build the fourth and present tower, of Talcott Mountain, at a point near Tariffville, overlooking the wild passage of the Farmington River through the mountain. It was erected in the spring of 1889, was constructed of wood, seventy feet in height, and connected with it is a large pavilion and bowling-alley. It is

LOOKING EAST FROM BARTLETT TOWER.

within a third of a mile of the P. R. & N. E. R. R., where a tower station has been built, and all passenger trains from Hartford stop, excursion tickets being daily sold.

This last tower is of easier access to the public, than any of the old ones; certainly by rail, and equally so by carriage. This year, the carriage road has been altered and grade improved, so that carriages can drive above the sheds, to within one hundred feet of the tower, and conveyance can be provided from tower station to the tower, for those not wishing to walk. Conveyance is also furnished those desiring to visit "Old Newgate," but a few miles distant. The view from its top is substantially the same as from the old towers; the eastern horizon-line being identical, measuring over one hundred miles in length, the nearest approach to which, is twenty miles distant. The immediate view is admitted by all to be more picturesque than any at the old towers. There is the same magnificent sweep of view over the valley of the Connecticut, reaching from below Middletown to the borders of Vermont and New Hampshire, covering at least 1,200 square miles, dotted with towns, cities and villages,—

186   THE TOWERS OF TALCOTT MOUNTAIN.

Hartford, Springfield and Rockville being prominent, while on the west, far below, the Farmington valley stretches away to the north and the south, bounded by a high range, similar to the one on which the tower stands; but

LOOKING NORTH FROM BARTLETT TOWER.

down hundreds of feet below are fields and groves and villages, spread out as if upon canvas, the laborers busy in the harvest fields, horses and oxen slowly drawing home loads of hay and grain, and trains of cars gliding swiftly along beyond the bright winding river — all appearing so diminutive in the distance, that they look like children's toys, spread out upon a rich green carpet.

The Bartlett tower stands in the same town, Bloomfield, where all the other towers have stood, although seven miles north. In the registers kept by Mr. Bartlett, we find the autographs of the late Ex-President Noah Porter of Yale, and Jackson of Trinity; Professors Fiske of Cornell, Brocklesby and Johnson of Trinity; Ex-Governors Hawley, Hubbard and Jewell; Ex-Senator Dawes of Massachusetts; Hon. Wm. Walter Phelps; Dudley Buck, the musical composer; Whitelaw Reid, the editor of the New York *Tribune*; Samuel L. Clemens, the humorist; "Buffalo Bill," or Hon. William F. Cody; Charles Dudley Warner, Elihu Burritt, Rose Terry Cooke, Charles Nordhoff, Frances Hodgson Burnett, Chin Lan Pin, ex-minister to the United States from China; Miss Fanny Hayes, daughter of the Ex-President; Miss Ellen Hernden Arthur, daughter of the Ex-President; Miss Alice, daughter of James G. Blaine, and many more. Here, in 1830, came John G. Whittier, and his memories of the place are found in the following lines:

To Mr Bartlett, who has robbed the historical Common and "Away with him to the Tower!" of all its terrors — this, With the grateful acknowledgments of

Mark Twain

Hartford, Oct. 1877.

Written on the leaf of a book presented Mr. Bartlett.

MONTE-VIDEO.

Beautiful Mount! with thy waving wood,
And thy old gray rocks like ruins rude
And hoary and mossy in masses piled,
Where the heart had thrilled and the dark eye smiled,
'Ere the spoiler's breath like a malin went
Over temple and tower and battlement.

I love to gaze from thy towered brow
On the gloom and grandeur and beauty below,
When the wind is rocking thy dwarfish pines,
And thy ruffled lake in the sunlight shines.—
Where the beautiful valleys look glad afar
Like the fairy land of some holy star,
By fancy seen — where the soul goes forth,
With an unchanged wing from the cold dull earth,
And the mists from its vision pass away
Like the shade of night from the glance of day!

'Tis gladness all — like a dream of love,
With a smiling forehead beaming above,
And a beautiful hand on the temples pressing,
As softly and sweet as an angel's blessing;
And a tone breathed low in the dreaming ear,
Like the chastened music which spirits hear.

Beautiful Mount! I may look no more
On thy ancient rocks and lake's green shore —
Yet the spirit's pencil has traced thy chart
Of wildness and joy on the human heart,—
And though my step may be gone from where
Thy pine-tops shake in the stirring air,
Yet oft will that chart before me pass
Like a shadowed dream in a mystic glass;
And thy form and features, as now thou art,
Live on in the secret depths of the heart.

TRIO AND TRIPOD

II. TO SALMON BROOK.

BY GEORGE H CARRINGTON.

"Isn't it most time for dinner?" asked John, as Sir Philip prepared to depart from the aqueduct. "Pretty soon," replied Sir Philip, "but we can go a few miles further. The dried beef is pretty fresh yet,"— and with a sad farewell, we gave one long last look at the spot where once glided "the heavy barges trailed by slow horses" and were on the road again. "There's a bridge; I must have that," said Huggins; and so began the series of those "long" waits that patient people like Sir Philip and John became accustomed to, for throughout the trip the bridges were many, and Huggins wanted to photograph nearly all of them.

Crossing to the east side of the river, we observed the legendary stream of "Cider Brook," and what more natural after thinking of cider,— mugs by the hearth on winter evenings, than to go into the land of Nod. Even here, Huggins must take another bridge; than we drove to East Avon, where we quartered our horses in a neighboring barn, spread our sumptuous repast of dried beef and crackers, on a grass plot by the mill, and sat down to enjoy the scenery and the banquet.

BRIDGE IN WEST AVON.

Avon street is a pleasant, quiet place, formerly part of the old Albany turnpike,— hence its direction east and west, instead of north and south, as is the main street of nearly every other town in the valley. Over sixty years ago Avon had several stores, carriage and blacksmith shops, and three hotels. From morning till night there was a "steady stream" of vehicles passing through the town. At the time the canal was put through, in 1828, Avon foresaw great business in store, and was incorporated as a town in 1830. Then, for a few years, were its busiest times. Since then traffic and business have gone largely in other directions.

At the west end of the street the house so high above us, across the pond, with its spacious grounds sloping down to the water's edge, its surrounding verandah and square architecture, giving it a comfortable, classical look, impresses us as an ideal place to visit in the summer, to read and dream, and doze,— provided that fuse-shop would not blow up, and interrupt our reveries. Just beyond the pond, around a bend in the road, we were shown the little house where two old ladies were murdered a few years ago, causing great excitement throughout the State at the time. Much as the deed is deplored, our sense of justice is further chagrined to learn that its perpetrators were never caught, thus adding to that list of crimes which so far exceeds the punishments for the same.

BRIDGE OVER THE FARMINGTON, EAST AVON.

From almost anywhere in this vicinity, the residents have looked to Talcott Mountain and seen, just above them, a tower upon its summit, until since the spring of 1893. How the people miss the old landmark. Doubtless, the sentiments of many were well expressed by the farmer, who said "he'd rather give ten dollars, than have that tower gone from sight." Our stay in Avon was short, and soon we were on our way northward, passing through West Weatogue, with its beautiful memorial fountain, upon which is this inscription:

IN MEMORY OF
FREDERICK A. WHITE, M. D.,
The beloved physician of this town for nearly fifty years, this fountain is erected by his wife Elizabeth Hungerford White.
Defunctus ad huc ministrat.

Next to photographing bridges Huggins' delight was in reading inscriptions in the cemeteries. The Simsbury cemetery was of especial interest, although he did not understand all that he read. Why,

"The memory of the just,
Shall blossom in the dust."

he seemed not to comprehend, and he construed the one which read, "Young Humphrey, died aged 76,"—to mean that Mr. Humphrey died young, aged 76.

He found that the Humphrey families were remarkable ones, and had many members, who, if names are an indication, must have teemed with genius: "Lurannah," "Starling," "Florella," "Dositheus," and "Lura," were all Humphreys. "Those names," quoth Sir Philip "are not rare or peculiar; my Aunt Kedijah, who lives in the Androscoggin district, has cousins on her paternal great-grandmother's side, with such names as those." As if to compensate for names he had never seen, Huggins found a familiar one. A large white stone near the center of the cemetery, bears upon its face, cut in clear, bold letters,—"The Grave of John Smith." Association of ideas, and his general absent-mindedness, led Huggins to remark,—"I don't find where Pocahontas was buried." After a while Sir Philip decided to go to the library, the others to follow soon. When Huggins and John went, they found out, before entering, that it was a private, not a public party there that day. Where was Sir Philip? As they sought the shade of a neighboring tree, he emerged from behind it, where he had retired to conceal his emotion. As our thirst for knowledge was not to be slaked at this place, we started to explore the surrounding country. We were now in what was formerly known as "Hop Meadow Street," named from the quantities of wild hops which the early settlers found growing there.

MILL, AVON.

AVON CHURCH.

Sir Philip carried a map with him to look up the names of towns, and to consult occasionally when he wanted to know what road we were on, and to see if the sun was in the proper position in the sky. The knowledge he could display, after looking at this map, was awe-inspiring.

Just here he used it, and asked a resident, "Where is 'Case's Farms'?" "'Case's Farms'? Case's Farms? Oh, ho! you mean West Simsbury. Haven't heard it called that for years. Oh, about four or five miles." So, getting the proper direction, we started. After going, as we supposed, the required distance, some huge barns by the roadside brought from Huggins, the query, "Is this 'Case's Barns'?" "Probably." At West Simsbury, some distance further, Huggins took nine hogs on one plate, which Sir Philip claimed was gluttony. At the creamery we all produced our handkerchiefs, it smelled so much like Cologne, according to the accounts we have read.

As the sun was sinking behind the mountain that shuts from this quiet little hamlet the region to the west, we

FOUNTAIN, WEATOGUE.

started onward, for it would soon be dark and we must find shelter for over night. A hospitable soul took us in. His hospitality was at the rate of one dollar a person, but as John was a small eater he would take the three for two dollars and a half. He had but one spare room, but would put a cot in that. At supper,—which Huggins noted as "fair," —our genial host had delegated his charming daughter to serve the viands. This made Huggins' appetite so delicate that he ate up all the cake. Sir Philip didn't seem to be affected at supper, but late in the evening he suddenly rushed down stairs to see her, claiming that he wanted a match. In an hour or so he came back with one. It was a *parlor* match. "Then why not take a flashlight?" This large, airy, upper chamber, being at least seven by nine, and containing only a four-poster, a cot, (Sir Philip's trundle-bed, we called it,) a bureau, a washstand, two chairs

"GLUTTONY."

and our baggage; we stood the camera outside in the hall, laid Huggins on the bed where he posed as "the retired photographer," had Sir Philip reading the history of "Case's Barns," leaving John to operate the camera and set off the flash. It was a brilliant event. But, alas! unlike most such events,

THE GORGE MILL — WEST GRANBY.

it was not a success. Huggins had his feet toward the camera and the room was invisible.

After changing our plates, we were soon asleep, dreaming of the pleasant experiences of the day. With confused ideas of a host of enemies applying the battering ram to our chamber door, we were aroused, only to find that "mine host" was in the kitchen below preparing the steak for breakfast. "Mine host" had a brawny arm and a pensive face, was smooth of speech and angular in appearance. We arose, and he told us the brook was down to the other end of the cow-lot. There we could wash. After breakfast, at which the steak was found to be "chewable," we got under way toward "Salmon Brook Street," as Sir Philip's antiquated map had it. The latter individual as he looked about him thus moralized: "You see that in the sandy soil of this region the white pine-tree flourishes with its evergreen foliage. Strange that the hardiest trees should grow in soil where there would seem to be the least nourishment. Yet, is it not so in life? The greatest wealth of character and mind is developed with meagre opportunities. The luxuriant tropical vegetation soon withers and dies." At Granby Street we met an acquaintance of Sir Philip, who took us under his guidance to see the beauties of Granby, and that he might keep watch of Sir Philip, as he cautiously intimated. This friend was a most genial and accommodating gentleman and it was rare good fortune to us that we thus met him. In hospitality he reminded us of the English country squire, so, as "The Squire" let him be known to us. He took us down to a pasture at the foot of a ravine, and chased cows around into picturesque attitudes for Huggins to practice on. After spending the morning visiting the various places of interest about the town, such as the old lock on the canal, the pumping station for the public water, and the cemetery, The Squire suggested that "The Gorge" at West Granby would be a good place to go to in the afternoon. It was so arranged. On the way there, The Squire showed us a place where a cloudburst had washed out about

THE GORGE.

a quarter of a mile of road a year or two ago, " and " said he, with a sigh that came from the depths of the pocket-book of a patriotic tax-payer, " it cost the town fifteen hundred dollars to fix it." It certainly was worth seeing, the havoc the water made on that road in one brief hour. Gigantic boulders hurled from their places as though but pebbles; great trees twisted and snapped off; the entire road-bed so utterly destroyed that a new road was made instead of repairing the old one.

"The Gorge" and its mill, for wildness and picturesque beauty, we found had not been overrated in The Squire's glowing description. For the artist, the photographer, the lover of nature, it is certainly an ideal place. The rocks here forming a narrow canon from thirty to fifty feet deep, show marks of water action to their tops. In the spring, with the water rushing through, the sight must be sublime. Well might Sir Philip attune his soul to the poetic as he clambered down the rocks repeating "Beneath the hill, there stands the mill," and when he had climbed up on the other side and looked down into the chasm, and on the ruggedness all around him, is it any wonder that he fell into the strains of the heroic, and declaimed:

> A place fit for the gods to dwell in of yore,
> When they waged their fierce battles and revelled in gore;
> This chasm so deep, once riven asunder
> When Jove intervened his lightning and thunder;
> These huge boulders standing from an earlier world,
> In tumultuous wars by those bold Titans hurled;
> And they sat at grim feasts, high up on the rock,—
> While the waters whirled under, their mad mirth to mock.

Maybe it was those same bold Titans that built the mill, for its looks have all the flavor of antiquity. It certainly could not be a more romantic place, with clearer, more crystalline water, than it is, had the Greek divinities planned it.

Our route homeward was taken by the road running between the "Barn Doors," that we might get a nearer view of those famous hills, and after supper, and a visit to the village store, we changed our plates, and planned to visit Newgate the following day.

(TO BE CONTINUED.)

"THE ONE SHALL BE TAKEN, THE OTHER LEFT."

STOCKTON BATES.

> I dream, dear wife, in sunset's afterglow,
>   That night will come and with it death and sleep;
>   That one will go and one remain to weep.
> Which one, dear heart, will be the first to go?
>
> Shall I lose thee? Dear God! forfend the blow!
>   I cannot bear the thought! Alone! To keep
>   Sad vigils day and night! What deeper deep
> Of suffering can anguished sorrow know?
>
> Should Death entreat me; comfort thy sad heart—
>   Say I but slumber longer—that I rest—
> But do not weep, for time will heal the smart.
>   But I—if thou obey Death's cold behest—
> What sophistry shall I employ? What art?
>   I can but grieve and beat my troubled breast.

SCROPE; OR, THE LOST LIBRARY.

A Novel of New York and Hartford.

BY FREDERICK BEECHER PERKINS.

CHAPTER III.

"So" said the old man, smiling indulgently as he spoke, to the younger one,—"so, cousin Scrope, you think one needs a good deal here below, and for a good while?"

"I do so,— I do indeed," replied the young fellow:—"Now, I should say, an, 'ouse here in the city,— yacht, of course,— place at Newport,— ah, sweet place, Newport, such soft hair, you know!— countwy seat on the 'Udson — say near Tarrytown — was up there yesterday — lovely countwy, I ashuah you. Went up there with Button — singular name that, Mr. Van Bwaam — Button, button, who's got the button?"

"Oh, I don't know," returned the old gentleman, (not meaning any ambiguity),— " Monsieur Bouton would seem quite fine, wouldn't it? By the way, I wonder why there has been no Mr. Scissors? But how do you like Button's first name?"

"Weally, I don't know it. T. Button, Esq., it said — Do you know, now, you 'ave a monstwous many hesquires in Hamewica?"

"Oh, he might call himself Baron Button of Buttonhole, and sign all instruments, and sue and be sued by that name, if he chose. And he might have any coat of arms he might fancy,— a coat all over gilt buttons, if he liked — on his seal, and on his carriage too, without being annoyed by the proud minions of the College of Heralds. He may tattoo himself and all his house — and grounds — all over, with any insignia he chooses, for that matter. This is a free country, cousin Scrope!"

There was something satirical in the old man's manner, as if he were half laughing at both Americans and English. He went on however:

"Tarbox Button, his name is; 'most musical, most melancholy!'"

"Most musical, most jolly, I should say," answered the young man. "But I can't imagine were'e got that name, do you know? Hit's certainly not in my copy of the Squope and Gwosvenor Woll. Bwummagem name I should fancy, Button, at any rate."

"Father," said the young girl, with a shade of grave motherliness and mild reproof in her manner — her mother was dead, and she was both mother and daughter to the old man —" Father, you musn't be bad, now, and make fun of Mr. Button. He has been too kind to us for that. What would you have to do, and where should we find so good a home to live in, and where should we visit at all, if it were not for him?"

striking liquid fulness like the lowest notes of a full-throated singing-bird. But it was neither sad nor glad; it had a certain indifferent or dreamy quality, almost as if the speech were that of a somnambulist; or perhaps it was an intonation of weariness.

"No harm, Civille,' said Mr. Van Braam; "I was observing upon his name, not upon him."

"Vewy well off is Mr. Button, I should say?" queried Scrope.

"Yes," answered the old man. "Here's this vacant piece of ground that this old house stands on,— why, it must be worth a quarter of a million dollars, and he finds it convenient to hold it unimproved and pay our New York taxes on it, until he has time to speculate with it in some way. Meanwhile Civille and I occupy one of the most valuable estates in the city," added the old man, laughing.

"Do you know, now," pursued Scrope, "I never should 'ave taken Button for one of the family if I'd met 'im by accident say in Gweenland? 'E 'asn't the style, at all."

"Why," said the old gentleman, "I've often thought of it myself. But he had a pretty hard time when he was a boy, like a good many other rich people, and he has made his own way, without any leisure to finish and polish himself. Besides there is a poor strain of blood in that branch of the family; those Gookins that his mother, old Mrs. Button came from were distillers and hard cases from generation to generation, by the town records;— rough, violent people,— a kind of natural-born pirates. And his wife's family, although they were decent enough, were narrow and small-minded, somehow. The fact is, that unless you take Button's executive ability as showing Scrope blood, there's only the record to prove that he has it. I don't know any of the rest of them that have so few of the family traits. And perhaps, as we are three Scropes here together, we may take Civille's and my Van Braam blood into our confidence and mention in strict secrecy that cousin Button's immense bragging about his Scrope blood is as near an absolute proof that he hasn't a drop of it, as any one thing could be. All the rest of us like to have it very well, but no other of us would advertise it so extensively."

"Now I should 'ave fancied," said Mr. Scrope, after having listened to all this with evident and close interest, "that Mr. Button's political hambition was more unnatuwal in one of our connection than is boasting."

"Very justly observed," answered Mr. Van Braam. "A good many of us have refused offices, and I know none of us except my cousin Button who wants them. But so it is; Mr. Button is proud of his descent, and he is terribly fond of being talked about, of having influence and holding offices. I fancy he likes all that best of all, moreover, because it is such a capital advertisement of his books. And he is so energetic and shrewd in managing, that, you may say, he ought to have influence and office, particularly as he is reckoned perfectly honest. 'The tools to him that can use them.' And he is very generous with his money where these two interests of his are concerned, and very sharp and close with it everywhere else. There, cousin Scrope — that is a pretty complete account of Mr. Button. It has only to be filled out with his minor traits; and those you can see for yourself."

"A vewy good man to 'ave on your side I should say," observed Mr. Scrope, smiling. "Indeed, he's given me some very good advice halready about horganizing the Squope Association. He knows exactly 'ow to manage people — exactly. 'E put me up to hall the dodges about the newspapers, and about cowwespondence, and influence and intwoductions. Do ye know, now, hi fancy I shouldn't 'ave been able to awange this matter at all without 'im."

Mr. Van Braam smiled and nodded, as much as to say, The most likely thing in the world. Scrope resumed:

"This other cousin now, Chester — your cowespondent about the genealogy,—'e's hanother sort of person, I imagine?"

"Why, yes," answered Mr. Van Braam. "He hasn't any money — that is, nothing except the little old place at Hartford where he and his great-aunt live together, and the income he earns. But an assistant-librarian doesn't have a very large salary, and I don't suppose his other revenues enable him to do much more than live comfortably. I guess Adrian is a pretty clear case of Scrope, though. He doesn't care much for money, he is fond of principles, he isn't afraid, he goes his own road, he has managed, by the help of a capital set of instincts of his own, to make himself a well-educated and accomplished young gentleman, he loves all manner of right thought and sound study, he is fond of fun, he is sweet-tempered, he likes pets and children, and old people, and they like him; and he likes to do things for others."

"Beg pardon," said Scrope of Scrope, "but if hit's a fair question, 'ow did 'e get hout of 'eaven?"

All three of the company laughed, and it was the young lady who answered this time: "The sons of God saw the daughters of men, that they were fair," she quoted. "It must have been my cousin Ann Button for whom Adrian came down to us."

"Oh," said Scrope; "then if 'e mawies her 'e wont need to twouble himself about money."

"Very true," replied Miss Civille; "and yet it would be a great mistake to suppose that Adrian wanted her money. I knew all about their engagement. Ann was never very much of a favorite with anybody in those days — I don't know that she is very much liked now. But then, she used to be really neglected and lonesome and miserable. Adrian just devoted himself to her because nobody else would; out of pure kindness; and so they fell in love."

Mr. Scrope bowed an acquiescence, but with a queer look, which Civille understood perfectly, and answered:

"Oh, you needn't think it — that was two or three years ago, when we were all younger and didn't think so much of money. Besides, Mr. Button was not nearly so rich then. It was afterwards that he made so much."

"Oh," replied Scrope;—"That does seem like it. But I don't suppose the money will make him like her any the less."

"I don't know about that," said Civille reverting to her dreamy manner, and looking out from great half covered gray eyes as if she was watching something beyond the walls of the room —"I don't know about that. If I know cousin Adrian, it's the likeliest reason in the world to repel him."

"I shouldn't wonder," observed the old man;—"it would be Scrope all over."

"If you'll allow me," said Scrope, "I'd like to suggest that that would be more suitable to the hold spelling than the new. S, c, ah, o, o, p, they used to spell it — Squoop, not Squope. Now Old Colonel Adwian the wegicide was so vewy particular that I say his name gave wise to the vewy term Squooples. He was full of 'em. And if my Yankee cousin is so squooplous, I don't know but I shall advise him to take the old-fashioned name again, and leave off the Chester entirely."

"I dare say he would like to do so," observed Mr. Van Braam. "I want you to see him to-night, however, if possible, so that you and he may know one another a little before the Association meeting. It may be of service to both. And my old-fashioned ways," added the old gentleman with a good-natured smile, " make me desirous that all those of our kin should know each other.—It's high time he was here, too."

"I can't honestly say I shall miss 'im," said Scrope, with a gallant look towards the young lady, " If 'e does not come. No man could be quite 'appy to see another hadmiwer in Miss Van Bwaam's pwesence; and I know no man can see 'er without being 'er hadmiwer."

At this not very elegant compliment one might have seen Mr. Van Braam's eyebrows give a curious lift, and he just glanced at the young man, but without moving what Mr. Scrope would call his 'ed. As for the young lady herself, she answered in her indifferent voice:

"Oh, thank you very much, Mr. Scrope, I'm sure. But your Yankee cousin will not be in your way. He is engaged already, as we were saying. Indeed, we here are not at all in society; you will be free of rivals, both with my father and myself."

"There, cousin Scrope," said the old man, "That's as much as to say that you may marry us both if you can get us!"

The young Englishman looked rather uneasy; even fewer Englishmen are good at taking jokes, good or bad, than at making them; and he answered quite at random, but as it happened quite well enough for such talk—

"Vewy 'appy, I'm sure!"

The perfect coolness and speed with which the two Americans carried forward his hint to such remote consequences had terrified him; for he could not be sure whether they spoke in irony or not, their manner was so entirely grave and impassive.

Mr. Van Braam laughed quietly, the daughter just smiled, while the old gentleman remarked,

"Not badly answered, cousin Scrope; but don't be alarmed; we neither of us propose matrimony at present."

The young man was silent for an awkward moment; when there was a ring at the door, a card was handed to Mr. Van Braam, who said "Show the gentleman in," and the absent kinsman entered. It was our young friend Mr. "Cash," of the auction room. As he came in, Mr. Van Braam rose and stepped forward to receive him, with hearty cordiality. Miss Civille and Mr. Scrope arose, as the old gentleman, leading the new comer toward the fire, presented him:

"I want you to be at home here at once, cousin Adrian," he said. "Civille, you knew your cousin better two or three years ago than now, but I hope you'll make up for lost time. Cousin Scrope, I know you and Mr. Chester will be friends, for you are kinsmen, and you have interests in common besides, at present, in this estate and association business."

Mr. Adrian Scrope Chester had enough of general resemblance to Mr. Van Braam and his daughter, and indeed to his five or six times removed English cousin, to pass very well for a co-descendant. That is, he was tall, erect, well-formed, quick and easy in movement, and of an intelligent and comely countenance. His brown hair, instead of the cometary horrors of Mr. Scrope's, was brushed in a conventional manner, and curled in large soft curls instead of persisting in the frizzle of the Englishman, and his beard and mustache were thick and fine. His eyes were of a clear dark blue, his lips at once full and sensitive, all his features delicate and yet not small; and whereas Mr. Scrope's bearing and presence gave an impression of good-nature, quickness, levity, fun, Chester's spoke of thorough kindness, instead of mere good nature; of penetration, of insight, instead of quickness; of sense and directness and strength rather than levity; of general intellectual activity, rather than of mirth only.

Comparatively speaking, the American seemed to possess large good qualities, of which the Englishman had only somewhat small imitations. And yet the English are very often what people sometimes call "singed cats—better than they look."

The young people tried to do justice to Mr. Van Braam's favorable introduction: but Miss Civille's manner was chilling enough, although she did not mean it to be, and indeed in spite of her intentions; so that Chester, barely touching her hand, which was cold and limp, said to himself, How did she come to dislike me? Mr. Scrope did rather better. He may possibly, in spite of the mild caustic that had just been applied to his demonstrations of jealousy, have felt some slight objection to the second young man in that company, or it may have been his ordinary awkwardness only that was upon him. However, he made his bow, shook hands, expressed his pleasure, and crowned the operation by taking from his pocket a card which he ceremoniously presented to Mr. Chester. Mr. Chester received it with thanks, delivered his own in exchange, as seemed to be expected, and then took time to peruse the legend upon that of Mr. Scrope. The phrase is correct—he took time. The card, a long one, like those sometimes sent on wedding occasions, contained the following composition: *

BRABAZON AYMAR DE VERE SCROPE OF SCROPE.

And at the point where an asterisk is put, there was moreover a most noble-looking coronet, printed in the three primary colors, very impressive to behold.

"I am sorry my daughter was absent at your recent visits to New York," said Mr. Van Braam, when the four had seated themselves. "You and I agree on so many points that I shall be glad to see you and her contending over them. She is always refuting her father."

But the kind smile and pleasant tone and half-mischievous expression with which the words were said gave them a second meaning directly opposite to their grammatical one.

"I am afraid of controversies with ladies," said the new comer. "They receive things by intuition, instead of groping to them by feeling along chains of reasoning. Reasoning will not induce a woman to agree with you; reasoning with women is like hunting wild ducks with a brass band. It scares them. I should never hope to convince a woman except by making her like me and then unintentionally on purpose letting her see what I thought."

"What treason!" exclaimed Miss Civille, this time with a sufficiently perceptible tone of interest.

"There you go!" exclaimed her father, amused.—"Thirlestane forever!"

"Thirlestane?" queried Mr. Scrope. "How Thirlestane?"

"Why," resumed the old gentleman; "don't you remember their motto? It's in the Lay of the Last Minstrel. 'Ready, aye, ready!'" Civille will always answer the trumpet call when it sounds for battle over Women's Rights!"

"Now father," she remonstrated; "are you going to quote every minute? How can I entertain the gentleman, particularly if you wish me to fight with Mr. Chester, if you open your broadside upon me too, like that miserable Frenchman against John Paul Jones in the Bonhomme Richard?"

"Well, well, my child—I'm dumb—*vox faucibus hæsit!*"

"But permit me to explain," said Chester, with some anxiety: "I had no treason in my soul. I do not mean that men have no intuitions, nor that women have no reason; but only that as between the two, women have most of one, and men of the other. It is just as it is with another couple of faculties

— or sets of faculties; I mean executive power and what people call goodness. I believe men have most of the former, and I believe women are better than men; I believe God put them into the world on purpose to be better than men; I do not believe that either of them is destitute of either faculty."

"I don't believe one single word of it," said Miss Civille, with a resolute tone. "If women are inferior to men in any particular or superior to them either, it's because they have been educated into going without their rights, and it's a great shame!"

"Well," rejoined Mr. Chester, pacifically; "Miss Van Braam will pardon me, I am sure, if I venture to act as if I were talking with a man in one particular?"

"I don't know about that," said the young lady, almost alertly — she had plenty of spirit, it would appear, under that cold languid manner, and the debate appeared not to be at all unwelcome; "what is it?"

"Why, only that really and truly, I do detest arguing and I tell you plainly, and say I'd rather not. I get so angry — or if I don't, I want to,— when I undertake to argue. But there's another reason for my begging off just now "— he looked at the two gentlemen —" I'll let you tread me into the very dust next time, but there are some things we ought to talk about."

As they all agreed that the apology was real, Miss Civille was graciously pleased to accept it.

"First," said Mr. Van Braam, "when did you come to town? I got your note only this afternoon."

"Yesterday, sir," said Chester. "I should have called last evening, only that I was too tired, and to tell you the honest truth I went to bed and slept all night long."

"The wisest thing you could do. Next, let us arrange about the Association meeting."

This meeting, however, as quickly appeared, was set for that day week; Scrope, moreover, in reply to their inquiries, showed them that under the experienced guidance of Mr. Button, all things had been put in such readiness that it only remained for the persons concerned to render themselves at the time and place appointed. Both Mr. Van Braam and Mr. Chester congratulated Mr. Scrope upon the thorough manner in which all these preliminaries had been adjusted, when there was once more a ringing at the door-bell, and once more a card was brought to the master of the house, who took it and read it, saddling his eye-glasses with an experienced little *jiggle* on the bridge of his nose, and looked puzzled. Then he read it again, very carefully, half shutting his eyes, cocking his head backwards, and focusing the object with a kind of trombone motion. Then his head dropped, and he looked around him like one who has received an unexpected affusion of cold water.

"Why," he said, rather to himself than to any one else —"what"— and he stopped, and said to the servant, with something of displeasure in his manner,

"Ask him to walk in."

Returning in a moment, the servant reported that the gentleman had only a word to say to Mr. Van Braam, and would trouble him but for a very little.

Still with the same wondering and half displeased look, the old gentleman arose and went out into the hall, leaving the door open. Listening, the three others heard some indistinct murmur of voices only. Then in a few minutes Mr. Van Braam said, speaking from the hall,

"Never mind me for a little while, young people!" and he shut the door. Evidently the business was to take rather more time than he had supposed.

CHAPTER IV.

Chester, when the door had closed, proceeded to make some further inquiries about the Scrope Association and its operations. All these were readily answered, becoming quite a debate on ways and means, and greatly enlightening the querist. The Association, it appeared, consisted, or was to consist, of the descendants of Adrian Scrope, son and heir of Colonel Adrian Scrope the Regicide, executed at Tyburn on the 9th or as others say the 17th October, 1660. To these descendants, it appeared, there now of right belonged a certain large sum of money representing property which had devolved to Adrian Scrope the younger after his flight to New England, and which still remained so situated that the heirs could certainly recover it upon making proof of their descent. Scrope of Scrope, being himself a descendant not of the regicide Colonel, but of a younger brother, could not inherit while there were direct heirs; but being fond of genealogical investigations he had come to a knowledge of the facts in this case. He avowed very frankly that he desired to make a profit by means of the affair, but he said that he was also partly actuated by the equally laudable motives of family pride and family liking. It was from these causes that he had come to America with the design of searching out the Scrope heirs, forming them into an Association, becoming their agent, obtaining from them the necessary funds, proving their claim, and receiving as compensation a proper percentage, to be allowed him when the heirs should be actually in receipt of their respective inheritances. This arrangement, of course, effectually prevented any malversation by the agent. In the prosecution of this undertaking, Scrope had first fortified himself with letters and documents, and had then come to the United States, where he had for some time been investigating, advertising and corresponding; and with much labor had advanced so far as to appoint the meeting referred to, in New York, one week from date, of a number of the American heirs.

Miss Civille Van Braam took little part in this discussion between the two young men, listening only, and even this was with the air of pre-occupation or fatigue or almost melancholy which was habitual to her. So, when all at once business matters having been sufficiently debated, Scrope of Scrope suddenly turned to her and asked for some music, she started almost as if from sleep.

"Oh! Excuse me!—What was it?—I beg your pardon!"

The request was repeated, and with an apology for her inattention, the young lady very readily went to the piano, and selecting some music, played, and then sang with good judgment and good execution, both instrumental and vocal, but without much emotion. The music she chose, apparently, was a graceful melody with lucidly arranged accompaniment, rather than crowded harmonies or technical difficulties; it was sufficiently good music, and at the same time simple enough for mixed society; safe music to play anywhere. There was a certain ease and truth of expression in her fingering and vocalizing however, which seemed to intimate the capacity of doing much more; and the peculiar vibrating fulness of her voice gave the impression of large passionate vehemence existing, though it might be asleep and unconscious of itself.

Having ended, she smilingly asked Mr. Scrope to take his turn, and he very readily complied. He sang one or two English ballads in a clear, not very expressive baritone or rather counter-tenor, and he sang without any embarrassment, sitting quietly on the sofa, simply explaining before he began that he knew no instrument. This style of singing is not very common in America, but it might well be; it requires and gives, a sort of self-reliance of ear and a peculiar completeness of style, exacted by the absence of accompaniment. The performance, indeed, was much better than any one would have argued from the exterior and general bearing of Scrope of Scrope; and he was applauded accordingly.

Next came Chester, externally much more easy in manner than Scrope, but in reality very much more shy. He would gladly have declined, but with some little effort he came up to the mark like a man, with the allowable apology that he could neither sing without an instrument like Mr. Scrope nor play like Miss Van Braam, and should therefore give them two inferior kinds of music together. So he went to the piano, and sang a little ballad of William Allingham's, whose words are sufficiently a specimen of that evening's performance to be worth giving.

THE CHILD'S THREE WISHES.

I.

Ring! ting! I wish I were a primrose?
A bright yellow primrose, blooming in the spring!
    The fleeting clouds above me,
    The little birds to love me,
The fern and moss to keep across,
    And the elm-tree for our king.

II.

Oh, no! I wish I were an elm-tree! —
A great royal elm-tree, with green leaves gay:
    The wind would set them dancing:
    The sun and moonbeams glance in;
And birds would house among the boughs,
    And sweetly sing.

III.

Nay, stay; I wish I were a robin! —
A robin or a little wren, everywhere to go, —
    Through forest, field or garden,
    And ask no leave nor pardon,
Till winter comes with icy thumbs,
    To ruffle up our wing.

IV.

Well, tell, whither would you fly to?
Where would you rest, — in forest or in dell?
    Before a day is over,
    Home would come the rover
For mother's kiss, — for sweeter this
    Than any other thing.

Chester was no player, and the air was nothing; but he sang the pretty little ballad, accompanying it by a few chords, with so much truth of intonation, with so much expression, and his voice, not noticeable except for clearness and sweetness, conveyed so much of intelligent sympathetic feeling, that his rendering was more effective than a great deal of the "best" singing, and he was rewarded with genuine praises. Miss Van Braam's were not very enthusiastic, and yet they conveyed an impression of restrained feeling which meant much; and Scrope's, somewhat over-eager and voluble as they were, still had sincerity enough in them to make them agreeable. They pressed him for another song, but he excused himself, saying, as indeed his flushed face, quick movements, and the evident tension of his nerves plainly enough showed, that he was easily excited by music, and adding that being unpractised, his fingers and his voice in such case quickly became uncertain. Nobody would have suspected the tall erect broad-shouldered fellow of being excitable. But he was, and the more so in proportion to the remoteness and spirituality of the exciting cause; that is more, for instance by music than he would have been by gambling or by a quarrel.

The conversation, which was now resumed, became lively, Scrope and Chester exchanging puns, jokes and nonsense, and Chester and Miss Van Braam finding that they had preserved in common many reminiscences of their previous acquaintance; so that the young lady after a time, bethinking her of her cool greeting, was a little pained in conscience thereat, and very prettily apologized:

"My health is poor this last year or two, since we came to live here, and my head aches a good deal of the time, cousin Adrian," she said; "I very often hardly know whether I am alive. I am having a severe attack to-night, and if I was rude to you at first, you will not misunderstand it, will you? I could hardly see or stand."

Chester hastened to make the proper answer; and Scrope hastened further to offer a remedy.

"P'raps you'd allow me to cure your 'edache," he obligingly suggested. "I've only to lay my two 'ands on top of your 'ed for a few minutes."

Miss Van Braam hesitated a moment. But she reflected, how absurd is that conventional idea that the touch of one human being differs from that of another! And again, she said to herself, why should it be any worse than waltzing — or as bad for that matter? Still, she did not so much welcome the experiment as force herself to acquiesce by reason; and her manner was a little cold — as often the case with shy and sensitive people — as she replied that she would be greatly obliged to Mr. Scrope if he liked to take so much trouble.

That gentleman however, assuring her that it was no trouble but a privilege ("I should think it was," said Chester to himself contrasting the features and bearing of the Englishman with the pale and spiritual face of the young girl), jumped up, and, stepping briskly to the back of her chair, laid his two hands upon the top of her head.

There was silence for a moment or two. Then Civille, who had been leaning in a tired way against the back of her great stuffed chair, suddenly raised herself, at the same time shaking her head violently, so as to free it from the touch of Mr. Scrope's hands, which indeed were almost tossed away in the vivacity of the rejecting movement.

"Oh! I can't! you'll kill me!" she exclaimed. Scrope of Scrope looked excessively displeased, but managed to say he was "vewy sowy, I'm sure!" and returned to his seat.

Civille suddenly threw her two hands up to her temples, uttering a low cry of intense pain, and resumed her leaning attitude, her head thrown far back.

"Oh!" she repeated, as if quite unable to repress the voice of physical anguish.

To persons of sympathetic temperament, and whose kindness is a genuine instinct, perhaps no emotion is so piercingly painful as to recognize the suffering of another. Both Scrope and Chester had much of this feeling, but Scrope's was a sense of his own personal discomfort and a good-natured readiness to help. Chester, however, at once strong and sensitive, possessed a share very unusual for a man of those spiritual endowments which are so little understood, and which are commonly termed intuitions. At the sight of the young girl's pain, he felt it, with a pang like a knife-thrust; he turned pale; his eyes filled with tears; and in his inexpressible longing to free her from it, without any distinct purpose or in fact consciousness, his left hand, which was nearest her, was held out towards her. With a quickness like the spring of an electric spark, she seized it and held it tight across her forehead. Her slender fingers closed upon it like iron, yet with a quiver that revealed a frightful nervous tension.

(TO BE CONTINUED.)

THE ROUND TABLE.

"The Knight's bones are dust,
And his good sword rust;
His soul is with the Saints, I trust."— COLERIDGE,

"There is no grander subject in the world than King Arthur."— TENNYSON.

THE AMERICAN TYPE.

The progress and perpetuity of races, as well as of individuals, illustrates the doctrine of the survival of the fittest. The evolution of humanity is based upon the permanency of the best race-elements. The English type combines the best ingredients of the Celtic, Saxon, and Norman races,— more virile and vigorous than any one of its constituents. It is the assimilation of the hardy low-German and Saxon-Danish peasantry with the grace and fervor of fiery Norman chivalry — an Alsace-Lorraine union of legions, but on a larger scale — the supple German sinews encased in graceful and elastic Norman armor.

The marvelous Celtic race gave us all the "glory that was Greece, the grandeur that was Rome" — our modern heritage of culture — and it distinguished itself further in fostering the hardy vitality and activity of the northern barbarians who over-ran these oases of civilization, and who were later to over-run the British isles, in successive waves of Angles, Saxons, Danes and Normans — all branches of one fruitful tree — to form the dominant race of to-day.

In the same way, America will produce a race derived from this sturdy Saxon stock, but stronger, greater, more glorious, because of the assimilation of other races. The German is stolid and phlegmatic, the Frenchman vacillating and vague, the Italian and Spaniard impetuous and spirited. The English is the blood of the world; the German, the thews and sinews; the French, the heart; the Italian and Spanish the nerves. In America we are receiving all the elements of vitality and virility, and raising up a higher and better type of manhood and womanhood; and this fact is being recognized more and more with each generation of our existence as a body politic.

The typical American will not be "a thing of shreds and patches" made from odds and ends of worn-out races. He will be a real product, a natural out-growth — one in whom nationality will not interfere with a true cosmopolitan aspect and spirit; and as he grows in racial and national stature he will more and more become truly a citizen of the world. He will gain this proud eminence, because ingrained principles of social equality, self-government, and the universal franchise, have raised him above the common herd of nations, whose citizens have no souls of their own but are merely undeveloped serfs of sovereignty. Over one hundred years of freedom, liberty, and equality have taught the American how to govern and be governed by his equals — a lesson that cannot be learned in a century or two in England and on the Continent.

Dean Hole was right in saying that in America must be developed the dominant type to govern the world,— the highest type humanity can produce,— the man of highest culture, broadest sentiment, deepest sympathy, and most consummate refinement : the perfect outgrowth of this land of magnificent resources.

It is strange with all this so palpable to the senses that we should still have Anglo-phobia, French frenzy and mimicry, and other insidious foreign fads in our land. It is galling to a true American's pride that our plutocrats should fawn upon foreign nobility, showering upon this decadent caste their ducats and their daughters, promiscuously. But it is idle to criticise the folly of the over-rich. One example of our sublime snobbery, not to say national "greenness," is the ready query invariably asked of a foreigner how he likes the country, even before he steps upon shore. Our own Mark Twain has been pouring "hot-shot" into the lockers of the departing Bourget, because of the latter's extravagantly realistic diatribe on America, "Outre Mer." And because Mark is furiously funny when he tries to be serious, some asinine Americans have undertaken to defend Bourget, and taking Mark seriously, to defame the American critic, to their own manifest detriment. The whole embroglio is unusually droll, and it only needs Max O'Rell to stir up the diverse ingredients with his spoon of satire ; and, to end the entertainment, the little Count Castellane to dance frantically, in despair, because he did not get the "dot" he desired and only the daughter.

"IT SMACKS OF THE SOIL." "While we are with the Americans we must as the Americans do," is the motto of most of our foreign visitors. Once it was the tendency to ridicule and raise a hue and cry about our ears thereby, after they had safely gotten home. Now, the other tack is taken. Since our World's Fair they have had their eyes opened to our immensity and grandeur: now it is the fashion to apostrophize, and salaam and gesticulate before our great national genius — like Aladdin before the wonder-genius of his lamp. We are all-wonderful, all-powerful; in fact, the whole country is a national Niagara, with cabinets of curios along its banks. So Bourget explores us, even down to the Everglades, looks into an alligator's mouth and draws deductions therefrom of the immensity of our domain. David Christie Murray, a fourth-rate fiction monger, comes here, and writes letters signed "A Cockney Columbus," to tell us things we already know. A member of the Comedie Francaise comes over for a week or two, goes to a few theatres, and stirs up the spleen of star-actors and managers with his envious shafts of criticism. The question is, why will our great, good-natured, healthy, infant Republic allow such nauseous emetics to be forced down its throat? "A burnt child dreads the fire," does not hold good here. How much longer will we suffer?

Is it not better my brothers and sisters of the quill, that we become acquainted with, really familiar with, our own country, in order that we may write about it graciously, thoughtfully, sincerely, ourselves? Is not a home criticism less stinging, after all; a domestic brawl preferable to calling in one's neighbors and gossips?

But you will say we have no such thing as a rational criticism, and no national literature; that our criticisms are superficial and provincial, our literature only given to illuminating bare, unfrequented spots, where travel is scarce and humanity scarcer. You will cite the fact that our greatest geniuses prefer to go off to some mountain fastness or remote parish, some country cross-roads or frontier settlement, and write of it in a tawdry "citified" style—as if a superior being was looking through a microscope upon some new parasite or microbe. You are right, there is no denying. We, like the foreigners, seek the inaccessible, the remote, the casual, the characteristic, odd, and trifling. The truth is we do not know our own minds yet, much less our own country. There is a missing link in our literature everywhere. This manner of writing is only patch-work; and there is no firm fabric between the patches to hold the whole garment together.

If we only had talented people all over our broad land, capable of writing of its beauties and attractions, its joys and sorrows, its significance and its short-comings, then might we look for a national literature — indeed, for the long-looked-for National Novel. Then would our land be as truly literary as England, France or Germany of to-day, as Shakspere's or Anne's England, as the age of Augustus or Pericles, of Alexander or Assur-banipal. We have seen only the beginnings of a national literature. We have had our Brockden Brown, Cooper, Irving, Willis, Poe, Bryant, and the poets of the beginning of the century; we now have our aging Howells; our Bret Harte and Crawford and James who are really foreigners; our Cable, Eggleston, Garland, and a group of women-writers who are more promising and productive than their male peers. Many more could be mentioned but this is enough to prove the case. We must look to our women-writers in future for our local, home-made literature, it is to be supposed. But it will not suffer in the hands of such writers as Mrs. Spofford Mrs. Rebecca Harding Davis, Mrs. Burnett, Mrs. Phelps-Ward, Miss "Octave Thanet" French, Miss Wilkins, Mrs. Deland, Miss Pool, Miss Murfree, Mrs. McLean Greene, Miss Jewett, and in criticism Miss Guiney and Miss Repplier.

We have often wondered why there have been so few story-writers in Connecticut, among such a number of writers in other lines. Rose Terry Cooke, Mrs. Sally Pratt McLean Green, Mrs. Stowe, and a few others that can be told upon the fingers almost, complete the list. Is it because the soil is sterile, the people barren of interest or incapable of idealization? Is it because the genius of our people runs to poetry, or history, or dry abstractions? Is the land devoid of charm? Has the day of productiveness passed? Is it not possible to awaken a new interest in this problem, to revive lethargic talent and develop later or new? We will welcome to our pages anything in this line that "smacks of the soil," that is truly of "the land of hasty pudding and wooden nutmegs"—anything that is up to our standard. But we deprecate the dialect story, which is not indigenous to Connecticut; the "stage Yankee" having gone into innocuous desuetude a generation ago, and besides there is a very tame and lame excuse for a story that depends upon dialect.

THE CHARM OF THE COMMONPLACE. What shall we write about? What is there to write about? Do you know how many things there are to write about, especially in an old and settled commonwealth or community, that you never thought or dreamed of before? Let us enumerate a few for your benefit? To this end we can do no better than quote a few lines from "The Art of Thomas Hardy," showing what he finds to write about in one of the oldest and most rustic parts of England. While we deprecate his morality, we certainly admire his art:

"He dwells in a dramatic meditation upon the earth's antiquity, the thought of the world's gray fathers and in particular upon certain tracts of land with which he has an intimacy; upon the human traditions of old time, upon the pageant of the past, upon the relics of long gone powers and forces; genealogies, rolls, tenures, heraldry; old names and old houses lingering in decay, unconscious of their age; pagan impulses, the spirit of material and natural religion, the wisdom and the simplicity, the blind and groping thoughts of a living peasantry still primitive; the antique works and ways of labor in woods and fields; the sense of a sacred dignity inherent in such things, in that immemorial need of man to till the soil for his daily bread; meditations upon 'the drums, and tramplings' of great armies, the fair forms of vanished civilities, the heroism and the ambition, the beauty and the splendor, long passed away, while still the old necessities remain, and still men go forth to their work and to their labor until the evening; meditations upon the slow sure end of all those evenings in the darkness and the pains of death; meditations upon the deep woods under the black starry nights, among the sounds of that solemn time, and upon the generations of laborers in their graves; meditations upon their stern or generous virtues, their patience, loving kindness, and self-sacrifice; upon their humors and habits, the homely pleasant features personal to each man of them; upon the great procession and continuance above and beyond those mortal lives of universal laws. And there is another side to his dramatic meditations: he loves to contemplate the entrance of new social ways and forms into a world of old social preference and tradition; to show how there is waged, the land over, a conflict between the street and field, factory and farm, or between the instincts of blood and the capacities of brain; to note how a little leaven of fresh learning may work havoc among the weighty mass of ancient, customary thought; to exhibit the mercurial influence of new things upon old, the frivolous fashion and light vulgarity of the seaside town, in contrast with the staid dignity and cumbrous strength of the gray village, the significance discernible in the intrusion of the jaunty villa among barns and dwellings and churches, old ' as the hills;' to built up, touch by touch, stroke upon stroke, the tragedy of such collision, the comedy of such contrast, the gentle humor or the heartless satire of it all, watched and recorded by an observant genius."

We have all this, and more too, to be developed in our commonwealth.

A WORD OF WELCOME. It only needs a glance through our pages to detect a revival of interest, in this State, in literature pure and simple. And we can say this perhaps without undue conceit. Already we have flocking into our fold a number of promising young poetasters and prose-writers who give us of their best; from sixteen-year-old Louis E. Thayer, who can do very creditable work already, to men of age and experience in both prose and numbers. We are well pleased that they have contributed their best work to our pages. We give them all a cordial welcome, and as many more as may come. They will have a large audience, at least: the present issue will be read by fully fifteen thousand and the next by perhaps twenty-five thousand. This is a phenomenally good start for a magazine.

It may not be considered bombastic if we call attention, in this little corner to some of our contributors. Miss Adele Greene is of an old Connecticut family formerly located at Haddam; she writes with a facile pen, and is familiar with and an enthusiastic lover of the old state. She is closely connected by kinship with Anna Katherine Green, the novelist, and some other charming writers and is equally at home herself in prose or poetry. Mr. Benjamin is of an old Granby family, a resident of Hartford, a lover of art, an inveterate book-worm and a close student of history and literature. He will be heard from in future papers. Prof. McLean, principal of McLean Seminay, is too well-known throughout the State as a geologist, historian, and lecturer to require introduction; we hope to hear from him on this class of topics at no distant date. It is seldom that father and son are addicted to poetry, but we have a brace of notable poems from such sources. Miss Larned is a constant contributor, and we are promised from her pen some attractive papers on semi-historical topics that will be sure to please. Mr. Chadwick is a new contributor, has only been writing for a year, but gives decided promise as a poet. Mr. Denton's stories are remarkable for their peculiar Poesque treatment, and as a poet has won his laurels already; we give two of his poems, the first a Walt Whitman impromptu, the second a sonnet, in which line he shows distinction and finish. Prof. Martin H. Smith, for a number of years at the head of the Connecticut Literary Institution, and now Judge of Probate at Suffield, writes entertainingly of his town, and we hope will appear often in our pages. He is a man of culture and refinement, a class-mate of Henry M. Alden, the editor of Harper's Magazine, a fine conversationalist and raconteur, and writes as cleverly as he talks. The other contributors in this number were introduced to the reader by our first issue, and hence will not require extended mention. We shall present some new writers in the next issue, who will please as well as profit their numerous readers. We invite others to contribute stories, poems, historical sketches, and anything of general interest; remembering always that "work is the genius that wins."

SOCIOLOGY AND CIVICS.

"The criminal classes are so close to us that even a policeman can see them. They are so far away from us that only a poet can understand them."

> "How best to help the slender store,
> How mend the dwellings of the poor,
> How gain in life, as life advances,
> Valor and charity more and more.—TENNYSON.

CHARITY ORGANIZATION AND MEDICINE.
In our last issue we had occasion to refer to the duties and obligations of the church in relation to charity with especial reference to the "Institutional Church." In the present issue, we wish to add a few words as to the inter-relations of the medical profession and the charity organizations. We can not do so in more fitting words than those of George M. Gould, A. M., M. D., of Philadelphia, President of the American Academy of Medicine, in his address before that body at its 1894 annual meeting:

"Ours is a missionary society at heart, but at its head it is a scientific one,—like medicine itself, indeed in these respects—and it is a peculiarity of our work that we should seek to determine intellectually the true bases and relations of professional and social progress. . . . Historically and presently, medicine is astonishingly self-forgetful, and most egregiously altruistic of all the sciences and arts. . . . If we do not strike hands with Lombroso and say all crime is due to the abnormality of organism, certainly crime and disease have some most intimate relations. What are they? What likewise are the subtle bonds that link together disease, physiologic or neurologic, with mental abnormalism? We do not seek to escape from our responsibility for much of the world's blindness; the idiot is physiologically defective; otology and laryngology have not said their last words as to deaf-mutism; every United States pensioner holds a physician's certificate (more's the pity!) Have the surgeons done all that is possible for the cripples? Have we no accountability for pauperism, no responsibility for the criminally high death-rates, and no guilt for the criminally low average length of life? In the mysterious tapestry of civilization, disease is weaving a thousand miscolored and rotten fibres that mar its beauty, spoil its design, and weaken its strength. Shall we long permit with careless consent such negligent and fateful weaving? Nay, shall we longer consent to be ourselves such weavers? . . . "In China the making of monstrosities was a regular business by putting children in pickling vats for years, by breaking and bending their bones, or by transplanting upon their bodies bits of the skin of animals. We are horrified at this, but are we not equally infamous with our dime-museum glass-eaters, our foundling asylums, and our patent medicine beastliness?" . . . One of the strangest and most dazing truths that soon becomes manifest is that charity as commonly practiced is SIN. The word, like many another, bears witness to the sad history of mankind. The beautiful Greek word is almost untranslatable into English. Its gracious compassion or tender pity has become simply almsgiving, a thing usually a double curse, degrading both to the giver and to the receiver. To relieve suffering is the delight and the duty of all good hearts, but we must see to it, 1, that the suffering is real and not fictitious; 2, that, if real, it is not deserved; 3, and most important, that by our methods, we do really relieve and do not increase the suffering. It is just here that we run across the first principle of the charity-organization societies, which is to make benevolence scientific. It has for years been my practice to give every street beggar a charity organization card with promise of relief, if he should be found worthy by the agent of the society. Only one has ever returned and he was set right without any alms giving." . . . "Mendicity is mendacity. The crimes of tramps and street-beggars are only surpassed by the crimes of those who give to them. Mendicancy, in all its forms and masks is not the result of poverty, but is the cause of poverty. All indiscriminate alms-giving. all wholesale crowd relief, or collective-relief of want or suffering is either a forged, to-be-protested promise-to-pay note of sympathy, or it is the payment of wages for something done. Nine times out of ten it is selfish charity or self-flattery. Foolish people love to flatter-themselves that they are kind-hearted. Benevolence is fashionable, and fashionable people —are fashionable! One of the most debauching and disgusting forms of selfishness is that of indiscriminate philanthropy. For downright diabolism witness the mutual hatreds of two rival professional philanthropists! Alms-giving on the other hand, is wages; by giving to beggars and tramps we pay for the continuance and increase of beggary and trampism; by Sunday breakfasts we increase hunger on Sunday mornings, and we also secure listeners for our pseudo-religious after-performances; by indiscriminate out-patient relief we stimulate the production of disease, hire patients to experiment on, increase our own reputation or that of our hospital, and at one fine stroke pauperize both the profession and the populace; by municipal workshops, State-aid to the unemployed and socialistic demagogism, we hire people to be unemployed, to strike, and to lessen the sum-total of production; by institutionalism gone mad, we hire the people to get rid of their personal duties to their dependents, and hire those on the borderland of breakdown, physical or mental, to give up the last instinct of self-help. We pay for these things and many like them when we give alms and taxes, and hire other people to be sympathetic for us. Of course, what we shirk doing ourselves, our hired agents will hardly do better. 'Like master, like man.'" . . . "Money given to the endowment or support of hospitals is likely to become a curse instead of a blessing to humanity unless certain provision is made against indiscriminate free treatment. . . . Indiscriminate medical charity is just as pernicious as indiscriminate alms-giving. . . . The nobler and infinitely more important sciences of public hygiene and preventative medicine are left unfurthered or are turned over to the non-medical world. Thus in this blind man's race we rush impetuously to a silly suicide." . . . As ordinary citizens and members of society we must each become members of the charity-organization societies, and as physicians we should use this method of therapeutics, just as we do hospitals, climate, nurses, food, or sanitation. In some respects, it seems a great pity that as a profession, we have allowed the beneficient exotic of charity organization to grow almost wholly out of lay ground, and not in the sacred soil of medicine. . . . There is a place and a possible useful occupation for every tramp and beggar. Most of them do not want to have their infirmity healed. Ours is the duty of unmasking at least the physical fraud.'"

Dr. Gould is undeniably right in his axiom that "Mendicity is mendacity." He gives some simple rules to follow : "1, Don't help frauds. 2, Help so as to make future help unnecessary. 3, Don't hire people to be miserable. 4, Prevent dependency." If physicians would only practice these rules also, it would be a great saving to themselves of time and money. They must clean house for themselves. "Physician, heal thyself," is not inapplicable here. There would be fewer cases of hysteria and hypochondria among the poor if the charity physician's aid was not free to all. How many hospitals there are that are simply training-schools for incompetent "sawbones." How many doctors there are that are willing to do mission-work in the slums for the miserable pittance of charity-societies,— rather than give up an untenable position in an overcrowded profession.

The greatest evil of modern society is dependency. It is part and parcel of socialism. Every dependent is an unnecessary and expensive burden on the community. The dependent is the product of disease mainly, and, curable or not, is the patient of society. He is also the patient of the physician who must either cure him or kill him off before society and the physicians are relieved of the burden. But, dependency is mainly due to, and is wholly aggravated by idleness. The inactivity of the occupants of our poorhouses and asylums breeds disease. Our descendants will cry out against us for housing our insane, epileptics, paupers, and criminals, in enforced idleness, at the expense of the thrifty outsider. Then again, charity driblets and "free soup" philosophy is despicable. Rather than cheap and free food we should teach the poor the proper choice, the proper cookery, and proper use of food. American families waste more food than would keep a French family of the same social status in comfort. But it will be long before people will listen to Edward Atkinson's advice in these respects.

Of course society should take care of the hopelessly idiotic, but study to prevent their recurrence; there are hundreds who are needlessly blind, and yet no law prevents the incapacity of the guilty practitioner; the crippled, the deaf, the senile, and the epileptic, appeal to our sympathy and receive it,—but are they not all more or less capable of partial self-support?" "Idleness," as Dr. Ferrier says : "increases the instability of the nervous system." As for the insane, therefore,— what a shame it is that many thousands of over-active, unstrung nervous wrecks are kept in idleness, hopelessly and expensively, at a great cost to the tax-payer, to the physician, and to the patient whose sufferings might be lightened or entirely removed by colonization, employment, and individualization. The cottage system is after all the best.

The charity-organization society has found remedies for nearly all social evils. It remains for us to help, to utilize, and to realize their nearly realized ideal. We must individualize our cases, and get into the personal relations with our dependents, (not lump them together as so many cattle); we must cure, and not simply endure our unfortunate brethren : we must give them employment; reward self-help; discourage dependency, and encourage self-respect.

The time will come when all charity will be organized and controlled by the State, and its recipients will bear their part of the burden.

SOLON.

THE CONNECTICUT SOCIETY FOR UNIVERSITY EXTENSION. The work accomplished by the Connecticut Society for University Extension during the winter months of this year has amply fulfilled the promise of last Fall. In four cities of the state as well as a large number of farming communities the work has been prosecuted with great earnestness, and we have every reason to be gratified, not only with the average size of the audiences, but also with the quality of the results accomplished.

The four cities which have done their work this year under the jurisdiction of the State Society are New Haven, Waterbury, Meriden and Hartford. New Haven was first in the field with a course by Professor Rosa, of Wesleyan, on "Electricity," which was listened to by an attendance averaging from 150 to 175 persons. With the ensuing course by Dr. Richard Burton, on "The History of Fiction," the size of the audiences rose to 250. The concluding course of this series was given by Professor McCook of Trinity, on "Some Pathological Aspects of Social Topics." Gratifying as these results are for the first year's work of a new "center," they have been surpassed at Waterbury where regular University Extension courses were also begun for the first time this season. The published programme of the Waterbury organization has a formidable appearance for the first year's work of a new "center." It includes courses by Professor Rosa of Wesleyan on Electricity, by Dr. Richard Burton on The History of English Fiction. The English Language and American Literature, by Professor Rice of Wesleyan, on Evolution, and Sandstones and Traps of the Connecticut Valley, by Dr. Anderson, of Yale, on Physical Culture and by Professor Conn of Wesleyan on The Study of Flowers.

There are upwards of 300 regular members and the audiences have averaged from 300 to 400 persons. Supt. Crosby, the chairman of the Executive Committee, in concluding his report says: "The success of the University Extension Movement in Waterbury has been quite beyond our early anticipations. We think we have done very well in furnishing twenty-one lectures at a cost to the members of less than fifteen cents for each lecture.

Even this record of attendance has been surpassed by the Meriden "center" which likewise began its work this year. But two courses have been given, by Professor Rosa, on "Electricity," and Dr. Burton on "The History of Fiction," but there have been over 600 subscribers, an attendance which has taxed the capacity of the hall where the lectures were held.

In Hartford we have had three regular University Extension courses: Professor Phelps of Yale on the Elizabethan Drama, Professor Winchester of Wesleyan on The Age of Queen Anne as seen in Literature and Professor Kuhns of Wesleyan on French Literature in the Nineteenth Century. The attendance at Professor Winchester's course averaged about 300, at Professor Phelps' course over 100, while Professor Kuhn's course which is now in progress promises about as well.

While these figures of attendance fall somewhat below those reported from one or two of the other "Centers," the average expense to the "members," that is the holders of season tickets, will not compare unfavorably with the result reported elsewhere. A notable feature of the season's work in Hartford has been the series of free organ recitals at the Center Church. These recitals form an important feature in the Educational work of the Hartford Society and their success is attested by the size of the audiences which have filled the old church to overflowing during the entire season.

Turning to another department of the state work I would speak in conclusion of the success of the lecture courses on agricultural subjects, given before different Grange audiences. One of the lecturers on our agricultural staff, Mr. George A. Mitchell, has already given, or arranged to give, a course on Crops, Soils and Fertilizers at seven different places and fifteen other Granges have applied for lectures by different members of the faculty of the Storrs Agricultural College.

Secretary.

SCHOOL OF SOCIOLOGY

The work of the School of Sociology is now so well known that no special introduction to it is necessary. The lectures for the term just closed have maintained a high grade of excellence. They have included a course by Prof. Falkner, of the University of Pennsylvania, on Statistics; the Evolution of Custom, by Prof. Ripley, of Columbia; the Evolution of Law by Prof. Erwin of the New York University Law School; two courses in Kulturgeschichte by Prof. Monro of the University of Pennsylvania, and Dr. Geer; The Social History of the United States, by Prof. Jameson of Brown; a theological discussion of the nation by Prof. Sloane. whose Life of Napoleon is now appearing in the Century; and a course in Ethics by President Hartranft. Questions of immediate practical interest were discussed by Prof. Rowe of the University of Pennsylvania, who spoke on Municipal Problems, and by Prof. Atwater, who considered the matter of Food Supply. In connection with this last a study was made of the dietaries of typical Hartford families, and other investigations of interest in connection with food supply were started.

Another important line of work, which has become more throughly organized during the past term is the friendly visiting which is carried on in connection with the Charity Organization Society, and which aims to bring about by personal contact a better understanding of those classes with which practical sociology finds its most immediate concern. Institutions of special sociological interest in Hartford and the vicinity have been studied by visits of personal inspection, and special facilities for examinations have usually been granted. The library has received constant additions, and a systematic attempt is being made to procure the reports and literature of all societies, public and private, in the country, whose work touches on Sociology.

In January, a meeting of Hartford women was called at the house of Miss Emily Morgan, for the purpose of organizing a Sociological Club. The Rev. Dr. Chester D. Hartranft presented a general outline of the purpose and methods of the proposed club which was duly organized, and has now a membership of over one hundred, with Dr. Hartranft as its president. The membership is fifty cents a year, and members are entitled to free attendance at the School of Sociology. The object of the Club is to promote the study of Sociology, and its practical development in Hartford. It aims to co-operate with all other institutional efforts which are being made to improve the city, and to consolidate, as far as possible, all of the Sociological organizations.

The club is divided into sections, according to the number of works undertaken. The sections devote themselves under the instruction of the Club, to separate Sociological work. and may discuss papers submitted by their members or engage specialists to lecture on specific topics descriptive of their fields. Sections have already been formed on Tenement Houses, the Settlement, Food, the Parish Burying Ground, and Women Wage-earners. The Tenement House Section and the Settlement Section. have been the most active so far. A house has been rented for Settlement work. Miss Woods is living there as head-worker. and one or two Hartford women are to be with her as "residents" for two or more weeks at a time. The tenement houses on many of the streets have been investigated, and the city laws regarding landlords and tenants have been type-written for the benefit of the section. Several houses have been reported to the Board of Health, and it is hoped that the efforts of this Section will procure practical results in the improvement of the tenement districts.

Arrangements are now being made for the second year of the School, and there is every prospect that there will be no falling off from the high standard already attained. Announcements of lecturers will probably be ready in the course of a month or two.

ARTHUR KENYON ROGERS,

Registrar.

CONNECTICUT HUMANE SOCIETY.

Five thousand miles of travel; three hundred complaints received and investigated — a record made of every case; relief given to 150 old people and children, and 1,000 animals; 31 convictions — resulting from 35 prosecutions; the distribution and sale of 1,000 copies of "Anna Malann,"— making 4,000 in all; the publication and distribution of 4,500 copies of the Society's Fourteenth Annual Report, together with correspondence and necessary details, is a modest summary of the work for the first quarter of 1895.

In the "Annual Report" just issued, the President calls attention to some facts that bring reflection to every thoughtful mind,— the wanton destruction of millions of beautiful birds to meet the demands of fashion, and the mutilating of man's most useful servant by docking. This year the Society presented a bill to the Legislature to prohibit the practice, and the measure bids fair to become a law.

The President also calls attention to the fact that the Connecticut Humane Society has rarely had occasion to apply for additional or amended legislation. Sometimes the ill-will of an offender or his friends are aroused, making itself apparent in the introduction of bills to impair the Society's usefulness. In the present Legislature, there has been introduced a bill to make the Society pay costs in cases where the accused is not convicted, or in any way released without payment of costs. The bill provided also, that the Society pay the defendant's counsel and witness fees. It hardly seems probable that so unreasonable a measure will become a law. None, except cruel men who neglect their families, beat their wives, and abuse or starve and neglect their animals, would rejoice at the passage of such a measure.

The Society is awaiting an important legal decision which may have some influence on its work in the future. A farmer, who had some starved and neglected horses, was visited by the General Agent who found them starved and valueless, and, after remonstrating without avail, legally condemned and killed the animals, to protect them from further cruelty and suffering. Evidence showed that the horses were valueless and the Agent had kept strictly within the law. The Justice, however, assumed to decide constitutional questions, and declared the right of eminent domain superior to any police regulation, and accordingly found against the Agent the amount of $35 — the owner's valuation of the animals — though he admitted he only gave $7 for one of them. An appeal was taken and the outcome in the higher Court is awaited with interest.

This Society entering upon its sixteenth year, can look back with gratification upon its growth and uniform success, yet humane work is only in its infancy. It was many years before public humane sentiment, in this country, broke the chains of every African slave. There is a force now at work — slowly, perhaps, but surely — that will inculcate in a humane public sentiment that will recognize the rights in this world of the lower orders of creation.

Chandler E. Miller

Secretary.

MUSICAL MELANGE.

"Other slow arts entirely keep the brain,
And therefore, finding barren practicers,
Scarce show a harvest of their heavy toil."—SHAKESPERE.

THE SPINET.

ELLEN BRAINERD PECK.

On the tinkling notes, and faint,
Of the spinet old and quaint,
Once pretty hands oft lightly strayed,
Coaxing gentle melodies,
From the slender ivory keys,
In days when dainty tunes were played.

In frock of dimity bedight,
Of a fashion then the height,
Perchance, some maid, demure and slim,
Practiced here a canzonet,
Or a graceful minuet,
In studied measure, queer and prim.

Now untouched the keys lie hid;
Silence sleeps beneath the lid,
And the voiceless spinet seems
Haunted with refrains of song,
That to other days belong
And eloquent of olden dreams.

INDIVIDUALITY IN MUSIC.

"Music has its foundation in the heart of nature. Wherever there is life, there is vibration, and wherever there is vibration there is some principle of music. Music is the sweetness of all sound. The art of music is the distillation of this sweetness from the ruder elements. Music is a language of moods; it conveys more directly the emotions of humanity than any other form of human expression. A man's true character is more distinctly shown in music than in any other art.

"Art is the mechanical expression of human thought and emotion. The Germans have called a musical composition a 'tone-picture.' The relation is good, but the comparison inadequate. A painting and a musical composition are as different as is a statue and the living being.

"Music is a part of life, not a lifeless imitation. The highest form of music is the direct expression of individuality. It is the vibration of musical sounds in perfect sympathy with the vibrations of emotions. The color of the mood must, by sympathy, color the tone.

"Individuality is as necessary to music as life is to the body. Life is not the outcome of form, but form is the outcome of life. Musical forms are created by the composer, and are the outcome of emotions, which must have a form through which they must find expression. You can never give that which you do not possess. No amount of practicing will make a musician of any note, unless the individuality is developed and taught to express itself. A great musician must be a great character.

"Life is but a grand symphony, full of joy and full of sorrow ; discord follows discord with a progression wonderful and incomprehensible. All that is, is grandest music, if our hearts could only hear.

FORREST CHENEY, in "Chips."

NEW YORK NOTATIONS.

"A chiel's amang ye takin' notes
And, faith, he'll prent it."—BURNS.

NEW YORK CITY, April 1, 1895.
The most brilliant operatic season that the metropolis has ever known is now a matter of history. For thirteen weeks, beginning in November last, the Italian and French Company of Abbey & Grau composed of some of the most illustrious singers of the world, held complete sway at the Metropolitan Opera House, and delighted the musical and fashionable world with the artistic excellence and the elaborate magnificence of their performances. From the very opening night, when "Romeo et Juliette" sang to the world "their old, old story," until the curtain was drawn upon the closing scenes of Goethe's "Faust," not a really false note was struck in the grand artistic ensemble. Twenty operas in all were produced during the season. Of these only two, "Falstaff," and "Elaine," were absolute novelties. Two others, "Manon" and "Samson et Dalila," were only comparative novelties, for they had been heard in New York before. It is undeniable that Verdi ruled the day, with some leaning also towards the French school, but it was equally noticeable that the German school, with the great Wagner, was almost entirely unrepresented, one single work only, "Lohengrin," redeeming the Vaterland from musical oblivion. It seemed especially appropriate, therefore, to read the announcement at the close of the Italian Opera triumphs, that our gifted young American Impressario, Walter Damrosch, would give a short season of Wagner's operas in German, beginning towards the end of February and lasting for four weeks.

On the evening of February 25th the season was begun before an immense audience with Wagner's "Tristan and Isolde," Frau Rosa Sucher appearing as Isolde, Frl. Maria Brema as Brangaene, and Herr Max Alvary as Tristan. Following closely upon this glowing, passionate love song came the other masterpieces of the famous composer, — "Lohengrin," "Tannhauser," "Die Walkure," "Siegfried," "Die Gotterdamerung," "Die Meistersinger,"—all the beautiful links that form the golden chain of the mystical Niebelungen Ring. And, as the dying notes of the swan are proverbially the sweetest, so it was that with both the Italian and the German Opera seasons, the closing nights of each being the most brilliant.

In the case of the first named, you will remember that on almost the last night of the season Verdi's latest work, "Falstaff," was produced after numerous postponements, delays, and disappointments. But how truly was it worth waiting for! What freshness, sparkle and spontaneity, all the more remarkable when you consider that the composer has passed beyond the allotted three score and ten, aye, even beyond the four-score milestone in his life's journey ! Produced at Milan in 1892, this opera met at once with immense success. From the very opening, the great Verdi seems to say, "Let us be happy and gay ; away with dullness and care," and the rising curtain discovers the Fat Knight in the Garter Tavern Inn, surrounded by his trusty companions, Bardolph and Pistol. A moment later we are transported to the garden of Ford's House, and here are Mistress Ford and Mrs. Page and Dame Quickly, all "Merry Wives of Windsor." And so the brilliant comedy goes on, and

" Love like a shadow flies when substance love pursues,
Pursuing that that flies, and flying what pursues "

The cast for this production was no less brilliant than the opera itself. M. Victor Maurel appeared as Sir John Falstaff, the role created by himself, and was perfection in the part. Mme. Emma Eames was a revelation to us as Mrs. Ford, and revelled in the comedy scenes with the ease and abandon of a finished comedienne. Mlle. Zelie de Lussan was a delight to the eye as "Sweet Anne Page," and Mme. Scalchi was excellent in the amusing part of Dame Quickly. At the fall of the final curtain, one of the most enthusiastic demonstrations ever witnessed in the Opera House took place. The artists were recalled time after time, and flowers, bouquets and wreaths were showered upon the stage in almost reckless profusion. As the immense audience reluctantly left the Opera House, one thought was uppermost in the minds of all : "Viva Verdi! Viva Italia!"

Quite as brilliant a scene as the one just described witnessed the closing nights of the German Opera season. The occasion was the celebration of Herr Max Alvary's one hundredth appearance as Siegfried, a role created by him on the stage of the Metropolitan Opera in November, 1887. Perhaps no better comparison could be made between the Italian school of Verdi, and the German school of Wagner, than to contrast "Falstaff" and "Siegfried." The one is a bright, gay comedy, breathing in every note of the sensuous amours of the fat Sir Knight. The other is tragic in the extreme, with mystical and legendary romances that concern the gods, not men. The climaxes of "Falstaff" are most ludicrous, and they find the "gay deceiver" either smothered in a buck-basket or dancing with the fairies in Windsor forest. The climaxes of "Siegfried" are most awe-inspiring and the death of Siegfried is perhaps the most overwhelmingly dramatic scene ever conceived by human intelligence. And this leads me to say that the greatest difference perhaps between the Italian and French operas and the Wagnerian operas presented this winter is that the first named are mainly historical and romantic, while the works of Wagner are almost entirely legendary and mythological. In fact, he chose the myth, because he believed that in the legends of nations, the heroic characters most suited to a perfect musical representation were oftenest found. He was influenced in this idea, perhaps, by the Greek Theatre, which he strove to emulate, for he had been able to see from the works of Æschylus and Euripides how closely the relations had been established between the lyric stage and the people. It was his conviction of the great musical and dramatic value of the myth that caused him to say: "In this and all succeeding plans, I turned for the selection of my material once for all from the domain of history to that of legend." The regular season of the German Opera closed on the 23d of March, but yielding to numerous requests for a few performances at popular prices, on the same plan as was followed with the Italian Opera, the management gave three extra performances with the same casts and company and with the same orchestral and scenic arrangements as prevailed on regular nights. The operas selected for this supplementary season were "Lohengrin," "Die Walkure," and "Tannhauser." The public testified to their appreciation of the courtesy by their liberal patronage, and it is safe to say that hundreds of persons were thus enabled to see one or two of Wagner's great musical dramas for the first time in all their lives

E. W. DeLeon.

TREASURE TROVE.

"Time hath, my lord, a wallet at his back,
Wherein he puts alms for oblivion."

"While place we seek or place we shun,
The soul finds happiness in none
But with a God to lead the way
'Tis equal joy to go or stay."— MADAME GUION.

THE LAST OF THE BLUE LAWS. The Sunday Laws in Connecticut have dwindled from the Old Blue Law times to the present day; but three or four such statutes were embodied in the revision of 1887, and the last of them are being repealed by the present Assembly. One of the last repeals permitted any Justice of the Peace having personal knowledge that a person was guilty of drunkenness, profane swearing, cursing, or Sabbath breaking, to render judgment against the offender without previous complaint or warrant. Another bill that has been reported from the Judiciary Committee, is to repeal the ancient statute denying the right of the swearer or Sabbath breaker to carry his case to the higher courts. This almost smacks of Russian temerity. Since the general revision of the statutes in 1808 there have been liberalizing tendencies. The fine for not attending church under the revision of 1808 was fifty cents, but this was repealed in 1814. Children under fourteen years of age were to be punished by their parents for profanation of the Lord's day, and a fine of fifty cents was imposed upon any parent neglecting duty in this respect. Idling in public inns after sunset, Saturday nights, was not permitted by a provision adopted in 1702. The law regulating the sailing of vessels on Sunday, practically prohibitive, was adopted in 1715. No vessels were allowed to sail out of any port or harbor in Connecticut, or to pass by any town or society on the Connecticut river, on Sunday, where there was public worship.

The general revision of 1838 dropped a good many of the old provisions, but sports, games, play, and recreation on Sunday were prohibited. Provision was then made for the carrying of the mails on Sundays. The courts of the State wrangled until 1850 over evidence admissible with regard to intent of riding on Sunday. The letting of a carriage for charity was permissible. Down to the general revision of 1866, tythingmen were allowed to be appointed annually by the churches, with power to bring offenders against the Sabbath laws to the courts. Meddlesome ministers and neighbors have frequently resorted to the statute just repealed by the present Assembly, for purposes of spite and revenge; and an instance occurred in Southington no later than the first of January, which led to its repeal. There has been some effort, this session, to abolish the laws practically prohibiting the running of Sunday trains for excursions; but this is one of the Sunday laws that Connecticut people revere; the Consolidated road has always opposed Sunday excursions. In the old days when a single car was run through to New York, the management discouraged local traffic on Sunday, by charging as much for a way-ticket as for one to the metropolis.

There has been no disposition here, as in Massachusetts, to abolish the Fast day appointed by the Governor; for over a century Good Friday has been observed as the annual Fast day. It is but just to say that these relics of Sabbath observance have been retained on the statute books, not from choice or desire, but by reason of neglect of the people to ask for changes more tolerant. The action of the present Assembly will place Connecticut on a par with other states in liberality. The day of the old Blue Laws has passed from our fair land; and only our true Connecticut blood retains its ultramarine or cerulean hue. ALGERNON.

CONNECTICUT HISTORICAL SOCIETY. The January meeting of the Society was entertained with a paper by Hon. Morris W. Seymour, of Bridgeport, on the "Hiding of the Charter." The reader reviewed the legendary stories, as well as all known facts relative to that event, and portrayed the character of Captain Joseph Wadsworth, showing his bold and daring spirit. After the reading, both gentlemen having expressed their willingness, it was voted that Mr. Seymour's paper and the paper recently read by Dr. Hoadly on the Hiding of the Charter should be both printed in an early publication of the Society. At this meeting, Dr. George Leon Walker presented a beautiful set of views of Hertford on the Lea, England, recently sent to him by Canon Woolmore Wigram, of St. Andrew's, Hertford. This presentation will serve to further strengthen the friendly ties existing between the senior and junior Hartfords.

At the opening of the February meeting, the president announced the recent death of Hon. Robbins Battell, of Norfolk, a former President and Vice-President of this Society. The paper of the evening was by Rev. George Leon Walker, S. T. D., on the Old Hartford Burying Ground, giving an historical description of the ground from the time of its first use for burial purposes, mentioning some of the notable people who lie buried there, calling attention to its present condition, and ending with a plea for an increased general interest in its care. Dr. Walker strongly advocated the clearing away of the row of dilapidated buildings at present standing between the old ground and Gold street.

Those present at the March meeting were much interested in a paper read by Rev. Joseph W. Backus, on Rev. Samuel Nott, D. D., of Franklin, Conn., which not only portrayed Dr. Nott himself, but sketched the life of a New England country pastor a century ago. The president made the pleasing announcement that the full text of volume three of the society's collections was in print, and only the printing of the prefatory pages and index and the binding were needed to complete the volume.

NEW HAVEN COLONY HISTORICAL SOCIETY. The annual meeting was held on the evening of November 26, 1894. Reports of various officers showed that the society was in an increasingly prosperous condition since the acquisition of its new building. The growth of the library during the year past was particularly noteworthy, the accessions numbering 460 volumes and 118 pamphlets. The following officers were elected: President, Hon. Simeon E. Baldwin; vice president, Eli Whitney; secretary, Henry T. Blake; treasurer, Dwight E. Bowers. Mr. Thomas R. Trowbridge, for many years the efficient secretary, declined a re-election, to the unanimous regret of the society.

The following papers have been read at the monthly meetings:

November 26, "The New Haven Green as a Political and Civic Forum;" December 31, "The English Commonwealth," by Rev. Burdette Hart; January 19, "The London County Council," by George L. Fox; February 25, "The Four Letters from a citizen of New Haven, published in 1788 at Paris, in Mazzei's Historical and Political Researches, in regard to the United States," by Hon. Simeon E. Baldwin.

DWIGHT E. BOWERS.

SONS OF THE AMERICAN REVOLUTION. The Connecticut Society of the Sons of the American Revolution, celebrated Washington's birthday for the sixth time, by a dinner at Norwich. The members of the Israel Putnam branch of the Society of Norwich, were the hosts of the occasion. During the morning the guests enjoyed the hospitalities of the Arcanum Club and had an opportunity to visit a special exhibit of paintings and colonial and revolutionary relics at the Slater museum. In the exhibit were included portraits by John Trumbull and Major Andre's letter to General Washington:

TAPPAN, Oct. 1, 1780.

Sir: Buoy'd above the terror of death by the consciousness of a life devoted to honourable pursuits and stained with no action that can give me remourse, I trust that the request that I make to Your Excellency at this serious period and which may soften my last moments, will not be rejected. Sympathy towards a soldier will surely induce Your Excellency a military tribunal to adapt the mode of my death to the feelings of a man of honor. Let me hope, sir, that if aught in my character impresses you with esteem towards me, if aught in my misfortune marks me as the victim of policy and not of resentment, I shall experience the operation of these feelings in your breast by being informed that I am not to die on a gibbet.

I have the honour to be Your Excellency's most obedient and most humble servant,
JOHN ANDRE,
Adj. Gen. to the British Army.
His Excellency General Washington.

The dinner was served in Lucas Hall at 1.30 p. m. and about two hundred members were present. Grace was said by the chaplain of the society, the Rev. E. H. Lines, of New Haven.

THE MENU.

Blue Point Oysters.
Radishes. Bouillon. Olives.
Boiled Kennebec river Salmon. Egg Sauce.
New Tomatoes. Celery.
Roast Turkey. Fillets of Beef.
Rice Croquettes. Potatoes. Cranberry.
Marmalade. Peas.
Chicken Salad
Roman Punch. Cigarettes.
Fruit. Cake. Confections.
Neapolitan Ice Cream.
Coffee. Crackers and Cheese. Cigars.

While the dinner was in progress, a large delegation from the Faith Trumbull branch of the Daughters of the Revolution appeared in the gallery and was received with applause.

After ample justice had been done to the menu, President Jonathan Trumbull called the assembly to order and introduced Dr. Robert P. Keep, who welcomed the guests in behalf of the Israel Putnam branch.

Judge Nathaniel Shipman, of Hartford, a son of Norwich, spoke with filial feeling to "The Old Town of Norwich." He opened by saying: "No man can do justice to Norwich; few men will undertake to do it, if they do, they will fail."

President Timothy Dwight of New Haven, also a son of Norwich, responded with delightful humor to "Good Old Yale." "In the revolution," said he, "Yale gave about one quarter part of all her graduates and students from 1765 to to 1781 to the American army."

"The Revival of Patriotism," was the subject treated by Colonel Norris G. Osborne, the brilliant editor of the New Haven Register.

Colonel Jacob L. Greene, of Hartford, read a scholarly paper on "The Duty of the Sons."

Mr. Walter Learned of New London, the poet, spoke to "The Day We Celebrate."

Captain Henry Goddard, a son of Norwich, formerly of Hartford, now of Baltimore, responded felicitously to "The South in the Revolution."

Mr. Bernard C. Steiner of Baltimore, but a son of Connecticut, librarian of the Pratt Free library, answered a call from the president. In the course of his answer he observed: "I have always felt that my two states of Connecticut and Maryland were states which on several occasions had lacked only one virtue, the virtue of self-protrusiveness."

The Hon. Edgar M. Warner of Putnam, made an appeal for the purchase and preservation of Putnam's Wolf-den.

The auditors indicated their pleasure by punctuating the remarks of all the speakers with frequent and hearty applause. The singing of "My Country, 'tis of Thee," closed the exercises.

Some hundreds of essays written by pupils of the schools of the state of Connecticut in competition for prizes offered by this society, have been received by the committee. It is expected that the prizes will be awarded on the anniversary of the battle of Lexington.

NOTES AND QUERIES.

SOCIETY OF THE DAUGHTERS OF THE REVOLUTION IN CONNECTICUT.

The chapters of the State were summoned to Meriden January 4, and assembled in the First Church. The attendance numbered several hundred, and the hospitality, graceful, particularly, if it is proper to make a discrimination, in the presence of a quartette of singers who, in giving old and new patriotic songs, brought out great enthusiasm.

Several subjects were introduced. One, the consideration of nominations of officers of the National Board, and for the office of State Regent. Another was a call for interest and actual investment in the Nathan Hale homestead in Coventry. This gave rise to the consideration of historic localities, and the attention paid to them. We learned of the interesting work of the Anna Warner Bailey Chapter of Groton and Stonington, in restoring and equipping, with a museum of relics, the Monument House, adjacent to the Groton Monument, which is dedicated to the heroes of the Fort Griswold massacre. The building was opened on the 113th anniversary of the battle.

January 4th was the day for a regular meeting of the Ruth Wyllys Chapter. The occasion was marked by the address of Rev. Dr. George Leon Walker on the " Old Hartford Burying Ground." It was written and printed in the hope that interest to improve the surroundings of the place might be aroused. The plan suggested is to purchase the strip of land called Gold street, "lucus e non lucendo" make a wide thoroughfare from Main to Lewis streets, giving a fine view of the park, and disposing of some most unsightly buildings.

At this meeting delegates were appointed to represent the Chapter in the Continental Congress.

This, the fourth of its kind, met in Washington, February 19, continuing through February 22.

The term of office of the State Regent having expired, Miss Susan B. Clark, was elected to the place. The new regent is from Middletown, where the first chapter in the state was organized.

Mrs. Keim, the retiring regent, was elected to the office of first Vice-President-General on a board of twenty. In a bright, patriotic address at the Congress she reported thirty-two Chapters in the state with a membership of 1.385 out of a national membership of 8,076, still holding her own as the banner state.

Julia Brattle Burbank

SOCIETY OF COLONIAL WARS.

The Third General Court of this Society will be held at the Connecticut Historical Society's rooms in Hartford, on Wednesday, May 1, 1895, at 3 o'clock in the afternoon, being the 258th Anniversary of the First General Court of the Colony of Connecticut held at Hartford on the first day of May. 1637 (O. S.), at which time the Sovereignty of the Colony was first asserted by the formal declaration of war against the nation of the Pequots. The annual election of officers, three successors to the members of the retiring class of the Council, and the Committees on Membership and Historical Documents will be held on this occasion. The meeting will adjourn in time to permit gentlemen to dress for dinner, which will be served at the Farmington Avenue Casino.

Chas. Sam'l Ward

Secretary.

NOTES AND QUERIES

" When found, make a note of."—CAPT. CUTTLE.

" It is a very sad thing that nowadays there is so little useless information."—ANON.

(In this department we propose to give genealogists a chance to settle mooted questions that arise in their researches. As space is valuable, a nominal charge of twenty-five cents for each query and its answer will be made,—neither to exceed ten lines. We welcome queries, notes on genealogical finds, new sources of data, and wish to keep a list of all genealogies in preparation by our readers.)

ABBOTT.—For this name see Hinman's "Puritan Settlers of Connecticut," Bond's "Watertown," (Mass.,) and "The Abbott Family" (1847). Robert Abbott came from England, to Watertown, thence to Watertown (Wethersfield,) Conn., 1641; juror in Hartford same year. Was a freeman of New Haven, 1642, and had land laid out in Branford, lived in New Haven till May, 1645. Name of wife and order of children unknown. Records of Branford taken to Newark, N. J., in 1665 and lost.

Seth Abbott, (supposed grandson of Robert the first, and probably a son of John or Daniel,) married, removed to Cornwall, Conn., and had Selah or Seeley, Nathan, Abel, Solomon, a son Seth or Samuel, Daniel, Sarah, and a daughter name unknown. The son Seth or Samuel is probably your ancestor, or the daughter name unknown may be Susannah. Seeley Abbott has descendants near Canistota, N. Y., of whom you can probably learn the facts.

BALDWIN.—Perhaps it may interest you to know that a bill is at present before the Legislature of the State " To establish Historical Localities." It is known as " Senate Joint Resolution No. 56," and is now in the hands of the Senate Judiciary Committee. A bill to mark forts and block-houses of early settlers prior to 1783, has passed the Pennsylvania legislature, and that body is now considering a proposition to expend $300 each in placing monuments upon the site of some 200 which have been selected by their commission

HENRY BALDWIN, New Haven, Conn.

BATTERSON.—Mary (Seeley) Battterson, I think, is probably daughter of Nathan and Deborah Seeley of Weston, Fairfield County, but am not certain. Would like to know if I am correct, and to know descent of her husband.

MRS. CLARA SEELEY PRINCE, 28 Vernon St., Hartford, Conn.

" My grandfather, Lebbeus Swords, married Reuamah (Ruhamah), Batterson, May 30, 1792. She was born October 23, 1765, and died July 9, 1835; was buried at Milltown, Putnam Co., N. Y., (near Danbury, Conn.) Can you inform me where she was born and where married. I think somewhere in Fairfield County.

J. F. SWORDS, 80 State St., Hartford, Conn.

BENJAMIN.—A descendant of Samuel Benjamin, senior, of Granby, Conn., informed the editor that he died in Granby in 1833 aged about 85, when he was a Rev. pensioner; and the easiest course to secure data is to write to the Pension Office, Washington, D. C., for a certified copy of all pension data relating to him which will be received as authentic by the S. A. R. The Rev. Roster of Conn., gives his services, but this is not exactly what is wanted.

BLAKESLEY.—BIRDSEYE.—CAMP.—FRANCIS. — Wanted, — Names of children of Samuel Blakesley, an original proprietor of Guilford; also of Eben. Blakesley, born 1664—Who was Rhoda, wife of Nathan Camp (4), of Milford and Durham, Joseph (3), Nicholas (2), Nicholas (1). Who was father of Joseph Francis of Wallingford, who married Sarah Hubbard June 8, 1726; first child Joseph, Jr., born June 11, 1728. Maiden names of the two wives of John Birdseye (4), Abel (3), John (2), John (1); Stratford records say "Hannah;" Middletown, "Sarah." He first appears in Middletown, 1734. Was second wife a Curtis?
MRS. G. W. CURTIS, Hartford, Conn.

CHAPMAN.—"I would say for those interested in family records and genealogies that the kindred 100ts of family names, (as carried through the various languages of Europe, etc.,) are often found under their proper heads in Webster's Unabridged and also in Prof. Whitney's Century Dictionary. This idea may help some in tracing out genealogies in all lands and in past ages. AARON B. CHAPMAN.
51 Hurlburt St., New Haven, Conn.
We never think of beginning a genealogy without first tracing the origin of the name in such works, also in Lower's "Patronymica Britannica," Wright's "Dictionary of Obsolete Words," Sir Isaac Taylor's works, "Names and Places," etc., and many more.

EDWARDS.—As a descendant of Jonathan Edwards's aunt, Ann, can you tell me where I can find data showing which of Richard's wives she was from? She married Jonathan Richardson, of Coventry, Conn.
F. L. HAMILTON, Meriden.
She was daughter of the first wife, viz.: Mary, Timothy, Abigail, Elizabeth, Ann, Mabel, and Martha. Six more children by second wife.

EDWARDS.—There has been for many years a large upright brown stone near the grave of Brainerd, to his "betrothed." I send you a copy of the inscription: "Jerusha, daughter of Jonathan and Sarah Edwards, born April 26, 1730, died Feb. 14, 1748. 'I shall be satisfied when I wake in thy likeness.'" The graves are in the old Northampton burial ground.
THOS. BRIDGMAN, Northampton, Mass.

FARRAND.—In a history of Norfolk it is stated, says a correspondent, that the Rev. Daniel Farrand, of South Canaan, was very kind to the Norfolk settlers, assisting them in various ways before they had a pastor, and helped organize their church, 1758-9. The Editor would like the names of his mother and grandmother, the wives of Nathaniel Farrand, Sr., and Jr., of Milford, Conn.

HALE.—The only connection that I remember of the Hales with the Millers was in this way: David Hale (son of Jonathan, of Samuel, of Samuel), was born June 11, 1727, married Mary Welles, and had a daughter Mabel who married Elijah Miller, all of Glastonbury, where some of the grand-children of Elijah and Mabel (Hale) Miller still live."
EDWARD WHITE HALE, Wethersfield, Conn.

MILLER.—Ancestors of Rev. Samuel Miller, pastor of Baptist Church, Wallingford and Meriden 23 years, whose son Rev. Harvey, filled same pulpit 18 years. Rev. Samuel had nine sons of whom Joel was father of Edward Miller, of Meriden; Rev. Samuel and Rev. Thomas, were sons of Jacob Miller and Eliz. (Fyler) of East Hampton, L. I., of Revolutionary times. Can Jacob be traced to the first John who came from Lynn, Mass., to East Hampton.
MRS. E. C. B. CURTIS, Hartford, Conn.

PECK —SANFORD.—DICKINSON.—DAYTON. Name and ancestry of wife of William Peck, born Hartford, 1686, son of Paul and grandson of Deacon Paul. Her name is given as Lois Webster, but this is probably incorrect. Name and ancestry of wife of John Sanford, Jr., (born New Haven, 1710) son of John Sanford and Hannah. Ancestry of Michael Dickinson of Litchfield, who married Abigail Catlin in 1765, daughter of Thomas and Abigail (Bissell) Catlin. Name and ancestry of the wife of Isaac Dayton, born 1720, died 1800, son of Isaac and Elizabeth (Todd) Dayton, and grandson of Isaac Dayton. GUY D. PECK, Greenwich, Conn.

SANFORD.—If the gentleman inquiring about the Atwaters will write Hon. W. C. Atwater, mayor of Derby, Conn, he may find what he seeks. There is also an Atwater family history which is scarce, and considerable about them in the Tuttle Family. The Editor of Notes and Queries, has collected considerable as to the English Atwaters, as they came from Kent, were near neighbors of the Hales, and intermarried with them. The Atwater book and Tuttle book have no answer to your query. We think it must have been Sarah, daughter of either John or Moses Atwater, of Wallingford. The Sanfords are given very fully in Todd's Redding and Mrs. Schenck's Fairfield, but no Mabel.—EDITOR.

SHEPARD.—As to the queries, when in a magazine like yours, they are perpetual. I have had letters in answer to an advertisement that was fifteen years old. In Wallingford, the other day, I found that a Dr. John Hull had sons John, Peter and Nimrod, names corresponding with three of the names on Hospital Rock. JAMES SHEPARD, New Britain.

Mr. H. P. Hitchcock informed us that Jeffrey O. Phelps, Senior, of Simsbury, was a Hospital Rock patient.—ED.

TUTTLE.—Can you trace the ancestors of Cecilia Moore, the wife of Timothy Tuttle, of Whippany, N. J., to determine if she has any "Dame of the Colonial period in her sufficient nose, to admit my daughter into the Society of the Colonial Dames."
REV. JOSEPH FARRAND TUTTLE,
Ex-Pres't. Wabash University,
Crawfordsville, Indiana.

BOOK NOTICES.

The ARMS PUBLISHING CO. is meeting with a ready sale for its "Continuous Family Genealogy" from all parts of the country, which shows that the importance of keeping family records is being more thoroughly realized, and that the subject of genealogy is becoming interesting in increasing ratio-everywhere. There is a demand for a practical and convenient book for permanent records, and this work meets all requirements. Their advertisement will be found on the front cover.

"Brook Farm, Historical and Personal Memoirs," by Dr. John Thomas Codman. (Arena Publishing Co, Boston), treats of the famous Brook-Farm experiment in communism, at West Roxbury, Mass., of George Ripley, Nathanel Hawthorne, Dr. Codman and others. We have had accounts in brief, or incidentally, of this undertaking, but nowhere has it been treated so fully or so carefully as in this book. It was in no sense a failure, for as the late George William Curtis said; "It is to the Transcendentalism, that seemed to so many good souls both wicked and absurd, that some of the best influences of American life to-day are due. The spirit that was concentrated at Brook Farm is diffused but not lost." The author of "Margaret Salisbury" adds: "It is a history that every thinking mind must value. Those noble souls who formed the little colony had the just idea; they lived a generation or two ahead of the masses. The trend of humanity is in their direction." We cannot help thinking that if the experiment were tried to-day again, it would succeed, with as good men at the helm: Ripley, one of the early editors of the *Tribune*, the veteran Dana of the *Sun*, Dwight, of "*Dwight's Journal of Music*," Curtis, and several others. It was here "the embattled farmers stood, and fired the shot heard round the world," in our own day and generation,—the most marvelous marksmanship of the present century!

We are indebted to the Board of Education for its report for 1894-'95, one of the most thorough and comprehensive state reports on the subject of education we have ever seen. It is very full on library, kindergarten and normal schools, manual training, private schools, and even cooking schools, proving that our Board is fully abreast of the times. It is to be commended for the interest taken in libraries.

Dr. Hoadly's latest addition to the archives of our Commonwealth has been received: "Records of the State of Connecticut, 1776--1777." This is the first of a series that will be carried down, probably to the time of the State Constitution, 1787, according to an act of the Assembly, if health and strength are given to the doctor to complete his task. Dr. Hoadly was born in 1828, graduated at Trinity, 1851, studied law but never practiced, and forty years ago, this April, began his duties as State librarian. In that time he has edited the New Haven Colonial Records (1638 to 1665 in two volumes, and the Colonial Records of Connecticut, volumes 4 to 15 (1689 to 1775), which was completed in 1877. The present volume is especially valuable to all who are looking up the services of Revolutionary ancestors.

"Stephen Lincoln, of Oakham, Mass.: His Ancestry and Descendants," compiled by Mr. John E. Morris, of this city, is a little volume of over 100 pages, giving portrait of Stephen Lincoln from a pencil sketch, and pictures of his old homestead at Oakham. He was a soldier in the Revolutionary war. Mr. Morris's plan is to trace the Lincolns of Hingham down to Stephen, then all the maternal and intermarried lines of his ancestry in all directions, tracing back from him to the first settlers and many lines running into the old country. Part II is devoted to the descendants of Stephen to the present day. In this "hour-glass" way, a genealogy may be compacted into 100 pages, without attempting to give all the descendants of an emigrant ancestor, which is a voluminous task. The blanks prepared by the editor of this department are peculiarly fitted for this method of compilation. Mr. Morris is a veteran compiler of genealogies,—the "Bontecou Genealogy" in 1885, "The Ancestry of Daniel Bontecou" in 1887, the "Resseguie Family" in 1888, (all old Huguenot families, and the "Felt Genealogy," 1893, as well as the present work. He is singularly well adapted to this work, which fills up a great deal of his leisure, being a thorough, painstaking, and untiring delver into antiquity, and his works are marvels of system and precision.

IN THE LINE OF ANNOUNCEMENTS:

For the remainder of the year, we shall publish; (not necessarily in the following order however):

SHORT BEACH AND "THE BUNGALOW," BY GARDNER A. RECKARD,
the artist, who will write of this favorite resort of New Haven and Meriden people, and illustrate it with some of his own paintings, including a fine frontispiece, and charming interior views of the "Bungalow," the summer home of Mrs. Ella Wheeler Wilcox.

CANTON, BY HON. WILLIAM EDGAR SIMONDS.
This graphic paper will delight all residents of Canton, the author's summer residence, with which he is familiar in all its aspects.

NORWALK AS A SUMMER RESIDENCE, BY HON. A. H. BYINGTON,
the well-known editor of the Norwalk Gazette, Washington correspondent, etc., who will describe Norwalk of which he is the recognized local historian.

CLINTON, BY MISS ELLEN BRAINERD PECK,
the poet, who will portray in a pleasing style, this modest and picturesque shore resort; it will be illustrated by fine prize views taken by the Rev. C. E. Barto, of Clinton.

BITS FROM GREAT GRANDMOTHER'S DIARY, BY MRS. ELLEN STRONG BARTLETT,
late of New Britain, details the reminiscences of her great-grandmother, who lived in Farmington and died a few years since at an advanced age. It gives a full insight into curious Colonial and Revolutionary customs, and will prove very interesting.

A LETTER FROM A REPENTANT ROYALIST, BY MISS ELLEN D. LARNED,
the historian of Windham County. This letter, dated April 13, 1784, affords another quaint glimpse of Revolutionary days, and, like its predecessor, will be welcomed by all antiquarians and historians.

THE "HENRY LEE" ARGONAUTS OF '49, BY FRANK LORENZO HAMILTON,
of Meriden, comes down almost to the present day, and treats in a pleasant, humorous manner of a party of gold seekers who went around the "Horn" in 1849, including some notable Hartford and Meriden people. It will be illustrated with portraits. This will be followed at a later date by

THE "WIDE AWAKES" OF '61, BY MAJOR JULIUS G. RATHBUN,
of Hartford, who was one of the original members and lieutenants, and accompanied this now historic party on all their patriotic forays and merry outings.

OLD TIME MUSIC AND MUSICIANS, BY PROF. N. H. ALLEN,
of Hartford, the Nestor among Hartford musicians, who has for a long time been preparing this interesting series of papers, which will commence in our Midsummer issue. He is peculiarly fitted for this work and with him it is truly a labor of love. It details the old days of psalmody, the introduction of instruments, (the spinet, harpsichord, virginals,) the quaint customs of old choirs and singers, and is replete with anecdotes and reminiscences of all the old musicians which he has carefully treasured.

MEMORIES OF MERIDEN, BY MRS. FRANCES A. BRECKENRIDGE,
of that city, a facile and interesting writer, favorably known for her historical and antiquarian contributions to the local press. It will be splendidly illustrated by fine views of the "Silver City."

POMFRET, BY HON. JOHN ADDISON PORTER,
editor of the Hartford Daily Post, who has promised a paper on his picturesque summer home in Windham County.

The present serial features will be continued during the present year, viz:

THE HARTFORD PARK SYSTEM,
of which the third paper, by Mr. H. W. Benjamin, will include "THE POPE AND POND PARKS," and the fourth, by Mr. James Shepard, "THE RESERVOIR PARK," to be concluded with a final paper by Judge S. W. Adams.

HISTORIC HOMES
will soon complete the Hartford list, and then be transferred to some other city.

TRIO AND TRIPOD,
will continue the amusing exploits of our trio of artists in traversing the State.

OLD COLONIAL CHARACTERS,
will grow more interesting as it advances, giving the pathetic careers of Aaron Burr and his beautiful daughter, Theodosia.

SCROPE
will increase in interest as it becomes localized in this State and present many amusing episodes.

In addition we shall publish STERLING STORIES, PLEASING POEMS, ATTRACTIVE DEPARTMENTS, FULL REPORTS OF SOCIETIES AND SCHOOLS, and numerous other new features.

THE CONNECTICUT QUARTERLY.

THE
WM. H. POST
CARPET CO.
1850-1894.

NEW STORE,

219 Asylum St.,
HARTFORD, - CONN.

Housefurnishing Specialties.

THE
WM. H. POST
CARPET CO.
(INCORPORATED.)

WM. H. POST,
President.
(Late WM. H. POST & Co.)

WM. STRONG POST,
Vice-Pres. and Sec.
(Late with RONX & Co., 5th Ave., New York.)

ARCHIE L. WHITING,
Treasurer.
(Late BROWN, THOMPSON & Co.)

Carpets, Draperies, Lace Curtains.

To Furnish your House Well,

Is more a matter of good taste and good judgment than a lavish expenditure of money.

STANDARD QUALITIES RECOMMENDED.   PRICES GUARANTEED.

THE WM. H. POST CARPET CO.,
New Stores: 219 Asylum and 15 Haynes Sts.

Please Mention THE CONNECTICUT QUARTERLY.

VISIT
THE BARTLETT TOWER,
TARIFFVILLE.

AND ENJOY ONE OF THE FINEST AND MOST EXTENSIVE OF NEW ENGLAND VIEWS— REACHING FROM NORTHERN MASSACHUSETTS TO SOUTHERN CONNECTICUT. EMBRACING BOTH FARMINGTON AND CONNECTICUT RIVER VALLEYS.

Excursion Tickets sold daily at Station of Phila. Reading and Central N. E. R. R., Hartford, good on all Passenger trains leaving Hartford, for one or more passengers stopping at Tower Station; where conveyance one-third of a mile, will, if desired, be furnished to Tower.

**TICKETS, 75 Cents both ways.
Children, 50 Cents.**

Including Tower Conveyance from Station to Tower, 10 cents.

Wednesdays and Saturdays, cheap days. **Excursion Tickets, 50 cents.**

Excursion Tickets also sold including Old Newgate.

M. H. BARTLETT, Prop.

McLean Seminary,
SIMSBURY, CONN.

"Shall we send our girls away from home to be educated?" This is a question which arises annually in the heart of many a parent, anxious for the best future of the child.

This query is not confined to those living at a distance from good schools. There are reasons why home, with all its advantages, is not always the best place for study; and parents often see the wisdom, sometimes the necessity, of sending their children away.

In America, the demands of society commence almost with childhood. Our youths must have their parties and receptions, receive and return calls, do their part in mission and church work, assist in fairs, festivals and amateur theatricals, attend concerts, lectures, and often theaters, operas and balls.

This constant interruption of study, and the great draft upon time and strength, break up all system and defeat the purpose and plans of the wisest teacher.

The frequent failure of health among young ladies is not alone due, as sometimes asserted, to over pressure of study, so much as to the attempt to combine a course of study with society life.

With regular habits of study and recreation, plenty of out-door exercise, pure air, wholesome food and sleep, a large amount of work can be accomplished with no danger to health.

The McLean Seminary offers advantages of a Superior Home School.

For Catalogue giving full particulars, address;

REV. J. B. McLEAN,
SIMSBURY, CT.

Fertiline.

**Liquid Plant Food—Odorless—
Easily Applied. Very
Effective.**

This article comes in liquid form and a small application every two weeks makes a wonderful change in appearance, besides increasing the blossoms. Ask your florist for it.

Lucien Sanderson,
Sole Proprietor,

NEW HAVEN, CONN.

VISIT . .
OLD NEWGATE PRISON
THIS SEASON.

**SEASON OPENS MAY 15, CLOSES
OCT. 15. CLOSED SUNDAYS.**

The Prison and Convict Caverns are wonderfully interesting. Experienced attendants, accommodations for picnic parties and good tennis court. Beautiful views from observatory covering a distance of seventy miles.

It is probable that a room of the old keeper's house will be devoted to a collection of valuable relics pertaining to the prison and revolutionary war. Everything will be done this season, to make it pleasant for visitors.

Excursion Tickets will be sold from Hartford to parties of four or more, at a low rate, including R. R. fare, admission to Bartlett's Tower, admission to Newgate, and conveyance to and from Tower to Newgate. It is expected that trains will stop at Copper Hill on the Northampton Div. of the N. Y. N. H. & H. R. R. during the season, a short walk from Newgate.

People wishing a complete history can secure one by sending 70 cents to the proprietor. Also souvenir books of sixteen views at 25 and 50 cents.

For further particulars, address:

S. D. VIETS, Prop.,
COPPER HILL, CONN.

Please mention THE CONNECTICUT QUARTERLY.

> *Many of the illustrations found in this issue are selected from the territory traversed by the Philadelphia, Reading & New England Railroad.*
>
> *If you contemplate summering in the country you will find that for health, pleasure and convenience Litchfield County and the Southern Berkshire has no equal.*
>
> *For a list of hotels, boarding houses, etc., procure a copy of our summer home book, containing upwards of 60 illustrations giving all information. The summer home book will be ready for free distribution at city ticket offices after April 16th, or will be mailed on receipt of 4 cents postage to*
>
> W. J. MARTIN,
> Gen'l Passenger Agent, Hartford, Conn.

1851   After Forty=four Years   1895

of business, **The Phoenix Mutual Life Insurance Company of Hartford, Connecticut,** is Stronger, Safer and Better than ever before.

Do not insure your life until you have seen our liberal contracts, embracing Extended Insurance, Loan, Cash and Paid-up values. The most liberal contracts issued by any life insurance company in the world. For sample policies, address the Home Office, Hartford, Conn.

JONATHAN B. BUNCE, President.
JOHN M. HOLCOMBE, Vice-President.
CHARLES H. LAWRENCE, Secretary.

The Springs of Connecticut,

Highland TONICA Water.

Has never failed to prove its value when used according to directions.

Note this Comparative Analysis.

HIGHLAND TONICA	THE HUMAN BLOOD
Contains in its natural state:	in its natural state contains:
Potassium, Lime,	Potassium, Lime,
Lime, Magnesia,	Lime, Magnesia,
Manganese,	Manganese,
Phosphoric Acid, Iron.	Phosphoric Acid, Iron.

A. W. K. NEWTON, M. D:—

"I have advised it for a large number of my patients. The effect has been wonderful."

Highland Rock Water,

"THE CLIMAX OF TABLE WATERS"

Is the purest ever analyzed.

CORRESPONDENCE INVITED.

The Tonica Springs Co.,

"HIGHLAND PARK,"   MANCHESTER, CONN.

HARTFORD AGENTS:
T. SISSON & CO., Main St.
TALCOTT, FRISBIE & CO., Asylum St.

The Life and Endowment Policies

—— OF ——

The Travelers

of Hartford, Conn.

Are the Best in the Market. Non=Forfeitable and World=Wide.

━━━ FORMS.

REGULAR LIFE.—The original and commonest sure way of leaving one's heirs in comfort instead of destitute. Even a mechanic can easily leave a fair estate behind him.

LIMITED=PAYMENT.—Concentrating payment into the working years of a man's life, and leaving him free from worry even if he is helpless.

REGULAR ENDOWMENTS.—Payable to the insured himself after a term of years, or to his family if he dies before the end of the term. The only means by which most men can save money for themselves.

ANNUITY PLAN.—Cheapest of all, and the only sure way of furnishing a regular income. Applied to either of the other forms. Principal sum payable in installments instead of in a lump, either to the insured (if Endowment) or his beneficiaries. If desired, they will be written so that in case of insured's death before the installments are all paid, his beneficiaries will receive the value of the remainder at once.

COMBINED LIFE AND ACCIDENT.—Combining any of these with weekly indemnity for disabling accident.

Also the Largest Accident Company in the World.

<u>LARGER</u> than ALL OTHERS in America together.

ASSETS, $17,664,000.   SURPLUS, $2,472,000.

Paid Policy-holders, over $27,000,000—$2,151,000 in 1894 alone.

———

JAMES G. BATTERSON, President.
RODNEY DENNIS, Secretary.

Most of them have been here

PRACTICAL
UP TO DATE
EDUCATION.

MORSE'S
ACTUAL
BUSINESS.

Hartford's Leading Business Men.

| 1895 | ARTISTIC PATTERNS | 1895 |

—— IN ——

FURNITURE

For the HALL, LIBRARY, RECEPTION ROOM, DINING ROOM and CHAMBER.

FINE REPRODUCTIONS FROM
Antique and Colonial Designs.

N. B.—Special attention given to the restoration of Antique Furniture.

LINUS T. FENN,

205 Main Street,   =   =   HARTFORD, CONN.

R. S. Peck & Co., Printers, Hartford, Conn.

Vol. 1 July, Aug., Sept., 1895. No. 3

THE Connecticut Quarterly.

THIS NUMBER CONTAINS

ILLUSTRATED ARTICLES

— ON —

Clinton,   Canton,
Norwalk,   Historic Homes,
Highland Park, Trio and Tripod,
Ella Wheeler Wilcox and the Bungalow,
The Henry Lee Argonauts of 1849,

And other valuable and interesting historical matter.

SEE CONTENTS ON FIRST PAGE.

50c. a Year   Hartford, Conn.   15c. a Copy

Connecticut General

LIFE INSURANCE CO.

HARTFORD, CONN.

Assets, January 1, 1895, ... $2,702,953.23

Liabilities, ... 2,159,308.08

Surplus to Policy-Holders, by Conn. and Mass. standard, . 543,645.15

Of which $289,548.69 is a special reserve due to Savings Endowment Policies.

THOMAS W. RUSSELL, *President.*

F. V. HUDSON, *Secretary.*

WHITE OAK.
Between PLAINVILLE AND NEW BRITAIN, on the N. Y. & N. E. R. R., and Central Railway and Electric Co.

Picnic Grounds for Sunday Schools.

An admirable place for Sunday-School Picnics—Boating, Swings, Flying Horses, Photo. Gallery, Restaurant, &c., &c. Large and Beautiful Grove. Ample accommodations for all. Special rates made for Excursion Parties from all points on the New England Road. Apply to Local Ticket Agents. Electric Cars from New Britain, Plainville and Berlin. Fare, 5 Cents.

...THE...
Connecticut Quarterly.

An Illustrated Magazine.

DEVOTED TO THE LITERATURE, HISTORY, AND PICTURESQUE FEATURES OF CONNECTICUT.

PUBLISHED QUARTERLY
By THE CONNECTICUT QUARTERLY COMPANY,
66 State Street, Courant Building,
HARTFORD, CONN.

GEO. C. ATWELL, General Manager.   W. FARRAND FELCH, Editor.

CONTENTS.

Vol. 1   July, August, September, 1895.   No. 3.

Frontispiece. "SHIPS THAT PASS IN THE NIGHT."		218
Bungalow Bay. From a painting by Gardner A. Reckard.		
Ella Wheeler Wilcox and the Bungalow.	*Gardner A. Reckard.*	219
Illustrated from paintings by Gardner A. Reckard.		
Sea Glow. Poem.	*F. C. H. Wendel.*	228
The Henry Lee Argonauts of 1849. Illustrated.	*Frank Lorenzo Hamilton.*	229
Clinton, once Killingworth. Illustrated.	*Ellen Brainerd Peck.*	233
Canton. Illustrated.	*Hon. William E. Simonds.*	239
Trio and Tripod. III. TO THE HARTLANDS VIA NEWGATE.	*George H. Carrington.*	250
Illustrated.		
Bits from Great-Grandmother's Journal.	*Mrs. Ellen Strong Bartlett.*	265
A Tribute to our Dead Poets. Poem.	*Louis E. Thayer.*	270
A Letter from a Repentant Royalist.	*Ellen D. Larned.*	271
Old Time Music and Musicians.	*N. H. Allen.*	274
A Midsummer Dream. Poem.	*Willard Warner.*	280
Ancient and Modern Norwalk. Illustrated.	*Hon. A. H. Byington.*	281
Historic Homes. III. HOMES OF STATE CRAFT. Illustrated.	*W. Farrand Felch.*	288
Highland Park, Manchester. Illustrated.	*Marie De Valcherville.*	298
A Day Dream. Poem. Illustrated.	*Clement C. Calverley.*	302
Scrópe; or the Lost Library: Serial.	*Frederic Beecher Perkins.*	303

DEPARTMENTS.

The Round Table.	*The Editor.*	307
Every Man an Antiquity.—Love of Nature.—A Word of Praise.		
Treasure Trove.	*"Algernon."*	310
The Half-way Covenant.—Connecticut Historical Society's Collections.—The Connecticut Society of the Sons of the American Revolution.—The Loyal Legion.—The Society of Colonial Wars.—Connecticut Historical Society.		
Sociology and Civics.	*"Solon."*	313
Connecticut Humane Society.—"The Fabian Essays."—The Messiah of the Apostles.		
Notes and Queries.		313

Copyright 1895 by THE CONNECTICUT QUARTERLY CO. (*All rights reserved.*)
Entered at the Post Office at Hartford, Conn., as mail matter of the second class.

IN THE LINE OF ANNOUNCEMENTS:

For the next issue we beg to submit the following "Menu":

MEMORIES OF MERIDEN, BY MRS. FRANCES A. BRECKINRIDGE.
The well-known writer, "Faith," of the Meriden press, will deal in a bright gossipy style with the "Silver City," in its early days, down to the last generation.

PICTURESQUE POMFRET, BY HON. JOHN ADDISON PORTER,
editor of the Hartford Post, who has kindly consented to give a graphic survey of the town he has chosen for a summer home.

THE HARTFORD PARK SYSTEM, IV. THE POPE AND POND PARKS, BY MR. HOWARD W. BENJAMIN
will resume the story of our picturesque chain of parks, illustrated with photographs by the author, and several drawings by Mr. Geo. F. Stanton, of Hartford.

TRIO AND TRIPOD, BY GEORGE H. CARRINGTON,
his facetious chronicle of our artists' pilgrimage will bring the party down the Connecticut Valley from Hartland to Bristol.

THE WIDE AWAKES OF 1860, BY MAJOR JULIUS G. RATHBUN,
of Hartford, one of the prime movers of this historic company, will detail its amusing history.

OLD TIME MUSIC AND MUSICIANS, BY PROF. N. H. ALLEN,
will be continued down to more recent days, treat of the introduction of musical instruments and the inauguration of church choirs.

YALE BOYS OF THE LAST CENTURY, BY MISS ELLEN D. LARNED,
will give extracts from some amusing college journals of the last century which prove that "Boys will be Boys," and were even in the old days.

OLD COLONIAL CHARACTERS, BY "FELIX OLDMIXON,"
will develop the romantic career of Aaron Burr and his beautiful daughter, Theodosia.

"THE GIRL FROM MASSACHUSETTS," BY MISS PAULINE PHELPS,
of Simsbury, is a pathetic little story of admirable local coloring, written especially for our pages, by this clever young writer, which will be welcomed by her many admirers.

AN ARTICLE ON NEW BRITAIN,
will be a welcomed addition, to be followed later on, by other articles on this enterprising little city.

SPECIAL ATTENTION WILL BE GIVEN TO NEW HAVEN
during the coming year; and finely illustrated articles will be presented, by MISS ELLEN 'STRONG BARTLETT, HON. JOHN ADDISON PORTER, and others are promised.

The usual DEPARTMENTS, POETRY, "SCROPE," and other interesting features, from time to time, will appear.

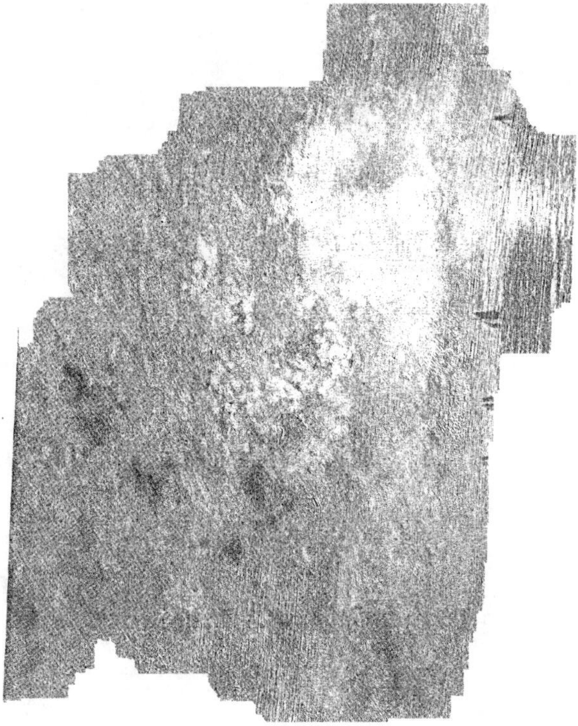

The Connecticut Quarterly.

"Leave not your native land behind."—Thoreau.

THIRD QUARTER.

Vol. 1   July, August and September, 1895.   No. 3.

ELLA WHEELER WILCOX AND THE BUNGALOW

BY GARDNER ARNOLD RECKARD.

  To a native of Short Beach, one of the most familiar questions propounded by the visitors to that breezy retreat is the query, "Where is the Bungalow?" This question from young and old, women and men, romantic misses and hard-featured elderly persons who would not be suspected of sentiment, indicates that all sorts and conditions of men and women are interested in the fair mistress of the Bungalow, and are curious to see the manner of house she inhabits.
  And surely few poets enjoy so ideal a home, with environments so inspiring to the muse, so artistic to the eye, so restful without a chance for a dull moment. But, before we enter the great stone gates, with their guardian griffins of bronze, it would be well to mention, parenthetically, that Short Beach is blessed in its location and in its public spirited and vigilant residents; there are no saloons, tramps, loafers, billionaires, or other public nuisances. The town is situated on a picturesque horse-shoe of golden sand, studded with bold rocks of pink and gray. On the west are the highest cliffs rising directly from the water, on the Atlantic coast from Key West, Florida, to the Thimble Islands. Midway between the points of the horse-shoe, is situated the Wilcox estate, and having passed the gates we enter Bungalow Court.

The Bungalow, like a great pelican perched upon its rocky home, has for its companions four cottages on the shore side of the lawn, like a row of "Mother Carey's chickens." These belong to the Wilcoxes, and are cosy cots, named "Sea-lawn, Mid-lawn, Rock-lawn and Oak-lawn," and are occupied by people of the literary, musical and artistic world who thus share a part of the Bungalow life; their relations being fraternal rather than financial. It is therefore a frequent occurrence for them to meet in the Bungalow and to contribute to the general fund of amusement, by music, song and the other accomplishments, and to join in the impromptu dances which almost nightly, in the height of the season, are liable to occur.

Imagine a great leviathan, stranded upon a pebbly beach, around which remnants of a former forest grew, with green grass almost to the water's edge,

THE BUNGALOW.

and a bay of sapphire stretching before you for a mile, where it is merged into the darker waters of the sound. Consider, then, the rock upon which the Bungalow is built as that leviathan; upon its gray back stands the house twenty-five feet above the water. The winds buffet it, and the angry waves thunder in impotent fury against its rocky base, the hurricanes lash it with the spray of the surf in vain. From the windows of the house you can look out, on stormy days, as you might from the windows of a light-house, observing the tremendous workings of the sea and wind. In stormy weather, one hears musical notes swelling like an organ through the wind-harps swinging in the breeze, then as they madly turn they blare as the wind increases, a strange weird accompaniment to the shrieking demons of the storm.

The front of the house faces the bay and sound to the south, and is reached by steps cut and built in the rock, or on the east side by means of a natural stair-way of rock which was left without any artificial touches, and with the rugged storm-torn cedars clinging in the crevices. The Bungalow was built, so to speak, by letter, Mr. Wilcox being absent. The writer of this article, who superintended the construction of the building, was happy in having a man of Mr. Wilcox's artistic temperament as a coadjutor; consequently not a tree was cut down, nor a rock chipped or blasted that was not actually in the way.

People living inland can hardly estimate the value of a tree at the sea-side, where their growth within a few feet of the salt water is so much retarded by storms and salt spray: so trees and sea and rocks are quite a precious and infrequent combination on the water's edge. Crossing the verandah, you enter the house through an oak Colonial door, with its quaint fastenings and latch; it

"THE FIRE-PLACE."

is as sound as the day it was made in Branford, one hundred years ago. If I were to pen a verse to place above this door, I should write,—

"Abandon care, all ye who enter here."

Having reached the old door, we give two or three resounding thumps on the old knocker, and if we listen will surely hear a cheerful, awe-dispelling voice bid us enter; and we raise the latch and find ourselves in a large room, full of vivid oriental color. Yes, the poet is in her "corner" and comes forward. She is a woman of gracious mein; she is clad in some diaphanous garment of East Indian fabrication; the effect is oriental, but for her fair complexion, and the gold-red glint of the Anglo-Celt in the hair. You find that her greeting is oriental, too, for she and her genial husband are as hospitable as Arabs. She does not consider that a literary reputation should make one haughty and depressing to others, but lives up to her famous verse,—

"Laugh and the world laughs with you;
Weep, and you weep alone."

And now that the introduction is over, you will doubtless find much to interest you in her abode, both in the plan of the interior, which is unique, and in the objects of art, curios, and books without number. You find that the room occupies nearly half of the ground floor, and that there is no ceiling to it; that although the day elsewhere is hot and unbearable, owing to the presence of water on three sides and the lofty room with dormer windows as ventilators, it is delightfully cool in this house. The other rooms are of course ceiled, but the space above, opening as it does into the front and screened by great rattan portieres, precludes the possibility of heat. It is the coolest house on the Sound, by virtue of its construction, and location.

No inky raven of insomnia to croak "Nevermore" above sleepless couches, on hot summer nights! The brow is fanned by zephyrs and a musical cadence of the lapping waves is the lullaby that brings sleep, — deep as that of childhood. Even your conscience cannot keep you awake at Short Beach, ordinarily — in the Bungalow, never. A conscience is a needless thing there; you might as well leave it in New York, Hartford or Boston, for all the good it would do you, for you could not live in the Bungalow and be wicked or unhappy: the thought is preposterous! You could not be an atheist, for no one would believe you or listen to you, in the presence of so much of God's creation; nor extremely orthodox, because no one would want to die and risk the harp-playing of Jones or Deacon Smith, while they could lie here in a hammock and listen to that Æolian harp; nor swear, for there is no cooking, and so no flies; nor covet your neighbor's property; nor steal — for you want nothing you haven't already.

Mr. Wilcox has been a great traveler in many parts

MOONLIGHT.

of the world, an indefatigable collector, and has many rare and beautiful curios. On one side of the big room, on a Navajo blanket, is a fine collection of American Indian relics. On the other, above a large and luxurious divan, is another of oriental arms and armor, — from a Damascus blade to a murderous, double-bladed dagger; curious wallets, with Mohammedan prayers on parchment; a rug from inaccessible Thibet; a strange little straw-and-wicker-gate to the stairway in the corner leading to the upper library, comes from Corea. Each corner, as well as each central panel, is instructive; over the piano a Bedouin tent; the south-east corner is the poet's own, containing a desk and a great ink stand that holds a quart: she evidently believes in plenty of ammunition, but like a good soldier she does not waste it.

The writer's memory lingers around the great open fire-place, with its andirons piled with huge chestnut logs,—drift-wood—that throws so radiant a light that the beautiful Viennese lanterns are extinguished in order that we may enjoy the genial glow the better; perhaps the autumn wind may be wailing, the waves beating on the rocks with a sullen roar; the small boats are safe behind the little break-water, the large ones, including the naphtha launch, "Robella," are anchored in the straits. All is snug alow and aloft, on sea and shore. Now, warmth and good cheer are at their height, for gathered around that glow are choice spirits of the literary or artistic world. Then it is that wit sparkles as it flies, and repartee from lip to lip is bandied like a shuttle-cock; while droll humor eggs on wit; or, if the wind moans and shrieks more dolefully than is its wont, and the drift-wood burns low and sheds a ghastly blue, then perchance some actor-friend may tell us some ghostly story that chills the marrow and makes our nervous friend throw on a pine-knot after the climax is reached; or maybe we hear the history of some book, old or new —how it went from publisher to publisher, from rejection to dejection, —how all has changed and the publisher (the ruffian) now has to grovel in the dust before the superior genius of "so and so;" or perhaps a thrilling yarn of the sea is told by some old "sea-dog;" or it may be Wilder, doing the balcony-scene from Romeo and Juliet, from the improvised balcony on the stairs.

Copyright, 1895, by Rockwood.
ELLA WHEELER WILCOX.

But, oh! the magnificent sunsets from the verandah; and the delightful languorous evenings, so frequent yet never commonplace, when the moon is more like a soft, subdued sun, so brilliant is it, and the gentle ripple made by the soft night breeze throwing a sparkle as of countless millions of diamonds in the moon's path. At such a

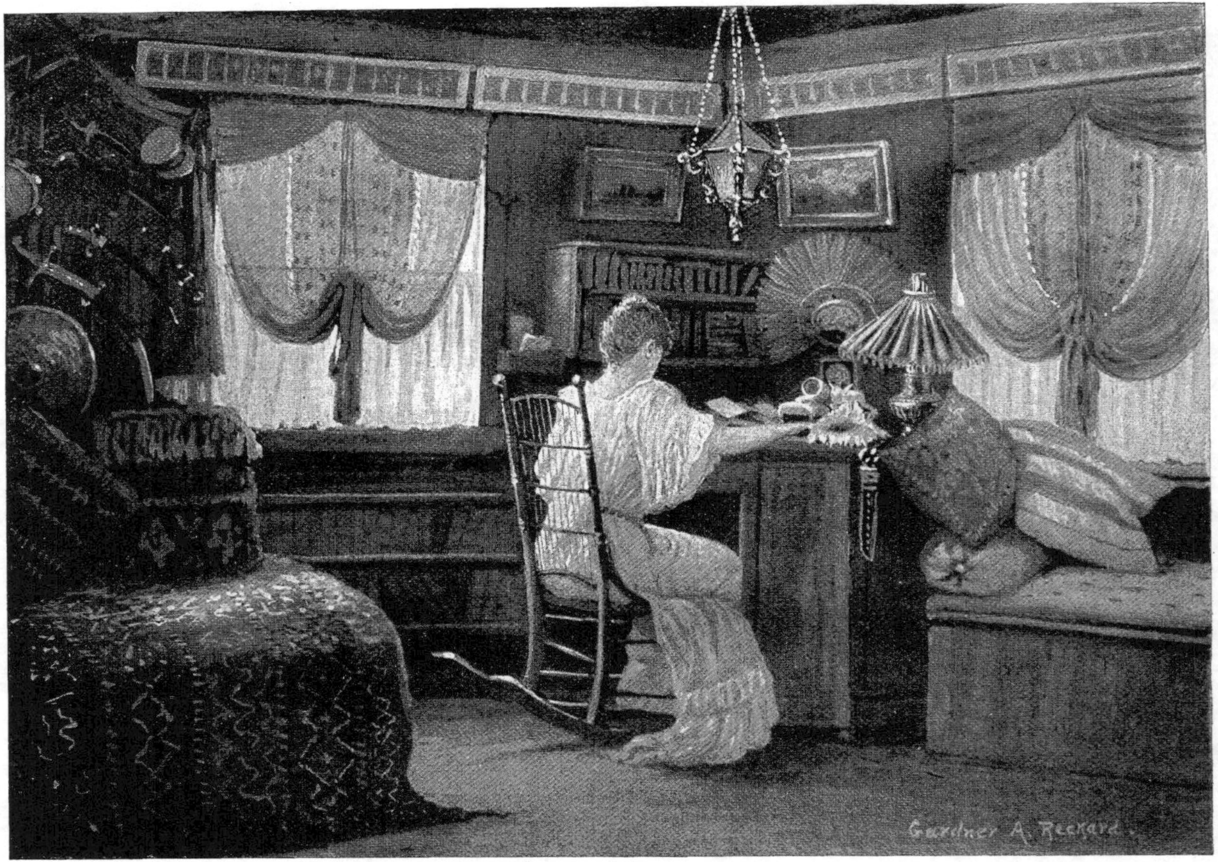
Gardner A. Reckard.

time, we may be rowed by some sons of Neptune, or in the swift launch, while the mandolins and banjos make troubadour music, as we glide in and out among the enchanted islands. On this little peninsula, the spectator always has a view of the rising and setting of the sun and moon across the water, thus having the full benefit of the gorgeous colors repeated in the mirror of the bay.

Naturally the Bungalow Hop is the event of the social season, by reason of the prominence of the hostess, and because there is an unusual number of dancing men present, which of course is proof positive that there is sure to be a bevy of pretty girls. One of Mrs. Wilcox's weaknesses is an extraordinary fondness for handsome girls, a fondness shared, as all of her pleasures are, by Mr. Wilcox — a reasonable weakness, a mild form of nympholepsy, most likely — shared too, by the writer, so he does not hesitate to appreciate the feast to the artistic eye which spreads itself through the Bungalow, on the spacious verandah and lawn, these "red-letter nights." The grounds are illuminated by a multitude of gay lanterns and colored fires. The wide verandah accommodates a swarm of brilliant dancers, as well as the Bungalow's great-room; while the lawns are fringed with those who are not fortunate enough to secure the coveted invitation.

Many visitors are here from the neighboring cities and from New York. During the evening it has become the custom to implore, inveigle, and cajole the poetess into dancing one of her graceful fancy dances. Mrs. Wilcox is a natural, easy dancer, and to that which nature has bestowed she has added art. The beautiful "fan" dance and other creations are wonderfully rendered; we had expected to be pleased; we are charmed and agreeably surprised at the high technical excellence of her dancing.

"LOVERS' ISLAND."
From a Painting by Gardner A. Reckard.

The little cove to the east of the Bungalow, is at high tide the meeting-place of a swarm of good swimmers, of whom Short Beach has a large number. The poser and the girl who never wets her bathing suit, would be discountenanced here, where aquatic sport is a fact not a myth. Consequently the bathers are more than usually gay and good-humored as well as athletic, the girls not a whit less than the men; and it is a pleasant sight to see frequent trials of distance-swimming by the latter. The writer has often accompanied Mrs. Wilcox and her swimming parties, and can vouch that as an amateur she is very expert. The swim to and from Green Island, a quarter of a mile away, and sometimes in rough water, is frequently made by her; she has a very beautiful stroke, is an excellent instructor in the art, and she has converted all her young dryad friends into naiads. Old Neptune owes her a heavy debt. Short Beach is truly nymphiparous. There are more Lurlines, naiads and mermaids here than you could read of in Greek or German mythology.

The Illumination Night is an annual holiday, peculiar to Short Beach. It consists of a night and day, set by a committee of the Short Beach Association; the night selected is one on which there is no lunar light. A programme is prepared and committees selected, for Amusement, Music, Yachting, Shore sports, and Finance. Boats and houses are covered with decorations, flags, and innumerable lanterns, which are kept in stock here and added to, year by year, by all cottagers. The yacht, naphtha, rowing, and swimming contests, are all for cups and prizes, presented by cottagers, including the Bungalow cups offered by Mr. Wilcox; the fine trophy of Mr. William H. Lockwood, of Hartford, for launches, is at present in the possession of Mr. Wilcox. These prizes are for the encouragement of local sports only, and are stimulating it greatly.

The illumination commences at dark and is marvellous in its beauty. It is the transformation of a pretty little seaside town into fairy-land. It is the result of seven or eight years of growth and development of the idea, and its beauty is partly due to the natural features,—trees, cliffs, and water, which when lit by thousands of lanterns on the trees, houses, piers, boats and rigging, and the colored fires on the rocky shores and islands, form a scene of enchantment which attracts visitors from all over the state. This is surprising in a place so small, but it is due to the harmonious efforts of all the cottagers. One of the events of last year was a creation of Mrs. Wilcox; a Colonial Float, with the Goddess of Liberty (impersonated by a well-known society lady of

From a painting by Gardner A. Reckard.   THE STORM.

New York, of superb Juno-like figure and face) surrounded by certain handsome damsels who posed as the thirteen original states.

Mrs. Wilcox can be described as neither a spasmodic nor a strictly methodical writer. She is very industrious, and although she has no regular Medo-Persian rules as to time, she generally writes some every day. She works with great intensity and earnestness; and what her literary conscience tells her has been neglected one day, she more than makes up the next day, being capable of rapid and effective writing under pressure of circumstances. She also possesses a happy faculty of concentration of mind, under conditions that would madden most persons. Ordinary conversation, music and laughter sometimes act as a stimulant. But at times, when some puzzling problems are disturbing her, I am sure that she is more often hindered than most writers are by well-meaning bores who unthinkingly or selfishly monopolize her valuable time by ill-timed or nonsensical conversation; or by occasional boorish idiots, who allow their curiosity to drive them to the indecent act of peering through windows, as if at some wild beast show. She writes most frequently without the use of notes or books of reference, and what is written generally stands, without much, if any, change or correction. After a good bit of work is done, she rises contentedly, and is as happy and gay as a child, joining in any of the pastimes or pleasures of the moment, like the merriest idler of them all.

But, before we leave this Arcadian retreat, let me describe our hostess to those friends who know her only through her writings. She is of medium height. The shape of her face is distinctly oval; the complexion fair; with a glint of red-gold in the waving hair; the eyes, deep topaz in their tinting, are at times dreamy, but more often sparkling with vivacity and life; their expression is full of candor, and they indicate the directness of purpose which is one of her strong intellectual traits. Her nose is regular, mouth very mobile and prone to betray her many moods, the chin that of an affectionate nature. The head indicates more than the physiognomy a strong will, the love of approbation of her friends, strong social and friendly faculties, well developed as to individuality and the intellectual faculties; a brain of good proportion and showing evidence of its fine quality; her temperament is a blending of the mental, motive and vital, in the order named. Her figure is girlish in appearance, when clothed in her pretty dresses, designed by herself, and which permit the freedom of limb movements and quick motion characteristic of her. One would hardly guess her weight or strength, for her appearance does not indicate it. She is athletic, and believes in health, beauty and love, for women and men.

Love is not more her theme in verse and prose than it is a part of her life. She is often called "the poetess of passion." But, I imagine that it is a pretty safe variety of passion; for she holds to that beautiful old way of bestowing love's choicest gifts upon her husband, who most happily deserves every morsel. With some writers, marriage ends the love-story. To her mind it is the mere beginning. It was not she, most certainly, that first put the query, "Is marriage a failure?" and her life is a romance of love that answers the question in the negative, decidedly.

Her husband is an inspiration to her; he is an artist and poet at heart, although to the world he may seem only a successful business man; and many a fine idea of his is embodied in her verse and prose. But, I must not open the Bungalow door too wide, and disclose so many of these secret little cabinets of the heart, even though Castle Wilcox is too new to have a delightful ancestral ghost, and has no spare closet for a skeleton.

SEA-GLOW.

F. C. H. WENDEL.

The sun has set upon our lee,
And phosphorescent glows the sea;
As, leaning o'er the vessel's stern
I watch the glittering waters turn.

Thrown in our wake, they seethe and swirl,
Like living flames they wreathe and curl;
Astern they stretch — a band of light
That grows most strangely, ghostly bright.

Dark is the sky and dark the sea,
Save where this ghostly sheen we see;
It breaks upon the vessel's prow,
And whirling, dashing, wildly, now,

Along her sides it takes its way,
A twirling stream of glittering spray.
It lights the sea with golden sheen,
That glimmers on the waters green.

Dark is the sea, and dark the sky,
Save that the myriad stars on high
Would marshal all that gathered light
To mingle with the sea-glow bright.

The sky above, the sea below,
Are lit with an ethereal glow,
That softly glimmers on the main,
Links sea to sky with golden chain.

Calm reigns, the winds are all asleep,
And not a breeze stirs on the deep;
While softly heaves the sea's long swell,
As if bewitched by night's soft spell.

THE "HENRY LEE" ARGONAUTS OF 1849.

BY FRANK LORENZO HAMILTON.

During the year 1848, the "Letter from California" was nearly as much in evidence in our newspaper columns as are the features of Napoleon in current magazines. The American flag was hardly unfurled over this recently acquired territory before the providential man made his initial bow to an eager public, and the hand of William Marshall beckoned us to the entrance of the "Golden Gate." At once the cry was "California Ho!" and even our steady-going young men of Connecticut abandoned for the time their "wooden nutmegs" to sit at the feet of golden eloquence. Occasionally a trite or waggish word of warning was interpolated, only to be relegated to the position of an unheeded criticism:

"Why seek far shores,
For precious ores?
  To me the case is clear;
We need not roam
At all from home—
  We've lots of 'owers' here."

Among the many companies imbued with the spirit of the time, was that of the "Henry Lee," organized by some of Hartford's representative young men, and recruited from the city and surrounding towns. After a lapse of half a century, it may prove interesting to recall the event which promised so well to the hopeful adventurers. The promoters were Philip Hewins, Carlos Glazier, Alfred E. Ely, Dean Alden, and R. Collins, (who subsequently dropped out,) but other enterprising

LEONARD H. BACON.

citizens came forward and "The Hartford Union Mining and Trading Company" was organized with the following officers:

Directors: A. M. Collins, Hoyt Freeman, Charles T. Webster, Noadiah Case, and Ezra Clark. The directors to remain in Hartford County.

Managers: Leonard H. Bacon, Hezekiah Griswold, Lorenzo Hamilton, Emerson Moody, Franklin Bolles, Erastus Granger, and Jared W. Smith. The managers to go out with the expedition.

Griswold and Granger later resigned, and Captain David P. Vail was added, who was also master of the ship. The Rev. O. F. Parker accompanied the expedition for the benefit of his health. He later administered to the spiritual wants of his comrades, and we are sure he found "a change" if not "an easy berth." The statistics show that this company at least had organized upon a solid business and financial basis, having a capital stock, paid-in of thirty-seven thousand dollars. The report states "The ship Henry Lee was purchased and re-fitted for the expedition, and after proving to be of great antiquity, with rotten bottom, a miserable sailer, and having gone through the fiery elements, was freighted and made ready for sea." Later events would seem to indicate that natural Yankee shrewdness previous to purchase must have had much to do with this unflattering report. Provisions were laid in for two years, with all necessary mining implements; the various tradesmen took full sets of tools, merchandise on consignment from stoneware to garden seed, together with boots, shoes and clothing, representing a total value of over fifty-four hundred dollars.

Regulations as to the future discipline of the ship were not overlooked. Of the character of the company, a New York correspondent of the day writes: "I have never seen a more noble looking, intelligent set of men on board vessel. They are quite cheerful, and in conversing with several of their number, I could not discover the least disposition to 'back out.'"

The sun shone brightly on the morning of February seventeenth, 1849, as those 128 sturdy souls (whose average age was only twenty-seven), representing all trades and professions known, was cheered by a throng that crowded pier 4, East River, and weighed anchor for a hard six months' experience around Cape Horn to the glittering gold fields of the Pacific. We can hear them now, as they sang their dedicatory song, (written by R. A. Erving,) to the tune of "Old Virginny," while the steamer alongside swiftly towed them out into "the bosom of the deep:"

LORENZO HAMILTON.

"Our buoyant bark is striding now upon the waters free,
With swelling sail and flashing prow, the stout old "Harry Lee;"
Oh, may their music never cease, but still around us roar
As she carries us o'er the mighty deep to California's shore."

* * * * * * *

"There, in that glorious valley, where Jove rained his golden showers
And each who will, may gain his share — we too will gather ours;
And when the good old ship is filled — is filled with golden ore,
We'll anchor weigh, and spread all sail, to see our homes once more."

We gather from "The Henry Lee Journal," printed on ship-board, (when the weather would permit,) that their tune was soon after changed, and the later birth of the composer alone, prevented "The land-lubbers, go down below," from becoming exceedingly popular. Of their experiences on board we can only summarize from this *multum in parvo* newspaper, the issues of which were distributed, preserved by many, and bound into an interesting little volume. Passing through the warm vapor of the Gulf Stream, to the music of "Flow gently, sweet Afton," the first heavy gales encountered made the Sabbath's services following, of decided interest, especially when, after the

Inaugural Ball to the honor of "Old Zack" Taylor, the elements, without warning, combined with the "artillery of heaven" to unnerve the stoutest hearts, and left the good "Old Harry" partially dismasted by the lightning's stroke and for a time a helpless wreck upon the ocean. We can appreciate the pathos of the scene, when a few days later, upon the morning air swelled the well-known anthem,

> "Safely through another week,
> God has brought us on our way."

The debating society which had been formed, "fully decided that the Government should restrict the free gathering of gold in California by foreigners," a decision from which we do not seem to have profited recently. Before sailing into the harbor of Rio Janeiro, their first landing place, the announcement was made of the election by them of Col. T. H. Seymour for Governor by a plurality of one vote over the Hon. Joseph Trumbull, the Free Soil candidate; Hon. J. M. Niles securing nineteen votes. We quote the following extract from the bill of fare, which was a very elaborate one:

> "Land-lubbers come and stay a week;
> We'll show you how to stuff the cheek.
> First, go below and see our toils,
> And have a finger in our broils.

CHORUS:—"If mush runs low or dundyfunk,
> We eat our fill of cold salt junk,
> Or down to beans or lobscouse stoop,
> Or, lower still, to smoked pea-soup."

The above parody, however, hardly agrees with a more definite and dainty *menu* given in a letter lying before me. The strict attention to old New England Sabbath observance, has been noted, but the Rio Janeiro Sunday attractions on shore (safe from watchful eyes), were too much for some of these young Puritans, and a passing notice of morning Cathedral attendance, is followed by a vivid description of a Brazilian bull fight, patronized during the afternoon.

Leaving the pleasures and courtesies of this land of tropical beauty, after interviewing a friendly school of whales, they were soon in the enjoyment of an ocean-race with "The Elizabeth Ellen," which, with cruel boasts of superiority, and earlier arrival at the "Gate," had preceded our boys from New York bay, with "Yankee Doodle" sounding from its deck. After two or three days of exciting interest, the "Old Harrys"

CAPT. DAVID P. VAIL.

took a last triumphant glimpse of their rival, far in their vessel's wake. Other vessels, sharing the same fate, the "pride that goeth before a fall," found them baffled for forty days, in a wilderness of tempests and seas, before this unrealized, with short days and long nights, alike spent in treacherous gloom; their only solace the thought that they survived, while others had found an involuntary port in vain attempts at "rounding the Horn."

As the month of July finds them in the vicinity, plans are laid for a grand celebration of Independence Day, on the Island of Juan Fernandez. Old Neptune, however, interferes, but as the event on ship-board was the crowning one of the whole trip, it requires due notice, and the printed programme for the day follows:

"National Salute and Ringing of the Bell at Daylight. President of the Day, L. H. Bacon. 1st, Prayer, by Rev. O. F. Parker; 2d, Songs for Fourth of July; 3d, Reading of the Declaration of Independence, by Col. William B. Dickinson; 4th, Music by the Band; 5th, Oration, by Lorenzo Hamilton; 6th, Benediction, by Rev. O. F. Parker; 7th, Dinner, Regular Toasts, Music, etc. Toastmaster, Capt. David P. Vail.

Services to commence at half past ten o'clock A. M.; A Gun at Sunset. Committee of Arrangements, E. Moody, L. Hamilton, L. H. Bacon. National Ball in the evening.

The mature thought and patriotic inspiration expressed in the toasts, as reported, which we would like to quote, did not space forbid, cause a contrasting reflection upon the young men of the present day. Conquerors over many a hard experience, we soon find our friends outstripping the contrary elements, and skimming along under clear and favorable skies, turning their eager attention towards ample provision for future wealth.

And now "The Temperance Club" swears a final pledge; the ingenious have put finishing touches to numberless useless inventions; the accounts of the Secretary have been audited and found correct; and gliding by the drowsy seals, through "the Golden Gate," while the "Stars and Stripes" burst upon their view, the command is given, "Stand clear; let go anchor," and the sturdy young captain of thirty-two, turns to say, "Well, gentlemen, I have done my best for you."

And what became of them all?

Divided into companies of three or four, they hopefully started out, many to encounter sickness, and find early graves; others to pluckily delve for a time and finally to join the ever increasing number of returning wanderers, some to settle down and call it "home;" but few, we imagine, realized their early anticipations of a golden harvest.

Lying high upon a San Francisco water-lot, and used for a time as a storeship, where the city has long since encroached upon the bay, the hull of the old "Henry Lee" lies, lost to sight but not forgotten, in the arms of Mother Earth, while her gallant captain, surviving most of his fellow-voyagers, and the last but one of the old-time whalers of sixty years ago, hale and "young of heart as ever," can still be found "at the helm, entrusted with the savings,

GOLDEN GATE.

and gifted with the esteem of citizens and friends, in the old home port of Sag Harbor—where he has at last chosen to cast his anchor.

CLINTON, ONCE KILLINGWORTH.

BY ELLEN BRAINERD PECK.

"Thus came the jocund spring in Killingworth
In fabulous days, some hundred years ago."
—TALES OF A WAYSIDE INN.

So sang the poet Longfellow, but the legend which blossomed forth at his touch into "The Poet's Tale," the years have almost folded within their silence, and it is now well nigh forgotten by those of the present generation whose ancestors founded Killingworth.

Old Killingworth of those early times, appears to-day in a new garb and under a new name; still, from amid the more modern surroundings, the face of the old town looks forth. It is said that men from Kenilworth, of the county of Warwick, in England, were among the first settlers, and Kenilworth,

WEST MAIN STREET.

not Killingworth, it was at the very first. But, in the lapse of time, through the vagaries of spelling and pronunciation, the settlement came to be called Killingworth, as though it would be entirely new and independent even to its name.

It was in the beautiful month of October, in the year 1663, that Killingworth began its existence as a tiny settlement of twelve planters. Here, in the year that seem to us so long ago, Uncas, the sachem of Mohegan, hunted in the pine-clad stretches, and along the gently flowing streams glided his canoe, where the reeds and rushes that whispered in the river sedges were weaved into mats for Indian wigwams. It was this chief, and his son Joshua, who yielded up their birth-right to the men of Killingworth. The tract of land which became the site of Killingworth was known among the Indians as Hammonasset, which name a small settlement between Clinton and Madison retains to-day. The Indians remained in large numbers around Killingworth until about the year 1740. "Old Else," the last of her tribe, who lived hereabout, is still remembered.

It cannot cease to be a regret that the town of Killingworth, honored in poetic lore, ever changed its name to Clinton, as it did in the year 1838, when Old Killingworth separated from North Killingworth. The town of Clinton, lovely in its quiet scenery, looks off on as dainty a bit of water view as can well be found. The irregular, picturesque harbor, and the placid streams meandering through the adjacent, low-lying meadow-land, with the soft blending of the

MEETING HOUSE HILL.

exquisite tints of land and sky and sea, give an almost dream-like beauty to the place. In the summer months, when nature revels in her vivid hues, all the scene glows in the warmth of brilliant color.

The town itself, with clustering New England homesteads grouped about the churches and the school, gives evidence of quiet thrift, and brings that feeling of rest and peace, nowhere more apparent than in the calm atmosphere beloved by the Puritan forefathers. To look down the reposeful length of the Main street, that stretches from east to west, and that lies on the main road between New London and New Haven, makes it hard to realize that less than half a mile to the south is the harbor leading to Long Island sound, and this beauty of a sequestered inland village, breathed upon by the fresh air of the sea, gives a double charm to Clinton. This is the main street of the original village of Old Killingworth, and it is beautified by lofty elms whose overarching boughs in the summer form a graceful leafy arcade.

About here were granted the thirty rights, and these included the rights for the minister and the right for the "support of the ministry forever." The grant of land where the church was built became known as "Meeting House Hill," which name it retains to-day, and now as then, the typical New England church crowns its eminence. There is a monument on this hill which attracts the attention of the passer-by as to its significance. It commemorates the spot where a building stood in which young men received instructions from the Rev. Abraham Pierson, the first rector of Yale College. Mr. Pierson, who was pastor of the Killingworth church, at the time of the founding of Yale College at Saybrook, found it impossible to go to Saybrook to give instruction, so the youths came to him in Killingworth. Abraham Pierson further benefited the then young institution by a gift of books. The cemetery extends back of the Congregational church, and it contains many old stones, among them the one

INDIAN RIVER.

that marks the resting place of Rev. Abraham Pierson. To-day, there are four churches in Clinton; but the larger portion of the community still clings to the Puritan faith.

Clinton is divided by the Indian river, which crosses the main street near the business center. The agora extends its small business thoroughfare about and near "The Corners"—where may be met the individual pith of the New England character, in its quaint and indigenous quintessence. Here tread a modern school of peripatetic philosophers. A short way to the west, along the main street, are the original "Old Corners." On the site of one of the present corners once stood a tavern, at which La Fayette regaled himself on his way through the town during his second visit to the United States.

Clinton is so quiet now, in respect to its traffic by water, that it requires some imagination to picture it as a busy little shipping-port, and to think of it as the locality of several prosperous ship-yards. This, however, is said to have been the case, in the last century and in the early part of this. Nearly all the young men in those days who did not till the land, in sailor phrase "followed the water." Near to the spot where the main street bridge crosses the Indian River, on the banks of this stream, were several ship-yards that launched from their ways many a staunch vessel; and at this time, also, Clinton had her modicum of trade with the West Indies. The harbor which to-day is very shallow, was then somewhat deeper, and where the sand-bar stretches westward across the harbor a pier once stood. Cattle which were to be shipped were driven out at low tide across the flats to the vessels. How changed the scene to-day when nearly all the boats that enter the harbor are pleasure yachts; for the railroad has quite taken the place of the water-roads.

THE OLD ACADEMY.

In the eastern end of the town, off from the main street, is the lower green, and here stands the old red brick academy, thrice rebuilded since Revolutionary times, that seems to tell anew the tale of "the battered desk, deep scarred by raps official." Now, this old schoolhouse remains silent and deserted alike by the surreptitious whisper and the merry, childish voice. The Morgan school, the gift of the late Charles Morgan to his native town, has for over twenty years taken its place. The majority of the houses in the village have an old-time look, and stand near the street. They are built in a simple style, with a plain exterior, breathing of the past as a page of bye-gone history, and neat and prim anear them glow, in the pleasant summer days, the old-fashioned gardens.

> In a fragrant garden,
>   Filled with radiant bloom,
> Dance the ragged sailors,
>   Waves the cockscomb's plume;
>
> Here ablaze with color,
>   A tall and stately row,
> Stand like gaudy sentinels,
>   The holly-hocks ablow.
>
> On the brier-roses,
>   Swing those murmurous guests,
> Laden bees a-crooning,
>   On golden honey quests;

Among the gay nasturtiums,
  They hither, thither dart.
Linger, musing lowly,
  Where droops the bleeding-heart.

Doris, of the blossoms
  Is weaving a bouquet,
Sprigged with coriander,
  And slim, green fennel spray.

From this quaint old garden,
  Where, just as long ago,
Stand, like gaudy sentinels
  The hollyhocks ablow.

Although the town does not equal many another in the quaintness of houses, abounding in nooks and recesses, so inspiring to romance, yet it does possess the primness and prettyness of a neat puritanic village, and has a charming symmetry and regularity of streets seldom found in so small a place.

In the war of the Revolution, Clinton bravely did her part and sent a regiment of men to aid in the victory. In the war of the year of 1812, Clinton again resounded to the tread of martial feet, and in regard to this war there are many anecdotes, more or less amusing, or so they seem to us when listened to from the lips of the story-teller. In the Civil war, Clinton sent forth a goodly number of volunteers.

There is a nook in Clinton that is rather apart from the rest of the town. It is reached by a narrow street, which was once a lane, that leads directly down to the water. Here is a small green, from which an unobstructed view of the sound may be had. This green is shadowed by elm trees, and about it are grouped a few old-fashioned houses. The spot is known as "Water-side." The grey stone docks, littered with their homely fishing gear, the boats swinging at their moorings, and the dilapidated time-marked bridge, whose foundation of unhewn stone was built in the latter part of 1600, all give an artistic

THE DOCK AT WATERSIDE.

value to the picture. Off to the southeast, the salt meadow lands stretch away to the low bluffs that shelve to the sound's shore. On the bluff known as the Big Hammock, which is the eastern point of the harbor, the sachem, Uncas, reserved for himself six acres of meadow when he signed away his lands to the men of Killingworth. On the green at Water-side, in the war of 1812, a small fort was erected, known as Fort Constitution. Near by was the soldiers' barracks, and daily upon the green the boys in blue went through their drill.

It was in this war of 1812 also, that some British tried to enter the harbor in a long-boat, but they were discovered and fired upon. On this same green, long years ago, a little tavern opened its doors to the way-farer, and it was, no

THE BRIDGE AT WATERSIDE.

doubt, the gathering-place of many jolly tars. There was a ship-yard too, at Water-side, and the first vessel built and launched from there was of goodly size and called "The Rising Sun." Among the pretty and interesting nooks in the vicinity of Clinton is the vigorous little watering-place, Grove Beach, which has lately sprung into life.

So Time, whose pinions are never still, has fluttered gently over the town, gradually obscuring old land-marks, and bringing into prominence the new. Tradition veils her face as the years go by, yielding more and more to the influence of the present, and the legendary romances and historical memories of Old Killingworth float back to us an echo from the olden days.

> Brought from the wood, the honeysuckle twines
> Around the porch and seems in that trim place
> A plant no longer wild; the cultured rose
> There blossoms, strong in health, and will be soon
> Roof high; the wild rose crowns the garden wall,
> And with the flowers are intermingled stones
> Sparry and bright, rough scatterings of the hills.

CANTON.

BY HON. WILLIAM EDGAR SIMONDS.

In 1630 a group of English families under the pastoral charge of Rev. Mr. Warham came over the seas to this new western world. For six years they abode at the place which was thereafter called Dorchester and which is now a part of Boston. Then in the spring of 1636 they traveled through a hundred miles of the solemn forest shadows and settled in Windsor, where the waters of the Tunxis blend with those of the noble Connecticut.

They were not slow to discover that the Tunxis was alive with salmon and that the "Falls," near the Tariffville of to-day, was the place of all others to take them. Sailing in canoes, on the smooth stretch of still water above that

CONGREGATIONAL CHURCH, COLLINSVILLE.

picturesque gorge, they found a broad open savannah on the west bank, with a certain fruitful vine growing there in wild luxuriance. Hopmeadow they named it on the instant, and Hopmeadow it remains to-day in the local vernacular, along with Terry's Plain, Weatauge, Westover's, Salmon Brook, and Turkey Hills; Hazel Meadow and Meadow Plain are little known outside the old records. The Indian name of the region thereabout was Massacoe, and a tribe of gentle Indians of that name held here their peaceful sway. A dweller in Simsbury street has within late years named his place "Massacoe Farm" as all who pass on the railway may plainly see.

Back of the savannah were great ranges of stately primeval pines, and straightway John Griffin, trader at Windsor, began to utilize them in the making of tar, pitch, turpentine, and candlewood; no small business this, for as late as 1728 a thrifty minister, the Rev. Timothy Woodbridge, sent five tons of turpentine to New York at a single shipment.

In 1648 Mannahooese, one of the Massacoes, kindled a fire which accidentally burned up some of Griffin's combustible goods; Griffin haled him to court at Windsor and the gentle Massacoes made haste to ransom him by a conveyance of all the Massacoe lands, " all the land from the foot of the hills on both sides of the river up to the brook that is called Nod Meadow." Needless to say that the General Court subsequently confirmed this shameful transaction.

Simsbury was incorporated as a town in 1670 "to runn from Farmington bounds to northward tenn miles; and from Windsor bounds on the east, to runn westward tenn miles," a tract of land including the Canton of to-day; and for the next one hundred and thirty-six years the history of Simsbury was also the history of Canton.

THE FARMINGTON, COLLINSVILLE.

Six years later, Sunday, March 26, 1676, the cohorts of Philip, King of the Pequots, burned to the ground the forty dwellings the Simsbury settlers had slowly and painfully erected during the quarter-century that just passed, the occupants having fled to Windsor and to Hartford the day before. Before labelling this deed as an inexcusable atrocity it is just as well to re-read, with the eyes of the red man, the series of Indian events in New England which began with the ravaging of Block Island by the whites in 1655; and it may possibly happen that we may come to look at Philip's final stand in behalf of his race as a supreme effort of pure patriotism on the part of one of the great men of the earth, ending with undying glory in the smoke and flame of the great "Swamp Fight" at Narragansett.

The next year after the incorporation of Simsbury, in May, 1671, it was voted, "to locate a meeting house at Hopmeadow," but it required thirteen years of controversy over the site — which was changed again and again — to get that meeting-house built. Finally the freemen met, and thirty-three of them signed an agreement which was placed on the public records beginning as follows:

"May ye 7th, 1683. Whereas there has been a difference arising amongst us, concerning ye setling the place of ye meeting house; that a setled peace may be obtained amongst us, to ye Glory of God, and the comfort of ourselves and ours, we whose names are unwritten do so agree and appoint as soon as may be comfortably obtained a day solemnly to meet together, in a solemn manner to cast lots for ye place where ye meeting-house shall stand."

CANTON STREET.

The next day "the lot that came forth was for ye west side of ye river," and there the meeting-house was built. The Rev. Dudley Woodbridge was ordained here November 10, 1697. The beef used on that occasion cost three cents a pound, the venison two cents, and the rum four and half pence a gill.

In process of time the first meeting-house was found too small for the growing community, and in 1725 an agitation began for the erection of a new one, whereupon the old fight broke out anew and with tremendous virulence. This quarrel, like the first one, lasted thirteen years, and was finally settled by the division of the town into three ecclesiastical societies; it estranged friends and separated families; at one time the ministerial association suspended the administration of the Lord's Supper, and for three years the General Assembly refused to appoint any justices of the peace for the town.

This bitter trouble was the occasion of the establishment, in 1736, of the Episcopal parish of St. Andrew's, whose church building is near the railway at the place long called Scotland and now known as North Bloomfield; its first rector was the Rev. William Gibbs, who has left behind him a sainted memory; but he fed four British soldiers who came his way a little before the Revolution and was taken to Hartford jail therefor, bound upon the back of a horse; he was over sixty years old, and he slipped from his seat and turned so that his head nearly dragged upon the ground; through carelessness or ugliness he was allowed to remain there so long that he became insane and died in that condition in 1777.

This same quarrel over the building of the second meeting-house in Simsbury was the occasion of the settlement of West Simsbury, now Canton, which began in 1737. Before that date two places in that general locality had

BAPTIST CHURCH AND GREEN AT CANTON STREET.

taken the names they bear to-day. "Cherry's Brook" and "Cherry Pond," the latter of which has given the name to Cherry Park. These two places were so called from an Indian chief "Waquaheag" who lived thereabout, but who occasionally appeared in Hopmeadow and was there familiarly known as "Old Cherry," probably on account of his fondness for cherry rum. The first burying-ground within the present town limits is near the Canton Center railway station; it is in a fair state of preservation, and it is to be hoped that at no distant date it may be re-adopted for the use of all the town, for which it has both historical and topographical fitness.

The oldest house now standing in Canton is the so-called "Page Place," midway between Collinsville and Canton Village, built in 1747 by Benjamin Dyer, schoolmate of Benjamin Franklin. The next oldest, neighbor of the

"BROOKMEAD;" RESIDENCE OF HON. WM. E. SIMONDS.

former, and the home of the writer, was built in 1756 by Thomas Dyer, son of the aforesaid Benjamin and grandfather of Thomas Dyer, afterward mayor of Chicago; it has descended from the original builder through an unbroken line of the ladies of the family to the present owner, who is of the same gentle persuasion. Its beams, as hard as iron, its floors put down with oaken pins, and its latch-bolts wrought by a skillful blacksmith and adorned with little brass knobs of the shape and size of a pigeon's egg, all attest its antiquity.

The people of West Simsbury held religious services from 1741 onward, the beginning of the Sunday session being announced by the beat of the drum; an ecclesiastical society was erected here in 1750, and the first meeting-house was built in 1763. In that year the society bought a pewter tankard and used it in the communion service; it is in existence to-day and bears this inscription: "Tankard used in the Communion service of the society who built the first meeting-house at West Simsbury in the year 1763. Rev. Gideon Mills, Pastor." The tankard had a lid; and each communicant drank from the top.

MAIN STREET HILL, COLLINSVILLE.

The pews were deep square boxes and the pulpit was high in the air. No fire was had, summer or winter, but the well-to-do brought foot-stoves. A committee to seat the people in the order of their social rank was chosen by vote; likewise a member to "tune the psalm" which he did with a pitch-pipe or a tuning-fork and a prolonged "do-o-o," in which the people joined before attacking the first verse. The attendants gathered during the noon-spell at a building hard by called the "cider-house," because it always held a barrel of cider free to all. Here they roasted the sausages they had brought with them, and with these and the doughnuts and the cider they fortified themselves against the afternoon freeze. Those who did not walk to church came on horseback, generally upon a pillion.

Darius Moses owned the first wagon, one of the lumber-box variety, but he did not dare to ride to church in it for a long time, because the community thought it frivolous. Later on the singing was led by a violin, base-viol and clarionet, and the music for a long time was of a higher order than was common elsewhere. Down to a revival in 1783 this church lived under the Half-Way Convenant, which allowed church membership and infant baptism to certain of the unregenerate who acknowledged the covenant.

The Rev. Jeremiah Hallock preached for this church from 1785 to his death in 1826, and the Rev. Jairus Burt, from 1826 to his death in 1857. Both were strong men; they made their lasting impress upon the people; and it is doubtless due in some substantial measure to them that Canton has continuously produced a race of men among whom character has been the chiefest of earthly possessions.

Canton was formally set off from Simsbury and incorporated as a town in 1806, the name — meaning a "division of territory" — being suggested by Ephraim Mills. The town is about eight miles long, north and south, by four miles wide east and west, and has a population of some 2,500 souls.

In the early days the largest number of houses was near the center of the town and came to be called Canton Center, but the most important highway in the old town of Simsbury, sometime the Albany Turnpike, with the Litchfield Turnpike branching off at "Suffrage" ran from east to west across the southern part of the present town of Canton; on it at "Suffrage" (now Canton Village) was established in 1798, the first post-office in the town of Simsbury; and, as

THE RIVER AT COLLINSVILLE.

a part of the Litchfield Turnpike, there was built across the Tunxis (now Farmington) river, the first town bridge in Simsbury, a mile north of the present Collinsville.

This was a famous old highway, enlivened by many a stage-coach drawn by four or six horses, and made musical by the merry winding of the drivers' horns. At Suffrage, at the forking of the two turnpikes, there stood for more than a century, the famous Hosford Tavern around which hangs a grewsome story. During the Revolution, a French paymaster left Hartford for Saratoga, with his stout saddle-bags filled with gold for the payment of the French officers in the American army. He was traced to this tavern for a night's rest and no further. The inn-keeper always avowed that he departed safe and sound, but it was probably heavenward, for no evidence of lateral travel was ever found, and a discovery made after the tavern burned down a few years ago tends toward a belief in his murder. This incident endowed the highway with the legend of a ghastly phantom, a headless horseman to be met at night in a

"BEL AIR," RESIDENCE OF J. HOWARD FOOTE.

neighboring pass where the trees shadow the road so completely that no sunlight penetrates even at midday.

Near the south line of the town, Captain Fred Humphrey built a grist-mill in 1805, a saw-mill in 1815, and within a few years afterwards four houses were to be found thereabout, including the not altogether reputable "Tim Case Tavern." In 1826 three young men, Samuel W. Collins, his brother David C. Collins, and their cousin, William Wells, came out from Hartford, bought the two mills with a few surrounding acres of land and began the manufacture of axes, each of the partners putting five thousand dollars into the enterprise. At that time no factory in the world made and sold axes as a business, and this undertaking was one of great audacity. Axes had been made by blacksmiths upon single orders and when an order was executed the purchaser had to spend half a day in grinding an edge upon his ugly looking tool. From the first, Collins & Co. put axes upon the market with an edge scarcely less keen than that of a razor and with side surfaces polished like a mirror. Not long before his death, Samuel W. Collins wrote out certain historical memoranda from which the following are extracts:

"1828.—Contracted with Oliver Couch to take his four-horse stage off the Albany Turnpike and run through Collinsville to Farmington and Hartford, and so got a post-office established at Collinsville. Built the first trip-hammer shop, etc. Commenced drawing axe-patterns, and making broad axes with trip hammers. Each man tempered his own, forging and tempering eight axes per day.

"1829.—Built the first shop ever used for Lehigh coal fires. This was the first use of hard coal for this purpose in America.   *   *   *   *   *

"1830.—Put up an office-building, a part of which was used as the only school for the children, as a public hall, and until 1836 the only church.   *   *   *   *   *

"1832.—Sold Sampson & Tisdale, of New York, thirty thousand dollars worth of axes—being the largest sale made at that time to any one firm. E. K. Root commenced work for us, and invented useful labor-saving machinery; he became our superintendent; and afterwards in 1849, went to the Colt's Fire-Arms Manufactory, of which company he succeeded, after the death of Col. Colt, to the presidency."

From this insignificant beginning, a few men, making each eight axes per day, the business has grown in nearly seventy years into a stock company with an invested capital of one million, with a large surplus, employing 600 men, producing 4,500 axes and tools per day, besides a large number of steel plows and wrenches. The annual consumption of anthracite and other coal is 11,000 tons; of charcoal 30,000 bushels; of steel, 1,100 tons; of iron, 5,000 tons; and of grindstones alone 600 tons, which are literally ground away in powder.

The original partnership of Collins & Company became The Collins Company of to-day; Samuel Watkinson Collins was succeeded in the presidency by E. B. Watkinson, he by William Jackson Wood now deceased, and he by Edward Hale Sears, who holds the reins with a masterly hand to-day.

The Congregational Church in Collinsville was organized with thirty-three members, June 25, 1832, "By Rev. Dr. Hawes, of Hartford; Rev. Mr. McLean of Simsbury; Rev. Mr. Burt, of Canton, and the Stated Supply." Joel Hawes, Allan McLean and Jairus Burt,—what a trio! The Rev. Joel Hawes was ordained pastor of the First Church in Hartford in 1818 and remained such until his death in 1867; the Rev. Allan McLean was ordained pastor of the church of Simsbury in 1809 and remained such until his death in 1861; the Rev. Jairus Burt was ordained pastor of the church in Canton Center in 1826, and remained such until his death in 1857. Together they waged war against the cider-brandy distilleries to be found on every farm, at a time when common hospitality demanded the maintenance in every household of a sideboard filled with liquors free to all, and they shot out winged arrows against the institution of human slavery at a time when the cost of doing it was the loss of pew-renters by the score. They did other things, not of the church militant, lovely and lovable, over which the writer fain would linger. Chaucer knew just such a man as was each of these when he wrote:

"He waytede after no pompe and reverence,
But Christes lore, and his apostle twelve,
He taught, but first he folwede it himselve."

The Rev. Charles B. McLean, son of Allan, was ordained pastor of the church in Collinsville in 1844; the writer grew from childhood to manhood under his teachings; his every sermon was a classic in style and in spirit a beatitude; tenderness and reverence not to be expressed exhaled from every thought of him.

The first name of Collinsville was South Canton and it took its present name against the wish and desire of Samuel W. Collins. That village — now lapping over into Burlington and Avon — lies upon the two sides of the Farmington

THE TWO VILLAGES.
Taken from the Place the Poem was Written.

river between two mountain ranges, each of which offers a most engaging view of the settlement below. Rose Terry had her chamber eyrie upon one of these mountain sides. As she looked from her window she saw the village of the living at her feet and straight across, high up on the opposing mountain side, the village of the dead. And she wrote these lines with truth as well as grace:

"Over the river, on the hill,
Lieth a village, white and still,
All around it the forest trees
Shiver, and whisper in the breeze;
Over it sailing shadows go,
Of soaring hawk and screaming crow;
And mountain grasses low and sweet,
Grow in the middle of every street.

Over the river, under the hill,
Another village lieth still,
There I see in the cloudy night,
Twinkling stars of household light,
Fires that gleam from the smithy's door,
Mists that curl on the river's shore;
And in the road no grasses grow,
For the wheels that hasten to and fro."

The town has seven school districts; the Collinsville district maintains a graded school of six departments, with hundreds of pupils, the finality of which is a high school of which George W. Flint is principal. The high school graduates small classes yearly, but the graduates go to the various colleges and are never "winged" on their entrance examinations.

Canton is not a showy town, but is emphatically one of substance. It is not in pressing need of the going reforms. Years ago the question of the sale of intoxicating liquors was taken out of politics and now it is not possible to drum up signatures enough to try on the question of license or no license in town meeting. Vote buying was never an industry there of any magnitude and to-day it is not an appreciable factor in any election. Canton has raised and sent out some useful and sturdy sons; Owen Brown, descendant of Peter Brown, who came over in the Mayflower, and father of John Brown the Martyr, was born there in 1771; he moved first to Torrington, Conn., where John was born, and then to Ohio, where he helped to build up the Western Reserve College, but when a negro applied for admission, and the trustees refused to take him in, Brown withdrew his support and helped to build up Oberlin. John Brown was a familiar sight in the streets of Collinsville after the troubles in Kansas and until his sacrifice at Harper's Ferry; he had made there the pikes he used in his raid on slavery.

Canton sent out the Rev. Heman Humphrey to be president of Amherst College, the Rev. Hector Humphrey to be professor at Trinity and afterwards president of St. Johns College at

COLLINSVILLE SCHOOL.

Annapolis, the Rev. Dr. Selah Merrill to be archæologist of the American Palestine Exploration Society, Solon Humphreys to be one of the chief builders of the Pacific railways, Merrill J. Mills to be Mayor of Detroit, Thomas Dyer to be Mayor of Chicago, and so on and so forth. Patriotism, stout and rugged as her hills, is native to the soil; in the French and Indian wars from 1744 to 1763, Canton furnished twenty volunteers of whom eight died at Louisburg and Havana; to the war of the Revolution she sent nearly eighty soldiers; in the French war of 1798 she had Oliver and George Humphrey on board the U. S. frigate Constitution in the action with the French 74-gun ship La Vengeance; to the war of 1812 she gave fifty men, and to the defence of the Union in 1861-5, at a time when her population was not more than two thousand, she contributed two hundred and eight of her citizens. "Deeds not words" has been the motto by which her people have lived and died. Nevertheless a great deal that is interesting remains to be said.

TRIO AND TRIPOD

III. TO THE HARTLANDS
VIA NEWGATE.

BY GEORGE H. CARRINGTON.

The proceedings of the day flitted vaguely through the minds of the trio in slumber,— glimpses of old mills high up on mossy banks mixed in delightful confusion with sounding water-wheels and a long-whiskered, dusty miller carrying a box mounted on three sticks and pointing it at mill dams, singing:

> "Der mill vill nefer grind
> Mit water dot ish past.
> Vell, who wants it to?"

Early in the morning the Squire appeared at our door and proceeded to map out our course for the day for us. "Planned for Newgate, have you?" said he. "Well, after Newgate, don't fail to go to the Crag Mill. For scenery, that's the place. Drive down through Copper Hill to Mechanicsville and squint across Cranberry Pond, then enquire the way to North Granby. From the Crag you can go westerly to East Hartland. On the way to East Hartland, find out where Rock House Hollow is, and go to it. It is worth a visit. There is a good place to cook your Irish stew there, and meditate on by-gone times." Huggins stowed these directions carefully away on the back seat of the carriage and started for the cemetery for a little quiet reflection before breakfast. It must have made him hilarious to read in several places in every cemetery he came to, these cheerful inscriptions:

GRANBY HOTEL.

> "Stranger stop, as you pass by,
> As you are now, so once was I;
> As I am now, so you will be,
> Prepare to die, and follow me."

And,—

> "Death is a debt to nature due,
> Which I have paid, and so must you."

He may have admired them for their veracity, for the charge of untruthfulness laid to so many epitaphs can never be imputed to these. Perhaps the most noteworthy stone in the Granby cemetery is over the grave of Daniel Hayes, who was captured by the Indians when a young man, remained in captivity about seven years, and after his release became a prominent member of the community. We were told that he was an ancestor of ex-President Hayes. The inscription on his tomb-stone is as follows:

HERE LIES YE BODY OF
MR. DANIEL HAYES,
who served his Generation in steady course of Probity and Piety, and was a lover of Peace, and God's Public Worship; and being satisfied with long life, left this world with a Comfortable Hope of life Eternal, Sept. 3d, 1756, in ye 71 year of his age.

After copying a few inscriptions, Huggins responded to the call for breakfast. John was not feeling very well and said he didn't want any breakfast, but was finally persuaded to take just a little food to keep him from getting faint. Not being a bit hungry, some oatmeal, a few fried eggs, a slice of steak, a veal cutlet, a little liver and bacon, fried potatoes, and coffee and rolls were all that he could worry down. But these kept him from getting faint until his appetite was better. John always had had trouble with his stomach. Since childhood it had bothered him, by getting empty, and when he tried to remedy this evil, he was troubled by its feeling uncomfortably full, before he had been at the table half an hour.

It would appear

EAST GRANBY CHURCH.

from the first illustration that Sir Philip was trying to skip his hotel bill. Huggins catching him thus in the act, thought it an ungrateful proceeding, and told John to go in and settle up, and John, realizing what good treatment "mine host and hostess" of Granby had given, cheerfully did so.

Thus, without the aid of a constable were we enabled to go to East Granby. John was feeling a little hungry here, and so all sat down to lunch by the church, which a summer boarder informed us was built in 1830 and cost four thousand dollars. The Granby churches are all of the same type, each with a square cupola surmounted by corner posts, the principal difference of the East Granby church from those of West Granby, Granby, and Copper Hill, consisting in its being built of stone, the others of wood. So each township has its own style of architecture, noticeable even in the bridges, which varied from the high boarded sides of those of Granby and Hartland, to the simple log sides of those of Canton.

It was on the way to Newgate, that Sir Phillip found the hole in an open field where Mr. Higley had mined his ore to make his forty-two-cent coppers, the location being described as about one-and-a-half miles south of the principal shafts of Copper Hill, over which are now the prison ruins. So he paraphrased the old lines as follows:

> "There lived and flourished long ago, in ancient Granby town,
> One Samuel Higley, a blacksmith, of genius and renown,
> 'Twas he who first taught Yankees how to make the copper ore,
> And manufacture money, which they'd never done before."

In 1705 it was reported at a town meeting of Simsbury that "there was a mine either of silvar or coper found in the town," and a committee was appointed to investigate. A mining company was formed in 1707, which was to give one-tenth of the proceeds to the town, "two-thirds of which was to go toward maintaining an able schoolmaster in Simsbury, and one-third to the support of the Collegiate School at New Haven." At the present time Yale College does not derive its sole support from these mines.

Mining was actively carried on until 1745, and a little was done until 1788, when it was finally abandoned. Two companies, The Phenix Mining Co., in 1830, and The Connecticut Copper Co., in 1850, endeavored to carry on the business, and spent considerable money erecting smelting furnaces, but the ore, although rich in copper, was, like most of the prisoners confined there, of a *refractory* character, and could not be economically utilized.

GATEWAY — NEWGATE.

In 1773, the mines were first used for the confinement of criminals, with the idea of turning their labor to profitable account in mining, and named Newgate Prison, to perpetuate the horrors in Tory minds of the famous London prison of that name, which was used for the most villainous and worst class of criminals. They were employed at mining but a short time, for they used their tools to dig out with, and escape, and the manufacture of boots

SENTRY BOX.

and shoes, nails, and barrels was substituted. As more light was needed for this work, buildings were erected above ground. These were added to and changed, from time to time, as found necessary. Of the buildings and ruins now standing, the wall was built in 1802. The ruins of the buildings on the

"THE VINE STILL CLINGS TO THE CRUMBLING WALL."

south side of the yard which contained the shoe shop, cooper's shop, hospital, kitchen, cells, and a chapel for divine worship are about eighty years old, and the stone building to the west which contained the treadmill, another kitchen, and more cells was built in 1824, thus making it about seventy-one years old. This was used but three years as in 1827 the prisoners were moved to Wethersfield. The warden's house and this latter building are well preserved to-day.

A writer in an article on "The Simsbury Copper Mines," published in the New England Magazine about 1886 thus summarizes the matter: "But the glory and the shame alike of Newgate have departed. The Simsbury Copper Mines are a source of wealth no longer. Even Copper Hill itself which in its historic period was part and parcel of the old town of Simsbury, has been transferred by successive legislative enactments into the towns of Granby and East Granby.

OLD DOOR.

"On the prison grounds, decay and change have done their work. The greater part of the old wall is still standing, though broken down in places; but the workshops are deserted, the treadmill is in ruins, the guard-house is crumbling to pieces. One of the buildings is somewhat less decayed than the others, and this is inhabited during the summer season by a guide, who, for a compensation, shows the curious visitor over the ruins, and lights him through the caverns, — but cannot tell him their history."

We, however, were shown about by a guide who had the history at his tongue's end, the place having come under other ownership.

The working of the treadmill, the shutes for the grain to slide to the floors below, the trough where the bread was kneaded by being gayly pranced upon by the bare feet of some of the convicts, gave a little idea of the culinary arrangements of the prison life. The bottom of the bread trough was full of dents, toe-nail prints, perhaps, where in excessive hilarity a big negro convict had put in some extra strokes, so Huggins imagined. But appetizing as it was to think of, we did not feel hungry for any of that bread. The cells in this building were fitted up with bunks, so arranged as to accommodate the greatest numbers in the smallest space. This was accomplished by "dovetailing" the prisoners, so each man's feet were near another's head, or as Huggins expressed

WORKSHOP WALLS ; FROM THE TOWER.

it, "One man's toes were in another man's mouth." The various insurrections and escapes were vividly described by our guide. Sir Philip disappeared for a few minutes, saying he had noticed an old door just around the corner, with some of the nails and bolts in it that had been forged in the blacksmith shop. He wanted to take a picture of it. He soon returned and we prepared with cameras and flash-light machines, to descend into the caverns. Later, Sir Philip *did* show us a picture of that door, but we also discovered in looking over his cash account the item "m — d — 15¢," which he said meant medicinal drugs. We were glad to have it explained, else we might have thought it to be "mixed drinks."

The caverns, darker than the Middle Ages, and damp and cool as an April shower, did not seem an ideal health resort, although the histories tell us, "that as a rule, the convicts enjoyed good health and that certain cutaneous diseases were cured by the confinement." But we have also read, "From other sources, however, come whispers of foul vermin, reeking filth and horrible stench, hard fare and cruel punishments. In the damp and filthy air of the dungeon, it is said, the clothing of the prisoners grew mouldy and rotten, and

THE DRAIN.—IN THE MINE.

fell away from their bodies while their limbs grew stiff with rheumatism." Whether these latter facts were true or not, they were as plausible and easy of belief as the former.

The sounding room, a small chamber hewn out of rock, has a peculiar reverberating echo, which Huggins, who was superstitious, thought was the agonized tones of the shade of the negro convict, who, when confined there, amused himself by drawing his fetters over the calves of his legs, was unable to

COPPER HILL AND MANITICK.

get them back, and his legs were amputated. John said that the blacksmith cut them off by mistake instead of the fetters, but we think that is false.

Huggins suggested how much more realistic that room would be as a "chamber of horrors," if a "wax-figger" of a negro, with tongue protruding and eyes bulging in awful agony, was chained to the ring stapled there in the rock. What a striking illustration of historical fact that would be. He also wanted John to pose in the drain as an escaping prisoner, while he took the picture; but John not having on his number eleven boots, declined. So he took it with only the hole, rocks, and pump in sight. We then went to the main room of the caverns, near the foot of the ladder where could be seen the remains of the planks, which had supported the bunks used by the prisoners. The platform which had once been above the prisoners to keep off the water which

THE MAIN CAVERN.

was continually dripping from the rocks, had long since been taken away. We spent some time getting our flash-light picture of this place, and wondered as we sought the upper world, how the convicts ever managed to get up and down that ladder, chained three together. It was all we wanted to do to get up singly, and we preferred the ordeal of having our pictures taken when we emerged from the stone jug, like any modern aspirants for a chance to decorate the rogues' gallery, than to trying any prison experiences of a by-gone time. So with prison garb, — the long linen dusters the guide furnished, — we lined up and were "took." This is one of the pictures we omit, for we are modest and do not court fame.

We looked back upon the ruins when driving away and pronounced them better than anything we had ever seen in Europe. Our stay there had been so long that it was near sunset when we looked down upon the Copper Hill settlement with its background of high, level-topped Manitick. Very expressive those Indian names. This one, according to Trumbull, was "a place of observation; a place for seeing (or to be seen) far off," and true to its parenthetical meaning to us, Manitick was in sight for many miles as we traveled toward the setting sun. We did not have much trouble in finding a stopping place for that night. Sir Philip drew upon his memories of the days of his commercial life, and proceeded to hunt up the little boy to whom he had given a stick of candy in one of those "years and years ago." Yes, fortunately he lived at the old homestead, and that stick of candy had been accumulating interest all those years, regardless of the fact that the boy had an older sister at the time it was given.

While Sir Philip chatted with his friend about old times, Huggins and John went out and sat on the piazza. The cool summer breeze stirred through the trees, bearing on its wings the music of the siren who was playing the piano in the house across the way. This reminded Huggins of old times also, for he murmured,

> "The breeze of the evening that cools the hot air,
> That kisses the orange, and shakes out thy hair,
> Is its freshness less welcome, less sweet its perfume,
> That we know not the region from whence it is come?"

" Blonde hair this time, not dark" thought Huggins, half aloud, and it was evident that Clara was present to his mind, although he had been very calm for the last two days. It did stir up a few yearnings, however, when at eleven o'clock, the siren appeared at the door to bid good night to her evening's company. This company was singular number, masculine gender. A hurried,

CRAG MILL FROM THE NORTH.

subdued conversation, a long interval of silence, then a short "good-night," the sound of quick footsteps growing fainter and fainter, and all was still. Huggins said it was getting late, and as the night air was a trifle chilly, he would go in. With a parting request to our friend that he pry the sun up early next morning over the southern point of the eastern mountain, we retired, to change plates, go to bed and remain in peaceful oblivion until morning. Only once were we aroused in the night by the horses kicking, in the barn, and when John

THE CRAG MILL.

inquired what that racket was, Huggins, too sleepy to realize that he was not at home, muttered, "Normals."

As we proceeded on our way to the northern wilds of the state, it was forced upon us what a distinguished company we were. The whole population turned out to greet us at Mechanicsville, and the mayor and his wife, for it could have been none others, as they were certainly the most prominent people

RAVINE, NEAR CRAG MILL.

there,—especially his wife,—and all the children of the place, took a great fancy to Sir Philip and followed him all around Cranberry Pond. One of the children, pointing to the camera, asked John if that was what people broke into houses with. It transpired that there had been reports come to them that a gang of burglars were working the state, and fearing we might be invited to stay to dinner, we departed for North Granby, for time was pressing. At the latter place, the people showed the same interest and they turned out in goodly numbers to greet us. The flattery we were bestowing on ourselves was unwarranted, however, for we had been mistaken this time for the stage, and the people's faces changed from that expectant, "I-hope-I've-got-a-letter" look, to a despondent, "how-mean-of-them" kind of expression, just as though it was our fault we were not bringing their last week's papers to them. So we passed

MANITICK FROM PHELPS' HILL.

quietly on to the Crag mill, where no one awaited us and there were none to criticize or eye us with suspicion. The mill was silent, and no sound disturbed the stillness of this veritable solitude, save the tumbling water and the rustling foliage moved by the wind,—a wild and romantic retreat presenting pictures to the eye from every direction.

While Huggins went abroad to secure views of the saw-mill, cider-mill, a few old bridges and a black calf, the others went down in the ravine where John amused Sir Philip by taking snap shots and was told by the latter that his pictures would be no good because there was not light enough there. John was

THE CHARCOAL BURNER.

a great success as a plate spoiler, and received prizes for the largest number of bad pictures at exhibitions. What attracted Huggins' attention most was a big snapping turtle that had his home beneath the dam.

BURNING PITS.

We looked at him wistfully and longed for soup, but he was out of reach, so we decided that we liked crackers and milk better, anyway. It was toward Hartland, as we journeyed westward from the Crag, that we met some charcoal wagons, and thus decided to get some pictures of pits in operation. Whether we had gotten into Hartland or not before we came to the place to turn into the woods, we could not tell; for our efforts at finding the town lines were not

THE CHARCOAL BURNER'S HOME.

always more successful than when in boyhood we looked on the ground for a big white chalk line to divide the towns. And why should we not find such a line? It was not our fault, but selectmen are too negligent as a rule, to keep guide-boards in proper condition, let alone mapping out the country in red, white and blue lines. Down through the woods, over the roughest of roads we came upon a clearing where in the midst was the charcoal-burner's home, which served to shelter himself and wife,

UNFINISHED PITS.

three children, and five hired men. The chicken yard had a pea-brush fence, and all the surroundings bore a rustic, "back-woodsey" aspect. It was interesting to study the construction of the pits, the way the wood was piled, the passage left to fire it, and the covering of all with dirt or turf. The burning of a pit occupies from two to three weeks and must be watched constantly, and ventila-

CHARCOAL PIT.

tion changed according to the wind. We were shown about by a son of the burner, a bright little fellow who spoke English, French and Italian. Some of the hired men were of one nationality, some another.

We were not far from Rock House Hollow and being fortunate in finding a gentleman well acquainted with the place who offered to take us there, we thought it best to heed the Squire's parting advice. Down through the woods for nearly a mile he led us, and there high up on one side of a deep gulch was "Indian Rock." This place, according to tradition, was a camping ground for the Indians when out on hunting expeditions or the war-path, and one better fitted by nature would be hard to find. An immense rock, projecting from the side of the hill, affording shelter for a number of people

CRADLING.

and an excellent natural fire-place for cooking, while but a short distance away is a good spring of water,—what more could the wily red man desire. According to a tradition of the day of frontier life in New England, the Indians after a raid on Suffield were pursued by the settlers to this spot and a lively skirmish took place. But let the gentleman who accompanied us relate it in his own language. He sat down beside Huggins under the rock, and told the following: "The Indians, living to the south and west of here were accustomed to making raids on the settlements every little while and hurriedly retreating through the woods. This was one of their stopping places for the night. Emboldened by their success, they at last kidnapped a young girl, the daughter of the most prominent man in the community. She of course was the most beautiful girl in the settlement. How they got her I do not know, but very likely she was out getting the cows. She was soon missed, and guessing the real state of affairs, an alarm

INDIAN ROCK.

raised soon brought together quite a band of settlers who determined on immediate pursuit. The Indians must be vigorously dealt with and taught an abiding lesson. The Indians had come to this place and were cooking supper when the whites overtook them. Cautiously creeping up, the whites hid behind those rocks over there on the other side of the gulch, and waited until near nightfall. The old chief of the tribe sat on that rock there. The captive was lying there, bound. The braves were preparing for the night, so they could be up and off early next morning. All was quiet, when suddenly a musket report

DRAYTON LOOMIS' SHOP.

rang out, and the old chief dropped dead, shot through the heart. The whites then charged, secured the girl, and hastily retreated, before the Indians could get re-enforcements. The old chief was buried where he fell I've been told, but I hardly believe that, for I myself came down here and spent a whole day digging for his bones, as you see by that hole there, but could find nothing," and sighing to think he'd been unable to dig up a skull, a tomahawk and a few arrow-heads, he led the way back to the road, where he showed us an old shop that had once been used for the manufacture of wooden plows by one Drayton Loomis. Continuing our way we still climbed the hills, and shortly after sundown came to a standstill on Hartland Green.

(TO BE CONTINUED.)

THE TROUTER'S PARADISE.

With slender pole, and line, and reel,
And feather-fly, with spring of steel,

Past noisy brooks in sunless glades,
And deeper streams in woodland shades,

We reach the trouter's paradise.
Among great hills it silent lies:

Where in the deep and darksome pool
The shy trout lurk serene and cool.

A quiet, wood embosomed nook,
Dim cloister of the chanting brook;

A cavern in the channeled hills
Wherein the crystal brims and spills—

By dark-browed hills it silent flows;
Or falls from clefts, like crumbling snows;

And purls and flashes all around
A soft, suffusing mist of sound.

BITS FROM GREAT-GRANDMOTHER'S JOURNAL.

BY MRS. ELLEN STRONG BARTLETT.

MAY, 1771. I must run down in the meadow to see old Moosuc and his wife. These are the last of the Tunxis tribe of Indians, and they live in a wigwam and raise corn and a few other things. They have the best samp, (yellow corn cooked whole) that I ever have seen and I seem to be quite a favorite with them, for they always have a gourd of "samp" for me to eat. In the river near their wigwam there is an island, and old Moosuc takes us to it in his canoe, and we get "ground nuts" there. These (wild artichokes) are nice in the spring. I feel very sorry for these poor Indians for they see how the white men are spreading over their country, that the hunting is useless and it is hard to get meat to eat. They do not think our way of living is the best.

The other day a bear came into our cornfield and I was glad that I had not gone there that day for young ears of corn to boil for the dinner. My brother went there on Sunday to get corn to roast and he saw the bear. Mother told him he should not have been in the field on Sunday.

Now that so many of the men are away, I have to go to the north meadow for the cows. One day, I saw a garter-snake. It made itself into a hoop and came after me and I ran as fast as I could, and got into the house exhausted, and mother killed the snake on the doorstep. She says that when the country is more cleared and settled we shall not have them in such numbers.

My great-grandfather was one of the original "Eighty-four proprietors" who settled here. They migrated from Windsor and Hartford, striking out into the woods west of the latter place. When they reached the brow of the hill east of us, and looked off on this beautiful valley, with the Tunxis river winding through it like a silver ribbon, they all exclaimed with delight and knelt with uncovered heads, to offer thanks to Him who had guided them through the trackless forest to such a delightsome place. This was the beginning of dear Farmington.

I am so glad that they bought the land of the Indians and did not cheat them, and that they lived peaceably together. Most of the Indians have gone where there are better hunting-grounds, and old Moosuc feels so lonely that I think he and his wife, (squaw, he calls her,) will soon follow them. There are no settlements west of us.

A man comes on horse-back every week with fish from the Connecticut river. We give him two pence for a large shad, but we have to buy a salmon too, because these are so plentiful that they must get rid of them, and shad come in the spring only. We have salmon in our river too, but they are building a dam for a mill and Father says that that will spoil the river for fish.

1772. I must write about our meeting-house. When our town was first settled, or rather, before it was settled and the land had been bought of the Indians, there was an Indian trail running north and south — and this is our main street; near the center, a lot was reserved for a house of worship, and a rude log house was built for that purpose. This, after a time, gave place to a framed building, with low seats in it without backs. Some of the women petitioned the authorities for permission to have backs put upon a few of the seats at their own expense, but they were refused, as those backs might be a source of envy and discontent to some, and might be thought to show a love of distinction in some, or a pride of wealth in others. They were asked to withdraw their request, and to be satisfied with such seats as the society provided for all.

Now our new meeting-house has been built, on the site of former ones and is considered very nice. Two of our leading men went up to Maine, and selected the timber, which is of the very best — the breastwork about the gallery is said to be very remarkable, for the broad panels, nearly or quite three feet wide, are each of one piece; and the shingles came from Maine also, and are nearly three feet long, and they have been put on with the greatest care, so as to last a great many years.* My Mother's cousin went up to the top of the spire to put in the weather vane. It was a fearful ascent and when he had accomplished it he found two holes in which it might be put, and in his doubt looked down to ask, lost his hold, and fell to the ground. He was killed instantly.

Mr. Woodruff, the master-builder, did all the handsome carving about the pulpit with a knife. The vine of grape leaves which is painted green is very natural on the white paint of the high pulpit. I wonder how the great high sounding-board was ever built above it. When the minister, Parson Pitkin, enters the church all the congregation rise and remain standing until he enters the pulpit. He carries his three-cornered hat in his hand. Families come from quite a distance to meeting and have to stay over the noon recess to attend the service in the afternoon. Back of the meeting-house is the "Sabbath-day house" to accommodate these. It is a one-story house, with two large rooms, a chimney in the middle, with a large fire-place in each room.

These families bring their lunch and go there to spend the hour between the two services and as the meeting-house is never warmed, these rooms make not only a comfortable place to stay in, but are used for cooking and also visiting.

My Mother used to have a woman come every Saturday afternoon to dress her hair very high, so that it would look well on the Sabbath at meeting. She wore a cap over it. But she had to hold her head straight up all night, so that the fine effect would not be spoiled.

One man, a Mr. Cook, comes from "White Oak district" with his large family, on a sled drawn by a yoke of oxen. He has bundles of hay for the oxen, and he covers a peck of potatoes in the hot ashes of one of the fire-places in the Sabbath-day house, before he goes into the meeting. After meeting, Mrs. Cook takes her frying-pan, cooks sausages, opens her basket of doughnuts, and the family feasts, and visits with the others who are doing similar things. This social hour seems very short and the long afternoon service a little duller than the morning, though I think it is because they cannot help thinking of the long ride home in the twilight of the short winter afternoon.

Sometime after the building of the church, this same Mr. Cook went into Duchess County in New York, just over the Connecticut line, and there saw the Dutch wagons used by the farmers. He thought that one would be very convenient to bring his family to meeting on the Sabbath, and that it would be a great improvement on the saddles and pillions then in use. So he bought a wagon, and on a Sabbath he really came to meeting, his wife, his children, and himself comfortably enjoying the unusual ride, but greatly to the wonderment of the people, for it was the first wagon that had ever been seen in Farmington. It all seemed very fine, but on Monday morning Mr. Cook was summoned before the authorities to answer to the charge of 'breaking the Sabbath,' because of the unseemly noise and disturbance of the peaceful quiet of the day.

---

* They are on the same roof now, one hundred and twenty-four years after.

MARCH, 1773. How fast news travels! Particularly, bad news. The messenger came through here to-day from Boston. His horse was reeking with perspiration and its sides were flecked with foam because of the rapid driving. Four days only from Boston, think of it! He was bearing to New York the news of the outbreak which had occurred between the British and the people of Boston. It seems that the inhabitants of that town, I ought to say the *men*, for women would not feel so, had resolved not use any more tea, because it was taxed; three ships had arrived from England, with the much discussed article on board, so a small party, disguised as Indians, went to the ships and threw the tea into the water. The consequence is that our town crier, Mr. Bull, has gone up and down our street, proclaiming the news, and to each house he leaves a command from some one who seems to have authority that no one is to use any more English tea. Every one calls it English tea, I suppose because it is brought to this country from England, although I have heard that it does not grow there but in a land on the other side of the globe, called China. The ships that bring it from there are many months in making the voyage.

I have heard Father say that he remembered the first tea brought to this town. His father kept a tavern about three miles from here, on the road to Hartford. One day, two strangers, Englishmen I think, stopped at the house and wanted dinner. One of them took from his portmanteau a little package of dried leaves, and told Grandmother that he wanted tea made. She had never seen any before, and so carefully soaked and boiled it all, threw away the water and served the leaves as a dish of *greens*, most carefully prepared with a small piece of boiled salt pork resting daintily in the middle. A disappointment all 'round! They say that the strangers called for their horses, and rode away muttering imprecations upon such a poor country as this. Well, it was a lesson for Grandmother, for Mother says she was very self-sufficient and independent, and she would not have asked how those leaves should be cooked lest she should not be thought to know everything. Uncle Solomon says I am like her, but I know he is mistaken, for I do not *feel* very independent, certainly not just now.

How I have wandered from my story! When the town-crier came to our house and told us we must not use any more tea, Mother sat down and cried; it was not really so much the loss of the tea as what all this was leading to. Poor Mother is very far from well, and she cannot eat some of our dinners of fat pork and turnips, (neither do I like them), and the cup of tea did help very much. We are beginning to have potatoes now. They are very nice when they are baked in the hot ashes on the hearth, and they help our salt-fish breakfast too. Then we have bread made of ground corn which is baked before the fire. Our tea is of sage or raspberry leaves or sassafras roots; but we will have the little pot of real tea for Mother. She sits at the end of the table where the drawer is, and keeps it in there. Yesterday, the town-crier came when we were at breakfast. He goes around to the houses most unexpectedly, to see if any one is so unpatriotic as to be really using English tea. I intended to have written that father remembers the first potatoes that were raised in this town. Before that, turnips were the staple vegetable.

JUNE 6, 1774. Birthdays are usually the time to set about performing the good resolutions which one has in mind for a long time. This is my birthday, but it is not bright and hopeful, for how can one feel happy where everyone is talking of our quarrel with England? What shall we do if there should be a war, for almost everything we wear comes from England, and then we really belong to it, and I cannot make it seem right for these colonies to break away from such a really good government. As I am a girl, I cannot help thinking that we had better pay that miserable little tax they call the "Stamp Act," for these small colonies would never use very much paper, nor have many documents that would have to be written on stamped paper, and not many newspapers, so that it would make but little difference to us.

But Father says it is the principle of the thing, that taxation without representation *is* wrong, and that we are going to be a great country which ought not to submit to oppression. He says that we cannot shout or sing "Long Live the King," for that would be disloyal to our great cause, and that every one must be willing to suffer, yes, and to die for it. I am afraid that much of the suffering will come to the poor women and children.

JULY 1775. How many days have passed since I wrote about the tea. A great deal has happened since. The war between the mother-country and the colonies has begun, and many of our friends have left their farms, taken their muskets, and gone to Boston, where the British are in great force. One young man from Lebanon, John Bartlett, left his plough in the furrow, unyoked his oxen, and hastened with other volunteers for Boston. It was a long, weary journey, and he was only sixteen, but when he arrived at night-fall, he, with others, helped to fortify a hill called Bunker's Hill. The grass had just been cut in the meadow below, and this was scattered on the road to deaden the sound of the carts which brought the earth for building the breast-work. He worked all night, walking close to the heads of the oxen and whispering his words of command to them. How circumstances help to develop character!

This is only the beginning of our dark and anxious days. Every Sunday. this same town-crier, Mr. Bull, goes through the street beating a drum to call people to meeting, and it is arranged that in any sudden emergency growing out of this war, the drum-beat shall be the summons for all the men to come to the meeting-house.*

1776. My brother Aaron was born July 4th, this year, the day our independence was proclaimed. I am afraid it will be a long time before we are really independent. Father has gone with a company of militia to New York. We cannot hear from him unless some soldier is sent back, and that we cannot expect as they have hard work to get men enough for soldiers, even if all should go. I know only one family of Tories in this town. They live in the house next south of the meeting-house, and their name is Mix.

DEC. 1776. We were glad to have Father come home last night. He, with others, have returned because it is winter and they are discharged or furloughed (according to terms of enlistment) until Spring. They walked from New York because the government had no money to pay its soldiers. They talk of issuing paper money, which will be called "Continental Currency," and the wise ones think it will be a poor substitute for the real silver and gold which it will pretend to represent. But, if it will buy our necessary food and clothing, we will be thankful, for we find it very hard to get along.

News has come this afternoon that some of our soldiers are over in the meadows beyond the bridge, unable to travel any further; so near home and yet too weary and foot-sore to reach it. They are returning from the north, where they have been fighting Burgoyne's army. My Father was there when Burgoyne surrendered, but he came back by New York, and these men have walked across the country through the deep snow.

The people of the town heard the news from two of the men, stronger and

---

* This drum is now in the Historical Society's rooms, Hartford.

more courageous than the rest, who pressed on across the bridge to the first house, where they sank down exhausted. Oxen were speedily yoked, the women piled the sleds with blankets and whatever could be hastily got together of provisions for the comfort of the half-starved and freezing men, and they soon had fourteen of them on the way to peace and comfort. It is said that their shoes were so worn out that the last two miles they traveled over the snow, could be easily tracked by their bleeding feet. They were given a glorious welcome, as they came through the street, and although they were soldiers, they wept when they saw the party of rescuers. I wonder if our independence will be worth all it is costing. So few seem to think of the mothers and children who are really bearing so much and in so many ways. I wish somebody would write about the "mothers of this infant republic" for we hear only about the fathers as making all the sacrifices. But the mothers could not have endured the privations that the soldiers have suffered. I do not like to hear my Father speak of it.

1777. There has been another call for soldiers, and as Mother is so ill, and there are so many dependent on Father, he has hired a man to go in his place in the army. It has been hard to get the money, which has to be paid in advance, three hundred dollars in Spanish coin. Now that Spring has come they will soon be on their way to headquarters in New York.

I get but little time to write, but things of interest are constantly occurring. A division of Washington's army passed through here, and in it was a regiment of French soldiers. I stood out by the gate to see them pass, and one of the men handed me an empty flat bottle, saying "No good, no good." This I shall keep. Another gave me a part of a dollar which had been cut in two with an axe. A part of the regiment was bivouacked in the south part of the town beyond the village, but there were many sick ones, and these quartered on the inhabitants without leave or question. We had eight of them, but we did not give them our nice, comfortable beds, for we never should have wanted to use them again. An abundance of clean straw was spread upon the floors for them. They were not like our own people who had left us but a short time before, for they were those who came from France with Gen. Lafayette. Mother was troubled to have those miserable, dirty people in her always tidy house, but they were sick as well as dirty, and so were cared for very kindly. One of them was sick from neglect more than from disease, and he was taken to the barn, provided with hot water and soap, and clean clothes. After a good supper and a night of rest on the clean straw, he seemed bright and well, and when he left, although we could not understand his words, he looked his thanks unmistakably.

1784. Another long interval of busy work and care. I have decided that I will teach this summer, and in Middlefield. I am to have one dollar a week, and am to board around — this means to board at the homes of the children a certain number of days for each child. Some of the places will be very pleasant, and some I shall simply endure.

Miss Becky Thompson has been here to make me a calico dress, and the rest of my clothes I shall make myself after I go to Middlefield. I shall have so much time, mornings and evenings, that I shall accomplish a great deal. This Becky Thompson is rather old and very deaf. She comes at seven o'clock in the morning and works until nine in the evening for a shilling a day. She can tell when it is about nine o'clock, and time to stop work, by the shortness of the candle. She says she wonders what people do with their old pins when they buy new ones! Hers are as yellow as gold.

1785. I have finished my teaching in Middlefield. Sewing was one of the branches to be taught, and I soon learned it was an adroit way for the mothers to get the family sewing done. Small children would appear, boys as well as girls, with difficult parts of dresses to be made, also trousers both large and small. Of course the teacher was expected to know how to do all kinds of sewing, and little boys and girls could not put in pockets and make button-holes, and that was a way to get the work done by the teacher. One day my table was loaded with fourteen pairs of trousers! I took garments home and worked morning and evenings at them, instead of doing my own sewing. I understand they are very sorry I will not teach longer.

NOV. 2, 1785. I have written one more date in this imperfectly kept journal, for yesterday was my wedding day, and we came immediately to this house which is henceforth to be my home. May our Heavenly Father bless us in this new life! A good many of the young people came here with us, most of them bringing some little useful article with their expression of kindness and good-will.

I intend to see my Mother a little while after supper every night so that she will not feel so desolate without me. The oldest of a family of six must be missed. Mother's mother comes to make her a visit every town-meeting day, and then I shall go to see her. They live on a farm three miles east. She rides on a pillion behind Grand-father, and as soon as she takes off her red riding-hood, she asks for yarn and begins a pair of stockings for one of the children, and always finishes it before she goes home at night.

And now, with new cares and an untried life before me, I must close my journal.

A TRIBUTE TO OUR DEAD POETS.

LOUIS E. THAYER.

We heard them sing; and wondered at their songs
So pure and sweet, but when each voice was hushed
Then only did we catch aright the notes
Of their sweet melody, and then alone
We sat and sadly strove to find again
Some thought or half forgotten strain
Of songs their lips had crushed.

They lived with us; they sang to us, but now
Their songs may sound in sweeter climes than this,
Yet still we mourn our loss, and gaze through tears
Down through the aisles of memory, and sometimes start
Perchance to hear some voice that seems to bear
The tones of those sweet singers; but, although the song is fair,
We find it but the murmur of a passing breeze.

Each voice is hushed; and as a tired bird
Flies for sure shelter to its nest,
They sang a parting song with chiming words
Then sought a silent grave for peace and rest.

A LETTER FROM A REPENTANT ROYALIST.

London, April 13, 1784.

BY MISS ELLEN D. LARNED.

Not a blind partisan, not a self-seeking office-holder, but a fair-minded, intelligent citizen of Connecticut, constrained by principle to remain loyal to king and government was the author of this epistle,—Joshua Chandler, of New Haven. The mass of Tories, during the American Revolution, was made up mainly of office-holders, monied men who feared the loss of property, and Episcopalians who honored the King as head both of Church and State. But there was also a class of moderate conservatives, who apart from personal considerations clung to the king, and believed rebellion unjustifiable.

The Chandler family at this date embraced all classes. Capt. John Chandler of Woodstock, (then in Massachusetts), was the most prominent citizen of Worcester county at the time of its organization, and his children and grandchildren held the highest offices in the gift of the government. As a matter of course, they were Loyalists of the most intense stamp, so bitter in opposition to the Patriot cause that out of six citizens of Worcester, sentenced to eternal banishment, enforced by the penalty of death if found a second time within the jurisdiction of Massachusetts, five were of this family connection.

On the other hand, Charles Church Chandler, whose father had remained in Woodstock, was a leading patriot, member of the Committee of Correspondence, and but for his early death might have filled the highest offices in the State of Connecticut. Another cousin, Thomas Bradbury Chandler, became at Yale college a convert to Episcopacy, entered upon holy orders, served acceptably as missionary and pastor, received a degree from Oxford and was offered the Bishopric of Nova Scotia. He and his family were devoted adherents of king and church, and by their position and wide influence, were able to give much aid and comfort to distressed Royalists.

Joshua, son of a fourth Chandler brother, after his graduation from Yale college, in 1747, remained in New Haven, engaging in the practice of law, and in extensive business operations, and acquired a large property. That he gained the respect and confidence of the community was manifested by public charges entrusted to him, and very notably by being placed first on the Committee of Correspondence in 1777. But, it was soon manifest that his sympathies were with the mother country. He could but think "his countrymen were in the wrong." His sons became, indeed, violent partisans of the Royal cause, even piloting British troops in their invasion of New Haven, so that their father was obliged to join the British in hot retreat from the town, leaving property valued at £30,000 to be confiscated by the State government. His prosperous career ended in "days of darkness." Repairing to England, after the close of the war, hoping to gain some equivalent for his losses in the Royal cause, he met but bitter disappointment. The subjoined letter* shows the innermost heart of one whose loyalty to the crown had wrecked his life and fortune. He felt that "the lost cause" had not been worth the sacrifice:

---

* Genealogy of the Chandler Family.

"To the Rev. Dr. Chauncey, New Haven, Conn.
              Reverend and Dr Friend;
    On my taking my Final and Everlasting Farewell of my Native Country, I addressed you and my Good old and Dr Friend, Mr. Whitney. I hope you Received that address as a Token of my Love and Friendship; as I flatter myself that you have a Friendship for me, and would be glad to know my Present Situation and Future Prospects in Life, I have taken the Liberty of once more Giving you the Trouble (I hope) the pleasing Trouble of this.

    I left New York on the 9th of October Last, with a Design of Calling at New Haven, and for the Last Time, to have bid adieu to that Delightful Spot, and to all my friends; but the Winds, but more the Feelings of my own Mind, and the Visible feelings of the Family forbid it. We had a most Terrible Passage to Nova Scotia, our Decks were swept of all our Stock, &c. &c. We arrived at Anapolis on the 23d. Mrs. Chandler was overcome with the Passage. She languished, mourned and Died in about 3 weeks after Landing. She is certainly Happy. She Died in the Death of the Righteous, and it is the first wish of my Soul, that her Family and her Friends might be as happy and composed as she was in the moment of her Death. Soon after the Death of Mrs. Chandler, I removed my Family about ten miles above Anapolis Royal. I provided as well as I could for them. I staid with them a few days. I then left them to the Gracious Protection of the Almighty, who I hope will be their God and their Comfort and Support. I left Halifax on the 9th of January, and Arrived, after a mixed Passage, in this Great Sink of Pollution, Corruption and Venality, on the 8th of February. I found the Nation in Great Tumults and Commotions. I found myself Perfectly Lost in Politicks, as well as in Compass; East was west and North is yet South.

    Before I left America, I supposed Lord North to be Rather attached to the Prerogatives of the Crown, and Lord Sidney and Mr. Pitt Rather Jealous for the Liberty of the People. But how Greatly was I mistaken. I found Lord North Decidedly against the Crown, in Favor of the Democratical Part of the Constitution to the Ruin of the Monarchial; and Mr. Pitt and Lord Sidney, &c. &c. &c. all in Favor of the Prerogative; these Political Squables you will see more Perfectly Depictured in the Newspapers, as also the Dissolution of Parliament, and the Calling of a new one; the Elections in many places have taken place, and the New Ministry will have a Great Majority in the New Chosen House; but their continuance cannot be long, the present Ministry are occupying ground that they are Strangers to; they stand upon Tory Ground, and are at Heart Republicans in Principle, if there is such a thing as Principle in the Kingdom, the existence of which I Greatly doubt. This Kingdom, without a miracle in its favor must soon be Lost; you can have no idea of their Corruption, of their Debauchery and Luxury; their Pride; their Riches; their Luxury has Ruined them; it is not in the Power of Human Nature to Save them, If they are saved, it must be by some Heavenly Power. I like not the Country, either their manners or even their Soil — the Soil is Nothing to America, you cannot see a single Tree but what wants a Flesh Brush — it is True that Agriculture and all the Arts are carried to great Perfection; but give America the means, and in one Half the Time she will Rise Superior to anything in this Country.

    My own prospects in Life are all Dashed, my only care is now for my Children; the Idea of a Compensation is but very faint. It is probable I may Have about £400 stg. per annum. My only effort now is to procure that Sum to be Settled on my two Daughters and my youngest Son for Life; my Son William Stands some Chance for a Separate Support for his Life. I find my Health on a Visible Decline; when I can Get my Little affairs Settled here, I shall go into Yorkshire or into Wales, to procure an Asylum for my Daughters and my two youngest Sons.

Thus this unhappy Controversy has Ruined Thousands; the Sacrificing the Prospects of my Family for life is not the only thing that fills my mind with distress. I yet have a very strong Affection to, and a Predilection for my Native Country; their Happiness would in some measure alleviate my Present Distress; but though I have found myself Greatly lost in Politicks, I cannot yet suppose my Country can be happy in their present state. A Democratical Government cannot long subsist in so great and extended a Country; the seeds of Discord I see Sown among you, former prejudices and future jealousies will cause Convulsions; the subversion of your present constitution cannot take place without bloodshed. I have sent in a small package to my Son, M. De Solme's (advocate in Geneva, Switzerland) History of the British Constitution; it is well wrote; I wish Dr. Stiles would admit it into the Library — it may be of some service to my Country in forming their new constitution, for a new one must be formed at some future time. In the hour of Contest I thought, and even yet think my Country wrong; but I never wished its ruin. I wish her to support a dignified character — that can be done only by great and dignified actions, one of which is a sacred and punctual adherence to public faith and Virtue. Men of your character may preach forever upon moral Virtue; but, if the people see and find that there is no public Virtue, your preaching will be like the Sounding Brass and tinkling Cymbal. I wrote to my Son a few days since; I wish you to enforce my regards to him, and also to remind him of sending the papers and documents I sent for. Tho' I am about to leave this city, and address to me, No. 40 Norton Street, near Portland Chapel, will always find me, *while I can find myself.* Pray remember me with the most sincere affections to your family, to all my friends. They must excuse my not writing to each one, neither my health or my feelings will permit; but let us all bear up under all our losses and separations with a becoming fortitude. My own time, and the time of my dear friend, is Short, very Short, in this world. My first and last prayers will be to meet where no Political disputes can Ever Separate from near and dear friends.

Your humble &c. &c.

JOSHUA CHANDLER."

Mr. Chandler's sad fore-bodings were too quickly realized. After his return to Annapolis he set out with his son, daughter, and a fellow-sufferer, for St. John, N. B., with all his books, papers, and evidence of colonial property, to be laid before the Commissioners and have their claims allowed. A terrible snow-storm drove their vessel upon the rocks. A slate-stone slab, in the old burying-ground, King street, St. John, gives the sequel to this sad story:

Here lyeth the Bodies of Col. JOSHUA CHANDLER, Aged 61 years And WILLIAM CHANDLER His Son Aged 29 years, who were Ship wreck'd on their passage from Digby to St. John on the Night of the 9th day of March 1787 & perished in the Woods on the 11th of said Month. Here lyeth the Bodies ot Mrs. SARAH GRANT, Aged 38 Years Widow of the late Major ALEX[r] GRANT; & Miss ELIZABETH CHANDLER aged 27 years, who were Shipwreck'd on their passage from Digby to St. John on the Night of the 9th day of March 1787 and Perished in the Woods on the 11th of said Month.

OLD TIME MUSIC AND MUSICIANS.

I.

BY N. H. ALLEN.

The history of music in New England, for two centuries after the landing of the pilgrims, is scarcely more than the slender story of psalmody in its rudest form. The future historian will devote more pages to the achievements of the last twenty, than to those of the first two hundred years. At the outset, before music was cultivated even slightly, it was barely tolerated, and was entirely restricted to the singing, in a dolorous fashion, of Henry Ainsworth's crude version of the psalter, or in some cases of the earlier one by Sternhold and Hopkins. A little later, the "Bay Psalm Book" was prepared by Rev. Thomas Weld, Rev. John Eliot, and Rev. Richard Mather. In this connection I quote somewhat freely from "Side-Glimpses of the Colonial Meeting-House," by William Root Bliss, (Riverside Press, 1894):

"Singing was not specified as a part of the service, although it was practiced, and so badly practiced that the 'speaking contemptuously of singing psalms' was notorious.

"A treatise called 'Singing of Psalms a Gospel Ordinance,' was published by John Cotton, of Boston, in the year 1647. The necessity for such a publication seems to imply that psalm-singing was not a general custom in meeting-houses. After all that was printed on the subject, there was, in the first century of New England, nothing that could be called a service of song; no harmonious band of singers 'to make one sound to be heard in praising and thanking the Lord, saying For he is good; for His mercy endureth forever.' The Bay Psalm Book, imprinted 1640, which was used in some parts of New England, was prepared by three ministers, neither of whom had a strand of music or poetry in his soul. It asks us to sing:

> 'Lift up thy foot on hye,
> Unto the desolations
> Of perpetuity:
> Thy foe within the Sanctuary
> Hath done all lewd designs.
> Amid the Church thy foes doe roare:
> Their Banners set for signes.'

"The best specimen of versification in the book is 'Psalm 137.' Yet it must have bewildered the rustics who launched themselves 'The rivers on, of Babilon' to learn where they were going to land:

> 'The rivers on of Babilon
> There when wee did sit downe:
> Yea even then wee mourned, when
> Wee remembered Sion . . . .'

"A much needed apology appears in the preface of this book, which reassures the stumbling singer in these words: 'If the verses are not always so smooth and elegant as some may desire or expect let them consider that God's altar needs not our polishings. *Exodus 20.*'

"Other hymn books known in New England were Ainsworth's 'Book of Psalms Englished both in prose and metre,' printed at Amsterdam in the year 1612. Older than this was the Sternhold and Hopkins hymnody which, during the reign of Queen Elizabeth, had been 'permitted rather than allowed' in the Church of England; it was bound in the covers of the Book of Common Prayer, and was rated as a work of superior excellence until the hymnal of Tate and Brady appeared in the year 1696. Then came hymns composed by Isaac Watts, which, in the course of time, crowded out all others. Up to the year 1781, forty editions of his psalms and hymns had been published in New England. . . . . His hymns, coming to the cheerless and shivering services of worship in the colonial meeting-house, were like the coming of a bright and hopeful guest to a disconsolate fireside. Some of them have been acknowledged to be the hymns of a true poet; and these are said to be more suitable for the service of divine worship than those of any other English composer. . .

"It may be said that Watts has written the songs of the church. For nearly two centuries his lyric poems have been sung, and are sung to-day wherever the English language is spoken. The reason for this must be that no other poet has so well expressed the devotional spirit, or has so closely sympathized with the experiences of a religious life.

"Are you penitent?   There is the hymn:
'Show pity, Lord! O Lord, forgive;
Let a repenting rebel live;
Are not thy mercies large and free?
May not a sinner trust in thee?'

"Are you truthful?   There is the hymn:
'Thus far the Lord hath led me on;
Thus far His power prolongs my days:
And every evening shall make known
Some fresh memorials of His grace.'

"Are you desirous of rendering a tribute of homage? . . .
'From all that dwell below the skies,
Let the Creator's praise arise;
Let the Redeemer's name be sung
Thro' every land, by every tongue.'

"And yet when the hymns of Dr. Watts appeared, many theologians of New England who had been laboriously singing from the Bay Psalm Book, or from the Sternhold and Hopkins version, stood still, not knowing, as they said, what hymns of Dr. Watts should be sung as sacred and what should be sung as profane. Some of them thought that carnal men should not sing at all. In the year 1736, ministers of Boston were discussing and doubting the propriety of singing any 'hymns of mere human composure,' and they objected to singing those which were not paraphrases of the Psalms of David.

"There appears to have been no scientific knowledge of music in New England until the early part of the last century. It is said that but five or six tunes were in use, and the only identity which these had, as used in different towns, was in the names. . . . . All tunes were like traditions handed down by ear, and so changed were they in the transmission that their original form was lost. In Old England the tunes had been left to the mercy of every parish clerk. Records of arch-deacons' courts show that the clerk was punished for singing the psalms in church service 'with such a jesticulous tone and altitonant voyce, viz., squeaking like a pigg which doth not only interrupt the other voyces but is altogether dissonant and disagreeing unto any musicall harmonie.' . . . ."

This is hardly to be wondered at, for Ainsworth, in the preface to his versification, writes:

"Tunes for the psalms, I find not any set of God; therefore, all people may use the most grave, decent, and comfortable manner of singing that they know."

Metrical psalmody, first introduced into the service of the church by Luther came tardily into use in England; and, beginning with Luther, melodies of many worldly, and it is said, even of licentious, songs, were pressed into service, so that when the practice became set in England this abuse was not lessened but rather increased; for, in the first case, it is supposed that Luther took melodies of earlier times, and such as were not known to the people in their original settings, while in England it is said that the airs of loose and ribald songs of much later periods were adapted to the psalms, and were sung alike as sacred and secular tunes. It is recorded that Sternhold was so shocked by this practice that he at once determined to provide the courtiers with his psalms "thinking thereby that they would sing them instead of the sonnet; but they did not."

It is easy, at this day, to speak of the efforts of the Puritans in England to suppress music as acts of fanaticism and vandalism, and mistaken they were of course, but when they prayed

"That all cathedral churches may be put down, where the service of God is most grieviously abused by piping with organs, singing, ringing, and trowling of psalms from one side of the choir to the other, with the squeaking of chanting choristers."

It may be that their indignation was aroused more by what they saw than by what they heard. This humorous but no doubt truthful description of the "chanting choristers," written in 1633, by Dr. John Earle, successively bishop of Worcester and Salisbury, may lend some weight to their view:

"The common singing men are a bad society, and yet a company of good fellows that roar deep in the quire, deeper in the tavern. They are the eight parts of speech which go to the Syntaxis of the service, and are distinguished for their noises much like bells, for they make not a consort but a peal. Their pastime or recreation is prayers, their exercise drinking; yet herein so religiously addicted that they serve God when they are drunk. Their humanity is a leg to the Residencer, their learning a chapter, for they learn it commonly before they read it; yet the old Hebrew names are little beholden to them, for they miscall them worse than one another. Though they never expound the Scriptures, they handle it much, and pollute the Gospel with two things, their conversation and their thumbs. Upon worky-days they behave themselves at prayers as at their pots, for they swallow them down in an instant. Their gowns are laced commonly with streamings of ale, the superfluities of a cup or a throat above measure. Their skill in melody makes them the better companions abroad; and their anthems abler to sing catches. Long lived for the most part they are not, especially the base, they over-flow their banks so oft to drown the organs. Briefly, if they escape arresting, they die constantly in God's service; and to take their death with more patience they have wine and cakes at their funeral, and now they keep the church a great deal better, and help to fill it with their bones, as before with their noise."

II.

It is said there were more among the Pilgrims who landed at Plymouth, that were brought up in the atmosphere of good music, and had some knowledge of it, than among the Puritans, who landed a few years later at Boston. Winslow, one of the Pilgrims, writes:

"We refreshed ourselves with singing of psalms, making joyful melody in our hearts, as well as with the voice, their being many of our congregation very expert in music, and, indeed, it was the sweetest music that mine ears ever heard."

---
* Anthony Wood.

It does not seem strange, however, that after a few years both companies should stand on the same level as to music; for with the struggle for a bare existence, the terrible losses by death, and the absence of printed music, the loss of skill in singing must be a foregone conclusion. It is fair to suppose that Mr. Hooker's company brought with them the Ainsworth Psalm Book, and quite likely made use of it long after the Bay Psalm Book had been printed, as this work was looked upon in many quarters as an unwarrantable innovation, and its first edition was but slowly taken. Another edition was printed seven years after the first, and to prepare the way for its more general use, Rev. John Cotton published his treatise, "Singing of Psalms a Gospel Ordinance," referred to by Mr. Bliss. In Dr. Walker's History of the First Church in Hartford one may read of a similar service rendered here eighty-five years later by Rev. Timothy Woodbridge. The whole account is so admirably given that permission has been asked and granted to reprint it in this paper:

Public services on the Lord's day began about nine o'clock. Congregations were called to the meeting-house by the beating of a drum, the blowing of a conch-shell or a horn, the display of a flag, or, if the community were so fortunate as to have a bell, by the "wringing of a bell." Hartford Church had a bell as early as 1641, and in all probability from the first, it being, with little doubt a part of the transported establishment from Cambridge. . . . .

After the scripture reading, "a Psalm succeeds. In some the Assembly being furnished with Psalm-books, they sing without the stop of Reading between every Line. But ordinarily the Psalm is read line after line by him whom the Pastor desires to do that Service; and the people generally sing in such grave Tunes as are most usual in the Churches in our nation." (RATIO DISCIPLINÆ).

The singing was, for the most part, more devout than melodious. Mather is able only to say of it, as late as 1727, when musical affairs in Massachusetts had already begun greatly to improve: "It has been commended by Strangers as generally not worse than what is in many other parts of the world." (Ibid). . . . . To add to the difficulty, no instrumental accompaniment, save the pitch pipe and tuning fork, was allowed; such assistance being supposed forbidden by Amos v. 23, "I will not hear the melody of thy viols," and other passages.

Many congregations did not attempt more than three or four tunes. The general custom was to use the Psalms in regular order; and the singing exercise which seems to have occurred usually but once in each service, was from a quarter to a half hour in its dolorous duration. About the first quarter of the eighteenth century, a general attempt was made to improve the music by the recall of "notes," and as it was termed "singing by rule." But it met with violent opposition. Many congregations were almost split on the question. The innovation was denounced as an insult to the memory of the fathers, and as tending to Papacy. "If we once begin to sing by note, the next thing will be to pray by rule, and then comes Popery." Ministers and people, deacons and congregation, were in many places, at open hostility on this burning question. The interposition of the civil authority was in some instances necessary to compose the disturbances arising from the proposal to "sing by rule."

The history of the matter in this First Hartford Society well illustrates the already well-established conservatism of this organization. . . . Doubtless affairs in a musical way had gone on here as generally, till about 1726 the subject of improved music began to be agitated in this region. The diary of Rev. Timothy Edwards, at East Windsor, and the records of the Windsor church show that the new method was disquieting this Israel.[*]

---

[*] Dr. Tarbox's "Windsor Church, 250 anniversary," pp. 97-100, also Judge Stoughton's "Windsor Farmes," pp. 96-98.

In 1727, the pastor of this Hartford church, Rev. Timothy Woodbridge, preached a "Singing Lecture" at East Hartford, in the pulpit of his nephew, Rev. Samuel Woodbridge. The uncle was now seventy-one years of age and the nephew forty-four, and both were obviously on the side of the new method. The lecture was printed with a preface signed "Per Amicum," written by the nephew, in which it is said: "The following Discourse was delivered at a Lecture for the encouragement of Regular Singing, a comely and commendable practice; which for want of Care in preserving, and skilful Instructors to revive, has languished in the Countrey till it is in a manner Lost and Dead; yea it has been so Long Dead, as with some it stinketh, who judge it a great Crime to use meanes to Recover it againe." . . . .

The same year the matter came before the General Association, met at Hartford, May 12th, a few days previous to the "Singing Lecture" just spoken of. Rev. Nathaniel Chauncey read a paper which the Association, over the signature of "T. Woodbridge, Moderator," ordered printed, entitled "Regular Way of Singing the Songs of the Lord." The subject proposed for discussion was "Whether in Singing the Songs of the Lord we ought to proceed by a certain Rule or to do it in any Loose, Defective, Irregular way that this or that People have Accustomed themselves unto." One of the reasons the essayist gives for the strong attachment to the old method is interesting: "Many will readily grant that they (the singers by ear) use many Quavers and Semi-Quavers, &c., and on this account it is that they are so well pleased with it, and so loathe to part with it: now all these Musical Characters belong wholly to Airy and Vain Songs, neither do we own or allow any of them in the Songs of the Lord."

But notwithstanding this committal of the old Pastor and of the General Association to the new way, the Hartford Church continued in the old several years longer. It sung as it had sung in Isaac Foster's day, till after the long pastorate of Timothy Woodbridge ended, and until he, after advocating the reform in vain, was gathered to his fathers. The year after Mr. Woodbridge died, however, the Society took action, on the 20th of June, 1733, in this cautious and tenative manner: "VOTED that this Society are willing and Content that such of them as Encline to Learn to Sing by Rule should apply themselves to the best manner they Can to gain a knowledge thereof. VOTED and agreed that after the expiration of three months, Singing by Rule shall be admitted to be practiced in the Congregation of this Society in their publick Worship on the Lord's day & until their annual Meeting in December next; & that then a Vote be Taken whether the Society will further proceed in that way or otherwise."

The two leaders of the opposing methods were then designated to "Take on them the Care of Setting the Psalm," for the periods specified: "Mr. William Goodwin as usual," and "Mr. Joseph Gilbert, jr., after the Expiration of the three months." Tried thus prudently for four months, the Society saw its way in December to vote "that singing by Rule be admitted and practiced in the Congregation of this Society in their publick Worshipping of God," and Mr. Gilbert was empowered to "sett the psalm." So that it was not long, probably, before it could have been said of the Hartford congregation, as Cotton Mather had quite exultantly said some years before of the improved condition of things in Massachusetts churches, that "more than a Score of Tunes are heard Regularly Sung in their Assemblies." . . . .

So it appears that only three or four tunes were being sung at the end of a hundred years, and the only progress that had been made in that time was the partial victory the advocates of singing "by rule" had won over their adversaries.

The tunes that were added to the Bay Psalm Book were twelve in number, and were named as follows: Litchfield, Low Dutch or Canterbury, York, Windsor, Cambridge, St. David's, Martyrs, Hackney or St. Mary's and the 100th, 115th, 119th and 148th psalm tunes. One of Mr. Bliss's "Glimpses" puts a quaint touch upon this old-fashioned singing in the meeting-house:

The fierceness of the controversy caused by the change in methods of psalm-singing may be seen in a petition sent by Joseph Hawley, of Farmington, to the legislature at Hartford, in May, 1725, which 'humbly sheweth' that 'Deacon hart ye Chorister one Sabbath day In setting ye psalm attempted to sing Bella tune — and your memorialist being used to ye old way supposed ye deacon had aimed at Cambridge short tune and set it wrong, whereupon your petitioner Raised his Voice in ye sd short tune and ye people followed him & so there was an unhappy Discord in ye Singing, and ye Blame was all imputed to your poor petitioner, and John Hooker Esqr sent for him & fined him for breach of Sabbath, and so your poor petitioner is Layed under a very heavie Scandal & Reproach & Rendered vile & prophane for what he did in ye fear of God.'"

In Chapin's Glastenbury (1853) this contention over singing by note or by rote is referred to, and in that town the question was settled as at Hartford and Windsor, by a compromise:

"The storm spent its greatest fury in Massachusetts, dividing congregations and arraying ministers and people, deacons and choirs, in the utmost hostility against each other. In Connecticut, the zeal of the combatants was less fervid and general. But even here the interposition of the General Court was required in many towns to quiet the disturbances arising from the introduction of singing by rule. In Glastenbury the matter was quietly and easily disposed of by a vote of the town in Feb. 1733, directing the congregation in the first society to sing one half of the day by 'rote' and the other half by 'rule' and to begin after the next election. . . . ."

This could only mean the ultimate triumph of the new way, and with it a demand for singing schools, and the introduction of choirs.

(TO BE CONTINUED.)

THE PENNYROYAL HYMN.

The operatic warbler may voice her culture rare
With Wagner, Rubinstein and Bach, or any high-flown air,
But still her notes are lacking they're so very straight and prim
By the side of that old melody, the pennyroyal hymn.

When Deacon Jones and Sister Prime in joyful tune did blend.
With many an extra here and there, and such a hearty end,
The church was filled with music up to the very brim,
When the chorus joined the choir in that penny-royal hymn.

The palsied organ creaked and wheezed, when soaring up on C,
And grumbled, groaned and trembled down along the depths of G;
But, never faltering its work, like a soldier, staid and grim,
It started out to wrestle with a pennyroyal hymn.

The boys would swell the rolling song to help the deacons out,
But keen would be the ear that told just what they sang about,
But words were never noticed, for they sang with mighty vim,
So their aid was very welcome in that pennyroyal hymn.

A MIDSUMMER DREAM.

WILLARD WARNER.

The golden year is in its summer gear;
   The world is sleeping in a cloud of luster;
And round the freighted altars of the year
   The blushing roses cluster.

Upon the hill-top sleeps the lambent light,
   While all the valley lies in deepest shadow;
The brooklet, murmuring at its languid plight,
   Creeps slowly through the meadow.

The fields are golden with their harvest crown
   That nods in every dewy breeze that passes,
The hardy apple trees are weighted down
   With golden fruit in masses.

And soft from branches of the way-side tree,
   The merry birds their matins carol, gladdening
The heart of nature with their melody,—
   Their mates with envy maddening.

The cow-boy seeks a sweet, noon-day repose,
   And rests beneath the apple-tree full-laden:
Among the clover-tops — a bed of rose —
   He dreams he lies in Aidenn.

He dreams that he alone, in cloud-land bright,
   Is set to keep the clouds from making battle.
The clouds seem all intent on showing fight,—
   Like great, unruly cattle!

But, down below, the gentle lowing kine
   Stand browsing in the riant, scented clover:
The cow-boy wakes, in ecstasy divine,—
   Then dreams the dream all over.

ANCIENT AND MODERN NORWALK.

BY HON. A. H. BYINGTON.

The town of Norfolk is one of notable antiquity as well as of modern thrift, enterprise and developed attractiveness. It was settled by the whites as early as 1640 when it was called by its Indian name "Norwake," and the next year, was formally established a town by its English settlers. Its location is upon the south-western hill-slopes that beautify the shores of Long Island sound, forty-two miles from the city of New York. Its population in 1860 was 7,582; in 1880, it was 13,956; in 1890, or in the last census, it was deemed to be about 18,000, and at the present time, a fair and moderate estimate puts its population at fully 20,000. Norwalk harbor is studded with numerous

NORWALK GREEN AND THADDEUS BETTS PLACE.

picturesque islands and the views from its surrounding hills are of unrivaled beauty. As a popular summer resort, its fame is wide-spread. A ride over its hills and along the saline shores, presents new charms in the constantly varying panorama of beauty and delight.

The New York and New Haven railroad runs hourly trains from Norwalk between the two cities, while a passenger steamer and two freight propellers daily ply to and from New York. A tri-weekly steamer also runs to and from Huntington, L. I., and scores of steam oyster boats, are engaged in Norwalk's great and profitable oyster industry. Trains over the Danbury and Housatonic divisions of the Consolidated system give convenient access to the interior of

WEST AVENUE, NORWALK.

the state and with south-western Massachusetts. Few New England towns possess such ample facilities of railroad and water communication, with all parts of the country.

Its parks, churches, beautiful homes and shaded avenues, with its two lines of electrically equipped street railways, its gas and two electric light plants, its two public water systems, ample sanitary sewer sys-

THE GOVERNOR BISSELL PLACE.

tem, several post-offices and free delivery, state armory, two public libraries, five national and three savings banks, society lodges, two Grand Army Posts, hotels and daily and weekly newspapers, added to its exceptional healthfulness,

THE ORRIS S. FERRY PLACE.

284   ANCIENT AND MODERN NORWALK.

TRYON'S HILL.

give Norwalk advantages and attractions as a place for desirable residence, business and manufactures, possessed by very few even of the most eligibly located New England towns. Its growth during the past decade has been phenomenal, and to-day Norwalk stands seventh in importance and population among the towns of the state.

Norwalk in its personal biographies is equally notable. It has been the birth-place and residence of statesmen, divines, judges, physicians, soldiers and philanthropists, almost innumerable and of historic renown. It was the home and is now the burial place of Governor Thomas Fitch of Colonial times; of Governor and Judge Clark Bissell; of U. S. Senators Thaddeus Betts and Orris S. Ferry, of Rev. Drs. Burnett (of revolutionary war fame), Buckingham, Hall, Mead, Weed and Beard. It is the present home of Maj. Gen. Darius N. Couch, who would have been in chief command of the Army of the Potomac at Gettysburg, had not his innate modesty, led him to resolutely decline the honor and responsibility. It is the birth-place and home of a daughter of Captain Hezekiah Betts of the Revolutionary Army, who still lives in the enjoyment of all her faculties. It was the birth-place and home of the parents of General, Judge and Senator Sherman, before their removal to Ohio, also of U. S. Treasurer James W. Hyatt, and is now that of U. S. Patent Commissioner John S. Seymour, and last, though by no means least, of Congressman Ebenezer J. Hill.

THE SHERMAN PLACE.

In ye olden times, Washington passed the night at one of our local hostelries; Franklin was a quite frequent visitor to the old Norwalk inn upon the church green and a voracious devourer of Norwalk's, even then, celebrated oysters. La Fayette halted here for supper and addressed his Norwalk admirers, on the occasion of his carriage ride through the state to Boston. It was burned by order of the British Commander Gen. Tryon, at the time of his raid into Connecticut, July 11, 1799, nevertheless it is to-day among the foremost towns of the state, in culture, modern enterprise and progress, in picturesque beauty of scenery and, as a summer resort, is justly believed to be unrivaled by any other town in New England.

The Norwalk Board of trade recently issued the following circular:

"The groups of Norwalk Islands, distant about a mile from the main land, form a beautiful and commodious harbor which receives the Norwalk River up which vessels of twelve feet draft can sail a distance of two miles. A passenger

THE ROBERTS MILITARY SCHOOL.

steamer runs daily to and from New York in the summer, and daily freight-boat during the entire year. There is also a tri-weekly boat to Huntington, Long Island, in the summer. Dorlon's Point at the eastern entrance to the harbor and Roton Point at the western are delightful summer resorts, and the drives over the hills and along the shore are unrivalled in beauty.

The New York, New Haven and Hartford Railroad furnishes hourly transit to and from New York city, and the Housatonic railroad with its western and northwestern connections brings Norwalk into easy communication with all parts of the country.

The town, lying for five miles along the valley of the Norwalk river and climbing up the splendid hills, that reach out on either side, with its magnificently shaded streets, the result of two hundred and fifty years of care and thought, is not only a town of beautiful homes, but by its location, its rail and water communications, and the advantages it possesses for all kinds of manufacturing industries, it has grown to the seventh in population in the State.

It has eight post-offices and a free delivery system, excellent telegraph and telephone service, twelve miles of street railroad, concrete and flag-stone sidewalks, a well organized and well equipped fire department and fire alarm system, gas and electric lights, a fine system of water-works, costing half a million dollars and now self-sustaining, a sewer system which has cost a quarter million of dollars, twelve public and five private schools, three daily and two weekly newspapers, three hotels and fifteen churches. It has two public libraries, five National banks with a total capital of $740,000, three Savings banks with 9,250 depositors and $3,162,000 of assets. It has two military companies and a fine State armory, a flourishing Young Men's Christian Association and thirty-one lodges, societies, and other social and benevolent organizations.

Its industries are diversified and extensive. The largest single one is the manufacture of fur hats, in which fifteen establishments employing about fifteen hundred persons are engaged. The second in importance is the cultivation of

STATE ARMORY.

oysters for which Norwalk has literally a world-wide reputation. In addition to these there are the following factories; 2 locks; 1 steam engines and air compressors; 2 straw hats; 1 corsets; 1 hatters' supplies; 2 furnaces and stoves; 3 cassimeres, worsteds and felts; 1 elastic fabrics; 3 shoes; 2 hardware novelties; 5 carriages; 1 shirts; 5 sash, doors and blinds; 3 paper boxes and packing-cases; 7 cigars; 2 fur cutting; 5 saw mills; 1 gas stoves and appliances; 2 iron fences; 2 cement pipe; 4 planing mills; 3 machine shops; 1 patterns."

In nothing however is Norwalk more notable than its shore and island sites for summer cottages. At Roton Point, Rowayton, Bell Island, Hickory Bluff, Piney Point, The Knob, and Fitch's Point, and upon the numerous picturesque outer Islands studding the harbor, there are several hundred of these beautiful summer homes, mainly owned and occupied by people from abroad, who have been attracted by Norwalk's unrivaled marine and shore scenery. The late noted Wall street Banker, LeGrand Lockwood built his two million dollar residence here and many other showy and costly edifices have been erected in recent years. The great majority of Norwalk's summer residences are, however, of the comfortable and unpretentious styles of architecture, rather than the gaudy and excessively ornamental structures, so frequently erected by shoddy or smart sort of people, who frequently migrate from our large cities and seek to impress their wealth and importance upon the more sober-minded and sensible

NORWALK YACHT CLUB HOUSE.

rustics. Norwalk is particularly blessed with a refined and cultured society and encouragingly exempt from the ignorant, vicious and degraded elements too common in other sea-port towns.

TO THE "BARD OF THE BUNGALOW."

JOHN PAYNE.

My day and night are in my lady's hand;
I have no other sunrise than her sight;
For me her favor glorifies the land;
Her anger darkens all the cheerful light,
  Her face is fairer than the hawthorne white,
When all a-flower in May the hedge-rows stand;
  While she is kind, I know of no affright;
My day and night are in my lady's hand.

All heaven in her glorious eyes is spanned;
Her smile is softer than the summer's night,
  Gladder than daybreak on the Faery stand;
I have no other sunrise than her sight.
  Her silver speech is like the singing flight
Of runnels rippling o'er the jeweled sand;
  Her kiss a dream of delicate delight;
For me her favor glorifies the land.

What if the Winter chase the Summer bland!
The gold sun in her hair burns ever bright.
  If she be sad, straightway all joy is banned;
Her anger darkens all the cheerful light.

HISTORIC HOMES.

III. HOMES OF STATE-CRAFT.

BY W. FARRAND FELCH.

We are all sufficiently familiar with the history of our country to tell on our fingers' ends the names of the principal heroes and leaders in its history — for instance, Governors Carver, Bradford and Winthrop, Miles Standish, Roger Williams, Thomas Hooker, John Eliot, and so on down to our day. But how little do we know of them personally, beyond the mere names and what they stand for. There is, however, a notable company of their descendants extending down to the present day that constitutes what Dr. Holmes, with great felicity,

THE GOVERNOR HOPKINS HOUSE.

called "The Brahmin-caste of New England," who were born leaders, brainy men, brilliant, straight-forward, steady-going people, all of them who fulfilled the promise given by their first ancestors on the soil. To this class belong such heroes as Israel Putnam, Nathan Hale, the Adamses, Winthrops, Edwardses, Hookers, and many others who come from the sturdy old stock of the founders of the Republic.

If it is so difficult for the average citizen of the republic to remember the worthies of national repute, how much more so to recall state celebrities who gain a local and limited repute merely. The average man can not recall the names of all the presidents, much less the governors of his native state in chronological order. These then, must be our excuses for presenting, as the last of this series, some data as to the homes of our governors and leading statesmen, in Hartford.

John Haynes, the first governor of Connecticut, came to this country in the same vessel with the venerable Hooker, in 1633, and was a member of his congregation in the original "Newtowne," in Massachusetts. He came from Copford Hall, Essex, England, and was a man of considerable wealth and evident culture. He was made governor of the Massachusetts colony, in 1635, and did not, in consequence, come to Hartford with the famous Hooker party, but soon after.

It is a tradition that the first written constitution of Connecticut was largely the work of Mr. Hooker and Mr. Haynes. It was adopted in 1639. Bancroft describes Mr. Haynes as a man of "large estate and larger affections; of heavenly mind and spotless life." He was chosen governor of the colony in 1639, and as he could not, by the constitution he had helped to write, hold the office more than one year at a time, he was elected alternate years as long as he lived, dying March 1, 1654.

The home of Governor Haynes was on Arch street, near the present gas works.

THE GOVERNOR TALCOTT HOUSE.

The same house was occupied by the sixth and seventh governors, John Winthrop, Junior, of New London and William Leete of Guilford. Arch street was then a noted thoroughfare, and withal historical.

Dr. Trumbull in speaking of the cause of the removal from Newtowne (Cambridge), to Newtowne in Connecticut (Hartford), considers that the relative popularity of Haynes and Winthrop, Cotton and Hooker was not without influence. Mr. Haynes, he says, "was not considered in any respect inferior to Governor Winthrop. His growing popularity and the fame of Mr. Hooker . . . . were supposed to have no small influence upon the general court in their granting liberty to Mr. Hooker and his company to remove to Connecticut.

Edward Hopkins was the second governor of Connecticut, and came with the New Haven colony, which reached Boston bay in 1637, four years after Haynes and Hooker. He married Ann Yale whose mother had married Theophilus Eaton, the first governor of the New Haven colony. He became a magistrate soon after coming to Hartford, and first Secretary under the written constitution, which would perhaps signify that he too was somewhat instrumental in its compilation, more perhaps than in the matter of chirography. He alternated with Mr. Haynes as governor and deputy-governor until Mr. Haynes' death. The May following, Mr. Hopkins was re-elected, although "absent," having gone to England, not to return. He had been in England several times before, but now that Cromwell was in full sway "at home," he saw fit to remain, became a member of parliament, and was made warden of the fleet, succeeding his brother. He died in England, in March, 1657, of consumption, aged fifty-eight, leaving his large property in New England to be devoted to the academic and collegiate education of young men. His wife was Ann, daughter of David Yale, of Denbighshire.* She is described by Gov. Winthrop, the elder, as "a goodly young woman and of special parts, who has fallen into a sad infirmity,

"GOVERNOR'S ROW," WASHINGTON STREET.

the loss of her understanding and reason which had been growing on her divers years by occasions of giving herself wholly to reading and writing, having written many books," and intimates that through the "tenderness and love of her husband, who was loth to deny her her favorite studies that her disease became seated and aggravated." About £2000 of his estate, plainly intended for Yale college fell into the hands of the trustees of Harvard, and three grammar schools at New Haven, Hartford and at Hadley, Massachusetts.

The home of Gov. Hopkins was on Governor street, traditionally the house

---

* David Yale, from Wales, New Haven 1637; Boston 1645, left sons David and Thomas and daughter Ann. Gov. Hopkins recommends to the care of David, his " poor distressed wife." She died Dec. 17, 1698 aged 83, insane. She was fifteen years her husband's junior. Elihu, son of Thomas Yale, first of New Haven, then of London, in East Indies twenty years and later Governor of Hon. East India Company, gave repeated and generous donations to Yale college which received his name. He died in London, buried in Wrexham, Denbighshire, 1721, aged 73. His daughter Catherine married Lord North; Ann married Lord Cavendish, son of Duke of Devonshire, and Ursula died unmarried.

of which a view is here given, hence the oldest existing home of an executive in this city. Governor Welles also resided on Governor street, and Thomas H. Seymour, one of our late governors who was akin to Horatio Seymour, Governor of New York state, both descended from the original John, of Hartford. The ancestral home of our Governor Seymour was on Arch street. The Ledyard elm, now standing south of the Lincoln iron works is on the original Seymour

RESIDENCE OF WILLIAM H. BULKELEY.

tract. John Ledyard, "the great American traveler," nephew of Thomas Seymour and cousin of the Governor, was born in Groton, and came to live with his uncle at the age of nineteen; he entered Dartmouth, 1772, and the next year came home from college down the Connecticut river in a canoe. This elm tree was planted in commemoration of the event. The property was deeded to the present owner, Mr. Lincoln, on condition that the tree should never be trimmed or cut in any way except by the Park commissioners. When it was struck by lightning a few years ago, the dead branches could not be removed except by the authority of the commissioners. We are indebted for this information to Mr. John Ledyard Denison, of Hartford, who adds that it is a striking example of "Woodman, spare that tree."

Governor George Wyllys, the third governor, lived on Charter Oak Hill, and was the original owner of the famous oak. Where it stood, a tablet has been placed, in the wall beside the street called Charter Oak Place. Ex-Mayor Wm. Waldo Hyde is the present owner of the estate.

Governor Wyllys came from Fenny Compton, county Warwick, England, leaving there a large estate. He was chosen deputy governor in 1641, governor in 1642, and died in March, 1644. Samuel Wyllys, his son, born in England, graduated at Harvard, married Ruth, daughter of Governor Haynes. He owned land in Glastonbury, and left a son Hezekiah who was Secretary of State from 1711 to 1735, whose son George was Secretary, 1735 to 1796, a period of sixty-one years; Gen. Samuel Wyllys, son of George, was Secretary of State from 1796 to 1809,—making a total of ninety-eight years the office was held by three generations of the Wyllyses! It is small wonder, then, as Miss Talcott says in her article on the Center church burying-ground, that one of the Wyllys family exclaimed that "if Connecticut could not remember the Wyllyses without grave-stones their memory might rot!" The family is now extinct in this town, Hezekiah being the last of the name to reside in the old mansion. He and his brother Samuel had children who died young or unmarried. Miss Peck, in her poem on The Charter Oak has embalmed the tradition which saved the Charter Oak to be a receptacle of the charter (or its duplicate, *vide* Dr. Hoadly). Ruth, daughter of Hezekiah Wyllys, married the third Richard Lord, brother of Elisha, who owned "Lord's Hill," now Asylum Hill. The Charter Oak estate was the residence of the late Isaac W. Stuart, ("Scaeva," author of "Hartford in the Olden Time,") son of Prof. Stuart, of Andover.

Governor Welles resided on Governor street, as noted. Thomas Welles probably came to Hartford from Saybrook, and is reported to have been private secretary to Lord Say and Seal before coming to New England. He was first treasurer of the colony, then secretary from 1640 to 1648, deputy

RESIDENCE OF LEVERETT BRAINARD.

governor in 1654, 1656, 1657, and 1659, and governor in 1658. He died January 14, 1660. He married for his second wife, Elizabeth, widow of Nathaniel Foote (of the famous Foote family, from whom descended the Beechers) and sister of John Deming. The governor's first wife was Elizabeth Hunt, whom he married in England. His son John went to Stamford to settle in 1640, carrying the Wethersfield records with him, claiming he had a right to them, a

HISTORIC HOMES. 293

practice quite common then which has caused no end of trouble to genealogists of to-day. Robert, son of this John, inherited the Governor's farm in Wethersfield, covering the ground where the state prison now is, and nearly half a mile further north. Samuel, son of the governor, inherited a farm in Glastonbury, or Naubuc, and from him came Hon. Gideon Welles, of Lincoln's cabinet. Thomas, junior, another son, settled in Hartford, and married the widow of John Pantry (another extinct name) and daughter of William Tuttle, of New Haven, (for whom see " Old Colonial Characters.") Sarah, daughter of the governor, married John Chester of Wethersfield, whose father was Leonard Chester, " Armiger," or 'Squire, who bore a coat of arms,— one of the few in Hartford — and came to this country before 1635. John Chester's daughter, Eunice, married Rev Timothy Stevens, first minister of Glastonbury, who with Hon.

RESIDENCE OF MORGAN G. BULKELEY.

Gershom Bulkeley (" Garsham Backly "), and Hon. Eleazer Kimberly (the first male child born in New Haven), Secretary of the Conn. Colony, 1696 to 1709, laid out the civil polity of that bailiwick.

Governor Joseph Talcott, the eleventh governor, resided on the east side of Main street at the entrance of what is now Talcott street. The present building occupying the site of this dwelling is commonly called " The Talcott house," and is probably the oldest house in town. The shingles on the south side have been in place for a century, and the old nails are of wrought iron. The house does not appear originally to have belonged to John Talcott. His house lot was on the opposite side of Main street. Talcott street was laid out in 1761 by Samuel Talcott. A part of the old Talcott building is said to have been built by John Talcott in 1646, and if so it is the oldest building in town. The Talcott interest was sold out as late as 1814, and since then it has had various owners. It has long been used for mercantile purposes.

The Talcott family is a very ancient one. The emigrant ancestor was John, who was born in Braintree, Essex, England, son of another John, and grandson of a third John of Colchester, Essex, living there in 1558, and his father, a fourth John, was from Warwickshire. The emigrant John, married Dorothy, daughter of Mark Mott, of Braintree, an eminent and ancient family, and brought his bride with him in "The Lion." Their son, Lieut.-Col. John (the fifth John in line) succeeded his father as treasurer of the colony, and was the father of Gov.

THE JEWELL RESIDENCE.

Jos. Talcott. Another son of John, the emigrant, was Samuel, ancestor of the Wethersfield and Glastonbury Talcotts, through his wife who was the daughter of Elizur and Mary (Pynchon), Holyoke of Springfield — distinguished names in Massachusetts — and was Secretary of State of Connecticut. His descendants intermarried with the Chesters, Demings, Hollisters, Bulkeleys, Wrights and Hales, and left a notable progeny.

We have already given the reader enough genealogy to ponder over for some time, and lest we shall weary him we will desist, remembering Tom Hood's famous lines on "Miss Kilmansegg":

"To trace the Kilmansegg pedigree
To the very root of the family tree,
  Were a task as rash as ridiculous;
Through antediluvian mists as thick
As London fog such a line to pick
Were enough in truth to puzzle Old Nick,
Not to name Sir Harry Nicolas,"—

meaning of course Sir Harris Nicolas, the eminent English heraldist and historian.

Oliver Wolcott, governor of the state from 1817 to 1827, resided on Main street a few paces south of Central Row. Governor Isaac Toucey lived at one time where the Aetna building now stands, on the corner of Athenæum street, succeeding to the estate of his father-in-law, Cyprian Nichols. Later he lived in the building now occupied by the Travelers Insurance Company, which must be seventy-five or more years old, and there he died, after the Civil war. He was in the cabinet of President Buchanan before the war. This building was also the residence at one time of Henry L. Ellsworth, who was United States Commissioner of Patents, twin brother of Governor William W. Ellsworth, the latter of whom resided in the old Captain Morgan house on Front street, still standing. Henry L. Ellsworth gave $700,000 to Yale College, which though failing in part, yet testified to his great regard for learning. On the opposite corner, where the Connecticut Fire Insurance Company's building stands, lived Governor Joseph Trumbull. On another corner lived Chief Justice Thomas S. Williams, now the residence of Mr. Parsons, his residuary legatee. On the remaining corner of Grove and Prospect streets lived Theodore Dwight,—this being a very historic corner fifty years and more ago.

THE HUBBARD RESIDENCE.

About this time Washington street became the fashionable quarter of the town, and what is now called "Governor's Row," was inaugurated, by the removal thither of Governor Ellsworth. In 1836 he built the house now owned and occupied by ex-Lieutenant Governor William H. Bulkeley. Governor Ellsworth was the son of the chief justice of the United States, Oliver Ellsworth, and his wife was the daughter of Noah Webster, the noted lexicographer, who resided with them for some years. For a generation, the Ellsworth mansion was one of the most charming social centers of the city. Mrs. Ellsworth died in 1861, and the Governor, January 15, 1868, at an advanced age. He was deacon of the Center church for half a century, and was one of the committee which selected Dr. Hawes as pastor. His son, Dr. Pinckney W. Ellsworth, resided in the house for two years when it was sold to Hon. Eliphalet A. Bulkeley, founder and first president of the Ætna Life Insurance company, and father of Governor Morgan G. Bulkeley, Lieut.-Gov. Bulkeley, Charles E. Bulkeley who was killed in the Civil war, and Mrs. Leverett Brainard, wife of the present Mayor of the city. This residence was the scene of brilliant receptions during the incumbency of General Bulkeley as Lieut. Governor, and is one of the most noted houses in the city.

During the administration of Gov. Andrews, the public receptions were given at the residence of Gen. Bulkeley, who was then on the governor's staff.

Public and State receptions have also been given at the residence of Hon. Leverett Brainard, formerly the home of Bishop Kip. When the buildings of Trinity College crowned Capitol Hill, efforts were made by the faculty to secure this as the place of residence of the president. It is a very imposing structure of the old Doric column style, so popular a century since.

The residence of Hon. Morgan G. Bulkeley which adjoins that of his brother, was erected by Thos. K. Brace. There have been a number of notable assemblages

THE BARBOUR RESIDENCE.

at this house, not the least remarkable being the reception given to Hon. James G. Blaine in 1888, when Mr. Bulkeley was the candidate for gubernatorial honors. A recent writer gives a glimpse of the interior of this house which is worthy of brief mention.

The rich antiques in the house, which the Governor and his wife have collected, would excite the envy of the oldest connoisseurs. Mrs. Bulkeley is an experienced collector of old china and art works, and has some of the most interesting specimens in the State. The souvenir plates with which the walls of the dining-room are decorated cannot be surpassed in Connecticut. The Governor himself has a cultivated taste in this direction and has recently acquired two of the most valuable specimens in the United States. One of them is an authenticated article from the table service of Thomas Hooker, "the light of the western churches" and founder of the Hartford colony. It is one of the rarest of old platters in the United States. The most elegant specimen in the Governor's collection is an invaluable plate that was owned by Governor Saltonstall. It is a unique work of art in itself. With this magnificent prize is a fragment of the dress worn by the wife of Governor Saltonstall when she was presented to the Queen. But the Governor's special interest is in old furniture. He is the owner of some of the most valuable specimens to be found In New England. One set of superbly-carved mahogany chairs in his possession can be traced back for 175 years. Tables and chairs of rare association and interest occupy the parlor and reception-rooms, and the house throughout is rich in art and evidences of culture.

Washington street has long been favored by the chief executives of the state, as a resident street. Hon. Marshall Jewell lived on the street before he became governor. Lieut.-Governor Albert Day passed his last hours in the Barbour residence, and Lieut.-Governor Francis B. Loomis in the one now owned by Mr. Joseph R. Cone, where his daughter, Mrs. Havemeyer then lived. Mr. Day resided during his official incumbency on Main street, near Sheldon.

Hon. Marshall Jewell, during his occupancy of the executive chair, lived in what is now known as the Niles residence on Farmington avenue. He was, in addition to Governor, Grant's Postmaster-General, and in charge of the national republican committee in one campaign. Gen. Grant came to Hartford in 1880, and the state militia in general, had rendezvous at Hartford to give him a rousing welcome. Gov. Jewell was further honored by the mission to Russia. He began life as a tanner's apprentice, like Grant, and by constant exposure of his arms in the steeping-vat he was, it is said, unable to sleep unless his arms were bare, a habit he retained all his life. As a journeyman-tanner he worked over-hours, day after day, and used to say to the laboring man:

"You have as fair a chance as any man in the world. Any working man who is industrious and temperate and ambitious can not only get on, but he will find the hand of the capitalist extended to him in many directions in order to help him get along. I tell you that the more there are of men of that kind the better capital will like it."

The residence of Governor R. D. Hubbard occupies a picturesque spot on Washington street. Part of the estate has been sold since his death, for building purposes, but the old residence is still standing. It was owned prior to his occupancy by Major Welles, first selectman of Hartford. Governor Hubbard has been "embalmed in bronze," the latest heroic-size statue in the capitol grounds.

The home of Lieut.-Governor Catlin has already been given in these pages, as the former home of Mrs. Sigourney, and since the article appeared it has been sold to a syndicate for business purposes.

Gov. Joseph R. Hawley resided on Sigourney street, during the year he held the executive reins, and there ex-Lieut.-Gov. E. Spicer Cleveland now lives. During one year of Gov. Lounsbury's term he lived in the Senator Dixon residence opposite the cathedral.*

The list might be extended and many facts of interest gathered concerning other noted residences in this "city of homes," but the few of the best known that have been treated in this series show us how time in his flight makes the life of yesterday the history of to-day.

---

* We are indebted for many facts to the Hartford Daily Times.

THE OLD PLACE.

JOSEPH TRUMAN.

A placid life hums through the homestead old,
    No modern mood aches here,
The peace of ages brood o'er wood and wold,—
    No village babbles near.

But all is openness, light, distance fair,
    And large majestic sky,
And through the silent heights of evening air
    The shouting rooks sail by.

A presence pure once moved through the hushed place,
    Stately and sweet and free,
Gave to its tongueless beauty vital grace,
    Lit the sequestered lea.

What images engaging gathered there—
    What warmth, what wit, what charm!
How filled with glory were those pastures bare,
    How glowed the homely farm!

That form has vanished, and the voice is still,
    The halo paled away:
Sunset is sad upon the lonely hill—
    The gold of morning grey.

HIGHLAND PARK, MANCHESTER

BY MARIE DE VALCHERVILLE.

Beautiful for situation are the Highlands of Manchester. Located amid the foothills of the Bolton range, which for romantic beauty are unsurpassed by any in New England, Highland Park lying about two miles easterly from South Manchester, is the gem of the surrounding country. The view to the south and east is obstructed by the wooded hills, but to the north and west, fifty miles of the Connecticut valley from Mount Holyoke on the north to the hills near Portland on the south may be seen from elevated points. Looking toward the west, occasional glimpses of the smooth-flowing Connecticut, the gilded dome of the Capitol glistening in the sunlight, the buildings of Trinity College, and in the extreme distance the heights of the Talcott Mountain range are visible.

A natural park forms the center of the village and is the first object of interest to the approaching tourist. To the south of this park are deep ravines with wooded sides, which form a pleasing setting for the two waterfalls which dash over the red sandstone precipices in masses of foaming spray. Two springs are situated near the upper fall, one of which has long been known to possess valuable healing properties. In fact it is said that the Indians were wont to resort here for their "medicine water," and a century ago it was a common occurrence to see a person on horseback with jugs on either side connected with ropes going to and from the spring. Only a few rods distant from this spring is another of clear, pure, sparkling water that

MINERAL SPRINGS.

is much used for table purposes. The glen below the second falls is thus described in the Memorial History of Hartford County. "Here the stream falls sixty-five feet over the rocks into the valley below, grass-covered, and enclosed for some distance by wooded bluffs,—a miniature Yosemite, admired by all observers. At the base of these bluffs are excavations that have been made for ore, (sulphide of copper), which, being found in limited quantity was supposed to indicate the existence of valuable mines. In the original division of the land, the place where the copper mines were supposed to be, was to remain undivided, 'to lye for the general benefit of the proprietors.'"

These "Wyllys mines" were operated to some extent in the first half of the century, and one across the brook from the valley still remains open for the investigation of those who have the temerity to explore its depths. This locality was once the old Wyllys farm, the property of Ephraim Wyllys, the founder of that family in this section and possibly a descendant of George Wyllys of Hartford, one of the early governors of Connecticut. His gambrel-roofed house still stands on the brow of the hill across from the mineral spring; the frame still remains intact, but it has been re-covered and its interior entirely remodeled by the present owner.

The whole vicinity of Highland Park in the early part of the century, was evidently a prosperous farming community, as the number of house cellars and old ruins attest, and history records the existence of a Baptist Church, formerly well attended, about a quarter of a mile to the east, where now only a triangular plot of ground remains to tell of the ancient house of worship. Although at the present time no descendant of any of the old families lives in the village, the name of Wyllys being perpetuated by the street name alone, good deeds often outlive family names, for a subscription paper recently found shows that Ephraim Wyllys in 1822 contributed seventy-five dollars to the building of a church, a considerable amount for a farmer to give in those days of large families and consequent rigid economy.

MOUTH OF THE MINE.

Since 1863, there have been extensive paper mills erected at Highland Park, by Case Brothers, furnishing employment to many of the villagers. On the site first occupied formerly stood a grist-mill, a picturesque affair with its ancient, overshot, wooden wheel, sixteen feet in diameter, the movements of which could be seen from the outside. Located in a little glen a short distance from the mill is a bottling house in the cottage style of architecture, so surrounded by trees that it is a surprise to the visitor approaching it for the first time.

In this secluded retreat, with the plashing of the waterfall, the purling of the brook, and the singing of the birds one might easily fall asleep, on a sum-

THE FALLS, HIGHLAND PARK.

mer's day, for "tired nature's sweet restorer, balmy sleep," seems to hold perfect sway in this delightful spot. Notwithstanding its rural surroundings, Highland Park keeps pace with the many modern improvements, having its own system of water-works, its electrical plant, and the first electric street lights placed in the town. It is rumored that the whirring of the trolley car will ere

RUSTIC BRIDGE.

long be heard in its quiet streets, but whatever concessions are made to the enterprises of human ingenuity, the natural beauty of the place can never be wholly effaced.

YOUR NATIVE TOWN.

JOSEPHINE CANNING.

"Oh, don't you remember the schoolhouse red
    Which stood far back on the hill,
And the great oak tree which lifted its head
    Close by? It stands there still.
You learned addition in that old place,
    And the use of verb and noun;
They have earned you much in life's hard race —
    Give some to the dear old town!

"You have wandered far from the hearthstone gray
    Where your infant feet first trod,
You have walked in many a devious way,
    But you worship your father's God.
For you'll never forget the lesson taught,
    When at night you all knelt down
In the home that you hold with the tenderest thought,
    In your own old native town.

"Ah! go when the summer solstice burns,
    And your city home is hot,
Go look where the winding river turns
    In the green old meadow lot.
Then ask the people what it needs,
    And count it life's best crown
To build it up with filial deeds,
    Your own dear native town!"

A DAY DREAM.

CLEMENT C. CALVERLEY.

Quaint old woodland, still I view thee,
As, in dreams, I wandered through thee—
When each rustling sound thrilled through me,
　Fraught with Nature's melody:
Whispering now, as in the olden
Days that Time has tinctured golden
　With thy mellow memory.

Through thy leaves are sun-beams straying:
In the brook are minnows playing;
Sweetest scents, the breeze delaying.
　Float at random on the air.
Where, among thy darkling spaces,
Light and shadow interlaces,
　In day-dreams, I, wandering, fare.

　　Here the trees, gaunt guardians, hover
　　O'er the brook, as if to cover
　　It from fond eyes, like a lover,
　　　Jealous of his lady's faith;
　　And the brook sweeps on, not caring
　　For the gracious shade, or flaring
　　　Sunlight, dancing like a wraith.

　　　　Singing, dancing, over ledges,—
　　　　Mosses, ferns, upon the edges;
　　　　Rippling softly through the sedges,
　　　　　Winding onward, dark and deep,—
　　　　Through the tangled thicket-bower,
　　　　Waiting for the dew-born shower,
　　　　　Still it wanders in my sleep.

　　　　And my soul is hushed in slumber,
　　　　Fondly dreaming of the number
　　　　Of the echoes that encumber
　　　　　Memories of voices gone.
　　　　Till my spirit wakens, glowing
　　　　With glad visions, over-flowing
　　　　　Dream-land into drowsy dawn.

　　Sweetest music now is filling
　　Atmosphere of dreamland,—thrilling,
　　Sad, and weird, and mournful,—stilling
　　　My soul with its symphony:
　　Thus, in day-dreams quiet gloaming,
　　Self and Soul are fond of roaming,
　　　Hushed by Nature's harmony.

　　　　　L' ENVOI.

　　Soul from Self we may not sever;
　　Life is but a day-dream ever:
　　Dreams are but the soul's endeavor
　　　To regain the life ideal.
　　All our life is but a seeming;
　　Death is but an endless dreaming;
　　　Dreamland is the "Land o' Leal."

A Novel of New York and Hartford.

BY FREDERIC BEECHER PERKINS.

CHAPTER V.

Old Mr. Van Braam found standing in his hall a monstrous fat, vulgar, oily-looking red-haired man with a vast face, of which a terrible over-proportion had gravitated into an elaborate apparatus of double chins. The old gentleman, a squeamish and delicate person, was about as much pleased as if he had been visited by a bone-boiling establishment; but he put on as good a face as possible, and said, as civilly as he could,

"Did you wish to see me, sir?"

"Yes sir," promptly answered this whale of a man, speaking in a thick wheezy gobbling voice, as if his larynx operated from under a pile of half-melted scrap-tallow, and puffing as he spoke. "Sorry to trouble you, sir, but it is necessary." And turning forwards the lapel of his coat he showed beneath it the broad silver badge of the Detective Service. At this corroboration of the professional name on the visitor's card, the old gentlemen was more annoyed and mystified than before. The detective's broad, impassive countenance did not change, and his head remained motionless; but his small, dull, grayish eyes just turned from Mr. Van Braam's puzzled face to the end of the hall and back,

"Haven't you some little side room where we could be quite alone for a few moments?" he asked.

Mr. Van Braam, without saying a word, showed the way into a small waiting-room, lit the gas, and handed his visitor a seat. He waddled over to a sofa, however, saying as he did so, in his fat wheezing way,

"Thank ye; but I take sofys ginrally when I can git um. Chairs ain't much 'count for a man o' my build, anyway."

The discomfort of the old gentleman arose to an extreme, as he sat waiting for this vast greasy man to reveal whatever horror there might be. But his conjectures were most wild. His own accounts and papers — he was, through the influence of Mr. Tarbox Button, Secretary of the Splosh Fire Insurance Company — he knew were correct. But had some defalcation been discovered in the office? Had either of his two servant-girls been caught in any evil-doing? Had his solitary old dwelling been marked down by burglars, and was he to be prepared for their coming? He strove in vain to imagine what the mystery might be. In a thousand years, however, strive as he might, the poor old gentleman would never have dreamed of what would be implied in the very first words of the vast fat man, who after divers signs of reluctance, broke out, with a clumsy abruptness where he had meant to begin from afar off —

"Is your daughter's health good?"

Mr. Van Braam started, and looked at the detective with a blank astounded face, whiter, if possible, than usual; his mouth open, without a word. The officer instantly saw that the old man, far more sensitive than he had imagined, had received one of those shocks which for the moment annihilate all consciousness. Discomfited, he could only wait. In a few minutes, his host had somewhat recovered. The detective, rough police officer as he was, was no brute, and he instantly decided upon what he saw was the only possible method with such nervous subjects; for, he reflected, if the old gentleman is this way, what must the young lady be? It was very important, he also remembered that he had been told at headquarters in Mulberry street, on account of the very great respectability of the parties interested, that no more annoyance should be caused to any one, than was absolutely unavoidable, and that everything should be managed in the most quiet possible manner. "I'll take the line of not believing a word of it," said the officer to himself, "and of acting on their side entirely." Accordingly, when he saw that the old man was in a situation to hear what was said to him, he began again:

"Ther ain't no 'casion to be troubled, Mr. Van Braam. No charges is made, and ther ain't no reason why ther should be. Fact is, I 'spose I might jest as well a sent the doctor as come myself."

"I'm not very strong," interrupted the old man, faintly, but gaining a desperate angry courage as he went on, "and she's my only child. I can't stand this long. For God Almighty's sake do be quick. Out with it. Why the devil don't you tell me what's the matter without toasting me in hell like that for an hour?"

"You're right, sir," said the man, without showing any ill humor — and indeed why should he? — "I will. Certain parties has intimated that Miss Van Braam, bein' delicate, and a little out of her head like, had accidently carried away a small passel o' lace from Jenks and Trainor's yesterday. Now it's very likely she ain't got it. Ef she has, of course she only took it by oversight. And thare's no disposition to make trouble. What's wanted is to prevent it. They's some parties that would be very troublesome in sech cases. Jenks and Trainor 've b'en plegged to death a'most with this kinder thing now for near onto a year, and they're out of all patience. But all that's necessary is to jest oversee the young lady quietly, and sorter let on in her hearin' about some o' these kleptermaniacs being took up, and it's goin ruther hard with 'em."

The long word which the detective evoked from the domains of modern sentimental criminality — or criminal sentimentality,— and which he flourished with an evident pride, like a strong man whirling a heavy Indian club, to show how easily he can do it, was the first out of all this singularly horrible discourse, that at all enlightened the shocked and confounded auditor. But when it came, it was enough. His anger disappeared as quickly as it had arisen, and an inexpressible sinking pain came in its stead. If any one can comprehend the terror, the agony, of a man who loves, who has but one to love, and who is old; of a father who sees his daughter, his only beloved, and the desire of his eyes, not merely suffering, not merely in sorrow, but in danger of becoming the very scandal and sport of the dirtiest of publics — that of a great city — who sees her certainly ill, possibly monomaniac, and at the parting of the two ways that lead to the mad-house or to the police station — if any one can imagine the sharp deep misery of such a prospect, the hint of it is even too much; and for any one who cannot, a library of detail could not paint it.

But the external signs of the pain that evil news inflicts, are seldom so marked as is often supposed. And persons whose characters are strong by nature, or solidified by hard experiences of life, are more likely to seem impassible even, than to show what they feel. Age, again, often contributes a real insensibility, which is perhaps, the unconscious acquirement of the soul from whose relations with material and embodied existence threads are already beginning to unfasten. Mr. Van Braam, as a person of even spirituality, delicate organization, both physically and mentally, was as easily startled, old man as he had become, as any wild bird. So he would soon have fainted under sharp physical pain. But neither of these weaknesses belonged to his mind, any more than delicate lungs would belong to his mind. Accordingly, although the experienced detective had correctly judged by the physical symptoms, that his suggestion inflicted a fearful shock at first, yet he was surprised at the promptness at which the distress was mastered, and the degree of steadiness with which the trouble was faced, by this white and slender old man.

"Well, Mr. Officer," he said, "you have done right to come to me. It is the first hint I have heard, of course. My daughter's health is not very strong, it is true"—

Here it suddenly struck him that the best thing he could do was to let her condition seem bad rather than good. Evidently if the persons concerned in this demonstration were—as they were said to be—inclined to avoid exposure if the annoyance should cease, the best way to co-operate with them was to promise the supervision suggested, and to acquiesce in the necessity of it. Evidently, also, to talk big and be indignant and threaten, would be to insure a scandal. All this Mr. Van Braam saw, not by wording it over at such length, but at one flash, in the instant's pause as he said "true"—and he went on: —"and I have been a good deal troubled at some of her symptoms and some of her actions. But it is equally important that a careful watch should be kept, whether or not she is as badly off as the gentlemen at your office seem to think. I will do my best; and if you employ some one, so much the better; only she musn't know it."

Some consultation now followed as to the sort of arrangement to be made; it was decided that a quiet and unobtrusive observation should be maintained by the police; and that some reason or other should be found for discontinuing or at least diminishing even the very modest actual indulgences of the young lady in what is called "shopping." And the officer further guaranteed that, if as he hoped (he said it with obvious sincerity), there was only a mistake, not another word should be heard about it by Mr. Van Braam or by anybody. And so the fat detective,—a singularly unsuitable person, Mr. Van Braam couldn't help thinking, physically at least, for such a profession—waddled away.

After seeing him to the door, Mr. Van Braam returned to the parlor. His distress was so great, the effort to control it was becoming such a strain, and the irritability that in such temperaments as his always accompanies displeasure, was rising so fast and so strongly with him, that courteous gentleman as he naturally and habitually was, he was strongly tempted to hustle the two young men instantly out of the house on any or no pretense except that they must begone.

He only came quietly in, however, resumed his seat; and begun mechanically to turn over his papers. He said not a word. He did not notice, in the whirl of his perplexed thoughts, the sense of monstrous evil, the violent struggle to control himself, that his daughter seemed to be asleep and that the two young men were sitting as silent as she—for Chester, after a little while, had quietly resumed his seat without any motion or resistance from Miss Van Braam. But they both saw that something was wrong, the moment he entered; and as he still turned and turned his papers mechanically, Chester, seeing what was proper, looked at his watch, exclaimed at the lateness of the hour, and arose to go. Scrope of Scrope, with creditable promptness, followed his example. The old man, arousing himself, gave them a very genuine invitation to call again and as often as they pleased, on the footing, indeed, he said, of well-acquainted cousins.

"Why, Civille," he exclaimed all at once; "are you going to let our friends go without saying a word?—I do believe she's sound asleep!" he continued, as she did not reply. He lifted the shade from the drop-light on the table and stepped over to her. She was perfectly still, her white teeth just showing between her lips, her head resting easily on the back of the chair, and breathing quietly and regularly.

"Why, Civille, my child!" he said, laying his hand on her shoulder; "You do make your cousins very much at home, I think!" And he shook her a little.

Chester spoke.

"Mr. Van Braam," he said, with embarrassment, "I'm afraid it's my fault. I never did such a thing before, but I think I put her asleep. I did not know it either, if it is so."

The old man looked at him in amazement. Chester then told him just what he had done, and that they had been sitting in silence, not knowing whether she were awake and in pain or asleep and therefore relieved, but supposing that quiet was kindest in either case.

Still with a confused look, Mr. Van Braam observed, "Asleep! put her asleep?"

"Magnetized," said Chester; "let me make some reversed passes. I've seen them do that; if I did put her asleep, I can awaken her, at any rate."

And holding his hands palms downward and flat, with the fingers towards her chin, he lifted them rapidly past her face throwing them apart above her forehead as if lifting and flinging back a veil. Half-a-dozen times he repeated the gesture, and paused. "Civille!" called the old man. They saw the pencilled eyebrows lift a little, as if in repeated efforts to open the eyes; a distressed look came over the face; and one finger of the hand that rested uppermost in her lap, moved in an odd and restless way.

Again Chester made the "reversed passes," saying at the last one, in a peremptory voice, "There; wake up!"

So she did; opening her great gray eyes wide, with an innocent puzzled look like a child's.

"Why, what is it?" she asked, startled at the three anxious faces gazing so intently at her. "Oh,—Cousin Adrian, you put me asleep didn't you!"

"It appears so," said the young man, gravely. "But I did not mean to. I wanted to relieve your headache."

"You did. It's all gone. But my head is so sore! It feels as if it had been pounded all over! But that's nothing. Oh, thank you!"

"Ah," said he, with a troubled voice,—"but please don't have any such pain again!"

She smiled quietly. "I shall though, often enough? But I will try not to trouble you with it."

"If I can cure it, Cousin Civille, please always trouble me with it!"

As they shook hands at going, Chester drew Mr. Van Braam one side, saying, just loud enough for the others to hear,

"About this meeting,"—and then dropping his voice, he quietly slid a card into the old man's hand, adding below his breath,

"I thought you might perhaps not choose anybody else to see this; I picked it up from the floor."

It was the detective's card; not engraved, but having on it in a sufficiently legible hand-writing, the words, "Amos Olds, Detective."

(TO BE CONTINUED.)

THE ROUND TABLE.

"The goodliest fellowship of noble knights
Of whom the world hath record."

EVERY MAN AN ANTIQUITY.

The present issue of this magazine will, we believe, be found to be more antiquarian in trend and scope than its predecessor. This is largely intentional, prompted by frequent advice and natural inclination to make it truly representative of the spirit of Colonial and Revolutionary days. We hesitated somewhat, wishing to make it as much a magazine for the younger folk as for the antiques and antiquarians; but the generous clientele it has already obtained, imbues us with the belief that all people are interested in "old things" nowadays.

The celebrated dictum of Bishop Warburton that "antiquarianism is to true letters what specious funguses are to the oak, which never shoot out and flourish till all the vigor and virtue of the grove are nearly exhausted," was doubtless true in his day, and true of the dry-as-dust pundits of his period. This opinion was given on the first appearance of Percy's "Reliques of Ancient Poetry," and was based on a false estimate of the aims and objects of literary antiquarianism. The modern antiquary, unlike his last century prototype, passes by dead, and seizes only living, issues. He can detect genuine literature under whatever form it is presented, and revivify the old days of "storm and stress" pioneering, in language as fitting as felicitous, knowing that the proper way to study the present is through the past.

"We, who from our youth up," writes Sir Walter Scott, "were accustomed to admire classical models, became acquainted, for the first time, with a race of poets who had the lofty ambition to spurn the flaming boundaries of the universe and to investigate the realms of Chaos and Old Night." Scott, himself, took a plunge into Chaos and his revival of chivalric legends was the result. Southey also dashed into the realms of Old Night, and revivified with his pen the Arthurian and other romances; he rediscovered to the world a new realm of beauty, brought back the reign of romance, and the ideal school began life anew.

And so, perhaps, in the beginning of the coming century, we shall have a reawakening in our country, as they in England in the beginning of the last century—a revival of our national literature, history, legends, and poetical inspiration—and mayhap one shall arise as great as Scott, in our land, who shall carry on the work which Irving and Cooper only commenced and Hawthorne merely outlined. Surely, none of our nowaday novelists seem equal to this task, even if they had the inspiration and ambition. One must become steeped and saturated, as was Scott, in the legends and lore of his native land. And so, perhaps, we are doing well to cultivate a still fallow field, if only in small measure, by our present efforts.

After all, is it not best to respect our forbears? Remember that the oldest form of worship in this world is ancestor-worship, and the most tenacious; it has not yet died out among all tribes of savagery. Besides, is it not true that we are all of us "antiquities"— for the world is very old? Bagehot, in a text we are fond of quoting, says;

"If we wanted to describe one of the most marked results—perhaps the most marked result —of late thought, we should say that by it everything is made "an antiquity." When in former times our ancestors thought of an antiquarian, they described him as occupied with coins and medals and Druid's stones,—these were then the characteristic records of the decipherable past, and it was with these that decipherers busied themselves; but now there are other relics,— indeed, all matter is become such."

"But what here concerns me is, that man himself has to the eye of science become 'an antiquity'; she tries to read, is beginning to read, knows she ought to read, in the frame of each man the result of a whole history of all his life, of what he is and what makes him so; of all his forefathers, of what they were and what made them so. Each nerve has a sort of memory of its past life,—is trained or not trained, dulled or quickened, as the case may be; each feature is shaped and characterized, or left loose and meaningless, as may happen: each hand is marked with its trade and life, subdued to what it works in; if we could but see it."

"It may be answered that in this there is nothing new: that we always knew how much a man's past modified a man's future; that we all knew how much a man is apt to be like his ancestors; that the existence of national character is the greatest commonplace in the world; that when a philosopher cannot account for anything in any other manner, he boldly ascribes it to an occult quality in some race. But, what physical science does, is, not to discover the hereditary element, but to render it distinct,—to give us an accurate conception of what we may expect and a good account of the evidence by which we are led to expect it."

"I do not think any who do not acquire—and it takes a hard effort to acquire—this notion of a transmitted nerve element will ever understand the 'connective tissue' of civilization. We have here the continuous force which binds age to age; which enables each to begin with some improvement on the last, if the last did itself improve; which makes each civilization not a set of detached dots, but a line of color surely enhancing shade by shade. There is by this doctrine a physical cause of improvement from generation to generation; and no imagination which has apprehended it can forget it; but unless you appreciate that cause in its subtle materialism,—

unless you see it, as it were playing upon the nerves of men, and age after age making nicer music from finer chords,—you cannot comprehend the principle of inheritance, either in its mystery or its power."

One could quote endlessly from this charming essay on "Physics and Politics" which so easily connects evolution and sociology — but time presses. It is too vast a subject for our pages. We commend the essay to all lovers of evolution (and can only add that Bagehot's works are found complete, in this country, solely in the "Traveler's Bagehot" collected by Mr. Forrest Morgan.) And now comes Prof. E. D. Cope, of the University of Pennsylvania, giving nine "missing links" or ancestors of man, tracing him back to paleozoic fishes; we have only a garbled report of his deliverance, in reportorial parlance, but it makes very interesting reading. His theory would combine the Darwinian descent of man with the Drummondian theory of the ascent of man—which would reconcile Science and the Bible and prove the most generally acceptable theory.

LOVE OF NATURE.

Next to a knowledge of himself, man should have a love of nature deeply planted in his soul. That reminds me of an appropriate sentiment in this connection: "This is a work-a-day world, and blessed be the man with the time and happy taste to gather and put before us the choice bits which reveal us to ourselves." This is from a booklet, "From a New England Hillside," by William Potts, under which prosaic name is a rare personality—a man who really communes with nature. A poet is one among ten thousand, but one who studies, admires, and really knows nature is surely as scarce as a true poet. There are many who write of nature off-hand, as of a side-show to life and humanity, and there are others who can only, parrot-like, botanize and specialize and classify; for the windows of book-stores are full of such books, telling us how to know wild-flowers and tame ones, the common birds and the uncommon ones, but what do they amount to except as a fad; and how little they are of use to the real lover of nature who enters into her life and spirit, and communes with her, and to whom she in return "speaks a various language"?

Of course it is necessary to know of these details of nature in order to understand her moods, but let it not end here. Let us quote him: "You cannot know how much more enjoyment you could find in flowers and trees until you have looked into their history, and studied their faces, learned their characters, their habits and their dispositions. You must lie down upon the same nill-side, look up at the same sky, drink in the same air. You must learn to feel your one-ness with them, and the strong family tie which makes everything that concerns them a matter of interest to you."

"Novalis called Spinoza 'a God-intoxicated man.' Intoxication is not a pleasant word,—enthusiasm is better,—en-the-osiasm,'—and it is this enthusiam, the gift of Nature and the imagination combined, the. offspring of poetry and fact, — that is the greatest, the richest. blessing of life. 'I do not see in Nature the colors that you find there,' said the lady to Turner. 'Don't you wish you could, madam?' was the reply. Suppose you try to look a little deeper, see a little further, turn the microscope upon your blossom, and discover a thousand beauties, the existence of which you never had suspected; turn your telescope upon the heavens, and find them bursting into bloom,—world beyond world receding into the vast unfathomable depths of space; believe me, you will not become blase with the extent of your knowledge, will not feel that the bloom is wholly gone from the peach, the perfume from the rose, the foam from the bounding wave."

Said a woman of straight-laced creed to a noted scientist: "Do you not think, Professor, that Dr. Soandso should stand facing the east at a certain part of the ritual?" The scientist called her attention to the magnitude of the universe, the distance of the sun. only one of a million of suns, stunned her dwarfed intellect with some grand figures, and then, as her breath was fast ebbing away with astonishment, he concluded, "Madam, I do not think the creator of this vast universe cares two straws which way Dr. Soandso stands or faces. Let us avoid cant and think only how insignificant we are and what a small part we are of nature." We have said that Mr. Potts is a man in direct sympathy with nature, as Thoreau, even Emerson at times, and as such we should appreciate him in our midst, for we have all too few genuine naturalists in the State. Mr. Burr of the Times is an enthusiastic lover of nature and his essay-editorials are altogether charming and timely when he deals with the daily aspects of nature, but an editor's life is too circumscribed to commune much with nature, and certainly too busy.

When there is one who loves nature and can describe it well and often accurately, there are thousands who have not this gift and can only stand in awe and admiration of the miracles of nature before them, and be dumb. There are so few real nature-poets. Longfellow and Whittier are gone, and Celia Thaxter gave too infrequent outbursts into song from her island-home; there are a few others but they are lost in the great whirl of the world, or their voices are drowned in the great Babylon of voices of the artificial and decadent poets, or else they live in the city's busy marts and have no chance to commune with nature or to get "near to Nature's heart." I mind me of a sweet singer, but just gone from our midst, the friend of Whittier, Holmes, Longfellow. Phillips Brooks. and although once but a simple factory girl and school-mistress to begin with, is surely entitled to rank with them in many ways. I mean Lucy Larcom. Years ago I read her simply autobiography "A New England Girlhood," and now am glad to learn that her life and letters have been published by the Riverside Press, and will no doubt be entitled to as many readers. She was a lovely soul, an American Jean Ingelow, and one whose works will be treasured in much the same manner as those of her English prototype, because of personal affections for, and rare sympathy with, her readers. One almost desires the old days back when such people could live their simple happy lives over again for our benefit and example. Then, there was Rose Terry Cooke, the poet of the Farmington valley, of whom Mr. Simonds quotes a couple of stanzas; we wish we had space here for the rest of the poem. "Thus sang Rose Terry in her cottage overlooking the river, with that vision always before her, I do not wonder that the song came to her. On the steep hillside the streets of white marble climb toward heaven from the busy manufacturing village, and their quietness in the broad glare of day contrasts as strongly with the bustle below, if not so impressively, as under the cold light of the moon." "The singer herself now reposes (as to the physical part) in that village on the hill where there's

Never a clock to toll the hours."

If the race of great nature poets is run, have we not some good prose writers extant who can preserve the communion with nature, or its tradition? Are there not some writers left who can describe nature as she exists, who are prose-poets in fact. In France we have Pierre Loti, in America (just now in Japan), we have Lafcadio Hearn. What a strange contrast to the quiet village-life of Lucy Larcom is that of this rare fleeting bird of passage, with brilliant plumage and flashing bravery! His life is eccentric, and exotic; he is a literary orchid. His style is as varied and brilliantly colored as the rainbow, and as evanescent. Imagine a quaint, dark-skinned, slight man, with a soft, shrinking voice, near-sighted, timid, and retiring. His father was an Englishman and his mother a Greek, and he was born at Smyrna, but fate cast him on our shores. He began life as a newspaper writer in Ohio, drifted down the Mississippi among the Creoles, and described them before Cable, and a great deal better, being so nearly akin in his own temperament. His work attracting the notice of a publisher, he was sent to the West Indies to write of the natives there. His amazing, dreamy sketches of the negroes, his familiarity with their patois, his pictures of their homes and habits, showed him a master of the pen and a genius. He seemed to have the mantle of Poe as a descriptive writer, and was just as indifferent to fame and fortune. Five years ago he went to Japan, married, and is there now, engaged as a teacher in a local college, and has a son of whom he is very proud. He has mastered their language, studied the Japanese with the same care as other semi-tropical natives he has written about, and his recent works on Japan are as thorough studies of that newly-awakened quarter of the globe as can be found. Lowell, Griffis, Pierre Loti, Bayard Taylor, Sir Edwin Arnold, have all told their tale, but do not enter into the personal life of the people as do the works of Hearn, of which he has written several. all of which show his sympathetic insight, thorough understanding of the people and country,—and all enveloped in his glowing, matchless style. As a stylist he has now, we think, no superior in this country.

A WORD OF PRAISE.

It is appropriate that we tender a tribute to those who have contributed to the present issue, to make it what it is, and "to render unto Cæsar the things which are Cæsar's;" and this we do gladly. The Short Beach article was a happy inspiration of the artist, Mr. Reckard, who has paid a delicate compliment in his pages to his poet-friend that she well deserves. It will be welcomed by her many admirers as a means of making her acquaintance. We also present several of his fine art-works, including another frontispiece.

Mr. Frank L. Hamilton, a former Hartford "boy," but now of Meriden, gives us an insight into the old Argonaut days, in his happy vein; among the people of whom he writes will be recognized the names of many citizens of both cities, most of them now dead or well advanced in life. Mr. Ezra Clark, Mr. Milo Hunt and others remain to corroborate the story. Clinton is treated by Miss Peck in a graphic manner, showing the same felicity in prose as in verse. She is achieving distinction and a wider hearing of late, that is very gratifying to her friends and to the modest "Colonial poet" herself.

Canton could not perhaps be treated better than by the pen of the Hon. Wm. E. Simonds, its distinguished citizen, who is thoroughly conversant with its local history. Mr. Simonds and General Franklin are the only two citizens of this vicinity entitled to wear "the red ribbon of France," the badge of the Legion of Honor. The author of "Trio and Tripod," who modestly insists upon hiding under a nom de plume, has given a complete and accurate account of Newgate and vicinity, in his gossipy style. "Bits from Great Grandmother's Journal" by the late Mrs. Bartlett, are fragments taken down from the lips of her grandmother, who used to live opposite Miss Porter's famous school. and written out for the benefit of her daughter, Miss Bartlett, of New Britain; this article will please antiquarians; the old may refresh their memories while the young will learn much of the old days. Of Miss Larned's sketch the same may be said, in equal measure, although more seriously historical.

We are fortunate in being able to present the first installment of Prof. Allen's "Old Time Music and Musicians," upon which he has been engaged for a long time, especially for our pages. He brings the record down to Revolutionary days and it will grow in interest as it proceeds. Hon. A. H. Byington, of Norwalk, has written graphically of his home, in the hurried intervals of an editor's life, and while making preparations to go abroad. "Historic Homes" will be found to be replete with stirring facts, and like its predecessors, disclose many new items which are unknown to the general reader. The poetry of the number, we believe is up to the average of previous issues. "Old Colonial Characters" is omitted until next issue, as also Mr. H. W. Benjamin's article on the new parks, for want of space. They will reappear in the next number. The departments are somewhat curtailed also, and the Musical department omitted entirely as Prof. Allen's article takes its place, we believe satisfactorily.

W. Farrand Felch

TREASURE TROVE.

"Time hath, my lord, a wallet at his back;
Wherein he puts alms for oblivion."

"While place we seek or place we shun,
The soul finds happiness in none
But with a God to lead the way
'Tis equal joy to go or stay."—MADAME GUION.

THE HALF-WAY COVENANT.

The admission into the churches of "covenanters" of "half-way covenant" members was the final outcome of a long and bitter ecclesiastical controversy, which waged throughout New England about the middle of the seventeenth century. A full account of this controversy would fill a volume, but, briefly stated, it is as follows:

Baptism was considered essential and all, even to the infant but a few days old, who died unbaptized, were firmly believed to be doomed to everlasting punishment. Children must be offered for baptism by a parent or other near relative who was a church member. After baptism they were considered as being under the watch of the church, and it was expected that upon arriving at mature years they would become members. An essential to membership, however, was a personal experience of divine grace. As many persons, though baptized, lacked this personal experience or regeneration, they were held to be unfit to become members of, and communicants with, the visible church; even though they believed, as many of them did, in all the articles of faith and doctrine of the church and lived lives that were above criticism.

To these unregenerate persons, believing as they did in all the doctrines of the church, especially in the necessity for baptism, the refusal of the church to receive their children in baptism was a hardship too great to be borne without strong protest. And so great was the pressure brought upon the churches in this matter, that they reluctantly consented to allow "all such persons, who are of an honest and goodly conversation, having a competency of knowledge in the principles of religion and shall desire to joyne with them in church-fellowship, by an explicit covenant; and that they have their children baptized." Thus it came about that the churches had two distinct classes of members — the one, members in the fullest sense of the word and communicants at the Lord's table — the other class, those who owned the half-way covenant, were members in that they acknowledged the creed and principles of the church, were subject to the rules and discipline, and could present their children for baptism; but they were considered as unregenerate and could not partake of the Lord's supper. Oftentimes, those who had previously "owned covenant," that is, the half-way covenant, would, "taking ye Vows of ye Lord upon them," be received into full communion.

CONN. HISTORICAL SOCIETY'S COLLECTIONS.

There has come to us since our last number was in print, a handsome octavo volume of 340 pages, which should be of universal interest to all students of the history of Connecticut. It is the third volume of the collections of the Connecticut Historical Society, which has been recently issued under the editorship of the Society's president, State Librarian Charles J. Hoadly, and at the expense of two Hartford citizens, ex-Governor M. G. Bulkeley, and General Wm. H. Bulkeley.

The major portion of the volume, and the part about which the chief interest centers, is the work written in 1692, by Gershom Bulkeley and printed for the first time in the collections of the Connecticut Historical Society. Mr. Bulkeley, the minister for some years at New London, and later at Wethersfield, both of which pastorates he was forced by ill-health to resign, was a man of more than ordinary abilities. Later, he took up the practice of law and medicine, and his writings show a trained legal mind. His book, here printed, "Will and Doom, or the miseries of Connecticut by and under an usurped and arbitrary power," is, in short, a political history of the colony, written in answer to several pamphlets which had been issued by James Fitch, and with a particular view to showing that the resumption of the charter government by the colony, after the accession of William and Mary to the throne of England, and the imprisonment of Sir Edmund Andros in Boston, was both legally and morally an arbitrary action and an assumption of power which could not be justified.

To begin the book is to read the whole of it, for upon reaching the text, after a somewhat dreary preface, the clear-cut and direct style in which the arguments and reasonings are given attracts and holds the attention, in spite of the biased and often prejudiced view which Mr. Bulkeley evidently takes, a view which makes one wonder if his long ill-health is not the result of dyspepsia. Beginning with the first settlement of the colony, he notes the making of their laws without authority and without allegiance to any power, and how, after the restoration of Charles II. they wisely petitioned him for a charter which was freely granted. This charter, although it granted the colonists power to erect courts, make laws, establish military, lay taxes, etc., was in itself only an instrument creating a highly privileged company and was, of course subsidiary in every respect to the power which had granted it — the

English throne. However, the colony, after receiving the charter, apparently considered itself as independent of the throne, and as a sovereignty in itself, equal to and not accountable to any. Its laws differed in many ways from the English laws and, even to the death punishment were executed in the name of the Governor and Company and not of the King. Soon after the accession of James the Second, the colony was served with a writ of quo warranto, and fearing that they might be united with one of the other colonies, they petition the king for a continuance of their present government, but if a change is to be made, they ask for annexation to Massachusetts rather than to New York. This is done, and Sir Edmund Andros is commissioned to govern Connecticut, with the other New England colonies. He comes with his guard to Hartford, is received with respect, causes his commission to be read, appoints the Governor and deputy Governor members of his council, gives commissioned offices to the other colony officials and takes the government into his own hands. Thus matters continue for eighteen months, but in the meantime, the people have been planning and plotting some way to resume the charter government, and at the news of the overthrow of Andros at Boston, a summons is hurriedly sent to the towns to appoint representatives to meet in general court. On the day previous to that fixed for the meeting, the deputies who had gathered held a solemn conclave as to what action should be taken and decided that those should be reappointed who were in office when Andros took the government. Thus was the charter government resumed, in direct opposition, says Bulkeley, to the actual desire of a large portion of the people. He then elaborates, in many pages, his reasons why the charter was wholly void, although it had never been given up and also the hardships which have befallen many on account of the tyrannical setting up again of this dead government. In spite of the shock which they give to our previous ideas upon the subject, it cannot be questioned that many of Mr. Bulkeley's points are well taken, and his arguments unanswerable.

In the volume of Collections is also printed for the first time, a "Memoir relating to Connecticut," written by the Hon. Roger Wolcott, when in his eighty-first year, in which he briefly traces the principal events in the history of the colony up to 1759. Directly contrary to the impression given by Bulkeley, is Wolcott's statement that upon the resumption of the Charter government, in 1689, "I never see a day of rejoicing in Connecticut like this."

The extracts from letters to the Rev. Thomas Prince, comprises forty-five pages of the volume. These extracts, made in 1772 by Rev. Benj. Trumbull, from letters written nearly forty years previously, give brief outline sketches of the principal events in each town in the colony; many curious facts and incidents are here gathered.

The writer of this feels unable to do justice to the remaining section of the Volume, "Some Helps for the Indians, showing them how to improve their natural reason to know the true God and the Christian religion," by the Rev. Abraham Pierson. This rare and curious tract of 237 years ago, is here reprinted with an introduction by that learned Indian scholar, Hon. J. Hammond Trumbull. It is the earliest effort of an early New England minister, aided by a London corporation, to bring the natives under the influence of the Christian religion. Mr. Pierson was the minister at Branford, Conn., and his catechism is the only book printed in any Indian dialect of that section, as well as the earliest book by a Connecticut author printed in this country.

While on the subject of revolutionary times we may mention that Charles Carleton Coffin, the well-known writer of war-stories, has gone back to revolutionary days and written a historical romance, "Daughters of the Revolution," which is a happy portraiture of the domestic, social and political life of the colonies. Most of the people were actual historical personages, or if not, they were at least typical and not far-fetched; it is in fact a blending of the real and ideal in proper proportions, and is in the main true to historical details and vraisemblance. We believe this work will be welcomed and widely read by all "D. A. R.," members, and we commend it as a style of writing which should have a new vogue, in which Scott and our own Mrs. Stowe were pioneers.

THE CONN. SOCIETY OF THE SONS OF THE AMERICAN REVOLUTION.

Prizes were awarded on the 19th of April, the anniversary of the battle of Lexington, by the Connecticut Society, to pupils in the schools of Connecticut, as follows: To pupils in the high schools, for essays on "The Share of Connecticut in the War of the Revolution." The awards were: J. Moss Ives, Danbury, the first prize, $20; Joseph Cooke Pullman, Bridgeport; Curtis Howe Walker, New Haven; Ray Morris, New Haven; Floyd H. Dusinberre, Bristol; Emma Comstock Bonfoey, Hartford; and Harry Davenport, Bridgeport. second prizes of $5. Helen Flora Newton, Woodbridge; Mark W. Norman, South Norwalk; and George Ellery Crosby, Hartford; honorable mention.

To pupils of common schools, the awards were: Lawrence Augustus Howard, Hartford, essay on "Nathan Hale," first prize, $20. Ruth A. Curtis, Hartford, subject "An Unknown Hero;" Robert Shannon, Hartford, subject, "Nathan Hale;" Joseph Hooker Woodward, Hartford, subject, "Benedict Arnold;" Mildred E. Camp, Hartford, subject, "Israel Putnam;" Bessie E. La Pierre, Norwich, subject, "William Williams;" and James J. Kavanaugh, Meriden, subject "Nathan Hale;" second prizes of $5. Phœbe Beale, Berlin, subject, "Connecticut Men of Mark of the Revolution;" Helen S. Partitz, Meriden, subject, "Captain John Couch;" John J. McCabe, New Hartford, subject, "Nathan Hale;" and Mabel S. Vaughn, Norwich, subject, "Nathan Hale;" honorable mention.

The annual meeting of the Society was held May 10, 1895, in Putnam Phalanx Hall, Hartford. President Jonathan Trumbull, Hartford, was in the chair, and delivered an address. The reports of the secretary, registrar, treasurer, and historian, were read and approved. Reports were also presented by the Committee on Necrology, Jonathan Flynt Morris, chairman, the General David Humphreys Branch of New Haven, the Captain John Couch Branch of Meriden, the General Gold Selleck Silliman Branch of Bridgeport, and the Israel Putnam Branch of Norwich. Officers for the ensuing year were elected as follows, viz:

President, Jonathan Trumbull, Norwich; vice-president, Edwin Seneca Greeley, New Haven; registrar, Frank Butler Gay, Hartford; secretary, Charles P. Cooley, Hartford; historian, Joseph Gurley Woodward, Hartford; treasurer, John Clark Hollister, New Haven; chaplain, Edwin S. Lines, New Haven. Board of Managers: Hobart L. Hotchkiss, Everett Edward Lord, William Erasmus Chandler, Franklin Henry Hart, New Haven; Jonathan Flynt Morris, Meigs Hayward Whaples, and Bennet Rowland Allen, Hartford; Edgar J. Doolittle, Meriden; Zalmon Goodsell, Rowland Bradley Lacey, Bridgeport; Henry Roger Jones, New Hartford; Francis Taylor Maxwell, Rockville; Frank Farnsworth Starr, Middletown; Loren A. Gallup, Norwich; and Rufus White Griswold, Rocky Hill.

Delegates to the National Society: H. Wales Lines, Meriden; Henry Baldwin Harrison, New Haven; Edward Morris Warner, Putnam; Frank J. Narramore, Bridgeport; Russell Frost, South Norwalk; John Hoyt Perry, Southport; Lucius Franklin Robinson, Hartford; Samuel E. Merwin, New Haven; William De Loss Love, Hartford; Alfred Hebard Chappell, New Haven; and Henry Woodward, Middletown. The year book, covering the years 1893-4, is nearly through the press, and, accidents excepted, it will be distributed to members shortly.

[signature]

Historian.

THE LOYAL LEGION.

While there is so much interest shown in societies basing their claims on revolutionary ancestry, it may not be out of order to call especial attention to one composed of officers of the late war, to which too little notice is paid in this section of the country. One or two decades from now there will be a scramble to get into this order or its junior branch, after all the old heroes are dead. This order was engendered, in the closing years of the war, in the active brain of Colonel Samuel B. Wylie Mitchell, now deceased, who had a genius for organization; he also instituted the Phi Kappa Sigma fraternity in college and was a prominent Mason, and a "jiner" of great note; as he facetiously said: He "belonged to almost everything but Mrs. Mitchell." It is much like the revolutionary order of the Cincinnati.

We give below the latest roster for this state: Stephen Ball, Second Lieut 12th. Conn. Infantry, Hartford; Morgan G. Bulkeley, member by inheritance from his brother, (private 13th H. A. N. Y. S. M.,) Hartford; George D. Chapman, Colonel 5th Conn. Infantry, Middletown; Frank W. Cheney, Lieut.-Col. 16th Conn. Infantry, South Manchester; Charles P. Clark, Acting Vol. Lieut., U. S. N., New Haven; Henry C. Dwight, captain 27th Mass. Infantry, Hartford; Joseph F. Field, 1st Lieut. Second Mass. H. A., Hartford; Charles J. Fuller. Capt. 13th Conn. Infantry, Hartford; Charles W. Harris, captain, 7th Mich. Infantry, Middletown; Charles F. Hildreth, surgeon 40th Mass. Infantry, Hartford; George C. Jarvis, surgeon 7th Conn. Infantry. Hartford; John B. Lewis, surgeon, brevet colonel U. S. V., Hartford; Matthew T. Newton, surgeon 10th Conn. Infantry, Suffield; Walter Pearce, Acting Master U. S. N., Hartford; George Pope, Lieut.-Col. 54th Mass. Infantry, Hartford; Edward V. Preston, major, paymaster U. S. V , Hartford; Alfred P. Rockwell, Col. 6th Conn. Infantry, brevet brigadier-general, New Haven; Henry P. Stearns, surgeon, brevet Lieut.-Col. U. S. V., Hartford; William H. H. Wooster, 1st Lieut. R. Q. M., 6th Conn Infantry. Mr. Henry Ellsworth Taintor, of Hartford, is the last member from this city.

THE SOCIETY OF COLONIAL WARS.

On the 17th of June, 1895, the Society of Colonial Wars celebrated the one hundred and fiftieth anniversary of the surrender of the fortress at Louisburg, Cape Breton, to New England troops, under Lieut.-General Pepperell, assisted by the British fleet under Commodore Warren. This is the most memorable occasion in the history of this young society. Addresses was made by the Governor-General of the society, Frederick J. de Peyster, Esq., representatives of the different states, Dr. J. G. Bourinot, C. M. G., representing the Royal Society of Canada, and others, including a descendant of Sir William Pepperell, Hon. Everett Pepperrell Wheeler. Not the least interesting feature of the celebration was the beautiful Tiffany medal, struck from the metal of an old brass cannon found upon a French frigate blown up in the harbor during the siege. It contains profiles of Sir William Pepperrell and Sir Peter Warren. The medals are two inches wide and some are suspended from the colors of the Society.—a scarlet moire silk ribbon, with a narrow white border.

[signature: Chas. Sam Ward]

We beg to congratulate Dr. Ward on the tasteful and appropriate literature gotten out for the Society under his supervision, which can best be described under only two words, choice and chaste! There can no fault be found with it, by even the most fastidious and sybaritic critic.—ED.

CONN. HISTORICAL SOCIETY.

At the opening of the April meeting President Hoadly presented to the society the newly published volume of "Collections," the third in number but the fourth to be issued. It was received with pleasure by the members and suitable votes of thanks were passed to Messrs. M. G. and W. H. Bulkeley, for defraying the cost of printing the volume, and to the president for his labors as editor. The paper of the evening was by Mr. P. H. Woodward on early marine insurance in Connecticut, in which sketches were given of many prominent business men of Hartford and vicinity, whose early efforts laid the foundation of the large insurance interests of the state.

The paper at the May meeting was by Mrs. Ellen Terry Johnson, on the Bermudas in 1792. It was based on the correspondence of the Wadsworth family of Hartford, and gave an interesting picture of domestic life on the islands, and of the difficulties of procuring many things which would here be considered as necessities. Mr. Jonathan F. Morris presented an interesting relic in the shape of a wooden maul used by Abraham Lincoln in splitting rails. Mr. Morris gave the history of the relic and read the documents and affidavits proving its authenticity.

At the annual meeting, on the 21st, the president and most of the other officers were re-elected. Mr. James Terry was chosen vice-president in place of Franklin B. Dexter, resigned, and T. S. Gold in place of Robbins Battell, deceased. The annual reports showed the society to be in a prosperous condition. The membership had increased since the last report; the use of the library is large; and the number of visitors to the exhibition hall is many.

The annual outing of the society occurred on June 11, when about fifty members and their friends visited the historic spots above New London and Groton. All reported an enjoyable time.

The library has received a valuable addition in the gift by Miss Clara Field, of Stockbrdge, Mass., of over four hundred volumes, besides valuable manuscripts, formerly belonging to the late David Dudley Field,

[signature: Albert C Bates]

Librarian.

SOCIOLOGY AND CIVICS.

"The criminal classes are so close to us that even a policeman can see them. They are so far away from us that only a poet can understand them."

CONN. HUMANE SOCIETY.

SECTION 4, in the Act Incorporating the Connecticut Humane Society, reads as follows: "The purpose of the society is to promote humanity and kindness, and to prevent cruelty to both men and the lower animals, by information, statistics, appropriate literature, and by any and all other lawful means which they may deem wise and best, and by assisting in the prosecution of crimes of a cruel and inhuman nature; and generally to encourage justice and humanity, and to discourage injustice and inhumanity."

ARTICLE 2, of the Constitution, reads thus: "Its objects are to provide effectual means for the prevention of cruelty, and especially of cruelty to animals, and to promote a humane public sentiment."

It is apparent that the opportunity for work is practically without limit. Complaints which are constantly made, are almost endless in variety. It is the purpose of the officers in charge to deal with those cases where there is cruelty — or injustice, which amounts to cruelty.

Children have been committed to the County Home on evidence that their surroundings were immoral. Some courts have held that such cruelty exceeded that of physical pain or punishment, because they might recover from the effects of cruel whipping but not from that of immoral influence. A law recently passed by the present legislature, places the expense of the care of neglected and dependent children on the towns to which they belong. Heretofore, such expense has been borne by the state.

The society has been uniformly successful in its prosecutions during the past quarter, having lost but three cases. One instance, where a man cruelly beat his horse until it finally died, the court imposed a fine of $2 — justice being tempered with mercy. A light penalty sometimes, however, has the desired effect, the object in view being to prevent rather than punish.

Electricity is relieving the society in the cities throughout the state, yet the demands upon it are increasing. Humane sentiment is growing, and gratifying as this may be, it is a fact that in matters humane we are yet far behind Great Britain and other European countries.

Chandler E. Miller

Secretary.

"THE FABIAN ESSAYS."

We have received a pleasing little volume under the above title, including essays on Socialism by the Fabian Society of England, edited by G. Bernard Shaw, and the American edition introduced by Edward Bellamy. The Fabian motto is: "For the right moment you must wait, as Fabian did, most patiently, when warring against Hannibal, though many censured his delays; but when the time comes you must strike hard, as Fabian did, or your waiting will be vain and fruitless." Some of these essays "strike hard," perhaps harder than is necessary at this stage, but at any rate they are earnest and often convincing. If one wishes to get a good idea of socialism in all its ramifications this little book, that slips easily into the pocket, is surely the vade mecum. Bellamy calls Socialism "the application of the democratic method to the economic administration of a people." But, before Socialism can prevail in the governmental administration of economic affairs, a most Herculean task must be accomplished, the complete cleaning of the Augean stables.

THE MESSIAH OF THE APOSTLES.

Mr. Charles A. Briggs, of heterodox fame, is engaged in the compilation of a series of volumes, which the Scribners are bringing out, and the third volume has just appeared, with the above title. The first was "The Messianic Prophecy," in 1886; the second, "The Messiah of the Gospels," in 1894; and it is his purpose to continue the series with "The Messiah of the Church," and "The Messiah of the Theologians," if life and health are given to him. This is a very elaborate and laudable plan, and we hope it will be accomplished. The present volume is the result of matured convictions and discipline of many years' duration, and he regards it as the ripe confession of his faith. It is at least worthy of more than transient study, in this transitional period of the creeds, analogous somewhat to the old Norse "twilight of the gods."

NOTES AND QUERIES.

"When found, make a note of."—CAPT. CUTTLE.

Please remember that a nominal charge of twenty-five cents is made for these queries, in advance, and they are not to exceed ten lines. We welcome queries; but we wish friends would help the editor to answer them, as his duties are onerous enough in other directions. Very little help has been given in this direction.

GARDINER—LEDYARD.—"In the article on the Center Church burying-ground, did not Miss Mary K. Talcott err in stating that Lyon Gardiner the first Lord of Gardiner's Island was there buried? Is it not his son David, the second proprietor? Also, was not Col. Wm. Ledyard murdered Sept. 6? B. C. A.

GORHAM.—Timothy Gorham, born 14 Sept., 1785, died 15 Jan , 1863. Wanted names of parents and grand-parents. This querist should at least give some locality for birth or death.

MASON.—Captain John Mason of Pequot war fame, had a son John who married Abigail Fitch and begat John 3d. The latter married his cousin Anne, (Samuel's daughter) who bore him John Mason 4th, at Lebanon, in 1702. He was baptized in Stonington in 1706. Can you give me any information respecting John 4th, where he settled, who he married, and when and where he died; it is for the Mason genealogy, being compiled by L. B. Mason, New York City.
J. K. MASON, M. D., Suffield, Conn.

Perhaps Jas. Fitch Mason, of Lebanon, can help you to the data.

MCDONOUGH.—We are informed that Commodore McDonough's grave at Middletown, is over-grown with sumac, fences are down, and it is badly neglected. The editor had a great-uncle who was chaplain under him, on Lake Champlain, and would like to see some society take hold of this matter, and keep the grave respectable. Also, can not his portrait be gotten for the Historical Society, formerly at the hotel in Middletown?

WILLIAMS.—Jos. Williams and his wife Mary lived at Norwich. He had recorded in the Norwich town records in 1750, the birth of eleven children, and was made a citizen of Norwich in 1702. Who was he? From whence did he come to Norwich? F. A. VERPLANCK, South Manchester, Conn.

THE CONNECTICUT
Building and Loan Association.

General Office, Charter Oak Bank Building, Hartford, Conn.

Has an authorized Guarantee Fund of $250,000, of which $50,000 in cash has been paid in.

OFFICERS.

GEORGE E. KEENEY, President.
ROCKWELL KEENEY, Vice-President.
EDGAR C. LINN, Secretary.
GEORGE W. HODGE, Treasurer.

ATTORNEY.

JOHN H. BUCK, Ass't State Attorney; with Buck & Eggleston, Attorneys, Hartford, Conn.

DIRECTORS.

HON. E. STEVENS HENRY, Rockville, Conn., Treasurer of People's Savings Bank; United States Congressman, First Connecticut District.
HON. PATRICK GARVAN, Hartford, Conn., Paper and Paper Stock Manufacturer; Ex-State Senator; Director State Bank.
R. B. PARKER, Hartford, Conn., President of Hartford Life and Annuity Insurance Co.; Director First National Bank; Cotton Manufacturer.
HON. GEORGE E. KEENEY, Somersville, Conn., Treasurer Somersville Manufacturing Co.; Ex-State Senator.
HON. GEORGE W. HODGE, Hartford, Conn., Treasurer of the State of Connecticut; Paper Manufacturer.
E. C. HILLIARD, Hartford, Conn., Woolen Manufacturer; Vice-President of the Hartford Life and Annuity Insurance Co.; Director First National Bank.
HON. E. C. PINNEY, Stafford, Conn., President of Stafford Savings Bank; Woolen Manufacturer; Ex-State Senator.
ROCKWELL KEENEY, Somersville, Conn., President of the Somersville Manufacturing Co.
E. C. LINN, Hartford, Conn., Secretary Connecticut Building and Loan Association.

Shareholders guaranteed against any loss of their Capital invested.

Maturity of Shares at once in the event of Death.

Cancellation of the Borrower's Mortgage at once in the event of Death.

No Membership, Admission or Entrance Fees.

Installment Shares, 50 cents per share per month A limited amount of 6 per cent. Coupon Shares for sale at par.

For further information, apply to the General Office.

WE PRINT

Law Blanks For Sale.

TRADE CATALOGUES,
GENEALOGIES,
GEER'S HARTFORD
CITY DIRECTORY.

BOOKS OF ALL KINDS. *Town Reports, Abstracts,*
MERCANTILE WORK OF *and Town*
EVERY DESCRIPTION. *Printing of every kind.*

We Solicit your Patronage, and will be Pleased to have you call on us.

OUR OFFICE IS 16 STATE STREET.
Our Telephone Number Is 649.

The Hartford Printing Co.,

Elihu Geer's Sons, HARTFORD, CONN.

EVERETT S. GEER, Prest.
ERASTUS C. GEER, Sec'y.
E. HOWARD GEER, Sup't.

We have a Library of City Directories of all the principal cities in the country; also, Foreign Directories, for free reference.

THE CONNECTICUT QUARTERLY.

Price 50 cents a year, (4 numbers,) payable in advance. Single copies 15 cents.

Remittances should be by Check, Express Money Order, P. O. Order, or Registered Letter. Money by mail at sender's risk.

All subscriptions taken with the understanding that they expire after four numbers have been sent, unless renewed by the subscriber. When change of address is desired give both the old and new address.

Agents wanted in every town in the State to get subscriptions. Write for terms, etc.

As the editions of Numbers 1 and 2 are exhausted, we are obliged to begin all subscriptions with No. 3. We can procure a few of No. 1 for persons desiring them at $1.00 each.

THE CONNECTICUT QUARTERLY CO.

P. O. BOX, 565, HARTFORD, CONN.

CAUTION.—Do not pay money to persons unknown to you. Our authorized agents have full credentials.

PALMER HAMMOCKS.

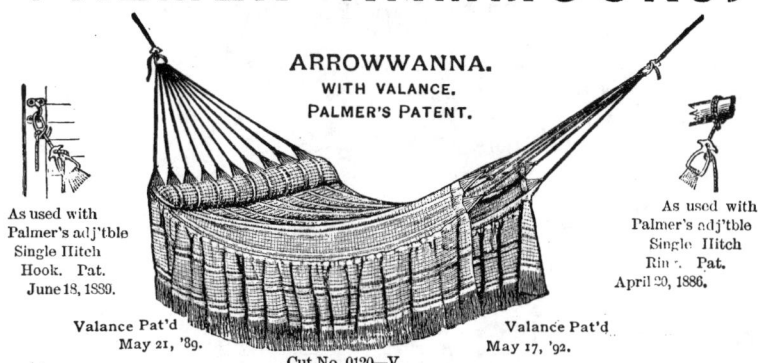

ARROWWANNA.
WITH VALANCE.
PALMER'S PATENT.

As used with Palmer's adj'tble Single Hitch Hook. Pat. June 18, 1889.

As used with Palmer's adj'tble Single Hitch Rin . Pat. April 20, 1886.

Valance Pat'd May 21, '89.

Valance Pat'd May 17, '92.

Cut No. 0120—V.

Palmer Hammocks have never been equalled. They are and always have been the standard in Material, Construction and Design. The continual efforts to imitate and infringe, have been without success and **Palmer Hammocks** still lead every make. Made in over 100 styles and in greater quantity than all others combined.

Be sure you get a "Palmer Patent Hammock." If your dealer does not have them be sure that he gets you one.

I. E. PALMER, Middletown, Conn.

Manufacturer of Canopies, Nettings, Hammock Attachments, Crinoline Linings, Etc. Trade supplied only.

THE ROGERS & HAMILTON CO.,
WATERBURY, CONN.

ALDINE COFFEE SPOON.

MANUFACTURERS OF

HIGHEST GRADE SILVER-PLATED WARE.

1794   OLDEST INSURANCE COMPANY IN HARTFORD.   1895

The Hartford Fire Insurance Company,
OF HARTFORD, CONN.

Has a Capital of One and One-quarter Million Dollars. Has a Net Surplus of over Two and One-half Million Dollars. Has Total Assets of over Eight and One-half Million Dollars. Has paid over Forty-six Million Dollars in Losses.

GEO. L. CHASE, President.

P. C. ROYCE, Secretary.   THOS. TURNBULL, Ass't Secretary. CHAS. E. CHASE, Ass't Secretary.

Metropolitan Department, No. 50 Wall St., New York. YOUNG & HODGES, Managers.
Western Department, Chicago, Ill. G. F. BISSELL, Manager; P. P. HEYWOOD, Ass't Manager.
Pacific Department, San Francisco, Cal. BELDEN & COFRAN, Managers.

Agencies in all the Prominent Localities throughout the United States and Canada.

Please mention THE CONNECTICUT QUARTERLY.

THE CO-OPERATIVE
Savings Society
OF CONNECTICUT,
HARTFORD.

GEORGE POPE, President.   Assets Over $650,000

Issues Six per cent. Coupon Certificates

In denominations of $200, $500 and $1,000, at $208 per share, (par value $200 per share). Certificates redeemable after one year at par, at option of holder.

For information address,
FRANCIS A. CRUM, Agency Manager,
at the Society's Principal Office, **No. 40 Pearl St., Hartford, Conn.**

VISIT THE
Bartlett Tower
TARIFFVILLE.

AND ENJOY ONE OF THE FINEST AND MOST EXTENSIVE OF NEW ENGLAND VIEWS—REACHING FROM NORTHERN MASSACHUSETTS TO SOUTHERN CONNECTICUT. EMBRACING BOTH FARMINGTON AND CONNECTICUT RIVER VALLEYS.

Excursion Tickets sold daily at Station of Phila. Reading and Central N. E. R. R., Hartford good on all Passenger trains leaving Hartford, for one or more passengers stopping at Tower Station; where conveyance one-third of a mile, will, if desired, be furnished to Tower.

TICKETS, 75 Cents both ways.
Children, 50 Cents.

Tower Conveyance from Station to Tower, 10 cents.

Wednesdays and Saturdays, cheap days. **Excursion Tickets, 50 Cents.**

Parties of ten taken from Tower to Newgate and return, including admission, 50 cents each person.

Parties of four, 75 cents each person.

M. H. BARTLETT, Proprietor.

VISIT
OLD NEWGATE PRISON.
Season closes October 15th.
CLOSED SUNDAYS.

The Prison and convict caverns are wonderfully interesting. Experienced attendants, accommodations for picnic parties and good tennis court. Beautiful views from observatory, covering a distance of over seventy miles. A room of the old keeper's house built in 1790, 37 years after Newgate was first used as a prison, has been devoted to a collection of relics pertaining to the prison and revolutionary war.

COME BY TRAIN.

Trains on the Northampton Div. Nos. 620 and 610 north bound, and 603, 621 and 625 south bound stop at Copper Hill, flag station, fifteen minutes walk from Newgate. From July 1st to Oct. 1st conveyance from station to Newgate by giving previous notice.

The Bartlett Tower and Newgate can be visited Wednesdays and Saturdays, by parties of ten or more, for $1.00 from Hartford. Tickets sold to Newgate every week day by Mr. Bartlett, to parties of ten or more for 50cts. Parties of four at a slight additional cost without giving notice.

Attractive illustrated lecture by the Rev. Duane N. Griffin of New Haven, on Newgate. Applications promptly attended to, and all questions cheerfully answered by the proprietor or the Rev. Duane N. Griffin.

EXTRACTS FROM TESTIMONIALS:

I have twice heard and seen it. Am ready for it again upon the first opportunity. CRANDALL J. NORTH, Presiding Elder, New Haven District, 361 George St., New Haven, Ct.

It is certainly one of the most interesting lectures to which I have ever listened. I advise all my friends to hear this lecture at the very first opportunity. JOHN KHEY THOMPSON, Pastor First M. E. Church, Meriden, Conn.

Complete history by mail. 70cts Souvenir books, 25 and 50 cents. For further particulars, address,

S. D. VIETS, Prop., Copper Hill, Conn.

Please mention THE CONNECTICUT QUARTERLY.

with our facilities and experience we guarantee satisfactory results.

Designing
Printing
Engraving
Embossing

We are General Printers and Engravers, and do not wish it understood that we print catalogues only, as we are fitted up to do **all kinds of Mercantile and Insurance Printing,** and a Bill Head, Circular or Announcement receives the same careful attention while in process, as larger work.

We invite correspondence from manufacturers and others who wish for Fine Drawings, Engravings or Printing of any nature whatever, and guarantee satisfaction in every instance, both as to price and quality of production.—Send for our catalogue.

☞Correct Styles in Wedding Invitations.

R. S. Peck & Co.
14 Ford St.,
Hartford, Conn.

THE CONNECTICUT QUARTERLY.

FOR SUPERIOR
HALF TONE PRINTING PLATES
CALL ON

THE HARTFORD ENGRAVING CO.

COURANT BUILDING, 66 STATE STREET,

HARTFORD, CONN.

The illustrations in this magazine were made by us.

> Many of the illustrations found in this issue are selected from the territory traversed by the Philadelphia, Reading & New England Railroad.
>
> If you contemplate summering in the country you will find that for health, pleasure and convenience Litchfield County and the Southern Berkshire has no equal.
>
> For a list of hotels, boarding houses, etc., procure a copy of our summer home book, containing upwards of 60 illustrations giving all information. The summer home books are now ready for free distribution at city ticket offices, of W. W. Jacobs, 293 Main St., and L. H. Colton, 18 State St., or will be mailed on receipt of 4 cents postage to
>
> W. J. MARTIN,
> Gen'l Passenger Agent, Hartford, Conn.

1851   After Forty=four Years   1895

of business, **The Phoenix Mutual Life Insurance Company of Hartford, Connecticut,** is Stronger, Safer and Better than ever before.

Do not insure your life until you have seen our liberal contracts, embracing Extended Insurance, Loan, Cash and Paid-up values. The most liberal contracts issued by any life insurance company in the world. For sample policies, address the Home Office, Hartford, Conn.

JONATHAN B. BUNCE, President.
JOHN M. HOLCOMBE, Vice-President.
CHARLES H. LAWRENCE, Secretary.

Please mention THE CONNECTICUT QUARTERLY.

The Springs of Connecticut,

Highland TONICA Water.

Has never failed to prove its value when used according to directions.

Note this Comparative Analysis.

HIGHLAND TONICA	THE HUMAN BLOOD
Contains in its natural state:	in its natural state contains:
Potassium, Lime,	Potassium, Lime,
Lime, Magnesia,	Lime, Magnesia,
Manganese,	Manganese,
Phosphoric Acid, Iron.	Phosphoric Acid, Iron.

A. W. K. NEWTON, M. D., says:—

"I have advised it for a large number of my patients. The effect has been wonderful."

Highland ROCK Water.

"THE CLIMAX OF TABLE WATERS"

Is the purest ever analyzed.

CORRESPONDENCE INVITED.

The Tonica Springs Co.,

"HIGHLAND PARK,"   MANCHESTER, CONN.

HARTFORD AGENTS:

T. SISSON & CO., Main St.

TALCOTT, FRISBIE & CO., Asylum St.

The Life and Endowment Policies

—— OF ——

The Travelers

of Hartford, Conn.

Are the Best in the Market. Non=Forfeitable and World=Wide.

—— FORMS.

REGULAR LIFE.—The original and commonest sure way of leaving one's heirs in comfort instead of destitute. Even a mechanic can easily leave a fair estate behind him.

LIMITED-PAYMENT.—Concentrating payment into the working years of a man's life, and leaving him free from worry even if he is helpless.

REGULAR ENDOWMENTS.—Payable to the insured himself after a term of years, or to his family if he dies before the end of the term. The only means by which most men can save money for themselves.

ANNUITY PLAN.—Cheapest of all, and the only sure way of furnishing a regular income. Applied to either of the other forms. Principal sum payable in installments instead of in a lump, either to the insured (if Endowment) or his beneficiaries. If desired, they will be written so that in case of insured's death before the installments are all paid, his beneficiaries will receive the value of the remainder at once.

COMBINED LIFE AND ACCIDENT.—Combining any of these with weekly indemnity for disabling accident.

Also the Largest Accident Company in the World.

LARGER than ALL OTHERS in America together.

ASSETS, $17,664,000.   **SURPLUS, $2,472,000.**

Paid Policy-holders, over $27,000,000—$2,151,000 in 1894 alone.

JAMES G. BATTERSON, President.
RODNEY DENNIS, Secretary.

Huntsinger Business College

AND
SCHOOL OF SHORTHAND AND TYPEWRITING.

This is the only school in Hartford which teaches Actual Business Practice from the Start, or learning to do by doing. The seventh school year, ending June 28th, shows the largest attendance and the most successful year in the history of the school. More graduates were placed in positions than by any other school in this State.

Many improvements will be made in the Course and the School for the fall opening, Sept. 2d. Call or write for new catalogue, etc.

30 Asylum St., HARTFORD, CONN.

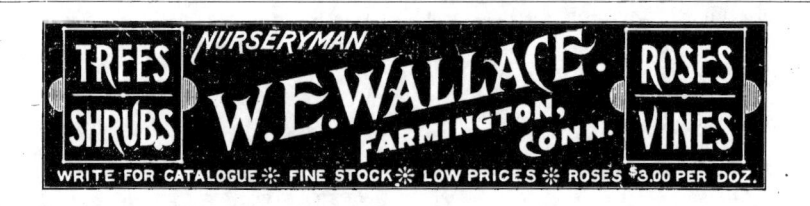

TREES — SHRUBS — W. E. WALLACE, NURSERYMAN, FARMINGTON, CONN. — ROSES — VINES
WRITE FOR CATALOGUE ❊ FINE STOCK ❊ LOW PRICES ❊ ROSES $3.00 PER DOZ.

Parsons' Advertising Agency,

71 ASYLUM ST., HARTFORD, CONN.

Advertisements placed in any paper or combination of papers at publishers' rates or below them, and at a large reduction in Parsons' Special List, embracing leading dailies and 12 best weeklies in Connecticut. On this special list we challenge competition.

No newspaper is worth so much to the general advertiser in proportion to its circulation as the well established country weekly. No other so effectively reaches the family, if so thoroughly read, or gives so much character to the advertisements in its columns. Our Special Weekly list is made up of the cream of these, the leading paper being selected in every instance, covering every important point in northern and central Connecticut, and at a price never before even approached in Hartford. The lists may be used entire or in part.

Papers always on file. Estimates for large or small amounts promptly furnished. Send for circular or, better, come and see us.

A. R. PARSONS,
Advertising Agent.

Fifteen years Editor and Publisher
Connecticut Farmer.

R. S. PECK & CO., PRINTERS, HARTFORD, CONN.

Vol. 1   Oct., Nov., Dec., 1895.   No. 4

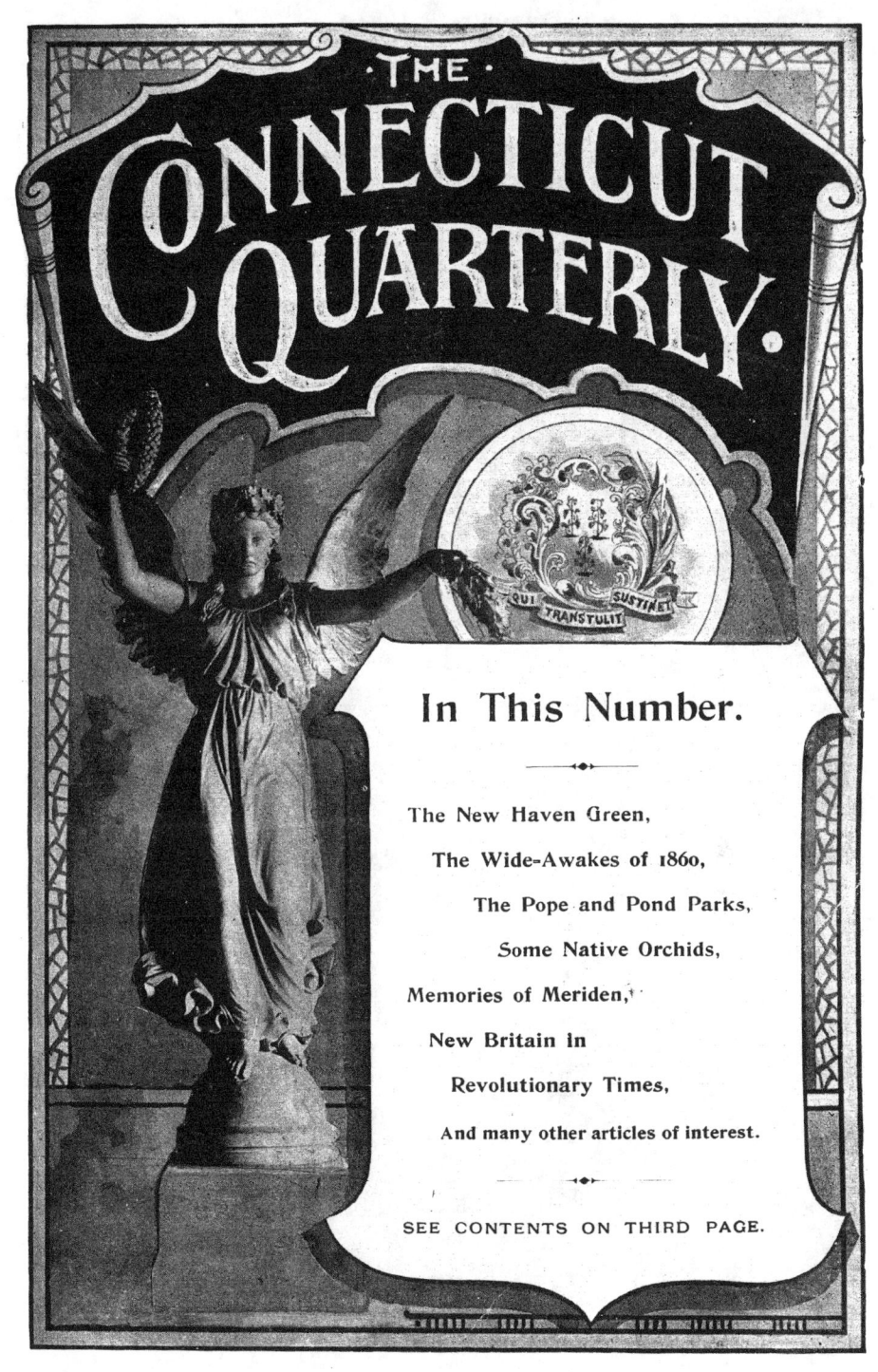

THE CONNECTICUT QUARTERLY.

In This Number.

The New Haven Green,

The Wide-Awakes of 1860,

The Pope and Pond Parks,

Some Native Orchids,

Memories of Meriden,

New Britain in Revolutionary Times,

And many other articles of interest.

SEE CONTENTS ON THIRD PAGE.

50c. a Year   Hartford, Conn.   15c. a Copy

The 19th Century Marvel.

The Secret of a Happy Home

lies in providing something new and attractive to make it an everlasting pleasure. **The Symphony** is a musical educator and entertainer for the whole family. A child four years old can operate it and produce an endless variety of music to suit all classes and ages. *The latest popular airs of the day, the works of the great masters, all can be rendered without the slightest knowledge of music.*

New York Parlors,
   123 5th Ave.
Philadelphia Pa.,
   1308 Chestnut St.
	**Thousands
	are daily
	in use.**
		Chicago, Ill.,
		   W. W. Kimball.
		Boston, Mass.,
		   Oliver Ditson Co.

One Opinion

A prominent Boston publisher said recently: "Of all the advertising journals printed (and I see them all), there is none which I enjoy reading so much as I do *Profitable Advertising*. It is, to my mind, the best one printed — the neatest, cleanest, most readable. I get valuable suggestions from it. It is worth many times its cost to me."

Profitable Advertising

is the advertisers' trade journal. The only one published in New England.

Every publisher, agent and ad-writer should have his announcement in its columns.
Every man who spends a dollar in advertising should subscribe for it.
Subscription price $1.00 per year.

KATE E. GRISWOLD,
Editor and Publisher.
13 School St., Boston, Mass.

The Philadelphia, Reading and New England Railroad

is offering Special Inducements for **Western Travel.**

The train leaving Hartford at 12.30 P. M. makes direct connection at the west termini of the line, at Campbell Hall, with fast expresses on the Ontario and Western and Erie roads. Tickets via this route are sold at from $1.00 to $3.00 less than via other routes and passengers arrive at Chicago via this line the following day at 9 P. M., being only one night on the road. Pullman sleepers and reclining chair cars from Campbell Hall.

THE ROUTE.

The route starting at Hartford, runs due west to the Hudson River at Poughkeepsie, N. Y., at this point they cross the great Poughkeepsie Bridge, largest in the United States, thence through the celebrated fruit and farming section of Ulster and Orange counties for thirty miles to Campbell Hall, N. Y., where direct connections is made with fast through Express trains for the west. The region traveled abounds in the picturesque mountains, lakes and valleys. From the time the train leaves Hartford until the travelers change cars at the western termini two superb panoramas of varied beauty are unrolled on either side of the embarrassed traveler, who is thus afflicted with the unusual annoyance of having just twice as much as he can profitably enjoy. To those who have never traveled through Western Connecticut the railroad ride will prove very interesting. The Litchfield Hills and Southern Berkshire, through which the road passes, are noted for their picturesque beauty.

For information, apply to W. J. MARTIN, General Passenger Agent, Hartford, Conn.

Mrs. Earle's Books on Old New England

THE SABBATH IN PURITAN NEW ENGLAND.
12 mo. $1.25.

BY MRS. ALICE MORSE EARLE.

"It is interesting, entertaining, instructive."—*Evangelist.*

"A graphic picture of the life of the Puritans."—*Boston Traveler.*

"A perfect mine of curious and interesting information. She has ransacked old records and chronicles with the richest results, and the picture she gives of old time observances is the most complete ever written."—*Boston Courier.*

CUSTOMS AND FASHIONS IN OLD NEW ENGLAND.
12 mo. $1.25.

BY MRS. ALICE MORSE EARLE.

"Mrs. Earle has made herself master of those archives of Old New England. She devotes this volume to the social side of the Puritan's life, picturing him from cradle to grave. Her style is delightful, and every page is interesting."—*The Critic.*

"Mrs. Earle has presented with a loving enthusiasm and a gentle and kindly humor the picture of the hard, harsh, and narrow life of our Puritan forefathers, ennobled by a sincere devotion and heroic self-sacrifice and enlivened by quaint, if unconscious, humor, and the ebullitions of human nature."—*Providence Journal.*

COSTUME OF COLONIAL TIMES.
BY MRS. ALICE MORSE EARLE.
12 mo. $1.25

"Aside from its usefulness the book is excellent reading."—*New York Times.*
"A charmingly quaint account of our foremother's time."—*Boston Times.*
"Lovers of old customs and costumes will find this book a treasury of delight."—*New York Observer.*

CHARLES SCRIBNER'S SONS,
153-157 Fifth Avenue, - - - - NEW YORK.

THE PUBLICATIONS OF LAMSON, WOLFFE, AND COMPANY,

6, Beacon Street, Boston.
Life Building, New York.

BAGBY, ALBERT MORRIS.
 MISS TRAUMEREI. A Weimar Idyl. 2d Edition. $1.50.
BOUTON, JOHN BELL.
 UNCLE SAM'S CHURCH; HIS CREED, BIBLE, AND HYMN-BOOK. 5th Edition. Cover in red, white and blue; or buff and blue. $0.50.
CARMAN, BLISS.
 BEHIND THE ARRAS; A BOOK OF THE UNSEEN. With designs by T. B. Meteyard. *Net,* $1.50.
ECHEGARAY, JOSE.
 THE GREAT GALEOTO, and FOLLY OR SAINTLINESS. Two plays done from the Spanish verse into English prose by Hannah Lynch. Brought out in connection with John Lane, of London. *Net,* $1.50.
HALE, EDWARD EVERETT.
 IF JESUS CAME TO BOSTON. $0.50.
 MY DOUBLE, AND HOW HE UNDID ME. Republished with a new preface and portrait of the author. $0.75.
HARRISON, MRS. BURTON.
 A VIRGINIA COUSIN and BAR HARBOR TALES. $1.25.
HOWE, MRS. JULIA WARD.
 IS POLITE SOCIETY POLITE? AND OTHER ESSAYS. With a new portrait of the author taken especially for this book. $1.50.
JOHNSON, E. PAULINE.
 THE WHITE WAMPUM: A BOOK OF INDIAN VERSE. Published in connection with John Lane, of London. *Net,* $1.50.
NODIER, CHARLES.
 TRILBY, THE FAIRY OF ARGYLE. Translated from the French by Minna Caroline Smith. 5th Edition. Scotch plaid cover. $.50.
ONGANIA, FERD. Venice.
 THE EARLY ART OF PRINTING. An elaborate and complete study from representative work during the Italian renaissance. *Net,* $5.50.
REVOLUTIONARY CALENDAR FOR 1896, lithographed in fifteen colors by Prang of Boston, and published under the auspices of the New York Chapter of the Daughters of the American Revolution. $1.00.
ROBINSON, CHARLES NEWTON.
 THE VIOL OF LOVE. Poems. Published in connection with John Lane, of London. *Net,* $1.50.

SAN MARCO IN VENEZIA (LA BASILICA DI.) Ferd. Ongania, Venice, Editor.
 Portfolio of complete lithographic plates.
 Portfolio of plates in black and white in ten (10) volumes. The complete text of description in Italian with three volumes of English translation. The price of this set, complete in sixteen volumes, was originally $466. A temporary offer is made for a few remaining sets at $300.
STREAMER, VOLNEY.
 I. IN FRIENDSHIP'S NAME. II. WHAT MAKES A FRIEND? Each, $1.25.
YALE WIT AND HUMOR.
 The wittiest things from the *Yale Record* 1889-1893. Arranged and edited by Edwin Ruthven Lamson. Illustrated. $1.50.

IN PRESS.

BOLTON, CHARLES KNOWLES.
 THE LOVE STORY OF URSULA WOLCOTT, being a Tale in Verse of the time of the "Great Revival" in New England. Illustrated by Ethel Reed. $1.00.
BRAZZA-SAVORGNAN, COUNTESS DI.
 OLD AND NEW LACE IN ITALY. Edition de luxe. Twenty-five copies. Illustrated. $3.00.
 TWO TYPES OF TO-DAY. "A Literary Farce" and "An American Idyl." With illustrations by the author. $1.50.
EMERSON, RALPH WALDO.
 Two unpublished essays; with an introduction by Dr. E. E. Hale. $1.00.
HALE, EDWARD EVERETT.
 A MAN WITHOUT A CITY. A new story inspired by the more modern patriotism of the need for better municipal government. $0.75.
 COL. INGHAM'S VISIT TO SYBARIS. A new edition. $0.75.
LUMMIS, CHARLES F.
 THE GOLDFISH OF GRAN CHIMU, AND OTHER PERUVIAN TALES. Illustrated. $1.50.
ROBERTS, C. G. D.
 EARTH'S ENIGMAS. AND OTHER STORIES. $1.00.
WETHERALD, ETHELWYN.
 THE HOUSE OF THE TREES AND OTHER POEMS. *Net,* $1.00.

Please mention THE CONNECTICUT QUARTERLY.

HOUGHTON, MIFFLIN & CO.

HOLIDAY BOOKS.

Mrs. Jameson's Works on Art.
Sacred and Legendary Art, 2 vols.
Legends of the Monastic Orders.
Legends of the Madonna.
Memoirs of the Early Italian Painters.

Edited by Miss ESTELLE M. HURLL, with a memoir and portrait of Mrs. Jameson. 5 vols., octavo, bound in simple but artistic style. Each volume contains nearly 100 illustrations, selected from the works of great masters. $3.00 a volume.

The Works of John Burroughs.
New Riverside Edition. With several portraits of Burroughs and engraved title pages. Printed from entirely new type, on paper of the best quality, and bound in a style combining simplicity and elegance. 9 vols., 12 mo, $13.50 net. (*Sold only in Sets.*)

Standish of Standish.
A beautiful *Holiday Edition* of this popular historical novel by Mrs. JANE G. AUSTIN, author of "A Nameless Nobleman," etc. With 20 exquisite full-page photogravure illustrations by FRANK T. MERRILL. 2 vols., 12 mo, tastefully bound, $5.00.

The Song of Hiawatha.
A *Popular Holiday Edition* of LONGFELLOW's unique poem, with 22 full-page illustrations by FREDERIC REMINGTON. Crown 8vo, $2.00.

The Courtship of Miles Standish.
A beautiful *Popular Holiday Edition* of LONGFELLOW's famous Pilgrim poem. With many illustrations. Crown 8vo, $1.50.

The Madonna of the Tubs.
New Popular Edition of one of Miss PHELPS's most striking and touching stories. With illustrations. Uniform with Mrs. WIGGIN's "The Bird's Christmas Carol." 75 cents.

BOOKS FOR YOUNG FOLKS.

Mr. Rabbit at Home.
A sequel to "Little Mr. Thimblefinger and His Queer Country." By JOEL CHANDLER HARRIS. With 25 illustrations by OLIVER HERFORD. Square 8vo, bound in very attractive style, $2.00.

Stories and Poems for Children.
By CELIA THAXTER, author of "Among the Isles of Shoals, etc. Edited by SARAH ORNE JEWETT. With a frontispiece illustration. 12 mo, $1.50.

Little Miss Phœbe Gay.
By HELEN DAWES BROWN, author of "The Petrie Estate," etc. With colored cover design and other illustrations. 16 mo, $1.00.

The Nimble Dollar, with Other Stories.
By CHARLES MINER THOMPSON. With a frontispiece illustration. 1 vol., 16mo, $1.00.

POETRY.

Last Poems of James Russell Lowell.
With a fine New Portrait and rubricated title and initials. Printed in artistic style, and bound in polished buckram. 12mo, $1.25.

Robert Browning.
Complete Poetic and Dramatic Works. *New Cambridge Edition.* A wonderful piece of book-making, printed from clear type, on opaque paper, and attractively bound. With Biographical Sketch, Notes, Indexes, a fine new portrait and a vignette of Asolo. Crown 8vo, gilt top, $3.00; half calf, gilt top, $5.00; tree calf. or full levant, $7.00.

Oliver Wendell Holmes.
Complete Poetical Works. *Cambridge Edition.* Uniform with the Cambridge Editions of LONGFELLOW and WHITTIER. With Biographical Sketch, Notes, Indexes, a Steel Portrait and engraved title. Crown 8vo, gilt top, $2.00; half calf, gilt top, $3.50; tree calf, or full levant, $5.50.

A Victorian Anthology.
Selections illustrating the Editor's critical review of British poetry in the reign of Victoria ["Victorian Poets"]. Selected and edited by E. C. STEDMAN. With brief biographies of the authors quoted, a fine frontispiece portrait of Queen Victoria, and a vignette of the Poets' Corner in Westminster Abbey. Large crown 8vo, bound in attractive library style, $2.50; full gilt, $3.00.

Mrs. Thaxter's Poems.
New Edition. Edited by SARAH ORNE JEWETT. 1 vol., 12mo, $1.50.

FICTION.

A Singular Life.
By ELIZABETH STUART PHELPS, author of "The Gates Ajar," etc. 16mo, $1.25.

The Life of Nancy.
By SARAH ORNE JEWETT, author of "Deephaven," "A Native of Winby," etc. 16mo, $1.25.

The Village Watch-Tower.
By Mrs. WIGGIN, author of "The Birds' Christmas Carol," etc. 16mo, $1.00.

A Gentleman Vagabond, and Some Others.
By F. HOPKINSON SMITH, author of "Colonel Carter of Cartersville." 16mo, $1.25.

The Wise Woman.
By Mrs. BURNHAM, author of "Sweet Clover," "Miss Bagg's Secretary," etc, 16mo, $1.25.

The Coming of Theodora.
By ELIZA ORNE WHITE, author of "Winterborough," "When Molly was Six." 16mo, $1.25.

Sold by all Booksellers. Sent, postpaid, by
HOUGHTON, MIFFLIN & CO., Boston; 11 E. 17th St., New York.

Please mention THE CONNECTICUT QUARTERLY.

...THE...
Connecticut Quarterly.

An Illustrated Magazine,

DEVOTED TO THE LITERATURE, HISTORY, AND PICTURESQUE FEATURES OF CONNECTICUT.

PUBLISHED QUARTERLY
By THE CONNECTICUT QUARTERLY COMPANY,
66 State Street, Courant Building,
HARTFORD, CONN.

GEO. C. ATWELL, General Manager.　　　　　W. FARRAND FELCH, Editor.

CONTENTS.

Vol. 1　　　　October, November, December, 1895.　　　　No. 4.

Frontispiece. "AUTUMN MORNING." From a painting by D. F. Wentworth.		314
The New Haven Green. Illustrated.	*Ellen Strong Bartlett.*	315
A Daughter of the Dawn. Poem. Illustrated.	*Will. Farrand Felch.*	326
The "Wide Awakes." The Great Political Organization of 1860. Illustrated.	*Major Julius G. Rathbun.*	327
The Pope and Pond Parks and Their Donors. Illustrated from photographs by the author and drawings by Geo. F. Stanton.	*Howard W. Benjamin.*	337
Some Native Orchids. Illustrated with drawings from nature by Alice M. Bartholomew.	*C. Antoinette Shepard.*	345
Memories of Meriden.	*Frances A. Breckenridge.*	352
An Autumn Rondeau. Poem.	*Ellen Brainerd Peck.*	354
Yale Boys of the Last Century. Extracts from the Journal of Elijah Backus.	*Ellen D. Larned.*	355
Departure. Double Sonnet.	*Robert Clarkson Tongue.*	361
The Girl from Massachusetts. Story.	*Pauline Phelps.*	362
Gentian. Poem.	*Joseph Archer.*	367
Old Time Music and Musicians.	*N. H. Allen.*	368
The Spirit of Beauty. Poem. Selected.	*Rufus Dawes.*	373
Old Colonial Characters. III Aaron Burr, Portrait of Aaron Burr, from a rare drawing from life.	*Felix Oldmixon.*	374
New Britain in the Days of the Revolution. Illustrated.	*Mrs. C J. Parker.*	379
The Old Farm Home. Poem. Selected.		390
Trio and Tripod. IV. From Hartland to Burlington. Illustrated.	*Geo. H. Carrington.*	391
Scrope; or the Lost Library: Serial.	*Frederic Beecher Perkins.*	399
New Haven Elms. Poem.	*Herbert Randall.*	402

DEPARTMENTS.

The Round Table. 403
　A Year Old.—A Former State Magazine.—The Growth of the Humane Sentiment.—"Civic Beings."—A Contretemps.—A Word of Retrospect.

Treasure Trove. 407
　Connecticut "Colloures."—Connecticut Society of Colonial Wars.—Connecticut Society of the Daughters of the Revolution.—Connecticut Society of the War for the Union.—New Haven Colony Historical Society.

Notes and Queries. 408
　Backus.—Graves.—Swords.—The Graves Reunion.

Book Notices. 410

Copyright 1895 by THE CONNECTICUT QUARTERLY Co. (*All rights reserved.*)
Entered at the Post Office at Hartford, Conn., as mail matter of the second class.

FOR THE ENSUING YEAR:

We propose to make THE QUARTERLY better and more attractive than ever. Special attention will be given New Haven and Fairfield Counties, as well as continuing in Hartford County, giving due attention to the rest of the State as soon as practicable. We have articles in preparation relating to the early history of different parts of the State, and it is our intention to make THE QUARTERLY the best historic, descriptive and picturesque work for standard reference and interesting reading of Connecticut.

There will be articles on New Haven in every number during 1896. Also a series of articles on Meriden will be given, of which the one in this issue, Memories of Meriden, is but introductory. The succeeding ones will be illustrated.

New Britain will also be continued through several numbers. It is our aim to give as complete an illustrated history of the various places as we can. Some of those already treated will have further attention at some future time.

PICTURESQUE POMFRET, BY HON. JOHN ADDISON PORTER,
  which was unavoidably delayed, will be an attractive feature of next number.

THE HARTFORD PARK SYSTEM, continued with an article on RESERVOIR PARK, BY JAMES SHEPARD,
  will claim our attention in the January number.

OLD TIME MUSIC AND MUSICIANS, III, BY PROF. N. H. ALLEN,
  will begin with the present century, and grow more interesting and popular as it approaches the present day and the living exemplars of the art.

YALE BOYS OF THE LAST CENTURY, BY MISS ELLEN D. LARNED,
  will continue her pleasing series of silhouettes of the last century, edited with appreciative [insight and fidelity.

A TYPOGRAPHICAL GALAXY, BY MR. MARCUS A. CASEY,
  Vice-President of the Case, Lockwood & Brainard Co., Hartford. This paper will commend itself to practical printers, journalists, publishers, and the more elderly readers of the QUARTERLY, giving a history of prominent leaders in the craft during this century, with portraits; also containing a letter and an extract from an early poem by Whittier, the latter written when he was a Hartford editor, which has never appeared in any collection.

IN THE DAYS OF OLD FATHER GEORGE AND HIGH BETTY MARTIN, BY MISS ESTELLE M. HART, OF NEW BRITAIN.
  This is the felicitous title of an amusing and gossipy article on last century amusements — games, contra-dances, huskings, quiltings — and festivals such as weddings. It forms a fitting *pendant* to Prof. Allen's musical memories, and showing the bright side of "the days of our daddies," after Puritan restraints had vanished.

Our plans for various interesting articles in the future, will make the succeeding numbers of surpassing value and interest. We cannot, of course, represent every town in one year, but we shall compass as much each year as possible.

TWO BOOKS
Of Interest to Connecticut Readers.

On The
Wooing of Martha Pitkin.
By Charles Knowles Bolton.

Hand-made paper, small octavo, seventeenth century binding, 75 cents. Thirty-five copies on large paper, full blind tooled leather, $2.00.

Dumb in June, A Book of Poems
By Richard Burton.

Small octavo paper boards, 75 cents. Thirty-five copies on Dutch hand-made paper, $2.00.

This book is the initial volume in a series of American Poets to be made in similar form and issued at irregular intervals under the name of OATEN STOPS.

COPELAND & DAY,
BOSTON.

History for Ready Reference
and Topical Reading.
By J. N. LARNED, *Ex-Pres't Am. Library Ass'n.*

☞ **Giving History on All Topics in the Exact Words of the Historians Themselves.** Not the opinion of one man, but the thoughts of many men, have been diligently sought out and arranged for the "Ready Reference" of the Reader.

"This book is a downright royal road to learning. It covers the histories of all epochs and of all countries."—SIDNEY S. RIDER.

"An encyclopædia of history has been greatly needed, but here is something much better. The work is equally happy in conception and execution."—PROF. RICHARD HUDSON, M.A.

"It is a veritable reference library of classics for historical research, and such a library, too, as no school has been fortunate enough to possess."—PROF. JOHN MCDUFFIE, A.M.

"It is reliable and up to date, and gives what an ordinary Encyclopædia does not."—RT. REV. J. WILLIAMS, D.D., LL.D.

"I desire also to express my satisfaction with the maps which illustrate the text. They are a distinct advance on anything heretofore produced in historic geography on this side of the Atlantic."—PROF. WILLISTON WALKER, PH.D.

Sold Only by Subscription. Send for Circular.

C. A. NICHOLS CO., Publishers,
Springfield, Mass.

THREE BOOKS.

History of the People of Israel.

By ERNST RENAN. Vol. V. Period of Jewish Independence and Judea under Roman Rule. With an index to the five volumes, 8vo. Cloth. $2.50.

Viewing the five volumes as a whole, their interest centres in Renan's interpretation of Hebrew history; and it may safely be said that nothing that he has done reveals the brilliancy of his mind and the greatness of his intellectual grasp as does this monument, which he was fortunately permitted to finish before his life came to an end.

From Jerusalem to Nicæa.

The Church in the First Three Centuries. Lowell Lectures. By PHILIP STAFFORD MOXOM, author of "The Aim of Life." 12mo, Cloth, $1.50.

"Can be read with profit and interest by the entire reading public."—*Boston Journal.*

The Aim of Life.

Plain Talks to Young Men and Women. By Rev. PHILIP S. MOXOM. 16mo, Cloth, $1.00.

"A noteworthy addition to the best reading for youth."—*Outlook.*

At all Bookstores. Postpaid on receipt of price by the publishers.

Roberts Brothers,
BOSTON, MASS.

Established 1838.

The Hartford
Printing Co.

ELIHU GEER'S SONS,

16 STATE STREET,
HARTFORD, CONN.

BOOK AND JOB

Printers.

Wedding Invitations and Announcements we make a specialty of.

Telephone number is **649.**

EVERETT S. GEER, Pres't.
ERASTUS C. GEER, Sec'y.
E. HOWARD GEER, Sup't.

We have a Library of City Directories of all the principal cities in the country; also, Foreign Directories, for free reference.

Please mention THE CONNECTICUT QUARTERLY.

THE CONNECTICUT QUARTERLY.

Price 50 cents a year, (4 numbers,) **payable in advance.** Single copies, 15 cents.

Remittances should be by Check, Express Money Order, P. O. Order, or Registered Letter. Money by mail at sender's risk.

All subscriptions taken with the understanding that they expire after four numbers have been sent, unless renewed by the subscriber. When change of address is desired, give both the old and new address.

Agents wanted in every town in the State to get subscriptions. Write for terms, etc.

As the editions of Numbers 1 and 2 are exhausted, we are obliged to begin all subscriptions with No. 3. We can procure a few of No. 1 for persons desiring them at $1.00 each, and No. 2 at 50 cents each.

As subscriptions have been taken only with the understanding that they are to be discontinued after four numbers have been sent unless renewed, we shall be glad to receive renewals for 1896 from all who began with No. 1. Otherwise we shall discontinue their subscription.

This number is not marked in any way denoting the expiration of your subscription, but if you have received the four numbers of 1895, please fill out and send the enclosed blank, with fifty cents, to us, or renew through your newsdealer.

. . . BINDING . . .

We have made arrangements with binders, so that we can supply our patrons with a durable and handsome binding for their Quarterly of 1895, with a **stamp of special design** on front cover.

Half Russia, 75 cts.; Half Morocco, $1.00; Half Morocco, extra fine, $1.25.

Samples can be seen at our Office, Room 25, Courant Building, Hartford, Conn.

On account of scarcity of Nos. 1 and 2, the price of bound volumes of 1895 will be $2.50 in Half Russia binding. Other bindings at a proportionally higher price. We have but a very limited number.

We wish to secure a large number of subscribers to The Quarterly for the coming year.

We have met with a liberal patronage during the last, our initial year, and wish to increase largely during 1896.

This we hope to do by keeping the standard fully up to its former excellence and surpassing it where we can, introducing new and valuable features. The expense of producing such a magazine necessitates a large sale.

We have put the price low, so that it is within the reach of all, and enables anyone to subscribe for themselves and one or more friends, thus giving a present that will be appreciated far above its nominal cost.

THE CONNECTICUT QUARTERLY,
Box 565, Hartford, Conn.

CAUTION.—Do not pay money to persons unknown to you. Our authorized agents have full credentials

---

1794   OLDEST INSURANCE COMPANY IN HARTFORD.   1895

The Hartford Fire Insurance Company,
OF HARTFORD, CONN.

Has a Capital of One and One-quarter Million Dollars. Has a Net Surplus of over Two and One-half Million Dollars. Has Total Assets of over Eight and One-half Million Dollars. Has paid over Forty-six Million Dollars in Losses.

GEO. L. CHASE, President.

P. C. ROYCE, Secretary.   THOS. TURNBULL, Ass't Secretary.
                                    CHAS. E. CHASE, Ass't Secretary.

Metropolitan Department, No. 50 Wall St., New York. YOUNG & HODGES, Managers.
Western Department, Chicago, Ill. G. F. BISSELL, Manager; P. P. HEYWOOD, Ass't Manager.
Pacific Department, San Francisco, Cal. BELDEN & COFRAN, Managers.

Agencies in all the Prominent Localities throughout the United States and Canada.

Please mention THE CONNECTICUT QUARTERLY.

Headquarters for Wedding Stationery

Printed or Engraved.

We use the very best quality and correct styles of paper and envelopes. . . . Our prices are more than satisfactory and the work of both engraved and printed Invitations, At Home Cards, Etc., is out of sight.

R. S. Peck & Co.

*14 Ford St.
Hartford, Conn.*

THE CONNECTICUT Building and Loan Association.

General Office: { Charter Oak Bank Building, Hartford, Conn.

Has an authorized Guarantee Fund of $250,000, of which $50,000 in cash has been paid in.

OFFICERS.

GEORGE E. KEENEY, President.
ROCKWELL KEENEY, Vice-President.
EDGAR C. LINN, Secretary.
GEORGE W. HODGE, Treasurer.

ATTORNEY.

JOHN H. BUCK, Ass't State Attorney; with Buck & Eggleston, Attorneys, Hartford, Conn.

DIRECTORS.

HON. E. STEVENS HENRY, Rockville, Conn., Treasurer of People's Savings Bank; United States Congressman, First Connecticut District.
HON. PATRICK GARVAN, Hartford, Conn., Paper and Paper Stock Manufacturer; Ex-State Senator; Director State Bank.
R. B. PARKER, Hartford, Conn., President Hartford Life and Annuity Insurance Co.; Director First National Bank; Cotton Manufacturer.
HON. GEORGE E. KEENEY, Somersville, Conn., Treasurer Somersville Manufacturing Co.; Ex-State Senator.
HON. GEORGE W. HODGE, Hartford, Conn., Treasurer of the State of Connecticut; Paper Manufacturer.
E. C. HILLIARD, Hartford, Conn., Woolen Manufacturer; Vice-President of the Hartford Life and Annuity Insurance Co.; Director First National Bank.
HON. E. C. PINNEY, Stafford, Conn., President of Stafford Savings Bank; Woolen Manufacturer; Ex-State Senator.
ROCKWELL KEENEY, Somersville, Conn., President of the Somersville Manufacturing Co.
E. C. LINN, Hartford, Conn., Secretary Connecticut Building and Loan Association.

Shareholders guaranteed against any loss of their Capital invested.
Maturity of Shares at once in the event of Death.
Cancellation of the Borrower's Mortgage at once in the event of Death.
No Membership, Admission or Entrance Fees.
Installment Shares, 50 cents per share per month. A limited amount of 6 per cent. Coupon Shares for sale at par.
For further information, apply to the General Office.

Please mention THE CONNECTICUT QUARTERLY.

Webster's International Dictionary

Successor of the "Unabridged."
Invaluable in Office, School, and Home.

Specimen pages, etc., sent on application.

Standard of the U. S. Supreme Court, of the U. S. Gov't Printing Office, and of nearly all Schoolbooks. Warmly commended by every State Superintendent of Schools.

THE BEST FOR PRACTICAL PURPOSES
BECAUSE

It is easy to find the word wanted.
Words are given their correct alphabetical places, each one beginning a paragraph.

It is easy to ascertain the pronunciation.
The pronunciation is indicated by the ordinary diacritically marked letters used in the schoolbooks.

It is easy to trace the growth of a word.
The etymologies are full, and the different meanings are given in the order of their development.

It is easy to learn what a word means.
The definitions are clear, explicit, and full, and each is contained in a separate paragraph.

G. & C. Merriam Co., Publishers, Springfield, Mass.

THE ROGERS & HAMILTON CO.,
WATERBURY, CONN.

ALDINE COFFEE SPOON.

MANUFACTURERS OF

HIGHEST GRADE SILVER-PLATED WARE.

IMPERIAL-GRANUM

Is Universally acknowledged the STANDARD and the BEST Prepared

FOOD

For INVALIDS and Convalescents, for Dyspeptic, Delicate, Infirm and Aged Persons. PURE, delicious, nourishing FOOD for nursing-mothers, infants and CHILDREN.

Sold everywhere. Shipping Depot, JOHN CARLE & SONS, NEW YORK.

AUTUMN MORNING.

From a painting by D. F. Wentworth.

The Connecticut Quarterly.

"Leave not your native land behind."—Thoreau.

FOURTH QUARTER.

Vol. 1   October, November, December, 1895.   No. 4.

THE NEW HAVEN GREEN.

BY MISS ELLEN STRONG BARTLETT.

When the forefathers marked out their famous nine squares, with that in the middle set apart as a "public market-place;" they fixed the center of the life of the city of Elms. The Green has been called the heart of New Haven. In absence, the name calls up stirring memories; on return, the sight of it stirs thrills of recognition. It is only a simple grassy square, surrounded and dotted by trees, divided by Temple street, crossed by many paths for the convenience of busy people; and enshrining three old churches. But the square has been there since Davenport and Eaton laid out the town in 1638; the trees have stood a hundred years; and around the churches are entwined the historic associations of the colony and the city.

The changes have been many. The alders and willows that over-hung pools of water, have gone; so, too, have the "market-house," the whipping-post, the buildings which one after another graced or disgraced its surface. The area is sixteen acres; it is not exactly square, because the surveyor who measured it in the midst of primeval wildness, was unable to be strictly accurate, but to the eye this is not apparent.

The surveyor was John Brockett, son of Sir John Brockett of Brockett's Hall, Herefordshire; and perhaps a little inexactness may be understood, if we believe the tradition that he had left all in England and had crossed the sea in pursuit of a charming girl among the Puritan band.

Around the Green were placed the houses of the leaders of the colony, which was the most opulent of those that left England; and thus the Green has always been before the eyes of the citizens, and has been the short-cut from one " quarter " to another. It is itself a token that the colonists came, not to seek adventure or to avoid the restraints of civilized life, but with a definite purpose to found a state, with a city at its head, that they intended to be graced by order and beauty. May the good intentions of good men be always thus carried out.

The building of the meeting-house, identified in New Haven so preeminently with the state, came foremost in their plans. The first Sabbath,

THE GREEN, SHOWING BRICK CHURCH AND CHURCH-YARD.
From a Painting in the rooms of the New Haven Colony Historical Society.

April 18, 1638, has been often described; and artists have been inspired by the chronicle to show us the spreading oak and the reverent company of Englishmen, women and children, assembled there for the worship they had crossed the ocean to maintain. This oak, under which John Davenport, the favorite London minister, preached on the temptation in the wilderness, was near the present corner of George and College streets, but the first house of God was nearly as possible, in the center of the Green. This was in 1638, and on this historic spot have been placed the successive buildings of the church, so appropriately known as the " Center." Even more than in other colonies was this a fitting situation, for the founders made the law that " the Church Members only shall be free Burgesses; and that they only shall chuse magistrates and officers among themselves to have the power of transacting all publique civil affairs of this plantation."

The "meeting-house" was a modest little shelter for sentiments like these. If was only fifty feet square, perfectly plain, with roof like a truncated pyramid, but on Sabbaths it must have been furnished nobly with keen intellect and high principle. We know all about the Sabbath then, the beating of the drum, the decorous walk through the Green to the meeting-house, the careful ranking of seats, the stationing of the guard to keep watch on lurking Indians. Those who go up now to worship may feel that they are literally following the footsteps of the fathers. Through the Green was the special path allowed to the first pastor, John Davenport, so that he might walk on Sundays from his house to the pulpit in the complete seclusion befitting his dignity. Here, later, was the first school-house, a little back of the church, and alas! in spite of all these privileges of religious and political liberty, before long a jail was necessary, that made a biot on the Green. The whipping-post was moved about until 1831, when it was exchanged for the less appalling sign-post for legal notices. And the public square was not too good in early days for a pound. The old almshouse stood on the northwest corner, near College street. For its convenience was a well of excellent water, and it is thought that it has never been filled up.

In 1639, Ne-pau-puck, a persistent enemy, was beheaded here, and perhaps this ghastly yielding of savage ferocity to Anglo-Saxon law is the darkest picture the Green has offered. After the English custom, the burying-ground adjoined the church, and there were laid the wise and good, the young and old, of the infant settlement. Martha Townsend was the first woman buried in this

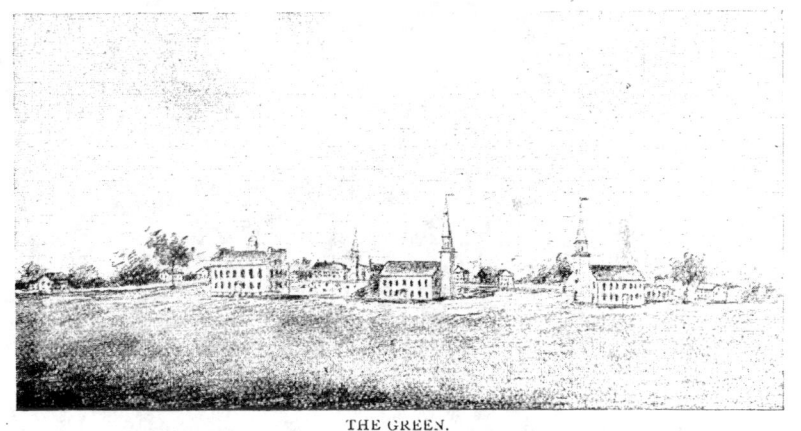

THE GREEN.
From a Drawing owned by the New Haven Colony Historical Society.

ground. Sometimes, at dead of night, apart from others, the victims of smallpox were fearfully laid here. The ground was filled with graves between the church and College street; sixteen bodies having been found within sixteen square feet, when in 1821, the stones were removed to the Grove Street Cemetery, and the ground was leveled. A few stones are left in their original places, while in the crypt of the church may be seen, in their original places, the monuments of more than a hundred and thirty of the early inhabitants. Back of the church are some small, dark stones, decidedly gnawed by time. Tradition used to ascribe two of these to the resting-places of Goffe and Whalley, the hunted regicides; and elaborate interpretations were given of the purposely brief and misleading inscriptions. Opinion now discredits this, and assigns the stone

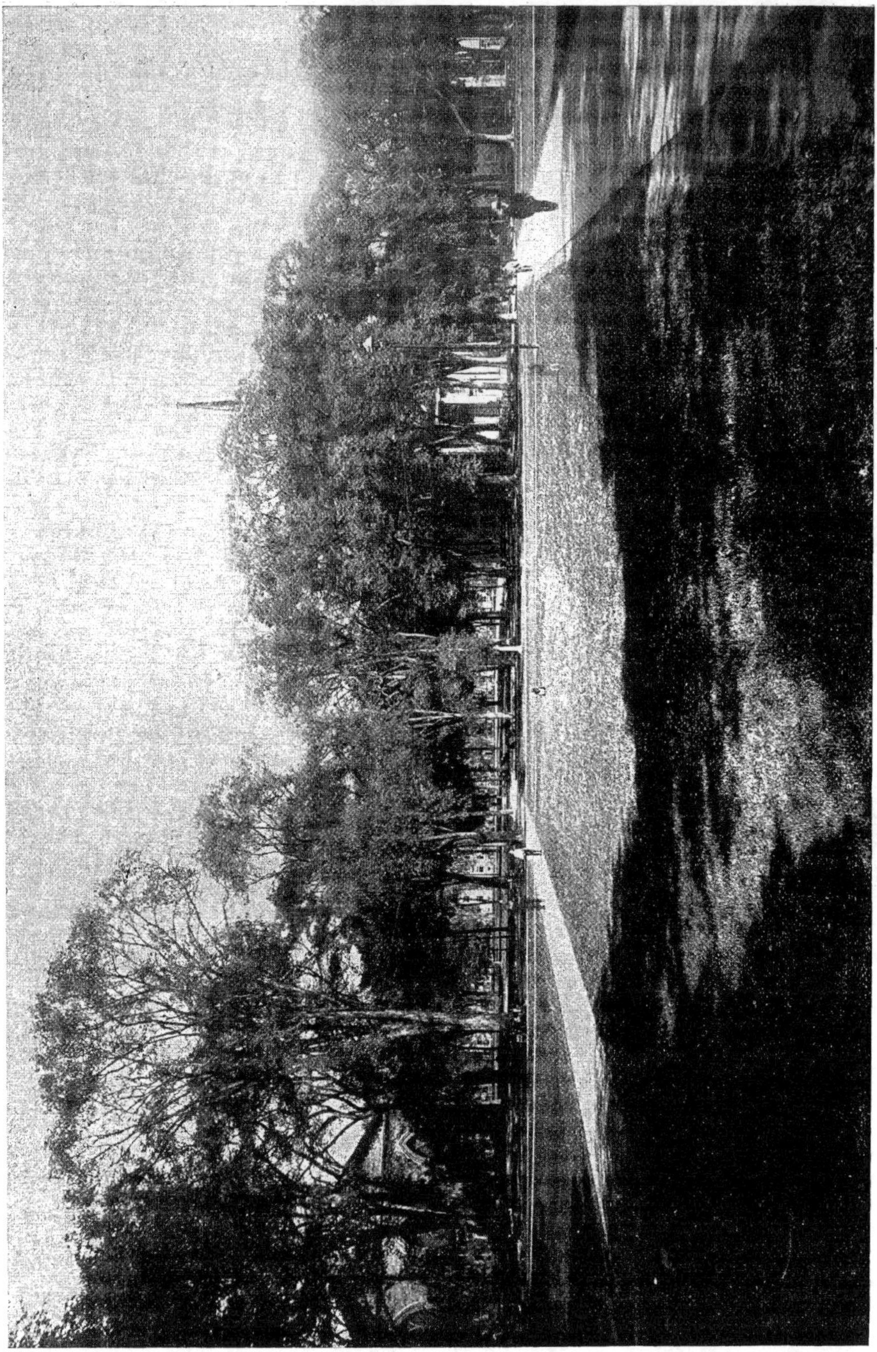

formerly called Whalley's to Martin Gilbert, Assistant Deputy. But there is no mistake about the grave of Dixwell, the third of the regicides, and the original stone, simply inscribed " J. D. 1688-9," etc., is plainly seen, while in the same enclosure is the monument erected in 1847, by the descendants of Dixwell. He had concealed his name under that of Davis. An inscription on the church-wall tells us that Theophilus Eaton, the noted founder of the town, lies near. Over the entrance of the church are the main dates and facts of the settlement of the town, and many a passer through the Green stops under the shade of the trees to read, and get a lesson in history.

THE GREEN.

From a Drawing owned by the New Haven Colony Historical Society.

As time passed, the Green was graded and cleared. Around it lived the Pierponts, the Trowbridges, the Ingersolls, and facing its upper side were the buildings of the infant Yale. They were very simple, and afford a great contrast to the elaborate and imposing array of to-day, but the forty boys were proud of their college.

The three churches on Temple street, in the very middle of the Green are an unusual and striking feature of a public square. The North Church now called the United Church, and Trinity Church, were built in 1814, as well as the present building of the Center Church, so that the three buildings were rising at the same time, during the troubled period of our second war with England. It is said that the ship which was bringing in material for Trinity was overhauled by a British cruiser, but that the enemy was persuaded to relinquish that part of the booty when its sacred destination was disclosed. Besides these, no buildings now stand within the inclosure, and no further encroachment is allowed. One after another, the various structures which a too accommodating public allowed, have been removed. The last to go was the " old State House," in 1887. Built in 1829, by Ithiel Towne, it was the successor of several State Houses which stood in different parts of the Green. Its removal was long discussed, and the friends and opponents of the measure were aroused to couch their arguments in decidedly vigorous language. Without the State House steps,

THE OLD STATE HOUSE.

classes and associations go hunting for a place for photographic groups. The classic columns of this copy of the Theseum, must figure in many a picture belonging to bye-gone days.

In the latter part of the last century, the Green began to put on its present appearance. The county-house and jail were taken away in 1784. In that year, a market-house was placed near the corner of Church and Chapel streets, but in 1798, it was taken down. At that time, the square was fenced, under the direction of James Hillhouse, David Austin, and Isaac Beers. In 1799, permission was obtained to level the surface at private expense. Evidently public spirit was stronger in individuals than in common councils. About that time the great planting of elms began. The two famous trees, which may have set the fashion, which caused Mrs. Tuthill to call New Haven the "City of Elms," were brought to town in 1686, by William Cooper, as a gift to the pastor, and were planted in front of the Pierpont house, where the Bristol house now is. There they flourished for more than one hundred and fifty years. They shaded the windows of Sarah Pierpont, that rare maiden who was "of a wonderful sweetness, calmness and unusual benevolence," who "sometimes went about singing sweetly, and seemed to be always full of joy and pleasure," who "loved to be alone, walking in the fields and groves," and whose charms of beauty, intellect, and good sense subjugated even Jonathan Edwards, the intellectual giant of America. Some one has said that in the shade of those trees, these famous lovers must have often lingered. Twenty-three years after their marriage, a platform was built under their pendent boughs and the "silver tongued" Whitfield preached to the listening crowd on the Green. The Pierpont elms lived for more than a century and a half. The last was cut down in 1840, having attained a circumference of eighteen feet. Two magnificent elms were also in front of the house and school of the Rev. Claudius Herrick, where Battell Chapel now is. They too, were a century and a half old, in 1879, when cut down. At the corner of Church and Chapel streets, is the

THE CENTER CHURCH.

TEMPLE STREET.

most noted of New Haven elms, the "Franklin Elm." Jerry Allen, a "poet and pedagogue" brought it on his back from Hamden Plains, and sold it to Thaddeus Beecher for a pint of rum and some trifles. It was planted on the day of Franklin's death, April 17, 1790. Its girth, two feet from the ground, is sixteen feet; its height is eighty feet. This noble tree spreads its graceful branches as a welcome and a shelter to all who make pilgrimage to New Haven. It seems a fitting gateway to the arcades that stretch athwart the turf beyond. In the shade of the Franklin elm is the "Town pump," one of the old landmarks which thirsty people would regret to see removed. It was given to the city long ago by Mr. Douglass of Middletown.

In 1784, the Common Council ordered the extension of Temple street to Grove, and in 1792, Hillhouse Avenue was laid out. Col. James Hillhouse,

THE DIXWELL MONUMENT.

ever enthusiastic in public works, besought the citizens to subscribe for beautifying the Green by planting trees. This was in 1787, and most of the trees were set between then and 1796. Most of them were brought from the Hillhouse farm in Meriden, and by the testimony of eye-witnesses, they varied from the size of whipstocks to a foot in thickness.

The zeal of Col. Hillhouse, who often took the spade in his own hands, inspired others. The Rev. David Austin was moved to plant the inner rows on the east and west sides of the Green, and many stories are told of the enthusiasm of boys in holding trees, girls in watering and tending them, all to help on the good work. The cool and shady streets of New Haven are a memorial of this widespread interest in Hillhouse's plan. Such men as Ogden Edwards, United States Judge Henry Baldwin, and President Day, were proud, in mature life, to look back on their boyish participation in the work.

A constant and varied succession of foot-passengers may be seen on the diagonal paths. There is no "age, sex, or condition" which is not to be found there during the day. Babies in summer, boys skating in winter, wise professors and students with book in hand, at all times, are surely there. Many times, thousands of children have been massed there, to add to the festivity of Fourth of July, Sunday-school, and centennial celebrations, and their choruses have carried the swelling voices of vast choirs to the cathedral arch of Temple street. Probably no famous man has ever visited New Haven without contributing his presence to the personal associations of this simple square. Nobles, scholars, poets, divines, statesmen, from all countries, have been there. Washington decorously attended church at Trinity. Lafayette reviewed troops here, and both were sometimes visitors of Roger Sherman who lived just above the Green. After the Revolutionary heroes, the place felt the tread of Madison and Monroe, of Andrew Jackson, of Van Buren. Then came the great men of the civil war; Grant, Sherman, Sheridan, Hancock, McDowell, and many more, have bowed to the cheers of thousands crowded on the Green.

Training days and county fairs must have caused the Green to smile, and even to laugh aloud, and whenever the feeling of the town has been stirred to its depths, the Green has been the spot to which every one hied to show his share in that feeling. Here the loyal subjects of George III. celebrated his majority, and some years later, made public rejoicing over the repeal of the Stamp Act. Here Benedict Arnold, after Lexington, assembled the Governor's Guard, to lead them to Cambridge, to swell the patriot army; here the citizens of a new republic crowded, to shout over the surrender of Cornwallis, and two years later, the gunners in long green gowns boomed the salutes for the treaty of peace with England. Here passed, in 1851, the barouche which contained all the survivors of the Revolution who could

ELM STREET.

be mustered for the Fourth of July parade. The year before that dirges were played here after President Taylor's death, and, ten years later, the Green was whitened by the recruiting tents of the Townsend Rifles; and the boys of the three months' regiments made their first bivouac here; too many, alas! afterward finding the "bivouac of death" on Southern fields. Here the New Haven branch of the Sanitary Commission was organized, and its chairman, Mr. Alfred Walker, sent out two hundred and eighty-seven boxes in the first month. In the State House, the New Haven Soldiers' Aid Association met for three years.

Under the trees, collations were given to returning soldiers, and sad crowds assembled to witness the funeral honors paid to New Haven's sons: to Theodore Winthrop, so early sacrificed, to General Terry and Commodore Foote, lost when ripened by experience. Great was the rejoicing when "the cruel war was over." Thousands assembled to cheer the news of the fall of Petersburg and Richmond. Then in the midst of joy came the blow of Lincoln's assassination, and a greater and a sadder crowd, hurried back to the old Green than it has ever seen gathered for any other occasion. Then, on the steps of the State House, Dr. Leonard Bacon voiced the lamentation of a city bereaved of its national head, and the elms sighed over a horror-stricken multitude.

THE FRANKLIN ELM.

It seems safe to feel that, after such a history, as long as life remains in the city, the "heart of New Haven" will beat on in its old place.

A DAUGHTER OF THE DAWN.

WILL. FARRAND FELCH.

She looks upon the lake's expanse—
Her hair wind-blown o'er eyes as blue
As mist that seems the waves to trance.
She watches the glad waves advance,
    Retreat, dance at her feet,—
    And then again retreat,—
In rhythmic, endless amplitude:
A priestess of the solitude.

Along the shore she steps in state,—
Her cheek glows with the rosy dawn
That now begins to dissipate
The morning's pearly dews that wait
    To greet, elate, her feet,
    And touch her gown, so sweet,
Then melt in balmy morning air,—
Like fragrance poured from chalice rare.

Her voice,— soft as the note that falls
From nesting bird, awake at night,
When to her drowsy mate she calls,—
Like music of the past, enthralls;
    Upsoars and falls, then soars:
    Like siren-songs, from shores
Of fatal Tyrrhencan sea,—
A flood of buoyant minstrelsy.

Her suave and gracious presence fills,
Complete the scene; her graceful mien
Enchants: like brightest dream fulfills
Its mission,— all the sense instills
    With light, then thrills delight
    Through all the inner sight.
Alas! she is but fleeting breath:
Twilight of Life! The Dawn of Death!

THE "WIDE AWAKES."

THE GREAT POLITICAL ORGANIZATION OF 1860.

BY MAJOR JULIUS G. RATHBUN.

This is in no sense a political article, and is written by request, in order to show just how, and where, the Wide Awakes originated, with a brief history of the "original thirty-six" of Hartford. The first campaign of the Republican party was that of 1856, the "Fremont and Jessie" campaign, in which the newly organized Republican party had shown great strength. In Hartford it had been hotly contested, and to a great extent it had been a bitter campaign. There was no public hall of sufficient capacity to accommodate the crowds which flocked to hear the eminent speakers, who were brought into the state, and in consequence the "Fremont Camp" was erected on a vacant lot, corner of Asylum and High streets, where the Park church now stands. It was roughly built, with common wooden benches, a seating capacity of perhaps two thousand but capable of holding many more, the main entrance being on High street at about the middle of the "camp." The population of Hartford at that time was about 25,000.

George P. Bissell was one of the most active of the young Republicans, and his old white hat, which he used to swing energetically, when calling for cheers for "Fremont and Jessie," was a feature of the meetings. Torchlight processions were quite common toward the close of the campaign; after the election was over and Buchanan had won the victory, the camp was taken down, and the well-worn torches were packed away for future use.

ORIGIN OF THE WIDE AWAKES.

The state campaign early in 1860, promised to be very lively, Hon. William A. Buckingham, of Norwich, having been nominated for Governor by the Republicans, and Colonel Thomas H. Seymour, of Hartford, by the Democrats. The former was comparatively unknown, excepting in the eastern part of the state, while Colonel Seymour was well known as a brave officer in the Mexican war, as well as minister to Russia, and enjoyed the respect and confidence of the citizens of Hartford; it seemed almost a hopeless task to beat him at the polls.

CAPT. JAMES S. CHALKER.

On Saturday evening, February 25, 1860, the spring campaign was opened with a meeting in Touro Hall, formerly the North Baptist Church, which stood where the Cheney block now stands, at which an immense audience was gathered to hear Hon. Cassius M. Clay of Kentucky, several hundred being unable to obtain admittance to the building. A torchlight procession had been arranged to escort the distinguish speaker to his quarters at the Allyn House, George P. Bissell, acting as marshal, wearing his famous white hat of the Fremont campaign of four years previous. The old torches were again brought out to do duty, many of them in a leaky condition, and as the right of the line was at the corner of Pratt and Main streets, in front of Talcott & Post's dry goods store, several clerks of that establishment in order to protect their clothing from dripping oil, went inside, tore of squares off black cambric, tied pieces of tape in the corners, and thus improvised capes which they wore. Marshal Bissell, noticing them, placed these young men at the head of the line, where the novelty of their "rig" attracted much attention, and after the parade was over, it was suggested that a company be organized to wear glazed capes and caps, and to provide better torches than those in use.

The young men who were thus the means of starting the movement, were Daniel G. Francis, James L. Francis, (brothers), Edgar S Yergason, Charles R. Hart and Charles M. Fairbanks.*

ORIGINAL MUSLIN CAPE.—Worn by E. S. Yergason.

Within the next few days, Silliman B. Ives, Horatio P. Blair, and Henry P. Hitchcock canvassed among the young men, and also had made at Roberts' tin ware shop on Kinsley street, a sample swinging torch, believed to be the first ever made, and a meeting was called for Saturday evening March 3d, in the rooms of J. Allen Francis over the City Bank, then on the southeast corner of Main and Kinsley street, at which meeting there were present thirty-six enthusiastic young Republicans, who proceeded to organize a marching club.

Through the courtesy of James P. Carpenter, now a resident of Boston, who has carefully preserved the records of the early meetings, though unfortunately not the original list of members, I am enabled to give verbatim the record of the preliminary meetings:

At a meeting of Republicans, held at Allen's rooms (over City Bank), Hartford, Saturday evening, March 3, 1860, the meeting was called to order by H. P. Blair, who announced the object of the meeting and moved the appointment of a chairman. Mr. Blair was nominated and elected, and having taken the chair, proceeded by stating that the first business in the formation of the club was to appoint a captain, and secretary and treasurer. Motion was made to appoint captain by ballot, which being put to vote and carried, we proceeded to ballot, which resulted in the election of James S. Chalker by upwards of two-thirds vote. At this stage of proceedings, Mr. Chalker made his appearance in the meeting, and upon learning of his election, declined the acceptance of it,

---

*D. G. Francis served in the 1st Conn. Vols. for three months, afterwards through the war in the 7th Conn. Vols. attaining the rank of captain. James L. Francis was a lieutenant in the 12th Conn. Vols and was killed in Louisiana. E. S. Yergason served in the 22d Conn. Vols. D. G. Francis now resides in West Hartford. Messrs. Yergason and Hart are prominent business men in Hartford. Fairbanks is supposed to reside in the west.

but being pressed by the "voice of the people" and the earnest wishes of his friends, he thanked them for their manifested regard in tendering to him so high an office among them, and accepted to the rejoicing of all present.

The next business was to appoint secretary and treasurer; James P. Carpenter being nominated, was elected.

A committee of six, whose duty it should be to transact the business of the club, was then appointed, consisting of Messrs. Newell, Stockbridge, Speare, Humphrey, Francis, and Carpenter. It having been voted to give the captain power to appoint his own aids, he then made choice of the following named persons as lieutenants to rank as they are called: Newell, Carpenter, Humphrey, Blair, Hitchcock, Francis. A motion was then made to give our club a name, and the name "Wide Awakes" being proposed, was adopted by a unanimous vote. It was then voted to adopt the glazed cap and cape as our uniform, and carry the swinging torch.

Discussions upon various topics, having occupied so much time, it was thought best to defer the adoption of resolutions, and all other business until the next meeting, and motion was made to adjourn.

Upon counting, there were found to be present 36, all "Wide Awake." Adjourned.

J. P. CARPENTER, Sec'y.

It is interesting to note how the name of this famous organization was adopted; the city editor of the Courant was William P. Fuller, and in reporting the Cassius M. Clay meeting he headed the article, "Republicans Wide Awake!" When the matter of a name for the new club was under discussion, H. P. Hitchcock spoke of the aforesaid article and proposed the name "Republican Wide Awakes." It met with favor, the name "Wide Awakes" was voted for, but at a later meeting was changed as above.

From later meetings recorded by Secretary Carpenter I will simply note a few items of interest; at a meeting held Tuesday evening, March 6th, the vote appointing six lieutenants was rescinded, the title of the officers changed to aids, and in their place the following were appointed: Chalker, Carpenter and Deming, a constitution and by-laws adopted and other business transacted. At a meeting held at Odd Fellows Hall, (Union Hall), March 12th, thirty-three names were added to the club, and then formed for drill by Lieutenant A. T. Hinckley of the Light Guard. A meeting was held March 14th, at City Hall, to make arrangements for an excursion to Waterbury, many more names being added.

Henry T. Sperry proposed the adoption of the following as the "Wide Awake" cheer and it was unanimously adopted. "Hurrah! Huzza! Hurrah! Huzza! Hurrah! Huzza!" At the close of the meeting the club paraded the streets arousing much enthusiasm. The club again met Thursday, March 15th, at 5.30 p. m., to take part in the trip to Waterbury with the "Republican Union." On Monday evening, March 5th, there was an immense gathering to welcome Abraham Lincoln, "the rail-splitter of Illinois;" a mass meeting was

THE YOUNG MEN'S REPUBLICAN UNION.

On the evening of March 10th, a Republican club was organized with the above title, to be distinct from the "Wide Awakes," although the members of the marching club were also members of the Union.

The officers were: *President*, Rowland Swift; *Vice-Presidents*, William H. Banks and forty-one others; *Corresponding Secretary*, Henry T. Sperry; *Recording Secretaries*, Joseph G. Woodward, Horace B. Winship; *Executive Committee*, Rowland Swift, George S. Gilman, E. R. Lee, Daniel F. Seymour, William H. Banks, Francis Fellows, Jr., James S. Chalker; *Finance Committee*, L. E. Hunt, Julius G. Rathbun, H. W. Conklin, Robert R. White, Solomon P. Connor; *Treasurer*, E. M. Bridgman; and thereafter the two organizations worked together, with headquarters at 311 Main street. On the evening of March 15th, the Hartford Republicans went to Waterbury to take part in a mass meeting held in Center square, in front of Brown's Hotel. The Wide Awakes numbered 100 in uniform, while the whole party, including additions along the route numbered 1,000; the procession in Waterbury numbered about 2,000, of which 500 carried torches, the officers carrying lanterns. As the Wide Awakes stood in line listening to the speeches, an assault with stones and other missiles was made upon them, by a howling mob, when Captain Chalker gave the order "About face! Wide Awakes do your duty! charge!" which order was obeyed with a will, and the mob was scattered.

The Second company in the state was formed in Waterbury, then others in New Haven, New Britain, and in very many other towns in the state patterning after the originals, which gave the Republican party a great boom. Money was quickly raised to build a temporary building for meetings, the lot on the east corner of Asylum and High streets, where the Batterson block now stands, was secured, V. W. Whiting, a leading carpenter employed, a call was made for volunteers with hammers, to assist, and an immense "Wigwam" was erected, capable of accommodating several thousands.

ABRAHAM LINCOLN. *

---

* From life size crayon made at the White House in 1863 by Silsbee, owned by H. T. Sperry, of Hartford.

Although not finished it was occupied on the evening of March 21st, to hear Hon. F. P. Stanton of Kansas, who was escorted by the "Wide Awakes." By March 24th we had 300 members who were organized into two companies, the First company under Captain J. S. Chalker, the Second company under Captain Julius G. Rathbun. The "camp" was dedicated Tuesday evening, March 27th, and was made the occasion of a great demonstration. The committee of arrangements was: J. D. Williams, George S. Gilman, W. H. D. Callender, H. C. Stocking, J. G. Rathbun, Charles C. Burt, H. T. Sperry, Rowland Swift, Charles G. Day, H. C. Beckwith, W. W. House, Edwin R. Lee and N. G. Hinckley. The speakers at this great meeting were Hon. "Tom" Corwin of Ohio, and Hon. Henry Wilson of Massachusetts; and the immense building could not contain one-half of those who desired to hear them. After the meeting there was a procession a mile long, 3,000 in line, with 2,000 torches, of which number 1,100 were Wide Awakes in uniform, 400 of them from New Haven. March 29th, about 400 went to New Haven and took part in a grand parade, where an attack was made by a party of roughs, and several injured.

THE STATE ELECTION.

Monday, April 2d, was state election, when the Wide Awakes throughout the state worked like beavers for the success of the Republican ticket. When it was certain that William A. Buckingham was elected, a salute was fired on the Park at 3 o'clock a. m. Tuesday, April 3d. The margin was a narrow one, the majority being but 561, and there is no doubt that the victory was gained because of the enthusiasm and hard work of the Wide Awakes. April 5th, in the evening, there was a grand glorification, a parade, cannon firing, fireworks, illuminations, and bonfires.

THE PRESIDENTIAL CAMPAIGN.

After the spring campaign, there was an interval of rest, until after the nomination of Lincoln and Hamlin in June 1860, when the Wide Awakes deemed it best to reorganize for the greater campaign before them; and a meeting was held at the City Hall, early in July. George S. Gilman was elected president of the club; James S. Chalker, captain of the first division; William L. Speare, captain of the second division, each having seven lieutenants and one aid. Henry T. Sperry was corresponding secretary, and had printed a circular with a history of the organization, constitution, description and cuts of uniforms, etc., and to show how extensive the movement was, it is only necessary to state that Mr. Sperry received upwards of 2,000 letters on the subject from all over the country. Captain Chalker and Aid C. V. R. Pond, opened a depot for the manufacture and sale of supplies, and had a lively trade. July 26th, was a memorable occasion, for on that evening 110 uniformed Wide Awakes from Newark, New Jersey, arrived on an excursion steamer, to visit and pay their respects to the "originals"; they were accompanied by a large number of prominent citizens and reporters from several New York papers, including the Illustrated News, which gave a history of the movement, illustrations of the grand parade and ovation given the visitors, pictures of Chalker, Pond, Sperry and others, all of which spread the flame throughout the entire northern states.

Our numbers grew rapidly and we promoted our captain to be Major Chalker, L. A. Dickinson was made adjutant, and Lieutenant Charles A. Stillman was promoted captain, while many of the earlier officers went on the staff. J. F. Morris agreed to join and carry a torch, when we should number 499, and very soon he became number 500, and faithfully carried his torch, throughout the campaign, as did "Joe" Hawley and many other leading citizens.

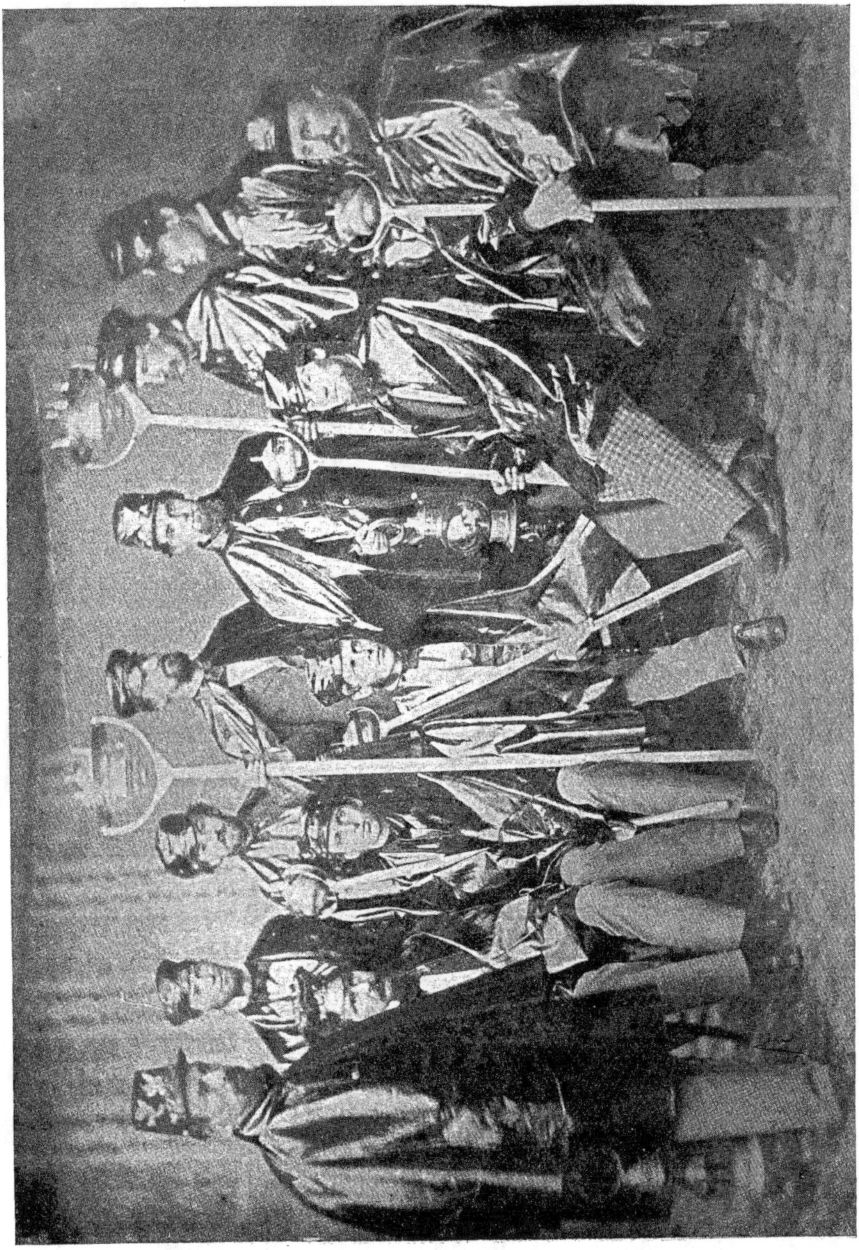

THE "WIDE AWAKES." 333

Among other interesting incidents connected with the banquet given to the Newark visitors, on the second evening of their visit, was the presentation to the Hartford Wide Awakes, by Joseph R. Hawley, in behalf of J. F. Morris, of a maul, used by Abraham Lincoln in splitting rails. It was obtained by Mr. Morris with the assistance of General Thomas S. Mather, of Springfield, Ill., and certified to as being genuine.*

By August 1st, there were upwards of 400 organizations in existence, and before the November election, there were upwards of 500,000 uniformed Wide Awakes in the northern states; our club was composed of four companies soon after July. With comparatively few exceptions, the uniforms were a cheap black cape of enameled cloth, cap and swinging torch, the officers wearing a longer cape or coat and carrying lanterns of red, white, blue and green. Some clubs, however, indulged in more style, and in many, the officers and staffs wore handsome long capes of brilliant colors. The originals were overwhelmed with invitations from all directions, but could accept few, the most prominent of which was that of October 3-4, to Newark and New York, on which occasion the batalion numbered two hundred under command of Major Chalker, Captains Speare and Stillman, H. T. Sperry and others as aids, J. G. Rathbun as first sergeant. We were accompanied by many prominent guests from Hartford, Providence, Springfield, New Haven and other cities, the Hartford Cornet band, J. P. King, leader, and Major Braun's drum corps. Leaving Hartford in the afternoon of October 3d, on the "Granite State," reaching Newark at 9.30 next morning; received by the Newark Wide Awakes, 200 strong; escorted, collated, and treated royally during the day; we left late in the afternoon; met at foot of Twenty-Third street, North River, New York city, by the Twentieth ward Wide Awakes, and a crowd of officers and aids; escorted to Broadway, and delivered to the ninth ward club, the "crack" organization of New York. This was probably the greatest political demonstration seen up to that time, clubs being present from several states; the line was *five miles long*. The Hartford boys were given the post of honor at the right of the line under the escort of the Ninth Ward club, which carried transparencies reading "We escort the original Jacobs," "How Jacobs has grown," and many others; it was a con-

MAUL, USED BY LINCOLN.

tinual triumphant march, ending with a collation, near Union Square, long after midnight, after which we were escorted to the steamer "Traveler," and were well on our way home when the sun rose; no one who took part in that trip will forget it.

Pressing invitations came from all directions, where they desired to see the "Originals," which could not be accepted; finally Major Chalker, Aid Sperry, Captain Valentine and Lieut. Riley went to Boston, acting as special aids to the chief marshal in a great parade. Providence would not take a negative answer; we must be present at a state parade just before election day; so five officers went, Major Chalker, Aids Sperry and Pond, Lieut. James L. Francis, and ex-Capt. Rathbun. These rode in an elegant barouche, handsomely decorated, and surrounded by a special body guard, and after the parade they were entertained at an elegant supper in the best Providence style.

---

*This maul having come again into the possession of Mr. Morris, was presented a few months since to the Connecticut Historical Society, where it can be seen by visitors to the rooms.

THE "WIDE AWAKES."

THE LAST AND BEST.

And then came the reward for our labors, the grand state demonstration, November 14th, after the election of Lincoln and Hamlin, to which every club in the state was invited. A great number came, also several from out of the state, and it certainly was a grand old demonstration. We had escorted Abraham Lincoln at the time of his visit in March, before his nomination at Chicago, and this is what the New York Tribune said: "The Hartford Wide Awakes who started this institution—this great feature of the campaign of

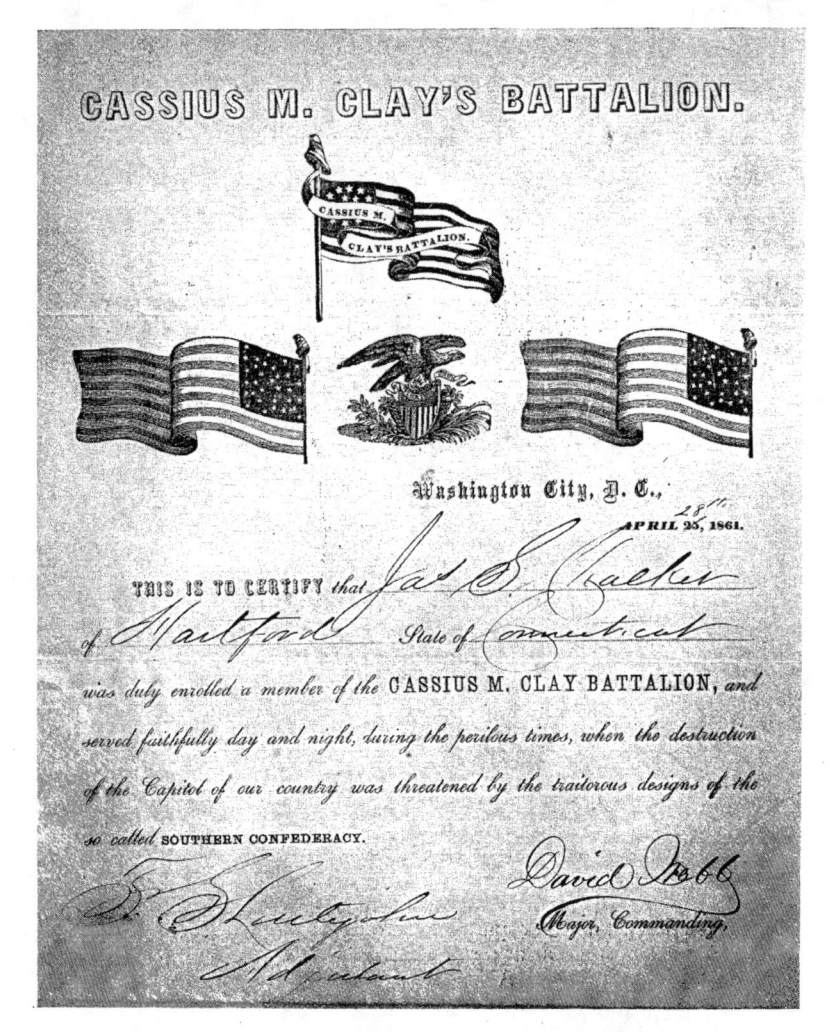

CASSIUS M. CLAY'S BATTALION.

Washington City, D. C., April 28th, 1861.

THIS IS TO CERTIFY that Jas. B. Walker of Hartford State of Connecticut was duly enrolled a member of the CASSIUS M. CLAY BATTALION, and served faithfully day and night, during the perilous times, when the destruction of the Capitol of our country was threatened by the traitorous designs of the so called SOUTHERN CONFEDERACY.

David Babb
Major, Commanding.

1860—will be entitled to the honor of escorting the President to the Capitol next March. They have given him escort heretofore; Abraham Lincoln and the Hartford Wide Awakes are old friends."

Well, we did not go down and act as his escort, but very many of the old club went to the front when he called for troops, and many, very many whose names were on our roll, never returned. It was universally conceded after the election that the Wide Awake movement, was one of the most important factors, in the success of the Republican ticket, at a critical period of our country's history; and it was acknowledged during the war, that the semi-military feature of the clubs, with obedience to the word of command, was of immense benefit to the tens of thousands of young Wide Awakes, from all parts of the north, who enlisted for the defence of the old flag.

After the election, Secretary Sperry received a letter from Abraham Lincoln, acknowledging the great services of the Wide Awakes during the campaign. This letter was loaned to Nicolay and Hay, who wrote the life of Lincoln, and was never returned.

When Fort Sumter fell, and war was declared, the capital of the nation was in peril, and for several days all communication with the north was cut off. The loyal residents of the city of Washington rallied to its defense, and among other companies formed was the "Cassius M. Clay's Battalion," to which was entrusted the defense of the capitol with its priceless possessions. Major Chalker happened to be in Washington at that time, and having volunteered his services, was duly enrolled as a member of the above battalion, as shown by a certificate of membership, in the possession of Mrs. Chalker.

Another highly prized document is a pass, a fac-simile of which is given; the signature will be recognized by many who are familiar with the early days of the war. Major Chalker, for many years, was in the customs service of "Uncle Sam," in New York city, and will be pleasantly remembered by many of his old comrades, who had occasion for his services, when returning from Europe. His death occurred at Clinton, Conn., July 19, 1890, at the age of 58 years, the burial being at Spring Grove cemetery in this city July 22d, many of his former comrades being present, the bearers being selected from the old officers of the "Wide Awakes." His mantle as the senior officer of the "Originals" has fallen on the shoulders of the writer of this article.

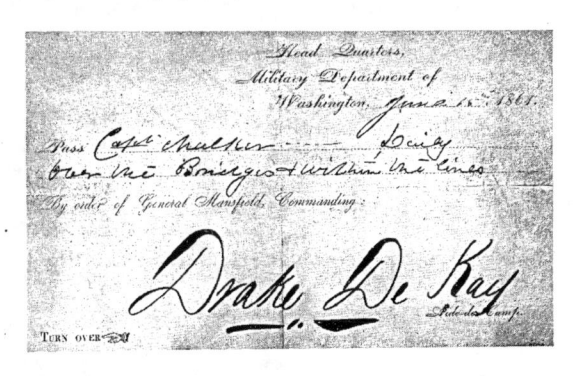

1880 — 1895.

In 1880 during the Garfield campaign, the Hartford Wide Awakes were called together, and re-organized, taking part in several parades, also in the campaigns of 1884, 1888 and 1892, with much of the old time enthusiasm, but more matured. Upwards of one hundred went to Washington in March, 1889, on a special train to take part in the inauguration of Benjamin Harrison, — himself a member of the organization in Ohio,— and were accorded a special reception at the White House, the morning after the inaugural ceremonies.

Thirty-five years have passed since the stirring times of 1860, during which the old campaign club did much toward shaping the destinies of these great United States. Surely, the five young dry good clerks wearing their black cambric capes, builded better than they knew.

SUMMER AFTERNOON IN POPE PARK.

BY HOWARD W. BENJAMIN.

Within the last few years a demand has arisen throughout the country for better or more extensive park facilities in our cities. Naturally, the greater cities first attempted to satisfy this demand by reason of the over-crowding within their limits. Next, the smaller cities and then the towns took up the refrain until there has scarcely been a chapter of town or municipal legislation during this time which has not had to do with a purpose of this kind. In some instances, and it must be confessed there are glaring examples, park lands have been both hastily and unwisely chosen, while large sums of public money have been expended in attempts to make nature vulgar and destroy the original beauty of the surface.

A city park, to fully fulfill the purpose which its name implies, should be both easy of access to those for whom it is designed, and preserved as far as possible in its original beauty. In all cases, it is true, that the first named consideration cannot be wholly realized, but the other should be a fundamental principle and as rarely departed from as the famous laws of the Medes and Persians. Waste land which could not be used for any other purpose has sometimes been considered suitable for park purposes; but nowadays the citizen wants the best and his eye is quick to see natural beauty or to note defects. Where such lands have been set aside for recreation grounds, they usually remain nothing but monuments to the stupendous folly of municipal boards or local legislators. On the principle that any park, however ill adapted to the wants of the public, is better than no park at all, they are perhaps justified in such selections, leaving out for the time being, the enormous expense involved.

All persons who have made a study of artistic surface decoration unite in agreeing upon the importance of a body of water as an accessory to the landscape in pleasure parks. In the treatment of this feature in the World's Fair grounds at Chicago, we have the most extensive application of this principle. If a tract of land is so situated that a stream or pond can be utilized in this manner, the surface of such a tract can be made attractive, where in itself the conformation would be somewhat undesirable. Another very good example of the application of water-ways in park decoration is Belle Isle park, near Detroit. Without the canals furnished by the water of Lake St. Clair, this park would lose much of its present attractiveness, and indeed, perhaps never would have been projected but for this feature.

The best example in this country of a park left almost wholly in its natural state is the Arboretum, near Boston. The peculiarly felicitous site of this park has enabled its keepers to preserve the surface in its original beauty. Wade Park, and Gordon Park, both in Cleveland, Ohio, belong also to this class, especially the latter. Central Park, in New York city, is almost wholly artificial, but this is so cleverly concealed that no stiffness results therefrom. Fairmount Park, Philadelphia, is one of the most beautiful sites in the country, at the same time one of the most extensive.

A PASTORAL.—POPE PARK.

Many parks throughout the country have had their origin by the gift of private individuals. This has, indeed, become a common form of benefaction within late years. In most instances, the intention of bequests or gifts of this kind has remained a secret until the death of the testator reveals, by a will more or less restricted, the purpose of the benefactor. Such a course is commendable in the extreme. In other instances, and these are of the rarer sort, park gifts have been made during the life-time of the donor, who can thus give his personal aid and advice to the fulfillment of his design. Where a gift is made in this manner, the original intention of the donor is always brought to a successful issue, while he receives and deserves the praise of all citizens irrespective of class. On the other hand, the instability of wills is a by-word, heirs are covetous, or executors fail to carry out the intention of the generous benefactor.

The city of Hartford has lately come into possession of two parks which conform closely to the conditions already mentioned. One is the gift of a private individual, made during the full possession of life and prosperity. The other is also the gift of a private individual, but whose generosity was only disclosed to the public by the terms of his will. In one, there is a valuable water-privilege which can be used to beautify the surface, after certain impediments are removed. The other has not this feature, but its sightly location and cultivation, render the want of it of little moment. Both are naturally attractive. Both are needed.* The city of Hartford cordially welcomes these additions to its comfort and attractiveness, and in the Pope Park and the Pond Park, notes many steps forward in municipal progress.

THE POPE PARK.—THE GIFT OF COL. ALBERT A. POPE.

About two years ago, Col. Albert A. Pope, of Boston, Massachusetts, first conceived the idea of presenting to the city of Hartford, a valuable tract of land for a public park. Colonel Pope, though not a resident of Hartford, is at the head of one of its largest industries. Perhaps no one manufactured article of commerce is more widely known than the Columbia bicycle. As this

ON PARK RIVER. POPE PARK.

bicycle has contributed materially to the wealth of Col. Pope, so Hartford has contributed materially to the making of it, and so Hartford is to be benefited by his generosity. The best idea that can be gotten of Col. Pope's gift is to be found in the text of his written offer as presented to the city government, on the 26th day of November, 1894:

"*To the Hon. Mayor and Court of Common Council of the City of Hartford:*

YOUR HONORS : I desire to submit for the consideration and action of your honorable body the following proposition of gift to the city of Hartford :

For many years I have taken a lively interest in the business prosperity and general welfare of Hartford. From the beginning of my financial connections with what is now one of your leading industries, I

---

*The city of Medford, Mass., with a population of 11,000, has 232 acres devoted to park purposes; Worcester, with a population of 84,000, has 364 acres in parks; Lynn, with a population of 55,000, has 2,054 acres; Springfield, with a population of 44,000, has 429 acres. In our own state, New Haven, with a population of 86,900, has about 950 acres; Bridgeport, with a population of 50,000, 232 acres; Providence, R. I., with 132,000, has 484 acres. *Hartford, population* 60,000, *less than 60 acres.*

THE RIVER IN THE PARK.

have been attracted by and have gradually acquired possession of a tract of land which is by nature peculiarly well adapted for a public park. In fact, I know of no other city where so large an area of beautifully undulating and well-watered land has remained unoccupied, especially within easy access of thickly populated districts.

I believe that a large part of the success of any manufacturing business depends upon the health, happiness and orderly life of its employees, and that in like manner a city thrives best by caring and providing for the well-being of its citizens.

Your city is in need of open breathing places and pleasure grounds which should be scattered in different regions and so laid out and arranged as to afford the means of recreation and pleasure to all classes of law-abiding citizens. They should be something more than public gardens, where even trespassing on the grass is properly forbidden.

Connected with such pleasure grounds there should be drives and walks, and if possible, groves of full-grown trees, where those not engaged in active sports may find other attractions.

I am informed that such parks in other parts of your city are already in contemplation by private parties.

In order that you may have an opportunity, if you deem it advisable, of establishing such a pleasure ground in the southern part of your city, I hereby offer to present to the city a deed of two tracts of land, comprising about 73 37-100 acres, to be held for park purposes only, a plat of which land is hereto attached, to which reference is made." . . . . .

Then follows a description of the property, which is situated in a most advantageous position for this purpose. It extends on both sides of Park street, westward from the Watkinson Juvenile Asylum and Farm School, taking in both banks of the Park river, which is here quite attractive. The river thus offers a good feature to the landscape gardener, and adds materially to the value of the park. The most important condition attached to this gift, and one

THE RIVER AT THE CAPITOL AVENUE ENTRANCE OF POPE PARK.

which its acceptance made necessary, was the acquirement by the city of certain tracts of land in the possession of the Watkinson Juvenile Asylum and Farm School, the Hartford Orphan Asylum, and the Hartford Real Estate Improvement Company. These tracts immediately adjoined the gift of Col. Pope, and by this acquirement would extend the proposed park from Park street to Capitol avenue, and from the Park river to Putnam street.

In a communication to the city government, under the same date as that of Col. Pope, the Hartford Orphan Asylum offered to sell to the city for $5,000, a strip of land extending from the Park river easterly to Putnam street, in all about four and a half acres. The Watkinson Juvenile Asylum and

Farm School, at this time also offered to convey to the city a tract of land extending easterly from the gift of Col. Pope, along the north side of Park street, about 425 feet and then northerly from that point on the east bank of Park river to the land offered by the Hartford Orphan Asylum. This transfer was to be made in consideration of the sum of ten thousand dollars. There remained, to be acquired, but a narrow strip of land along Park river, from Capitol avenue south to the land owned by the Hartford Orphan Asylum, to complete the conditions attached to Col. Pope's gift. The strip was owned by the Hartford Real Estate Improvement company, and was formally tendered to the city on November 26, 1894. Hartford had thus the opportunity to acquire a most beautiful park, and nothing remained but to ratify the acceptance of the gift, and vote the necessary funds for the purchase of the two tracts of the Orphan Asylum and Farm School. A committee of the city government, consisting of the Mayor, three aldermen, and eight councilmen, together with three members of the park commission, was appointed to look into the matter, and who reported by the following resolution, dated January 7, 1895:

RESOLVED, That this city accepts the tracts of land offered by Albert A. Pope, November 15, 1894, for the uses and purposes stated in said offer (as now on file), and subject to the conditions and reservations therein set forth; the same to be a public park of this city.

RESOLVED, That the tracts severally offered for like purposes by the "Watkinson Juvenile Asylum and Farm School," the "Hartford Orphan Asylum" and by the "Hartford Real Estate Improvement Company" respectively be, and they are hereby, accepted by this city, each on the terms and subject to the conditions contained in the written offers of said tracts respectively, as now on file. And said tracts, together with that tract offered by Col. Pope north of Park street, shall constitute collectively another public park for this city.

AND WHEREAS, It is, or may become, necessary that the foregoing resolutions be approved, ratified and adopted by the legal voters of this city in a meeting to be called and held for that purpose, therefore be it further

RESOLVED, That His Honor the Mayor be, and hereby is, requested to call a meeting of the legal voters of this city, to be held on the 30th day of January, A. D. 1895, at the proper voting places, then and there to vote by ballot and check list upon the question of the approval, ratification and adoption of the foregoing resolution as a whole; *provided*, that in the call for said meeting a copy of these resolutions be inserted. And in said meeting each voter in favor of the adoption of said resolutions shall deposit his ballot with only the word "Yes" written or printed thereon. And each voter opposed to the adoption of said resolutions shall deposit his ballot with only the word "No" written or printed thereon. All of which is respectfully submitted."

In the board of aldermen the report was accepted and resolutions passed. The common council board concurred. On the 30th day of January, 1895, the voters of Hartford* legalized the formation of this new public park.

What Hartford will do in completing this generous design remains to be seen. One has but to note the beauty of its surface, comprising undulating meadow and woodland, to believe that the future will show the foresight of Col. Pope. Certainly, we know of no section of our city in which a public park could be established more advantageously. And, furthermore, we know of no tract which by its natural attractiveness could more fully satisfy all intelligent citizens. All honor to the generous donor, whose name the park will perpetuate, and to the institutions which have made possible the acceptance of this gift.

---

*It appears by the returns on file in the office of the clerk of the city that there were cast 1,253 votes in favor of said resolutions and 130 against said resolutions."

THE POND PARK.—THE BEQUEST OF HON. CHARLES M. POND.

The history of this generous bequest is as yet but a short one. For many years, the intimate friends of Mr. Pond had been aware of his benevolent intentions toward the city of his residence and the scene of his life-long career.

In conversations which occurred at different times prior to his decease,† he had made no secret of the plan which his will disclosed to the public. He was fully conscious of the many attractions which his homestead and the property surrounding it had for a public park. In order that the carrying out of his plan should not be a burden to the city, Mr. Pond accompanied this bequest with the addition of one-half of his personal estate, the same to be used in caring for and improving this property, and for the procurement of additional land, if thought advisable. The money value of this one-half of his personal

---
†He died August 30, 1894.

estate amounted to nearly $180,000. The market value of the land and buildings thereon thus given to the city, was estimated by the executors of Mr. Pond's will at $68,000 — a grand total of $248,000. Very few people understand the possibilities which can be undertaken by the command of such a sum of money. Since the founding of Hartford, we know of no gift or bequest of a public character which approaches it. We give entire, herewith, the portion of the will of Mr. Pond which refers to this bequest:

"I give to the city of Hartford this gift to take effect one (1) year after my death, and on its acceptance by the court of common council of said city, all the land connected with my residence, including all the land upon the east side of Prospect avenue. The same is bounded: East part, north by Asylum avenue, east by estate of Solomon Porter, south, by Herbert C. Bingham, and west by Prospect avenue. The west part is bounded north by Asylum avenue continued, west by Quaker Lane, so called; then south by Gaines, then west by Gaines and by Joel L. English, then south by George B. Foster, then east by land of Burdette Loomis, and by Samuel H. Allen, then south by land of Samuel H. Allen, then east by Prospect avenue, to Asylum avenue, and containing in all about ninety (90) acres, and with all the buildings thereon and rights, easements, and appurtenances connected with said land or any of it, the same with such additions to it as are hereinafter provided for as otherwise may be hereafter made in behalf of the city, to be forever held and used as a public park, or for such other lawful public purpose of health, culture or improvement as may be determined upon by the city through its court of common council. In such determination I desire that the city will consult with my friends, Henry C. Robinson, Francis Goodwin, Charles M. Joslyn, Thomas O. Enders, and Charles F. Hildreth, some of whom are quite familiar with my purposes in this gift. No restriction upon the removal or other disposition of buildings is designed. My wish, which, however, I do not enforce upon this gift, is that this land may be associated with the name Elizabeth, in memory of my beloved wife.

All the rest and residue of my estate I give unto the Hartford Trust Co., in trust, as follows: Onehalf thereof to be paid over to the city of Hartford to be used in connection with the city in putting the land hereinbefore given to the city in good and seemly condition to accomplish the object of the gift, as by laying out streets and walks, grading, draining and landscape gardening, and to purchase additional land, to be added to the tract hereinbefore given to the city and for the same purposes, this gift to the city to take effect at the same time as I have attached to the specific gift of land hereinbefore made to said city."

This communication was presented to the city government on the 26t day of November, 1894. On January 28, 1895, the special commission t whom this bequest was referred, reported as follows:

. . . . "That it has had said will of Mr. Pond, as well as the communication of Charles M. Josly and Lucius F. Robinson, executors of said will, relating thereto (which communication is dated Novembe 10, 1894) under consideration and are of the opinion that the estate devised and bequeathed by said wi to this city should be accepted with due acknowledgment (which at some time in the future should tak the shape of a suitable memorial) and recommend the passage of the following resolution.
Respectfully submitted, LEVERETT BRAINARD, Chairman.

"RESOLVED, That the City of Hartford hereby gratefully accepts the several gifts, devises and b quests made to it, or for its use and benefit, by the last will and testament of the late Hon. Charles M Pond, dated January 29, 1894."

The report was accepted and resolution passed unanimously.

Thus the Pond Park (or "Elizabeth Park"?) became one of the family parks which are to encompass the city of Hartford. While the situation of thi park does not render it of easy access to the poorer sections of the city, it wi certainly adorn a portion of Hartford which is being resorted to more an more every year by great numbers of its well-to-do citizens for homes.

From almost any part of Mr. Pond's bequest, a most magnificent view the city can be had, together with a considerable portion of the far-famed valle of the Connecticut. Various plans for the improvement of this park have bee promulgated, but it seems to be the impression that for the present at least tl surface will remain undisturbed. It is unfortunate in many respects that t generous intentions of Mr. Pond should be disregarded, or rather attacked, l contestants of his will. All patriotic citizens trust that the outcome of the legal proceedings will be favorable to the original project of Mr. Pond. He h certainly furnished a most praiseworthy example to his wealthy townsmen.

Some Native Orchids

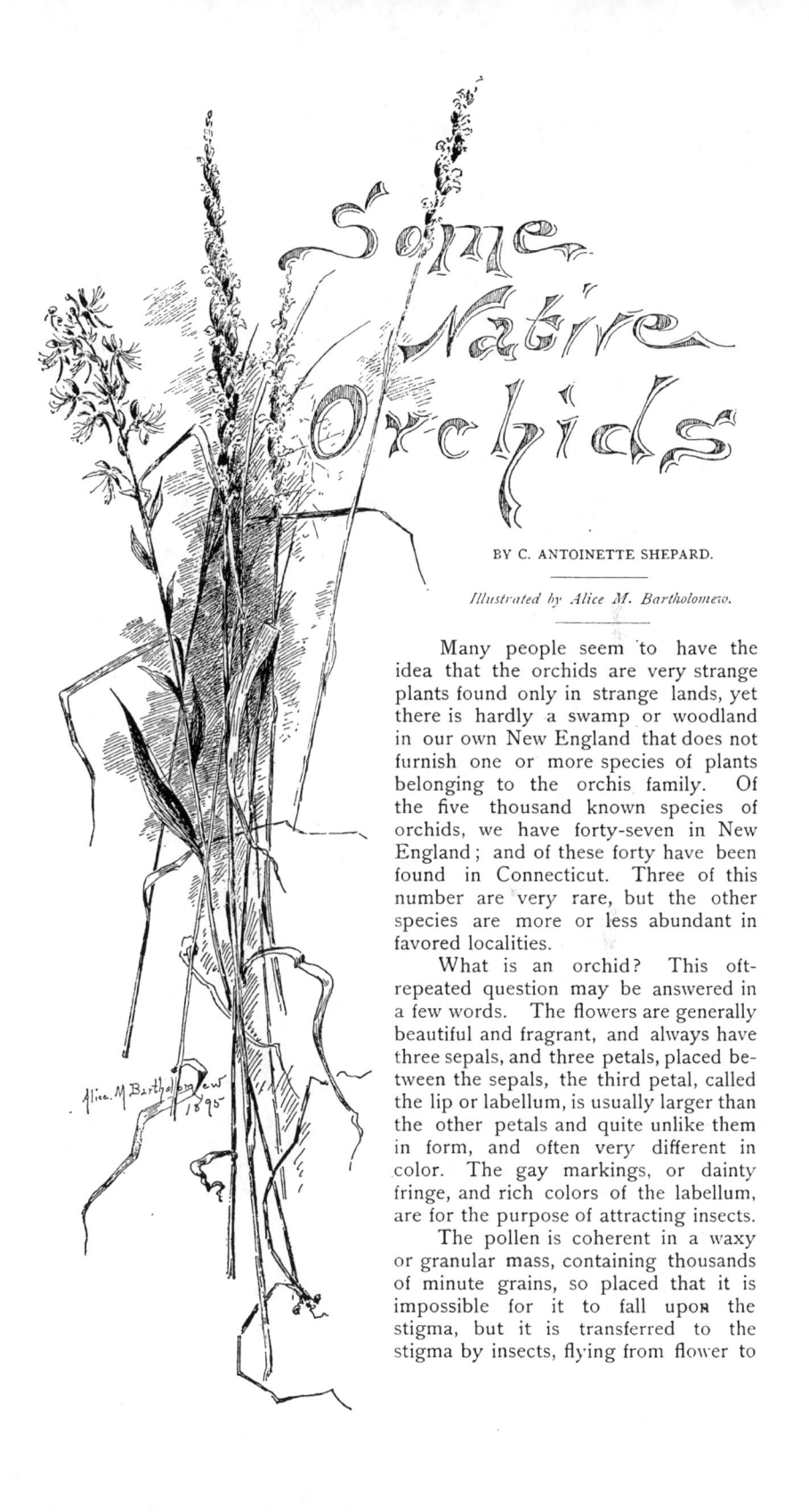

BY C. ANTOINETTE SHEPARD.

Illustrated by Alice M. Bartholomew.

Many people seem to have the idea that the orchids are very strange plants found only in strange lands, yet there is hardly a swamp or woodland in our own New England that does not furnish one or more species of plants belonging to the orchis family. Of the five thousand known species of orchids, we have forty-seven in New England; and of these forty have been found in Connecticut. Three of this number are very rare, but the other species are more or less abundant in favored localities.

What is an orchid? This oft-repeated question may be answered in a few words. The flowers are generally beautiful and fragrant, and always have three sepals, and three petals, placed between the sepals, the third petal, called the lip or labellum, is usually larger than the other petals and quite unlike them in form, and often very different in color. The gay markings, or dainty fringe, and rich colors of the labellum, are for the purpose of attracting insects.

The pollen is coherent in a waxy or granular mass, containing thousands of minute grains, so placed that it is impossible for it to fall upon the stigma, but it is transferred to the stigma by insects, flying from flower to flower and carrying some of the pollen with them, perfecting the work known as cross-fertilization. The order owes its chief peculiarities to the consolidation of stamens and pistil into one common mass called the column. The plants grow from short creeping root-stalks tubers, thickened fibrous roots, or bulbs. The leaves are undivided, (that is, they have an unbroken margin,) and are paralleled-veined. A multitude of very fine seeds are inclosed in the seed capsules.

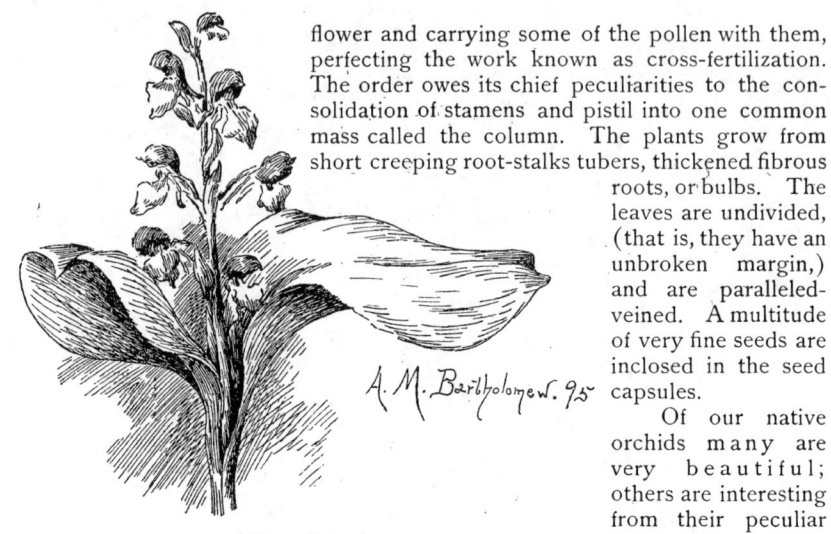

Of our native orchids many are very beautiful; others are interesting from their peculiar construction; and a

SHOWY ORCHIS.

few are very small, known and loved only by the botanist, who always has the greatest respect for every member of this royal family of plants. Orchids are never so beautiful when plucked from the parent stem, as they are when growing "on their native heath," or on some thickly wooded hillside, amid the plants of earliest spring, where the ferns are fast coming on, pushing their way out of the moist earth "fists up," and the Trilliums are unfolding their great leaves by the big rocks. In such a sheltered nook, we saw for the first time the Spring Orchis, blooming in the perfection of its beauty. Words fail to express the pleasure of finding such treasures for the first time; we may find better flowers and more of them, but they never seem quite equal to these first surprises. This "Gay," "Showy," or "Spring" Orchis, all in pink and white, is sometimes called "Preacher-in-the-Pulpit," (not to be confounded with Jack-in-the-Pulpit, which is not an orchid), from the anther cells under canopied sepals and petals suggesting two clergymen overshadowed by a "sounding-board." The dainty purple-pink and white flowers are set off by two large silvery-green leaves.

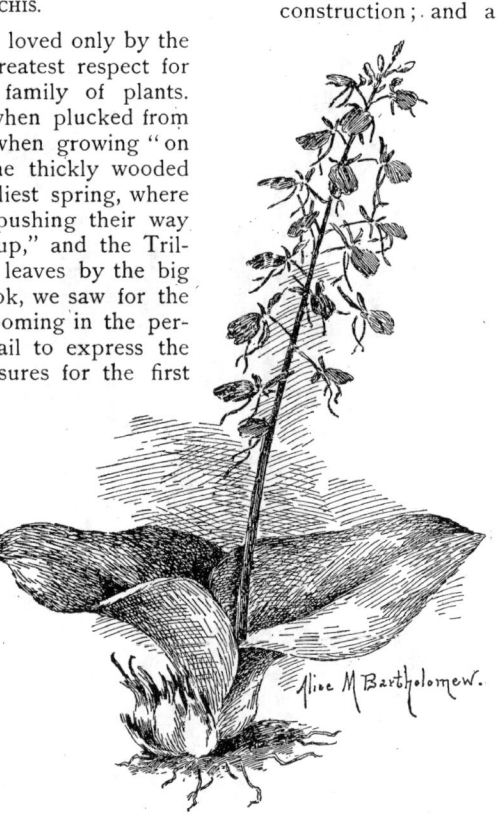

PURPLE TWAYBLADE.

In May, we visit the "Great Pine Swamp"; passing through thickets of birch and pine, coming out into open spaces walled in with trees, and carpeted with moss, lichens and fragrant pine-needles. We are sure to get lost and wander about, not knowing whither we go, but we will come out — somewhere. As we pass along from one of these open spaces to another, we find the mossy carpet decked with sweet Sand Violets, and the Pink Cypripedium. Very gay they look, setting there beneath the trees, their broad, dark-green leaves contrasting finely with the large pink flowers. The color varies from pale rosy pink to deep pink, and sometimes we are surprised to find a pure white flower. These albinos are very dainty and beautiful, but are not as unusual as generally believed.

Who does not like to drive miles from home and come back laden with Pink Cypripedium? But, right here, let me drop a word of caution. The plants live only two years, and if we pick all the flowers they will soon be exterminated. Plants can not be reproduced unless some flowers are left to furnish seeds. "The habit of purposeless or careless destruction is a bad one. It is barbarism to deface a beautiful page of nature."

Elaine Goodale describes this flower in her lines to the Indian's Moccasin:

"Shy and proud among the forest flowers,

* * * *

One true-born blossom, native to our skies
  We dare not claim as kin,
Nor frankly seek, for all that in it lies,
  The Indian's Moccasin.

WHORLED POGONIA.

Graceful and tall the slender drooping stem
  With two broad leaves below,
Shapely the flower so lightly poised between,
  And warm her rosy glow."

More rare, but scarcely less beautiful than the Pink, are the two species of Yellow Cypripedium. One having a large pale-yellow flower, the other with smaller, brighter yellow labellum, and long, curiously twisted sepals of rich purple-brown. This little orchid is considered rather rare. Both of the Yellow Cypripediums are far more shy than their Pink sister, and should be most carefully guarded and protected. The children call these flowers "Whippoor-Will's-Shoes," but when I was a child these flowers, nodding and swinging on the top of their tall stems, seemed more like little yellow birds, just ready to fly away. Children always have some name for the flowers they love, often names that are expressive, if not at all scientific. Somewhere the children have given the Pink Cypripedium the names of "Indian Moccasin," "Old Goose," "Camel's Foot," and "Noah's Ark," but who gave it the name of "Venus Slipper?"

In early July, two orchids may be found growing together in sunny swamps, or wet meadows, and about the margin of ponds. They are Calopogon and Pogonia. A cluster of from two to six pink-purple flowers, beautifully bearded with white and yellow, surmount the slender stem, and, nodding above the grass

PINK CYPRIPEDIUM.

and sedge, seem to beckon us to come. When we reach these gay flowers, we find growing at their feet the more dainty Pogonia, with one or two beard-

SMALL YELLOW CYPRIPEDIUM.

crested and fringed; pale rose-colored or white flowers full of rich violet-like odor. The white Pogonia is considered rare, but we have found many pure white flowers during the past three or four years. A difference in color only, does not make a different species. Thoreau says, speaking of these orchids,—"They are flowers without a name, Pogonia! Calopogon! They would blush still deeper if they knew the names man has given them."

We have another species called Whorled Pogonia. It is rather rare, and seldom noticed except by the botanist. It is more curious than beautiful; at the top of the stem is a whorl of silvery-green leaves, and a purple-brown flower. The sepals are very long and sharply-pointed, giving the appearance of three long horns.

All the Habenarias are interesting; the best known of this class are the two rose-purple fringed-orchids. There are several species with white flowers, and several more with green or greenish-white flowers. The Habenaria that appears in our title cut, is known as the Ragged Orchis. The fringe is so finely-cut and the whole flower so dainty, it deserves a better common name. It is quite common, but growing with tall grasses and sedges it is easily overlooked.

The most beautiful of all the Habenarias is the *Yellow Fringed Orchis*. This is the gem of orchids in Eastern United States. It is rare in New England, but is said to grow in some of the swamps of New York and New Jersey, as "thick as common weeds." It is sometimes found along the margin of brooks amid the grasses, or in wet pasture-lands and swamps in Connecticut. The plants grow about two feet high; the leaves are oblong or lanceolate, the upper ones passing into little pointed bracts. The plant is surmounted by an oblong spike of many flowers, and what beautiful flowers they are! Of the richest shades of orange-yellow, or sometimes passing into a delicate shade of apricot color. The oblong lip beautifully fringed with long, and very fine silken fringe, such as only an orchid or gentian is permitted to wear.

It is indeed a royal flower, "fit symbol of the wealth and glow of August," "admitting but one rival, the Cardinal flower." Mr. Baldwin says, "If I had my way, it should never grow in bogs among coarse pitcher plants; but in ferny meadows bordering a sandy brook, as it does in a jealously guarded spot I know of—and if I ever write a romance of Indian life, my dusky heroine, Birch Tree, or Trembling Fawn, shall meet her lover with a wreath of this Orchis on her head."

We are all familiar with *Goodyera pubescens;* commonly called "Rattlesnake plantain"—so often found growing with partridgeberry vines and ferns under hemlock or pine trees. The deep green leaves reticulated with white, are like a bit of dainty embroidery. The plant is very hardy; the leaves remaining fresh all winter, untouched by snow or frost. Its flowers are small, greenish-white, and hardly noticeable as a flower, the beauty of the plant being entirely in leaves.

The Purple Twayblade has two broad root-leaves, and rising from them

CALOPOGON AND POGONIA.

a low scape, covered with curious little flowers resembling insects. It is a charming little plant, the petals are green, and thread-like, the lip long and wedged-shaped, of rich brown-purple; sometimes almost bronze-colored. This small plant more closely resembles the orchids of the tropics in the curious form and coloring of the flowers, than any other species.

We have several species of Spiranthes, commonly called "Ladies' Tresses." They all have little flowers, on curiously twisted flower-stalks. The flowers are white, waxy in texture and of pearly luster. Some of the species bloom in summer, but the most beautiful of them all blooms late in the season. They are the most fragrant of all our native orchids. We often find them growing in company with the Fringed Gentian, fit companions during the last days of the floral season.

They are:

> "Flowers that linger after frost,
> Tell us of the summer lost,
> Gentian of the richest blue
> Sky reflected deepest hue,
> While from the Spiranthes white
> Richest odors fill the night."

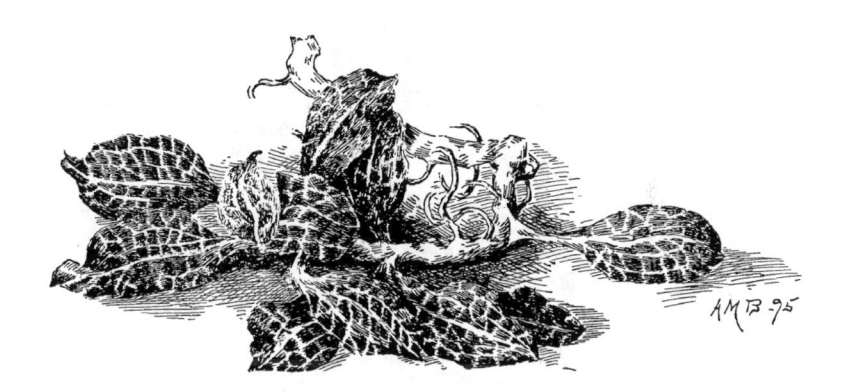

MEMORIES OF MERIDEN.

I.

BY MRS. FRANCES A. BRECKENRIDGE.

The traveler, passing through Meriden by the railroad, sees really nothing of the brisk, bustling, diversified, country-city. The transit, as with most railroads, is at the rear of almost everything. From it the beautiful Hanging Hills are not visible. Scarcely is a glimpse given of the many handsome dwellings; the churches cannot be seen; the town hall and Soldier's Monument are almost invisible. The buildings of the Connecticut School for Boys are conspicuous; but the spacious and well-kept grounds surrounding them are hidden. Only the most superficial view can be had of the business center through which the road passes. But, a few rods, either east or west, and the locality changes its aspect. The ground rises — at some points rapidly; the horizon widens, and the blue hills and fells appear. A walk or ride of less than a mile and a scene of twenty miles in extent expands before the beholder. Upon a clear morning, the reflection of the sun upon the windows of the old church in the town of Prospect has been seen from Broad street. This would happen of course in the days of shutterless church windows.

A gentleman familiar with the noted points of European scenery, once said that water was the only feature lacking in Meriden. The Mountain reservoir and Hanover lake now amend that deficiency. Of hillside springs and mint and wood-violet bordered rivulets flowing therefrom, there were plenty once. But we are a busy and a utilitarian folk, and these once bright, clear waters are now confined in stone reservoirs, hemmed in by stone walls or viaducts; or, alas! desecrated by being made to do duty as sewers. A profanation of Nature's good gifts! Within the memory of persons not far advanced beyond middle life, the whole tract where now is the railroad and its station, with all the contiguous streets east and north, the great buildings, manufactories, stores, public halls, and newspaper publishing-houses, was a morass, nearly always under water, and green with the waving blades of Indian calamus or "sweet-flag." The present surface of the ground is now far above the original plane. In the spring of the year, the highway that crossed it was a quagmire, a "Slough of Despond," into which the pilgrim was certain to sink, and his raiment bore the stains thereafter, for Meriden mud was, and is, tenacious, and the soil so tinctured with iron that no laundry could efface the traces from a garment once stained with it.

The only manufactures of importance were of tin-ware, ivory combs, and coffee mills. A few brass and wooden combs were made; chiefly for the Southern negro trade. The nucleus of the present immense trade in silverware was in a small shop in which any of the smallest departments in any of the present factories would be cramped for room. Wood was the only fuel in the old days. The venders thereof were kept in excellent order by the experienced housewives, who could tell at a glance if the despised elm or hemlock were mixed in a load presumed to consist of hickory, oak, or maple. When coal came in with the railroad, the perplexed housekeepers were divided in their minds as to the utility of the new combustible. Most of them did not believe it would burn, and would not try it. One woman proved to her own satisfaction its worthlessness: "She put two lumps into the stove with the wood, and there they staid all day, just as black as ever." The first stationmaster, among whose multifarious duties was attending to the fire, was much exercised by the mysterious nature of the coal; he considered that a substance so hard and black required all the afflation possible, and was horrified to find his stove red-hot and just ready, he thought, to melt. To avert such a catastrophe, he threw the contents of a pail of water on the glowing mass. The providence that watches over a certain class of individuals, prevented a probable tragedy.

The first printing-office was a little one-room building — just about opposite the spot where the substantial building of the Meriden Daily Journal is now located. Access to the tiny premises was over a plank laid across a deep gutter, or rather ditch, always full of water and tin-chips. This ditch, with its black contents, extended several rods on the north side of what is now East Main street. Until the railroad was built, the newspapers read here were the New Haven Palladium, and the Register; and the Hartford Times, and Courant; the fortnightly supplement of the latter was eagerly looked for. One firm took for their office, the New York Journal of Commerce, and one of the firm subscribed, in its first year, for Godey's Lady Book, and continued to take it as long as it was published in the old form; these he had bound, and they are now valuable as exponents of the customs and social observances of nearly a century ago.

Sunday was a day of rest to everybody but the minister. He was expected to preach two sermons never preached before, — he was carefully looked after in this matter, — to superintend the noon Sunday-school; also to conduct a Bible class at the close of the day, and to open the evening prayer-meeting. All respectable families went to "Meeting," except a very few who went to "Church"; these few were the only observers of Christmas. The only holidays generally recognized were election day, Fourth of July, and Thanksgiving. A sort of go-as-you-please ball-playing on the green, in front of the Congregational church, was indulged in by the apprentices who were allowed a three days' holiday. The games were played seriously, with little hilarity, and probably as little science. The tone of all social functions was attuned to a low-spirited key. The singing of hymns was a very usual feature at weddings. It is told that at the marriage of a belle of the village, the bride proposed the singing of what she said was her favorite: "Come, ye Disconsolate."

In 1836, the school-houses in the several districts had advanced and improved in external aspect and interior comfort, from the little red-buildings of an earlier time, with their open fire-places. They had larger seating capacity, were painted white, and were warmed by box-stoves, for which the large boys, and sometimes the teacher, cut the wood, which was deposited in a pile by the door. In the winter the routine of study reached a climax at "Daboll's Rule of Three." In the summer, the feminine element predominated, and did not aspire to such flights. Reading, spelling, puckered-up patch-work, and a tangled arrangement of woolen yarn and long steel-needles, miscalled knitting, kept the teacher busy, and enabled her to earn her one-dollar-and-a-half a week. A select school was also kept, where the "extra six-pence to learn manners," was required.

By 1836, our world had moved a little. The bass-viol had become a factor in choir singing. The Episcopalians, who were considered rather heterodox

Christians, admitted the violin and flute. In 1842, the St. Andrew's Episcopal Society set up the first church organ in town. The instrument cost four hundred dollars. A few years after, this organ was sold to the Roman Catholic Society of St. Rose, then in its infancy, and was the first organ owned by them. None of those costing thousands, in the various places of worship in our city, has ever been listened to, with the delight and enthusiasm which greeted the first notes of the sweet-toned instrument; or, with deeper devotion, than when it upheld the voices of the choir, in the long full notes of the grand old "Gloria in Excelsis."

But this article is exceeding its limits. Another time must serve to mention some points of interest in which the historical and modern are intermixed. Among which are the mountains, in particular West Peak,— once owned by the Johnson family— now known as Percival Park, on the summit of which William Catlin owns, and in summer occupies, a commodious cottage. Upon the highest point on the peak, a few feet from the cottage there lies a large flat rock, on which are cut the names of many persons now passed out of sight. From this rock extends a view reaching from Long Island Sound to Mount Tom, at Holyoke, Massachusetts.

(TO BE CONTINUED.)

AN AUTUMN RONDEAU.

ELLEN BRAINERD PECK.

When days are weaved of dreamful light,
The leaves are waving, red and gold,
So from the trees, in hosts untold,
Like oriflammes of Autumn bright,
Along the path of Summer's flight
Their farewells fluttering manifold,
When days are weaved of dreamful light,
The leaves are waving red and gold.

The crickets chant their music trite,
Quaint, black-robed singers, as of old,
And in dim, grass cathedrals hold,
At eve, the masses of the night,—
When days are weaved of dreamful light.

YALE BOYS OF THE LAST CENTURY.

"The Journal of Elijah Backus Junior, at Yale College, From Jan. ye first to Dec. 31, 1777."

EDITED BY MISS ELLEN D. LARNED.

A neat leather-bound volume, shaped like an old-fashioned singing book (four by six and a half inches), preserves intact the daily jottings of this young gentleman, son of that worthy patriot, Elijah Backus, of Norwich, whose iron-works at Yantic were doing such good service in the patriot cause. Though not quite eighteen years of age, our student was in his senior year at college, in the largest class that had been enrolled at Yale. He was a sober, pains-taking youth, duly interested in current events. It is not an inspiriting chronicle that he gives us, and for that very reason more faithfully depicts the time.

Apart from the slow progress of the war, the atmosphere of Yale was peculiarly depressing at that juncture. There was uncertainty of college continuance, difficulty in finding board, high prices, a small-pox scare, dissatisfaction with President Dagget, who figures in these columns as "Old Tunker." But our journalist may tell his own story:

"*Norwich*, Jan. 1, 1777. We have entered upon another year. I am preparing to set out for New Haven next Monday. 3. We have most certain accounts which come in the New London paper that Gen. Washington crossed the Delaware the night of the 25th of December and attacked a body of Hessians. . . . . After an engagement of 35 minutes, he routed them and took upwards of 900 of them prisoners, besides killed and wounded. 4. We have the yesterday's news confirmed. 5. I was at meeting to-day at Woodbridge's at noon, and there saw a copy of Gen. Heath's letter, confirming the above account. 6. Set out for New Haven, a little after sunrise, with Avery and Tracy; very cold and windy. We had not gone above four miles when we saw a man fall off his horse and it hurt him considerably; we rid about three miles further when Tracy's horse fell down with him; did not hurt him very greatly but came very nigh killing the horse. We arrived at Middletown and as the taverns were all full we went to Col. Talcott's and staid gratis; left our horses at a tavern. 7. We sat out from Col. Talcott's, and when we had ridden about three-fourths of a mile Avery's horse fell down upon him, but did not hurt him. We rode as far as Durham and saw Gen. Arnold, who came from Gen. Washington and was going to Providence; from thence came to New Haven.

New Haven. 8. I am turned out of my lodgings at Mrs. Todd's and am obliged to seek for others. I stopped at Mr. Edwards' last night with Tracy, and am going to live there till I can get another. 9. There has happened an eclipse of the sun to-day, beginning near 9, and lasting till noon. 10. There has been an express through town from Gen. Parsons bringing an account

---

For a brief account of the Backus family, see Notes & Queries. Prof. Dexter of Yale expresses much interest in this diary as a rare and valuable discovery.—ED.

that Gen. Washington has had another engagement and has taken 500 more prisoners. 11. We had a recitation in Avery's room. The right honorable Barnabas Baldwin was here to-day. Because I did not pay him more for the use of his horse he refused to pay me what it cost me for shoeing him, and threatens to go to Tunker and complain of me. 12. Sabbath. I heard Tunker preach in the chapel; cold weather. 13. The first part of the class disputed to-day, but I did not, because I did not know that there was any question put out. 14. I feel a little off the head to-day; was not at the recitation at noon, and there was none in the afternoon. We have it reported that there has been another engagement, regulars all killed or taken prisoners and we have all their baggage and thirty field pieces. 15. Am rather suspicious that yesterday's story is not trustworthy. 16. Hopkins came down last night, and I went to sleep with Hillhouse; have tried to-day in vain to get a place to live at. 17. Bushnell has come down and we can't get a place so we have come to Mrs. Todd's and made up a fire but don't board there. 18. It is very cold and I board in the Hall, and am very sick with the headache. 19. I heard the President preach in the Chapel. We hear that Fort Washington is retaken by our troops. 20. The yesterday's story is a falsehood. There are 200 prisoners brought into town. 21. I have got a load of wood at $2. Bushnell and I have begun to board at Deacon Ball's, at 7s. a week. I have the constant unhappiness to undergo a series of very disagreeable reflections."

What with his headaches and his "disagreeable reflections," our youngster is evidently a little bilious. He certainly is not hurting himself by study, and gives no hint of home-sickness. A contemporary journal-writer from Thompson, born the same year, and now driving Continental teams and hunting Tories over in Fairfield County, gets a great deal more fun out of life than our Yale student, but things may brighten now that he has a chum and steady boarding-place.

"23. We hear that Gen. Putnam has taken a great number of wagons loaded with baggage. 25. Adj. Gen. Huntington was through town to-day. I paid Col. Fitch £7, 14s., and still owe him now £3. N. B. I got my hair cut off and *Pudit me magnipire visu.* 26. Sabbath. I heard Tunker preach in the Chapel. Gen. Parsons was in town yesterday and there is an express after him to-day with orders to go immediately back to the army. 30. Town meeting to-day to regulate the price of articles. I and Bushnell began to study the Greek Testament this evening.

Feb. 1. To-day we began the 3d vol. of Locke and I got a quart of rum at Atwater's at 2s. per quart. 3. Expect to declaim soon; read arguments to-day and drank a mug of flip at night. 4. Declaimed this morn. and plainly showed to the wondering scholars my immense eloquence. 8. The present nocturnal assemblies and the tumultuous and riotous proceedings of the mob in this town are sufficient to strike any sensible person with horror and raise his indignation against a set of men that not only disgrace the name of *Whig* by being called by it, but human nature. 11. Began to read last night Vol. VII. Rollin's Ancient History, having finished Elements of Criticism. There is a very dangerous practice in college of those scholars who have had the smallpox going down to see those who are sick with it in town, by which those who have not had it are greatly exposed. 15. Bought two loads of woods for 20s. We have an account of a battle in the Jersies, in which our people have killed 300 of the enemy. 18. Headquarters are transported here where we live, and if I may be allowed the expression we are under guard. 22. There was a frigate of 36 guns anchored off this harbour and sent in a flag of truce after

March 1. I, Pond and Marcy went down to Isaac Jones's to buy books. I bought a book called "View of the Invisible World" and 3 singing books for 14s. 8. A very warm, pleasant day. Mansfield and several others were taken last night in a barn with about 300 counterfeit money. They had come from Long Island. "O lost to virtue, lost to manly thought; and all the noble sallies of the soul." 9. There was a man shot at last night by the sentry at the gate because he would give no answer to him. I disputed to-day before Tunker concerning witches. 11. Hear our people have had a fight and killed 500. 13. There was a printed paper stuck up in the Chapel this morn concerning the Captives of Napthali. Col. Fitch says he cannot keep the commons any longer than the quarter and the Corporation are sent for to determine about it.

17. The Plutonians have their anniversary to-day; went in solemn procession and somebody tolled the bell for them. Mr. Dwight gave us a very sensible lecture upon history; heard that Hillhouse had gone home after receiving account that his mother lay at the point of death. 20. It is in my opinion very dangerous living in town on account of the small-pox and 'tis very likely college will be dismissed or removed next week, for Col. Fitch positively affirms he won't keep up Commons unless the Corporation will give him 12 or 14 shillings per week, for he says he has already lost £100 and loses still £9 per week. I hear that Dunbar was hanged yesterday, who is the first that has fell a victim to the injured Americans: "Is there not some hidden vengeance in the Stores of Heaven to blast those men that attempt to make their fortune by their country's ruin." 21. The great day came on this afternoon, when there were exhibited the best exercises that ever have been since *fuit funda mintum Collegii*. 22. The President has notified the scholars that college will break up next Wed. in order that they may send for their horses. He further says that when the Corporation come together he shall resign his presidentship and has given the scholars an affecting speech, so that their tune is turned, for it used to be "old damned Tunker," but now *bona praeses*. 23. I was not at meeting this P. M. on account of sending a letter home by Mr. Flint. 26. I read the Elements of Criticism before Mr. Dwight. They say College is to be dismissed to-morrow. 27. The new college was set on fire this A. M. by some of the scholars who have burnt straw in it, and this P. M. there was a large house in town set on fire and most of the roof consumed. 28. Cold weather. College was dismissed this A. M. Our horses are not come to-day. 29. The scholars are almost all gone. Mr. Dwight thinks that college won't be called together again in this town, and that our class won't be called together at all.*
He has been talking with some of the class to know their minds whether if he should call them together in his own name they would be willing to meet at any place he should appoint.

April 1, Bushnell's horse came and he set out about nine. My horse came about 1 p. m. (brother James came to bring it). Tracy's horse came

---

*Arrangements had then been made for the dispersion of the students — the Freshmen going to Farmington under Tutor Lewis; the Sophomores and Juniors to Glastonbury under Prof. Strong and Tutors Buckminster and Baldwin; the Seniors to Wethersfield under Tutor Dwight, the future President.

too. Lathrop brought it. Breed's brother has not sent a horse for him, but he has hired one here. April fools are not as plenty to-day as the pigeons were yesterday, for they flew over in such numbers that we may reasonably expect to be plentifully supplied with them this season. 2. Tracy, Breed, James, and myself set out from New Haven this morn, and after various incidents, viz.: stops, drams entirely composed of flip, a plentiful dinner and a large quantity of childish conversation, we arrived at Colchester, where we had a warm fire, a good bowl of egg-punch, an excellent supper, a good bed to lie on, and your petitioner farther saith not.

Colchester, April 2, 7 p. m. In general Congress assembled. To all to whom these presents may come, greeting: *Whereas*, it may happen in the course of human events that mankind may be ignorant of the true causes and reasons of our delay at this place at the present time, and *Whereas*, several disaffected and evil-minded persons have taken occasion from it to misrepresent and abuse us, all which is contrary to our dignity and the grandeur of our exalted station — Be it known unto you that the question was proposed: Whether we should proceed to the town of Norwich, the 2d instant or not, when after a very long and warm debate, we for several weighty and important reasons, in our great wisdom, concluded and resolved, *nimine contradicente* to tarry here till the 3d and then forward to the place above mentioned. Given under our hand, April 3, 1777.

ELIJAH BACKUS, President.

3. Sat out from Colchester about 6 o'clock and arrived at Norwich about 9, where we ate breakfast. Just as we arrived home it began to rain. 5. *Pater* had orders from government to make another cannon. *Libertatem habeo* to go and have the small-pox."

This fashionable expedient for forestalling an attack from a dreaded enemy was looked upon in advance as something in the nature of "a lark," though our student finds it a very serious affair.

6. Was at meeting to-day and heard Rev. Mr. Williams of Pomfret preach. 7. James and I sat out from Norwich this morn, the sun about an hour high, and went to Mason's and found that he was gone. We accordingly went as far as a tavern, about 4 miles from Windham, towards Canada (Hampton), and while our horses were eating, Bushnell, Mason and Tiffany rid up and dismounted. When we had staid here a sufficient time we embarked and rode as far as Pomfret and dined; at this place I saw Dr. Waterman and Beriah Bill. We again embarked and with but two more stops arrived at Uxbridge at Dr. Willard's, where not being able to get entertainment, we went to Col. Reed's tavern and put up. I am very tired and have a great pain in my breast and left arm. 8. Feel something better. We have been inoculated. 9. Storrs came to the doctor's last night and is to live here and is inoculated. 11. As nothing worthy of notice happens shall omit several days. 14. Walton went to the hospital to-day. Our inoculation has all taken except Bushnell's. 16. Mr. Uxbridge was at the doctor's this morn. About 10 o'clock, Bushnell, Mason, James and myself sat out from Dr. Willard's attended by Abraham Willard. We have Mr. Williams' horse to carry our packs and Jemmy rode on it as he was the smallest. We walked about four miles when my symptoms came on so hard that I was unable to go afoot, so James dismounted and I rode the other two miles as far as Col. Smith's where we left our things and proceeded to the hospital about 12 o'clock, where we were shown the hospital and its inhabitants, particularly Huntington, who was the most horrible sight I ever saw. Here we found Mr. Williams, Col. Dyer's son, and several others we were acquainted with. The melancholy, the mournful, and the death-like

aspect of this place, the dismal looking flags that were hung in the air to keep off all comers to our habitation, attended with the sickness with which I was afflicted, made the place destined to be the receptacle for persons in my condition appear more like the infernal regions than any other place I ever had any idea of. For three days I continued sick, waiting with longing expectation for the appearance of the pock. 21. My symptoms have left me and I feel much better. 22. I have about two or three hundred pock and James about the same number. Walton is broke out and has thousands of pocks but he bears them with bravery and patience. Bushnell is broke out, the last of our number. 24. Morley and several others have entered the hospital. 27. Mr. Deming, Dyer and Amory went out to-day, Mr. Williams and his nephew yesterday. 29. Mrs. Vedder has sent me the second part of my pies and says she has sent them all. I sent 4 quarts of apples to her and she sent back about 3 quarts of apple pies, crust and all, those poor miserable things. *O tempora! O mores!* 30. We have been in the hospital two weeks and have not had one clear, warm day. Benjamin and Christopher Backus and Eliphalet Huntington came to Mendon last night and were at the hospital this morn and we are to ride their horses back. Bushnell, James and I washed up and deserted the land of the ragged visionaries. Bushnell staid at Col. Smith's and we took the horses and proceeded to Dr. Willard's at Uxbridge. After several attempts, an old gentleman, Col. Spring, agreed to keep our horses till next Monday and we went to our lodgings.

May 1. Fast day through Mass. government. James has been very unwell since he came from the hospital. His ancle has been very much swelled but is much better. There is one, Dr. Walton of Killingley, here (a bitter Tory) and one Mr. Fogg a church-priest from Brooklyn, Conn., under inoculation *ambo inimica patria.* 2. Storrs went down to Mendon with Conant and others who were going into the hospital. This day have I completed my eighteenth year, and what am I?—an awkward, foolish boy—conducted from infancy by an unseen hand through various dangers, seen and unseen, fed and clothed by its bounty, and brought to the present time, sensible of my own littleness and inability to perform anything either to the service of my Master, or greatly to the advantage of mankind. 3. We had news of the Regulars destroying the stores at Danbury and of the engagement our people have had with them, in which we had the misfortune to have Gen. Wooster mortally wounded and several others killed, among whom is Dr. Atwater of New London. The Regulars have retreated to their ships. 5. Col. Spring brought our horses about 9 o'clock and we sat out and rode about twelve miles to dinner (Thompson) and from thence we rode about six miles and parted from Bushnell, then rode to Killingly, South Society, baited our horses, drank, ate, and proceeded to Eaton's (Plainfield) where we arrived about 8 o'clock. Got supper and went to bed very tired. 6. Sat out from Eaton's about 7, arrived home about 10; after dinner went to see the cannon fired. 8. I sat out about noon to carry Mr. Lord's horse back; thence went to Capt. Kinsman's in search of a new hat, but being disappointed went to Jewett's and got our cloth and came home. 9. John Hilhouse was at our house and brings news that Gen. Wooster is dead. 10. The old militia men go down to N. L. in droves in order the more handily to pursue the laudable exercise of fighting. 11. Uncle Isaac Backus came here yesterday and preached at the upper meeting-house to-day. 12. Upson, Little, and Bushnell here and staid long enough to drink up a little of our muddy wine. 14. I went to fetch Aunt Loudon up to our house and heard of the famous Tory plan that is brought out. There were seven Tories caught last night at New London and North Parish. As I was riding home with Aunt in the chaise, there appeared upon his full march to the court house, the famous Darius Morgan honored by a guard of two men. 15. The examination of the Tories continues but not with the greatest success. 17. We have a rumor about that the Regulars at Newport and the Tories are embarking. 21. Woodbridge came from Hartford to-day and brought news that there were forty sail of ships with a number of flat-bottomed boats coming down Sound—their destination unknown. 22. There are great quantities of stores, both public and private exported out of the town every day.

"Before the passing bell begun,
The news through half the town has run."

23. I carried my gun up to Weston's to have a bayonet put on it. . . . .

June 18. Tracy and I set out for Wethersfield this morn; came as far as Lebanon where we added Bushnell to our number and arrived at W. about 7. 17. We have at last, after much difficulty got in at Capt. Welles's. 20. John Mix rode my horse home to-day. 21. The scholars come into town, but slow. 22. I was not at meeting, *quia non vobis*. 23. There are 17 or 18 scholars in town and 'tis likely there will not be much over 20. 24. We attend exercises regularly at the school-house. 25. I brought in a composition this evening . . . "If you are highly unhappy either in your person, your abilities, or your fortune, wait not for miracles to change you but conduct yourself under your present circumstances in such a manner as will be most for your own advantage.—Backus." 27. Warm day. We had a most terrible thunder-storm at night. It struck an house about 40 rods from my lodgings about 10 at night and damaged it very much.

July 1. There are rumors of wars in the latter ages. We recited English grammar this p. m. 2. We hear the Regulars have gone across the lake and intend to come around Fort Ticonderoga and so down North river. We also hear that those who retreated out of the Jersies have gone back again. 9. There was a singing-meeting to-night at Mrs. Porter's. 10. We have had news upon news concerning our people being taken in Fort Ticonderoga but it is impossible to know what to believe—the accounts are so different. 13. Hear that about forty of our men took Gen. Prescott out of his bed at Newport and brought him to Providence. 13. We have news that may certainly be depended on that Ticonderoga and Fort Independence are both in the hands of the Regulars and that Gen. Prescott is taken by our people. 15. I heard that our people had had an engagement with the enemy at Fort Anne, and that they (the enemy) retreated, leaving 300 dead upon the field. Also that Gen. Feller's had engaged another party and taken 700 of them. 18. Ives came into town this p. m. and brought two sheets of parchment, which was a present to our class from Tunker. 19. Warm day. Tunker is in town and I am afraid will preach to-morrow; went in swimming this p. m. with several others. 20. Mr. Dwight preached here to-day concerning the necessity of early piety. 21. James brought our horse for me to-day. 22. Our exercises began *tertiam horam* p. m., and was not ended till about 6."

And here ends the college life of our Yale student. The brief exercise noted above took the place of the usual commencement examination and exhibition. In September the Corporation met, voted degrees to fifty-six students and elected Ezra Stiles president. Backus writes of riding to Lebanon with Havens (Jonathan N.) to get Bushnell to promise "that he would write our diplomas," but we find no note of its reception.

The Journal drags on through the year in perfunctory fashion with brief weather notices, excerpts from classic and standard authors and many *nihil dignum motari accidit*. Public events still excite interest.

Woodbridge brought an account from Hartford which is confirmed by Brown, the post, that the two armies at the northward have had an engagement and have killed and wounded a thousand of the enemy with the loss of not 150. Oct. 19. Hear that Gen. Burgoyne and his whole army, numbering 4,500 men, are cut up and will be surrendered as prisoners of war."

A few unimportant items close the year's public record, diversified by many melancholy mortuary reflections in blank verse, apparently original, like this final entry:

"Dec. 31. 'I'm swiftly wafted down the Tide of Life ;
And soon shall enter on the endless scenes
Of the huge Ocean of Eternity
Where never ceasing rolls the vast Abyss.'—*Backus*."

DEPARTURE.

DOUBLE SONNET.

ROBERT CLARKSON TONGUE.

Two friends of late passed from me; one to roam
In old-world countries far beyond the sea.
O younger friend! would I might trace with thee
The golden paths we dreamed of here at home:
The storied North, cliff-bound and scourged with foam,
The softer spell and tender mystery
Of climes where song and summer never flee;
Vast, noble cities, rising dome on dome,
And hoar cathedrals, lifting to the light
The pristine beauty time can ne'er efface;
And sky-ward soaring mountains, calm and white,
Above the people's surging at their base,—
These we would share; and every wished for sight
Would gain new meaning from thy voice and face.

Friend, on whose brow the many years had pressed
Their solemn seals; the heavy night was old,—
The gray mist wrapped the valley, fold on fold,
And dimmed the pale stars lingering in the west,
What time we parted. I, who loved thee best,
Saw all the eastern sky awake in gold,
The glories of the maiden dawn unrolled,—
And thou wert gone upon thy lonely quest.
Would I had passed with thee, O soul serene!
Swiftly to mount upon that star-strewn way,
Beyond the earth-mist and the cloudy screen,
Together we had hastened through the gray
And untried port of night, together seen
The golden upward-flushing of the day!

THE GIRL FROM MASSACHUSETTS.

BY MISS PAULINE PHELPS.

Sara Morton, spinster, sat beside the open window in the dining-room, where, by only turning her eyes, she could look out upon the shaded front yard, with its myrtle carpet, its trim flower beds, and the rows of box-wood bordering the path to the wide veranda. There was the smell of honeysuckle in the warm air, and bees hummed a drowsy accompaniment to her voice.

"Lucy Davis was the only out-of-town teacher we ever had," she said, reflectively, "An' she didn't stay through a year; it prejudiced some against hirin' you, thinkin' of the time we had then. She wa'n't over twenty, though, an' that makes a difference. Now I shouldn't wonder but what you're old enough, so you'll suit first rate."

I bowed in recognition of the doubtful compliment, with a vague pity for my predecessor, who had been too young to please. "Did she come from a distance?" I asked.

"From Cambridge, Massachusetts; that's across from Bostin, you know. She was third cousin to the Pettibones, though they hadn't never met, an' when her uncle died she wrote to Tom about gettin' a place to teach. He happened to be committee-man for our district that year, an' he sent an' hired her. It seemed a natural thing enough to do. I never heard of anybody that objected beforehand but Sam Perkins, an' he objects to everything, an' has ever since he was old enough to talk. He can't look out the window an' see a clear blue sky without objectin' to it because it's a weather breeder, an' I s'pose he had to object to the school teacher to keep his name up, though he hadn't a chick nor child in the world. He made me a call, the day before she come, to talk it over. 'If Pettibone wants to have the responsibility of hirin' a Massachusetts young gal to take charge of that school-room, an' then wake up some mornin' an' find the whole buildin' set on fire an' a mass of ruins, he can do it,' says he, 'But I shouldn't like to be in his shoes. You never can tell what a day'll bring forth, when you try to have school without government.'"

"I didn't see why a Massachusetts girl couldn't keep just as good government as one brought up right here in town, an' I told him so, but he was as positive as if he'd had a fore-ordination."

"'They lack *staminy*,' says he, bringin' down his hand. 'Staminy an' grit. There ain't nobody but what's born an' raised in Connecticut that's got staminy an' grit enough to teach a Connecticut school, an' she bein' from Bostin won't have so much as most Massachusetts folk. The more I think on't, the more I think she won't have *any*. She'll cackerlate on oat-meal for breakfast before she can eat her meat an' pertater, an' ten chances to one you'll be 'bliged to make up her bed for her; an' if there don't somethin' serious happen to them children before the winter's out — a fire or some bad accident — it'll be surprisin'. But,' says he, as if thinkin' on't brought him a pile of comfort, an' I don't doubt it did, 'Whatever comes, they can't say I didn't tell 'em 'twould beforehand.'"

"An' I guess that was true of every calamity since the world begun, for he'd be'n prophesyin' so much he'd hit 'em all, one time or another."

"And the teacher, did she answer his description?"

"No, she didn't. I was afraid she'd be too cityfied at first, for she was as pretty as a picture, an' looked like a fashion plate too, with her brown dress an' big hat, an' yellow hair all kind o' fluffed around her head, an' done up in back in a — a — wait a minute, I always have to think of mowin'-machine to get the right word — scythe — scythy — scyk — that's it, 'Psyche' knot. But she made herself right to home in the house, as if she'd be'n used to drawin' water from a well instead of gettin' it out of a facet all her life; an' before she'd stayed a week she told me she cut all her own dresses. I wa'n't afraid but what she'd have government, after that. Maybe her looks helped her some with the older boys, come winter, but the young ones was kept in order too, an' everybody agreed 'twas as good a school as there'd be'n in years. There wa'n't but one fault to find — an' that was on account of her flirtin' ways."

"Her *flirting* ways."

"Maybe I oughtn't to call it that. Maybe she didn't mean it, an' 'twas just on account of her bringin' up. But bein' from the city, an' so pretty an' full of fun, give her the pick of all the boys; an' seein' there's never be'n enough to go around in town, it did seem as if 'twould be'n fairer to settled on one, an' let the other girls have a chance with the rest. But that wa'n't her way. One night she'd walk home from meetin' with Fred Smith, an' Fred would feel as if he'd got the inside track, an' then when he asked her to sleigh-ride she'd be goin' with Frank Adams; an' maybe in a week 'twould be a party with Burt Simonson. An' every fellow she went with she'd laugh an' talk an' act as if she was havin' so good a time she couldn't possibly have any better, an' you'd think 'twas a settled thing — 'til you saw her again with some-body else. It made feelin' of course. I didn't care so much about Frank Adams an' Phil Slocum, an' maybe her treatin' Fred Smith that way was good for his conceit, though his mother hain't forgiven her to this day. But I was real disappointed about Milton Hoskins, for his folks thought she was goin' to marry him sure, an' invited her there to tea; an' he was studyin' for a doctor, an' the best match in town. I made up my mind after she stopped goin' with him she wouldn't ever think serious of anybody around here, an' I didn't pay much attention to her other friendships, 'til she picked up Jim Merritt. That was a different matter.'"

"That was *serious*, I suppose?"

"'Twas serious for him. I hadn't worried but what the other boys would get over their fancy as soon as Lucy was out of sight, but he was five years older than the rest of them, an' never went with a girl before steady in his life. We all thought that was the reason she took such pains to make him like her, at first; an' after that — well, maybe 'twas to see what she could do. But knowin' how 'twould turn out, we hated to see it. His aunt use to tell him what a fool he was for bein' taken by her flirtin' ways, when we knew they didn't mean anythin'; an' so did a good many others. You couldn't say much to her. For all her fun an' liveliness, she wa'n't ever one of the confidential kind. I did try a few words about Jim once, but I might just as well have saved my breath. She stopped me before I got half through, her lips all wreathed in smiles. 'Why, Aunt Sarah,' she said — she'd got into the way of callin' me that from hearin' the other young folks — 'You're mistaken about it altogether. He don't care any more about me than I do about him. Wait until I see something that makes me think he does, and then I'll stop; I promise you.' Lookin' at me with her big, laughin' blue eyes, as if she wa'n't any more responsible for her mischief than my grey kitten would be when it tumbled over the work-box."

"It went on that way for as much as two months. All the neighborhood was talking about what a shame 'twas, an' one afternoon when she was at school Sam Perkins stopped into the house to put in his say, too. He'd kept away as long as things was goin' smooth. 'I told you they'd regret ever havin' an' out-of-town teacher,' says he. 'An' now you see my words hev' come true. Makin' fools of the other fellows was bad enough, an' ought to have satisfied her; but no, she must go flirtin' with Jim Merritt, as sober an' sensible a man as there is in town, an' work till she's got him so he worships the ground she walks on. An' what is she doin' it for ? Jest to gratify her vanity. It's woman's natur'— woman's natur' the world over.'"

"'Perhaps she'll marry him,' said I. I didn't believe it, for I'd about made up my mind the girl hadn't any heart to speak of, but his way of talkin' vexed me. It's always old bachelors, with the least chance to know anything about women's natures, that say the most against them; you'll find that out.'"

"'Marry,' says he. 'Why, she's set her heart on a millionaire. Milton Hoskins wa'n't good enough for her, an' she wouldn't think a feller like Jim enough acquaint to wipe her old shoes on, for all he owns a nice farm. She'll jilt him jest as soon as she gits a little tired of the fun, an' you mark my words, he ain't the kind to take a thing like that easy. I shouldn't be surprised to hear of his doin' somethin' desp'rit.'"

"'Twas that very night, as I sat there thinkin' about it, that Lucy danced into the room. She'd be'n sleigh-ridin,' an' her hair was all kind of tumbled around her face, an' her eyes shinin' like stars. 'I suppose, Aunt Sarah,' says she, 'You'll be relieved to hear Jim says he ain't comin' any more ?'"

"'Did you — did you let him know you didn't care,' — I began."

"'Oh, he didn't ask me. I told you he wasn't interested. But we quarrelled a little; I don't approve of quarrelling, so I suggested we should say good-bye while we could do it pleasantly, and he jumped at the chance. He might have shown more feeling, out of consideration for me, don't you think ?'"

"I didn't believe her, but I knew she'd sent him away for good, never mind what she took for an excuse. She commenced goin' with Fred Smith again, an' they was out 'most every night, sleigh-ridin' or gettin' up parties an' candy pulls; an' if there was any difference in her actions it was that she was livelier an' talked an' laughed more than ever. It seemed odd she should be in such spirits, for from all accounts her school wa'n't the easiest one in the world to manage, them days. The boys had behaved well enough before, so I s'p'ose 'twas hearin' the old folks criticize her started it, an' they said Jim Merritt's cousin was the leader. But there wa'n't anything, from singin' songs en' drawin' pictures on the blackboard to writin' letters signed with his name, sayin' he was goin' to kill himself, that those children didn't think of, to torment her with, durin' the last two months of school. An' she took it as if she didn't care a straw."

" And Jim — how did he take it ?"

"You ca'n't tell so much about a man, you see. The neighbors said he acted about the same, but it ain't always those that cry out the loudest that are hurt the worst. I hadn't never be'n afraid of his doin' anything rash; I knew he'd keep along someway an' get over it, but there's apt to be more sufferin' put in the 'gettin' over' than to make up for all the comfort you take afterwards. I've lived enough to know that, an' yet I'm an old maid, an' if you ask the neighbors they'll say they don't believe I ever cared for anybody in my life."

She laughed, but there was something besides laughter in the faded eyes; and she looked for a long moment at the sweet peas gaily nodding their heads outside, before she went on with the story.

"'Twas the last of February Jim stopped comin', an' Lucy's school was out in April. She was goin' home for good then. 'I don't believe teachin' is my vocation, Aunt Sarah,' she said, an' I didn't urge her to try another term. I couldn't feel quite the same since she treated Jim that way, an' then I thought a rest would do her good. She'd grown real thin durin' the last few weeks. There ain't many can stand workin' days an' goin' every night.'

"The way it had all turned out I didn't even want them to give her a surprise party the night before she left, but I couldn't refuse; an' after I'd said yes, I went ahead an' planned everything I could to help them have a good time. It had be'n rainin' steady for three days, an' the flood was up so you couldn't cross Guldrain bridge, but there was over thirty come, for all that. Dick Mathers brought a whole load in his boat, an' Fred Smith rode through on horseback, an' borrowed Will Black's suit of clothes after he got this side. They was a mile too big for him, but he didn't mind that so long as he got to the party. Sam Perkins was with the rest, of course. He keeps 'bachelor's hall' at home, an' folks say he never misses a surprise party because it's the only chance he has of gettin' something decent to eat. He was about as cast down an' discouraged as I ever remember him. Said the doctor had been to see Antoinette Case, his third cousin on his father's side, an' she'd got a Palestine in her nose."

"'Polypus, I guess you mean, don't you?' I asked. I wa'n't surprised at his gittin' the name wrong. He was always so busy borryin' trouble he never had time for an education."

"'Mebbe so, mebbe so; but they're terrible painful, whatever they be. Start with a numbness, an' then burn like a red-hot coal o' fire. I hain't a doubt but what I'll hev' one before the summer's over. I don't say anything about it, but my nose has be'n feelin' kind of queer for two or three weeks. An' them sort of things allers run in families.'"

"But he was the only one acted out of sorts, an' the rest just had a jolly time. They played blind-man's buff, an' dumb crambo, an' hide the thimble, an' Lucy was the gayest of the lot. She'd slipped away after they come an' put on a grey dress fixed up with pink ribbons, an' she looked like a picture. I felt glad Jim wa'n't there to see her. He'd had to go to town that afternoon, they said, but if he got home time enough he'd drop in later."

"''Twas just as we'd begun to pass the cake that I heard some one steppin' on the veranda. 'There's Jim!' says Dick Mathers, an' they all commenced to shout. 'Not much left for you, Jim.' You'll have to hurry if you get any cake. Better late than never.' But when the door opened, it was old Mr. Thomas stood there, an' something in the look on his face stopped the laughin' in a minute."

"'Have you — you hav'n't heard about Jim Merritt, have you?' he asked."

"'Jim? No! What—'"

"'I don't want to frighten ye,' he said, 'But maybe you wouldn't like to think of how ye laughed through the ev'nin' afterwards, if anything did happen. He went to town with the hired man about four o'clock, an' the hoss' just come home alone. They must have tried to cross Guldrain bridge for some reason or other, though he ought to know the flood was up. The wagon's lyin' just this side o' the drain' kicked half to pieces. 'Twas a dark night, an' you a'l know how the water rushes in there, an' what a current——'"

"Yes, we knew. We'd talked about the place often, an' the selectmen meant to fix the road, but they hadn't got to it. Everybody looked at Lucy. Of course her jiltin' Jim didn't make him any more liable to be drowned, but it seemed as if it did; an' while we was wonderin' how she could take it so unconcerned, she sprung to her feet with a cry like you'd struck her, an' then fell forward on the floor.

"We wa'n't frightened much at first. We thought it was just an ordinary faint, an' worked with camphor an' cold water to bring her to. It wa'n't until she opened her eyes, an' looked around on us as if we was thousands of miles away, an' begun to talk of Jim, an' where he was, an' why didn't he come, that we thought of sendin' for the doctor. It wa'n't until he'd be'n there twice, an' there wa'n't any chance for a mistake, that we could realize 'twas brain fever. She hadn't much vitality, the doctor said. He thought it must be she'd be'n worryin' more than she showed. 'An' hadn't we noticed she was runnin' down! Hadn't we noticed she seemed over-excitable?' No, he couldn't promise to save her. He would do his best, but it was a bad case. Perhaps if the young man she talked about proved to be all right, an' she could see him —'"

"The flood went down, an' boats were out all day huntin' for his body; an' some said they wouldn't find it 'til it rose, an' some said they didn't believe he was drowned at all, but had gone crazy an' wandered off; an' still others thought the hired man had killed him an' run away with the money. The days went on, an' the hope that we'd ever see him alive grew fainter an' fainter — an' all the time Lucy was lyin' there, talkin' of 'Jim! Jim!' always 'Jim!' Of the good times they used to have, an' the foolish quarrel; an' how when she got vexed an' said somethin' she didn't mean he took it in earnest, an' went away. 'He wouldn't if he'd cared,' she said. 'He didn't care; it was only me. But I want him to know how sorry I am — I want him to come, so I can tell! Oh, if he knew how I cared, don't you believe he'd come?' An' we that watched used to sit an' listen an' wipe our eyes to think how we'd misjudged her; an' wonder if it wasn't our talk that had made Jim so ready to take her words in earnest, an' if we'd ever have a chance to make it up."

"For a week she lay there just the same, only growin' weaker. It was the mornin' of the eighth day that she seemed to be a little more quiet, an' they left me for a few minutes all alone. I remember sittin' lookin' at her, an' wonderin' if she'd ever looked so pretty when she was well as she did then, with her pink cheeks, an' her hair curlin' all around her face, an' her blue dress. She'd talked so much about shrouds an' coffins that we'd slipped on a wrapper of Mary Hewins', thinkin' the color might take her mind off, but it hadn't done any good. She lay there with closed eyes, always a murmurin', 'Jim, Jim!' just above her breath."

"Maybe I'd dropped off a minute; I hadn't had any sleep for three nights. But some movement she made brought me to myself, an' I turned around with a start. She was out of bed, standin' up, an' the look on her face made me think of the pictures of angels. 'It's Jim,' she says softly. 'He's coming. I hear him.'"

"For a second I thought she was struck with death, an' lookin' into Heaven; then I started toward her, but she motioned me back. 'It's Jim!' she cried louder. 'I tell you I hear his voice.' The door opened! I couldn't speak.' 'Twas time for the body to rise, an' I thought it was his ghost that stood there, but she sprang like a flash. Ghost or human, it wouldn't 'a mattered to her. 'Jim! Jim!' she gasped. 'I wanted to tell you!' An' then — it was Jim in the flesh that stood there, an' his arms that caught her as she fell!

"An' so — an' so — Why, my dear, I didn't mean to get you wrought up. She wa'n't dead, though we thought she was for a long time, while we worked to bring her to; but she begun to mend from that day. I don't know what I am cryin' for, I'm sure. Only the look on her face always brings it back to me — an' there's so many make just such awful mistakes, an' so few that ever get the chance to set them right.'"

"And Jim? Tell me how he escaped?"

"Why, Jim wa'n't with his team at all. He run across a man he knew that day in the city, just startin' out for a few days' trampin' an' fishin', an' he wanted Jim to go too. It seemed a funny time of year for it, but 'twas a doctor's prescription, an' Jim caught at any excuse for gettin' away just then. He sent the man home with the team an' the message, an' maybe he got drunk an' drove the horse into the flood, an' then run away to save payin' for the wagon. All we ever knew about that part of it was that he wa'n't drowned, for Dick Mathers see him six months afterwards down Farmington way. An' Jim stayed with his chum trampin' an' fishin', an' probably havin' a good time too — for love don't make the world for a man like it does for a woman — 'till he read of his disappearance in a weekly paper. 'Twas that started him for home."

"So it turned out all right. There couldn't anybody do enough for Lucy while she was gettin' well, an' Jim didn't want her out of his sight. They was married in June, right in this house. 'Twas a pretty wedding, with lots of presents, an' the only one not pleased was Sam Perkins. I stood on the steps with him after the rest was gone, lookin' at the rice an' old shoes spread over the grass. 'It seems to me,' says I, thinkin' of the look on their faces as they drove away, 'that they're about the happiest couple I ever saw.' I didn't expect him to agree with me."

"'Mebbe they're happy enough now,' he grumbled, 'But this fallin' in love is something like sailin' around in one of them new fangled flyin' machines I read about in the paper. It's all well enough up in mid air, but it must be a ter'ble shock when you strike level ground ag'in. Jim's deservin' a sensible wife, an' he hain't got her. Any sensible woman would have waited an' found out whether a man was killed or not, 'fore she hed brain fever over it. He's made a bad bargain, Miss Morton, an' you mark my words, he'll live to regret it.'"

"Maybe he will, but they've be'n married over a year, an' I hain't seen any signs of repentin' yet. I was invited there to spend the day last week. Lucy makes a first rate housekeeper — an' such green-currant pies I never tasted."

GENTIAN.

JOSEPH ARCHER.

Gentian, beautiful, pure,
  Hid in the deep of the grass,
Down in thy coverture,
  Off from the haunts that allure,
Hunt to thy tangled morass,—

Deep in the mud and the wet,
  Sprinkled and sparkling with dew,
Generously, o'er thy net,
    Gentian!

OLD TIME MUSIC AND MUSICIANS.

III.

BY N. H. ALLEN.

"There is a little formula, couched in pure Saxon, which you may hear in the co⟨rner of⟩ the yard of the dames' school from very little republicans: 'I'm as good as you be⟨.' It is the⟩ essence of the Massachusetts Bill of Rights and of the American Declaration of Inde⟨pendence. It⟩ was at the bottom of Plymouth Rock and of Boston Stone; and this could be heard ⟨in⟩ the petitions to the king, and the platform of the churches, and was said and sun⟨g in the⟩ Psalmody of the Puritans."— EMERSON.

Letting the bars down for the devil to come in, may have ⟨been,⟩ but this little formula, still heard " in the yard of the dames' schoo⟨l, I'm⟩ as you be," was at the bottom of all this fuss over singing by r⟨ule in⟩ the churches. Our Puritan forefathers did not readily yield any⟨thing,⟩ slight, without demonstrating this with emphasis. But it was ⟨the⟩ Puritan minister who urged this better way of singing, and the peo⟨ple opposed⟩ it. Excessive repression always reacts, and after this great strug⟨gle, when⟩ peace again began to reign, it is fair to suppose that secular mus⟨ic had its⟩ share of attention, and instruments came into general use. The ⟨violin,⟩ in what the Rev. Nathaniel Chauncey frowns on as "Airy an⟨d light,"⟩ with their many "quavers and semi-quavers;" and indeed in t⟨hat day,⟩ if a better knowledge of music did not exist than was allowe⟨d to be⟩ exercised, why was the singing of psalms, as then practiced, s⟨o con-⟩ temptuously as to be notorious?

Where the instruments were first procured I am unable t⟨o say;⟩ they were of foreign make there can be little doubt. The first ⟨manufac-⟩ tured in this country came from Massachusetts, and were made ⟨by one⟩ Stafford, a transported convict, who, with two hundred others o⟨f his⟩ standing, was landed in Massachusetts in 1691. Stafford, who ⟨was a⟩ fiddle-maker" in London, is described as a notorious ruffian, ⟨who made⟩ "fiddles" and no end of trouble here. Governor Fletcher ⟨of N. Y.⟩ sought to utilize these convicts as protection against the ⟨invading⟩ French; but once armed they became free-booters rather th⟨an soldiers. The⟩ desperate gang, with Stafford as leader, struck out across cou⟨ntry⟩ near Albany, where it was a perpetual terror. Because of ⟨their⟩ assaults upon several Indian settlements, Fletcher, in a fit of ⟨vexa-⟩ tion, sent for Stafford to come to New York and consult w⟨ith about an⟩ Indian campaign; but Stafford soon forfeited his patron's favo⟨r, and was⟩ ually hanged to a tree by a Dutchman, upon whom he h⟨ad committed⟩ robbery*.

In the early days, nothing was used in the churches to ⟨aid in⟩ striking the right key; the pitch-pipe and tuning-fork were ⟨not used till⟩ some time in the eighteenth century.† But there must have ⟨been music⟩ of some sort in the colony, even in the early days, for John ⟨...⟩

---

*Spillane.

†Two of these pitch-pipes may be seen in the Historical Society's collection.

refers to them in his "Singing of Psalms a Gospel Ordinance," (1647) but permits the use of them, with a condition. He says:

"We also grant that any private Christian who hath a gifte to frame a spirituall song may both frame it and sing it privately for his own private comfort and remembrance of some speciall benefit or deliverance. Nor doe we forbid the use of any instrument therewithall: so that attention to the instrument does not divert the heart from attention to the matter of song."

At the two hundred and fiftieth anniversary of the First Church of Hartford, in 1883, Mr. Rowland Swift read a paper on "The Meeting Houses of the First Church," from which I get some information on this point:

"In October, 1769, a society of singing-masters 'voluntarily associated with a view to encourage Psalmody in this Government,' invited the public to the South Meeting-House to hear several new pieces of music performed with voices and instruments, and a sermon preached on the occasion." *

It would be interesting to know what instruments were used at this performance. All the notices of William Billings, the first Yankee composer of any pretension, give him the credit of introducing 'viols' in the music of the church, and Billings had scarcely grown to manhood when this 'Society of Singing Masters' entertained the people of Hartford.

With the introduction of choirs, some difficulty was experienced, here as elsewhere, in assigning them seats. Mr. Swift speaks of the church in Medford, Massachusetts, which refused to grant seats to singers at all, as late as 1770; and at Hollis, N. H., in 1784, it was agreed, "that twelve feet of the hind body seats below, next the Broad aisle be appropriated to the use of singers, on condition that a certain number of them will give the Glass necessary to repair the windows."

They were placed at the front and at the back, and perhaps at the sides, before they were finally landed in the galleries; and even then it seems, in view of modern requirements, not always to stay.

Dr. Franklin published the first edition of Watts' psalms and hymns which came into general use, in 1741, at Philadelphia. In 1784 this advertisement appeared in the Connecticut Courant:

Dr. Watts' Imitation
of the
Psalms of David,
Corrected and Enlarged
By
JOEL BARLOW.
To which is added
A Collection of Hymns.
The whole applied to the state of the Christian Church in general.
Under the patronage of the General Association, Rev. Messrs.
Timothy Pitkin, John Smalley and Theodore Hinsdale,
Committee.

In the adjoining column is this closely printed and characteristic advertisement, which shows that the spirit of competition was alive, even in those slow days:

"The subscriber has just printed a neat edition of Dr. Watts' Psalms which have since the peace been revised, altered and amended in such a manner as not to mention the king, Great Britain, &c., in our churches; but instead now mention Congress, United States, America, &c. This book has been perused by numbers since, and allowed to be very nicely and ingeniously altered. Dr. Watts has made so good a collection of Psalms that few can excel them; and the good people of this and the neighboring states, it is hoped will, if they approve of these alterations, continue the same in their churches, notwithstanding any individual that would wish to alter them otherways, in order to monopolize the sole printing and vending such a work at extravagant prices. For the public well know, that where every printer has a right to print

---

*We learn from Dr. Parker's History of the South Church that this "Society of Singing Masters" was organized in Wallingford, and came to Hartford to hold this meeting.

a book, it is the only way to have it cheap; and if one printer has a right to print one and not the rest, he, human nature like, will get as great a price as he can, and when the book is established and people must have them, it is as easy to say 3s. for Dr. Watts' Psalms as 2s. or 1s. 6d. The subscriber is willing to let any clergyman have one to peruse, before they recommend them to their church, and if approved of and will send for any quantity of six or above, they shall have them bound at 1s. 6d. each, and if 500 are sent for at one time, they shall have them at 1s. 4d. They are now retailed at 2s. single, which is enough for such a book. NATHANIEL PATTEN.

N. B. The rapid sale that this impression has already met with, gives the subscriber great hopes that it will be approved of. Since the impression was finished, 1,300 have been sent for from the city of New York. Hartford, Dec. 24, 1784.

Judging from the price of the book, and the number of words in this advertisement, it is evident that rates for space in the Courant have been changed since 1784. In January of the above year, the following advertisement appeared for the first time in the Courant:

"Just come to hand, and now selling by the printers hereof.
THE CHORISTER'S COMPANION,
Church Music Revised, etc., etc."

A year later a book was advertised which was evidently a Hartford compilation, " Brownson's Collection of Music, to be sold by the dozen or single. At his house, or at Benham's, in New Hartford." There was also a collection of music, "sold by the printer hereof," compiled by Law, and advertised with that of Brownson. Oliver Brownson, whose name was as often spelled Brunson or Bronson, published his book in 1783, and gave it the name " Select Tunes and Anthems." Several of Bronson's original tunes were copied from this book into later collections. Andrew Law was born in the town of Cheshire, 1748. He received a liberal education and adopted music teaching as his life work. He was active as a singing-school teacher for many years in the New England states, and also lived at Newark, N. J., where he devised a new method of musical notation which enjoyed a brief popularity. Mr. Law published " The Musical Magazine," the first musical periodical issued in this country. This was continued about five years. Some years before the Revolution, the making of singing books began in Massachusetts, and Ritter in his " Music in America " speaks of one Daniel Reed, who came to Hartford from that state. He made combs by day and devoted his evenings to singing-school teaching; and in 1771 published a little singing-school manual. Ritter has evidently made a mistake in dates, as he gives 1757 as the year of his birth, and 1793 the year in which he published a second book. He was the composer of the well known tune, *Windam.*

But, after the " peace," these singing books came thick and fast, and Connecticut did her share in producing them. Before 1786, all the books printed were from engraved plates, but in that year Isaiah Thomas, of Worcester, Massachusetts, imported a font of music-type, and his next book was announced as "printed typographically," and the new way soon became general.

In 1795, Mr. Amos Bull, who kept a general store near the South Church in Hartford, and was then chorister of that church, published a collection called " The Responsary," a copy of which Dr. Parker now has in his possession. Mr. Bull announced the Responsary as

"containing a collection of Church Musick, set with second Trebles instead of Counters, and peculiarly adapted to the use of the New England Churches."

Moore in his " Encyclopedia of Music " mentions a book published in 1794 by Mr. Bull, called " The Repository." Mr. Moore was a great collector of these old books of psalmody; but it is quite possible he has erred in giving the title, and the book referred to is " The Responsary." It matters little at the present time whether there were two books or only one; for, as Dr. Parker says of " The Responsary,"

"It was quite as good as any book of that period, but its tunes and anthems were composed in utter ignorance of the rudiments of musical science, and the performance of them by any modern choir would prove excruciating to the congregation."

About this time the South Church was appropriating from sixty to one hundred dollars a year for its music, and Dr. Parker gives the names in his history of the above-named church, of six choristers who served prior to the engagement of Mr. Amos Bull, which began in 1795 and continued nearly a quarter of a century. The names were David Isham, Horace Meecham, Eli Roberts, John Robbins, Loring Brace, and Alfred Goodrich.

IV.

It is not easy to get exact information about the progress of instrumental music in Hartford during the last century. Andrew Law both played and taught the violin and flute as early as 1770 in this state, and was probably well known in this city. It is a fact, too, that such instruments as the spinet and virginal (fore-runners of the piano-forte), were owned by people of wealth in New York city as early as the beginning of the last century; and even before the Revolution a good many harpsichords were to be found there. These were nearly all imported from England, a very few having been made in New York and Philadelphia. In view of the lively trade that was carried on with other parts of the world, it would be surprising if some of the aristocratic houses of Front street did not contain these instruments. The first *piano-forte* that was brought to this country, so far as known, was on board a British merchant vessel bound for New York, which was seized in 1779 by the continental privateering frigate *Boston*, and brought into the port of Boston. The cargo of general merchandise included this "London-made piano-forte," and a lot of flutes and harpsichord supplies, all of which were sold for the benefit of the National Treasury. It seems improbable, but may be taken for a fact, that the British occupany of New York at this time was highly beneficial to the place from a musical point of view; and the English influence was dominant until the Germans came in large numbers and introduced higher standards, with the present result that New York is one of the most musical cities in the world. Scarcely any of this growth is traceable in its beginning to the Dutch settlers.

The chief trade in New England at this time, however, was in fifes and drums. After the war, the English piano-fortes were imported extensively,* and the Marquis de Chastellux expressed surprise at the state of musical culture in the wealthy Boston families. But Ritter gives a list of pieces that were in vogue at the time, and it may be doubted whether the Marquis was above criticism as to musical taste. I give a few of these titles: "White Cockade," "Irish Howl," "Duchess of Brunswick," "Nancy of the Mill," "Ossian's Ghost," "Dead March in Saul," "Every inch a Soldier," etc.

The Courant of 1785 has this advertisement: "Imported by Wheelock & Co., a Collection of Songs," etc. This was undoubtedly of the class of music above mentioned, and there must have been instruments and players enough, as well as singers, in Hartford, to warrant the importation. I had for several years in my possession, a quaint, little five-octave London piano that had been in one family at Colchester several generations. It has since been restored, and is known to be at least a hundred years old.

Mr. Griffith, "dancing master from New York," advertised in the Courant, May 7, 1787, that he would teach "at Enos Doolittle's large room in this city." Enos Doolittle was a brass founder, but made the casting of bells a specialty.

---

*John Jacob Astor began the business in 1789, and continued it until his fur business crowded it out.

Late in the century the firm was known as "The Hartford Bell Foundry." A few years after Mr. Griffiths' advent, the popular dancing master in Hartford, as well as in some of the towns of Litchfield and Tolland counties, was J. C. Devero, "late from Europe." His Hartford school was held in Mr. Goodwin's ball room. He advertised to teach "plain and fancy, Minuets, Cotilions and Pettycotees, Irish Jiggs, and Reels in their various figures, the much admired Scotch Reel, first, second and threeble Hornpipe, Country-Dances, &c., in the most modern and elegant stile."

Dr. Parker alludes briefly to the social pleasures and amusements in vogue a century ago. He says:

"Dramatic exhibitions found their way into Hartford as early as 1776, and flourished in the latter years of the century. In 1795, a theater was built on what is now Temple Street, and was patronized by the best citizens, but in May, 1800, the General Assembly passed an act to prevent all theatrical exhibitions, imposing a fine of fifty dollars, on all offenders, and for a while the theater was in abeyance here. But amusements flourished. There were dancing-schools in abundance, and weekly balls and 'assemblies' of the most innocent and brilliant sort."

The theater flourished chiefly in midsummer. A troup known as "The Old American Company" played in Hartford during the month of August, on Mondays and Thursdays. Their last engagement was in 1794. They generally gave a comedy and a farce each evening; but they had singers with them, and occasionally gave a comic opera. After the Temple Street theater (known as New Theater) was built, a company from New York, under the management of Hallam and Hodgkinson, opened on the night of August 3d, 1795, and played Mondays, Wednesdays and Fridays, until Oct. 14th. Mr. Hodgkinson was a member of the company, and Mr. Hallam business manager. Tickets were sold at the Post Office, at the following prices: "Boxes, one dollar; Pit, three-quarters, and Gallery, half a dollar." Previously, doors had been opened at six, and the performance began at seven o'clock. With the advent of the new company, doors were opened at half-past five, and the performance began at half-past six o'clock; and the request was made that "Ladies and Gentlemen send their servants by five at the FARTHEST, to keep place in the boxes." Another announcement was that "Ladies who chuse to sit in the Pit, are respectfully informed that there is a Partition railed off for their accommodation." Before the opening of the New Theater, on July 25, 1795, a "Grand Concert" was given in the Court House, by the orchestra of ten men, and members of the opera company. There were orchestral pieces, a clarinet concerto, harp solos, a French horn solo, and various vocal pieces. Tickets were sold at one dollar. The last performance that year was on October 14th, and was the "Benefit of Mrs. and Mr. King, and Mrs. and Mr. Cleveland." As an extra inducement it was announced: "At the end of Act 3d, Mr. King will sing a celebrated song, written by Dibdin, called *Tom Bowling*." After the performance, the company hurried away, and opened the following week in New York for the winter season. They returned the next summer, and the business instinct of Mr. Hallam caused the following announcement to appear on the play-bills: "The Ladies and Gentlemen of East Hartford, East Windsor, Glastenbury, &c., are respectfully informed the Ferrymen have contracted to attend regularly every evening after the performance is concluded;" and yet there are some who have supposed that theater parties from East Windsor and Glastonbury were hardly possible before the advent of the trolley.

Mr. Hallam, who had had like experience in England, was manager of the first regular theatre in New York. It was a stone structure, built in 1750, in the rear of the Dutch church in Nassau street, near Maiden Lane. Previously, theatrical performances had been given in many curious places for such a purpose. One of the favorite early resorts was a store on Crugers' Wharf, near Old Slip. Mr. Hallam had a tolerably good company, which he recruited from the provincial theaters of England, and gave many of the sterling English tragedies and comedies. After a time, however, he received such flattering invitations from Jamaica that he was induced to take his company thither, and the theatre was pulled down. When the John street theatre was built, Hallam returned to New York with a much stronger company, and became its manager. In 1798, the Park Theatre was built, between Ann and Beekman streets, fronting the Park. Mr. Hodgkinson was one of the early managers of this establishment.*

As has been said, the style of plays given was of the laughter-provoking kind, but occasional exception was made, and the Hartford public was now and then given a chance to shudder at tragedy. The music, as indicated by the programmes of the *grand* concerts with which the successive seasons were opened, was very flimsy, and would in these days sound absurd. The company of actors was chiefly English and Irish, while the names of the instrumentalists indicate Frenchmen and Italians, but no Germans.

It is a pretty bare record for the space of one hundred and eighty years that notes little else than the making of a parcel of tune and anthem books by uneducated or ill-educated persons, whose music would now be "excruciating," and the earlier defeat of those mistaken persons who would have prevented the growth of scientific music in New England because of a verse or two in the fifth chapter of Amos.

Glance a moment over those same years in the musical history of Europe. What a glorious epoch it was! Bach and Handel, Mozart and Haydn are associated with it; and before them Monteverde had accomplished his great work in Italy, and Purcell his in England. Beethoven may be included too, for in 1795, he published his Opus I. What has been done in America, along true lines of development, comes well within the space of a century; and they of the old world may in turn wonder at a growth and activity that are without precedent.

Hartford has been in musical matters as in all things, conservative, but steadily growing; and the paper which is to follow will bring before the reader many interesting persons and enterprises, as also several portraits and other illustrations.

---

* See Description of the City of New York, by James Hardie, A. M., 1827.

THE SPIRIT OF BEAUTY.

RUFUS DAWES.

She hovers around us at twilight hour,
When her presence is felt with its deepest power;
She silvers the landscape, and crowds the stream
With shadows that flit like a fairy dream;
Then wheeling her flight through the gladdened air,
The spirit of beauty is everywhere.

OLD COLONIAL CHARACTERS.

III. AARON BURR.

BY FELIX OLDMIXON.

On Burr's return from Quebec, Washington breveted him Major and made him one of his aids. But Burr soon became dissatisfied with a life of inactivity, perhaps expecting greater advancement. He was on the point of resigning his commission when John Hancock induced him to accept a position as aid to Gen. Putnam. It has been said that a disreputable affair " similar to that with the beautiful and unfortunate Margaret Moncrieff which occurred some months afterwards, was the cause of the disagreement with Gen. Washington." There is not a shadow of evidence to prove this, as stated by a writer in the Atlantic Monthly in 1858, who, however, advances a more tenable theory: " But aside from any such cause there was ground enough in the character of the two men. Discipline compelled Washington to hold his subordinates at a distance of implied, if not asserted, inferiority; and Burr never met a man to whom he thought himself inferior."

The name of Burr was soon after associated in an infamous manner with that of Margaret Moncrieff, a daughter of Gen. James Moncrieff, who was brother-in-law of John Jay and of Governor Livingston, and uncle of Gen. Richard Montgomery. She was about fourteen years of age, but a woman in development, with the vivacity, piquancy, and beauty of maturity. They were thrown much together, being in the same household, Gen. Putnam's, until, to avoid scandal, she was removed to King's Bridge — not by order of Gen. Washington, as has been asserted, but by Gen. Putnam, and at the request of Burr himself. Out of these simple facts Burr has been held up to execration as a monster of turpitude, a seducer of innocent virtue, and condemned with malicious invective. But Sabine in his " History of the American Loyalists" says, referring to the touching tribute paid to him by Margaret Moncrieff, " Upon this written evidence, Burr, be his reputation for intrigue as it may, is to be acquitted of the ruin of Margaret Moncrieff, since the only proof is from her own pen, and she, instead of accusing him as the author of her woes, looked back to her relations with him as to the happiest moments of her life."

Her last days were as melancholy as those of Burr himself, and we may with justice to both attribute it to the same causes. Her father, Col. James Moncrieff, had been offered the command of the army for the invasion of Canada, subsequently given to Montgomery, but he adhered to the Crown. He died in New York, after memorable and commendable service, in 1791, and was buried in Trinity churchyard. His daughter Margaret was married to Capt. John Coghlan of the Eighty-ninth Foot, and this ceremony was the last official act of the Rev. Dr. Auchmuty as rector of Trinity church, as he died in 1777; at this time she was only sixteen, while Burr had just attained his majority. How different, perhaps, would have been the fate of either had their lives together flown, as was natural and inevitable but for the interference of parental authority. Captain Coghlan drove his young wife into the arms of a lover by his brutality, and her after career was as a creature of shame. She expressed herself that she had led a strictly virtuous life until after having been led, or rather forced, into a marriage with a man she loathed, and who treated her with harshness and cruelty. She parted from him to become the mistress of the Duke of York and afterwards of several other noblemen, and for fifteen years from 1780, she made no inconsiderable noise in the fashionable circles of Great Britain and France, alternately reveling in wealth and sunk in squalid poverty, until at last she died a broken-hearted woman. Capt. Coghlan's end was no less bitter and unenviable. He was the son of a London merchant of great wealth. He entered the British navy as a midshipman and went with the famous Captain Cook around the world. Disliking the sea, he turned his attention to the bar, and then to the church, but finally procured a commission in the army. After the close of the American war for independence, he obtained permission to serve in the Russian army; but domestic misery in 1783, led him into, or accelerated, dissipation until he broke down. As a wretched outcast he became an inmate of St. Bartholomew's Hospital, in London, and died there in 1804, in his fifty-fourth year. His relations both in England and Wales were very respectable, and hence his body was retained in the deadhouse for eight days in the hope that some one of them would claim and give it decent burial; but the charity of a stranger furnished the means of burial in the hospital grounds. It is said that Capt. Coghlan was one of the handsomest men of his time; he was social, convivial, and in his charities, when he had means, liberal to a fault. One cause of the difficulties between himself and his wife was political, she sympathizing with the Whigs. A novel called "Margaret Moncrieffe," founded on this affair was written by C. J. Burdett, and published in New York. Mr. Burdett was a *protege* of Col. Burr, and was educated for him, at Col. Partridge's Military school at Middletown, Conn.

Col. Burr's military record is too well known to need further mention. In later years when slanders, political and personal rivals and enemies robbed his name of almost every claim to the consideration, sympathy, or fellowship of mankind, Burr himself remarked: "If they persist in saying that I was a bad man they shall at least admit that I was a good soldier." And this was undoubtedly true, although his record is not without blemish; but given greater opportunities he would have distinguished himself as a leader of men and a valiant chieftain. The moral of Wellington's saying, says a late writer, that "When my life is written many statues must come down," has a universal application.

In 1782 Burr, while on duty in Westchester county, married a widow, Mrs. Theodosia (Bartow) Prevost, who was then ten years his senior and the mother of two sons; she died in 1794, leaving an only daughter born to them, June 23, 1783, named Theodosia, the only daughter and heir of his house. The mother was descended from a French Protestant refugee to England in 1685, thence to America, Gen. Bertaut. His son, Rev. John Bartow was the first rector of St. Peter's Episcopal church in Westchester county, New York, and married Helen Read, a sister of Col. Read, governor of New Jersey. Rev. John had a son Theodosias, who inherited land and lived in Shrewsbury, New Jersey, and married Anna Stillwell; their daughter Theodosia married (1) Frederick Prevost and (2) Col. Aaron Burr.

Theodosia, the only child of Col. Burr was carefully educated under the direct and constant supervision of her father; and became perfect in the Greek, Latin, German, and French languages besides the usual accomplishments. At the age of fourteen she was installed as mistress of her father's mansion at Richmond Hill, and entertained his distinguished guests with grace, charm, and dignity. She was freely acknowledged the most beautiful and accomplished woman of her time. She married in Albany, in 1801, Joseph, son of Hon. William and Rebecca (Motte) Alston, of South Carolina, who was born 1778, educated as a lawyer but did not practice, and was for several years a member of the South Carolina legislature, general of the state militia, and later governor of South Carolina. His father was a cousin of the famous painter, Washington Allston; and his grandfather married Rebecca Brewton, a remarkable woman, one of whose daughters married Gen. Thomas Pinckney and another married his brother, the famous Charles Cotesworth Pinckney, sons of Chief Justice Pinckney.

Burr's subsequent career, as lawyer, legislator, attorney-general of the state of New York, founder of the Manhattan bank, manager of the Holland Land Co. judge of the supreme court of the United States, senator, and latterly intriguing for the Presidency, is too well known, as part of history, to need extended mention here. We are simply concerned with the inner man as visible in his extraneous efforts in narrower spheres. His life is the most romantic, without doubt, of any American citizen who rose to similar heights of distinction and who fell so ingloriously from his great eminence.

Of all the forms of human love, one of the tenderest, strongest and most beautiful is that of the father for his daughter. Theodosia Burr was an only daughter, losing her mother in childhood, and without brother or sister, her father had filled the place of both her parents, as well as teacher and companion. He despised the vain pursuits and frivolous accomplishments of the women of his time and started to realize in Theodosia his ideal of a well-educated woman in all respects. He succeeded admirably. In South Carolina she maintained her place at the head of society with dignity and without vanity, a model of purity, intelligence, and loveliness. She admired and loved her father and none knew him better. Thus she compared him with others: "My vanity would be greater had I not been placed so near you; and yet my pride is not in our relationship." The abuse, slander, odium and calumny constantly heaped upon him served but to intensify her admiration and love. "Indeed," she writes, "I witness your extraordinary fortitude with new wonder at every new misfortune. Brave the storm; if the worst comes I will leave everything to suffer with you, I would rather not live than not to be the daughter of such a man." He was sure of one welcome in America; one door was open to him. Associated with his daughter in all his thought was his little grand-son, Aaron Burr Allston, of whom he invariably spoke under the endearing diminutive of "Gamp," an abbreviation of grandpa, which the baby lips had formed, and Burr came to use the pet name, applying it to his grand-son and himself indiscriminately.

Soon after his acquittal at Richmond he went to England with the object in view of negotiating with England for the emancipation of Mexico from the Spanish government, and his enterprise had some prospect of success at one time. But the year 1807 saw the culmination of Napoleon's power, and the British government taking alarm at the military reputation of Burr, who it was apprehended might run a similar course in South America, warned him to leave the country and Burr was requested to name the place to which he would go. He suggested France, then Ireland, then Russia, or South America. No, was the answer to all these suggestions. The government then named Heligoland, a barren island in the German ocean, but Burr absolutely refused and declared that the British government had not power to carry him there alive. Sweden was then determined upon. Thither he went and at Stockholm he was received in the highest circles and enjoyed himself thoroughly for six months. From Sweden he proceeded to Germany, then to Scotland, then Holland, and finally Paris, and was everywhere received with marked attention. By the French government he was however viewed with suspicion and was detained in Paris nearly a year, almost without hope of release, until he became absolutely destitute. His funds were exhausted; no remittances or letters arrived from America; he at last got permission to leave the country, crossed the Channel to England, set sail for Boston in June, 1812. On arriving in Boston he was in destitute circumstances; among his effects were some valuable books he had brought from Europe. Mr. Jonathan Mason, an old classmate of Burr's, now a retired merchant, was living in Boston and to him Col. Burr offered his books for sale, or if preferred as security for a loan. He was informed by Mr. Mason that he had withdrawn from commerce and that it was not convenient to make advances. Thus coldly was he received in his own home.

Theodosia was in South Carolina. She was to meet her father at New York. About a week previous to Burr's starting from Boston little "Gamp" had died, June 30, 1812, at the age of ten. The health of Mrs. Allston had been delicate for years. As early as 1805, apprehensive of an early death she had prepared a letter to be given to Gov. Allston after her decease, which was in the nature of a will and was found among her papers after her death. It breathes a spirit of tender affection and betrays a pious, delicate, noble nature.

AARON BURR.

By the death of her son, Mrs. Allston was greatly prostrated. On the 30th of December, 1812, however, she embarked at Georgetown, S. C., in the schooner "Patriot" bound for New York.

The vessel did not arrive. For months her father waited in hopeless suspense. He entreated Gov. Allston to give him some hope that the vessel had put into some other port and would yet be heard from. No tidings, however, came. Hope slowly gave way to despair. From this blow he never fully recovered. At the time it was commonly supposed that the vessel foundered at sea in a heavy gale, a few days after leaving port. Many believed that she was captured by pirates which infested southern waters, and the crew and passengers murdered.

In 1879 the Washington Post contained an article in regard to the death of Theodosia Burr Allston, to this effect: In 1850, an old man, who, years before, had been a sailor, and then was an occupant of the Cass County poor house at Cassopolis, Michigan, had in conversation with a lady, the wife of the Methodist minister, told of his past life, full of wrong-doing and crime; he said that the act which caused him the most remorse was the tipping of the plank on which Mrs. Allston, the daughter of Aaron Burr, had walked into the sea. He said: "I was a sailor on a pirate vessel. We captured the vessel in which this lady was. When told she must walk the plank into the sea, she asked for a few moments alone, which was granted her. She came forward, when told her time had expired, dressed beautifully in white, the loveliest woman I had ever seen. Calmly she stepped upon the plank. With eyes raised to the heavens and hands crossed upon her bosom she walked slowly and firmly into the ocean without an apparent tremor. Had I refused to perform my work, as I wish with all my heart I had, my death would have been sure and certain.' This is the testimony of an almost dying man, and the confession of the most terrible act of his life. It seems to me that when an old man bemoaning his life filled with sin, makes such a confession without any other provocation whatever than to unburden his soul during his preparations for another life — for death came soon after — that there must be some truth in his statement.*

After the death of his wife and son, a settled despondency took possession of Gov. Allston, from which nothing could arouse him. He died at Charleston, Sept. 10, 1816, aged 38 years.

Soon after his arrival in New York, Col. Burr opened a law office, though something like a combination was brought to bear against his returning to the bar. The great reputation of Burr as a lawyer, his familiarity with the records and with the ancestry of prominent families, and the tenure of titles, secured for him at once a large and profitable business. He was employed on almost every land case in the docket, and his income would have been sufficient for the acquisition of a large fortune, but for his great liberality, and his carelessness in the use of money. He acted as if he were guardian and trustee of a large patrimony for the benefit of his protegees, while he lived abstemiously, and slept on a settee, uncomfortable enough for a friar of La Trappe.

The remaining years of his life are soon told, although a volume of interesting incidents might be filled. He was unpopular from the start. His business fell off gradually. He used to pass whole days in his dingy offices in Reade street, with his head sunk upon his breast, apparently absorbed in melancholy reflections. When he walked the streets, he acquired the habit of looking about furtively without raising his head, to see if the approaching acquaintance would cut him, which was generally the intention. It was a period of almost complete loneliness, mournful memories, and social ostracism, which however did not embitter his feelings.

W. H. Seward speaks of him in 1831, when he met him in Albany, in a fourth-class hotel: "I could not but think of him, when I ascended the narrow dirty stair-case to his lodging in the small two-bedded room in the upper story, of the contrast between his present state and that he enjoyed when he contended so long, even-handed with Jefferson for the Presidential chair, in the second election after the retirement of Washington. He had lost property, fame, character, and honor. Once so fashionable in his dress, so fascinating in his manners, so glorious in his eloquence, and so mighty in his influence, how altered did he seem when he met me, drawing a coarse, woolen surtout over his other clothes, his coarse cotton shirt and cravat struggling by a form of modern fashion to display the proud spirit of the wearer; his few gray hairs filled with powder, put on as thickly as paste, wet down and smoothed over his head; his form shrivelled into the dimensions almost of a dwarf; his voice forgetful of its former melody; while naught remained to express the daring spirit of his youth but his eagle-like brilliant black eye. He approached me with the air and demeanor of a gentleman of the old school, and as I shook his shrivelled and trembling hand I felt a thousand recollections come to my mind of the most unpleasant nature."

---

*For another version of her death see one of the last issues of Worthington's Magazine.

NEW BRITAIN IN THE DAYS OF THE REVOLUTION.

WRITTEN FOR THE "ESTHER STANLEY" CHAPTER, D. A. R.

BY MRS. C. J. PARKER.

To look up the story and achievements of our ancestors is our first duty as members of this organization, a duty that is a pleasure as well, for we feel a pardonable pride in tracing our descent from brave men and women. But to acquaint ourselves with the deeds of our particular ancestors does not satisfy the historic instinct newly aroused within us, and we question how it was with New Britain those early days and what was its share in the great struggle for liberty. We feel sure that, in common with every village and hamlet in the

THE JUDD ELM.

state, it had its story of patriotic men and women, whose names and deeds are now partially forgotten.

The early records contain few historic incidents, and so impress me with the *newness* of this city, that in preparing this sketch I am tempted to adopt Eugene Field's method of writing a life of the poet Horace. He found so little material suitable for his purpose that he introduced his biography with this frank declaration: "I am going to write a sentimental life of Horace that will be interesting. We know very little about him; there is really little to tell, but

380 NEW BRITAIN IN THE DAYS OF THE REVOLUTION.

what I don't know, I'll *make up!*" A little margin of that kind would greatly improve this chronicle, for in point of fact New Britain did not exist as a town until the present century, and previous to that time its history is interwoven with that of the older towns about us in a most confusing way.

In these days of intense interest in Revolutionary history when every place is jealously claiming its heritage of honor, the historian of New Britain, with Farmington on one side and Berlin on the other, is steering between Scylla and Charybdis, and, if wise, will strictly follow the chart, which says once for all, this is not historic ground. To be sure there were early settlements in this vicinity, for Farmington, of which New Britain was originally a part, was incorporated as a town in 1645, and its history during Revolutionary days is full of interest and incident, which we would gladly claim. Well may that beautiful old street have a dignity and serenity all its own, conscious of the historical interest that attaches to many of its quaint homesteads and lofty trees, and remembering, too, that once upon a time it was the largest town in the county and included even New Britain within its borders!

THE THOMAS HART HOUSE.

The rapid increase of population in the southern and eastern sections necessitated a division of the town, and in 1785 the parish of New Britain was divorced from Farmington and espoused by Berlin, which relation continued until 1850, when New Britain shook off all early entanglements and began an independent existence. It could never have been anticipated that New Britain, when "set off" from Farmington, was destined to become a village — much less a city — for its natural advantages were not so great as to promise future growth. Our forefathers were ambitious only to make it a society where suitable schools might be established, gospel services maintained, and in time a church organized. It was a community of industrious, law-abiding, God-fearing men, with strong hands and honest hearts, to whose enterprise and high character New Britain owes the prosperity it now enjoys. These early settlers were heads of large families, and in many instances all the children remained at home, building near the homestead. This was notably the case in the western part of the town, where the sons and grandsons of Deacon Elijah and Judah Hart all located near the homes of their sires, thus giving to that section the name of "Hart Quarter," by which it has ever since been known. There were similar instances among the Stanleys in Stanley Quarter, the Judds and Smiths on East street, and the Andrews in the western part of the town. Sometimes a father with his eight sons, all full-grown men, could be seen in the old meeting-house, all members of the church and representative men in the parish. Society was a unit, having similar aims and occupations, and, aside from the few negro servants it was then allowable to own, the inhabitants were of one race.

Now the people of American birth and descent are but a handful, compared with the other nationalities that throng our streets, but it is worthy of note that so many descendants of the old stock are here; and the names so prominent on the earliest records of the place are names familiar to us to-day in the social, business, and church-life of the city.

THE HEZEKIAH ANDREWS PLACE.

It is difficult for us to imagine New Britain as it was in 1775. It consisted of three small settlements — Stanley Quarter, East street and Hart Quarter — all of which had been peopled by thrifty farmers several years before the war began. In what we call the Center there were only a few scattered houses, stretches of woodland,

THE HOUSE OF ELIJAH HART, 3rd.

large farms and running streams, and much land that was productive only of swamps or ledges. It was by no means an ideal place in which to found a city, and the pioneers had little to encourage them in the way of soil, location or surroundings.

The few residents were Nathan Booth, the first man to build after a clearing in the forest was made and the largest landholder; Col. Isaac Lee, called the "Father of New Britain," of whom mention will be made later; Joshua Mather; James Booth; James North, father of Seth,[*] Alvin, William and Henry North, all men of character and influence; and John Judd, Sr., who lived on West Main street, where five generations of the Judds have had their home. As if to designate this place, a descendant of John Judd, in his boyhood, planted a noble elm, which in the course of years has become one of the most beautiful objects in the city, its branches drooping with their wealth of

THE HOUSE AND STORE OF ELNATHAN SMITH.

foliage, as if in benediction over the throngs that pass to and fro under its shadow. Such trees, so strong and stately, typify all that is enduring in nature, in silent contrast to the generations of mankind that so quickly come and go.

Far out on West Main street, which was then only a crooked path going over the hill, was the home of Thomas Hart, and a little farther west, that of Moses Andrews, who, to his lasting honor be it recorded, gave six of his nine sons to his country's service, the youngest a lad of sixteen, enlisting after the oldest son had perished in the army. Out on the Plainville road there were a few settlers, including Hezekiah Andrews, ancestor of Deacon Alfred Andrews, famous for his Memorial of New Britain, which is a *sine qua non* to all interested in our early history.

---

[*] As Major Seth North belongs to the next generation, mention of him and his vital connection with the various interests of New Britain, will not be in place here; unless, indeed, we put him in the same category as did President Andrews of Marietta College, once a resident here. When asked by a western man, what natural advantages New Britain had to account for, the great success of its manufactories, etc., he answered,—"Major North!"

NEW BRITAIN IN THE DAYS OF THE REVOLUTION. 383

Perhaps you would like to know what houses are now standing near the center having special interest for us because they ante-date the Revolution. They are as follows: The house built and occupied by Col. Isaac Lee on North Main street; James North house near Dr. Comings'; the James Booth house now on Walnut street; the Elijah Hart house on Kensington street; the Thomas Hart and Moses Andrews places on West Main street, and the Nathan Booth house on Arch street, which originally stood on the present site of the South Church.

We cannot but wonder at the sameness in style of all these old houses. In those days what was good for John was equally good for Mary, and — more remarkable yet — what suited the father also suited the sons, for when they left the paternal home they proceeded to build others like unto it! Probably there

HOME OF JOSIAH LEE.

was variety of individual taste then as now, but it certainly found no expression in the architecture.

Some of the houses of the early inhabitants have been so changed, taken from, added to, and built over, that but little of the original structure remains, although proudly pointed out to me as land-marks. I could but think of the pocket-knife the old gentleman carried and valued so highly, because it was the knife of his boyhood — to be sure it had had a new handle, and a new blade, but to his fond imagination it was the same old knife. So I found it to be with some of the houses of long ago, very precious in the eyes of the owner, but not having enough of the original to give them the flavor of antiquity.

I do not know that any of these places are of special historic interest, but they are rich in the associations of family and home, and we love to see them here and there in the city, just as we love to meet the few old people still spared to us, who can speak of by-gone days and generations. They stir the memory and imagination, and touch a chord in our natures that otherwise might never be awakened, for in this busy nineteenth century we live so intensely in the present that we sometimes forget what we owe the past.

Having rambled around the center of the place, let us take a brief look at the three districts, Stanley Quarter, East street, and Hart Quarter, which constituted the New Britain of that period. The principal "business center" was East street, where were large and thrifty farms, a mill and blacksmith shop, and the only store in the parish. This was kept by Elnathan Smith, who lived in the old Rhodes place, and for many years used one room of this house for a store, where "groceries, pins and needles" were kept. We may believe that "trade for cash only" did not greet the eyes of the occasional shopper in this place, for money was a scarce article in those days, and the principal business of a store was barter, exchanging a few dry goods, groceries, etc., for corn, wheat, rye and other products of the farm. Not only was trade conducted in this way but ministers' salaries, doctors' bills, and traveling expenses were paid in these commodities. (The story is told of a young man in New Britain taking his lady to Middletown to a party — both mounted on one horse, and back of the pillion a bunch of carded flax to pay for the supper. What an equable division of labor there was! He furnishing conveyance and "driving team," and she paying expenses with the work of her own hands.)

DOORWAY OF THE LEE HOUSE.

South of this store Joseph Smith, father of Elnathan, was keeping a tavern, the most noted in the place and a popular resort for soldiers and officers. This word tavern does not convey to us the meaning it had to our fathers. It was in those days the secular meeting-house, second only in importance to the

A STANLEY HOMESTEAD.

THE NOAH STANLEY HOUSE.

STREET IN STANLEY QUARTER.

church, a place where all affairs of the moment were planned and discussed. They suggested unbounded hospitality and good cheer, and were centers of attraction for all classes of people as well as travelers. Other residents on East street were Dr. Smalley, who owned a house and large farm, Ladwick Hotchkiss, and Ezra Belden, who owned land extending nearly to the center. At the north of the street were the homes of the Judds, Lees, and Gen. John Paterson, and the old home of Josiah Lee, (now called the Skinner House.) This is spoken of in the records as one of the "largest and grandest" in the place, and it is probably the oldest, as it had been standing thirty-five years when the war began. There is no end to the associations and suggestions of this old house, on whose walls the suns and storms of a century and a half have left their traces. Here in the years gone by many a story of love and sorrow and death has had its course, and varied scenes pass through the mind as we conjure up the people of long ago. The old place looks weary with the burden of age, and prosaic enough to dispel all reflections of a romantic past, but down that narrow stair-case, glimpses of which we see through the open door, there once stepped as lovely a bride as one would wish to see. This was Elizabeth, only daughter of Deacon Josiah Lee, who in June, 1766, was married to the young lawyer, John Paterson, afterwards Major General in the American army and an intimate friend of Washington.

In the Paterson biographies we read of the courtship of the young couple,

THE "STATE HOUSE."

VIEW IN HART QUARTER.

388 NEW BRITAIN IN THE DAYS OF THE REVOLUTION.

the beauty of the fair-haired bride, of the wedding celebrated at this house with festivities and rejoicing and of the happy married life that followed.

As we read the "old, old story" we have a feeling akin to wonder that in the rugged, toilsome lives of our forefathers, there could have been any touch of sentiment or any time for joy. But we know that human nature and the needs of the human heart are ever the same, and that even in those days of hardships, anxieties and perils also, there must have been some compensating pleasures.

After John Paterson and family removed

THE BENJAMIN HART PLACE.

to Lenox, the house was bought by John Richards,* and later by the Rev. Newton Skinner, who occupied it until his death in 1825; since which time it

THE JUDAH HART PLACE.

has passed through many changes, until now, time-worn and neglected, it is interesting only for what it suggests of the people and life of earlier times.

(*Great-great-grandfather, of the writer.)

NEW BRITAIN IN THE DAYS OF THE REVOLUTION. 389

From East street we pass to Stanley Quarter, which, as its name implies, was peopled mainly by the Stanleys, a family prominent in New Britain history from the earliest days until now, and honorably identified with all that pertains to its growth, development and prosperity. Here were the homes of Thomas Stanley, the original settler, and his four sons, including Col. Gad Stanley of Revolutionary fame, a sketch of whom will be given later. Only two of the homesteads remain, that of Noah Stanley being notable, because it was occupied by three successive generations of the same name, and at the time of the war was one of the three famous taverns of the place. Other residents were John Clark, Stephen Hart, grandfather of the late George Hart, and Levi Andrews, whose homestead and farm are still occupied by his descendants. He was the father of Prof. Ethan Andrews, LL. D., celebrated as the author of valuable text-books, particularly a Latin Grammar and Latin Reader, the very mention of which recalls our school life, when we used to " die daily " with these same books.

A CORNER IN THE BOOTH HOUSE, WALNUT STREET.

The old places along this road are now embowered in trees, and the highway to Hartford has beauty and charm for us as well as historic associations. Verily we find here the one bit of historic ground over which we may grow reminiscent, for it was along this old road to Hartford that a body of French troops marched at the close of the war in 1781. Backward over the years we send them a grateful thought, remembering that under foreign skies they and their countrymen had been fighting America's battle for freedom and independence — blessings that might have been long delayed but for their timely aid. Weary and footsore they must have been, as they marched along the rugged way, but we believe they were a jubilant company withal, rejoicing that their enemy and ours, obstinate old King George, was finally conquered.

A glance at Hart Quarter and our little journey is ended. Here there were a number of large farms, less richly productive, perhaps, than those of Stanley Quarter, and a group of sturdy farmers of one name and blood, all descendants of Stephen Hart of Farmington. Quite remote from the other sections of the parish, they led peaceful, industrious lives, adding to the strength of the church and the character and solidity of the place. Is there not a hint in the natural environment of these two large and influential families that may account for the oft-quoted remark of Dr. Smalley's, that he "looked to the Harts for grace, and the Stanleys for money." Whatever the cause of this old-time saying, if Dr. Smalley found such desirable things in numerical proportion to the families mentioned, we are not surprised that he remained here more than fifty years!

Within a radius of half a mile we may see seven of the houses built by the original settlers, including the "state house," which has had a more varied history than its common-place exterior suggests. At the time of the war it was a tavern kept by Elizur Hart, later it was a favorite resort with the young people for parties and balls, and after the great revival in 1821, which a few now living may remember, it was used for religious services, until the new meeting-house was finished a year or two later. All these old houses are slowly going to decay, taking their own time, for in Hart Quarter the "old is not rudely jostled by the new." The years have wrought but little change here, and as we leave the noise and bustle of the city to tarry a while among these homesteads, we feel as if we had stepped back into the eighteenth century. Verily, it seems as if the electric railway felt its incongruity here, for it only comes upon the street, gives one look at the old, old house of Judah Hart, then takes a sudden turn and speeds away to Plainville.

We have now a little idea of New Britain as it was in 1775. We have been introduced to its inhabitants, and by looking around the city we may see for ourselves many of the homes they occupied. At our reception in June we were shown rare old china from their corner cupboards, samples of their needle-work and home-spun draperies, treasures of silk and lace from their wardrobe. Surely we are getting acquainted with these people of the olden time, these ancestors of ours, who have always seemed so unreal and far-away to us. Could we summon them from the mists and shadows of the past, with pride would we bid them look on this fair and prosperous city, whose foundations were laid by them in the midst of hardship and toil, and we would say to them, "ye builded better than ye knew."

(TO BE CONTINUED.)

THE OLD FARM HOME.

We are proud of our house on the city street,
   With its noble height and size.
It is furnished with care with fittings rare,
   And the choicest that wealth can devise.

But the sight of this house so stately and grand,
   No matter how far we may roam,
Does not give us the thrill that comes over us still
   When we think of our old farm home.

TRIO AND TRIPOD

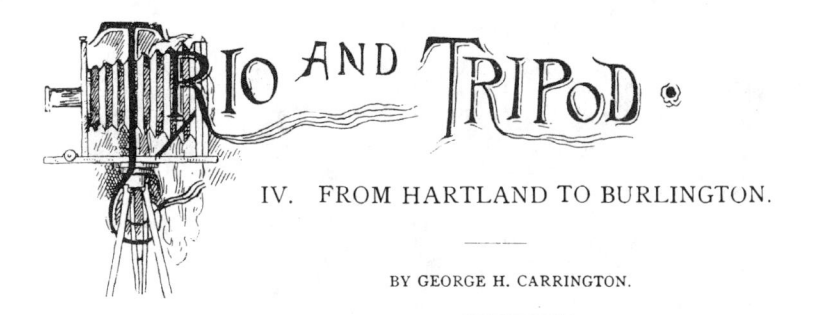

IV. FROM HARTLAND TO BURLINGTON.

BY GEORGE H. CARRINGTON.

We were on Hartland Green by the East Hartland church and by the oldest house in the town built by Uriel Holmes about 1761. The churches of Hartland are on the hills and as the people from below climb upward of a Sabbath, they must get into a devout frame of mind; they certainly get above most earthly things. A resident of the lowly regions of Chippen's Hill, Bristol, once had occasion to visit Hartland and his account of it was, "I went up and up and up until I bumped my head and then turned around and came back, and I had on a low cap, at that."

Upon calling a halt there in the twilight Huggins was appointed ambassador to a near residence to negotiate for food and lodging. He inquired of the

HARTLAND GREEN.

woman who answered the door for the man of the house, but the man promptly referred the question back to the woman. They hadn't very much on hand, "they were not cooked up," but they would keep us if we could put up with what they had, and we decided to try it.

The air was cool, so cool that they claimed John had to sleep with his clothes on, but in truth it was only because he dropped down for a short nap and did not wake up until four o'clock in the morning, then he undressed and went to bed. The winds blow so hard there, they leave no dilapidated buildings standing, but sweep them all away, and Sir Philip's window rattled all night,— because he was too sleepy to get up and wedge it. Huggins came near packing with his belongings, the bureau pin cushion, because it had an H embroidered thereon,— which John explained to him, did not stand for Huggins, but for Henrietta, the oldest daughter.

"SHAD" FENCE.

" We had a small game,
And Ah Sin took a hand :
It was euchre.   The same
He did not understand ; "

The cool, bracing breezes make this a delightful summer resort and our host tried to sell us his place for a summer residence. "Why," said he, "there was a man in New York wanted just such a place as this, and

"*But the hands that were played
By that heathen Chinee,
And the points that he made,
Were quite frightful to see*" —

advertised for it in the New York Sunday — Sunday Sun, I believe,— Is there such a paper as the Sunday Sun? Yes? — Well, someone told me a man down there wanted to buy this place, but I wouldn't sell it then, but I'd sell it now to you for fifteen hundred dollars. 'Twould be a nice place to spend the summer." Yes, we thought it would, and we also thought it would be a better place to spend the summer than the winter. But they who weather the Hartland winters are a vigorous race, and the place has sent out sturdy men into the world who have achieved renown.

All along the route the people had complained of the drought, and were perfectly willing to have us get wet. We, on the other hand, while deploring the dry weather were willing to wait for the rain until we got home, or if it must come, let it be in the night, — so the horses could rest. But not so did it happen, and before we were through breakfast the next morning it clouded and began to drizzle, soon came harder and rained steadily all the morning. We had settled for the day, Sir Philip reading the history of Hartland, and now and then reading a passage aloud, as something interesting caught his eye, and

Huggins, pondering whether he should write the great American novel then and there, or photograph the mistress of the house washing the breakfast dishes, suddenly exclaimed, " I have it, let's illustrate a poem."—

"Well, I vum," said Sir Philip, "just listen. In an extract from the Connecticut Courant of 1796, and copied into Barber's History, it tells of a man then living here, Mr. Jonas Wilder, in the ninety-seventh year of his age, still hale and seldom losing a day from work. He had two wives, both of one name, both Christian and maiden, the last of which he lived with sixty-five years. He had twelve children, never having lost any, the oldest seventy-three, the youngest forty-seven at that time, and his seven sons had all held important offices.

"Pretty good record. Hartland air evidently agreed with him. What's that I heard! Did you say something about illustrating a poem?"

"Yes," said Huggins, "one with figures, so we can pose as the characters." But when the family library of poetry was discussed from " Maud Muller " and " The Barefoot Boy " to " Bingen " and " Casabianca," he objected to taking the

*" Till at last he put down a right bower,
Which the same Nye had dealt unto me."*

part of Maud or being blown up as Casabianca, and though Sir Philip had been called the old boy it was a young one we wanted to represent Mr. Whittier's poem. The accessories for most of the poems were too difficult to procure, and it was not until we came across Bret Harte's, " Plain Language from Truthful James," that we found one suitable. Here the number of characters was just right, the make-up comparatively easy, the loft room would make a good mining camp, and the horse pistols that the family's ancestors carried in the Revolution would do for "Colt's Navies." Soon settling upon the role for each, the preparations began and as in amateur theatricals the most fun is at the rehearsals, the getting ready was real sport. The results are explained by the accompanying pictures better than they could be in words, and we leave the reader to imagine who took that particularly villainous looking part of Bill Nye. We were not sorry after all that the morning had been rainy.

* * * * * * * *
* * * * * * * *

By noon it had cleared and we took a trip to "the bear's den," a name given a cave a few miles to the south, in the deep woods, in one of the wildest and rockiest gorges to be found in Connecticut. The hardy native who guided us thither regaled us with accounts of his own and his family's exploits, from shooting wildcats to picking huckleberries. His wife earned eighteen dollars a week all summer long at the latter occupation, which certainly was remunerative, if not exciting work. The bear was by no means a myth, as he told about it. He had very nearly come into close contact with bruin, for one night when he was "down there coon hunting," he treed a huge, dark looking animal that "must have been a bear, it growled like one," and he kept it in the tree all night, and wouldn't have let it down then, only he got hungry and had to go to breakfast. This was the part of wisdom, whose ways were pleasanter and whose paths were more peaceful, than to have sat down to a feast at which he could have eaten nothing. For his services as guide he charged us nothing, and for his stories a paltry one dollar bill sufficed, which was cheaper than we could have hired a lawyer, and was really quite reasonable for four hours' steady talk of a man who could tell some of the tallest stories of any one in the county. We met three men in the town, each of whom denounced the other two as prodigious liars, and it seemed as though they had really told the truth for once. We returned to our stopping place of the night before, and after supper, Huggins,

NORTH CANTON CHURCH.

ever intent on getting suitable material for his note-book, visited the cemetery, and propounded the usual question to a native whom he met: "Are there any old or curious inscriptions on these stones?" "Wall, I dunno,— there's the stun to old Squire M——, he used to seem to be toler'ble old,— great big

HARTLAND HOLLOW.

feller,— never used to do nuthin but stan round and chaw terbacker,— I allers supposed he wuz nigh onto ninety,— but I see the stun don't give no sech age. As fer curus eppetafs, I saw one here 'tother day that wuz a derned old curus one. I committed it to mem'ry, it was so curus. It went, 'as, — as, — as you wuz once, so now,' — no, thet wuzn't it, — wall it's strange I can't remember thet,

BURLINGTON CENTER.

I learned it once, — it was a derned curus one, anway." Huggins assured him 'twas all right, to never mind — he'd try and get along without it, and he sadly put away the note-book that he had so eagerly pulled out at the prospect of a new inscription.

The next morning we looked from the church belfry southward through the valley when Sir Philip exclaimed, "There's West Peak, Meriden!" "Are you sure?" asked John. "Oh, yes, you can't fool me on that. I drove cows

THE VINEYARD FALLS.

up there all one summer when a boy. I can tell that by the shape anywhere." And so from near the northern boundary of the state, we were but "two looks" from the sound. After gazing at a large part of Connecticut and Massachusetts, and waiting for Huggins's usual farewell cemeterial visit, we started southward, first to go to West Hartland then to come back to the Hollow and go down through the edge of Barkhamsted to Canton, and from there to Burlington. There may be longer and steeper hills in Connecticut than those of Hartland, but we have never found them. It seemed miles to the Hollow from both Hartlands, and the roads were so steep that we *almost* had to tie the horses' tails to the dash-board to keep them from turning somersaults. We

DUNNELL'S FALLS.

thoroughly believed the first phrase in the account of Hartland in Barber's History. "Hartland is an elevated township" was his mild way of expressing it.

In the Hollow Sir Philip got a good picture of a side-hill or "shad" fence, and farther down toward Barkhamsted, such a vision of loveliness floated before our eyes for about half a mile of the distance, that the place is known to us this day as "the blue-dress region."

From cursory observations through Canton we decided that it was the land of C's,—for we saw cameras, carrots, cats and Cases. We had time for but a hasty glance at the different parts of this town, and proceeded across the river to the Burlington hills. This rugged country abounds in waterfalls, especially through "the vineyard." Late in the afternoon, as the cows came winding down a distant hill in single file, the tinkling of the leader's bell wafted to our ears from afar, a dreamy, reposeful feeling took possession of us, and we drew rein by the Burlington store.

(TO BE CONCLUDED IN NEXT NUMBER.)

SCROPE; OR, THE LOST LIBRARY.

A Novel of New York and Hartford.

BY FREDERIC BEECHER PERKINS.

CHAPTER VI.

"No one can know," said Mrs. Tarbox Button with deep feeling, and a suitable separate emphasis on each word — "no one can know what Perfect Happiness is, until they have attended a Female Prayer-Meeting. Of course I shall be there, and Anjesinthy too, Doctor Toomston. I have been there, and still would go, For 'tis a little heaven below."

"And you too then, let me hope, my dear young Female Timothy, my example of the believers. You will accompany your good mother, thy mother Eunice?"

Thus asked further the Reverend Doctor Toomston of Miss Ann Jacintha Button — the "Anjesinthy" of the first speaker, who always gave her daughter both names. He asked the question, — no, he did not so much ask, or speak, as utter. He uttered this overture — the Doctor was a Presbyterian — with his invariable majestic manner, and with the same forth-putting, roomy articulation as if he had been speaking from what he always called " the sacred desk." He always spoke from the sacred desk, even if he were talking to a baby. He had the sacred desk, in fact, as the slang phrase is, "about his clothes;" indeed, nearer still. He walked abroad in the sacred desk; he slept in it; if he had been stripped to the skin and forced to dance a death-dance by the Modoc Indians, he would have danced it in the sacred desk.

"Oh yes, indeed, Doctor," replied the young lady. "I feel it a great privilege."

They have in theatres what they call the Leading Lady. She is the chief actress, who does the heavy heroine business, such as queens' parts. So they have in churches. Mrs. Tarbox Button was the leading lady in the Reverend Doctor Toomston's church.

Churches are in some things a good deal like some other institutions composed of human beings. There are things to be done, people to do them, and people to take charge of doing them. And as in politics, it is very commonly the case that there is an official organization to stand up and look well, and by the side of it or mingled with it, informal powers that do a great part of what is to be done.

In a church, there is the regular course of obligatory religious observances proper, and there is also a semi-official and semi-temporal series closely parallel with this; and there is besides these — in large cities particularly, — what may be called the optional or volunteer course. The stated preaching of the Gospel is the regular course. Along with it, it is true, goes the Worship of God, which Protestants have been so good as to admit to a place in their religious rites only inferior to that occupied by the Sermon. And the Sunday School belongs in this series. The semi-official and semi-temporal series includes the business meetings of the church; the week-day prayer-meeting; the teachers' meeting; the rehearsal by the choir; and the like. And the optional or volunteer course includes any charity schools, sewing societies, organized helps for the poor or afflicted, picnics and parties for the Sunday School children, donation parties;—in short the charity and amusement department, being pretty much all that gives enjoyment or relieves suffering.

The minister and his officials,—deacons, ruling elder, treasurer of the society, or what not, along with the chief musician and Sunday School superintendent,—govern for the most part the two former of these three currents of action and influence. The ladies of the church commonly conduct the third, under a more or less definite chieftainship by the Leading Lady, and with whatever recourse they may wish or can obtain to the purses and counsels of their husbands and fathers. Be it understood always, moreover, that according to strength and wisdom, the ladies use more or less of influence in the two other departments of church activity also.

Mr. Tarbox Button was the richest man in Doctor Toomston's church, and the most energetic, practical and efficient also. In fact, he had been the chief agent in bringing this sound conservative divine to the city, and in the whole strenuous and laborious campaign which established the church. He was the Doctor's right hand man, his tower of strength and unfailing resource in every strait. And Mrs. Button, a shrewd, hard-working New England woman, fortified always by the counsels of her experienced spouse, was at once the Doctor's chief stay and support and her husband's powerful and successful auxiliary in all church matters, as she was in all social matters also. The distinction exists, the fact is, in American religious circles, only after the wholly imaginary manner of those estates which lawyers call "one undivided half."

Among all the good works which were so remarkable a feature of this well known metropolitan church (as the newspapers called it), it was of course that one and another should be engineered by one and another chief executive. It will be found that Sewing Societies, Flower Missions and Companies for Executing Classical Music to the Afflicted, as much as in insurance companies, associations for recovering estates in England, civil governments or war administrations, the successful ones proceed on the principle of having one executive to do things, and a board or chorus or ministry to consult, indorse, help along and keep watch. Thus it was in Doctor Toomston's church. The Doctor was a thoroughly good and kind hearted man, a regular old-fashioned verbal inspirationist and textual preacher, a strict orthodox Calvinist, a well read theologian, and a steady sermonizer, good for ninety honest new sermons every year (deduct two months' summer vacation, and you have left forty-four "Sabbaths" —as he called them,—to which add Fast and Thanksgiving, at one discourse each); but he did not know this practical rule so as to state it, nor perhaps did Mr. or Mrs. Button; but things took that shape simply because these able managers had that unconscious faculty of complying with the universe which constitutes "tact and sense in getting along."

Mrs. Button, accordingly, was often consulted by the executive ladies of all the beneficent enterprises of the church, and she was wise enough to let them use her advice while she kept out of sight; it was the power that she liked, not the show. She had also her own pet or predilection among these, which she along with her Anjesinthy managed pretty much as they pleased, but always with the same dextrous deferential treatment of the other members of their board. This pet or predilection was called by the pretty fanciful name of The Shadowing Wings. It was a little institution established in a poor quarter of the city, which abounded in tenement houses, surplus sewerage, piles of filth, evil smells, rum shops, and small dirty children, and not very far from the high-lying and airy cross street on Murray Hill where Mr. Button inhabited a stately undistinguishable slice of a long row of brown stone front houses exactly alike.

The Shadowing Wings included two — wings, so to speak; being indeed, the usual number, and as few as the plural will justify. One was for supplying to needy mothers having new born children, what the French call a *layette.* The other was what the French call — really, it seems as if those benighted Romanists had invented some handy names, destitute as they may be of a pure Gospel — what the French call a *creche;* a neat little room or two where mothers too needy to lose their days' works might leave their little babies under competent care during the day-time. The two ladies were on their way to The Shadowing Wings, where they met Doctor Toomston, and answered his inquiry about the female prayer-meeting for the week, as aforementioned. This done, the pastor and the ladies parted, the doctor to go about some clerical errand, the ladies to their ordinary Wednesday's inspection at The Shadowing Wings.

Deftly they went, tiptoeing along as every well-dressed Christian must among the dirt and wet of this world, their neatly gloved hands holding their embroidered white skirts carefully up from contact with the various unclean things by the way. Over the ill-cleaned gutters of the Third Avenue they tripped, and then through a terrible Thermopylæ where the wide double sliding doors of a great livery-stable gaped upon a cobble-stoned break in the sidewalk, and a sloping gulf yawned below, leading to the basement where horses stamped and whinnied. A "bret" and a buggy were paraded before the door, while a red shirted hostler with a pipe in his mouth swashed and squirted Croton water, in utter defiance of the city ordinances, from a hose, over the vehicles and all about them. Close to the street edge of this perilous way were crowded a great red-wheeled furniture van and a truck; the reek of horses and harnesses and all things horsy, with the mighty incense of the groom's tobacco floating upon it like wreaths upon a river, seethed in the place, a very Phlegethon of smell.

Past this and other equally noble street monuments of American civic civilization, the unterrified ladies proceeded on their errand of mercy, until they reached the humble doors of The Shadowing Wings, which for the time being were outspread in the second floor of a great brick tenement block. It was a most suitable place; for it was one of those localities where in summer time it seems as if the very substance of the immense edifice crawled with children, as cheese does with mites. They are heaps upon heaps, in doorways and entries; they squeal and chatter out of every window; they overflow upon the sidewalk, into the black sloppy filth of the cobble-stoned street itself; the very air is one screeching din of sharp childish voices.

Even now a good many of them were playing about in the chilly wintry sunshine. None of them, however, paid any attention to the two ladies, except to move — a little — to let them pass. The attention business, and the penny-begging business, had long ago been tried upon them to the uttermost. As soon take Gibraltar by casting cut flowers at it. Both ladies were principled against giving money in the street, and against encouraging street childhood at all; for they were of that healthy and severe New England training, which justly reckons the receipt of charity always a misfortune and commonly a shame, and begging a crime; and they knew that children should be either at home or at school. Still, if they had been very fond of little children some would have run along with them, dirty or not dirty. But they kept them off without the least difficulty, and went upstairs to the rooms.

As they opened the door an infant's screech, coming out, met them, and a voice said, " Give me the dear little thing, doctor. I can quiet it."

" I declare," observed Miss Button to her mother, stopping short with her hand on the door-knob, " I do believe Civille Van Braam lives in these rooms! Adrian sha'n't see her here, anyhow!" She spoke in a low voice, and with obvious discomfort or displeasure, over and above the intimation of jealousy — if jealousy it were — as much as to say, I'm sure I don't want to see her !

"Oh, never mind," answered Mrs. Button, adding, with evident references to some previous consultation or discussion as to something that might be supposed to change their previous relations, " we are to meet her jest the same, you know." Then, as if enforcing a moral lesson from a fact in point, she said, with serious emphasis, "And by the way — remember that, too, Anjesinthy! Tain't right to set in judgment on your neighbor."

"Yes, ma," said the young lady, and they went in.

TO BE CONTINUED.

NEW HAVEN ELMS.

HERBERT RANDALL.

When intermingling sounds of Spring,
  Ring out, in joyful tide ;
As robins sing their litanies
  Through arches glorified,
That span, like great cathedral domes,
  The vista to the skies;
I cross my heart and count my beads,
  Then, kneeling, lift my eyes
Up to Eternity, and say:
  "The shadows grow more dense;
But summer needs the tender shade
  Across her way, and hence,
Were souls forever nurtured in
  Emotion's smiling sun,
This shelter and the hush of peace
  Thou giv'st, Eternal One,
Inspired no portion of their faith,
  Nor were the melody
Of Spring's returning tiding-bells,
  Hallowed by memory."
Responsive to my spirit's dream,
  Up to my feet I rise,
And, through the mullioned arching elms,
  I read upon the skies
The immortality of love —
  Its wealth without alloy,
And for the angels of this world,
  Its sacraments of joy.
My heart sends forth its gratitude,
  Keyed to majestic chords ;
I kiss the rosary and cross,
  Forgetting minor words ;
Lifting Love's chalice to my lips
  I drink its fragrance in ;
Upon Life's altar try to lay
  My sacrifice of sin.

THE ROUND TABLE.

"The goodliest fellowship of noble knights
Of whom the world hath record."

A YEAR OLD.

Our little Quarterly is a year old, with this issue. It is usual in such instances to feel a trifle proud, like a boy in his first "unmentionables." Some magazines, even advertise the fact extensively, and crow a bit. We do not think it necessary, however, for there was no apparent reason why we should not live a year, nor in fact many years. It was a rather lusty infant to begin with, and has been carefully nourished from its birth by its editor and its publisher. Perhaps too carefully and conservatively, but then we wanted it to live.

We assumed at the start that there was no comparison between it and the sturdy metropolitan magazines, but that ours was rather a comely country maiden, modest and somewhat dainty. We do not care to make any comparisons now, for they are always odious, or as Mrs. Malaprop says—"odorous." But we do feel a trifle vain over the fact that ours is the only State Magazine with any just pretensions to take rank with the older and larger Magazines in point of fulness of illustration or popular trend of reading. The majority of State Magazines, hitherto, have been as dry as baskets of chips and about as succulent, —dreary details, endless dates, tedious history, uninviting topics, prosy biographies. Not a spice of variety or an indication of virility or vitality.

We contend that there is no good reason why a local magazine, or for that matter a local weekly or daily newspaper, whether in city or country, can not be made intensely interesting, highly "popular," and even literary and cultured in its scope and significance, if only its promoters choose to make it so. There is too much brain-fag and intellectual slothfulness abroad; even editors are sometimes too tired or too indifferent to think for themselves. The average editor starts out as a frank imitator of a myriad predecessors, and has not ingenuity enough to raise himself out of the rut of routine into which they have fallen. His efforts alternate between the paste-pot and the shears, with only an occasional dip into a sluggish ink-well, not often stirred to its depths.

There is no reason why a periodical of the scope of ours should be all history any more than it should be all society chatter and local puffery. If it is not popular it will not win readers. If it is too heavy and tedious it will not secure them. If it is too local it will not gain wide circulation. On the other hand, if it slops over the State boundaries, and becomes too general and far-reaching it will not acquire sufficient prestige to help it much. It must preserve a happy medium, and suit the average reader, and moreover it must be supremely patriotic as far as the State is concerned. We try to be all this and to take suggestions kindly, but we are once in a while criticised for making it too dry; and perhaps the next person will say it is the reverse and not heavy enough. "Who shall decide when doctors disagree?"

A FORMER STATE MAGAZINE.

We have on our desk, as we write, a thin board-bound book, very decrepit, containing all that remains of the first magazine ever printed in Hartford. It is yclept "The Rural Magazine and Farmers Monthly Museum, Devoted to History, Biography, Agriculture, Manufacture, Miscellany, Poetry, and Foreign and Domestic Intelligence,"—surely a wide-enough field to venture into. It was edited by "S. Putnam Waldo, Esq., (compiler of 'Robbins' Journal,' author of 'President's Tour,' and 'Memoirs of Jackson.') With the assistance of other gentlemen. Hartford: Published by J. & W. Russell, Roberts and Burr, Printers, 1819." It was published only six months, February to July inclusive.

It started out with a flaming prospectus: "Proposals for Publishing in the city of Hartford, a Periodical Work, to be entitled," etc., etc. It ends with a note from the "Editor's Closet,"—almost a wail: "The assistance of other gentlemen was promised but has not been realized. The work has been solely furnished by the Editor, except a few original poems. This is mentioned as an excuse for its want of interest. We have omitted our Poetical Department 'on account of the weather.'" He is not the only editor who has found that it was necessary to write most all the "copy," often under numerous aliases, and to resort to many subterfuges to keep up the interest,—as witness Poe, Edward Eggleston and others.

This Hartford magazine is interesting—at least now, because it is so queer, quaint, and pedantic. It is as full of italics as a woman's love letter. In comparing his magazine to larger ones he is pleased to reflect that "little Iulus" was permitted "at least to follow Anchises." It contains a "Miniature History of Connecticut" which is a model of perspicuity, and a department called "The Social Companion," containing a series of papers of which it says: "The reader involuntarily compares them with the Spectator of Addison, The Rambler of Johnson, The Essays of Goldsmith, The Lounger of our own beloved Dennie, and the Brief Remarker of Sampson."

Oh, those delightful old days of literary leisure, when such essays, foppish, pedantic, far-fetched, could be written at ease without the press thundering at one's heels as now; and when Addison could stop the press to remove or insert a comma, without maledictions falling on his precious head! "Ye editor" of now-a-days can not even find time to write conscientiously. "We hope" he adds, "our Poetical Department will be furnished with the efforts of native genius, as well as the finished productions of the sons of the European Muse. But few can hope to be Cowpers or Byrons." How soon he was to find how flat, stale and unprofitable a drug poetry is, and how scarce the genuine article; no wonder he had to take that department in out of the rain at the last !

What a strange medley it is; "hifalutin" history. puffed-up biography. bucolic lectures, even Alexander Hamilton's own oratory or Noah Webster's budget of sage remarks, — immediately followed by accounts of cattle shows with premium lists. and of new inventions such as Eli Whitney's cotton gin, the printing press of John I. Wells of Hartford, Cobb s Grammatical Expositor on the plan of an orrery, Porter's patent churn, last but not least, Utley's remedy for tooth-ache, made from shrubs in Connecticut. Truly an admirable anti-climax! Reviews of Trumbull's state History, Tytler's General History, (printed by "Peter Parley," in Hartford) and "Sketches of Universal History," (by Cooke & Hale, in Hartford,) besides anecdotes without end. Miss Huntley, later Mrs. Sigourney, had just brought out a volume of poems at Norwich ; Noah Webster at this time published in the Courant a series of Addisonian essays called "The Prompter," afterwards put in book-form, and this led Ezra Sampson to use the same channels for his " Brief Remarker." But where are these books now? Surely Dudley Warner had sufficient precedent for his "Back-log studies" and his "Summer in a garden."

Here we have a dissertation on alewives, and a notice of a new corn-sheller, followed by a turgid poem on "Africa," and another "Zembo and Nila."— faint echoes of the shades of Tom Moore, — and at the head of the "Poetical Department" is the line: "Columbian Muse, advance and claim thy right!" We hope she did. Who are the "Harriet" and the "Maria" that trip so lightly in "The Social Companion?" Surely not Mrs. Stowe, that is to be, and some girl-friend chaffering each other for sport.

How times have changed since then! It is not necessary to offer our own magazine as a comparison, more or less invidious, for the times are so altered that there is really no similarity. We of the present generation can laugh at Dickens' American Notes, which made our ancestors of a generation or two ago foam at the mouth. Time makes a myth of everything, — in, sometimes less than a century. Even Washington is becoming in some sense a myth ; in time he will be a demigod, then a god. So it is also with Napoleon, as witness the late outburst of hero-worship. ad nauseam. It requires only a century for us to forget our own grand-parents — even their names — and a half-century to efface the lineaments of our own parents from the tablets of our memories ; they are utterly gone from us and forgotten. Or if they continue to live, how old-fashioned they have become, entirely out of the swing of our own high-pressure every day life.

Did you ever take up a family album of wartimes and back of that, to study and grin over your old forbears and bye-gone relations. How straight, stiff, and mechanical the posings ; the dress, so ridiculously out of style ; the cut of hair, so formal and outlandish, straight-combed over the ears ; and the features so rigid, expressionless, ungenial, aye unhandsome. Look at the "Wide Awake" group for instance, — all genial and worthy gentlemen, grant you — but those now living would hardly recognize their own old counterfeit presentments, if it were not that a lens can not lie. It seems to me that in the last twenty-five years there have come into our lives so many humanizing and uplifting influences, so much of business rush and bustle and confusion to sharpen the wits, and so many civilizing avenues for us to tread, that faces have changed, as well as clothes, habits, methods of thought and living. It is an electric age and we are only entering upon it, galvanized into an undue activity that is new to us and unexpected. But how soon even this will be old style.

HUMANE SENTIMENT.

The President of the Connecticut Humane Society. Mr. Rodney Dennis, in a recent address before the ministers' association of this city, spoke feelingly of the "Tardy Growth of Humane Sentiment," in words which we are permitted to quote briefly, as they have an especial bearing upon this Commonwealth:

"Perhaps, owing to several most exciting and absorbing questions in our political. social and religious life, on which men's minds were occupied— questions vital at the moment — the claims of humanity toward the animal race in particular, were postponed a half century in this country beyond the time when they earnestly engaged the attention of the best men and women in England, as well as that of the English Parliment. . . . This may, however, be fairly and intelligently accounted for, when we consider the fact that in Great Britain the domestic animals, as well as the land, are owned mainly by the few. The dogs of the rich are kenneled and fed and exercised daintily, while their studs of horses fare sumptuously every day.

" In cases where a poor man is fortunate enough to own a single horse or cow — possession of which is an important factor in contributing to the support of the family—great care and kindness are exercised toward them. The cabins of the poor, in the tight little island, as well as those in Holland, Belgium, and other continental districts — shelter the one cow or pony, whose welfare is so important to the comfort and maintenance of the family, often under the family roof. Generous food, cleanliness and kindness are the rule.

"In this country,—in our own State—notably on isolated farms, in the loneliness of by-roads. often indicating a receding civilization—in these lonely places, on farms large in acreage, almost worthless in quality, worked unthriftily and ignorantly, all the conditions of life are hard. Discouragement, indifference and thoughtlessness beget cruelty, both in the family, stable and byre. The houses are comfortless often, for the family, and the shelter for the animals, which are always too numerous for the provision made for them, is wholly wanting or inadequate. The result is suffering, and not unfrequently starvation. . . .

"Thousands of cattle and horses are owned in this country by a class of persons who in Europe own very few, and who have long since learned that the way to secure the largest products of labor and milk is to bestow the best care. The contrast which exists in many parts of this country is certainly very great. Here numbers are ignorantly regarded as of more importance than quality ; and if the Conn. Humane Society had no other function, no other work on its hands, but to educate these people to carry the Gospel of Kindness and Compassion into these dark places, its right to existence and perpetulty would be established."

The growth of this humane sentiment in our state is largely due to the constant and systematic efforts of one man, the President of the Connecticut Humane Society, who by dint of earnestness, enthusiasm, example, and precept, has raised the humane sentiment — which is innate in every breast, no doubt — to the level where it rightly belongs; its general recognition in this state by all Christians, churches, societies, law courts, employers and laborers — in fact a leavening of the whole lump of humanity. The influence of one such man, who lives so blameless and upright a life that no one can say aught against him, in any path of his career, is mightier than that of many ministers of fame and power — although there may not seem, at first blush, to be any comparison between the saving of human souls and the saving of animals from suffering and torture.

It is mightier for these reasons: That the influence is farther reaching; is constantly progressing, in its elevating and humanizing elements, in arithmetical progression, ever widening like the circles in a pool; and that once started it never ceases to act as a leaven for righteousness and tolerance, charity and good feeling toward the dumb and servile. Surely there must be something wholly good and praiseworthy in a life that is so largely given to the amelioration of the condition of those creatures who cannot speak for themselves but can only plod and slave and serve their masters forever, without even the expected recompense of a kind word or caress. If there are really "nature's noblemen," the insignia and heraldry of that order must, first of all, be granted to such men as Henry Bergh, Charles Loring Brace, George T. Angell, and Rodney Dennis, as readily as to the Beechers and Spurgeons, Ballington Booths or Pere Hyacinthes, or any of the knight-errant evangelists of the truth in our latter days.

While we are on the topic, so fruitful one does not wish to stop, we must announce with great regret the discontinuance of our department of Sociology and Civics, for the present at least, because the exigencies of space and publication forbid us to devote so much room to departments that are so ulterior to our general plan. The people have come to regard this as a historical magazine pure and simple — and so it must be to please them, or they will say us nay. We have been gradually drifting to that phase of the project; and so announced in our last. But in order to introduce new features in that particular line, and to make the magazine more historical and genealogical, in the future, we find we must curtail some features that are of general interest only. We sacrificed the Musical Department, gladly, when we found that Prof. Allen's careful and well-digested history of music in this state would so ably and amply take its place. We must now sacrifice another department to make room for some new ideas to be evolved in the future.

"CIVIC BEINGS."

The phrase is not ours, but that of a London contemporary, and means Citizens, which for some reason or other unknown to us, prefers to say "Civic Beings." He uses it in discussing the latest fad, "Collectivism," or in other words, "Socialism on the largest scale." Socialism, however, requires, first of all a complete change in the nature of man. The peculiar kind of men or "civic beings" necessary for the working out of a complete system of socialism has not yet been produced. Ants and bees, probably also wasps, form their communities upon strictly socialistic principles; but that is because "it is their nature to." But their nature is not very high up in the scale of evolution, nor according to the very close observations of Sir John Lubbock and others, does it appear that their socialism makes them entirely happy. Ants seem to have no conscience and no heart; they are known to keep slaves; if an ant is hurt, the others simply drag it to one side to die, and carry out their monotonous task as before.

As a matter of fact, there is no stronger proof of incapacity for suggesting or carrying out real and tangible improvements, than the disposition so characteristic of quick shallow minds, of forming large schemes for renewing the face of the whole earth. It is in this spirit that resolutions are passed by bodies of workingmen and socialists that no one ever dreams of carrying into effect. Passing them makes a limited sensation, but does not strike terror into the hearts of the enemy — the sober, industrious man. He is the best friend of the workingman who aids him in his present adversity, instead of deluding him with expectations which he can never realize.

It is not often that a man puts more just and discriminating thought into a few sentences than Mr. Arthur Balfour did the other day in a speech at Newcastle, in which he said that "Socialism is a fallacious system of thought, because it concerns itself only with distribution and forgets that men must first of all produce something to distribute; and that the majority is not always 'the People' because the majority changes, while the people endure," Our own Prof. Richard T. Ely says, on this subject: "The difficulties in the way of Socialism seem to me to be insuperable. First of all, there is the difficulty in the way of the organization of agriculture, which has never yet been squarely faced by Socialists. Then, Socialism once organized, there remains difficulty in securing that distribution of annual income which would give general satisfaction, and at the same time promote progress."

A CONTRETEMPS.

It is not often that an editor is caught napping, if he keeps his eyes open. We feel that we must apologize for a sin of omission. In our last was a poem called "Your Native Town," by "Josephine Canning," which came to us in a round-about way from a western writer An Eastern writer of the same name, not a nom de plume, wrote to know the origin of the poem, surprised that another of the same name was also a writer of poetry as she had been herself for years. Later we received a copy of a periodical giving the same poem signed by its true author, Kate Upson Clark, a well-known Brooklyn writer. We are glad to make apology to her for the oversight. She wrote the verses "Your Native Town," many years ago, especially to influence Mr. Potter of New York to give something to his native town of Charlemont. "As he at last gave a fifteen hundred dollar clock, I consider that I received that sum for the verses." So, there was considerable romance about the poetry; and we may add, considerable merit, or else they would not have been plagiarized by some unknown bard.

A WORD OF RETROSPECT.

In looking back over the year, there may have been shortcomings that we recognized afterwards, or that so-called friends told us of after the damage was done; but all such counsels we will keep to ourselves, as that is the safest plan. We can say, however, frankly, that the magazine is not an experiment, was not started as such, and is already a success in more ways than one. We have tried to keep it to a certain level of excellence, and to gradually improve it and evolve better ideas. But when it comes to be bound up and put on the shelf, we shall not be ashamed of it. Would you? Best of all, however, to us is the large list of friends that we have found and made, not only among contributors, but subscribers and readers at large ; and they are of the kind that stays with us. We try to retain our friends and give them a fair return for their friendship and assistance in all lines of work.

We are also glad to note that our little periodical, as it becomes known throughout the state and surrounding states, has wakened up a strong and virile chorus of singers, sturdy and graphic prose-writers, and warm friends, who, although not writers are of infinite help in many ways. If we have done any good service to literature in general we are proud ; if we have simply selected and segregated a corps of able writers and cemented them together in a homogeneous whole we are just as proud. As it is they have become so numerous that it requires time and space to mention them all, but to each and every one we give a welcoming hand.

In the coming year the magazine will be more historical and genealogical in the departments, and perhaps, more so in the body of the magazine. We desire to bring down the history of the leading local families from their first settlement in the state to Revolutionary times, if our subscribers will help us; to do this we shall begin with names beginning with letter A, and continue indefinitely until completed, on the plan somewhat of "Hinman's Puritan Settlers" of the state. Will you aid us?

A glance at our Index and the list of authors and artists who have contributed to our pages the past year, will convince the reader that the little magazine has served as a magnet in attracting considerable talent during its short life ; and what is better, as it ages, the clientele grows more meritorious. "Good wine needs no bush," hence we say no more.

In the present issue we introduce some new contributors, in whom we have a sincere degree of interest : Miss Ellen Strong Bartlett, daughter of the editor of "Bits from Great Grand Mother's diary," and long a resident of New Haven and New Britain, now of the faculty of Oxford College, Oxford, Ohio, who delights to honor the heart of the Elm City, with her facile pen ; Major Julius G. Rathbun, "the historian of Lord's Hill" in the old days, has depicted the remarkable growth of the "Wide Awakes," with which he won glory and renown ; Miss C. Antoinette Shepard, daughter of Mr. James Shepard, of New Britain, and one of the leading botanists of the state, gives a fine paper on a fashionable form of vegetation,—beautifully illustrated from nature by Miss Alice M. Bartholomew ; Mrs. Frances A. Breckenridge, the well-known writer "Faith" of Meriden journalism, opens a delightful vista of memory of the old times in that city ; Miss Pauline Phelps, of Simsbury, a rising young writer, who has also won honors histrionic and elocutionary hitherto, writes a pathetic story that shows great promise for future work ; Mr. Joseph Archer, a local bard and epigram writer ; Mrs. C. J. Parker, of New Britain, gives a thoroughly interesting paper on New Britain Revolutionary life ; Mr. Robert Clarkson Tongue, formerly of Trinity College, Hartford, now of Berkeley Divinity School, Middletown, a poet of great promise and perfection whose work has already found its way largely into leading periodicals, and who writes in the semi-didactic or Wordsworthian strain of William Watson ; and Mr. Herbert Randall, a New Haven artist and poet, who is about to embalm his muse, in so far as it refers to the city of his residence, in a finely illustrated volume, "Elm City in Picture and Verse,"—the entire artistic and literary conception being his own composition,— published by Prang,—which will prove a delightful holiday surprise to the citizens of New Haven. These, in addition to authors, introduced in previous issues, gives us hope of gradual growth and perfection in our enterprise.

We shall add new features from time to time, and new writers, but they will in no wise fall below the level of attainment we strive to reach.

W. Farrand Felch

TREASURE TROVE.

"Time hath my lord, a wallet at his back,
Wherein he puts alms for oblivion."

"While place we seek or place we shun,
The soul finds happiness in none
But with a God to lead the way
'Tis equal joy to go or stay." — MADAME GUION.

CONNECTICUT "COLLOURES."

Samuel Crampton of Salem agreed to furnish "ye towne of Saybrook in ye county of New London with a pr of colloures fitt for ye company of duble scarlet red with a white field to show the red cross, a flagstaf & tassels suitable, to be sent the first oppurtunity after the first of May next & upon y receipt whereof wee whose names are underwritten doe ingage to pay unto ye sd Samuel Crampton or his order the sume of five pounds in pease & rye at three shillings pr bushel provided yt ye sd collours be of ye sd kind one yard three quarters on ye staff, 2 yards & ¼ flourish with a blew ball in ye sd collours, which said payment is to mad at or before the 1st day of October next ensueing ye date heareof as witnes our hands this 30 March 1675.
WILLIAM PRATT.
ABRAHAM POST."
[Essex County Mass. Land Records, Vol. 4, p. 414.]

The above document, copied by Mr. Frank Farnsworth Starr, of Middletown, the veteran genealogist, has been forwarded to the Editor of the QUARTERLY. It would be interesting to know the source of the insignia and colors used; also how long they were in use and what became of them.

THE SOCIETY OF COLONIAL WARS.

The first Council meeting since the summer vacation was held September 19, 1895. Much business was done of a purely executive character.

Time did not permit of the consideration of names of new applicants for membership but they will be acted upon later in the month of October.

The initial number of what promises to be a most interesting series of publications will soon be issued by the society.

The following minute concerning the late Professor Eaton was adopted:

Daniel Cady Eaton, the first Governor of this Society, died at his residence in New Haven on the morning of June 29th, 1895.

This being the first meeting of the council since that date. we deem it proper to place on our record the fact of his death, and to express briefly, the sense of our great loss by this sad event.

Governor Eaton was a man of rare nobility and loveliness of character, so that all became attached to him who came within the sphere of his influence. His ideals were high, his convictions clear, his judgment sound, and his courage unwavering. Whatever success this Society may have attained, is mainly due to his wisdom and fidelity in the formative period of its history. The patient care and thought which he gave to every article of its constitution, and to all its rules and methods of procedure, and which he afterwards strictly but judiciously enforced in his official position as its presiding officer, stamped upon it his character of historical scholarship, patriotic devotion, social dignity, and moral worth.

We trust that on some fitting occasion the Society may be presented with a full memoir of his life, so that those who come after us may unite with us in revering his memory, and may strive to imitate his example.

Chas. Sam'l Ward
Secretary.

DAUGHTERS OF THE REVOLUTION.
(Ruth Wyllys Chapter.)

The attendance of the chapter is unusually good, and a larger number than the average came together to hear Mrs. C. F. Johnson read again her paper on "The Wadsworth Family" on the 25th of April. The records of this family are rich in number and quality, and the life of the refined, intelligent and high-minded Colonel Jeremiah Wadsworth is worth picturing to the present generation. The family residence was on the site of the present City Library, and gave graceful hospitality to strangers and to home friends. Mrs. Johnson added many pleasant things about the family, of some of whom she had pictures in miniature and other styles.

The vagaries of fashion have brought into vogue the styles of a century ago, and a modern belle would call even the dress of the figures in these pictures graceful and attractive. At the business meeting which followed, a reception for Miss Clark, the newly-elected Regent was arranged. This accordingly took place June 7th, at the Library buildings, the Picture Gallery, Historical Room and Art Gallery being opened for the occasion. The ladies invited the Sons of the Revolution, and the spacious rooms interesting themselves, were decorated with flowers, and seemed never so attractive before.

Miss Clark, Mrs. Holcombe, Mrs. Smith, and Mrs. Coffin, wife of the Governor of the Stat·, received the guests, who entertained themselves with the interesting objects in the different rooms, and sooner or later found their way to tables where ladies served tea and coffee and other dainties. The day was bright, the attendance large, and the occasion one that it will be pleasant to recall to mind; and adding a charm to historical associations not originally anticipated.

John Brattle Burbank

We regret not being able to chronicle anything with regard to the "Sons," owing to a paucity of data on the subject.

We are also obliged to omit a report of the Conn. Historical Society, on account of the serious illness of the librarian, Mr. Albert C. Bates, at his home, East Granby, where he has been confined for over two months with typhoid fever. At one time his illness was very serious, and his life despaired of, several doctors and three trained nurses being in attendance; but at latest accounts he was rapidly recovering We could ill afford to spare so promising a historian as Mr. Bates, and so genial and obliging a gentleman.

The position held by Mr. Bates has been most acceptably filled, during the interim, by Mr. George Hoadly and Miss Alice Gay.

THE SOCIETY OF THE WAR FOR THE UNION.

This new society, an outgrowth from Lafayette Camp, No. 140, Division of New York, Sons of Veterans, was organized on December 19, 1894. It grew out of the dissatisfaction manifested by a number of the members of Lafayette Camp with the ritual, and other features of the Sons of Veterans. The Camp had, at its November meeting, unanimously passed a resolution in favor of establishing a purely social organization upon the basis of descent from a soldier or sailor of the Union Army, in the late Civil War. The constitution provides that: "All male citizens of the United States of over eighteen years of age, who are lineally descended from an ancestor who bore arms in the service of the United States in the War for the Union, are eligible to membership."

The By-laws provide that: "The initiation fee shall be five dollars (suspended for one year), and the annual dues five dollars, payable in advance, except that any member of the Sons of Veterans in good standing, or who shall have an honorable discharge therefrom, may be admitted without the payment of an initiation fee." The object of the new society is stated in the Constitution to be "to promote mutual acquaintance, and friendship among the descendants of the men who fought for the preservation of the Union, to keep green their memories, and to perpetuate the principles for which they fought." There are to be three or four meetings a year, at least two of them being small dinners, for which there will be no extra charge. A new by-law permits the election of non-resident members, on payment of two and one-half dollars annual dues. Present membership 35. The President is Mr. P. Tecumseh Sherman, second son of General Wm. Tecumseh Sherman. All interested in the society, or in forming a New England Chapter, may address the Rev. Dr. F. C. H. Wendel, East Granby, Ct.

NEW HAVEN COLONY HISTORICAL SOCIETY.

The regular monthly meetings of the New Haven Colony Historical Society during the past six months have been held on April 29th, May 27th, and September 30th. On these occasions the following papers were read: April 29th, "New Haven Green from 1638 to 1862, as a Religious and Ecclesiastical Arena," by Mr. Henry T. Blake, secretary of the society. May 27th, "A Biographical Sketch of Professor Henry Bronson, M. D.," by Dr. Stephen G. Hubbard. September 30th, "The Blue Laws of New Haven Colony," by Hon. Henry G. Newton. On the 20th of August, a special meeting of the Board of Directors was held for the purpose of adopting resolutions upon the death of Mr. Eli Whitney, Vice-president of the society. — "In whom the society has lost a faithful officer, a staunch supporter, and a generous friend."

It is a noteworthy fact that Mr. Whitney presided at the last meeting of the society previous to his death, during the absence of the President, Judge Simeon E. Baldwin. Some valuable donations have been added to the society's collections, also a number of books, pamphlets, etc., to the library.

KATHERINE H. TROWBRIDGE,
Asst. Librarian and Curator.

NOTES AND QUERIES.

"When found, make a note of."— CAPT. CUTTLE.

BACKUS.—Wm. Backus, Senior, is supposed to have been living at Saybrook as early as 1637. He married (1) Sarah, dau. of John Charles (2) Mrs. Anne Bingham, before leaving Saybrook; he brought with him to the new settlement three daughters, two sons, and Thos. Bingham, his wife's son. Lt. Wm. Backus, Jun., married Elizabeth daughter of Lt. Wm. Pratt of Saybrook. Dea. Jos., and Nathaniel, younger sons of Wm. 2d remained in Norwich. Dea. Jos. married Elizabeth daughter of Simon Huntington, Jun., of Norwich. Their sons Jos. Jun., and Simon, were the first two of the name to graduate at Yale, and they also married into the famous Edwards family. Jos. Jun., md. 1721-2, Hannah, youngest dau. of Richard Edwards, Esq., and half-sister of Rev. Jonathan. The former was for years called "Lawyer Backus of Norwich," probably having studied under his father-in-law. Rev. Simon born 1701, Yale 1724, succeeded Elisha Williams as pastor at Newington when the later became Rector of Yale. Simon married Eunice, dau. of Rev. Timothy Edwards, niece of the wife of his brother Jos. Simon was chaplain at Louisburg where he died, aged 45; his widow brought up a family of seven children and died at East Windsor, 1788, aged 83.

Elijah Backus senior, owned the iron works at Yantic, Norwich, so serviceable to the country in the Rev. war, and was a grand-son of Jos. He married Lucy, dau. of John Griswold of Lyme. His son and son-in-law Dudley Woodbridge were among the first emigrants to Ohio. James, one of his sons, as Agent of the Ohio Company made the first surveys at Marietta and built the first regular house there; he returned to Norwich where he died in 1816. The second Elijah, brother of James ("Jemmy") is the hero of our diary. Elijah Jun. was for several years Collector of Customs at New London. His first wife was Lucretia daughter of Russell Hubbard, who died at New London in 1787, aged 25. Her epitaph is in Latin, showing her husband's fondness for that tongue, *vide* his diary. He afterwards married Hannah, dau. of Guy Richards, and removed with his family to Marietta, Ohio, where he died in 1811. His daughter, Lucretia, born at New London in 1787, married Nathaniel Pope of Kaskaskia, Ills., Mem. Congress from Ills., in 1816, and Judge of the U. S. District Court. Maj. Gen. John Pope, U S. A. is their son, born Mar. 12, 1823. Another descendant of this family is George A. Backus, actor, author and dramatist, an old school-mate of the editor of the Quarterly, and who has personated over sixty different *roles* in the past ten years.

The "Uncle Isaac" of the diary was Rev. Isaac Backus, A. M., of Middleboro, Mass., born at Norwich, 1724, died 1806.

He was first a Separatist, afterwards embraced Baptist principles, and was author of several historical works relating to the diffusion of that faith in New England.

GRAVES-SWORDS.— First Generation in America: Rear Admiral Thomas Graves of Charlestown, Mass., born at Ratcliffe, England, July 6, 1605; married in England, Katharine Gray, daughter of Thomas Gray and Katharine Myles; came to the New England colonies about 1637. He died July 31, 1653; widow died Feby. 21, 1681. Second Generation: Joseph Graves, son of the Admiral, born Feby. 3, 1645; married Jany. 15, 1665-6, Elizabeth, daughter of John and Mary (Axtell) Maynard; residence, Sudbury, Mass. She died June 5, 1676. He married second, Mary Ross, in 1678. Third Generation: Richard Graves, born April 7, 1672; married Joanna ——— ———, who died Septr. 10, 1726. Fourth Generation: Lebbeus Graves, born June 20, 1705; married October 14, 1730, Amity (Amittai) Whitney; removed from Sudbury, Mass., to Killingly, Conn. Fifth Generation: Amity (Amittai), born July 7, 1734; married Francis Dawson Swords, 1762, at or near Stamford, Conn. Information desired. Sixth Generation: Lebbeus Swords, born at Redding, Conn., June 21, 1769; married Ruhamah Batterson, of Fairfield, Conn., May 30, 1792, daughter of William and Grisel (Blackman) Batterson. She was born October 23, 1764, and died at Milltown, Putnam Co., New York, July 9, 1835. He died at same place, October 20, 1848. Seventh Generation: Henry Swords, born at New Fairfield, Conn., December 9, 1797; married at New York City, April 24, 1829, Mary Smith, daughter of Bartholomew and Hannah (Forsyth) Smith, of Colchester, Conn. She was born at Colchester, Conn., December 16, 1805, and died at Yonkers, New York, November 28, 1866. He died at Brooklyn, New York, June 13, 1884. Eighth Generation: Joseph Forsyth Swords, born New York City, August 8, 1842. Residing at Hartford, Conn.

We shall be glad to publish lineages like the above, at a merely nominal rate for space occupied, of any persons who have collated them for admission into societies, or for any similar purpose. We are glad to have Mr. Swords break the ice.

THE GRAVES FAMILY.

REUNION AT HATFIELD, MASS.

(Correspondence of The Courant.)

HATFIELD, MASS., Sept. 12.

A representative of "The Courant" alighted from the Connecticut River Railroad train at Hatfield Station this morning and found awaiting him a fine team, which conveyed him to the Congregational Church on Old Hatfield street, where the descendants of that Thomas Graves who went from Hartford to settle Hatfield in 1642 were in session. If ever Hatfield street had appreciation of the fact that its line of ancestry dated from Hartford, it was demonstrated on this occasion, for the spreading elms and gigantic oaks vied with the shapely maple trees to welcome the Graves family, members of which were present from Connecticut, Massachusetts and Wisconsin. The church was admirably festooned and decorated with flowers, the altar piece stretching from side to side bearing the inscription in variegated colors, "Graves— 1642-1895." Below the organ, and almost the most prominent of the decorations, hung the coat-of-arms of the Graves family — a shield bearing a golden eagle rampant on a field of red, with the family motto, "Aquila non Captat Muscas" (an eagle does not catch flies.)

The exercises opened with prayer by the pastor, the Rev. Mr. Woods, followed by the address of welcome by Thaddeus Graves, Esq., of Hatfield. Mass., the response by Hollis D. Graves, Esq., of Sunderland, Mass.; then a hymn written for the occasion by Mrs. M. E. Graves Miller of Deerfield, Mass., was sung by the congregation to the grand old tune of Coronation. By this time it was high noon and all were invited to a basket lunch in the vestry, which proved to be ample and self-sufficient, and then the local photographer mustered the aged sires, their children and grandchildren, in front of the church, and after he had pressed the button decided that there were no flies on the crowd that stood for that picture.

Then followed the business meeting and the election of officers, the retiring president A. H. Graves, Esq., of Hatfield, at his own request, being succeeded by Thaddeus Graves, Esq., of Hatfield; secretary, W. C. Graves, Esq., of Williamsburg; treasurer, Hollis C. Graves of South Deerfield, Mass.; with an executive committee composed of A. H. Graves of Hatfield, H. D. Graves of Sunderland, N. S. Graves of Amherst, G. A. Graves of Florence and James M. Crafts of Orange.

The historical address, which was to be delivered by General John C. Graves of Buffalo, N. Y., who was unavoidably absent, was read by the president. A. H. Graves, and was in itself an almost complete genealogical biography, tracing the descent of the family from Rear Admiral Thomas Graves of Boston, Salem and Charlestown, Mass., in colonial times, who commanded the Trial, the first American vessel built at Boston (in 1625), and following the line of descent to Marshal George Graves, who is buried in Middletown, Conn., Thomas of Hartford, John of New Haven, and other members who settled at Guilford, Stamford and Litchfield. The genealogy of President Cleveland and Senator George F. Hoar of Worcester, shows a line of descent from a female member of the Graves family, while by intermarriages there is a family connection with Senator John Sherman, General William T. Sherman and the Hon. William M. Evarts.

An original poem which was written and delivered by the Rev. H. C. Graves, D. D., of New Bedford, Mass., paid a glowing tribute to those members of the family renowned for associations connected with church and state. Another poem by Mrs. Emily Graves Lapey of Buffalo, N. Y., descriptive of the coming of three brothers of the good old name of Graves to settle New England. Singing followed by solos and duets by Miss Laura Halstead Graves, of New York city, and Mr. Murray B. Graves, of Hatfield. An address by Charles E. Graves, Esq., of New Haven, treasurer of Trinity College, referred to Daniel Graves, of Vermont, one of the most prominent of the anti-slavery agitators of his time, and spoke feelingly of the interest awakened by the historical researches he had been impelled to undertake so late in his life by a visit to the home of his boyhood, and the graves of his ancestors, pioneers representing the best blood in the country, patriots, soldiers and statesmen every one. The venerable James M. Crafts, of Orange. Mass., told of the labors he had shared with General John C. Graves in gathering together nearly 20,000 names of the family, soon to be compiled in three volumes, the first to be issued by January 1, at a cost of $5 per volume to those who wish to subscribe, stating that subscriptions could be sent to any member of the executive committee.

In all there were about 200 representatives present, those from Hartford being Mr. and Mrs. George A. Graves, of Barbour street, and Joseph F. Swords, who are descendants of Real Admiral Thomas Graves, as are also Miles W. Graves, Esq , vice-president of the Connecticut River Banking Company, and Joseph A. Graves, Esq., principal of the South District School. Some of the Hubbard family were present and feelingly referred to the association of the late Stephen A. Hubbard with "The Courant," which was a welcome visitor through the Connecticut Valley, and stated that Mr. Hubbard's grave was kept in good condition by loving hands.

The session was adjourned on invitation of Myron Graves, Esq., of Springfield, Mass., to that city, the next reunion to be held on September 12, 1896, at Graves's hall, the proprietor kindly placing the hall at the disposition of the executive committee free of expense.

A vote of thanks was heartily given to the lady members of the committee, Mrs Thaddeus Graves, of Hatfield, and Mrs. H. L. Graves, of Williamsburg, who contributed so much for the welfare of visiting members of the family.

(Republished by Request.)

LITERARY NOTES.

While America bemoans the decline of the drama, Spain has developed a theatre whose plays are literature.

Jose Echegaray, the monarch of the Spanish theater is one of the most interesting personalities in Europe. Born in 1832, he was forty before he wrote one of the fifty or more dramas which are played in Spain, and already belong to the classic literature of Europe.

He is the photographer of Spanish life, — its Quixotic chivalry, its shadow, and most of all its sense of modern need. He is also a terrible voice of contempt, exhibiting the degenerates in their shame.

Spaniards declare that not for two hundred years — not since Lope de Vega — has their drama produced a serious rival to this man.

Lamson, Wolffe & Co. take keen pleasure in introducing this remarkable dramatist to Americans. They present in one superb volume two of his most characteristic plays, "The Great Galeoto" and "Folly of Saintliness," — preceded by an appreciative, critical introduction by Hannah Lynch, the distinguished translator. No small part of the charm of these plays lies in the happiness and fluency of the English rendition.

This volume is of some 200 pages, heavy paper, uncut edges, and delicately bound in light pink buckram, used for the first time in binding books. For sale by all booksellers. Or sent upon receipt of the price — $1.50 — if ordered from the publishers direct.

It is doubtful if there is in existence another book which even attempts what a forthcoming volume, "The Poor in Great Cities," aims to do — to give a view of the whole problem of mitigating the evils of poverty in England and America, and to bring together the best experience in dealing with it. The authors contributing to the volume are Walter Besant, Oscar Craig, W. T. Eising, Joseph Kirkland, J. W. Mario, J. A. Riis, E. R. Spearman, Willard Parsons, W. J. Tucker, Robert A. Woods, all of whom have been for years among the best known students of the great social problems. The work is fully illustrated and contains an appendix on tenement-house building by Ernest Flagg. It will be published by the Scribners.

In his new book, in press with the Scribners, "The Art of Living," Mr. Robert Grant has given new proof of his happy wit and fancy. He has taken up the practical problems that beset every man in America who desires to live as near as he can to the opportunities of our civilization, without running into its extravagances, and he attacks such problems as income, the dwelling, living expenses, education, etc., from the point of view of such a man. The book will be charmingly embellished by 135 illustrations by C. D. Gibson, B. W. Clinedinst and W. H. Hyde.

Messrs. Lamson, Wolffe & Company have brought out a volume of Indian-lore poems, by Miss E. Pauline Johnson (Tekahionwake), entitled "The White Wampum," and published simultaneously in Boston, London, and Toronto, which they offer to the public as a distinctly individual contribution to the poesy of the day.

Miss Johnson is an Indian princess of one of the proudest of the old tribes. At the same time she is a flower of Canadian culture and high breeding. But with all her social accomplishments and prestige, she has always retained her hold on the life of the forest. Equally at home in her canoe or in exclusive London society, she is perhaps the only Indian who has ever succeeded in giving with adequate grace an English expression to the deep imagination of her people.

Her poems present a series of pictures of the life of the first Americans, executed with wonderful sympathy and color, as well as precision

"An Old New England Town," by Frank Samuel Child, is a book which Charles Scribner's Sons will put upon the market in October. Among the subjects treated in a popular way by the author are, Pioneer Days in Connecticut; the Witchcraft Craze; the Congregational Churches as a State religion; the Capture of General Silliman by the British; the Marriage of John Hancock, President of the Continental Congress; the Family of Aaron Burr; the Burning of Fairfield; the War of 1812; Judge Roger M. Sherman, etc. The book is a setting forth of the important relations which the New England towns have borne to the progress and triumph of the American people, and will therefore have a special interest to members of such organizations as The Colonial Dames, The Sons of the Revolution, The Daughters of the Revolution, etc. The book will be handsomely illustrated, and there will be an edition de luxe, limited to 300 copies.

Messrs. Lamson, Wolffe & Company announce the publication of new editions of two collections, entitled respectively: "In Friendship's Name" and "What Makes a Friend?" Both have been compiled by Mr. Volney Streamer.

These books appear in uniform binding of Imperial Vellum, and are printed on dekled edge Holland paper, with uncut leaves.

From HOUGHTON, MIFFLIN & CO., The RIVERSIDE PRESS.

Little Miss Phœbe Gay, by Helen Dawes Brown. With three full-page illustrations and a cover design by Miss S. J. F. Johnston. Square 16mo, $1.00.

A wholesome, bright little book with a delightful play of humor running through the narrative. It is made up of fifteen little stories, each recording a special event in the life of Miss Phœbe when she was about ten years old.

A Blockaded Family, by Parthenia A. Hague. Life in Southern Alabama during the Civil War. 16mo, $1.00. The author was a governess in a southern family during the war. Her task has been to detail the innumerable devices of herself and friends to supply cloth, shoes, hats, thread, dyes, hoop-skirts, buttons; to find substitutes for coffee, tea, raisins, starch and medicine.

Is there any boy or girl who failed to be interested in "Little Mr. Thimblefinger, and his Queer Country," the successor to "Brer Rabbit" by Joel Chandler Harris, as it appeared serially. Here we have all the fanciful inventions of this charming author, Sweetest Susan, Buster, John and Drusilla.

The Story of Mary Washington, by Marion Harland. Illustrated. 16mo, $1.00. This little volume was prepared at the express request of the National Mary Washington Memorial Association, and gives all the available information in regard to its subject, and is a reverent tribute to the memory of a woman who should be better known and esteemed by her country women and the nation.

The Dwight Slate Machine Co.

Manufacturers of and Dealers in

Machinery and Machinists' ... Supplies.

Drilling
Machines
a Specialty.

Special
Machinery,
   Model Work.

Fine
Instrument
Repairing,

   Gear Cutting,
   Hangers,
   Shafting,
   Pulleys and
   Supplies.

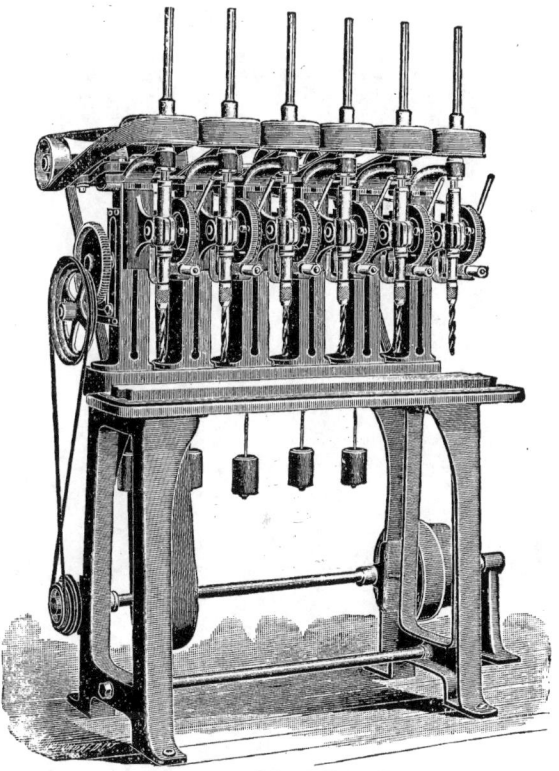

Automatic Worm Feed Dri'l.

Machinery Moved, Set Up, and Millwright Work Given Prompt and Careful Attention.

Wareroom and Office, **13 Central Row.** Factory adjoining.

Long Distance Telephone, No. 147-4.

Please mention THE CONNECTICUT QUARTERLY.

THE CO-OPERATIVE
SAVINGS SOCIETY
OF CONNECTICUT,
HARTFORD,

Assets, Over $750,000.00

GEORGE POPE, President,

Offers for sale **$500.000 Five per cent. Coupon Certificates.**

In denominations of $200, $500 and $1000.
Selling price par ($200 per share) and accrued interest.
Certificates redeemable at par after one year from date of purchase,
at option of holder.

Securities consist of Non=negotiable First Mortgages.

For information address,
FRANCIS A. CRUM, Department Manager,
at the Society's Principal Office, **No. 49 Pearl St.,**
HARTFORD, CONN.

R. S. Peck & Co.
Hartford, Conn.

Embossed Catalog Covers
Designs submitted.

DESIGNERS
ENGRAVERS
PRINTERS
EMBOSSERS

ARTISTIC
PRINTING

We would be glad to quote upon anything in our line upon advice of your requirements. Correspondence solicited. Send for our elegant catalog.

Please mention THE CONNECTICUT QUARTERLY.

of Hartford, Conn.

Best either for family protection or investment of savings.

Non=forfeitable, World=wide,
Lowest Cash Rate.

Assets,	$18,501,000
Liabilities,	15,875,000
Surplus,	2,626,000

Largest Accident Company in the world,
Original and only large
and successful one
in America.

Covers Accidents of **Travel, Sport or Business**
All around the Globe.

Paid Policy=holders, $28,000,000.
$2,151,000 in 1894 alone.

JAS. G. BATTERSON, President.
RODNEY DENNIS, Secretary.
JOHN E. MORRIS, Assistant Sec'y.

---

*WE do not put an illustration here to show our work, but if you want to see what kind of a cut we can make when we have a good copy to work from, turn to **page 326** of this magazine.*

THE HARTFORD ENGRAVING CO.,

*Manufacturers of Superior
Half-Tone Printing Plates.*

OFFICE: Room 23, Courant Building,
66 State Street, HARTFORD, CONN.

OUR CONSTANT AIM—
TO MAKE THE
FERRIS HAMS
The FINEST!

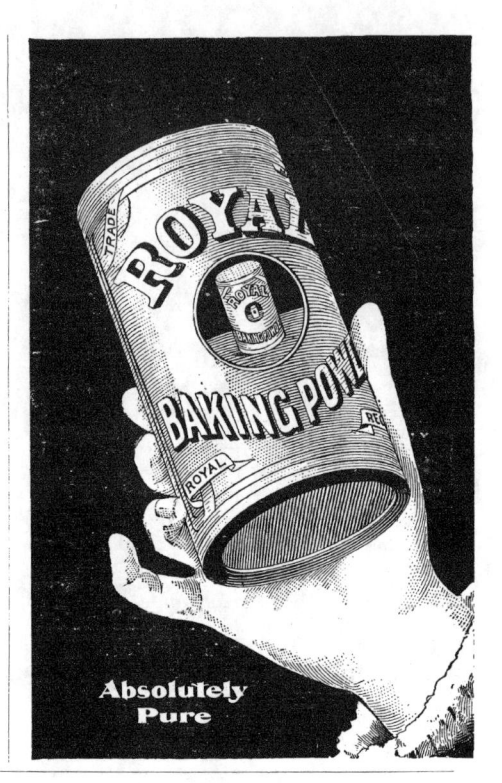

(Royal Baking Powder — Absolutely Pure)

Ye Olde Arm Chair

We have it & high-backed, cozy and inviting, & with many others built on the exact lines of those quaint old colonial chairs that

Our Grandfathers used

We shall take pleasure in showing you our fine reproductions of old-time designs, & also some originals, which have justly given us such a high reputation for restoring and finishing antique.

& & & Furniture.

LINUS T. FENN,

205 Main Street,
Opposite the Athenaeum,   Hartford, Conn.

R. S. PECK & CO., PRINTERS, HARTFORD, CONN.